The
Edinburgh Critical History
of
Middle Ages and Renaissance
Philosophy

The Edinburgh Critical History of Philosophy
General Editors: Howard Caygill and David Webb

Titles available
The Edinburgh Critical History of Nineteenth-Century Philosophy
Edited by Alison Stone

The Edinburgh Critical History of Middle Ages and Renaissance Philosophy
Edited by Andrew LaZella and Richard A. Lee, Jr.

Forthcoming volumes in the series

The Edinburgh Critical History of Greek and Roman Philosophy
Edited by Giuseppe Cambiano and Alexandra Lianeri

The Edinburgh Critical History of Islamic Philosophy

The Edinburgh Critical History of Early Modern and Enlightenment Philosophy

The Edinburgh Critical History of Early Twentieth-Century Philosophy

The Edinburgh Critical History of Contemporary Philosophy

Visit the Edinburgh Critical History of Philosophy website at:

www.edinburghuniversitypress.com/series/ECHP

The Edinburgh Critical History of Middle Ages and Renaissance Philosophy

Edited by Andrew LaZella and
Richard A. Lee, Jr.

EDINBURGH
University Press

Edinburgh University Press is one of the leading university presses in the UK. We publish academic books and journals in our selected subject areas across the humanities and social sciences, combining cutting-edge scholarship with high editorial and production values to produce academic works of lasting importance. For more information visit our website: edinburghuniversitypress.com

© editorial matter and organisation Andrew LaZella and Richard A. Lee, Jr., 2020, 2024
© the chapters their several authors, 2020, 2024

Edinburgh University Press Ltd
13 Infirmary Street
Edinburgh EH1 1LT

First published in hardback by Edinburgh University Press 2020

Typeset in 10 / 12 Ehrhardt MT by
IDSUK (DataConnection) Ltd

A CIP record for this book is available from the British Library

ISBN 978 1 4744 5080 5 (hardback)
ISBN 978 1 4744 5081 2 (paperback)
ISBN 978 1 4744 5082 9 (webready PDF)
ISBN 978 1 4744 5083 6 (epub)

The right of Andrew LaZella and Richard A. Lee, Jr. to be identified as the Editors of this work has been asserted in accordance with the Copyright, Designs and Patents Act 1988, and the Copyright and Related Rights Regulations 2003 (SI No. 2498).

Contents

General Editors' Preface vii
Howard Caygill and David Webb

Editors' Introduction 1
Andrew LaZella and Richard A. Lee, Jr.

Part I Bodies/Pleasures: Embodiment, Affect and Forms of Life

1. *Augustine of Hippo in Medieval and Contemporary Dialogues on Embodiment* 21
   Karmen MacKendrick

2. *Disability, Ableism and Anti-Ableism in Medieval Latin Philosophy and Theology* 37
   Scott M. Williams

3. *The Art of Excess as a Medieval Aesthetic* 58
   Lisa Mahoney

4. *A Classroom of One's Own: Medieval Conceptions of Women and Education* 74
   Maggie Ann Labinski

5. *Shame: A Phenomenological Re-examination of Aquinas's Analysis* 97
   Daniel Dahlstrom

Part II Soul and the World/Soul Beyond the World: Experience, Thought and Language

6. *Experience in Monastic Theology and Philosophy in the Eleventh and Twelfth Centuries* 117
   Emmanuel Falque (translated by Ian Alexander Moore)

7. *Medieval Neoplatonism and the Dialectics of Being and Non-being* 142
   Dermot Moran

8. *Medieval Semiotics and Philosophy of Language (Ninth to Fourteenth Centuries)* 160
   Costantino Marmo

9. *A Path to Identity: Meister Eckhart's Ascesis of the Soul* 185
   Alberto Martinengo

10. *The Enigma of God and Dialogue in the Midst of an Epochal Threshold: The Case of Nicholas of Cusa (1401–1464)* 200
    Peter Casarella

Part III Politics/Community: Justice, Injustice and Power

11. *Cosmopolitanism in the Medieval Arabic and Islamic World* 217
    Josh Hayes

12. *Intellectual Virtues and the Attention to* Kairos *in Maimonides and Dante* 234
    Jason Aleksander

13. *Ethics of Property, Ethics of Poverty* 249
    Pascal Massie

14. *Humanity, Nature, Science and Politics in Renaissance Utopias* 272
    Georgios Steiris

15. *Religion and Just War in the Conquest of America: Sepúlveda, Las Casas and Vitoria* 283
    Felipe Castañeda

Part IV Repetitions: Tradition and Historical Inheritance

16. *A Gaping Lacuna: Gersonides's Apparent Silence About Aristotle's Ethics/Politics in the Context of the Judeo-Arabic Tradition* 301
    Idit Dobbs-Weinstein

17. *Founding Body in Platonism: A Reconsideration of the Tradition from Origen to Cusa* 317
    Wayne Hankey

18. *'Medieval Ethics' in the History of Philosophy* 332
    Mark D. Jordan

19. *The Structural Causality of Specific Difference from Medieval Thought to Deleuze and Althusser* 344
    Eleanor Kaufman

Notes on contributors 357
Index 361

General Editors' Preface

All forms of inquiry are enriched by an appreciation of their own history, and this seems especially true in the case of philosophy. The study of past thinkers and their works continues to sustain and to renew philosophical thought, shaping the way that even the most concrete of contemporary problems are seen, and how they are tackled. If one of the hallmarks of philosophy is a reflection on the limits of what it is possible to think at any time, then the history of philosophy is at once an indispensable resource, a testing ground, and a reminder that we are never really done with thinking.

The Edinburgh Critical History of Philosophy places itself in the European tradition of philosophy, without being bound to any single vision of what philosophy should be. It treats the history of philosophy from its beginnings in Ancient Greece to the present day as composed of many threads, breaks, borrowings and intrigues that cannot be unified in a single narrative. Often, the orthodox classification of philosophy into themes and sub-disciplines has been set aside, since it does not always reflect the way problems and themes first emerged. In turn, consideration of this emergence has sometimes allowed for the inclusion of figures who may not be well known outside specialist circles, but whose work was significant in shaping later developments.

Although the idea of critical philosophy properly speaking has passed through many reformulations since originating with Kant, the idea of philosophy as an ongoing reflection on its limits has become almost commonplace and goes beyond any adherence to this or that methodology, school or tradition. The aim of the series is to present a historical perspective on philosophy that matches this broad critical outlook. As such, it recognises that 'Western Philosophy' has developed through exchanges across its geographical borders; that historically speaking, not only are limits hard to define, but periods are sometimes linked in multiple and unexpected ways; and that what is taken to define a given period, movement, or sub-discipline within philosophy is often not indigenous to it. In the same way, philosophy has often taken up problems from other disciplines, transforming them, and sometimes being transformed by them, in the process. Ignoring these movements across and along borders can obscure the multifaceted development of problems and themes as they feed into, and off, one another. It can also tempt one to regard the subject matter of philosophy as simply given, as though its history were merely a record of increasing clarification. Similarly, although there are essays in this series dedicated to individual philosophers, this is not the default choice. Instead, the critical perspective adopted in this series tries to keep in view how the problems and themes of a given period took shape, and in turn gave shape to the philosophical work around them. Wherever possible, we have encouraged volume editors and authors to consider that links may exist between different essays within volumes, and across volumes. However, for good reasons, this could not become their central preoccupation, and so many of these links remain implicit, and even unintended. It is our hope that this may add to the richness of the work as a whole and that the reader will take pleasure in their discovery.

As general editors of the series, we have enjoyed working with volume editors who are outstanding subject specialists, and who have brought great imagination and dedication to the task. The series as a whole owes a great deal to all of them. Special thanks goes to Carol Macdonald at Edinburgh University Press, whose patience, care and determination has made all the difference.

Howard Caygill
David Webb

Editors' Introduction

Gerrymandered Epochs? Challenge to Periodisation

It seems that a volume on 'Medieval and Renaissance Philosophy' presupposes that there is such a thing. To say 'Medieval and Renaissance Philosophy' implies a natural unity; or, if this is not a single unity, then each name by itself denotes a unified historical period similar enough to the other so as to be treated in a single volume. This leads us to ask: what are those conditions by which historical periods are at all possible? Are these conditions natural to the history of philosophy as such? Or are they generated as the result of other factors on account of which epochs in the history of philosophy are 'carved up'? We see a task of a *critical* history to ask after such conditions of possibility, to which we will return in Part III. A 'critical history of philosophy' that is also divided by epochs in the history of philosophy presents a multiplicity of complicated questions.

Let us begin by asking: is there some real basis for classifying a period that spans from CE 476 to roughly 1450 temporally, and spatially from the Samanid Persian dynasty – in what is currently Uzbekistan – to Ireland, under a single name 'Medieval Philosophy'? Consider for the moment the following: roughly the same amount of time separates Thomas Aquinas (a medieval philosopher) from Boethius (another medieval philosopher) as separates Aquinas from us; or William of Ockham is further in space from Ibn Sina than he is from those of us working in the eastern United States. What sort of unity – whether proper, specific or even generic – can one possibly assign to such a temporo-spatially diverse set of philosophers? How can one bundle them together under anything but the most gerrymandered of sets (Haslanger 2005)?

The term 'gerrymandering' refers to the practice in US politics of drawing congressional districts to favour a given political party. Looking at a map of such districts, one sees shapes whose lines zig and zag in every which way reaching out to include the vastest expanse of landscape then contracting to include only the narrowest of slivers (the origin of 'Gerrymander' arose from the fact that such an odd district looked like a salamander and was drawn up by Elbridge Gerry, Governor of Massachusetts). The enclosed districts appear to have no natural or essential unity. Even while cutting against the grain, so to speak, what unifies them are political operations.

The image of gerrymandering has been deployed by social ontologists. In discussing race and gender, Sally Haslanger, for example, distinguishes between gerrymandered sets, objective types and natural kinds (Haslanger 2005). For Haslanger, one of the most important questions, if not *the* most important, is the *purpose* for which such sets are constructed. By pointing to the purpose, Haslanger intends what she calls an 'ameliorative' account. However, her argument can also help uncover those non-ameliorative projects that have brought about such sets or kinds. This is an important project insofar as the processes by which such sets are constituted remain hidden from view. While Haslanger rejects treating either race or gender as a natural kind (i.e., an essential unity), she resists thinking of them as mere gerrymandered sets. Rather, she argues, they are objective types (i.e., a similarity class).

Objective types share a property in common, which accounts for their unity. Haslanger's examples include red things, things on my desk, things weighing exactly ten pounds, and so on. They are objective in the sense that they are mind-independent unities and not mere fictional classifications (e.g., unicorns or centaurs). Unlike natural kinds, however, their reason for sharing their unifying property is not the same or essential. Tomatoes are red for a different reason than Mars is red. Compare this to the case of electrons, which are unified on account of sharing a negative charge. Whereas objective kinds classify, natural kinds identify.

With respect to the matter at hand, it seems clear that the historical epoch 'The Middle Ages' is not a natural kind. Whether it is an objective type, merely a gerrymandered set or something else remains to be seen. In addition to the spatio-temporal diversity discussed above, the Middle Ages also encompasses at least three 'major' religious traditions (i.e., Judaism, Christianity and Islam), perhaps more depending on where we start our designation of the Middle Ages. These traditions themselves are not homogeneous, but belie multiple internal debates, variations and struggles. In Islam, there is not only the differentiation of Sunni and Shia, but also the battle between the 'theologians' (*Mutakallimun*) and the philosophers, and the contest between Sufis and their 'rationalistic' antagonists (*falasifa*). In Christianity, there is not only great differences concerning the Trinity, but also many who considered themselves 'good or even 'true' Christians found themselves at one point or another labelled as 'heretics' (e.g., the Beguines, the Cathars, the Brethren of the Free Spirit, not to mention the Franciscans). Within Judaism, the situation is even more complex as there is no central authority or authorities to whom to appeal for the 'right' or 'orthodox' understanding of the faith – Judaism is, by the Middle Ages, a diffuse body of thought.[1]

The linguistic landscape is even more diverse. Medieval philosophy includes texts written in Greek, Arabic, Hebrew, Latin and 'vernacular' languages (e.g., Persian, French, German, Italian, English). Matters grow even more complex when we consider that much of Jewish philosophy was written in Arabic and that Maimonides wrote in Judeo-Arabic (Arabic written in Hebrew characters).

The political, cultural and institutional structures of medieval philosophy complicate this picture even further. Philosophers teaching in a European university in 1290 have different audiences, practices and external pressures and limitations than a Jewish rabbi writing to teach his congregation. An Islamic commentator on the texts of Aristotle (Ibn Rushd), commissioned by the caliph Abu Yaqub Yusuf, works in a context and for a purpose that is entirely different than a Christian preacher (Meister Eckhart) giving sermons to nuns living in the Rhein Valley. We have attempted to illustrate the diverse landscape of this nominally unified period. And up to this point, we have only been focusing on the 'Middle Ages'.

Adding in Renaissance philosophy makes the unity of the volume even more suspect. Renaissance philosophy is that sliver of philosophy that does not quite fit in the arid climate of medieval thought; nor, however, does it enjoy the clarity of Cartesian Modernity. In one sense, Renaissance philosophy sets itself in opposition to medieval scholasticism. Figures such as Ficino, Pico della Mirandola, Erasmus or Machiavelli (just to name a few of the most obvious) hearken back to an ancient humanism seemingly lost in the Middle Ages. These thinkers are easily characterised as 'Renaissance', while 'Scholastic' philosophers such as Suarez (born 16 years after Erasmus's death) and Cajetan (overlapping both Erasmus and Luther) are often not seen as pure exemplars of 'Renaissance thought'. In another sense, Renaissance

---

[1] One could argue that 'rabbinic' Judaism, i.e., the Judaism that emerges in exile and away from the temple and its priestly structure, is already a body of thought without a centre and central authority.

philosophy continues the trends of medieval thought. Suarez or Cajetan would be at home in the European universities of the thirteenth century. Cusanus, who died a year after Pico della Mirandola was born and overlaps with Ficino, blends elements from both medieval scholasticism and Renaissance humanism.

So what, if anything, unifies the subject matter covered by this volume? If the names 'Medieval' and 'Renaissance philosophy' refer to gerrymandered sets, what forces were at play in constructing them? Perhaps the so-called 'Middle Ages' and 'Renaissance' are merely the leftovers after the rest of the history of philosophy has been carved up into neatly delineated epochs. Once this great landgrab has run its course, these remaining areas fit in the category of 'Other'.

Part of this othering is written into the very names of these epochs. This is most prominent with respect to the *middling* of the Middle Ages. It should go without saying, but seldom is said, that no thinker in the 'Middle Ages' was aware of their epoch as 'medieval', the age in the 'middle'. Rather, this classification was invented after the fact to set it apart from what came after and to differentiate the then present (*modernus*, modernity) from this stale past.

The claim that the 'Middle Ages' were invented is nothing new. The historian Norman Cantor, for example, titled one of his books *Inventing the Middle Ages* (Cantor 1991). In it, he chronicles how twentieth-century historians were responsible for bringing about our idea of 'The Middle Ages' or 'The Middle Age'. Even if the term 'medieval' enjoys older ancestry than the twentieth century, it was derived well after the Middle Ages to designate that time that came before.

Here we can identify a distinct moment in this process of 'middling' the period or epoch. This process begins by setting the 'Renaissance' apart from its predecessor, whether due to the former's own self-fashioning or that of historians who followed. To call a period a 're-birth' entails that something once living has died. This leaves that which comes before it as a dead corpse of a previous civilisation. In order for this construction of the history of Western philosophy to function, something must die. This is the role traditionally assigned to the Middle Ages.

One might identify a secondary moment whereby both the Middle Ages and the Renaissance are lumped together as pre-*Modern*. That is, whereas the Renaissance benefited from a distinction from the Middle Ages *aesthetically* (i.e., the art of the Renaissance is generally celebrated as a triumph over the art of the Middle Ages), *philosophically* it formed part of pre-modernity against which Descartes and modern philosophy could rebel. This philosophical break – not to mention the break in natural philosophy, which we nowadays call 'science' – sets itself apart from everything 'pre-modern', including much of the philosophy of the Renaissance period. 'Modernity', as the first moment of historical self-consciousness, requires that everything that came before is simply 'pre'. The moment when Descartes announces that he will build his philosophy on a new foundation is the moment when 'modernity' is conscious of itself as an epoch and, therefore, must mark and name every previous epoch – but mark it as, at best, past, at worst, dead. In this way, modernity might have inaugurated 'Medieval and Renaissance Philosophy' as a gerrymandered set in that it is only 'held together' by the pronouncement of modernity.

If we treat the question of 'what unifies?' more optimistically, and, therefore, as something more and also less than a gerrymandered set, we might find an answer from a 'grand narrative' approach to the history of philosophy.[2] In such a scheme, as in any unified narrative, the Middle Ages and Renaissance have a role to play, albeit as secondary characters. Two elements oftentimes associated with such grand narrative schemes are progress and inevitability. Greek

---

[2] We take this phrase from Jean-François Lyotard's *The Postmodern Condition*. See, especially, pp. 31–41 (Lyotard 1979).

philosophy marks progress over the mythical worldviews both at home and abroad (e.g., Egyptians, Babylonians). We celebrate Socrates's martyrdom against ignorance and wickedness; even though he was put to death, his legacy lives on and has achieved immortality. When the march of progress stalls (e.g., the Fall of Rome), it struggles through the darkness to find rebirth and light after long periods of dormancy. There is an inevitability to this march. The views of a thinker or a period are the outcome of what preceded it. Plato emerges from tensions inherent in Parmenides and Heraclitus; Kant provides the necessary momentum to overcome the limitations of continental rationalism and British empiricism.

To view the history of philosophy according to a grand narrative means imposing a grid of intelligibility by which to link together various thinkers and ideas. The history of philosophy thus forms a narrative with a beginning, an end and a middle. The very names of the two periods in question play into the grand narrative scheme of the history of philosophy. The *middling* of the 'Middles Ages' mediates two extremes in time. The middle plays an important role in linking together the beginning and the end, but the middle must leave resolution for the final act. As such, the middle is always giving way to the next – in fact, to the last. In an unending series, there is no middle. Once the middle has been established, it is dead on arrival – such is the role of the middle. A rebirth is necessary in order to bring about the 'final act' of the history of philosophy.

To this point, we have considered approaches to medieval and Renaissance philosophy that either categorise them as *Other* or use them to link more 'essential' periods together in a unified grand narrative. In what follows, we will show that, despite the diversity of medieval and Renaissance philosophy, these periods – like all periods in the history of philosophy – can be considered *epochally*, i.e., as unified by means of a principle organising the various thinkers of a period. After deriving elements from the work of Heidegger and Schürmann, we will establish what we'll come to call a *critical* epochal history of philosophy.

Does the Centre Hold?

Does the history of philosophy fall so neatly into periods? If it does, then a 'period' should have a 'principle' around which it is gathered – that is, a centre that allows one to see all thinkers as belonging to the 'period'. As we have argued, time and dates alone do not seem to function as such a principle. The concept of a 'gerrymandered set' displaces the question of principle in important ways. To see what is at stake, we should first understand the concept of period or epoch that is based on such a principle.

Heidegger, for example, has argued that the 'principle' that grounds the epochs of the history of philosophy might be linguistic. Philosophy first spoke Greek, then was translated into and learned to speak Latin, and, lastly, came to speak in the 'vernacular'.[3] There is an obvious Eurocentrism to this periodisation. Heidegger rarely, if ever, speaks of the influence of Ibn Sina (Avicenna), Ibn Rushd (Averroes), Maimonides or Ibn Gabirol (Avicebron) on the development of philosophy after the fall of the Roman Empire. Furthermore, Reiner Schürmann, looking to both rescue and critique Heidegger's 'epochalisation' of the history of philosophy still looks for an internal principle, i.e., that around which the thought of a period turns (Schürmann 1987: 25–43).

---

[3] While Schürmann frequently refers this idea to Heidegger, we have been unable to locate any passage where Heidegger says this. See Schürmann (1987: 58, 2003: 348).

Heidegger on Epochal History

From the beginning of his career, Heidegger is convinced of two interrelated theses: (1) the tradition or history of philosophy is still alive and at work in our current thinking and our current modes of philosophising; and (2) that the human, truth and being are thoroughly historical. The first thesis is on display in Heidegger's early teaching when he turns to Aristotle, Augustine, Aquinas, Leibniz, Plato, the Pre-Socratics, etc., as thinkers who are still 'alive' in the sense that their thought still has something to say to us. The conclusion, perhaps, to which this early move leads him is that this history or tradition cannot be simply 'brought back into play' but has to be 'retrieved' (*wiederholt*). If, for example, we simply assume that the texts of the history of philosophy are transparent, open and accessible to us, we fail to understand them in their own historical context, a context which is no longer ours.[4] That is, if we assume that some 'rational kernel', '*philosophia perennis*', or a-historical content is what is most important, decisive or, even worse, interesting about the texts of the history of philosophy, we run the risk of failing to confront two important ways in which the tradition is still living. First, we risk losing something like the meaning of key terms, concepts and arguments because we fail to understand them in their own context. To take one example, if we read late ancient or medieval texts on the Trinity of God, and we do not understand that the term 'person' is a translation of the Latin *persona*, a legal term, which, in turn, was a translation of the Greek *prosopon*, a term from Greek drama, we risk losing the sense of the thought and the 'semantic fields' in which the terms played. For Heidegger's earlier thought, this 'retrieval' required more than just an understanding of or 'attentiveness' to 'historical context'. It required, first and foremost, an understanding of what history is and what role it plays in philosophy today.

This leads to the second point. If it turns out, for example, that medieval thinkers were accustomed to assume that there are angels, that angels have a role to play in the world and the cosmos, and that, therefore, philosophy in the Middle Ages is fundamentally different from philosophy in ancient Greece or in modern France, then the first task of philosophy is to figure out just what constitutes that difference. In other words, the medieval world and our world might not be *the same world*! Already, we can begin to see a complication. We speak about history only to mark just this kind of difference – if the Middle Ages are historical, that means there is some difference that makes them other than today. One does not think of last year, for example, as historical. In this way, history seems to point primarily, if not exclusively, to some differences by which we mark the present from the past and some past time (the Middle Ages) from another past time (ancient Rome). A first insight, therefore, emerges: what makes up the 'essence'[5] of history is differentiation. And then a second insight emerges: if history is this differentiation, then it is also constituted by breaks or interruptions. If we can recognise that we are not medieval, then there must be a break that separates our age, our time, from another. And now a third insight emerges: if history is constituted by interruptive breaks, then we must be able to point to something that 'holds together' a time, an age, an epoch in such a way that we can recognise when it has been interrupted. Drawing all this together, we see that there is an emerging conception of history that requires a thinking of how history is made up of differences that interrupt epochs.

To this point, we have been speaking vaguely of 'a time' or 'an age'. The insights that have emerged above now come together to require that we understand what characterises such a time

---

[4] This is similar to what Gadamer refers to as the 'historical horizon'. See Gadamer (1991: 302–3).
[5] At the moment, we mean by 'essence' only what answers the question 'What is it to be X?' Whatever answers the question 'What is it to be history?' is the essence of history.

or age. We can say, first, that the differences and interruptions point to a stoppage, a ceasing, that in Greek could be called an ἐποχή. Therefore, history is 'epochal' in the sense that it is differentiated by means of interruptions. There are, therefore, historical epochs or, better still, history is epochal. So, we can now rephrase the question as 'what constitutes an historical epoch?'

As Heidegger will come to express it in 1946:

> What are merely historiographically constructed philosophies of history supposed to tell us about history if they only dazzle us with a review of the material they adduce; if they explain history without ever thinking the foundations of the principles of explanation out of the essence of history, and this from out of being itself? (Heidegger 1977: 326; 2002: 245)

In this, there are two important points. The first is what we might call Heidegger's critique of historiography, namely his critique of the notion that we can 'get' history if only we can gather enough material. While he does not draw this critique out here, we can say that there is an argument – and not just from Heidegger – that if we assume we can come to understand, for example, the Middle Ages, simply by gathering philosophical, religious, juridical, political, literary, etc., texts from the epoch, we must already understand what constitutes that epoch. If we want to understand Thomas Aquinas's *Summa Theologiae*, and we think that this means we must gather other texts of the epoch – philosophical and extra-philosophical – to assist us, this means we already know what constitutes that epoch. We need, therefore, a way of enquiring into what constitutes the epoch.

Here, and this is the second point, Heidegger points out that, if we agree that history 'matters', we must give an account of the 'foundation of the *principles* of explanation' (emphasis added). For Heidegger, history is ontological in the sense that it is related to being at the most fundamental level. More precisely, being simply is historical for Heidegger. This conclusion is based on Heidegger's insight that whenever we say that something is, or that X is Y, the 'is' in each case refers to that which is neither a thing nor a characteristic (i.e., to use the language of Aristotle and his medieval followers, is neither a substance nor an accident). Yet to what can this refer? Heidegger's answer is that it refers to or uncovers being. This must mean that being is epochally – and, therefore, historically – differentiated. In order to understand how this can be the case, we must first understand how being is differentiation.

Short Excursus into Duns Scotus

Duns Scotus is famous for two main philosophical positions: (1) the irreducibility of singularity in the notion of *haecceitas* and (2) the univocity of being.[6] It turns out that, for Scotus, these two positions are fundamentally related – or, perhaps, the same proposition in reverse. That is, if, as Heidegger insists, being differentiates itself epochally, then we need to think through what it means to say that being is always 'just being', but, more so, how it is differentiated. For Scotus, the 'univocity of being' means that whenever being is predicated of anything – God, an accident, the planet Jupiter, a rock – the 'content' of the concept is always identical. Yet clearly God is not identical to the planet Jupiter. Therefore, there must be something other than 'being' that, along with being, constitutes any thing that is. If we take the example of 'The Porphyrian Tree', we can begin to see what this means (Fig. I.1).

---

[6] Deleuze claims that the 'univocity of being' is 'the only ontological proposition'. See Deleuze (1968: 52, 1994: 35).

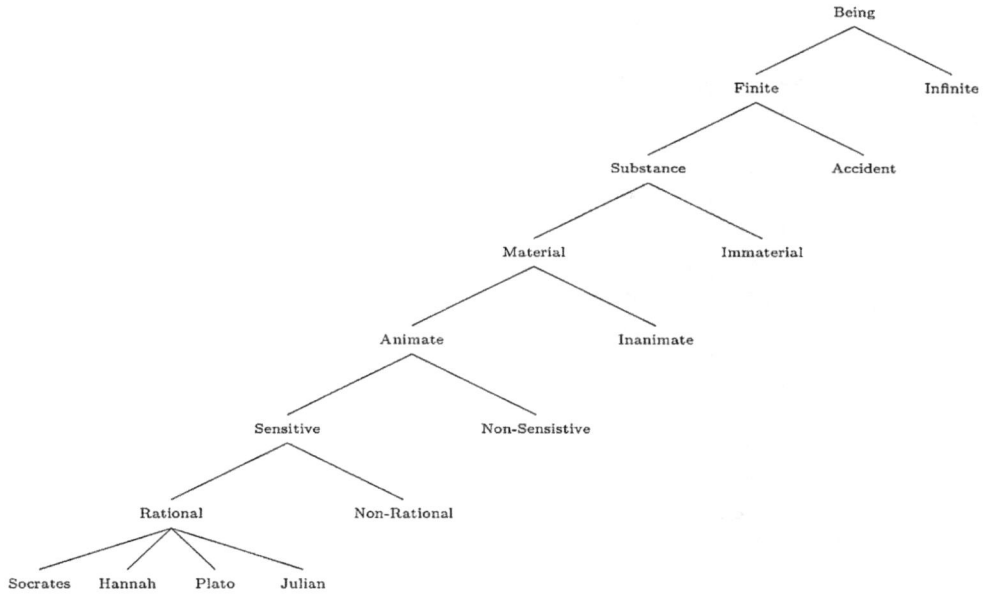

Fig. I.1 The Tree of Porphyry (editors' own)

What Scotus draws from thinking through this 'coordination of predicates' is that the highest level – for him, being – must be completely determinable while the lowest – *this* – must be completely determinate, i.e., in no further way able to be determined. Scotus comes to think of determinability as a kind of [*quasi*] potentiality and determination as a kind of [*quasi*] actuality. As completely determinable, 'being' is empty in that it indicates everything that is not nothing and does so indiscriminately. Therefore, there is nothing that is simply 'being' or 'a being'. Every being is determined by something. What the tree illustrates, then, is that schema of determination. The schema is brought about by means of differentiation in that what determines being to be something – and there is nothing that is not something – is difference. The higher levels of the schema are brought about by means of a difference that results not in individuals but rather in kinds, i.e., in genera and species. At the lowest level, there is a differentiation that results in individuals. Since being is completely determinable and this last difference completely determining, we can say that this last level exhibits the 'highest actuality'.[7]

While Scotus's position on the univocity of being and the role of differentiation is much more complex than we have presented it here, we can draw a few main points that are relevant to our reading of being as epochal in Heidegger. First, Scotus does not insist that being is irrelevant because of its emptiness or indiscriminate pointing to everything. If being were irrelevant then only differentiation would be metaphysically relevant. In that case, we might wonder what is being differentiated. What is more, if there were only differentiation, then it would be impossible, both logically and metaphysically, to distinguish the kind of differentiation

---

[7] We draw this from various areas of Scotus's thought. For a full scope of the argument, see LaZella (2019).

that results in a group such as 'animals' from the differentiation that results in individuals. There are, in short, different ways or types of differentiation.[8]

Second, at each level, all the way up to being, the resulting genera, species or individuals *just are* what is differentiated. Paul, Hannah and Julian *are* human, their being is human being. Similarly, humans *are* animals. There is, therefore, a kind of identity that is running through the entire tree. While it may seem obvious, that identity is precisely what being is or means. However, the reverse of this is that being is or means just this schema of differentiation because there is no being that is not a coming together of determinability and determination. Being, in short, is differentiation, because anything that is has been determined to its actuality by differentiation.

Therefore, third, Scotus is the most sophisticated thinker of the coordination of being and difference, which is also to say the coordination of being and determination. While not always or even entirely thinking of Scotus, Heidegger points to just this same issue: the way in which any being 'is' must be directly related to the way in which being is differentiated, the way in which, as differentiated, being is 'exhibited', and, in 'showing itself', is 'captured'. This is just another way of saying that being is only relevant to the extent that it is something. Both Heidegger and Scotus show why being – i.e., what is – has its way of being from differentiation and that is another way of saying 'enclosed'. There is a fundamental connection between Scotus's thinking through of differentiation and the 'Epochalisation of Being'.

Epoch as Differentiation of Being

Heidegger's argument which we began to trace above is that being is differentiated historically and the result is the various epochs of being. To continue with Scotus's language, we can say that, for Heidegger, being is determined and the differentiation that provides the determination is historical. Heidegger links the 'gathering' of being – what above we called both 'determination' and 'capture' – to the question of truth and what he calls the 'essence of being'.

> The being of beings gathers itself (λέγεσθαι, λόγος) in the ultimacy of its destiny. The hitherto prevailing essence of being disappears into its still concealed truth. The history of being gathers itself in this departure. The gathering in this departure, as the gathering (λόγος) of the utmost (ἔσχατον) of its hitherto prevailing essence, is the eschatology of being. As destining, being itself is inherently eschatological. (Heidegger 1977: 327, 2002: 246)

Being 'gathers itself' [*das Sein versammelt sich*], i.e., comes to appear in a determinate way. In this new mode of gathering, what constituted being – the essence of being [*Das Wesen des Seins*] – withers and passes away [*untergeht*]. Yet Heidegger insists that this perishing is a movement into its truth that it still concealed [*in seine noch verhüllte Wahrheit*]. This movement into a truth that remains concealed turns on Heidegger's rethinking of the concept of truth already beginning in the 1930s. Heidegger begins that investigation by assuming the traditional (and, it seems, perennial) concept of truth as correspondence, or, as Aquinas puts it, '*adequatio intellectus et rei*'.[9] Heidegger shows that this definition of truth can only function as a definition if it itself is true. Yet, what is the correspondence involved in this truth, namely that truth is a correspondence between proposition/intellect and thing? The truth of the proposition that truth is a correspondence must be 'self-evident' to us and it is this self-evidence that *guarantees*

---

[8] This is also why Scotus was insistent on the importance of 'modal distinctions'. If, e.g., being a lion is a *way* [*modus*] of being an animal, then the difference between them would be modal.
[9] Sancti Thomae De Aquino (1970), *De Veritate*, q.1, a.1c.

truth as correspondence. However, this means that it is self-evident *to us*. Therefore, *we* become the guarantors of truth. We must ask, therefore, '. . . are *we* and what is self-evident to *us*, the ultimate and primary criterion [of truth]?' (Heidegger 1997: 6, 2002: 4).[10] The self-evidence of the essence of truth now requires a measure, and that measure is us. However, how we are the measure of truth is not equally self-evident. Therefore, truth has become incomprehensible and thus we need to gain some distance. That distance, Heidegger argues, can come from an investigation into the history of the essence of truth.

In the return back [*der Schritt zurück*] to the beginning of the notion of truth, Heidegger finds that, for the Greeks, truth is α-λήθεια understood as a privative: un-hiddenness or unconcealment. As he comes to read Heraclitus, Plato and Aristotle, truth does not name a property of propositions but names the very way in which a being *is*. In other words, truth is not an epistemological issue but an ontological one. Yet what does it mean to say that truth is unconcealment? At first glance, this might be taken as indicating that truth is a certain revelation of what something is.[11] However, if we take it in this sense of 'revelation', truth is once again inserted into a question of knowledge or perception. Rather, for Heidegger, this coming into unconcealment is just what it means for a being to be.

The coming into unconcealment has a twofold aspect. First, it means that a being comes out from the mass of other beings. You go to see and cheer your brother on as he runs the Chicago Marathon, in fact his first marathon. You stand along the route as masses of runners come towards you and pass by. None of them is an individual as each of them belongs to the clump of 'not-hims'. You then see a familiar feature – a moustache, a roundness of the face, etc. – and then, not all at once but eventually, your brother emerges from out of the concealment that was the mass of all beings. In this way, a being is a being when it comes out from 'behind' all the other beings. Second, a being comes into unconcealment when it 'gathers itself' in a certain way.

As an example of this 'gathering,' we can point to the Church of Saint Mark (*Chiesa San Marco*) in Florence, where there is an altar that is the resting place of, according to a card placed nearby, 'the uncorrupted body of St. Antoninus' (*Atlas Obscura* 2019). There is, of course, a way in which the claim that his body is uncorrupted is not true. However, given a certain factical life, the body of San Antoninus comes to the fore and comes to be present precisely as uncorrupted. By 'factical life', we refer to Heidegger's early thinking in which philosophical questions – such as truth and being – are thought from out their emergence in day-to-day life.[12] While this life is not always and not entirely steeped in the theoretical concerns of the philosophical tradition, if that philosophical tradition is meaningful, then the clues, questions and concerns of those who make their way through what is given – the root of 'facticity' and the 'factical' [*factum*] – are that from which philosophy emerges and, therefore, should be that

---

[10] It is important to note that many medieval thinkers distinguished between what is self-evident in itself [*per se nota in se*] and what is self-evident for beings like humans, i.e., rational beings who are limited in the understanding both by being finite and by being embodied. Here, Heidegger does not seem to recognise this distinction. However, his point is that the self-evidence of the truth of the definition of truth, namely that truth is correspondence, depends on it being self-evident to us and, therefore, we become the measure of truth *tout court*.

[11] In his *De Veritate*, Anselm distinguishes between truth and a true thing. While truth belongs to a proposition, the truth of that proposition depends upon the prior 'being true' of a thing. 'This is a triangle', e.g., is true not merely because it corresponds to what is the case but also because the thing that is spoken of is a 'true triangle' or, we might say, 'truly is a triangle'. This last formulation shows clearly what Heidegger is after in his argument.

[12] See for example (Heidegger 1999), especially p. 5.

for which philosophy is responsible. From out of the life of someone for whom the saints provide an everyday entry or opening to the divine, San Antoninus is an opening, and therefore is opened up as just that opening. San Antoninus's flesh is also clearly corrupting, but not in the same factical life. The uncorrupted body of San Antoninus comes, like the brother in the marathon, from out of the mass of beings and it comes out so as to appear, so as to come to presence, as the thing it is. Yet, in order for it to appear as, let us say, holy, an object of veneration, and, therefore, as 'uncorrupted', other ways in which it can come to appear recede or are hidden. In this way, its coming to be is unconcealment that is always, necessarily, also concealment.

Unconcealment is therefore always and at the same time concealment. The holy relic does not come forth while the scientific object (i.e., the obviously decomposing body) is present. Heidegger's argument is that this unconcealment is truth and is what the 'object' is. There is, of course, no contradiction between the scientific appearance of the body and the holy relic. The venerable 'object' comes forth, it shows itself, and is unconcealed not from a 'perspective', but from a way of being – a way of its being and a way of our being. That one who sees the apparent corrupted body might be in the same space at the same time as one who understands that San Antoninus's body is uncorrupted does not mean the two are in the same world.

We can now return to Heidegger's insistence that the history of being gathers in the 'departure' [*der Abschied*].[13] If we take as an example the coming-to-an-end of modernity, we can note that only after its going away can philosophers come to recognise the way in which it was an epoch in which beings came into presence – were unconcealed – in relation to the self-possession of the thinking subject.[14] While this epochal principle (self-consciousness) 'held sway', i.e., was active as an organising and ordering function, it remained hidden. We can note this if we pay attention to the fact that Descartes's *Meditations* are *Meditations on* First Philosophy, i.e., 'Meditations on metaphysics'. He did not set out to reduce all of being to the being-present-for-self-consciousness, nor did he take this to be the achievement of his project. The truth of being – being is being-for-self-consciousness – was concealed while it brought all things into unconcealment as present to consciousness. As Schürmann argues,

> The establishment of a principle is its institution at the beginning of the period for which it will serve as ultimate point of reference, of recourse, thus dominating that era. Such a first becomes thinkable however only when its grip begins to loosen. The establishments bequeathed us are talked about and questioned as they collapse, so that we know history primarily by its reversals. (Schürmann 1987: 30)

Schürmann here argues that Heidegger's insistence that the history of being gathers in the departure means that '[t]he reversals of history are what makes it intelligible' (Schürmann 1987: 30). In other words, the hegemonic[15] hold that a principle has over its epoch 'goes without saying' until it no longer is the ultimate referent of that epoch. Only in withering and passing are epochal principles intelligible. What is more, the very claim about epochal principles as such is intelligible – by the same argument – only on the condition that history has ceased to be epochal and, therefore, that epochal principles no longer function to 'hold together' an epoch. We are, on Schürmann's account, able to think, for the first time,

---

[13] The German here means not only a going away but a marking of that going away. It is as a 'waving goodbye', or a 'taking one's leave' and not a mere 'slipping away unnoticed'.
[14] This is what Schürmann calls the 'hypothesis of closure' (Schürmann 1987: 33–43).
[15] In his final work, *Des hégémonies brises* (*Broken Hegemonies*), Schürmann shifts from speaking of 'principles' to speaking of 'hegemonic fantasms'. We will discuss this more fully below.

anarchically, without *arche*, i.e., without epochal principles. Yet even though we are able to be outside epochal history, it is nonetheless the case, for Schürmann, that history is still epochal and its epochs are determined by principles.

Towards a Critical History: On Critique and Rescue

How can such an epochal history be critical? Given our observations in section 1, it would appear that a critical history would be opposed to an epochal one. This is because epochs seem to be as essential as (if not more essential than) the natural kinds we argued against in section 1. There, we exposed the difficulty of gathering the incredible diversity of medieval and Renaissance thinkers around a singular principle. That difficulty must be brought to bear on the notion of epochal history we investigated in section 2. However, there are important issues that the Heideggerian (and perhaps more so, the Schürmannian) notion of epochal history raises.

Epochal histories are organised around an ultimate referent as a principle. As Schürmann explains in *Broken Hegemonies*, an epoch is a fantasmic organisation instituted by language. The fantasm makes *e pluribus unum* (Schürmann 2003: 4–8). Schürmann goes on to note: 'A fantasm is hegemonic when an entire culture relies on it as if it provided that in the name of which one speaks and acts' (Schürmann 2003: 7). The hegemon, as the chief-represented, functions as the mechanism by which singulars are classified and inscribed in and under an authoritative norm. This norm determines what may appear during the epoch; it constitutes the phenomenality of phenomena.

We have raised arguments to show compelling reasons why periods in the history of philosophy can be understood only as the most gerrymandered of sets. Epochs, it would seem, claim too great a unity. In terms of the epoch at issue for this volume (medieval *and* Renaissance), Schürmann argues that the period speaks Latin. This epoch marks a break from its Greek-speaking predecessor. The hegemonic fantasm of the one (*hen*) organises the latter, nature (*natura*) the former (self-consciousness is then the fantasm that follows in the so-called 'Modern' epoch of the history of philosophy whose language is 'the vernacular').[16] Not only does the unity 'medieval *and* Renaissance' seem ill-fitted for a single epochal-sending of being, but even 'medieval' taken by itself names a multiplicity of trajectories, not all of which *speak Latin*. Is there a single hegemonic fantasm that makes the complex geographical, temporal, linguistic, cultural, religious and institutional landscape of medieval and Renaissance philosophy *e pluribus unum*?

The answer to these questions might be yes if we understand the *unum (e pluribus)* in terms of what Schürmann calls an ultimate referent rather than a supreme one. That is, to understand the conditions of the possibility under which an epoch is constituted, we must not turn to one appearing measure among others, but instead to a non-appearing measure. Schürmann explains:

> The history of hegemonic fantasms is the history of *ultimate* referents, which are, quite literally, 'nothing', *non-res*. A 'supreme' standard, in political economy, would be a standard commodity (gold, oil); an 'ultimate' standard would be the variable relation of goods to a factor that is itself variable. A fantasmic economy is a result of the variable relations among beings, large or small, to a referent that is itself diachronically variable; a relational referent that does not appear among beings. The doctrine of principles treats of these ultimate authorities. (Schürmann 2003: 8)

---

[16] While there might be difficulties surrounding Schürmann's identification of *natura* as the organising principle of medieval *and* Renaissance philosophy, we will argue presently that the epoch(s) might actually resist Schürmann's framework altogether.

For Schürmann, an epoch is best understood as an economy. An economy is a relation of things determined to have 'value', and that value allows movement of and relation between things. It also allows a circulation.

Following Marx, Schürmann sees that the value that is the condition of the possibility for exchange, i.e., the condition for the possibility of 'appearing' within that economy, only functions to the extent that it is outside of the exchange (i.e., the appearing) and circulation (i.e., relation) of value. In other words, corn and iron can only confront one another[17] if they are brought to appear *in a certain way*. What allows them to appear to one another is a third thing that is not part of the exchange. There is, therefore, a standard on the basis of which corn and iron can be seen as exchangeable. Corn and iron, on this example, appear to one another and also appear in an entire economy. That appearance, however, is based on a measure or standard. Yet that standard does not appear. It is a referent in that corn and iron both *refer back* to a 'non-thing' (because not appearing) that is their own condition for appearing. In this way, the referent (at this stage in the analogy, abstract labour power) brings around itself all other beings and makes them what they are. This referent is ultimate, according to Schürmann, if it is also variable. What Schürmann uncovers is that from *within* an epoch such a referent must 'go without saying' if it establishes the economy of the epoch. However, from the perspective of this *history of epochs*, the referent is itself variable, i.e., comes to be, withers and falls away. In its passing away, a principle becomes intelligible.

Critique retraces the process by which the unsaid of a given epoch, or its ultimate referent, is constituted. In this way, Schürmann goes some distance towards such a critical history of philosophy. As we will argue below, a critical history unearths how a multiplicity of disparate elements comes to be constituted as a set of factors belonging to a single 'economy' in the sense described above. On the way towards uncovering a critical history, we can ask: how does a multiplicity of disparate elements come to appear together under an unseen measure? How do they come to move together for a time around a centre that is no thing, but not nothing?

To answer these questions, the notion of 'apparatus' [*dispositif*] that Foucault uses to find the middle ground between an 'internal' and 'external' principle of gathering a period together seems a more fruitful approach to a critical history, while at the same time maintaining the insights of an epochal history.

> What I'm trying to pick out with this term [*dispositif*] is, firstly, a thoroughly heterogeneous ensemble consisting of discourses, institutions, architectural forms, regulatory decisions, laws, administrative measures, scientific statements, philosophical, moral and philanthropic propositions – in short, the said as much as the unsaid. Such are the elements of the apparatus [*dispositif*]. The apparatus [*dispositif*] itself is the system of relations that can be established between these elements. (Foucault 1980: 194)

We can note that, for Foucault, a *dispositif* is both heterogeneous and an 'ensemble'. In this sense, the 'unity' of an apparatus, a *dispositif*, arises not, as it were, internally, but emerges from the very relations that are established from the elements that belong to it. Second, the *dispositif* includes both explicit elements – the 'said' – and implicit elements – the 'unsaid'.

---

[17] Schürmann's 'economic' language calls to mind the argument that Marx makes in *Capital* that exchange value is the *Erscheinungsform* of a reality that is distinct from it. In other words, there are social conditions for the appearance of a use-value as commodity, conditions that are themselves historically variable. See Marx (1976: chapter 1).

From this perspective, the 'Middle Ages' as much as the 'Renaissance', and more so the conjunction of 'medieval and Renaissance philosophy' might be a 'system of relations' between elements that, of themselves, have no direct ontological or epistemological relation. Thinking epochs as other than essences or natural kinds, we must conceive of them as temporal ensembles of disparate elements. *For a time*, these disparate elements revolve around a common centre. As suggested above, this common centre is not one more being among others; it is not one more thing. Rather, this non-thing (*non-res*) is an ultimate referent in the sense that *for a time*, the disparate elements circle around it.

Perhaps the best image to capture an epochal ensemble that is a something, but not a what, is a hurricane. A hurricane is not a what, it possesses no stable centre or core. And yet, for a time, certain disparate elements move together around a centre that is not itself a thing. These elements move together for a time, until they are released from this ensemble into their own. Where a hurricane begins and ends, which elements are internal and which ones are external, cannot be decided by an absolute measure. Furthermore, only after the fact can the full trajectory of the hurricane, which bears a proper name (e.g., Andrew, Katrina, Irma), be understood. Even the best predictive models cannot accurately forecast its trajectory, speeds or point of impacts as it is happening. Given the total impact caused by the event that is a hurricane, it only seems right to baptise it with a proper name. And yet a proper name, usually applied to seemingly stable substances, here belies what is really a temporal ensemble. That is, *for a time* the disparate multiplicity moves together and reinforces the centre that is not itself a thing, but that is not nothing.

Relying on this image of a hurricane, we might say that epochal history unearths more than arbitrary, gerrymandered sets. The sets are not merely constituted by historians of philosophy *ex post facto*. Epochs, like hurricanes, are obviously something; they have real effects in the world and engage with the world around them in real time. But, epochs, again like hurricanes, are not essences or natural kinds. (Heidegger might overplay his hand at times in describing epochal history as a sending of being.) Epochs are not things with an essential nature, but ways in which an ensemble of things moves together for a time before it falls apart. The centre holds, not as a supreme something, but instead as an ultimate referent that is itself no thing.

As discussed above, a time or an age, that is, an epoch, can be defined in terms of interruptions or differences by which the epoch can be seen as a gathering force (or 'sending') around which disparate elements are positioned. Positioned beyond essences and/or natural kinds, on the one hand, and gerrymandered sets, on the other, *epochs* serve as the object of critical history. Critical history shows the conditions of the possibility under which several elements (some pre-existing, some generated along the way) come to hold together for a time around a centre that is no thing but not nothing, then such elements are gradually released into new ensembles or as free radicals.

Taken in abstraction, such elements may appear to be the same. For example, both Anselm and Descartes offer what Kant will later come to dub 'an ontological argument' for the existence of God. Likewise, both al-Ghazali and David Hume are sceptical about our ability to derive the necessity of cause and effect from observation of constant conjunction. And yet, either element (i.e., the Ontological Argument or Critique of Causation) must be properly understood within its context (i.e., temporal ensemble). One seeking to derive a standard logical argument from Anselm's *Proslogion* does violence to this text. Making a beeline to Chapter 2, while ignoring the preparatory remarks, misses the point. In a similar vein, to treat al-Ghazali's causal scepticism in purely epistemological or ontological terms, while bracketing his views on the divine attributes (in particular, the attribute of Power) or Ash'arite atomism, risks misunderstanding these rich arguments. A critical history unearths those conditions under which a seemingly similar element, such as the ones mentioned above, comes to hold around disparate epochal centres.

A critical history of philosophy emerges at what seems to be an impasse. If an epochal history of philosophy insists on a principle around which the thought of an epoch turns then, as we have argued, there is an insufficiency in that such a history cannot gather together all the philosophers of that epoch. Against this, the Foucauldian notion of a *dispositif* showed more promise in that it did not rely on a merely internal principle. This is because such a critical genealogy destabilises essences and shows that they emerge as contingent happenings, which nevertheless take hold and produce real effects in the world (Foucault 1977). Between an internal epochal principle and the mere relations among elements for which there is no principle, a critical history of philosophy intervenes.

A critical history of philosophy not only engages in critique but also in rescue (Adorno 1998: 34, 2001:19). That is, on the one hand, it shows the conditions of the possibility under which a certain epoch (or archive) is constituted. On the other, it also seeks to retrieve or repeat possibilities in the history of philosophy that have been obscured or covered over by a history that demands that each thinker is put in their 'place'. This seemingly rational demand, a demand that creates the 'history of philosophy', appears in multiples guises: it may appear as a certain 'grand' teleological narrative that leads from the past to the present; or it may appear as curatorial histories or historiographies (*Historie*, not *Geschichte*) that put everything back in place as it was; or it may appear as analytic histories of philosophy that go back to the past in order to mine it for hidden gems and resources that may prove valuable in the present.[18]

Rescue does not mean to justify, rewrite or revise a bygone past. Rather, rescue entails blasting through the reality of history as a solid-state object in order repeat a lost possibility that is obdurate against such presentism. Adorno explains: '[t]he means employed in negative dialectics for the penetration of its hardened objects is possibility – the possibility of which their reality has cheated the objects and which is nonetheless visible in each one' (Adorno 1973: 52, 2003: 62). Critical history rescues insofar as it retrieves or repeats a past possibility covered over in an ossified reality. Critical history must win back a possibility cheated historical objects by their reality. Reality is nothing but sedimented history and, as such, the spoils of the victors. A critical history, according to Adorno, penetrates this sedimented reality by means of possibility, opening up this history against what has actually become the case.

The role of possibility stands at the core of a critical history of philosophy. But we ought to be clear on what we mean here by 'possibility'. Otherwise, one might worry, with W. V. O. Quine, that possibility might overgrow into a Meinongian Jungle. *How can we tell apart the possible fat man at the door from the possible bald one? How can I distinguish my possible sister from my possible best friend?* Such an overgrown ontology seems to call for Ockham's razor to trim the fat (not to mix metaphors).

Critical rescue requires that we avoid rendering the fat of the 'possible' into the lean of the actual (or the real). This is because, as Marcuse shows in *One Dimensional Man*, such an exorcism (to invoke yet another metaphor) leads to ghosts. Marcuse begins the final section 'The Chance for Alternatives' by calling out the situation of contemporary analytic philosophy. 'The commitment of analytic philosophy to the mutilated reality of thought and speech shows

---

[18] It is interesting to note that in each of the cases we speak about here, a certain principle establishes an impermeable reality and, therefore, all of them share a feature with the Heideggerian/Schürmannian notion of epochal history.

forth strikingly in its treatment of *universals*' (Marcuse 1964: 203). Analytic philosophy remains haunted by the ghosts of those metaphysical problems it attempts to exorcise. The haunting occurs because logical and linguistic analysis, the staples of analytic reduction, cannot account for the full scale of meaning for the terms it attempts to eliminate: mind, will, self, good.

Marcuse goes on to argue that 'even in this battle of the ghosts, forces are called up which might bring the phony war to an end' (Marcuse 1964: 204). He explains that despite the best attempts of Gilbert Ryle or W. V. O. Quine to reductively translate such universal terms as 'nation', 'state', 'the British Constitution' to the particular entities from which they emerge, these attempts fail. He explains 'the way in which such things and people are organized, integrated, and administered operates *as* an entity different from its component parts – to such an extent that it can dispose of life and death, as in the case of the nation and the constitution' (Marcuse 1964: 205). A *real ghost* emerges as the specter haunting an unrealised set of possibilities.

Critical rescue entails showing that *there is more* in the abstract noun than merely the sum total of the quality: there is more in Beauty than in beautiful things; in Justice than in just things. Asking whether the *possible* bald man at the door is identical with the *possible* fat man at the door, à la Quine, misses the point entirely. Rather, Marcuse adds, 'The possibility of an entirely different societal organization of life has nothing in common with the "possibility" of a man with a green hat appearing in all doorways tomorrow' (Marcuse 1964: 216). Possibility, as obdurate, stands against that which reality/actuality as the imperfect state of current of affairs does not offer us. Without it, and without realism, how we can go beyond the present?

A critical history of philosophy, therefore, takes seriously what Schürmann calls the 'phenomenology of historical epochs' in that it sees how – to a certain extent – the history of philosophy in the West does move, historically, between periods in which thought seems organised by principles/fantasms that 'go without saying' and, therefore, remain unsaid. It attempts to bring the unsaid to a certain visibility. More than that, and countering the Heideggerian/Schürmannian tendency, it sees within an epoch the moments in which other possibilities were voiced, even if *sotto voce*. Such a critical history, therefore, works to uncover those unrealised possibilities and it does so by means of positioning thinkers and concepts in new constellations.

Bringing thinkers and concepts into new constellations is not a mode of explaining 'the history of philosophy' but, rather, a way of bringing to the fore what would otherwise remain invisible. In so doing, a critical history of philosophy attempts a certain *fidelity* that is other than 'what actually happened' and other than the gathering of 'facts' of a historicism. At its best, a critical history of philosophy will bear witness to the fragments, broken voices, excluded and 'peripheral' thinkers who also form the 'history of philosophy'.

Overview of the Volume

The chapters in this volume each take up various themes, trajectories, movements and thinkers in the medieval and Renaissance periods with a view towards what makes the periods living contributions to philosophy. They do this, sometimes explicitly, sometimes implicitly, with a hermeneutic framework that is critical in the ways we have exposed.

The essays in 'Part I Bodies/Pleasures: Embodiment, Affect and Forms of Life' engage in a rethinking of the range of issues relating to human life in its embodied condition. In fact, one of the reasons why these periods are 'skipped over' in this history of philosophy is the perceived 'denial of the flesh' that belongs to a Christian notion of sin and salvation or to various forms of Islamic ascetic practice. In cases where salvation also has to do with 'the resurrection of the flesh' (which is the case for some forms of Judaism, Christianity, and Islam) that redeemed flesh will, so the account goes, be perfected and freed from 'defect', 'desire', 'pleasure' and the need for sexual expression. In Chapter 1, Karmen MacKendrick challenges these notions in relation to Augustine of Hippo and the traditions upon which he is drawing. By tracing a path through Augustine's own intellectual development, MacKendrick not only unveils the role of matter and embodiment in the various late ancient schools with which Augustine engaged; she also begins a re-examination of his complex views on desire and delight in our embodied, intercorporeal state. Scott Williams recovers a way of thinking disability in the Middles Ages. In Chapter 2, he shows how medieval thinkers thought about disability and ability in relation to sin and salvation in the 'intersection' between medieval thought and contemporary theorists of disability. In Chapter 3, Lisa Mahoney uncovers a notion of creativity in the production of art in relation to its function. She shows that creativity often finds expression in the 'margins' of texts (literally) and other works of art. This creativity is an expression of the pleasure of creating but also visually aids the viewer to come to a religious or theological pleasure. Maggie Labinski engages in a rethinking of the status and role of women by looking at the education of women in Augustine, Peter Abelard and Thomas Aquinas. Through education, she is able to show the ways in which women were positioned in terms of intellect and the possibility of achieving knowledge of the truth. Finally, Chapter 5 looks at moral affects and the notion of sin by investigating the concept of shame. Daniel Dahlstrom argues that shame, particularly in Thomas Aquinas, is a complex emotion or passion that is at once individual and social, bodily and spiritual.

'Part II Soul and the World/Soul Beyond the World: Experience, Thought and Language' brings together chapters that discuss various modes by which we humans not only access ourselves and the world around us, but also seek an otherworldly transcendence. As these chapters show, medieval and Renaissance thinkers were attuned to both the possibilities for and limitations of what we might call access to truth. By what mechanisms do we humans know ourselves, the world and God? What are the limits of our cognitive and linguistic abilities, both in their natural conditions as well as their supernatural, or perfected, states?

In Chapter 6, Emmanuel Falque looks to the notion of experience developed in thinkers reflecting on monastic life. He develops this notion of experience in conversation with the philosophy of experience in contemporary phenomenological and hermeneutic thought and shows that the medieval understanding forces us to understand the fundamental unity of hermeneutics and phenomenology. In Chapter 7, Dermot Moran traces the dialectic between being and non-being in the medieval tradition of Neoplatonism. Neoplatonism in general, the chapter's primary representative of this tradition (that is, John Scottus Eriugena) in particular, devises an original approach to the question of God's nothingness in its attempt to think divine transcendence. Eriugena's *meontology* offers an insightful glimpse into the much-overlooked concept of nothingness in Western thought. Costantino Marmo engages the role of language as part of a broader medieval conception of semiotics. Unlike our narrower focus on philosophy of language – a focus that oftentimes influences our readings of medieval philosophy – Chapter 8 traces the development of a general semiotics throughout the Middle Ages. In Chapter 9, Alberto Martinengo explores the role of *ascesis* in medieval mysticism as a path for grounding identity. For medieval mystics, such as Meister Eckhart, ascesis functions as a process of granting being, an event rather than a thing. As an event, being is a being called to being and happens. It is not a certain type of thing (e.g., a substance). Martinengo shows how, despite a contested identity among scholars, Meister Eckhart's proto-evental conception of being carries much resonance for twentieth-century continental philosophy (e.g., Martin Heidegger, Reiner Schürmann, etc.). Peter Casarella rounds out this section by exploring the power of language with respect to the challenges of dialogue. Chapter 10 shows how Nicholas Cusanus derives 'an enigmatic' theory of dialogue through his speculation on the divine absolute. Amidst Cusanus's contested legacy, and in dialogue with such 'post-modern' thinkers as Gadamer, Derrida, Agamben and others,

Casarella argues that Cusanus's theory of dialogue offers a path to interrogate the excesses of modern rationalism.

Another way in which the medieval and Renaissance periods are occluded in our understanding of the history of philosophy is through the implicit notion that political theory, or any genuine understanding of politics, is either entirely absent or only sporadically present in less than systematic ways (Marsilius of Padua, Ockham, Machiavelli and Grotius). 'Real' political theory is often understood to begin in modernity with the rise of the social contract tradition. The chapters in 'Part III Politics/Community: Justice, Injustice and Power' recover the rich thinking of community and the body politic in the Middle Ages and Renaissance. In Chapter 11, Joshua Hayes investigates the tradition of cosmopolitan thought in medieval Islamic thought to show how thinkers in that tradition exposed the 'unity' of all humans as members of the community that results from a proper understanding of the cosmos. In Chapter 12, Jason Aleksander looks at the relation of the 'intellectual virtues' that are presented in Aristotle's *Nichomachean Ethics* (*techne*, *sophia*, *episteme*, *phronesis* and *nous*). Through Moses Maimonides and Dante, Aleksander shows how a rethinking of these virtues opens up a rethinking of the relation of religion/politics to philosophy. This thinking of both virtue and community are brought together in Chapter 13. Pascal Massie shows how the Franciscan insistence on poverty and the reaction against that insistence help to uncover a notion of property and dominion that challenges the human relation to things. An insistence on something such as poverty as both an ethical and a spiritual virtue/value can easily lead to a positing of a notion of a community that is not of this world or of this place. Georgios Steiris argues, in Chapter 14, that during the Renaissance there was both a renewed interest in the science of nature and a profusion of the production of utopias. He shows that there is a connection between the thinking of a utopia and the thinking of nature as a living whole. Finally, Chapter 15 shows the challenges to the notion of the human and the human community that were posed by the conquest of the Americas. Felipe Castañeda investigates the intense debate among (primarily) Spanish theologians and philosophers concerning the status of the indigenous people of the Americas. Casteñeda exposes the tension between a developing notion of (universal) natural rights and a duty to evangelise.

'Part IV Repetitions: Tradition and Historical Inheritance' situates the Middle Ages and Renaissance with respect to its past and future. How did these thinkers receive and transform the traditions they inherited? These traditions include both that of the oftentimes 'pagan' philosophy of the ancient world, as well as the various religious traditions in which the thinkers were situated. With respect to the future, we might ask: how have these epochs been received and transformed by thinkers who have come after them, including us? In other words, why go back to the Middle Ages and Renaissance when doing philosophy? Why not, as with Descartes, wash our hands of this heritage and start from scratch?

In Chapter 16, Idit Dobbs-Weinstein shows that what appears to be a 'gaping lacuna' in the philosophy of Gersonides, that is, that he did not produce a commentary on Aristotle's *Nichomachean Ethics*, is actually filled through a careful reading of his *Commentary on Ecclesiastes*. Gersonides's reception of the Aristotelian text is not straightforward and shows that Gersonides is writing between a materialist natural science and a modern ethics/politics. In Chapter 17, Wayne Hankey challenges dominant misconceptions of Platonic and Neoplatonic understandings of matter and the material world. He shows how despite these misconceptions, French philosophy of the last 150 years has been inspired by the radical incarnationalism of various Platonists and Neoplatonists. Mark Jordan uncovers a richer variety of 'medieval ethics' by rethinking the question in terms of its periodisation, language and cultural geography; the genres and methods of medieval ethics; and the topics and disciplines of medieval ethics. Chapter 18 provides three illustrations of 'etho-poetic projections' to expose the question:

how do I expect myself to be re-subjectivated by enquiring into the history of medieval ethics? Perhaps more than any other concept, difference has been the focus of twentieth-century 'continental' philosophy. In Chapter 19, Eleanor Kaufman traces the link between medieval and contemporary French treatments of difference. Bringing together Gilles Deleuze's scattered remarks on difference in medieval philosophy with Louis Althusser's less apparent, but no less important, treatment of the subject, she makes the case for the need to return to medieval philosophy and its robust thinking of difference.

References

Adorno, T. (1973). *Negative Dialectics*. Trans. E. B. Aston. New York: Continuum.
Adorno, T. (1998). *Metaphysik: Begriff und Probleme*. Nachgelassene Schriften: Vorlesungen, Vol. 1. Frankfurt: Suhrkamp.
Adorno, T. (2001). *Metaphysics: Concept and Problems*. Trans. E. Jephcott. Stanford: Stanford University Press.
Adorno, T. (2003). *Negative Dialektik*. Frankfurt: Suhrkamp Verlag.
Atlas Obscura (2019). 'The Relic of St. Antoninus' (n.d.). Retrieved 16 March 2019 from <https://www.atlasobscura.com/places/the-relic-of-st-antoninus-florence-italy>.
Cantor, N. (1991). *Inventing the Middle Ages: The Lives, Works, and Ideas of the Great Medievalists of the Twentieth Century*. New York: William Morrow and Company.
Deleuze, G. (1968). *Différence et Repetition*. Paris: Presses Universitaires de France.
Deleuze, G. (1994). *Difference and Repetition*. Trans. P. Patton. New York: Columbia University Press.
Foucault, M. (1977). 'Nietzsche, Genealogy, History'. Trans. D. F. Bouchard and S. Simon. In *Language, Counter-Memory, and Practice*, pp. 139–64. Ithaca: Cornell University Press.
Foucault, M. and C. Gordon (1980). *Power/Knowledge: Selected Interviews and Other Writings 1972–1977*. New York: Pantheon Books.
Gadamer, H.-G. (1991). *Truth and Method*. New York: Crossroad.
Haslanger, S. A. (2005). 'What are We Talking About? The Semantics and Politics of Social Kinds', *Hypatia*, 20/4: 10–26.
Heidegger, M. (1977). *Holzwege*. Ed. F.-W. von Hermann. Gesamtausgabe, Vol. 5. Frankfurt: Vittorio Klostermann.
Heidegger, M. (1997). *Vom Wesen der Wahrheit*. Gesamtausgabe, Vol. 34, abt. 2. Frankfurt: Vittorio Klostermann.
Heidegger, M. (1999). *Ontology: The Hermeneutics of Facticity*. Bloomington: Indiana University Press.
Heidegger, M. (2002). *The Essence of Truth: On Plato's Parable of the Cave Allegory and Theaetetus*. Trans. T. Sadler. London and New York: Continuum.
LaZella, A. (2019). *The Singular Voice of Being: John Duns Scotus and Ultimate Difference*. New York: Fordham University Press.
Lyotard, J.-F. (1979). *The Postmodern Condition: A Report on Knowledge*. Trans. G. Bennington and B. Massumi. Theory and History of Literature, Vol. 10. Minneapolis: University of Minnesota Press.
Marcuse, H. (1964). *One-Dimensional Man*. Boston, MA: Beacon Press.
Marx, K. (1976). *Capital*. Trans. B. Fowkes. Harmondsworth: Penguin Books.
Sancti Thomae De Aquino (1970). *Opera omnia iussu Leonis XIII P. M. edita, t. 22: Quaestiones disputatae de veritate*. Roma: Editori di San Tommaso, Vol. 1, Fascicula 2.
Schürmann, R. (1987). *Heidegger on Being and Acting: From Principles to Anarchy*. Bloomington: Indiana University Press.
Schürmann, R. (2003). *Broken Hegemonies*. Trans. R. Lilly. Bloomington: Indiana University Press.

Part I

Bodies/Pleasures: Embodiment, Affect and Forms of Life

1

Augustine of Hippo in Medieval and Contemporary Dialogues on Embodiment

Karmen MacKendrick

Few early Christian thinkers have had such lasting influence as Augustine of Hippo. Librarian Paul Schrodt's (2001: 169) remarks from 2001 are exemplary:

> It has often been remarked that the history of western philosophy can easily be construed as a series of 'footnotes' to Plato, for Plato's insights seem so rich that nearly every philosopher after him can be understood in terms of how his or her thoughts relate to the seminal insights of Plato. In a similar and somewhat oversimplified vein, we would state that the history of theology in the West can analogously be construed as a series of 'footnotes' or annotations to the articulated thoughts and theology of Augustine.[1]

Born in 354 in what is now Algeria, Augustine studied and taught rhetoric in Carthage, Rome and Milan, eventually returning to Algeria to serve as a bishop until his death in 430. Though Augustine's life unfolded within the Roman Empire, his thought developed in relation to both Roman and Hellenic philosophy, especially as the latter emerged from the vibrant philosophical exchanges in Alexandria during the preceding centuries. By the time that Augustine began his education, the intermixture of philosophical schools was thoroughgoing, though members of those various schools insisted all the more on their differences (Engberg-Pedersen 2010: 5).

Troels Engberg-Pedersen (2010: 1) sets up some of these antecedents, describing Alexandria as 'a place where dogmatic, nonskeptical Platonism began to develop into Middle Platonism' in the first centuries CE. He credits Eudorus of Alexandria (first century BCE), who added a Neopythagorean twist to the work of 'new Academician turned Stoic' Antiochus of Ascalon (130–69/68 BCE). Our knowledge of Antiochus's ideas comes largely through one of his pupils, the Roman orator Cicero (106–43 BCE), whose work first turned Augustine towards philosophy (Engberg-Pederson 2010: 2).[2] Among the schools, Platonism became the dominant philosophy even before Augustine's time, but by then it had thoroughly absorbed many other influences. The resulting eclectic Platonism is now labelled Neoplatonism, though those given the label simply understood themselves as faithful interpreters of Plato.

Augustine, for all the variety in his antecedents, is generally understood as a Neoplatonic Christian, an understanding that runs something like this: holding on to Platonism's unwavering

---

[1] Cf. (Helm 2004: 11). The comment on Plato is by Whitehead (1978: 39): 'The safest general characterization of European philosophy is that it consists of a series of footnotes to Plato.'
[2] Cicero writes glowingly of Antiochus (Cicero 1933: 91, 235).

dualism and conviction of the inferiority of the flesh and the senses, Augustine's Christianity imposes stringent standards of behaviour, condemning the body, disapproving of the pleasures of the flesh and any devotion to them, and demanding instead an austere devotion to God – but not *so* austere as to draw undue attention to embodiment (he even approves of marriage, though granting that it is not quite as good as virginity).[3] This hostile anti-carnality comes to typify so much of Christianity that Friedrich Nietzsche will put the hatred of pleasure and the flesh at the centre of his furious criticisms of Christians and their 'slave morality' (see Nietzsche 1988). Hostility to bodies is also read into the classical philosophies that influenced Augustine – Neoplatonism, but Stoicism as well, particularly as the Roman Stoics come to emphasise ascetic self-control. In other words, Augustine inherits a hatred of bodies and pleasure, intensifies it and passes it on to Christianity ever after.

This description has been debated in recent decades. In 2005, Margaret Miles (309) argues that it is 'caricatures and misconceptions of Augustine's teachings [that] have contributed to western societies in which all bodies – human and non-human – are the helpless victims of the joyless pursuit of sex, power, and possessions'. She has in mind theologians such as Uta Ranke-Heinemann (1990: 75, 78) who writes, 'The man who fused Christianity together with hatred of sex and pleasure into a systematic unity was the greatest of the Church Fathers, St. Augustine', who 'equat[es] pleasure with perdition'. Though arguing that Augustine turns from love to hatred of pleasure upon his conversion to Christianity, she includes 'Augustine, Thomas, Jerome, the Stoics, Philo', in 'the whole antipleasure tradition' (Ranke-Heinemann 1990: 82). Martha Nussbaum (1990: 365–91) too reads Augustine's ideal as dehumanised, an effort to reach the disembodied life of an angel.

For centuries, the view that Augustine rejected the body in favour of the soul seemed perfectly fine. But eventually even philosophers, abstract lot though we are, begin viewing bodies a little more positively. The result is that the image of Augustine's thinking as anti-corporeal and anti-hedonic remains, but the evaluation of it alters. Paul Helm ruefully comments,

> the tendency at present . . . is not so much to damn [Augustine] with faint praise as to damn him because he is thought to present a bloodless, passionless idea of the Christian life that is hyper-intellectual and that finds no proper place for the physical and, in particular, for the embodied. He is said to be a Platonist, a dualist, even a Manichean – even though he avowedly repudiated Manicheism. (Helm 2004: 11)

I suspect that Augustine's complex and contradictory views of bodies, in their very contrariness, actually tell us something that resists our urge for simplification. Let us see why these accusations matter.

Augustine as Manichaean

While studying rhetoric at Carthage, Augustine read Cicero's *Hortensius*, probably as a standard part of the curriculum. He declares that Cicero changed his life, turning him towards a love of philosophy and the search for truth. This search in turn led him to Manichaeaism, which he

---

[3] 'Therefore, marriage and fornication are not two evils, the second of which is worse; but marriage and continence are two goods, the second of which is better', '*Non ergo duo mala sunt coniubium et fornication, quorum alterum peius, sed duo bona sunt, conubium et continentia, quorum alterum est Melius . . . "De bono coniugalia"*' (Augustine 1955: §8).

embraced for the next nine years (Augustine 1991b: 3.4.7–8). Jason BeDuhn (2009: 1.31) notes that North African Manichaeaism 'looked more like a philosophical system than a religion – and that was an important part of its appeal'. Certainly this was part of its appeal for Augustine. Manichaean teachers, he writes, 'promised to make Christianity intelligible[;] . . . not to resort to superstitions that overawed the unsophisticated among the faithful, and . . . not [to] intimidate smaller fry. They vowed to . . . appeal to reason, pure and simple. Who would not be seduced by such promises?' (Augustine 2006 [1891]: 809–10). In fact, the faith's founder, Mani, claimed to establish his religion on a comprehensive, solid science, rather like L. Ron Hubbard (Kaufman 2012: 810).

Although claiming themselves to be Christian, the Manichaeans held that the world's creator was an evil demiurge, who fought with the good god of Light and imprisoned the immaterial soul in the inferior matter of the body. Rigorous asceticism was necessary to free the divine spark of the soul from the trap of flesh. They regarded the body of Christ as a pure appearance; the notion of a material or materialised god was absurd to them, and so too the notion of flesh that is itself good. Augustine was never a Manichaean of the innermost circle, which would have required him to be celibate, but he did take up more moderate ascetic practices, such as vegetarianism.

Augustine had many reasons for eventually leaving the Manichaeans. As Peter Iver Kaufman points out, the Manichaean elect sought followers and celebrity status, and attracted them charismatically – but they did not have particularly good answers to deep questions: 'They kept saying "truth, truth," and told me that they had much to reveal, yet there was no truth in them' (*et dicebant: 'veritas et veritas,' et multum eam dicibant mihi, et nusquam erat in eis, sed falsa loquebantur non de te tantum, qui vere veritas es . . .*) (Augustine 1991a: 3.6.10). Augustine was especially dismayed by the quarrelsomeness and low ethical standards among the elect, finding asceticism no match for arrogance and dishonesty.[4] The Manichaeans lacked not only answers but, perhaps more importantly, intellectual as well as personal humility, as Kaufman points out. The humility that Christianity values as a virtue (contrary to classical pride) is also essential to dialogue. Without it, dialectical discussion becomes one-sided lecture – and Augustine had been drawn to Manichaeism precisely for the conversations (Kaufman 2012: 810–11). He also valued the Socratic form of humility, claiming that the ability of humans to grasp truth is limited, and that God's unlimited truth is beyond our comprehension (see Augustine 2005; Plato 1966: 20d–e, 23a–b).

Augustine went on to write extensively against the Manichaeans, rejecting their claims that the created world is evil in favour of the claim by the God of Genesis that it is in fact 'very good'. Despite this, scholars sometimes wonder if his rejection was motivated by political expedience, as imperial Rome increasingly pursued and persecuted this suspiciously Persian faith (see BeDuhn 2009: 136; Kaufman 2012: 811). Or they suspect that he was unable to shake the Manichean influence entirely – that it appears in a turn away from physicality. Even when he insists that the body is neither evil nor a trap for the soul, Augustine may suggest that the soul is superior to the flesh, and that the latter presents numerous temptations (see Augustine 1933: 13.22). According to Judith Chelius Stark (2007: 22), 'He . . . wrestled to extirpate from his thinking the Manichaean position that claimed the material world and the human body were the sites of the evil force in the cosmos, attempting to overcome the good by entrapping it in matter.' BeDuhn (2009: 56) also argues that Augustine's inward turn, widely credited as a founding moment in the creation of subjectivity, is an echo of a Manichean concern with interiority, an interior construed as mind and not as flesh.

---

[4] This point is central in Kaufman.

Sceptical Interlude

In his disenchantment with Manichaeaism, Augustine, like the final members of Plato's Academy, turned to scepticism. The Academic Sceptics valued Plato's dialogical style but denied that it could lead to conclusion. Truth might exist, but it is beyond our knowing (in contrast, the earlier Pyrrhonian Sceptics had acknowledged that the claim that nothing was knowable with certainty was itself not certainly knowable). Academic scepticism appealed in turn to Cicero, and to Augustine, for its open-mindedness and flexibility, along with its insistence on holding positions on the basis of reason rather than emotion (see Cicero 1913: 2.7–8, 3.20; 1927: 1.8, 4.83, 5.33, 8.82; 1928: 1.36; 1933: 2.7–9, 2.65–6, 2.134; Augustine 1991a: 5.14). Given Augustine's rejection of Manichaeaism for its ungrounded and arrogant assertions, we can see the appeal of a dialogical, carefully uncertain philosophy.

The scepticism that appealed to Cicero and then Augustine, though, was less purely doubtful. At the end of the sceptical period of the Academy, Antiochus had moved towards a newly syncretic 'Middle Platonism'. Dialogical back-and-forth remained essential, but he felt that it was possible to recognise truth through a cognitive impression of the sort hypothesised by the Stoics.[5] He condemned Academic scepticism for its certainty about uncertainty, even as he valued its openness to new possibilities. Cicero followed Antiochus in his preference for this more limited scepticism, and Augustine followed Cicero similarly. It is not quite clear how deeply Augustine's own scepticism ran during this brief period. Like Cicero and Antiochus, he sought truth; like Socrates, he believed there are limits on our knowing it. His understanding of the reach for truth seems to be interpersonal even when it is written rather than spoken; his work has a strong sense of *address* even though it is not usually in dialogue form, as if he were teaching, or preaching, or praying.

Because of its insistence on both sides of any argument, scepticism provides us with no particular position on bodies or pleasures. Even among sceptics who thought that truth was ultimately knowable or findable, there was no consensus on these matters. Soon enough, however, Augustine was drawn again to a more decided position. Like Platonism, he moved on.

Augustine as Platonist

Throughout his philosophical pursuits, Augustine had been unimpressed with Christianity. Though his mother was a devoted Christian and his father a deathbed convert, Augustine (1991a: 3.5) considered Christian scriptures to be too much like a series of stories for children. But in Milan, perhaps under maternal influence, he heard sermons by the bishop Ambrose, whose Christianity was philosophically infused with a sophisticated Neoplatonism (Augustine 1991a: 7.9).[6] Intrigued, Augustine (Augustine 1991a: 8.2) turned to certain 'books of the Platonists' (*quosdam libros Platonicorum*), probably those of Plotinus and his student Porphyry.

---

[5] According to James Allen, much of our evidence about Antiochus comes from Cicero: 'He defended the veracity of the senses. He seems to have argued that in order even to possess a concept of the truth we must indisputably apprehend some truths in a way that is possible only if there are cognitive impressions (1933: 2.33). He argued that probable impressions are a wholly inadequate substitute for cognitive impressions (1933: 2.35–6), so that the charge that by abolishing the cognitive impression (as they think) the Academics deprive human beings of a basis for action stands (1933: 2.31, 33, 54, 62, 102–3, 110). And he argued that, in maintaining the skeptical position, the Academics must take themselves to know at least one thing, viz., that nothing can be known (1933: 2.28–9, 109)' (Allen 2018).

[6] See Little (1949: 70): 'Neoplatonism was christianised when Augustine, won over to the philosophy of Plotinus, recognized that he had been won over to all that had hitherto dismayed him in Christianity, and he became a Christian carrying with him his philosophy.'

Plotinus proposed a highly abstract cosmology, centred upon the One, a perfect principle of unity that overflows into the various levels of creation and to which creation flows back – though from the perspective of eternity, this circular 'flow' always *is*. The aim of living is to know that return, which is beyond the movement of time; the way to that knowledge is contemplation. Because the body too is an emanation from the One, it cannot be bad, but materiality is the most distant level of emanations, and its inferior pleasures are too ready a distraction from higher goods.

Despite its complexity, Neoplatonism is widely accused of rejecting physicality. Plotinus's anti-materialist reputation rests heavily on the interpretations of his work by his pupil Porphyry (1991: 1), who begins his brief 'Life of Plotinus' with the declaration, 'Plotinus . . . seemed ashamed of being in the body'. Plotinus did once describe his body as a 'prisonhouse', and wrote to a friend, 'Purify your soul from all undue hope and fear about earthly things, mortify the body, deny self – affections as well as appetites, and the inner eye will begin to exercise its clear and solemn vision' (Plotinus 1905: 101). That inner eye can finally surpass even reason to the revelatory experience of oneness, a realisation that the soul is essentially one with its source. It may be in response to Porphyry that Augustine (1991a: 7.9) writes in the *Confessions* of the many parallels he found between Platonic thought and various passages from John's Gospel – 'But that "the word was made flesh and dwelt among us" (John 1:13–14) I did not read there' (*sed quia verbum caro factus est et habitavit in nobis, non ibi legi*).

In a related criticism, despite Plotinus's unwavering emphasis on unity and union, Neoplatonism is widely regarded as the source of a dualism that turns against the body and proscribes its pleasures. Miles (1979: 50) notes Plotinus's practical and moderate attitude towards the body. But Ranke-Heinemann (1990: 81) presents the more common perspective:

> Plotinus combined Gnostic flight from the world and recognition of its futility with knowledge of the one true and good God . . . Augustine's ascetical Neoplatonic bent, his urge to break away from everything earthly and beloved on this earth, his turn toward the one true God was finally shifted to an escapist version of Christianity. . . .

Stark (2007: 22) presents a similar perspective:

> From the Platonists, he inherited the tendency to view the material world with a great deal of suspicion, at times moving perilously close to downright rejection . . . [H]e did not entirely escape the Platonic suspicion of matter, including, indeed especially, a suspicion of the human body. In appropriating Platonism, Augustine believed that human beings are composed of two entities, the soul and the body, and there is no question which one is to be preferred.

Even those who acknowledge some of Christianity's more positive influences may still believe that the Neoplatonic negatives in Augustine are strong. Laurie Jungling (2007: 324) argues, '[A]lthough he rescued the *created* body from the evils of the Manichaean and Platonic flesh, the order he arranged returned a *sinful* body to a place of suspicion and renunciation'. Augustine, we are given to understand, takes Platonic dualism into Christianity, however awkwardly it might seem to fit with either a divine incarnation or a perfect One, and urges his followers to devote themselves not to flesh or its senses or pleasures, but to a purely abstract creator God whom they are certain, nonetheless, to disappoint (Little 1949: 70–1) (see Jungling 2007: 317).[7]

---

[7] Several of the texts cited in Schrodt (2001: 171–5) make similar arguments, citing the Platonic and Plotinian influence.

All of this, however, ignores the powerful sense of unitive eros that is central to Platonism. A key text is Plato's *Symposium*, in which Socrates presents a speech at once fascinating and bewildering. He attributes it entirely to the fictive Diotima, though Plato drops enough hints for the reader to know that she too is Socrates's creation (see esp. Plato 1989: 305e, 212c). In finishing 'her' speech, Diotima takes us up a ladder of loves, beginning with the desire for a single beautiful body and culminating in an incomprehensible revelation of the Beautiful itself, a love beyond philosophy, which, she teases, Socrates may be unable to understand (see Plato 1989: 209e–210a).

This speech may be received as a lesson in leaving behind the worldly and the individual; each step on Diotima's ladder is less corporeal and more universal than the preceding – from one body to aesthetic appreciation, one soul to the laws of virtue, and so on. But it may also be that in each subsequent stage, the necessary previous step is enriched and transfigured rather than abandoned. Similarly, in the *Phaedrus*, Socrates declares that it is the desire for bodily beauty that first reminds our souls of the heavens, where beauty is at its most pure (Plato 1995: 250d–252c). And even in the letter in which he calls his own body a 'prisonhouse', Plotinus numbers among the ways to the 'experience' of the infinite 'the love of beauty which exalts the poet'. His descriptions of beauty in the *Enneads*, though they too end with an ascent to the unsayable, begin with musical harmony, bodily proportion and colour (Plotinus 1991: 1.6.1). For both Plato and the later Platonists, then, an ability to perceive and desire the world, to be astonished in 'the flash of a trembling glance' (*in ictu trepidantis aspectu*) (Augustine 1991a: 7.17) is not only a way towards the divine, but quite possibly essential for any progress in the divine direction.

Augustine too affirms the traces of divine beauty in the material world. He offers a particularly strong affirmation of this beauty just as he argues that God is not a material thing: having queried the earth, sea, wind, heavenly bodies and animals as to whether they are God, he asks them, 'Tell me of my God . . . And with a great voice they cried out: "he made us" (Ps. 99:3). My question was the attention I gave to them, and their response was their beauty' ('. . . *dicite mihi de deo meo, quod vos non estis, dicite mihi de illo aliquid'. et exclamaverunt voce magna : "ipse fecit nos". interrogatio mea intentio mea, et responsio eorum species eorum'*) (Augustine 1991a: 10.6). The beauty in the very form of things tells us God, not argumentatively, but astonishingly, like sight of the beautiful boy that unfurls the wings of Platonic remembrance or leads one up Diotima's revelatory ladder. For Augustine, the problem with our desire for material beauty is not that it is so intense, but that we stop short in it, instead of letting it draw us to a revelation of the unspeakable beauty of its maker, in dialogue with the world itself.

In an important distinction, for Platonists the world's beauty draws us towards remembrance of the heavens and earlier incarnations, while for Augustine it draws us in anticipation towards the final perfection of all flesh. Helm (2004: 19) writes, 'If . . . Augustine is a baptised Platonist, then one might expect that he would look forward to death because at the point of death, the soul leaves the body forever. But not a bit of it. In fact we find in Augustine a very strict understanding of the idea of the resurrection of the body . . . .' Miles (2005: 314) also highlights the importance of the resurrection of the body: 'Augustine said that Porphyry's advice to "flee all bodies" was intended as a direct rebuttal of the Christian teaching of the resurrection. Augustine's views largely repeat those of his Christian predecessors, but he went beyond scripture and earlier authors . . . .'

Prior to the Fall (the first occasion of sin), humans, on Augustine's analysis, enjoyed all sorts of bodily talents due to the perfect harmony of body and will; likewise, they enjoyed sex without being driven mad by desire. Even in our fallen state, bodies can do remarkable things (see Augustine 2003: Book 14). After the (bodily) resurrection, flesh will again be a site of pure enjoyment; the beauty of bodies will be such that it will cause the risen to sing praise to the creator. To be sure, there will be no sexual intercourse, which may make this joy appear suspiciously attenuated. Miles (2005: 309–12) points out, however, that this probably has to do with the lack of need for reproduction, and that if we accept the extension of sexuality beyond the genital, thinking instead of the intense pleasures of bodies, then this joy may be its own form of eros. The sense of the goodness of matter in harmony with will (and reason) reflects both Augustine's reading of Paul's claims for resurrection and yet another influence, that of Stoicism.

Augustine as Stoic

Scholars once argued that Augustine went through a Stoic stage, but it seems more likely that he encountered Stoic ideas in a less sequential way, through their influence on his many other sources (Colish 1985: 153). John Rist (1996: 13) argues that in addition to Stoic ethics, which Augustine would have known through his readings of Cicero and Seneca, Augustine knew something of Stoic physics and logic (see Augustine 1991a: 5.6). Augustine's use and knowledge of Stoicism is more diffuse and harder to locate than his use of Neoplatonic ideas, but scholars seem increasingly to be aware of its importance.

Stoicism changes over its long history, but its physics is always materialist and immanentist. God is Nature, the rational guiding principle within all that exists. Thus divinity can be found everywhere in nature; it is Nature itself (Long 1982: 36).[8] As Marcia Colish (1985: 152) points out, this high opinion of materiality might be more compatible than some modes of Neoplatonism with a creation whose God saw that it was very good.[9] Physics is most important in early Stoicism; by the time of the Roman Empire, the Stoic focus is more narrowly ethical. The strictness of Stoic ethics may be part of its appeal to Augustine, especially after his disappointment with the pettiness of the Manichaeans.

In keeping with a world formed by divine reason, Stoic ethics emphasises rational self-formation. It holds that emotions, especially negative emotions, are often based on poor judgements, confusing the truly valuable with the insignificant, and it emphasises attention to one's role in the social and natural system. Stoicism's popular reputation derives especially from its ideal of *apatheia*, imperturbability even in the face of trauma, the governance of reason over any emotion. While Augustine cannot be accused of taking an anti-materialist perspective from Stoicism, he can be, and is, seen as taking from it an undue love of reason over emotion (Helm 2004: 17).[10] This devalues body as well, putting reason in charge of the senses and refusing intense physical pleasures (Stark 2007: 23).[11] Augustine's suggestions that pre-lapsarian sex

---

[8] 'All things in the Stoic universe are combinations of god and matter, stones no less than men. But if god and matter in association fail to tell us what is human about persons, that is no cause for immediate alarm. The Stoic god, in its constant conjunction with matter, can make rational beings as well as stones.'
[9] '[H]is Neoplatonism, for all its force, was colored by Augustine's anti-Manichaean need to declare that the material creation is good and that it has been redeemed by Christ, a position that he often calls upon Stoicism to reinforce'.
[10] 'One indirect way in which Augustine's allegedly low view of the body and its functions is reckoned to show itself is in the claim that he thought that the Christian's duty was the cultivation of a Stoic-like freedom from emotion.' As Helm points out, this is a misapprehension (ibid.).
[11] 'Augustine was convinced that the senses should be under the direction of reason'.

never escaped wilful control, and heavenly sex does not exist, raise these suspicions. In a highly Stoic description, Jungling (2007: 323–4) argues,

> one might say that for Augustine, order itself rather than sexuality represented the ultimate erotic pleasure . . . This was an order created by a rational God who loved not with human emotion but with an ordered will . . . And because this order was perceived first with the external senses, the physical world became the criterion for understanding the order and thus God's love. Order, centered on proper use of the material world, was Augustine's ultimate criterion for defining and structuring all relational love, including sexual love.

Thus, even a view so positive towards matter can read as constraint. But in a world that is formed by divinity, whether or not so immanently as in Stoicism, the sense of joy seems to burst as much as to bind.

When considering Stoic doctrines, it is important to remember that ancient Stoicism is less a purely intellectual pastime than a way of life. John Sellars (2009: 33) points out the Socratic origin of this view: 'In antiquity philosophy was often conceived as something that would transform an individual's way of life (*bios*) . . . Throughout the *Apology* it is repeatedly made clear that Socrates' principle concern is not with argument or definition or rational understanding, but rather with life (*bios*).' Pierre Hadot (2009: 35) begins his exploration of philosophy as a way of life in what he calls 'the spiritual exercises' of Plotinus as well as those of Stoic emperor Marcus Aurelius. But he adds: 'In ancient philosophical sources the idea of an art of living is primarily associated with the Stoics.' In the third century CE, Sextus Empiricus writes, 'the Stoics say straight out the practical wisdom, which is knowledge of things which are good and bad and neither, is an art relating to life' (Sellars 2009: 55, citing Sextus Empiricus 1949: 11.170).

The focus on rationality as emotionally repressive misses the important materially positive aspects of both Stoicism and Augustinianism. Reason is not something distinct from and repressive of the flesh; it is a principle of nature itself and is divine. Rational joy is joy nonetheless. For all its macho reputation, Stoicism is perhaps the pre-eminently relational philosophy; its ethical stance is coherent with its cosmology of systematic interconnectedness among all things.

Augustine the Misogynist

From all of these influences, then, Augustine is widely regarded as having gathered an anti-corporeal, indeed anti-material, and anti-hedonic ethical and metaphysical view, though I hope already to have shown that this requires some lazy reading. Some of the strongest condemnations and some of the most vivid changes have appeared in feminist theorising about Augustine. Simone de Beauvoir (1972: 11) already writes in 1949, 'the authority of St. Augustine . . . is called on' to claim that 'the wife is an animal neither reliable nor stable' and must be under her husband's control. In 1976, Margaret Farley (1976: 186) lists Augustine among her 'sources of Christian misogyny', who are 'entrenched in sophisticated theologies of original sin, in anthropological theories of higher and lower nature, of mind and body, rationality and desire . . .'.

Though there remain exceptions, these views gradually gain complexity. By 1989, though noting that it 'is usually the case in feminist theology' that 'blame for the scapegoating of women for sexual sin is fairly laid at Augustine's door' (Grey 1989: 480), Mary Grey (1989: 487) argues for a more nuanced view, and suggests that Augustine would not have been happy with the more repressive aspects of his legacy. In 2007, Jane Duran (2007: 665–6) both insists on 'the masculinist nature of the Platonic and Plotinistic thought' that influenced Augustine and argues that he can give us tools for feminist thinking.

Among attentive scholars, particularly those less inclined to analytic philosophical methods, matters continue to improve for Augustine's reputation. By 2015, Elizabeth Johnson (2015: 152) can offer a reading that draws on Augustine to bring together feminist and ecological concerns:

> Can the truth of incarnation be communicated using Wisdom/Sophia language, which is grammatically and imaginatively feminine? Augustine, for one, thought so. Writing of Christ being sent into the world, he did not hesitate to say of divine *Sapientia:* 'But she is sent in one way that she may be with human beings; and she has been sent in another way that she herself might be a human being.' In other words, Jesus Christ is the human being Sophia became. Unless something in line with this gender-inclusive view can be achieved, the notion of deep incarnation will but project an unjust view of male predominance into the whole universe. (citing Augustine 2012: 4.20.27)

Here the identification of woman with earth or earthiness takes a complex and lovely theological turn on Augustinian grounds. Turning us again towards Augustine's anticipation of risen bodies, Margaret Miles (2005: 315, citing Augustine 2003: 22.17) similarly emphasises the sustained differences in perfected flesh: 'His mature writings emphasised repeatedly and in detail the continuity – the concrete fleshiness – of women's and men's present and resurrected bodies.' Augustine's views may even offer 'the possibility of beginning to dismantle attitudes toward bodies that continue to fund economic injustice, ecological irresponsibility, and oppression based on race, class, and sexual orientation' (Miles 2005: 308).

Joyful Bodies

To think more carefully about the differences among bodies, we may return our attention to the future, where bodies are perfect. Miles points out that resurrected bodies, having no needs, have no 'use' for the world; they can and do purely enjoy it.[12] And there is actually a model for that enjoyment in our lives already – the very beauty that reveals God to Augustine, the One to Plotinus, Nature's ordered perfection to the Stoics. In *City of God*, Augustine (Augustine 2003:22.29, 22.30, citing 1 Corinthians 15:28) summarises:

> It will not be as now, when the invisible realities of God are apprehended and observed through the material things of his creation, and are partially apprehended by means of a puzzling reflection in a mirror ... He will be seen in every body by means of bodies, wherever the eyes of the spiritual body are directed with their penetrating gaze. The saints' spiritual bodies will see God 'wherever we turn our eyes,' for 'God will be all in all'. (We see God *quam rerum corporalium species, quam per oculos cernimus corporals*, as *omnia in omnibus.*)

It is not that one body will be wandering among the other bodies, and *that one* will be identifiable as God, but that the divinity that bodies reveal to us will appear, not on rare and uncertain occasions, but always. 'The "miraculous loveliness" of the world, he said, causes wonder,

---

[12] On the distinction between use and enjoyment see particularly Augustine (2005: 1.3–5).

astonishment, and pleasure. The beauty presently visible is permanent, whereas utility applies only to the present . . .' (Miles 2005: 317). That is, in our present bodily state, it is joy at beauty, not grim disincarnation, that anticipates for us a life immersed in divinity.

Though sexual intercourse will not be part of this life, sexed bodies will – bodies will lose none of their parts. Rather than serving the useful purpose of reproduction, these bodies, genitalia and all, will serve as the impetus to songs of praise, simply through enjoyment of their beauty (Augustine 2003: 22.17). Hadot's description of the *Confessions* is relevant here; its intent, he says, is 'to sing the work of God in the world and in humans' (Hadot 2009: 64). Unlike our current enjoyment, the heavenly version will never give way to boredom or distraction. But even our current enjoyment is amazing, as Miles points out, 'The continuity between present and resurrection bodies was based on the astounding miracle of present bodies' (Miles 2005: 321, citing Augustine 2003: 22.24).

The sense of eros is here, with its astonishment and delight; it is not reproductive nor even genital, but rather visual and tactile, sonorous in the outburst of joy, resonant across bodies rather than contained within subjects. Miles (2005: 322, citing Augustine 2012: 9.3.3; and Miles 1983: 127) calls it a 'distributed sexuality', distributed across both a body's senses and places and the multiplicity of bodies. The life Augustine sees as heavenly is an intensification of the joys of present, complex, multiple bodies.

Oddly Bounded Bodies

The multiplicity is stranger than it might seem, and the boundaries of these bodies less certain. God 'will be seen in every body by means of bodies, wherever the eyes of the spiritual body are directed with their penetrating gaze' (*Deus . . . uideatur et per corpora in omni corpore, quocumque fuerint spiritalis corporis oculi acie perueniente directi*) (Augustine 2003: 22:29).[13] The idea of the gaze as penetrating evokes early optical theory, in which visual rays stream from both perceiver and perceived. Though this no longer fits our views of physics, it retains some experiential validity. Maxine Sheets-Johnstone writes, 'The natural power of optics is not strictly a *visual* lure; whatever attracts us visually or whatever we long to see is not purely a visual datum but something that encompasses or spills over into other sense modalities, most specifically, *touch*' (Miles 2005: 323, citing Sheets-Johnstone 1994: 28). For Sheets-Johnstone, what we might think of as intersubjectivity becomes *intercorporeality*; 'social relations are always intercorporeal relations . . . meanings engendered and/or articulated by living bodies'. As Miles (2005: 313–14, citing Sheets-Johnstone 1994: 57, 329) explains, 'The first task of intercorporeality is "reflecting on what it is like to be that other body . . . educating ourselves in the deepest possible sense on what it is to be a human body".' Among risen bodies, Augustine argues, 'Mutual recognition will occur . . . "not just because they see faces" but by "a deeper kind of knowledge"' (Miles 2005: 323). Bodies enter one another by means of vision.

To take up and go beyond Miles's arguments, the risen body is uncontainable, indeed excessive, in its own right as well. Augustine (2003: 22.12–20) worries about what happens to the cut nails or hair, the shed skin cells, and decides that all are reincorporated into the risen body; matter that was ever yours is always yours. But far from locking in 'mineness', this means that bodily boundaries are made even more uncertain: we share matter throughout our lives, from the immediacy of mother's milk to the slow absorption of a corpse's minerals into an edible plant.

---

[13] As cited in Miles (2005: 322).

Augustine's own descriptions multiply and enlarge. Bodies might all be very big (with their reincorporated matter). He offers multiple possibilities for the age of resurrected bodies: they might be at some ideal age; they might be the age they were at death. For those who died in childhood, perhaps age will be added on, so that the body is able to attain its perfection (Augustine 2003: 22.14–18). Wanting to describe the range of abilities that will be possible when the will and the flesh are no longer at odds, he turns again to our present bodies, as we have seen, apparently unable to stop himself from multiplying the list of examples for both ordinary and saintly flesh (Augustine 2005: 14.24, 22.24). As this overspilling prose suggests, the body that, through its senses, offers us in the world a model of perfect divine joy is also the body that is itself written. Here, somewhat surprisingly, Augustine appears at his most feminist.

Bodily Speech

The multiplicity and overflow of Augustine's language about bodies mirrors those bodies themselves. Not all readers delight in this. Hadot (2009: 59) remarks, 'I have always been struck by the fact that the historians say . . . "Saint Augustine writes poorly".' His language, that is, does not follow logical orderliness. He interrupts himself, perhaps to exhort God or to mention one more amazing bodily skill. He returns to themes without resolution – the location of God, the structure of time, the proper objects of love. He shrugs off argumentative precision – 'Why not rather say both', he writes of scriptural interpretation, 'if both are true?' (. . . *cur non utrumque potius, si utrumque verum est* . . .) (Augustine 1991a: 12.31).

George Lawless notes that Augustine often seems to be quite intentional in his ambiguity: 'He oscillates by coming down on both sides of the binomial at the same time, or at different times depending upon the particular context' (Stark 2007: 175, citing Lawless 1990: 175). Lawless (1990: 175, as cited in Stark 2007: 24) notes the importance of recognising the 'antinomies' of Greek and Roman thought, in order to avoid the 'impression that Augustine's reasoning is partial, biased and one-sided'. Certainly, some of Augustine's apparent inconsistency has to do with his own philosophical development over the many decades during which he wrote, and some, undoubtedly, he simply overlooked – it was not so easy then to review copies of one's earlier files. But could some of it have an intentional value, and might this say anything to us about the flesh? And why come down on both sides at all? After all, Augustine was clearly not one to shy away from controversy, nor from correction of his own earlier views. In this concluding section, I wish to raise the possibility that there is something fruitful in Augustine's irresolvable comments on bodies and their pleasures.

We may begin with a return to feminist thought. Augustine can scarcely be part of what Hélène Cixous (1976: 882) characterises as 'the unifying, regulating history that homogenises and channels forces, herding contradictions into a single battlefield'. His prose is rarely 'boring in its pointedness and singularity' (Tong 2009: 276). These characterisations of a dominant written style as orderly, logical and masculine come from Cixous's work describing *écriture féminine*, women's writing, a term generally used in the French because it originates in French feminism of the 1970s.

Even as we are happily becoming more open to shifts, ambiguities and multiplicities in gendering, I am not going to try to claim that Augustine was a woman. For some of these feminist writers, however, the feminine in writing need not come only from women writers. As Cixous (1976: 879) notes, there are and have been men who write in this way, 'failures' within 'the phallocentric tradition', of which she writes, 'Nearly the entire history of writing is confounded with the history of reason, of which it is at once the effect, the support, and one of the privileged alibis.' These failures may seek instead 'what cannot be represented' (Kristeva 1974: 21).[14] They may write 'badly'.

Writing that happily says 'both' is characterised by the multiplicity that also characterises women's bodies and pleasures. Claiming that masculine sexuality 'engender[s a] centralised body . . .', Cixous (1976: 889) adds, 'woman does not bring about the same regionalization which . . . is inscribed only within boundaries. Her libido is cosmic . . . .' Luce Irigaray (1985: 28) similarly declares, 'woman has sex organs more or less everywhere', indicating not a monstrous multiplication of genitalia but rather that a woman 'finds pleasure almost anywhere', rather than at a single bodily site. In connection to this erogenous multiplicity, women's language 'sets off in all directions leaving "him" unable to discern any coherence of meaning' (Irigaray 1985: 29). Multiple meanings and pleasures not only create language 'somewhat mad from the standpoint of reason' (Irigaray 1985: 29), and 'articulate the profusion of meanings that run through it in every direction' (Cixous 1976: 885), but even speak 'the language of 1,000 tongues which knows neither enclosure nor death' (Cixous 1976: 889).

In brief: this 'women's' writing is bodily, multiple, multiply pleasurable or polymorphously erotic and erogenous, sometimes contradictory, generally ambiguous or inconclusive. It opens onto possibility rather than foreclosing; it is of life rather than death. It speaks from many different bodies at once. It is remarkably like the prayer of the *Confessions*, or the singing risen bodies of the *City of God*, all bursting in song at the sight that shifts the bodies in and among one another. Such a language might sing forth from innumerable bodies and their mutually transparent beauty that tells the divine without darkness, or even madly from the world whose many beauties answer questions entirely by their forms.

Writing Relationally

We do not have to be quite so anachronistic to see a kind of feminist writing at work in Augustine. He may not inherit the carnality of his writing (the fleshiness of his words) from his intellectual ancestors, but he does inherit a strongly intersubjective style, one that combines with bodiliness to become, at least arguably, intercorporeal as well. Both Stoics and Platonists – certainly Plato himself – wrote dialogues, not always exclusively, but extensively (and Academic scepticism is dialogical almost by definition). When they did not, they often wrote letters, or essays dedicated to particular readers, or lectures – forms in which address and interchange are evident and important. Aristotle's works are almost entirely developed for his students (or even, when the works were lost, created out of their notes). Plotinus's *Enneads* read as if they were philosophical or mystical essays, but in fact he wrote in order to teach, at his students' request (see Hadot 2009: 52–5). Marcus Aurelius wrote to himself, addressing his exhortations to 'you' as he strove for Stoic calm in the midst of war. Seneca wrote both dialogues and letters as well as essays, and Cicero's *Hortensius*, which Augustine found so conversionary, is one of several dialogues that Cicero created. In fact, as Hadot (2009: 55) points out, 'The Latins, when they spoke of a philosophical writing, called it a *dialogue* . . .'.

Though Augustine is not primarily a writer of dialogues, he is known for keeping his audience in mind, for addressing with a seductive directness and urgency. Here we may turn again to Miles, whose 1992 reading of *Confessions*, titled *Desire and Delight*, marked a turning point

---

[14] 'By "woman" I mean that which cannot be represented, what is not said, what remains above and beyond nomenclatures and ideologies. There are certain "men" who are familiar with this phenomenon.' As cited in Barnes and Henessy (1995: 72).

in scholarship on Augustine. That reading emerges from an explicitly feminine and feminist perspective. Miles considers *Confessions* as a work both of and about pleasure, a work that reconsiders what pleasure itself is. Though he acknowledges that sensory pleasures can be dangerous, tempting one to attend to them in disregard of other pleasures or obligations, 'Augustine concludes his scrutiny of the dangerous pleasures of the senses by suggesting daringly that the pleasures of the physical senses can be contiguous with the spiritual senses. In fact, they provide the most accurate and precise analogy for the greatest pleasure, enjoyment of beauty itself' (Miles 1992: 104, citing Augustine 1991a: 10.27). Nor does Augustine dualistically separate body and soul; 'the body is not a metaphor for the psyche, but both are irreducibly interwoven' (Miles 1992: 104, 115). Miles has several criticisms of the *Confessions*, especially of the last four books, but the most influential aspect of *Desire and Delight* may be not simply that it is a feminist reading, but that it is a feminist *way* of reading – a very corporeal one. Miles (1992: 708) begins by outlining the sensuous circumstances of her reading:

> I went with three dear friends for a month to the blue-and-white Greek island of Paros, taking with me the *Confessions* in Latin. In the mornings I read Augustine excitedly, making copious notes, examining Augustine's language and grammar in detail. Afternoons, we went to a beach where I sat under a tree and pondered the morning's reading, sometimes writing pages of ideas I had about it, sometimes writing nothing, but letting ideas float in and out like the softly lapping Mediterranean – the same sea that touched Ostia and Hippo Regius.

She adds, 'Reading the *Confessions* is a pleasure: this is perhaps the most straightforward reading of my claim that it is a text of pleasure' (Miles 1992: 9). The pleasure is importantly interactive, and Miles notes that she must 'recognize the necessity of analyzing my side of the conversation I have had with Augustine's text' (Miles 1992: 10). Miles's 'conversation' may not be more 'right' than an argumentative reading, but it is perhaps closer to what Augustine had in mind. Particularly in the *Confessions*, he is well aware of both the interactivity and the physicality of reading. He notes his surprise at seeing Ambrose reading silently (Augustine 1991a: 6.3). His conversionary reading of Paul is motivated by a child's voice, telling him 'take and read' (*tolle, lege*). Upon that reading, his heart is filled with light (Augustine 1991a: 8.12).

This way of reading meets with some resistance. Reviewing *Desire and Delight* for the journal *Speculum*, Carole Straw (1993: 1176) writes, 'Broadly speaking, two trends inform contemporary religious studies. A historical school analyzes a work in its historical context, tracing the traditions that shaped it and coming to terms with previous scholarship on the subject.' By historians' standards, Augustine writes poorly. Straw continues,

> A more recent trend employs theories of modern literary criticism, particularly those of deconstruction. Casting doubt on the possibility of securing valid historical conclusions, this school exalts the primacy of the text as a timeless artistic creation. The possibility of multiple meanings, intended and unintended, is acknowledged, and priority is given to the commentator's own exegesis and reactions to the text. Professor Miles's 'new reading' of Augustine's *Confessions* represents this second trend. (Straw 1993: 1176–9)

More than a decade later, Aideen Hartney reviews *Feminist Interpretations of Augustine* by noting, 'most of the authors begin with the premise that Augustine's view of women as inferior has shaped Christian misogyny'. However, she continues, 'There are articles where the authors . . . attempt to prove that Augustine actually celebrated aspects of the feminine in his writings' (Hartney 2009: 693). These are characterised in a way remarkably like Straw's description of *Desire and Delight*: 'These discussions seem born out of a much more personal space than the literary theory or historical analysis . . . And while the urgency of their quest can be understood and empathised with, their argument seems less than convincing . . .' (Hartney 2009: 693). What may intrigue us here is the sense that these personal engagements make bad arguments. They make bad arguments, perhaps, because they make such good conversations, with the humility inherent in inconclusion.

And in this, they make good philosophy after all. Julia Annas writes of Plato, 'One of the advantages of the dialogue form, and one that Plato exploits to the full, is the ability to bring different kinds of philosophical consideration together in a single discussion, without raising the question of their relationship' (Annas 1997: 37). When Socrates speaks, we can also see the advantage of dialogue in being able to meet his listeners where they are, leading them gradually out their limited understanding (Annas 1997: 33–4). But as Annas (1997: 24) continues, 'The history of Platonic scholarship shows how the advantages of the dialogue form become disadvantages once philosophy becomes more professional and precise about its own concerns.' The benefit of dialogical conversation, its speech in many tongues of many possibilities, resists what philosophy becomes: 'But we find that . . . the people whom we call Middle Platonists start interpreting Plato as a philosopher with a system of positive doctrine (in the way that has been standard in the twentieth century)' (Annas 1997: 24). As John Dillon (Dillon 1985, as cited in Annas 1997: 24) puts it, '[N]o later Platonist . . . could be strictly "orthodox", since Plato does not leave a body of doctrine which can be simply adopted, but rather a series of guiding ideas, replete with loose ends and even contradictions, which require interpretation.' Hadot (2009: 151) remarks more broadly, 'It does not surprise me that there are rather contradictory positions in the ancient philosophers. For precisely, these are not systems.' Of Augustine specifically, he writes,

> Above all, the work, even if it is apparently theoretical and systematic, is written not so much to inform the reader of a doctrinal content but to form him, to make him traverse a certain itinerary in the course of which he will make spiritual progress. This procedure is clear in the works of Plotinus and Augustine, in which all the detours, starts and stops, and digressions of the work are formative elements. (Hadot 1995: 64)

This is writing meant to mutually form our flesh. Augustine's attitudes towards embodiment, with its trials and delights, are complex, and they develop over the course of his work. They come out of his own immersion within and meditations on traditions that are themselves complicated and occasionally contradictory. We simplify the contradictions out of preference for a systematicity that Augustine is unlikely to have sought. His are, in fact, attitudes that are characteristic of bodies once we think of them beyond containers for individual subjects: of intercorporeal, interconnected, sensual flesh that is multitudinous enough to contradict itself.

Bibliography

Allen, James (2018). 'Antiochus of Ascalon'. *Stanford Encyclopedia of Philosophy*: <https://plato.stanford.edu/entries/antiochus-ascalon/>.
Annas, Julia (1997). 'Is Plato a Stoic?'. *Méthexis*, 10: 23–38.
Augustine (1933). *The Measure of the Soul*. Trans. Francis E. Tourcher. Philadelphia: Peter Reilly Company. (Translated from *De quantite animae*, facing text in the same volume.)
Augustine (1955). 'The Good of Marriage'. In *Treatises on Marriage and Other Subjects*. Ed. Roy J. Deferrari, Washington, DC: Catholic University of America Press, pp. 5–54. (Translated from 'De bono coniugali et De sancta virginitate'. Ed. and trans. P. G. Walsh, Oxford: Oxford University Press, 2001.)

Augustine (1991a). *Confessions*. Trans. Henry Chadwick. Oxford: Oxford University Press.
Augustine (1991b), 'De Genesi Contra Manichaeos'. In *On Genesis: Two Books of Genesis Against the Manichees, and on the Literal Interpretation of Genesis, an Unfinished Book*. Washington, DC: Catholic University of America Press, pp. 47–90.
Augustine (2003). *City of God*. Trans. Henry Bettenson. New York: Penguin.
Augustine (2005). *On Christian Belief*. Trans. Edmund Hill, OP, Ray Kearney, Michael G. Campbell and Bruce Harbert. Hyde Park, NY: New City Press.
Augustine (2006 [1891]). *De utilitate credendi, De duabus animabus, Contra Fortunatum Manichaeum, Contra Adimantum, Contra epistulam fundamenti, Contra Faustum Manichaeum*. Corpus Scriptorum Ecclesiasticorum Latinorum, Vol. 25.1. Ed. J. Zycha. Vienna: Austrian Academy of Sciences Press.
Augustine (2010). *Revisions*. Trans. Roland Teske. Hyde Park, NY: New City Press. (Translated from *Retractationes*. The Fathers of the Church, Vol. 60, Catholic University of America Press, 1999.)
Augustine (2012). *The Trinity*. Trans. Edmund Hill. Hyde Park, NY: New City Press. (Translated from *De trinitate*. Opera Omnia S. Augustini, Vol. 3, Post Falls, ID: Mediatrix Press, 2015.)
Barnes, Gill Gorell and Sharon Henessy (1995). 'Reclaiming a Female Mind from the Experience of Child Sex Abuse: A Developing Conversation Between Writers and Editors'. In *Gender, Power, and Relationships*. Ed. Charlotte and Bebe Speed Burke. New York: Routledge, pp. 69–85.
Beauvoir, Simone de (1972). *The Second Sex*. Trans. H. M. Parshley. New York: Penguin Books.
BeDuhn, Jason (2009). *Augustine's Manichean Dilemma, Vol. 1: Conversion and Apostasy, 373–388 CE*. Philadelphia: University of Pennsylvania Press.
Brickhouse, Thomas and Nicholas D. Smith (1995). *Plato's Socrates*. Oxford: Oxford University Press.
Burnyeat, Myles (1997). 'Antipater and Self-Refutation'. In *Assent and Argument: Studies in Cicero's Academic Books*. Ed. B. Inwood and J. Mansfeld. Utrecht: Brill, pp. 277–310.
Cicero (1913). *On Duties*. Loeb Classical Library Vol. 30. Trans. Walter Miller. Cambridge, MA: Harvard University Press.
Cicero (1927). *Tusculan Disputations*. Trans. J. E. King. Cambridge, MA: Harvard University Press.
Cicero (1928). *On The Laws*. Loeb Classical Library Vol. 213. Trans. Clinton W. Keyes. Cambridge, MA: Harvard University Press.
Cicero (1933). *On the Nature of the Gods and Academica*. Trans. H. Rackha. Cambridge, MA: Harvard University Press.
Cixous, Hélène (1976). 'The Laugh of the Medusa'. *Signs*, 1/4: 875–93.
Colish, Marcia (1985). *The Stoic Tradition from Antiquity to the Early Middle Ages, Vol. 2: Stoicism in Christian Latin Thought Through the Sixth Century*. Leiden: Brill.
Dillon, John (1985). 'Orthodoxy and Eclecticism in Middle Platonism'. In *On and Off the Beaten Track: Studies in the History of Platonism*. Ed. T. G. Sinnige. Nijmegen, Netherlands: Nijmegen University Press, pp. 31–50.
Duran, Jane (2007). 'A Feminist Appraisal of Augustine'. *New Blackfriars*, 88: 665–77.
Engberg-Pedersen, Troels (2010). 'Setting the Scene: Stoicism and Platonism in the Transitional Period in Ancient Philosophy'. In *Stoicism in Early Christianity*. Ed. Tuomas Rasimus, Troels Engberg-Pedersen and Ismo Dunderberg. Grand Rapids: Baker Academic, pp. 1–14.
Farley, Margaret A. (1976). 'Sources of Sexual Inequality in the History of Christian Thought'. *The Journal of Religion*, 56/2: 162–76.
Foucault, Michel (1980). *The History of Sexuality, Volume 1: An Introduction*. Trans. Robert Hurely. New York: Vintage.
Grey, Mary (1989). 'Augustine and the Legacy of Guilt'. *New Blackfriars*, 70/832: 476–88.
Hadot, Pierre (1995). *Philosophy as a Way of Life: Spiritual Exercises from Socrates to Foucault*. Trans. Michael Chase. Oxford: Wiley-Blackwell.
Hadot, Pierre (2009). *The Present Alone is Our Happiness: Conversations with Jeannie Carlier and Arnold L. Davidson*. Trans. Marc Djaballah. Stanford: Stanford University Press.
Hartney, Aideen (2009). 'Review of Feminist Interpretations of Augustine'. *Journal of Theological Studies*, 60/2: 692–3.
Helm, Paul (2004). 'Will the Real Augustine Please Stand Up?' *Crux* 11/4: 11–21.

Irigaray, Luce (1985). *This Sex Which is Not One*. Trans. Catherine Porter with Carolyn Burke. Ithaca: Cornell University Press.
Johnson, Elizabeth A. (2015). 'Jesus and the Cosmos: Soundings in Deep Christology'. In *Incarnation: On the Scope and Depth of Christology*. Ed. Niels Henrik Gergersen. Minneapolis: Augsburg Fortress Press, pp. 133–56.
Jungling, Laurie A. (2007). 'Passionate Order: Order and Sexuality in Augustine's Theology'. *Word and World*, 27/3: 315–24.
Kaufman, Peter Iver (2012). 'Augustine on Manichaeaism and Charisma'. *Religions* 3: 808–16.
Kristeva, Julia (1974). 'La Femme, Ce N'est Jamais Ca'. *Tel Quel*, 59: 19–24.
Lawless, George (1990). 'Augustine and Human Embodiment'. In *Collectanea Augustiniana*. Ed. M. Lamberigts, B. Bruning and J. van Houtem. Louvain: Leuven University Press.
Little, Arthur, SJ (1949). 'Neoplatonism and the Growth of Christian Philosophy'. *Studies: An Irish Quarterly Review*, 38/149: 63–72.
Long, A. A. (1982). 'Soul and Body in Stoicism'. *Phronesis* 27/1: 34–57.
Miles, Margaret R. (1979). *Augustine on the Body*. Missoula, MT: Scholars Press.
Miles, Margaret R. (1983). 'Vision: The Eye of the Body and the Eye of the Mind in St. Augustine's De Trinitate and the *Confessions*'. *Journal of Religion* 63/22: 124–42.
Miles, Margaret R. (1992). *Desire and Delight: A New Reading of Augustine's Confessions*. New York: Crossroad Publishing.
Miles, Margaret R. (2005). 'Sex and the City (of God): Is Sex Forfeited or Fulfilled in Augustine's Resurrection of Body?' *Journal of the American Academy of Religion* 73/2: 307–27.
Nietzsche, Friedrich (1998). *On the Genealogy of Morality*. Trans. Maudemarie Clark and Alan J. Swensen. Indianapolis: Hackett Publishing.
Nussbaum, Martha (1990). *Love's Knowledge: Essays on Philosophy and Literature*. New York: Oxford University Press.
Plato (1966). *Apology*. Trans. Harold North Fowler. London: William Heinemann.
Plato (1989). *Symposium*. Trans. Alexander Nehemas and Paul Woodruff. Indianapolis: Hackett Publishing.
Plato (1995). *Phaedrus*. Trans. Alexander Nehemas and Paul Woodruff. Indianapolis: Hackett Publishing.
Plotinus (1905). 'Letter to Flaccus'. In *Cosmic Consciousness: A Study in the Evolution of the Human Mind*. Ed. Richard Maurice Bucke. Philadelphia: Innes and Sons, pp. 101–3.
Plotinus (1991). *Plotinus: The Enneads*. Trans. Stephen MacKenna. New York: Penguin Books.
Porphyry (1991). 'On the Life of Plotinus and the Arrangement of His Work'. In *Plotinus: The Enneads*. New York: Penguin Books, pp. cii–cxxv.
Ranke-Heinemann, Uta (1990). *Eunuchs for the Kingdom of Heaven: Women, Sexuality, and the Catholic Church*. Trans. Peter Heinegg. New York: Doubleday.
Rist, John (1996). *Augustine: Ancient Thought Baptized*. Cambridge: Cambridge University Press.
Schrodt, Paul (2001). 'Augustine in Recent Research'. *American Theological Library Association Summary* 55: 169–85.
Sellars, John (2009). *The Art of Living: The Stoics on the Nature and Function of Philosophy*. Bristol: Bristol Classical Press.
Seneca (1920). *Epistles 66-92*. Trans. Richard M. Gummere. Cambridge, MA: Harvard University Press.
Sextus Empiricus (1949). *Against Professors*. Trans. R. G. Bury. Cambridge, MA: Harvard University Press.
Sheets-Johnstone, Maxine (1994). *The Roots of Power: Animate Form and Gendered Bodies*. Chicago: Open Court.
Stark, Judith Chelius (2007). 'Introduction'. In *Feminist Interpretations of Augustine*. Ed. Judith Chelius Stark. University Park: Pennsylvania State University Press, pp. 1–45.
Straw, Carole (1993). 'Review of Margaret R. Miles, Desire and Delight'. *Speculum*, 68/4: 1176–78.
Thorsrud, Harald (2009). 'Cicero: Academic Skepticism'. <https://www.iep.utm.edu/cicero-a/>.
Tong, Rosemarie (2009). *Feminist Thought: A More Comprehensive Introduction*. Boulder: Westview Press.
Whitehead, Alfred North (1978). *Process and Reality*. New York: The Free Press.

2

Disability, Ableism and Anti-Ableism in Medieval Latin Philosophy and Theology

Scott M. Williams

Introduction

Contemporary scholars of medieval philosophy and theology have discussed many important topics that arise from the medieval texts. For example, *The Cambridge History of Medieval Philosophy* (2009, 2014), which runs to 1,218 pages, is divided into nine sections (Fundamentals, Logic and Language, Natural Philosophy, Soul and Knowledge, Will and Desire, Ethics, Political Philosophy, Metaphysics, and Theology) and consists of fifty-six chapters. In the 'Introduction', Robert Pasnau (2014: 3–6) reports his asking several scholars (of diverse backgrounds and interests) about what they believe are desiderata for future research in medieval philosophy. Many interesting and important research topics are identified, thirty in total. None of these, however, mentions or refers to disability. 'Disability' or any terms like it are not found. Still, Pasnau (2014: 7) concludes saying,

> Although few philosophers know very much about medieval philosophy, it is now widely recognized as fertile ground for historical inquiry. There is, then, no longer any need for special pleading regarding the merits of medieval philosophy; that case has been made by the labors of prior generations. All that remains for us is to go out and do that work.

A few scholars of medieval philosophy and theology have recently begun investigating the intersection between contemporary philosophy and theology of disability and medieval philosophy and theology. There are several reasons that this particular intersection is useful (henceforth, 'the Intersection'). Why *contemporary* philosophy and theology of disability? First, it draws attention to the relevant diverse phenomena and explananda that are referred to by the term 'disability'. Second, it provides conceptual frameworks for understanding the diverse phenomena and explananda that are called 'disability'. Third, it provides arguments for competing (moral) evaluations of 'disability' and for competing definitions of 'disability'. If a scholar of medieval philosophy or theology were to engage with the medieval texts without the various tools and concerns that are raised in contemporary philosophy and theology of disability, then the scholar's analysis of the medieval text(s) may be impoverished, underdeveloped or framed in ableist (discriminatory) ways without realising it. Consequently, contemporary philosophers and theologians of disability, who read what scholars of medieval philosophy and theology would publish, would not be given an accurate presentation of the issues (interpretive and evaluative) that arise from a close and attuned reading of the medieval texts. Scholars working in the Intersection suggest that familiarity with contemporary arguments and concerns can help the medieval scholar become a closer and more sophisticated reader of the medieval texts. One historian expresses it like this, 'The modern theories of disability do not work for the student of medieval history as such, but the conceptions are helpful in the attempts of detecting not only the paradigms of medieval society, but also the attitudes of the historians trying to reach them' (Kuuliala 2013: 3). When a scholar working at the Intersection is mindful of various models of disability, he or she is better situated to understand the relevant medieval texts and their implications; this sort of engagement reveals medieval philosophical and theological texts to have rich and nuanced things to say about what we call 'disability'. As I see it, there are two general hermeneutical tasks. First, there is the goal of understanding the medieval texts. Second, some scholars working at the Intersection may wish to use medieval texts in order to construct a new theory or to inform our own practices (ecclesial, moral, social or political). In some cases, one may use implications from a medieval text that the medieval author did not articulate, develop or discuss. If the former task is understanding (or the pursuit of the medieval text's meaning), then the latter might be called overstanding (a reader's pursuit of the text's significance for the reader's interests) (see Vanhoozer 1998: 263).

With regard to disability studies, scholars of medieval philosophy and theology are, by and large, behind scholars of medieval history, literature and law (see Walker Bynum 1995; Metzler 2006, 2013, 2016; Wheatley 2013; Kuuliala 2016). There has been a growing field within Disability Studies that looks to the medieval worlds for understanding how 'disability' was conceptualised, evaluated, how human beings with disabilities were interpreted and treated, and how medieval beliefs and practices influenced later periods. It is time for scholars of medieval philosophy and theology to contribute. Fortunately, a few have begun this work. Part I below surveys discussions in contemporary philosophy and theology that are commonly referred to, and used, by scholars of medieval philosophy and theology working at the Intersection. Part II surveys recent examples from work in the Intersection on the theme of the conflation of disability and sin. Part III is on Disability and the Sacraments. Part IV is on Causal Explanations of Mental Disorder and Free Choice of the Will.

Part I: Contemporary Philosophy and Theology of Disability

What is meant by 'disability'? In the twentieth century there were two major rival answers to this question: the medical model and the social model. Each model arose out of specific historical circumstances. The medical model arose out of responses to veterans of World War I. With certain advances in medicine, soldiers who otherwise would have died came home after the war. But many of them came home missing arms or legs or had lost their vision or other sensory modalities. A general response to wounded veterans was to care for them by trying to heal or fix their wounded bodies so that they might regain (to an approximation) the lost functions. A term for this wide range of lost limbs and functions was 'disability'. These are disabled veterans who deserve their governments' interventions to try to fix or heal them. One assumption here is that one's disability is entirely a matter of one's *intrinsic* properties. So, a soldier who lost his legs might be given a wheelchair so that he can move around when he wished; this voluntary movement is only an approximation to functioning legs. Another assumption is that not having functioning legs is evaluated as always making a bad difference to one's life, no matter what else is going on in one's life. The medical model consists of these two claims: a definitional claim and an evaluative claim. A disability is defined with reference to one's intrinsic properties and a disability is evaluated as intrinsically bad.

By contrast, the social model arose out of the disability rights movements in the 1970s and 1980s (see Oliver 1990). Wheelchair users argued that their disability is not based on the status of whether they have functioning legs, but rather on the social conditions in which they find themselves. They claimed that the social conditions caused their disability, that is, building designs were the cause of their disability. One slogan was, 'Disabled by society, not by our bodies!' (Shakespeare and Watson 2001: 11). A building designed in such a way that one can access it only by climbing stairs is discriminatory because it excludes those who cannot access the building in that way. The assumption here is that the disability, that is inaccessible building designs, is bad and should be fixed. The disability is not located in an individual's body but rather in the social circumstances. The social model consists of these two claims: a definitional claim and an evaluative claim. A disability is defined with reference to one's social conditions, and a disability is evaluated as intrinsically bad – that is, social conditions that discriminate are bad and ought to be removed. There is another piece to the social model, namely that being a wheelchair user does not in itself make a bad difference to one's life; rather, it is the conjunction of being a wheelchair user plus discriminatory social conditions that is what makes a bad difference to one's life. The badness comes from this conjunction. Further, there was need to give a name for one's not having, for example, functioning legs. Consequently, some philosophers of disability distinguish 'impairment' and 'disability'. 'Impairment refers to a biological or physiological condition that entails the loss of physical, sensory, or cognitive function, and disability refers to an inability to perform a personal or socially necessary task because of that impairment or the societal reaction to it' (see Berger 2013: 6). So, while a wheelchair user has an impairment with regard to, for example, walking, he or she has a disability with regard to the personal or social expectation that he or she *ought to*, for example, climb stairs. Furthermore, those in the medical community have developed 'prosthetics' in order to enable an impaired individual to approximate the personally or socially expected function (see Berger 2013; Garland-Thompson 2013). A wheelchair is a prosthesis that assists an individual in moving oneself. A prosthetic leg may assist someone in walking or assist one in appearing to others to have two legs (and so pass as 'normal'). Likewise, if one has a mental disability and takes medication for it so that the individual can do personally or socially expected tasks, then the medication is a prosthesis. A prosthesis can remove a disability, even if it does not remove the impairment.[1]

Contemporary philosophers of disability have an ongoing debate about the definition of 'disability'; to name a few, there is a medical model, a social model, a welfare model (see Kahane and Savulescu 2009), modified social models (see Shakespeare and Watson 2001), a capability approach (see Terzi 2009; Nussbaum 2010), and an extensional account based on group solidarity (see Barnes 2016). It is significant how one defines 'disability' in part because of evaluative judgements that come along with one's proposed definition. An advocate of a medical model would negatively judge a wheelchair user and believe that one should have pity on, or feel sorry for, the wheelchair user. But suppose a wheelchair user lives a more or less happy life. The advocate of a medical model would believe that the individual's life remains suboptimal because the lack of use of one's legs is judged to make a bad difference to one's life no matter what. The wheelchair user may protest against such evaluations, 'My life is good! I have friends who are wheelchair users and our shared experiences have contributed to our happy lives. How dare you say that my lack of functioning legs makes my life worse!'[2] If the advocate of the medical model disbelieves or distrusts the testimony, then the question arises 'What is the basis of this disbelief or distrust?' Epistemologists have pointed out that such cases might be instances of epistemic injustice. The medical model advocate may try to justify his or her

---

[1] For a different account of the impairment/disability distinction, cf. Cross (2011).
[2] For discussion of 'adaptive preference' and the importance of first-person testimony, cf. Barnes (2009: 1–22).

negative evaluation by claiming that the wheelchair user has an adaptive preference, according to which an individual has a desire for something but because one cannot do or have that thing, then one lies to oneself by thinking 'I didn't really desire that thing anyway.' An advocate of the medical model would claim that wheelchair users lie to (or deceive) themselves in order to make the best out of a bad situation. But what is pernicious about assuming that another has an adaptive preference is that one ignores or denies the testimony of (for example) the wheelchair user as being a reliable source of information, all other things being equal. While adaptive preferences may happen in various cases, it is imperative that philosophers of disability attend to, and care about, the testimonies of those about whom they are theorising. A slogan in the disability community has been 'Nothing about us without us!' (see Barnes 2016: 183–4).

The social model has come under criticism in recent years because political advocates who used it downplayed individuals' experience of their own impairment(s). Philosophers of disability are paying closer attention to the testimony of individuals with impairments (and disabilities). In many cases, having an impairment is hard, frustrating or annoying (see Barnes 2014). The question arises: does this imply that being impaired in itself makes a bad difference to one's life? Philosophers of disability disagree. There are many things that are hard, frustrating or annoying, but we would not (and should not) claim that they are bad for someone. Some common examples are menstrual cramps, going through puberty, not being able to do some activity one wishes to do, and being able to run a four-minute mile. If it is right to say that some things that are hard, frustrating or annoying are not thereby bad-difference makers to one's overall life, then are impairments in the same category? Philosophers of disability disagree among themselves. Some contend that what I'm calling 'impairments' make a mere-difference to one's life, but others that they make a bad-difference to one's life – even assuming that social conditions are accommodating and non-disabling (see Barnes 2016: 54–77).

Having surveyed 'disability', 'impairment', 'prosthesis' and the two major rival models of disability, I turn to 'ableism'. Ableism is akin to racism, sexism and heterosexism. Ableism is a discriminatory belief or practice (whether interpersonal or systemic) against someone on the basis of their disability (or impairment) (see Berger 2013: 14). The social model activist would claim that disabling building designs are expressions of ableism – a discrimination against those who are not able to climb stairs. Ableism can be expressed in many ways. If one is ableist, then one might not believe that someone with a disability could be one's friend or potential romantic partner (see Berger 2013: 113–44). If one is ableist, one might laugh at someone with a disability because they look or act differently (see Berger 2013: 198–203). The key feature of ableism is that it is discrimination against someone with a disability (or impairment) because of the disability (or impairment).

Ableism in the modern world typically endorses a distinction between 'normal' and 'abnormal' human beings. In contemporary English we have the term 'normal' and, at least since the nineteenth century, some English speakers have said things like 'that is a normal human being' and 'that is an abnormal human being'. The term 'normal' has a descriptive feature and an evaluative feature. The descriptive feature is that there is some statistical average with regard to (for example) human beings, and that if an individual does not fall within the range of average human beings, then that individual is not 'normal'. The evaluative feature is that goodness is associated with being statistically average, and badness is associated with being below the statistical average. So when an ableist says, 'that human being is not normal', he or she is making a descriptive claim and an evaluative claim: 'that human being *is* different and *should not* be different'. Lennard Davis has pointed out that an exception had to be made in cases of individuals who are above average (for example, in IQ scores). These human beings differ from the statistical average but are not associated with badness. So, these are not called 'disabled' individuals, but rather something like 'geniuses'. To show this statistically, statisticians came up with quartiles to express the *value* that those below average should not be that way, and those who are average or above average are 'good' or 'okay' and should be that way (Davis 2013: 1–12). Davis argues that using 'normal' to express evaluative claims is ableist. This is easy enough to understand from a historical perspective because 'normality' was used in concert with social Darwinism to bring about political policies that promoted eugenics and oppression (for example, forced sterilisation, forced institutionalisation, exclusion from society and family, and stigmatisation), and in some cases mass murder (see Hubbard 2013; Feder Kittay 2016).

In order to work at the Intersection, the scholar of medieval philosophy and theology should be familiar with these contemporary discussions and arguments. One should understand (1) that there are competing definitions of 'disability' and the arguments for those definitions; (2) that there is a distinction between 'impairment' and 'disability'; (3) that there is debate about the moral status of disabilities, whether in themselves they make a good-difference,[3] bad-difference or mere-difference to one's life; (4) that there are problems with conflating disability and sin; (5) that there are problems with interpreting disability as 'virtuous suffering'; and (6) that appealing to what is 'normal' as a basis for settling a question is likely to be question begging. Points (1)–(6) are jointly vital for hermeneutically sophisticated engagements with texts in medieval philosophy and theology.

The term 'disability' is of recent coinage and (obviously) cannot be found in the medieval Latin texts. Nevertheless, the putative referents of this term can be found if we look for certain Latin terms (and how they are used in context). What Latin terms should scholars working at the Intersection look for? Miguel Romero (2012) has identified 'infirmitatis corporis' (for bodily 'disability') and 'amentia' (for mental 'disability'). Vesa Hirvonen (2006: 173) has identified several additional terms connected with mental disorder, 'alienatio', 'amentia', 'furia', 'insania', 'fatuitas' and 'phrenesis'. He says that, '"Amentia" and "insania" were general terms for madness. The other terms were, in principle, more specific, referring to different kinds of mental disorders, but even they were not often used with great precision.' Richard Cross (2017a: 318) adds that scholars should look for the term 'defectus' and investigate whether a certain use of it overlaps with how 'disability' or 'impairment' are used in contemporary discussions.

Part II: Conflation of Disability and Sin

What does it mean to say that one conflates disability and sin? It can be interpreted in more than one way. It can mean that disability as such is sinful or wrong, or that a disability is a punishment for one's having sinned or done something wrong (and so disability is a sign of one's sinning or wrongdoing), or it can mean both. Some call the conjunction of these the 'religio-moral' construction of disability (see Goodley 2011: 5–10; cross-reference Cross 2017a: 317). (See the discussion of Thomas Aquinas on original sin and disability below.)

Kristi Upson-Saia and Brian Brock have written on Augustine and disability and have located passages in which Augustine associates bodily wounds, scars or mental disorders with sin or badness. Upson-Saia reports that Augustine (and some Christian authors before him) worried about how human bodies in this life are corruptible but human bodies in the resurrection are incorruptible. The thought is that resurrected bodies will not have 'deformities'

---

[3] Berkman (2013: 81–96) contends that those who have profound intellectual disabilities and are baptised are icons of the heavenly life, whereas everyone else who is baptised is not. It seems that the former's cognitive impairment makes a good-difference, and the latter's lack of this cognitive impairment makes a bad-difference. I worry whether there is an implicit ableism at work in the sense of interpreting such individuals as more special than everyone else; it's a positive stigma of those who are special. For a brief discussion of the claim that an impaired human being is 'special', see Berger (2013: 93–4).

because they will be incorruptible. The assumption is that 'deformities' in this life are associated with one's being corruptible. In this vein, disabilities (physical and mental) are evaluated as intrinsically bad. Augustine had another reason to doubt whether resurrected bodies will have deformities: aesthetics. 'For Augustine, deformities and defects were troublesome not only because they were inconsistent with the incorruptibility that characterized the heavenly space, but also because they were unsightly and ugly' (Upson-Saia 2011: 100; cf. Berger 2013: 7). Augustine seemed to accept a traditional Greek aesthetic value by exclusively associating beauty with symmetry. Deformed and scarred bodies are not symmetrical, and so are not beautiful given this aesthetic value.

> Moreover, we might also assume that Augustine and his contemporaries were concerned with beauty of heavenly bodies because of the conventional link between aesthetics and virtue. Informed by physiognomy – the science of physical appearance – Greeks and Romans held that the disposition of the soul showed itself on the surface of the body through physical signs. It was possible, therefore, to interpret an individual's character and temperament purely from his or her physical appearance. According to physiognomic taxonomies, beauty and virtue were inextricably linked, so that one man's handsome, well-proportioned looks were evidence of his praiseworthy character, while another man's ugliness and deformities were proof of his depravity and immorality.
> [. . .] For these reasons, Augustine holds that heavenly bodies ought to be beautiful in keeping with the aesthetics of the heavenly space and as evidence of the perfected character and virtue of its saintly inhabitants. (Upson-Saia 2011: 101)

Augustine seems to have a bad-difference view of (what we call) disability when writing about resurrected saints. However, Augustine has more to say about wounded and scarred bodies of resurrected saints who were martyrs. In *City of God*, Augustine (1984: 1061–2) writes,

> Now we feel such extraordinary affection for the blessed martyrs in the kingdom of God we want to see on their bodies the scars of the wounds which they have suffered for Christ's name; and see them perhaps we shall. For in those wounds there will be no deformity, but only dignity, and the beauty of their valour will shine out, a beauty in the body and yet not of the body. And if the martyrs have had any limbs cut off, any parts removed, they will not lack those parts at the resurrection; for they have been told that 'not a hair of your head will perish'. But if it will be right that in that new age the marks of glorious wounds should remain in those immortal bodies, for all to see, then scars of the blows or the cuts will also be visible in places where limbs were hacked off, although the parts have not been lost, but restored. And so the defects which have thus been caused in the body will no longer be there, in that new life; and yet, to be sure, those proofs of valour are not to be accounted defects, or to be called by that name.[4]

---

[4] See Augustine (1955: 839, 66–80): 'Nescio quo autem modo sic afficimur amore martyrum beatorum, ut uelimus in illo regno in eorum corporibus uidere uulnerum cicatrices, quae pro Christi nomine pertulerunt; et fortasse uidebimus. Non enim deformitas in eis, sed dignitas erit, et quaedam, quamvis in corpore, non corporis, sed uirtutis pulchritudo fulgebit. Nec ideo tamen si aliqua martyribus amputata et ablata sunt membra, sine ipsis membris erunt in resurrectione mortuorum, quibus dictum est: *Capillus capitis uestri non peribit*. Sed si hoc decebit in illo nouo saeculo, ut indicia gloriosorum uulnerum in illa inmortali carne cernantur, ubi membra, ut praeciderentur, percussa uel secta sunt, ibi cicatrices, sed tamen eisdem membris redditis, non perditis, apparebunt. Quamuis itaque omnia quae acciderunt corpori uitia tunc non erunt, non sunt tamen deputanda uel appellanda uitia uirtutis indicia.'

Kristi Upson-Saia (2011: 94) comments on this passage saying,

> Augustine's evaluation of bodily deformities [. . .] deviates notably from his contemporaries. While he certainly agrees with the prevailing contempt for disabled bodies when he argues that *most* deformities are gross malformations that will need to be healed in the heavenly realm, Augustine surprisingly argues that other deformities will be a part of the perfect spiritual body, entirely worthy of the heavenly space. Thus, he calls into question the conventionally wholesale denigration of all bodily deformities and defects that pervaded the literature of his time.

The important point that Augustine makes is that bodily marks, scars, wounds, etc., can be signs of virtue, and if such is a sign of virtue, then it is aesthetically beautiful and we should expect to find these in (e.g.) the martyrs who are resurrected saints in heaven. By interpreting such bodily marks as signs of virtue, Augustine reframes the Greco-Roman way in which such marks are perceived. But are signs different than things? Should we interpret Augustine as suggesting that such marks are only *extrinsically* beautiful because of their relation to a state of affairs (e.g., one's virtuous actions, one's suffering physical harm, and linguistic representations of these) or that they are *intrinsically* beautiful? What, exactly, is a sign? Can a scarred or wounded body itself be a sign? In *On Christian Teaching*, Augustine (1996: 106–7) distinguishes things and signs, and then signs into sub-classes.[5] In the following passage he distinguishes 'natural signs' and 'conventional or given signs'.

> Among signs, then, some are natural, some conventional. Natural ones are those which have the effect of making something else known, without there being any desire or intention of signifying, as for example smoke signifying fire. It does not do this, after all, because it wishes to signify; but through our experience of things and our observation and memory, we know that fire is there, even if only smoke can be seen. And again, the [footprint] of a passing animal is this kind of sign; and the expression of an angry or sad person signifies his mood, even without the angry or sad person wishing to do so [. . .] Conventional or given signs, on the other hand, are those which living creatures gives one another in order to show, as far as they can, their moods and feelings, or to indicate whatever it may be they have sensed or understood. (Augustine 1996: 129)[6]

Some signs are 'natural' in the sense that they are things that automatically reference something else for those who are familiar with the thing because of previous experience of the thing. Some signs are 'conventional' in the sense that one creature intentionally uses a sign to communicate something to another creature. What kind of sign, then, is a wound or scar in a resurrected saint who is a martyr? It clearly must be a natural sign. This makes a difference to

---

[5] See Chapter 8 in this volume by Costantino Marmo.
[6] See Augustine (1962: 32, 12–33, 20, 33, 1–3): 'Signorum igitur alia sunt naturalia, alia data. Naturalia sunt, quae sine uoluntate atque ullo appetitu significandi praeter se aliquid aliud ex se cognosci faciunt, sicuti est fumus significans ignem. Non enim uolens significare id facit, sed rerum expertarum animaduersione et notatione cognoscitur ignem subesse, etiam si fumus solus appareat. Sed et uestigium transeuntis animantis ad hoc genus pertinet et uultus irati seu tristis affectionem animi significat etiam nulla eius uoluntate, qui aut iratus aut tristis est [. . .]. [. . .] Data uero signa sunt, quae sibi quaeque uiuentia inuicem dant ad demonstrandos, quantum possunt, motus animi sui uel sensa aut intellecta quaelibet.'

how we should interpret Augustine's association of beauty and valour with a wound or scar in a resurrected saint. If it is the linguistic or conventional representation of the wound or scar that is beautiful, then the wound or scar itself would not be beautiful but rather a linguistic expression about it would be beautiful. On this interpretation, the wound or scar would be extrinsically beautiful, that is, by its extrinsic relation to linguistic signs that reference it. But by taking the wound or scar to be a natural sign, we would find Augustine to be saying that the scar or wound itself is beautiful. The former interpretation downgrades the beauty of the wound or scar itself, and such an interpretation is consistent with ableism. But the latter interpretation has it that the wound or scar in itself is beautiful, or the wound or scar itself is a part of the saint's virtuous actions. This interpretation is consistent with anti-ableism.

Moreover, in writing about 'monstrous human births', Augustine (1984: 16, 8, cited in Brock 2009: 88) again suggests an anti-ableist view.

> For God is the Creator of all things: He Himself knows where and when anything should be, or should have been, created; and He knows how to weave the beauty of the whole out of the similarity and diversity of its parts. The man who cannot view the whole is offended by what he takes to be the deformity of a part; but this is because he does not know how it is to be adapted or related to the whole. We know of men who were born with more than five fingers or five toes. This is a trivial thing and not any great divergence from the norm. God forbid, however, that someone who does not know why the Creator has done what He has done should be foolish enough to suppose that God has in such cases erred in allotting the number of human fingers. So, then, even if a greater divergence should occur, He whose work no one may justly condemn knows what He has done.
>
> There is at Hippo Zaritus a man who has crescent-shaped feet with only two toes on each; and his hands are similar. If there were any race with these features, it would be added to our list of the curiosities and wonders of nature. But are we for this reason to deny that this man is descended from that one man who was created in the beginning?[7]

This passage suggests that 'divergences' among human beings should not automatically be interpreted as bad-differences. Rather, there is a beauty in each part of the whole human race. This suggests that beauty is to be associated with all 'divergences'. Moreover, Augustine claims that human beings with trivial or significantly different bodily configurations are of the same human family by virtue of common descent. According to Brian Brock (2009: 76), '[Augustine] suggests that what may look like a deformity may actually be an artefact of sinful inability to see God's working in all people to create a beautiful whole'. (Compare Augustine's position with John Locke who distrusts the fact that a child is born from a human parent as a basis for ascribing 'humanity' to that child.

---

[7] See Augustine (1955: 509, 31–46): 'Deus enim creator est omnium, qui ubi et quando creari quid oporteat uel oportuerit, ipse nouit, sciens uniuersitatis pulchritudinem quarum partium uel similitudine uel diuersitate contexat. Sed qui totum inspicere non potest, tamquam deformitate partis offenditur, quoniam cui congruat et quo referatur ignorat. Pluribus quam quinis digitis in manibus et pedibus nasci homines nouimus; et haec leuior est quam ulla distantia; sed tamen absit, ut quis ita desipiat, ut existimet in numero humanorum digitorum errasse Creatorem, quamuis nesciens cur hoc fecerit. Ita etsi maior diuersitas oriatur, scit ille quid, egerit, cuius opera iuste nemo reprehendit. Apud Hipponem Zaritum est homo quasi lunatas habens plantas et in eis binos tantummodo digitos, similes et manus. Si aliqua gens talis esset, illi curiosae atque mirabili adderetur historiae. Num igitur istum propter hoc negabimus ex illo uno, quia primus creatus est, esse propagatum?' Aquinas discusses the beauty of diversely configured bodies in *ST* I, 96, 3, ad 3.

Locke (1979: 454) writes, 'if several Men were to be asked, concerning some oddly-shaped Foetus, as soon as born, whether it were a Man, or no, 'tis past doubt, one should meet with different Answers'.) This passage reframes how we should interpret Augustine's saying that resurrected saints will be healed of their wounds and made 'perfect'.

Augustine's claim that all human beings are beautiful because they are created by God, in conjunction with his claim that resurrected martyrs will have wounds and scars as signs of their virtue, encourages us to be wary of asserting that Augustine expresses an ableist position when affirming the aesthetic value of symmetry. It is more accurate to suppose that Augustine says things that imply, or if not are at least consistent with, an anti-ableist view. To this extent we should be wary of supposing that Augustine conflates sin and disability. Augustine's texts do not easily fit with the 'religio-moral' construction of disability.

Another way into the theme of conflation of sin and disability by medieval theologians is by looking at their discussions of the consequences of original sin. According to Richard Cross (2017b: 76–7), Thomas Aquinas's interpretation of disability, or what Aquinas calls a *defectus*, necessarily is a punishment for original sin. For Aquinas,

> Adam's fall forfeited original justice, and thus the teleologically normative ordering of substance and powers that original justice secured. The lack of original justice, and thus the universal punitive absence of certain teleologically normative powers and activities, is inherited by Adam's progeny. On this view, then, all human beings descended from Adam are automatically guilty of original sin, and deserving of punishment. And Aquinas claims that the defects that are the automatic consequences of the loss of original justice are included among the relevant punishments. 'The removal of original justice has the character of a punishment. [. . .] Therefore also death and all the consequent bodily defects are particular punishments for original sin [. . .] ordered according to the justice of God who punishes.' [. . .] This view has, as a consequence, the claim that there could be no *pure* nature, by which I mean no nature lacking both original justice and punishment for sin. The only morally acceptable explanation for the absence of original justice is that this absence is a punishment for sin.[8]

Cross later points out three things about Aquinas's account of physical 'defect' as punishment for original sin. First, every human being is to some extent 'defective' or subject to teleological failure because of original sin. 'Teleological failure' implies that one's body is not perfectly subject to one's rational soul, and that one's rational soul is not perfectly subject to (or oriented towards) God as it ought to be. In short, all human beings are to some extent teleologically disordered as a punishment for original sin. In effect, Aquinas normalises human 'defects'; there is no contrast between 'normal' and 'abnormal' human beings – all (except for certain theological counter-examples) are 'defective'. Comparing this with what Lennard Davis has shown regarding the invention of a statistical norm for human beings and their various functions, we should note that there are no 'normal' human beings in contrast to 'abnormal' human beings. All human beings are subject to teleological failure (excluding certain theological counter-examples, e.g., Christ) (cf. Cross 2017a: 329–30).

Second, Aquinas allows for ameliorative responses to human suffering from various bodily 'defects' because they provide the opportunity for human beings to love their neighbour (cf. Aquinas 1981: II-II, 32, 3, ad 2; Romero 2002: 119–20; Cross 2017a: 337). Although 'defects'

---

[8] Also, see Cross (2017a: 332, note 70).

are punishments for original sin, for Aquinas this does not imply that we should not care for those who suffer from such 'defects'. This suggests, then, that disabilities are bad because they are punishments for original sin. Nevertheless, Aquinas holds that while 'defects' are punishments, they are not necessarily only punitive punishments; Aquinas allows that 'defects' can also be non-punitive (restorative) punishments (Cross 2017a: 335, note 78). So, a human being can look to God for help in response to their experience of their own bodily 'defect'. This can play a role in the process of one's conversion (by grace) towards reordering oneself to God.

Third, Aquinas needs to explain why there is a diversity (in kind and intensity) of human 'defects' if the ultimate cause of everyone's 'defects' is the same original sin. Aquinas's response is that once original justice (the right ordering of human body to soul and soul to God) left Adam and Eve, human bodies were 'left to themselves' to develop in diverse ways (see Aquinas 1981: I-II, 86, a. 4, ad. 1).[9]

In 'Duns Scotus on Disability: Teleology, Divine Willing, and Pure Nature', Richard Cross compares Duns Scotus to Thomas Aquinas with regard to disability, original sin, and whether there is a conflation of sin and disability. Cross (2017b: 73–4) writes,

> Now, while [the punishment] approach to disability is found pervasively in the Middle Ages, it is not universal. Here I attempt to show that Duns Scotus rejects the strong punishment view found in Aquinas. He agrees that there is de facto a punitive element to disability in the context of a theology of original sin, but he disagrees with the view that it is a necessary feature of disability. He considers various counterfactual situations in which we can find disability in the absence of sin, and thus in the absence of punishment. Scotus develops, instead, a theory according to which disability could simply be part of the divine plan, and in which disability might indeed have its own particular intrinsic beauty. It is, in other words, a fully natural state, one that God could have caused quite independently of human sin, and have done so on the basis of some beauty perceived by God in the relevant bodily configurations.[10]

One thing to note is that Duns Scotus echoes Augustine's discussion of beauty in the diversity of human bodily configurations: an individual bodily configuration, including a disabled bodily configuration, can be beautiful in itself. On Cross's reading, Duns Scotus holds that while various bodily 'defects' are *de facto* punishments for original sin, Duns Scotus denies that such bodily 'defects' can only be punishments. Consequently, for Duns Scotus bodily 'defects' are contingently extrinsically associated with sin (because they are punishments for original sin) but not intrinsically associated with sin. In light of contemporary discussions of bad-difference views of disability, it is clear that in this context (at least) Duns Scotus does not imply a bad-difference view because he denies that a bodily 'defect' in itself is a punishment. To translate Duns Scotus's view into contemporary terms, he seems to have a kind social model according to which a bodily 'defect' in relation to a complex state of affairs (God, God's commandments, original sin) is where the association with sin is found; in contrast, Thomas Aquinas may be translated as having a kind of medical model of physical 'defects' according to

---

[9] Latin available at <http://www.corpusthomisticum.org/sth2085.html#37226>: 'Sic igitur, remota originali iustitita, natura corporis humani relicta est sibi [. . .].'

[10] In footnote 7 Cross writes, 'For the role of the aesthetic in Scotus's moral thinking more generally, see in particular Ingham (1995: 825–37); Ingham (2012: 95–113), and the literature she cites there. See also Cross (2012a)'.

which a bodily 'defect' in itself is a punishment (because it is intrinsically associated with sin). Still, for Aquinas all human beings in this life (except, e.g., Christ) have bodily 'defects' such that there are no 'normal' or 'abnormal' human beings.

Part III: Disability and Sacraments

What we call 'disability' also shows up in medieval philosophical theologians' discussions of the conditions required for receiving a sacrament. For example, they ask whether one must consciously assent to certain propositions in order to be baptised or receive the eucharist. In what follows I survey what has been written recently about what Thomas Aquinas and Duns Scotus have to say about the requirements for baptism.

Richard Cross compares and analyses what Thomas Aquinas and Duns Scotus have to say about what is required for a human being without the use of reason (what contemporary philosophers would call a severe cognitive impairment) to receive the sacrament of baptism (see Cross 2012b; see also Romero 2002: 115–16). Both theologians held that what a person receives through baptism is grace, e.g., a theological habit of faith. This is an inclination to believe propositions of faith.[11] They disagreed, however, on the conditions required for receiving this habit of faith.

Both have a general discussion of what is required for baptism, and then apply those general conditions to different cases that involve those without the use of reason. The cases that both discuss include infants without the use of reason, children without the use of reason, children with the use of reason, adults without the use of reason, and adults with the use of reason. For Aquinas, baptism can happen only if the person to be baptised has an explicit (occurrent) act of faith or a sponsor for the person to be baptised has an explicit (occurrent) act of faith that stands on behalf of the person to be baptised (see Aquinas 1981: II-II, q. 2, a. 5, cited in Cross 2012b: 430–1). In the cases of infants and children without the use of reason, if their parents wish for them to be baptised and a parent has an explicit act of faith then the infant or child may be baptised. In the following passage Aquinas (1981: III, 68, 12) identifies different situations of adults without the use of reason (*amentia*).

> In the matter of imbeciles and madmen a distinction is to be made. For some are so from birth, and have no lucid intervals, and show no signs of the use of reason. And with regard to these it seems that we should come to the same decision as with regard to children who are baptized in the faith of the church. But there are others who have fallen from a state of sanity into insanity. And with regard to these we must be guided by their wishes as expressed by them when sane; so that, if then they manifested a desire to receive baptism, it should be given to them when in a state of madness or imbecility, even though then they refuse.
>
> If, on the other hand, while sane they showed no desire to receive baptism, they must not be baptized. Again, there are some who, though mad or imbecile from birth, have, nevertheless, lucid intervals, in which they can make right use of reason. So, if then they express a desire for baptism, they can be baptized though they actually be in a state of madness. And in this case the sacrament should be bestowed on them if there be fear of danger otherwise it is better to wait until the time when they are sane, so that they may receive the

---

[11] For differences between them on the epistemic status of propositions of the faith, cf. Aquinas (1981: II-II, q. 1, a. 1); co.; Duns Scotus (1969: 511–12). Also, cf. Williams (2017: 428).

sacrament more devoutly. But if during the interval of lucidity they manifest no desire to receive baptism, they should not be baptized while in a state of insanity. Lastly, there are others who, though not altogether sane, yet can use their reason so far as to think about their salvation, and understand the power of the sacrament. And these are to be treated the same as those who are sane, and who are baptized if they be willing, but not against their will.[12]

There are several things to note. First, Aquinas maintains that one should not be baptised against one's expressed will or against one's parents' expressed will if one is an infant or child without the use of reason. Second, if at some time one expresses one's desire to be baptised but later lacks the use of reason, then one can and should be baptised because of one's prior expressed desire to be baptised. Third, while it is not clear whether the names 'amentes' and 'furiosos' are supposed to track the different situations of those without the use of reason, the important thing is that Aquinas identifies these different situations. (In part IV below, I quote Peter John Olivi who stipulates how certain terms should be used.)

Duns Scotus likewise identifies these different situations in relation to when it is permissible to baptise someone (see Hirvonen 2006: 181–2). But he disagrees with Aquinas's stipulation that an explicit (occurrent) act of faith is required for an individual to be baptised. According to Cross (2012b: 423–33),

> [. . .] Scotus goes much further than Aquinas. He holds that implicit faith is required of all – even those incapable of the use of reason – but he argues that, in the absence of explicit faith, implicit faith is present just so long as the relevant habit is present. So he identifies implicit faith simply as the infused disposition to believe (i.e. the *habit* of faith), and expressly claims that implicit faith – the disposition – is sufficient for salvation, even in the absence of any explicit or occurrent faith: 'It was necessary in every dispensation to have an implicit act about all [the articles of faith]. *For in that case an act is had implicitly when a habit is had.*'

There is an important conceptual distinction from Aquinas, and I have emphasized it in the last sentence: the presence of a habit is sufficient for an (implicit) act irrespective of any further internal or external condition. Aquinas, of course, concedes that habitual faith

---

[12] See <http://www.corpusthomisticum.org/sth4066.html#50149>: 'Respondeo dicendum quod circa amentes et furiosos est distinguendum. Quidam enim sunt a nativitate tales, nulla habentes lucida intervalla, in quibus etiam nullus usus rationis apparet. Et de talibus, quantum ad Baptismi susceptionem, videtur esse idem iudicium et de pueris, qui baptizantur in fide Ecclesiae, ut supra dictum est. Alii vero sunt amentes qui ex sana mente quam habuerunt prius, in amentiam inciderunt. Et tales sunt iudicandi secundum voluntatem quam habuerunt dum sanae mentis existerent. Et ideo, si tunc apparuit in eis voluntas suscipiendi Baptismum, debet exhiberi eis in furia vel amentia constitutis, etiam si tunc contradicant. Alioquin, si nulla voluntas suscipiendi Baptismum in eis apparuit dum sanae mentis essent, non sunt baptizandi. Quidam vero sunt qui, etsi a nativitate fuerint furiosi et amentes, habent tamen aliqua lucida intervalla, in quibus recta ratione uti possunt. Unde, si tunc baptizari voluerint, baptizari possunt etiam in amentia constituti. Et debet eis sacramentum tunc conferri si periculum timeatur, alioquin melius est ut tempus expectetur in quo sint sanae mentis ad hoc quod devotius suscipiant sacramentum. Si autem tempore lucidi intervalli non appareat in eis voluntas Baptismum suscipiendi, baptizari non debent in amentia constituti. Quidam vero sunt qui, etsi non omnino sanae mentis existant, in tantum tamen ratione utuntur quod possunt de sua salute cogitare, et intelligere sacramenti virtutem. Et de talibus idem est iudicium sicut de his qui sanae mentis existunt, qui baptizantur volentes, non inviti.'

is, in certain circumstances (e.g., *amentia*), all the individual requires *intrinsically*. But he makes this habitual faith dependent on the actual faith of others. Scotus denies this, and makes salvific faith consist simply in the presence of a disposition to believe, independent of the explicit or occurrent faith of any other person – since the disposition to believe itself supplies, or entails, the relevant and requisite implicit faith.[13]

The differences between Thomas Aquinas and Duns Scotus on whether explicit or occurrent faith is required for baptism has an important implication for those with *amentia* (cf. Cross 2012b: 437). In Aquinas's view, those with *amentia* depend on another church member's explicit faith in order for one with *amentia* to receive the sacrament of baptism, and so receive the habit of faith. This implies that there is an asymmetrical dependence of the *amentia* on those with explicit faith. This suggests that those with *amentia* are akin to second-class members of the Church. Whereas for Duns Scotus there is no such asymmetrical dependence because no one requires an explicit act of faith in order to be baptised and so to receive the habit of faith. This implies that those with *amentia* do not have a second-class status in the Church.

> If Scotus is correct, we might be able to say a little more than [saying that those with *amentia* only can give their presence to others]. The habits and dispositions that the medieval theologians talk about are fundamentally matters of human orientation: toward the good or toward the evil. Those with profound cognitive impairments are unequivocally as capable of being oriented by God as any one else is, and this is as true of cognitive states as it is of affective ones. (Cross 2012b: 438)[14]

In effect, Duns Scotus's view conforms with the goals of some contemporary philosophers and theologians of disability who argue for the equal status of 'disabled' human beings (see Eiesland 1994; Yong 2007; Vanier 2008). Cross (2012b: 437) draws a lesson from work at the Intersection, namely that,

> [...] medieval theologians offer rich insights, I believe, because their theological speculations – sometimes thought to be overly inquisitive or rationalistic – are so densely textured. In this case, we can uncover a theology of dispositions that can make it wholly clear why cognitive (dis)abilities turn out to be irrelevant to a capacity to participate in the life of the church – albeit without flattening the variety of ways in which human persons, with all of their differences, can so participate.

Part IV: Causal Explanations of Mental Disorders and Free Choice of the Will

Medieval philosophers and theologians give accounts of the causes of a human being's lack of the use of reason (*amentia*) and how that impacts a human being's free choice of the will. In part III, I quoted Aquinas on when it is permissible to baptise someone; there Aquinas says that an individual can be baptised if they express their will to be baptised. Free choice of the will plays an important role in this question. Moreover, medieval philosophers' and theologians' different theories of free will play a role in their analysis of whether a human being with

---

[13] Cross quotes Duns Scotus, *Lectura* 3, d. 25, q. un. n. 19 (Vatican, XXI, 163).
[14] The text in the square brackets refers to Reinders (2008: 377–8).

amentia, or *phrenesis* or *alienatio* or *raptus*, can make free choices, including choices having to do with the sacraments (see Hirvonen 2006: 174–5, 177, 182–3; see also Olivi 1922: 551). Peter John Olivi's account of the causes of mental disorder is somewhat representative of the field. According to Vesa Hirvonen (2006: 175–6),

> In mental disorders, the problem is, according to [Peter John] Olivi, an immoderate direction of imagination. In mad men, the imagination or cogitation functions, but it is immoderately inclined or directed to the species [that is, representation] of its object. The wrong direction in the superior powers, that is, in the intellect, follows from this. Olivi goes on to say that there can be two causes for such a direction in the imagination. It can be caused either by a natural bodily cause, or by a separate spirit. In both cases, the change is spiritual, not local or substantial. If the cause is bodily and natural, and it can only be removed with difficulty, the person is said to have amentia (*amentia*). If it can be removed easily, he or she is said to have frenzy (*phrenesis*). If the cause is a separate spirit, it is a question of alienation (*alienatio*) or rapture (*raptus*). Olivi remarks that sometimes the organic or humoral bodily states can affect the mind very suddenly, as happens, for instance, in the case of the conjugal acts, according to Augustine and Cicero.

Olivi posits different kinds of cause for mental impairment. A mental impairment is either naturally caused or caused by a separate spirit. For Olivi (and others), a separate spirit can directly affect what and how one imagines something, and this is the source of one's imagination not being directed in the right way. Further, the type of mental disorder is determined by its temporal duration or by the ease of removing it. (Presumably, a medical doctor may assist in removing such a mental disorder.) It is important to observe that Olivi does not assign a general value on such mental conditions – some might make a bad-difference, or a mere-difference, or a good difference.

Although Olivi stipulates that those with 'amentia' are those with a naturally caused mental disorder that can only be removed with difficulty, he allows that there can be another use of the term 'amentia'. Olivi comments on *The Acts of the Apostles* where the Apostle Paul writes that,

> We are fools for the sake of Christ, but you are wise in Christ. We are weak, but you are strong [. . .] To the present hour we are hungry and thirsty, we are poorly clothed and beaten and homeless, and we grow weary from the work of our own hands. When reviled, we bless; when persecuted, we endure; when slandered, we speak kindly. We have become like the rubbish of the world, the dregs of all things, to this very day. (1 Corinthians 4:10–13)

Olivi (1922, 2001: 419–20) says that the Apostle Paul had

> a holy and spiritual mindlessness according to 1 Corinthians 4:10, 'We are fools because of Christ.' Therefore, he is counted as insane because he passed beyond common human use and sense, extending himself to what is arduous and strange; he seemed to care about himself and his temporal goods as if [they were] nothing. This world holds him to be insane.[15]

---

[15] 'Sed tamen haec est sancta et spiritalis amentia iuxta illud eiusdem I Ad Corinthios 4, 10: *Nos stulti propter Christum*. Vel ideo insanum reputat, quia ultra communem hominum etiam peritorum usum et sensum ad tam ardua et insolita se extendens de se ipso et suius temporalibus commodis quasi nihil curare videbatur. Hoc enim mundus pro insania habet.'

In addition to the previous passages where Olivi used 'amentia' to refer to those with a disordered imagination, this passage shows that Olivi uses 'amentia' for someone who behaves in ways that 'the world' considers strange, foolish or insane, that is, individuals who do things that lead to being poorly clothed, homeless and hungry. Although we should not consider Paul 'mentally impaired', what we should observe is that Olivi recognises that 'amentia' can refer to certain sorts of social outcasts. In effect, those with 'amentia' may be stigmatised by 'the world'.[16]

Olivi is well known for his libertarian account of free choice of the will (see Yrionsuuri 2002; Kaye 2004). His discussion of cognitive impairment in relation to free will is illustrative of his analysis of free will. Olivi raises an objection against the claim that those with, for example, 'fury' [*furiosi*] have free choice of the will. The objection reads: 'Freedom is nothing other than a full faculty of those things, in relation of which it is freedom itself; but where there is a full faculty, there can be a use of such a faculty at once; therefore, etc.' Olivi replies saying,

> It should be said [. . .] that there is an equivocation between 'freedom' and 'faculty', according to which there is freedom according to essence and according to habit and according to aspect or use. Therefore, free choice, when it is under such an impediment, there is a deficit from freedom, faculty, and power according to use or according to aspect.[17]

What prevents a cognitively impaired human being from exercising free choice of the will is that the object is not cognitively present to the human being under the right or 'due' aspect.[18] The upshot for Olivi is that cognitive impairments (or 'disorders') can remove from one an opportunity to exercise one's free will, but such cognitive impairments do not remove one's essential or habitual faculty of free will.

Regarding the causation of mental 'disorders', Duns Scotus agrees with Olivi that separate spirits can causally affect a human being's imagination. According to Vesa Hirvonen (2006: 173),

> Duns Scotus discusses whether an angel (good or evil) can cause something in a human being's intellect. His view is that an angel cannot enrapture (*rapere*) the intellect to have an intellectual vision of something purely intelligible, but it can enrapture the imagination to imagine something imaginable. This imaging can become so intense that it leads to insanity. This too intensive imagining, according to Scotus, is rather a question of fury than rapture. While having an intense imagination experience of something, a person may seem to have an intellectual vision of it, but that is not the case. An intense imagination experience of something, however, is naturally accompanied by an intellectual cognition of the imagined thing. In this way, through phantasms, the devil can affect the intellect.

---

[16] On stigmas and disability, see Berger (2013: 8, 43–8).

[17] See Olivi (1922: q. 59, pp. 518, 558): '[L]ibertas nihil aliud est quam plena facultas eorum, respectu quorum est libertas ipsa; sed ubi est plena facultas, ibi statim potest esse usus talis facultatis; ergo et cetera [. . .] Ad quartum dicendum quod [. . .] est aequivocatio libertatis et facultatis, secundum quod est libertas secundum essentiam et secundum habitum et secundum aspectum vel usum. Liberum igitur arbitrium, quando est sub tali impedimento, deficit a libertate, facultate et potestate secundum usum vel secundum aspectum.'

[18] Olivi (1922: q. 59, p. 558): 'Ad tertium, dicendum quod etsi potentiae non sunt debilitatae quoad essentias suas, deficiunt tamen a debito modo existendi et aspiciendi. Et hoc sufficit ad hoc quod agere non possint, saltem debito modo.'

Note that Duns Scotus has a general position according to which an angel, good or evil, can causally affect a human being's imagination. A good angel may try to help a human being from sinning, but a bad angel may try to tempt a human being into sinning.

Hirvonen (2006: 180–2) also cites passages in which Duns Scotus identifies natural causes for various mental disorders.[19] In *Lectura* 2, dist. 14, q. 3, Duns Scotus asks, 'whether the corporeal stars have efficacy or a certain influence on the inferior things?' He responds saying that the stars act on the elements and that the sun affects the generation, vivification and death of plants. Duns Scotus then turns to claims by astrologers. He concedes that they can make certain judgements about natural effects such as when sea tides occur,[20] but not about, for example, when rain showers will occur. Duns Scotus infers 'how much more in the life of a human [being]' will an astrologer not be certain. 'Although, corporeal stars can act on a human body, organs, and imagination, and so impede the action of the intellect and make a human frenetic, it is entirely false that they have an immediate effect on the intellect and will.'[21] In *Reportata* 2, dist. 14, q. 3, he says a little more about the stars' effects on human beings.

> [The stars] can dispose [one] regarding sanity and illness, inasmuch as to the proportion of the humours, and so, they can alter an animated body, and in this way there can be an indisposition of the soul and then death occurs. Also, they can act on organs by bringing about a quality that is a due grade or by removing [it]. And so, it is said that an intellect is ruined by a certain internal corruption in us, as is the case of lunatics who are sometimes badly disposed and sometimes well [disposed]. But the organ of the sensitive appetite seems the same because some are more disposed toward desiring this than that. Nevertheless, the will is purely free. Therefore, although a sensitive appetite inclines toward one [alternative], the will can elect [its] contrary, because no star, nor some creature, can efficiently cause an act in the will except itself.[22]

For Duns Scotus, natural causes can affect one's sensory organs, including the organ of the imagination, but the freedom of the will cannot be directly affected by any other creature. This holds for 'frenetic' and 'sane' human beings. A key assumption is that the will is not located in any corporeal organ (see Adams 1987: 633–69; Cross 2014: 73–7). The implication is that if it could be affected by natural causes, then it is located in an organ. But since it is not located in an organ, it follows (by modus tollens) that it cannot be affected by natural causes

---

[19] See Duns Scotus, *Lectura* 2, d. 14, q. 3, n. 36 (Vatican 19, 126); *Ordinatio* 1, d. 3, p. 1, q. 4, n. 252 (Vatican 3, 153).

[20] In Duns Scotus (1969: 2, d. 14, q. 3, n. 3, p. 342), Duns Scotus says that the moon causes the sea tides.

[21] Duns Scotus, *Lectura* 2, d. 14, q. 3, n. 36 (Vatican 19, 126): 'Unde licet corpora caelestia possint agere in corpus humanum et in organum et in phantasiam, et sic impedire actionem intellectus et facere hominem phreneticum, – sed quod habeant actionem immediate circa intellectum et voluntatem, est omnino falsum.'

[22] Duns Scotus (1969: 2, d. 14, q. 3, n. 5, p. 342): 'Et sic possunt disponere quantum ad sanitatem et aegritudinem ut quantum ad proportionem humorum, et sic possunt alterare corpus animatum ita ut sit indispositio animae et tunc accidit mors. Possunt etiam agere in organa intendendo qualitatem ad gradum debitum vel remittendo. Et ideo dicitur quod intellectus corrumpitur corrupto quodam interiori in nobis, et sic Lunatici aliquando peius disponuntur aliquando melius. Sed idem videtur de organo appetitus sensitiui, quia magis disponuntur aliqui ad appetendum hoc quam illud. Tamen voluntas est mere libera. Et ideo quamquam appetitus sensitiuus inclinet ad unum potest voluntas eligere contrarium, quia nulla stella, nec aliqua creatura potest causare effectiue actum in voluntate, nisi ipsamet.' William Ockham also uses 'aegritudo' to refer to what we would call mental impairment. See Hirvonen (2006: 184, note 56, for references).

including other creatures' natural efficient causation. (A full assessment of different medieval philosophers' and theologians' analyses of the ways in which separate spirits can causally affect human beings in relation to disability – and health – remains to be seen. Still, there are several important studies on the historical period (see Laine-Frigren et al. 2009; Katajala-Paltomaa and Niiranen 2014)).

Hirvonen (2006: 182, 185) also discusses the way in which William of Ockham understands the relation between mental disorder and free choice of the will.

> In the *Various Questions*, q. 8, Ockham says he 'firmly believes' that a fool and a furious person cannot have some acts of the intellect, especially judging ones. There cannot be in them acts with respect to complex objects, since in order to have such acts, there has to be a concurrent act of the will.
>
> In a fool and a mad person's will, there still are, according to Ockham, acts, but not free ones. Their volitions may even be directed to good things because of virtuous habits generated when they were healthy. Such acts are not, however, virtuous, because these people do not know what they do. Because of the lack of the use of reason, the wills of mentally disordered people are incapable of performing their due functions, such as controlling sensory passions. Therefore, they may have desires, sorrows and joys which they cannot control.[23]
>
> [Moreover,] Ockham thinks that the functions of the intellect and the will are not in order in fools and mad people because of wrongly ordained imaginations, which, in their turn, originate at the bodily level.

It is a commonplace among medieval Aristotelians to locate the causal impediments to one's use of reason and one's exercise of free choice of the will in one's body (including one's 'humours') and sensory organs, and whatever may affect them so as to cause various cognitive disorders.[24] But, even more, it is a commonplace among these philosophers and theologians to deny that the power of intellect and the power of will are located in any bodily organ. This allows them to maintain that all human beings, whether they are temporarily or permanently 'insane', 'phrenetic' or 'mindless', have the same basic powers of intellect and will (see Pasnau 1997; Romero 2002: 103–7; Cross 2014; Frost 2020).[25] This has welcome consequences for medieval theologians who theorise about those with 'amentia' and, for example, the sacrament of baptism. In short, the implication is that even those with 'amentia' have an intrinsic capacity to receive an intellectual habit of faith from God, despite any disordered senses or a disordered imagination.

Furthermore, Ockham concedes that someone without the use of reason [*in illis non est usus rationis*] nevertheless can have desires, sorrows and joys that arise from one's sensory cognitive powers located in one's corporeal organs. Ockham also concedes that someone without the use of reason can have non-complex intellectual acts and voluntary acts. This concession reflects Ockham's – and many other medieval philosophers' and theologians' – Aristotelian analysis of human beings' cognitive powers. This concession serves as a guideline for scholars working at the Intersection; they should be sensitive to the way in which medieval philosophers and

---

[23] Ockham, *Quaestiones Variae*, q. 8 (OTh, VIII, 427), ln. 401–15.
[24] This is consistent with, e.g., medical texts which predominantly focus on natural causes of illness. Cf. Scott Nokes (2018: 136–40). For a history of 'health' as it relates to ancient and medieval philosophy, cf. Pormann (2019: 43–74), Allen (2019: 103–35), both of which are in Adamson (2018). Compare with later medical and spiritual interpretations in Vacek (2015).
[25] For discussion of 'personhood' in relation to cognitive powers, cf. Williams (2019a, 2019b).

theologians describe those 'without the use of reason'. This phrase can be used to refer to (1) someone temporarily without the use of reason, (2) someone permanently without the use of reason, (3) someone with acts of intellect but no (second-order) intellectual acts by which they make complex judgements, or (4) someone with simple acts of intellect and consequent volitions based on those simple acts of intellect but with no (higher-order) complex acts of intellect or will. What these different referents of 'lack of the use of reason' show is that medieval theologians' texts are just as Cross (2012b: 437) claimed, 'medieval theologians offer rich insights, I believe, because their theological speculations – sometimes thought to be overly inquisitive or rationalistic – are so densely textured'.

* * *

This survey of the intersection between disability and medieval philosophy and theology has shown several things. First, for a scholar of medieval philosophy or theology to do excellent work in the Intersection, they should be familiar enough with debates going on in contemporary philosophy and theology of disability. This familiarity is an advantage because it helps attune the scholar to the many complexities of 'disability' and (questionable) assumptions one may have when researching a history of the philosophy or theology of disability in medieval philosophy or theology.[26] Second, scholars of medieval philosophy or theology now have a new research area in which to engage. Third, not only does the Intersection help scholars to understand better what is going on in the medieval texts, but if a scholar were so willing, they may 'overstand' medieval insights and develop them into new contributions in contemporary philosophy or theology of disability.[27]

Bibliography

Adams, Marilyn McCord (1987). *William Ockham, Volume II*. Notre Dame: Notre Dame University Press.
Adamson, Peter (2018). 'Health in Arabic Ethical Works'. In *Health: A History*. Ed. Peter Adamson. Oxford: Oxford University Press, pp. 103–35.
Allen, James (2019). 'The Soul's Virtue and the Health of the Body in Ancient Philosophy'. In *Health: A History*. Ed. Peter Adamson. Oxford: Oxford University Press, pp. 75–94.
Aquinas, Thomas (1981). *Summa Theologiae* Trans. Fathers of the English Dominican Province. New York: Ave Maria Press.
Augustine (1955). *De Civitate Dei*. Turnhout: Brepols.
Augustine (1962). *De doctrina christiana. De vera religione. Corpus Christianorum Series Latina v. 32*. Ed. K. D. Daur and J. Martin.
Augustine (1984). *City of God*. Trans. Henry Bettenson. New York: Penguin.
Augustine (1996). *On Christian Teaching*. Trans. Edmund Hill. Hyde Park, NY: New City Press.
Barnes, Elizabeth (2009). 'Disability and Adaptive Preference'. *Philosophical Perspective*, 23: 1–22.
Barnes, Elizabeth (2014). 'Valuing Disability, Causing Disability'. *Ethics*, 125/1: 88–113.
Barnes, Elizabeth (2016). *The Minority Body: A Theory of Disability*. Oxford: Oxford University Press.
Berger, Ronald J. (2013). *Introducing Disability Studies*. London: Lynne Rienner Publishers.

---

[26] For a more wide-ranging discussion of the Intersection, see Williams (2020).
[27] At the end of part III I reported Cross's claim that Duns Scotus's insights can be used to develop a better theology of disability for, e.g., the Catholic Church. There are two additional recent examples: Cross (2011) and Williams (2018).

Berkman, John (2013). 'Are Persons with Profound Intellectual Disabilities Sacramental Icons for the Heavenly Life? Aquinas on Impairment'. *Studies in Christian Ethics*, 26: 81–96.

Brock, Brian (2009). 'Augustine's Hierarchies of Human Wholeness and Their Healing'. In *Disability in the Christian Tradition*. Ed. Brian Brock and John Swinton. Grand Rapids: Eerdmans.

Cross, Richard (2011). 'Disability, Impairment, and Some Medieval Accounts of the Incarnation: Suggestions for a Theology of Personhood'. *Modern Theology*, 27/4: 639–58.

Cross, Richard (2012a). 'Natural Law, Moral Constructivism, and Duns Scotus's Metaethics: The Centrality of Aesthetic Explanation'. In *Reason, Religion, and Natural Law: Historical and Analytical Studies*. Ed. Jonathan Jacobs. Oxford: Oxford University Press, pp. 175–97.

Cross, Richard (2012b). 'Baptism, Faith and Severe Cognitive Impairment in Some Medieval Theologies'. *International Journal of Systematic Theology*, 14/4: 420–38.

Cross, Richard (2014). *Duns Scotus's Theory of Cognition*. Oxford: Oxford University Press.

Cross, Richard (2017a). 'Aquinas on Physical Impairment: Human Nature and Original Sin'. *Harvard Theological Review*, 110/3: 317–38.

Cross, Richard (2017b). 'Duns Scotus on Disability: Teleology, Divine Willing, and Pure Nature'. *Theological Studies*, 87/1: 72–95.

Davis, Lennard (2013). 'Introducing Disability, Normality, and Power'. In *The Disabilities Study Reader*, 4th edn. Ed. Lennard Davis. New York: Routledge, pp. 1–12.

Duns Scotus, John (1969). *Reportata Parisiensis* in *Opera Omnia*, XI.I. Ed. Luke Wadding. Hildesheim: G. Olms, pp. 511–12.

Eiesland, Nancy (1994). *The Disabled God: Toward a Liberatory Theology of Disability*. Nashville: Abingdon Press.

Feder Kittay, Eva (2016). 'Deadly Medicine: Project T4, Mental Disability, and Racism'. *Res Philosophica*, 93/4: 715–41.

Frost, Gloria (2020). 'Medieval Aristotelians on Congenital Disabilities and Their Early Modern Critics'. In *Disability in Medieval Christian Philosophy and Theology*. Ed. Scott M. Williams. New York: Routledge.

Garland-Thompson, Rosemarie (2013). 'Integrating Disability, Transforming Feminist Theory'. In *The Disability Studies Reader*, 4th edn. Ed. Lennard J. Davis. New York: Routledge.

Goodley, Dan (2011). *Disability Studies: An Interdisciplinary Introduction*. Los Angeles: Sage.

Hirvonen, Vesa (2006). 'Mental Disorders in Late Medieval Philosophy and Theology'. In *Mind and Modality: Studies in the History of Philosophy in Honour of Simo Knuuttila*. Ed. Vesa Hirvonen, Toivio J. Holopainen and Miira Tuomiinen. Leiden: Brill.

Hubbard, Ruth (2013). 'Abortion and Disability: Who Should and Should Not Inhbait the World?' In *The Disability Studies Reader*, 4th edn. Ed. Lennard Davis. New York: Routledge.

Ingham, Mary Beth (1995). 'Duns Scotus' Moral Reasoning and the Artistic Paradigm'. In *Via Scoti: Methodologica ad mentem Joannis Duns Scoti*. Ed. Leonardo Sileo. Rome: Edizioni Antonianum.

Ingham, Mary Beth (2012). *The Harmony of Goodness: Mutuality and Moral Living According to John Duns Scouts*, 2nd edn. St. Bonaventure, NY: Franciscan Institute.

Kahane, Guy and Julian Savulescu (2009). 'The Welfarist Account of Disability'. In *Disability and Disadvantage*. Ed. Kimberly Brownlee and Adam Cureton. Oxford: Oxford University Press, pp. 14–53.

Katajala-Peltomaa, Sara and Susanna Niiranen (eds) (2014). *Mental (Dis)order in Late Medieval Europe*. Leiden: Brill.

Kaye, Sharon M. (2004). 'Why the Liberty of Indifference is Worth Wanting: Buridan's Ass, Friendship, and Peter John Olivi'. *History of Philosophy Quarterly*, 21/1: 21–42.

Kuuliala, Jenni (2013). 'In Search of Medieval Disability'. *Lectio Praecursoria*, 16/2: 1–6.

Kuuliala, Jenni (2016). *Childhood Disability and Social Integration in the Middle Ages: Constructions of Impairments in Thirteenth- and Fourteenth-Century Canonization Process*. Turnhout: Brepols.

Laine-Frigren, Tuomas, Jari Eilola and Markku Hokkanen (eds) (2009). *Encountering Crises of the Mind: Madness, Culture, and Society, 1200s–1900s*. Leiden: Brill.

Locke, John (1979). *An Essay Concerning Human Understanding*. Ed. Peter H. Nidditch. Oxford: Oxford University Press.

Metzler, Irina (2006). *Disability in Medieval Europe: Thinking about Physical Impairment in the High Middle Ages, c. 1100–c. 1400*. New York: Routledge.

Metzler, Irina (2013). *A Social History of Disability in the Middle Ages: Cultural Considerations of Physical Impairment*. New York: Routledge.

Metzler, Irina (2016). *Fools and Idiots?: Intellectual Disability in the Middle Ages*. Manchester: Manchester University Press.

Nussbaum, Martha (2010). 'The Capabilities of People with Cognitive Disabilities'. In *Cognitive Disability and Its Challenges to Moral Philosophy*. Ed. Eva Feder Kittay and Licia Carlson. Oxford: Wiley-Blackwell, pp. 75–95.

Ockham, William (1983). *Quaestiones Variae*. In *Opera Theologica*, vol. 8. Ed. Joseph C. Wey, Girard J. Etzkorn and Franciscus E. Kelley. St. Bonaventure, NY: Franciscan Institute of St. Bonaventure University.

Oliver, Michael (1990). *The Politics of Disablement: A Sociological Approach*. New York: St. Martin's Press.

Olivi, Peter John (1922). *Quaestiones in Secundum Librum Sententiarum*, vol. 2. Ed. Bernardus Jansen, SJ. Quaracchi: St. Bonaventure College Press.

Olivi, Peter John (2001). *On the Acts of the Apostles*. Ed. David Flood. St. Bonaventure, NY: The Franciscan Institute Press.

Pasnau, Robert (1997). *Theories of Cognition in the Latter Middle Ages*. Cambridge: Cambridge University Press.

Pasnau, Robert (2014). 'Introduction'. In *The Cambridge History of Medieval Philosophy*. Ed. Robert Pasnau and Christian van Dyke. Cambridge: Cambridge University Press, pp. 3–6.

Pormann, Peter (2019). 'Medical Conceptions of Health from Antiquity to the Renaissance'. In *Health: A History*. Ed. Peter Adamson. Oxford: Oxford University Press, pp. 43–74.

Reinders, Hans (2008). *Receiving the Gift of Friendship: Profound Disability, Theological Anthropology, and Ethics*. Grand Rapids: Eerdmans.

Romero, Miguel (2012). 'Aquinas on the *corporis infirmitas*: Broken Flesh and the Grammar of Grace'. In *Disability in the Christian Tradition*. Ed. Brian Brock and John Swinton. Grand Rapids: Eerdmans, pp. 101–51.

Scott Nokes, Richard (2018). 'Reflection: The Rationality of Medieval Leechbooks'. In *Health: A History*. Ed. Peter Adamson. Oxford: Oxford University Press, pp. 136–40.

Shakespeare, Tom and Nicholas Watson (2001). 'The Social Model of Disability: An Outdated Ideology?' In *Exploring Theories and Expanding Methodologies: Where We Are and Where We Need to Go*. Ed. Sharon N. Barnartt and Barbara M. Altman. Bingley: Emerald Publishing Group.

Terzi, Lorella (2009). 'Vagaries of the Natural Lottery? Human Diversity, Disability, and Justice: A Capability Perspective'. In *Disability and Disadvantage*. Ed. Kimberley Brownlee and Adam Cureton. Oxford: Oxford University Press, pp. 86–111.

Upson-Saia, Kristi (2011). 'Resurrecting Deformity: Augustine on Wounded and Scarred Bodies in the Heavenly Realm'. In *Disability in Judaism, Christianity, and Islam: Sacred Texts, Historical Traditions, and Social Analysis*. Ed. Darla Schumm and Michael Stoltzfus. New York: Palgrave Macmillan.

Vacek, Hether H. (2015). *Madness: An American Protestant Response to Mental Illness*. Waco: Baylor University Press.

Vanhoozer, Kevin J. (1998). *Is There a Meaning in this Text? The Bible, the Reader, and the Morality of Literary Knowledge*. Grand Rapids: Zondervan.

Vanier, Jean (2008). *Becoming Human*. New York: Paulist Press.

Walker Bynum, Caroline (1995). *The Resurrection of the Body in Western Christianity, 200 1336*. New York: Columbia University Press.

Wheatley, Edward (2013). *Stumbling Blocks before the Blind: Medieval Constructions of a Disability*. Ann Arbor: University of Michigan Press.

Williams, Scott M. (2017). 'John Duns Scotus'. In *The Oxford Handbook of the Epistemology of Theology*. Ed. William Abraham and Frederick Aquino. Oxford: Oxford University Press, p. 428.

Williams, Scott M. (2018). 'Horrendous-Difference Disabilities, Resurrected Saints, and the Beatific Vision: A Theodicy'. *Religions*, 9/52: 1–13.

Williams, Scott M. (2019a). 'Persons in Patristic and Medieval Christian Theology'. In *Person: A History*. Ed. Antonia Lolordo. Oxford: Oxford University Press.

Williams, Scott M. (2019b). 'When Personhood Goes Wrong in Ethics and Philosophical Theology: Disability, Ableism, and (Modern) Personhood'. In *The Lost Sheep in Philosophy of Religion: New Perspective on Disability, Gender, Race, and Animals*. Ed. Blake Hereth and Kevin Timpe. New York: Routledge.

Williams, Scott M. (2020). *Disability in Medieval Christian Philosophy and Theology*. Ed. Scott M. Williams. New York: Routledge.

Yong, Amos. (2007). *Theology and Down Syndrome: Reimagining Disability in Late Modernity*. Waco: Baylor University Press.

Yrionsuuri, Mikko (2002). 'Free Will and Self-Control in Peter Olivi'. In *Emotions and Choice from Boethius to Descartes*. Ed. Henrik Lagerlund and Mikko Yrionsuuri. Dordrecht: Kluwer, pp. 99–128.

3

The Art of Excess as a Medieval Aesthetic

Lisa Mahoney

From a modern perspective, there was no art in the Middle Ages. Indeed, medieval works, small or large, were the products of an anonymous group, not a named individual, that created by means of skills learned and according to a patron-determined design rather than by inspiration and imagination (see Dean 2006). Whether or not this holds entirely, a simpler and more essential definition of art – as something that exceeds in form what is required by function – certainly allows such an assessment to be called into question. This chapter looks at the ways in which we see this excess. It does not, however, look at descriptions of beauty in extant texts that identify required components of the aesthetically pleasing or that suggest more general aesthetic principles. Instead, it looks at medieval visual culture itself, underlining the ways in which material, line, mass and colour are able to point to value in the explicitly unnecessary. Such an analysis will rely, on the one hand and perhaps unexpectedly, on establishing the functional as a requirement in the medieval world, a requirement demanded by the prohibition against human beings creating anything 'in heaven . . . in the earth beneath . . . or in the waters under the earth' (Exodus 20:4) and, moreover, by the medieval workaround that found in images a capacity to instruct the illiterate. This allowance had an effect deep and broad, extending even to non-figural works. On the other hand, this analysis will rely on finding evidence for 'art' as defined here in unlikely and easily overlooked corners, in under-regulated margins, in the decorative, and in the use of precious materials. In other words, it will rely on finding evidence for the centrality and the celebration of the non-functional. The fact that enormous human and financial resources were dedicated to such creations suggests their importance within the medieval world and, accordingly, for any understanding of it.

Art as Functional: The Problem of Images

An essay on medieval aesthetics in a volume treating the history of philosophical thought finds a nice beginning with Immanuel Kant. Indeed, no medievalist would deny that a conception of beauty much like his existed in the Middle Ages, wherein the sights most pleasurable to the senses were those that provoked spiritual transcendence. This conception of beauty can be found in the texts of medieval philosophers and theologians, Dionysius the Pseudo-Areopagite principal among them.[1] In the *De divinis nominibus*, written c. 500,

---

[1] On Pseudo-Dionysius and beauty, see, for example, Ivanovic (2014). For an introductory discussion of Pseudo-Dionysius and art, see Eco (2002: 17–27). For a concrete example of Pseudo-Dionysius's influence on the production of art in the Middle Ages, see Elsner (1994).

Pseudo-Dionysius's contemplation of divine beauty brings about a mind 'away from passion and from earth' until 'we shall be united with him and, our understanding carried away, blessedly happy, we shall be struck by his blazing light . . . our minds . . . like those in the heavens above' (*De div. nom.*: 1.4).[2] Such an experience is echoed by medieval historians like Procopius, more or less a contemporary of Pseudo-Dionysius, who characterises the Hagia Sophia in the sixth century as indescribably beautiful and credits that beauty to its forms and materials and, even more, to the effect of these forms and materials, for

> whenever anyone enters this church to pray, he understands at once that it is not by any human power or skill, but by the influence of God, that this work has been so finely turned. And so his mind is lifted up toward God and exalted, feeling that He cannot be far away [. . .] (Procopius 1987: I, 1, 11.54–61)

About 600 years later and half a world away, Suger, abbot of Paris's St Denis, advocates a similarly ecstatic function for the gems in his new church:

> Often we contemplate . . . these different ornaments . . . when – out of my delight in the beauty of the house of God – the loveliness of the many-colored gems has called me away from external cares, and worthy meditation has induced me to reflect, transferring that which is material to that which is immaterial, on the diversity of the sacred virtues: then it seems to me . . . that, by the grace of God, I can be transported from this inferior to that higher world in an anagogical manner. (*De admin.*: XXXIII, 62–5)[3]

Figures like Procopius and Suger make Pseudo-Dionysius's abstract ideas about beauty concrete and move us out of the realm of philosophy and into that of art history. Their words point to an understanding of material's potential that derives from the earliest arguments for the presence of art in sacred spaces, arguments necessitated by the Second Commandment:

> You shall not make for yourself an idol, whether in the form of anything that is in heaven above, or that is on the earth beneath, or that is in the water underneath the earth. You shall not bow down to them or worship them; for I, the Lord your God, am a jealous God. (Exodus 20:4–5)

Augustine underlined the dangers of even mental representations, pointing to the many false appearances that result, since 'one represents the features and figures of those bodies in one way, and another in a different way', and encouraging a recognition of such appearances as a distraction from the more exalted aims of devotion – 'our faith is not busied there with the bodily countenance of those men, but only with the life that they led through the grace of God' (Augustine 2002: VIII, chapter 4, p. 10). The Kantian-esque solution to the problem of art will be articulated by Pope Gregory the Great at the turn of the seventh century in a letter written to Serenus, Bishop of Marseilles, who has recently had the images in the churches of

---

[2] All Pseudo-Dionysius translations are taken from Luibheid (1987).
[3] Translation and Latin found in Panofsky (1979). On the relationship between Pseudo-Dionysius and the potential of the material described here, see Kidson (1987). Suger seems to have confused Pseudo-Dionysius with the patron of his church (Kidson 1987: 4).

his diocese destroyed. Gregory condemns the bishop's iconoclasm and, more important for the history of art, defends images for provoking a metaphysical turn in its beholder,

> for it is one thing to adore a picture, another through a picture's story to learn what must be adored. For what writing offers to those who read it, a picture offers to the ignorant who look at it, since in it the ignorant see what they ought to follow, in it they read who do not know letters. (Chazelle 1990: 139–40)[4]

This will look more like Kant in the expression of later Gregory-influenced thinkers. In his *Opusculum de conversione sua*, Herman-Judah seems to record an actual debate on the nature of idolatry. To his interlocutor, the twelfth-century theologian Rupert of Deutz, Herman-Judah charges, 'In your temples (*sic*) you have set up as objects of adoration for yourself, huge images elaborately wrought with the arts of painters and sculptors . . . Either set forth for me the authority for this abominable worship . . . or . . . confess . . . that you cannot . . .' (*Opusculum*: 80).[5] Rupert responds by pointing to the affective, or metaphysical and transporting, value of the objects against which Herman inveighs.[6]

The foregoing, although brief, reveals my area of expertise, namely Latin Christian ideology and argument related to images. This ideology and argument were not alone. Orthodox theologians such as John of Damascus were similarly disposed, defending images, for example, both because of their instructional and their evocative capacity, because they made the invisible visible or, better, because they so effectively elicited their prototype. Indeed, images were of issue for the Abrahamic religions in general during the Middle Ages, and all shared a fundamental concern with misuse and a fear of idolatry, to which they responded in varied but related ways. According to one hadith, for example, Muhammed objected to the appearance of figures on curtains but allowed for them on cushions, marking the potential for image worship in the vertical but not the horizontal display.[7] Within the Jewish tradition, rabbinic texts drew distinctions between subject types and underlined the seductive power of plastic arts especially (Bland 2000; Mann 2000).[8] All of these apprehensions and misgivings led to carefully circumscribed image use across the board and, moreover, carefully described image use, whether as educational or ecstatic or both.

Art as Excessive: The Possibility in Images

I have not provided here anything like a comprehensive or even sufficiently detailed assessment of arguments made on behalf of images within Latin Christianity during the Middle Ages, nor have I offered an exhaustive catalogue of statements connecting images with transcendence.[9] Rather, I have attempted simply to lay out one approach to medieval aesthetics, the approach that has determined the interpretation of the subject within the history of art. This approach

---

[4] This is from the second of two letters. For the original Latin, see Chazell (1990).
[5] Translation from Morrison (1992).
[6] This dispute took place in 1128 but was not recorded until the middle of the twelfth century. On the relationship between Rupert's argument and Gregory the Great, see Kessler (2010: 152).
[7] For a more subtle and substantial discussion of this issue, see Grabar (1973) and Allen (1988).
[8] A relatively recent and richly varied treatment of this subject is Pearce (2013).
[9] For a more comprehensive treatment along these lines, start with Eco (2002) and Kessler (2010) for the West and, for the East, Michelis (1964), Mathew (1971), James (1996), Maguire (1999), Schibille (2014), Barber (forthcoming). For Islamic art, see Grabar (1995).

privileges reception, or at least an intended reception, and is well supported by primary texts. In what follows, I propose instead to focus attention on the creators of works of art in the Middle Ages, and to use art itself to see them.

This focus allows us a different, and differently illuminating, perspective on medieval aesthetics. Before truly beginning, however, it is necessary to define what is meant by the term 'creator' here and to fend off its potentially anachronistic modern associations. If we take the creator to be the person who caused a work of art or architecture to come into being, defining or even identifying this figure proves a far more daunting and tangled affair than it might seem at first blush. For the project at hand, it suffices to say that such a word would have no single referent in the Middle Ages. The person who caused a work of art or architecture to come into being could be the initiator of the work, someone usually called a patron or donor, who paid for the commission, selecting and requesting elements of design (medium, material, kind of imagery) as desired or as financially entitled.[10] Or this person could be the head of a workshop or scriptorium, who finalised designs, oversaw their execution and ensured their uniform appearance despite the heterogeneity of the workshop or scriptorium itself. Or, finally, this person could be someone who laboured in the workshop or scriptorium, who worked according to the dictates of a commission and as part of a collective effort as directed by the workshop's or the scriptorium's master (Alexander 1992; Priester 1993; Byng 2017).[11] None of these agents were able to guarantee that the work they made was the work received, of course. The viewer, then, was yet another 'creator' (Mathews 2000).

Modern, Western ideas related to the creation of art and architecture privilege innovation. The lines from Augustine quoted above, which complain about mental images and difference, prepare us for an alternative view. In fact, innovation in images was especially problematic. Both Gregory's insistence on their instructive potential and Rupert's insistence on their affective potential (via Herman-Judah) assume the employment of pre-existing, known forms and details of forms (or iconography). In a world where images communicated doctrine and inspired faith, those images needed to be readable in order to be comprehensible. In other words, it is useful to think of images like words in a language and so see how innovation might lead to unintelligibility. Texts such as the *Pictor in Carmine*, which prescribes subject matter and its location within ecclesiastical spaces, reveal a concern for consistency that can only ever be implied in images themselves (James 1951). And beyond the worry of innovation leading to unintelligibility or miscommunication, there was the terrifying prospect of false doctrine and, ultimately, heresy. In the thirteenth century, Lucas, Bishop of Tuy, railed against artists for rendering the Crucifixion with three rather than four nails, among other things (Gilbert 1985: 128). A well-known miniature of God creating the world with a compass in a thirteenth-century Bible moralisée underlines another danger (Vienna, Österreichische Nationalbibliothek, MS 2554: f. 1v).[12] It is one thing to use and thereby celebrate a talent for making beautiful things – a talent that has been given by God – another to imagine oneself God-like, fashioning *ex nihilo*.[13]

---

[10] Jill Caskey points out that there is no noun matching our 'donor' or 'patron' in the Middle Ages. Instead this person or group of people is described verbally, indicating what they effect or bring about. See Caskey (2010: 197). For monographs on this type of creator, see Panofsky (1979) and Weiss (1998). On the financial role of whole towns in creations, see Kraus (1979).
[11] Annemarie Weyl Carr has suggested an alternative non-workshop-centric model of (manuscript) production, wherein a single scribe, in possession of exemplars, approached different illuminators according to the different demands of patrons; see Carr (1987: esp. 12–28 and 50–69).
[12] For a reproduction, see Tachau (1998).
[13] See, for example, Theophilus (1979). On artists acting like God, see, among others, Hassig (1990/1991: esp. 144).

Whether or not innovation and originality are to be found nevertheless in the art and architecture of the Middle Ages is a question for a different essay.[14] The preceding paragraphs are meant simply to show that artistic creation in the Middle Ages is easily understood as an exclusively utilitarian activity and that this understanding finds abundant support in contemporary texts. Given this, we would expect to find a corpus of art and architecture that relies on images, for example, and on forms, for another, that are themselves utilitarian. What we find instead is a corpus of art and architecture wherein images and forms exceed what is required by function. The remainder of this chapter looks at the ways in which we see this excess, for it is precisely here that we might find the principles of medieval aesthetics operating.[15]

A particularly compelling place to begin such a discussion is in margins. The margin belongs perhaps most literally to manuscripts. Within such objects, the space surrounding text was a logical and convenient location for commenting on that text.[16] Word and image did this alike. The edges of the folia of a ninth-century prayer book called the Khludov Psalter (Moscow, State Historical Museum, MS D.129) provide a quintessential example of this particular image function. Here, a section of the Psalms is juxtaposed with a scene of the Crucifixion. Blue wavy lines indicate the section of text in relation to which this image is to be viewed.[17] It reads, 'They gave me gall for my food; and in my thirst they gave me vinegar to drink' (Psalm 68:22). The Crucifixion scene shows Jesus on the cross at the moment when he is given vinegar mixed with gall by a soldier (Matthew 27:34). The matching details of text and image are quickly understood to clarify the text's significance, namely that the New Testament event was foreseen in the Old Testament, a typological understanding of the Bible that defined medieval theology.[18]

The conception of the margin as a space allowing for commentary morphed easily into a space allowing for expression in general. What's more, the possibilities afforded by the literal margin of a book, i.e., the partial liberation from doctrinal and utilitarian constraint, extended quite naturally to any non-central, non-principal space in art and architecture: frames, archivolts, capitals, misericords, rooftops. The floor of Chartres Cathedral, for example, contains a thirteenth-century circular path that ends at an open scalloped space (Fig. 3.1). This scalloped space is meant to be Jerusalem, something once announced clearly, perhaps, in a now-missing plaque (the ghost of which remains in bolt-holes) and still announced obliquely by the scallops themselves, which recall the decoration of the Last Supper's table, a relic of which could still be seen by pilgrims to the Holy Land during the Middle Ages (Connolly 2005: 297–8). The whole was sized to be inhabited, providing an opportunity thereby for an ersatz journey to Jerusalem, where the salvific sacrifice foreseen in Jesus's final meal with the Apostles had taken place. A crenellated wall surrounds this path, a wall unnecessary to the path's function. It is easy to write this wall off as an

---

[14] And one dealt with long ago by Schapiro (1947).
[15] Schapiro (1947) looks at the unnecessary in medieval art as well, but from a different impetus and with different conclusions.
[16] The introduction to Tribble (1993) is particularly useful as a concise history of the glossed margin.
[17] For a reproduction, see Corrigan (1992).
[18] The painting of the Crucifixion inspires additional commentary in the lowest border of the folio, where two men who look like the men crucifying Jesus whitewash an icon of Jesus that looks exactly like the Jesus being crucified (the circular frame recalling even his nimbus). The commentary is, of course, that those who whitewash images (iconoclasts) are like those who crucified Jesus.

Fig. 3.1 Pavement, Notre Dame Cathedral, Chartres, Frances, c. 1220 (photo: Sonia Halliday Photo Library)

anticipated component of the city of Jerusalem, and yet the fact that it contains but one gate, when Jerusalem importantly had twelve according to scripture (Ezekiel 40–8) and eight in reality, suggests that this particular frame is doing something more than imitating Jerusalem's walls. Indeed, the crenellated wall makes the central circular path read less like, say, a shaped garden maze and more like a built labyrinth. And its creators read like the famous first architect, Daedalus, accordingly.[19]

A similar boldness can be observed in the throwaway surfaces of ecclesiastical painting programmes. At the Church of the Resurrection in Abu Ghosh, Israel, which was built around the middle of the thirteenth century for the Knights of the Hospital of St John (the Hospitallers), dados, pillars, arches and window splays are painted in imitation of more expensive and more difficult to acquire coloured marble slabs (Carr 1982; Kühnel 1988; Fishhof 2017; Fig. 3.2). This is a centuries-old practice, with compelling examples found in the well-preserved painted interiors of sites like Herculaneum and Pompeii. There is something particularly interesting about its implications within a Christian space, however. The focus of the programme within the body of the church is depictions of individual saints and elaborate scenes dedicated to important moments in the life of Jesus and the life of the Virgin, as one might expect. These paintings find their organising function in communicating Christian doctrine in general and the redemptive power of this space in particular. The dominant modern and Western judgement that the best art is realistic art had no place in this world, where pains were taken to ensure that viewers did not mistake a painted figure with actual presence. Accordingly, it was not the goal of the medieval artist to create realistic forms.[20] The realism that has inspired the faux marbled dados, pillars, arches and window splays is thus especially interesting, for it

Fig. 3.2 Wall paintings, Church of the Resurrection, Abu Ghosh, Israel, c. 1170
(photo: Rory O'Neill)

---

[19] Murray (1996: 170–3) sees the crafty labyrinth at Notre Dame to do this same thing. Connolly (2005: 285–314, esp. 296–7) understands the crenellations to refer to Jerusalem's actual walls.
[20] On the meaningful absence of realism in medieval works of art, see Maguire (1989) and Freeman and Meyvaert (2001).

demonstrates an ability to make things that look like things in the world. If we recall the function of the margin as a gloss on a centre, it also suggests that these areas are meant to remind a viewer of the power of paint and to not be too drawn in by it.

Other clearly marginal spaces include the archivolts of church tympana, those outer arches that envelop the portal scenes that prepare an audience for its transition into a sacred space.[21] The Romanesque Church of Sainte-Foy in Conques, France has a large and elaborate Last Judgement scene in this location, which announces, 'Sinners, if you do not change your ways, know that a hard judgement will be upon you', according to the lowest band of text (Kendall 1989: 169).[22] Christ in Majesty is in the centre, with right hand raised to save those on his right (our left) and left hand lowered to condemn those on his left (our right). The scene is inspired especially by the Books of Matthew and Revelation, a connection made emphatic by the text that is reproduced on available flat surfaces whether or not it could be read.[23] This text does not account, however, for all of the scene's details, not Charlemagne among the processing saved, for example, the emperor who had donated the abbey's land, nor the poacher roasted alive by a hare-demon among the damned. This alternately hopeful and harrowing scene has at its outermost edges, nearly out of sight, a series of fourteen figures who peek out from above unfurling scrolls, as if simultaneously revealing the Last Judgement and drawing attention to the act of revealing. Although the identity of these sculpted figures is unclear, it is not much of a stretch to see them as the creators of this locally inspired eschatological event and, thus, as playing an unexpectedly vital role in the drama of the church façade.[24]

Michael Camille long ago argued for the vitality and importance of the marginal, and art historians such as Lillian Randall and Thomas Dale have long demonstrated the extent to which imagery of the margins is polyvalent (Randall 1966; Camille 1992; Dale 2001).[25] For the project at hand, the additive potential of the margin, freed of the obligations of the centre, allows it to point to the very excesses that interest us here and to see in these excesses shadows of their creators. Bernard of Clairvaux bemoaned just this in his oft-quoted *Apologia* (c. 1125):

> To what purpose are those unclean apes, those fierce lions, those monstrous centaurs, those half-men, those striped tigers, those fighting knights, those hunters winding their horns? . . . [S]o many and so marvelous are the varieties of divers shapes on every hand, that we are more tempted to read in the marble than in our books, and to spend the whole day in wondering at these things rather than in meditating the law of God. (Rudolph 1990: 282–3)

The larger text to which this passage belongs indicates that Bernard's main concerns are with artistic distractions in the monastery, but his list of famously well-observed imaginative and unorthodox forms is instructive nonetheless.[26] In short, then, the above examples show, at least on one level, creators using marginal spaces to say something about the creator, on the one hand, and about the creative practice, on the other.

---

[21] A good place to start with imagery of this kind is Camille (1992: 56–75), especially the chapters on images in the margins of the monastery.
[22] For a reproduction of this tympanum, see Hearn (1981).
[23] On the effect of illiteracy on reception, see Mathews (2000). On illiteracy in general, see Bäuml (1980).
[24] On the performative aspect of tympana, see, for example, Cahn (1992) and, more recently, Castiñeiras (2015). On the role of the artist in the creation of this tympanum, see Huang (2014).
[25] Scholarship on this subject is voluminous. These sources also provide particularly good historiographical analyses.
[26] The meaning of Bernard's words has been much debated, see, for example, Viollet-le-Duc (1859: II, 283–301), Schapiro (1947), Rudolph (1990) and Kessler (2012). Rudolph (1989, 1990: 13–16) gives a systematic overview of the scholarship (up to 2000).

Having found such traces of artistic creation in marginal spaces, we might then move towards the centre. The so-called 'carpet pages' of seventh- and eighth-century Anglo-Saxon manuscripts are striking examples of foregrounded (non-utilitarian) decoration; indeed, it is this foregrounded and vast decoration that has led them to be associated with luxurious carpets.[27] Meyer Schapiro's modernist leanings inspired him to locate artistic genius in just these folia, folia that had previously been treated as beautiful but rote works of ornament (Schapiro 2005: 29–53). Schapiro argued that the creators of these manuscripts' patterned pages were aware of an audience and of the expectations that that audience had of ornament, offering sly irregularities in colour, shape and orientation in place of the regularity that ought to belong to them. He also argued that these patterned pages were similar to works that are recognised products of artistic genius – like painted landscapes and figural reliefs, like architecture and music. In this way, Schapiro demonstrated that even works that appear to be the most wholly, the most singularly, the most manifestly decorative, held within them a space for something beyond what was required, a space for excess. One example from the Lindisfarne Gospels (c. 715) shows, in particular, the musical quality of 'decoration' (London, British Library, Cotton MS Nero D IV; Fig. 3.3). This is not a carpet page but the beginning of the Book of Matthew. The phrase 'Liber generationis ihu xpi filii david filii abraham [The book of the genealogy of Jesus Christ, son of David, son of Abraham]' covers the available surface entirely. As the letters move from left to right and top to bottom, they become smaller, thinner, less densely decorated and closer to one another (Schapiro 2005: 34–7). These changes suggest an increased agility and speed and, thus, animate the presumed inanimate. If this effect is missed in the first letters, the last make it clear. Here 'abra' piles on top of 'ham' as if pushed there by the impact of the 'Liber generationis ihu xpi filii david filii' that precedes them. The apparent force of all of these characters has even dented and begun to break the page's frame. Beyond its analogy with music, which Schapiro names 'ingression' and defines as 'the process of entering into a powerful, dynamic, and musical way', this painted page is peculiarly illuminating because the purpose of its content seems so straightforward – to present the first words of the Book of Matthew (Schapiro 2005: 36). In the Lindisfarne Gospels, however, formal manipulations serve to manifest the power of the scribe or illuminator who has painted these words, for they have the ability to make something seemingly self-evident and fixed, nuanced and flexible.

The Lindisfarne Gospels, then, point not only to the excesses of the centre, but also to the excessive potential of essentially nonrepresentational forms. The Procopius and Suger quotes with which this chapter began testified already to the unintuitive promise of the nonrepresentational, of course, the former with regard to the Hagia Sophia's incomprehensible structure and the latter to St Denis's kaleidoscopic materials, and both with regard to transcendence. These seemingly one-dimensional forms could be both ecstatic and expressive sites, however, something one sees particularly acutely in Cistercian grisaille stained glass and Hrabanus Maurus's figured poems.

The Cistercian order was born as a reform movement in 1098. It was characterised by a return to the self-sufficiency and austerity that lay at the heart of the Rule of St Benedict, the rule that dominated monastic life in medieval Europe.[28] The Cistercian commitment to austerity affected their built environment noticeably, encouraging formal simplicity and forbidding colour and imagery. One result of these controls was grisaille stained-glass windows with abstract motifs (see, for example, Fig. 3.4). The colourless windows and regularly repeating floral and geometric shapes were deliberately stripped of distraction, of

---

[27] For an overview, see Karkov (2011).

[28] Of the many sources that might be given here, see Rudolph (1987, 1997) and Talbot (1986).

Fig. 3.3 Incipit from the Gospel of Matthew, Lindisfarne Gospels, c. 715 (London, British Library, Cotton MS Nero D IV, f. 27r) (photo: The British Library Board)

Fig. 3.4 Cistercian glass, Eberbach, Germany, c. 1180 (Wiesbaden Museum, Wiesbaden, Germany) (photo: Michael Palmen/Stiftung Kloster Eberbach)

course – of the vibrant colour and of the biblical and hagiographical narratives that conventionally characterise stained glass – but in its place offered conspicuously outlined forms that concentrated thought by way of immersive patterns.[29] In this way, these windows belong to a long tradition of strategically designing windows in spaces used by clergy to facilitate mediation, albeit by distinctly Cistercian means (Caviness 1992; Kessler 2000). Their grisaille, however, involved an expense that is unintuitive for historians, and irregular for Cistercians (Gage 1982; Parsons Lillich 1984: 218). It was also unnecessary. Even if the colourless-ness of the windows made their lead-lined forms conspicuous, it also placed the impressively rhythmic floral and geometric shapes and their intricacy centre stage and, thereby, underlined their admirable artistry. The Cistercian windows, thus, offer an example of excess that is monetary and, more important, chromatic.

In the early ninth century, Hrabanus Maurus (d. 856) composed his *De laudibus sanctae crucis*, a series of twenty-eight *carmina figurata*, or figured poems (Sears 1989). Each poem consists of hexametrical verses equal in length. Each line of each of these poems consists of thirty-five to thirty-seven characters. Within the character field of each poem are additional poetic phrases that work like a crossword puzzle, only here the borrowed letters of the main poem become an image. The most frequently reproduced of these poems contains at its centre a word-based image of Jesus in cruciform (Rome, Biblioteca Apostolica Vaticana, MS Reg. lat. 124; Fig. 3.5). His halo is formed by the letters 'REXREGUMETDOMINUSDOMINORUM [King of kings and Lord of lords]',

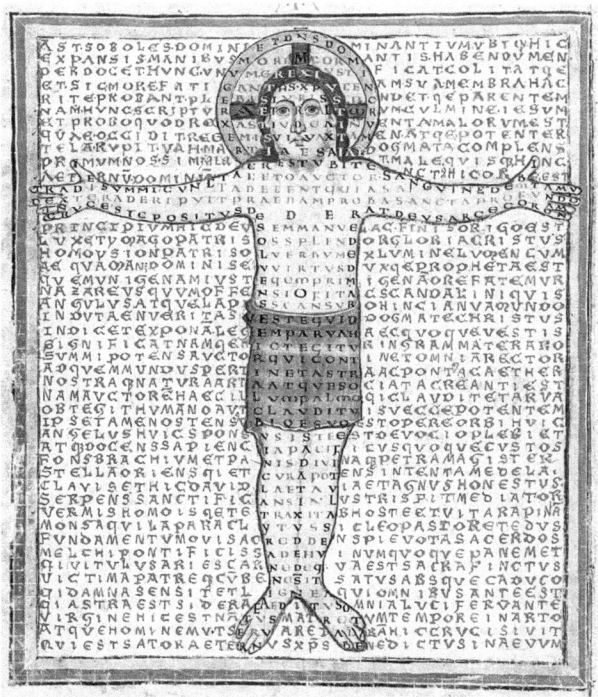

Fig. 3.5 Hrabanus Maurus, *De laudibus sanctae crucis*, second quarter 9th c. (Rome, Biblioteca Apostolica Vaticana, Vatican MS Reg. lat. 124, f. 8v) (photo: 2019 Biblioteca Apostolica Vaticana)

---

[29] On these windows and their capacity to direct meditation, see Parsons Lillich (1984: 7–54, esp. 218–22).

his hair by the letters 'ISTEESTREXIUSITIAE [This is the king of justice]'. This spectacular fusion of word and image performs fundamentally the Church's position, namely that text (and not, say, the pictures produced by way of the imagination of an artist) underlies and provokes spiritual meditation. According to the contemporary *Libri Carolini*, an impassioned response to the discussion of the veneration of images that had taken place in the seventh ecumenical council of Nicaea (787), text is, in fact, the only thing human-made capable of provoking spiritual meditation (Chazelle 1986: 181).[30] With this thinking in mind, Maurus's Jesus appears intentionally ethereal, without the details of historical, geographical and narrative setting one might expect. This aligns remarkably with the volume's project, each of its poems and the collection of poems as a whole intended to inspire mediation on the holy cross, on the Crucifixion, as implied by the title – *De laudibus sanctae crucis*.[31] The meditation, then, is aided by the poetic phrases, which initiate the move from profane to sacred things as the reader considers their relationship to the main poem and to the shapes they evoke (Sears 1989: 341).[32] But, as with the grisaille of the Cistercian windows, the paint that joins the poetic phrases into a recognisable formal whole is expendable and, ultimately, draws attention to Maurus's pictorial way with words.

Conclusion

The preceding paragraphs offer but a suggestion of the ways in which we can see a medieval aesthetic, or the ideas that guide the design of art and architecture. Rather than being led by a reading of texts that insist function determines form, which would incidentally also give us a medieval aesthetic, this discussion has been led by an analysis of the seemingly inconsequential spaces, inert motifs and unnecessary material components that suggest otherwise. The selection of works has been guided by the goal of considering different kinds of arts and their different excessive possibilities. The result is neither encyclopedic nor comprehensive, something especially obvious in the emphasis on the middle of the Middle Ages, on the West and on religious contexts.[33] What is more, the analysis of the selection offers but one way of seeing a medieval aesthetic, when the impulse to imitate, for example, to order form according to rules of proportion, to value variation, to employ one master rather than another would likewise serve as available indicators of the creators' aesthetic principles (Schapiro 1932–3, 1947; Krautheimer 1942; Brenk 1987).[34] The particular site for locating a medieval aesthetic that has been advanced is not radically new, scholars have long looked at the margins, at ornament and at material to uncover the individual within the communal, freedom within the carefully circumscribed. Nevertheless, the specific works of art and architecture presented here and the different ways in which these works point to the non-utilitarian, to that which is not required and to excess encourage a way of looking at medieval visual culture that the unexpected is illuminated and attention is drawn to the creators themselves, however obliquely. In so doing, I hope to have highlighted a particularly medieval aesthetic matter.

---

[30] This is too simple a presentation of the Carolingian position on images. For one more complex, see, for example, Freeman (1957), Chazelle (1986, 1995), Freeman and Meyvaert (2001). On the special status of text that is described here, see especially Chazelle (1986: 181).

[31] On the cross and the *Libri Carolini*, see Chazelle (1986: 165–70).

[32] These relationships were aided by a commentary (Sears 1989: 342). See also Reudenbach (1984) and Chaganti (2014).

[33] On the different expectations and requirements of non-religious art, see, for example, Hassig (1990/1991) and Maguire (1999).

[34] Caviness's (2010) essay on reception in *A Companion to Medieval Art* offers a substantial historiographical discussion on the issue of art appreciation.

References

Alexander, Jonathan J. G. (1992). *Medieval Illuminators and Their Methods of Work*. New Haven: Yale University.
Allen, Terry (1988). 'Aniconism and Figural Representation in Islamic Art'. In *Five Essays on Islamic Art*. Sebastopol, CA: Solipsist Press, pp. 17–37.
Augustine (2002). *On the Trinity*. Trans. Stephen McKenna. Cambridge: Cambridge University Press.
Barber, Charles (ed.) (forthcoming). *Texts on Byzantine Art and Aesthetics*. Cambridge: Cambridge University Press.
Bäuml, Franz H. (1980). 'Varieties and Consequences of Medieval Literacy and Illiteracy'. *Speculum*, 55: 237–65.
Bland, Kalman P. (2000). *The Artless Jew: Medieval and Modern Affirmations and Denials of the Visual*. Princeton: Princeton University Press.
Brenk, Beat (1987). 'Spolia from Constantine to Charlemagne: Aesthetics versus Ideology'. *Dumbarton Oaks Papers*, 41: 103–9.
Byng, Gabriel (2017). *Church Building and Society in the Later Middle Ages*. Cambridge: Cambridge University Press.
Cahn, Walter (1992). 'Romanesque Sculpture and the Spectator'. In *The Romanesque Frieze and Its Spectator*. Ed. Deborah Kahn. London: Harvey Miller, pp. 45–60.
Camille, Michael (1992). *Image on the Edge: The Margins of Medieval Art*. Cambridge, MA: Harvard University Press.
Carr, Annemarie Weyl (1982). 'The Mural Paintings of Abu Ghosh and the Patronage of Manuel Comnenus in the Holy Land'. In *Crusader Art in the Twelfth Century*. Ed. Jaroslav Folda. Jerusalem: British Archaeological Reports, pp. 215–43.
Carr, Annemarie Weyl (1987). *Byzantine Illumination, 1150–1250: The Study of a Provincial Tradition*. Chicago: University of Chicago Press.
Caskey, Jill (2010). 'Whodunnit? Patronage, the Canon, and the Problems of Agency in Romanesqu and Gothic Art'. In *A Companion to Medieval Art*. Ed. Conrad Rudolph. Oxford: Wiley Blackwell.
Castiñeiras, Manuel (2015). 'The Romanesque Portal as Performance'. *Journal of the British Archaeological Association*, 168: 1–33.
Caviness, Madeline H. (1992). *The Bible in the Middle Ages: Its Influence on Literature and Art*. Binghamton, NY: SUNY.
Caviness, Madeline H. (2010). 'Reception of Images by Medieval Views'. In *A Companion to Medieval Art*. Ed. Conrad Rudolph. Oxford: Wiley-Blackwell, pp. 65–85.
Chaganti, Seeta (2014). 'Figure and Ground: *Elene's* Nails, Cynewulf's Runes, and Hrabanus Maurus's Painted Poems'. In *The Arma Christi in Medieval and Early Modern Material Culture*. Ed. Lisa H. Cooper and Andrea Denny-Brown. Earnham, Surrey: Ashgate.
Chazelle, Celia M. (1986). 'Matter, Spirit, and Image in the *Libri Carolini*'. *Recherches Augustiniennes*, 21: 163–84.
Chazelle, Celia M. (1990). 'Pictures, Books, and the Illiterate: Pope Gregory I's Letters to Serenus of Marseilles'. *Word & Image*, 6: 139–40.
Chazelle, Celia M. (1995). '"Not in Painting but in Writing": Augustine and the Supremacy of the Word in the *Libri Carolini*'. In *Reading and Wisdom: The* De doctrina christiana *of Augustinein the Middle Ages*. Ed. Edward D. English. South Bend, IN: University of Notre Dame, pp. 1-22.
Connolly, Daniel (2005). 'At the Center of the World: The Labyrinth Pavement of Chartres Cathedral'. In *Art and Architecture of Late Medieval Pilgrimage in Northern Europe and the British Isles*. Ed. Sarah Blick and Rita Tekippe. Leiden: Brill.
Corrigan, Kathleen (1992). *Visual Polemics in the Ninth-Century Byzantine Psalters*. Cambridge: Cambridge University Press.
Dale, Thomas E. A. (2001). 'Monsters, Corporeal Deformities and Phantasms in the Cloister of St-Michel-de-Cuxa: A Response to Saint Bernard'. *Art Bulletin*, 83: pp. 402–36.
Dean, Carolyn (2006). 'The Trouble with (the Term) Art'. *Art Journal*, 65: 24–32.
Eco, Umberto (2002). *Art and Beauty in the Middle Ages*. New Haven, CT: Yale University Press.

Elsner, Jas (1994). 'The Viewer and the Vision: The Case of the Sinai Apse'. *Art History*, 17: 81–102.
Fishhof, Gil (2017). 'Hospitaller Patronage and the Mural Cycle of the Church of the Resurrection at Abu-Ghosh (Emmaus): A New Reading'. In *The Military Orders*. Ed. Jochen Schenk and Mike Carr. London: Routledge, pp. 81–93.
Freeman, Ann (1957). 'Theodulf of Orleans and the Libri Carolini', *Speculum*, 32: 663–705.
Freeman, Ann and Paul Meyvaert (2001). 'The Meaning of Theodulf's Apse Mosaic at Germigny des-Prés'. *Gesta*, 40: 125–39.
Gage, John (1982). 'Gothic Glass: Two Aspects of a Dionysian Aesthetic'. *Art Bulletin*, 5: 36–58.
Gilbert, Creighton (1985). 'A Statement of the Aesthetic Attitude around 1230'. *Hebrew University Studies in Literature and Art*, 13: 125–52.
Grabar, Oleg (1973). 'Islamic Attitudes toward the Arts'. In *The Formation of Islamic Art*. New Haven: Yale University Press, pp. 72–98, reprinted 1987.
Grabar, Oleg (1995). *The Meditation of Ornament*. Princeton: Princeton University Press.
Hassig, Debra (1990/1991). 'Beauty in the Beasts: A Study of Medieval Aesthetics'. *RES: Anthropology and Aesthetics*, 19/20: 137–61.
Hearn, M. F. (1981). *Romanesque Sculpture: The Revival of Monumental Stone Sculpture in the Eleventh and Twelfth Centuries*. Ithaca: Cornell University.
Huang, Lei (2014). 'Le Maître du tympan de l'abbatiale Sainte-Foy de Conques: état de la question et perspectives'. *Études aveyronnaises*: 87–100.
Ivanovic, Filip (2014). 'The Eternally and Uniquely Beautiful: Dionysius the Areopagite's Understanding of the Divine Beauty'. *International Journal of Philosophy and Theology* 74: 188–204.
James, Liz (1996). *Light and Color in Byzantine Art*. Oxford: Clarendon.
James, M. R. (1951). 'Pictor in Carmine'. *Archeologia*, 94: 141–66.
Karkov, Catherine E. (2011). *The Art of Anglo-Saxon England*. Woodbridge: Boydell.
Kendall, Calvin B. (1989). 'The Voice in the Stone: The Verse Inscriptions of Ste.-Foy of Conques and the Date of the Tympanum'. In *Hermeneutics and Medieval Culture*. Ed. Patrick J. Gallacher and Helen Damico. Albany: SUNY, pp. 163–82.
Kessler, Herbert (2000). 'The Function of *Vitrum Vestitum* and the Use of *Materia Saphirorum* in Suger's St-Denis'. In *Spiritual Seeing: Picturing God's Insibility in Medieval Art*. Philadelphia: University of Pennsylvania Press, pp. 190–205.
Kessler, Herbert (2010). 'Gregory the Great and Image Theory in Northern Europe during the Twelfth and Thirteenth Centuries'. In *A Companion to Medieval Art*. Ed. Conrad Rudolph. Oxford: Wiley-Blackwell.
Kessler, Herbert (2012). '"They preach not by speaking out loud but by signifying": Vitreous Arts as Typology'. *Gesta*, 51: 55–70.
Kidson, Peter (1987). 'Panofsku, Suger, and St. Denis'. *Journal of the Warburg and Courtauld Institutes*, 50: 1–17.
Kraus, Henry (1979). *Gold was the Mortar: The Economics of Cathedral Building*. London: Routledge and Kegan Paul.
Krautheimer, Richard (1942). 'Introduction to an "Iconography of Medieval Architecture"'. *Journal of the Warburg and Courtauld Institutes*, 5: 1–33.
Kühnel, Gustav (1988). *Wall Painting in the Latin Kingdom of Jerusalem*. Berlin: Gebr. Mann.
Luibheid, Colin (trans.) (1987). *Pseudo-Dionysius The Complete Works*. New York: Paulist Press.
Maguire, Henry (1989). 'Style and Ideology in Byzantine Imperial Art'. *Gesta*, 28: 217–31.
Maguire, Henry (1999). 'The Profane Aesthetic in Byzantine Art and Literature'. *Dumbarton Oaks Papers*, 53: 189–205.
Mann, Vivian B. (2000). *Jewish Texts on the Visual Arts*. Cambridge: Cambridge University Press.
Mathew, Gervase (1971). *Byzantine Aesthetics*. New York: Harper and Row.
Mattews, Karen Rose (2000). 'Reading Romanesque Sculpture: The Iconography and Reception of the South Portal Sculpture at Santiago de Compostela'. *Gesta*, 39: 3–12.
Michelis, P. A. (1964). 'Comments on Gervase Mathew's "Byzantine Aesthetics"'. *The British Journal of Aesthetics*, 4: 253–62.
Morrison, Karl F. (trans.) (1992). *Conversion and Text: The Cases of Augustine of Hippo, Herman Judah, and Constantine Tsatsos*. Charlottesville: University Press of Virginia.

Murray, Stephen (1996). *Notre-Dame, Cathedral of Amiens: The Power of Change in Gothic*. Cambridge: Cambridge University Press.
Panofksy, Erwin (ed. and trans.) (1979). *Abbott Suger on the Abbey Chirch of St.-Denis and Its Art Treasures*. Princeton: Princeton University Press.
Parsons Lillich, Meredith (1984). Monastic Stained Glass: Patronage and Style'. In *Monasticism and the Arts*. Ed. Timothy Gregory Verdon. Syracuse: Syracuse University Press, pp. 207–54.
Pearce, Sarah (ed.) (2013). *The Image and Its Prohibition in Jewish Antiquity*. Oxford: Journal of Jewish Studies.
Priester, Ann (1993). 'Bell Towers and Building Workshops in Medieval Rome'. *Journal of the Society of Architectural Historians*, 52: 199–220.
Procopius (1987). *On Buildings*. Trans. H. B. Dewing. Cambridge, MA: Harvard University Press.
Randall, Lillian M. C. (1966). *Images in the Margins of Gothic Manuscripts*. Berkeley: University of California Press.
Reudenbach, Bruno (1984). 'Das Verhältnis von Text und Bild in "De laudibus sanctae crucis" der Hrabanus Maurus'. In *Geistliche Denkformen in der Literatur des Mittelalters*. Ed. Klaus Grubmüller, Ruth Schmidt-Wiegand and Klaus Speckenback. Munich: Wilhelm Fink, pp. 282–320.
Rudolph, Conrad (1987). 'The "Principal Founders" and the Early Artistic Legislation of Cîteaux'. *Studies in Cistercian Art*, vol. III. Ed. Meredith Parsons Lillich. Kalamazoo: Cistercian Publications, pp. 1–45.
Rudolph, Conrad (1989). The Scholarship on Bernard of Clairvaux's *Apologia*'. *Cîteaux: Commentarii Cistercienses*, 40: 69–111.
Rudolph, Conrad (1990). *The 'Things of Greater Importance:' Bernard of Clairvaux's* Apologia *and the Medieval Attitude Toward Art*. Philadelphia: University of Pennsylvania Press.
Rudolph, Conrad (1997). *Violence and Daily Life: Reading, Art, and Polemics in the Citeaux* Moralia in Job. Princeton: Princeton University Press.
Schapiro, Meyer (1932–3). 'Über den Schematismus in der romanischen Kunst'. *Kritische Berichte zur Kunstgeschichtlichen Literatur*, 5: 1–21. (Reprinted as 'On Geometrical Schematism in Romanesque Art', in *Romanesque Art: Selected Papers*. New York: George Braziller, 1977, pp. 265–84.)
Schapiro, Meyer (1947). 'On the Aesthetic Attitude in Romanesque Art'. In *Art and Thought*. Ed. K. Bharatha Iver. London: Luzac, pp. 130–50. (Reprinted in *Romanesque Art: Selected Papers*. New York: George Braziller, 1977, pp. 1–27.)
Schapiro, Meyer (2005). 'The Capret Page and the Giant Initial'. In *The Language of Forms: Lectures on Insular Manuscript Art*. New York: Morgan Library and Museum, pp. 29–53.
Schibille, Nadine (2014). *Hagia Sophia and the Byzantine Aesthetic Experience*. Earnham, Surrey: Ashgate.
Sears, Elizabeth (1989). 'Words and Images in Carolingian *Carmina Figurata*'. In *World Art: Themes of Unity and Diversity*. Ed. Iriving Lavin. University Park: Pennsylvania State University Press, II, pp. 341–5.
Tachau, Katherine H. (1998). 'God's Compass and *Vanu Curiositas*: Scientific Study in the Old French *Bible Moralisée*'. *Art Bulletin*, 80: 7–33, fig. 1.
Talbot, Charles Hugh (1986). 'The Cistercian Attitude Towards Art: The Literary Evidence'. In *Cistercian Art and Architecture in the British Isles*. Ed. Christopher Norton and David Park. Cambridge: Cambridge University Press, pp. 56–64.
Theophilus (1979). 'Prologue'. In *On Divers Arts: The Foremost Medieval Treatise on Painting, Glassmaking, and Metalwork*. Trans. John G. Hawthorne and Cyril Stanley Smith. New York: Dover, pp. 11–13.
Tribble, Evelyn B. (1993). *Margins and Marginality: The Printed Page in Early Modern England*. Charlottesville: University of Virginia Press.
Viollet-le-Duc, Eugene-Emmanuel (1859). *Dictionnaire raisonné de l'architecture française du XIe au XVIe siècle*. Paris: B. Bance.
Weiss, Daniel H. (1998). *Art and Crusades in the Age of Saint Louis*. Cambridge: Cambridge University Press.

4

A Classroom of One's Own: Medieval Conceptions of Women and Education

Maggie Ann Labinski

Introduction

The presence of women within higher education remains a source of ongoing contention. Across the United States, colleges and universities are considering new policies that would disproportionately hinder those students and faculty who identify as female. These considerations have raised a host of enquiries: does the diversification of 'the canon' mark the beginning of the end of democracy (Stephens 2017)? Should practices intended to protect survivors of sexual assault be abandoned (DeVos 2018)? Is the need for gender-based scholarships a thing of the past (Bauer-Wolf 2018)?

Such issues have largely originated in conjunction with recent statistics regarding the academic achievements of women. After a long tradition of exclusion from most formal educational settings, women have begun to make up much-needed ground. Studies suggest that female students are more likely than ever to complete a bachelor's degree, master standardised tests and participate in college preparatory work (Marcus 2017). As Janet Mulvey (2018) argues: 'The 21st century is becoming the era of the woman . . . Even in the hard sciences and engineering, where men traditionally have dominated, the margin is narrowing.' While some might regard this as a victory, an example of what it looks like to defy systemic oppression, others have expressed concerns. Most notably, a select group of scholars and pedagogues have maintained that the success of women in the classroom has negatively impacted the lives of men. Bernie Froese-Germain (2005) explains:

> 'What about the boys?' has become the rallying cry of critics who believe schools are failing young males. Some feel [. . .] that gains for girls have been made on boys' backs. 'Feminization' of the curriculum, school culture and teaching profession, so the argument goes, has worked against the interest and strengths of boys.

By extension, many have called for sweeping pedagogical changes that would 'balance' the gender scales, 'de-feminise' the classroom and return crucial resources to their 'proper' place (Osaat and Okenwa 2018).

The either/or logic behind this sentiment raises serious questions about popular notions of educational progress. It also highlights the practical consequences of our assumptions about gender. To claim, for instance, that women are better served by a 'feminised' curriculum implies a certain understanding of the essence of 'women' themselves. So, too, the conclusion that feminine experience is somehow detrimental to the promise of teaching and learning is nothing new. As Patricia Cayo Sexton (1965: 57) states, the topic of women's pedagogical place is an 'ancient conflict' with an extensive history (see Grumet 1981; Griffiths 2006;

Maher 2012). In order to elucidate at least part of this history, in what follows I will investigate how three philosophers from the medieval era – Augustine, Abelard and Thomas Aquinas – broached the intersection of gender and education. Special attention will be paid to the ways in which their theories about gender shaped their receptivity to women in the classroom. My intention in turning to these figures is not to suggest that they offer exemplary answers to such (disappointingly) relevant problems. Rather, my goal is simply to underscore the importance of critically examining the connection between our ideas about gender and those who occupy our classrooms. As such, and by way of conclusion, I will gesture broadly towards some of the avenues we might explore when it comes to the subject of women and education today.

Augustine

Neutered Homo

Perhaps the most influential aspect of Augustine's (354–430 CE)[1] understanding of gender can be found in his analysis of the *imago dei* – that is, the notion that human beings reflect the likeness of the Christian God (Matter 2007: 210). Throughout the third and fourth centuries, the Christian Church was engaged in a variety of debates about the parameters of the *imago dei*. (Power 1996: 131–4). Of particular concern was whether or not women share in this divine gift. For Augustine, the issue was partly scriptural. Augustine was committed to the idea that, as the one true word of his one true God, the Christian Bible presented one consistent message. However, certain key passages seemed to offer conflicting ideas about the status of women. Rosemary Radford Ruether (2007: 54) explains:

> Part of the problem was how to interpret an apparent contradiction between two key texts: *Genesis* 1:27, which seemed to give women the image of God with men and *1 Corinthians* 11:7 where Paul declared that men should not cover their heads because they are the image of God, whereas women should cover their heads because they are only a secondary reflection.

Augustine found himself, thereby, caught between a theological rock and a hard place. While Genesis extended the *imago dei* to all human beings, 1 Corinthians suggested that women fall short.

Augustine's response to this quandary reflects his desire for exegetical continuity and offers insight into his conception of gender. Augustine encourages readers to divide women in two – to 'neuter' them (Chelius Stark 2007: 231). He suggests that insofar as women, like men, are spiritual/rational beings (*homo*), they fully reflect the image of his God. However, insofar as women have female bodies (*femina*), they do not:

> But because she differs from the man by her bodily sex, that part of the reason which is turned aside to regulate temporal things could be properly symbolized by her corporeal veil; thus the image of God does not remain except in that part of the mind of man in which it clings to the contemplation and consideration of the eternal reasons, which, as is evident, not only men but also women possess. (Augustine 2002: 12.7.12)[2]

---

[1] Translations noted in end-of-chapter references. Latin editions of Augustine's texts are from Citta Nuova's *S. Aurelii Augustini Opera Omnia*. Available at <www.augustinus.it.htm> (last accessed 20 March 2019).
[2] 'Sed quia sexu corporis distat a uiro, rite potuit in eius corporali uelamento figurari pars illa rationis quae ad temporalia gubernanda deflectitur ut non maneat imago dei nisi ex qua parte mens hominis aeternis rationibus conspiciendis uel consulendis adhaerescit, quam non solum masculos sed etiam feminas habere manifestum est.'

Consequently, Augustine argues that one need only read the Christian Bible from the correct perspective to see the uniformity of its position. When the author of Genesis proposes that women are the *imago dei*, he writes from the standpoint of *homo*. When Paul infers that women are not, he operates on the side of *femina*.

As Kari Elisabeth Borresen (1990: 411–27) explains, Augustine's acknowledgement of women as *homo* would likely have been considered revolutionary. It was uncommon for thinkers at this time to grant women equal footing with men in any capacity, especially within the lofty heights of the interior realm. Unfortunately, as others have observed, Augustine's account would also seem to harbour significant misgivings about women and their bodies. For, Augustine does not maintain that male participation in the *imago dei* is similarly contingent upon any such separation from the corporeal. It is only women who are in need of 'neutering'. It is only female bodies that fail to mirror the likeness of his God.

By extension, this inconsistency would appear to reinforce the continued subordination of women in the social/political sphere – a place where human beings exist with their bodies. As Judith Chelius Stark (2007: 235) contends, Augustine's contribution to this tradition of misogyny remains despite his own self-stated preference for the spiritual/rational:

> It could be argued that at least Augustine has provided the grounding for a fuller articulation of women's *imago* status by placing it in the spiritual realm, which is, after all, the most important reality for him. Even granting this point, Augustine has done this in the most minimal way possible, according women some acknowledgement as human beings, but providing very little leverage to challenge women's subordinate status in the social, political, or legal realms.

In other words, the problem is that, whether Augustine likes it or not, human beings do not exist as free-floating *homines*. Within the material world, Augustine's reconciliation of Genesis and 1 Corinthians fails to move women beyond the margins. So understood, his conclusions about gender would seem to be, at best, complicated – revolutionary in tone, but potentially oppressive in practice.

The Banquet

This complexity is evident in Augustine's early dialogue, *The Happy Life* (*De beata vita*). After quitting his teaching post in Milan, Augustine travelled to the countryside of Cassiciacum to devote himself to the study of philosophy (Augustine 1948b:1.2.5). While there, he chartered an informal school and invited select friends and family members to join him. Augustine claims to have had some of their more productive lessons transcribed (Augustine 1948b:1.2.5), and *De beata vita* represents one such transcription.

The main subject the interlocutors explore in this text is the terms of human happiness, the condition of 'the full satisfaction of souls'. Most generally, Augustine (1948a: 4.35) argues that the happy life is to be found in the Christian God: 'This, then, is the full satisfaction of souls, this is the happy life: to recognize piously and completely the One through whom you are led into the truth, the nature of the truth you enjoy, and the bond that connects you with the supreme measure.'[3] The issue, Augustine explains, is that such 'pious' acknowledgement is

---

[3] 'Illa est igitur plena satietas animorum, hoc est beata vita, pie perfecteque cognoscere a quo inducaris in veritatem, qua veritate perfruaris, per quid connectaris summo modo.'

easier said than done. While many seek the truth, few have yet discovered it. As a result, those present at Cassiciacum are compelled to investigate the plight of the individual who seeks but does not rest with 'the One' – i.e., the student.

In this way, both the form and content of *De beata vita* offer insight into Augustine's philosophy of education (Marrou 1982). More specifically, within this dialogue Augustine describes the process of teaching and learning as a kind of banquet for the soul. Augustine suggests that all those who 'hunger' for the truth, who chase after his God, are in need of sustenance. Such spiritual 'nutrition' is precisely what the classroom provides. Furthermore, Augustine (1948a: 2.8–9) explains that those who have joined him in the country are about to participate in a special feast:

> There exists, believe me, I said, a certain real sterility and hunger of the soul. For, as the body when its nutrition is withheld is generally ill and scabious, bodily faults that indicate hunger, so are souls filled with ills through which they betray their impoverishment [. . .] On the strength of this, I think that on my birthday I ought to serve a somewhat richer meal, not only for our bodies, but also for our souls, since we all agree that man consists of two things: body and soul.[4]

Augustine maintains that the topic of human happiness, the state of the student, deserves an even grander banquet than usual. It is this 'richer meal' that he, on the occasion of his birth, is eager to serve.

There are multiple parallels, if not coincidences, between traditional early Roman dinners (Dunbabin 2003) and the structure of *De beata vita*. For example, in order to best accommodate their guests, Roman hosts tended to limit themselves to a maximum of nine attendees – the number Augustine invited to his school. Such meals usually involved three courses – the number of days that Augustine instructed his students. Finally, part of what made Roman gatherings distinct from their Greek versions was that men and women were often permitted to dine together. This may well explain the presence of a woman at Augustine's banquet – namely, his mother Monica.

Our Mother

Augustine (1948a: 1.6) is clear that Monica is no ordinary student. Throughout each day of feasting, Augustine gives his mother – 'our mother' – a position of privilege. Monica is the first name on his course roster, the first guest on his list. Augustine (1948a: 1.6) suggests that this is because she is the most 'meritorious' student in attendance at his banquet. More specifically, Augustine argues that Monica's excellence is particularly evident in the demonstration of her intellectual skills. Her desire to know has given her 'mastery of the very stronghold of philosophy' (Augustine 1948a: 2.10).[5] Monica's abilities are similarly acknowledged by her fellow invitees. Her peers direct questions to her, agree with her and tend to give her the last word in their debates.

---

[4] 'Ista ipsa est, inquam, crede mihi, quaedam sterilitas et quasi fames animorum. Nam quemadmodum corpus detracto cibo plerumque morbis atque scabie repletur, quae in eo vivam indicant famem; ita et illorum animi pleni sunt morbis quibus sua ieiunia confitentur [. . .] Quae cum ita sint, arbitror die natali meo, quoniam duo quaedam esse in homine convenit inter nos, id est corpus atque animam, non me prandium paulo lautius corporibus nostris solum, sed animis etiam exhibere debere.'
[5] 'Cui ego arridens atque gestiens: Ipsam, inquam, prorsus, mater, arcem philosophiae tenuisti.'

The source of Monica's exceptionality has been a matter of great scholarly interest. The majority has argued that Augustine attributes his mother's gifts to her relationship with the Christian God (Clark 1999; Boersma 2016). As Elizabeth Clark (1999: 17) explains, while Augustine had, at this point, only recently converted to Christianity, his mother had been immersed in the faith for quite some time. As such, it is not surprising that Monica would serve as the emblem of the faithful, the paradigm of the spiritual. In this vein, Augustine (1948a: 4.27) proposes that Monica's rational capacities originate from a decidedly spiritual place. Her insights stem from the lessons of an internal 'source':

> When, at this point, all had expressed their admiration, and I myself was filled with joy and delight because it was she who had uttered that truth which, as gleaned from the books of the philosophers, I had intended to bring forward as an imposing final argument, I said: Do you all see now that a great difference exists between many and varied doctrines and a soul that is devoted to God? For from what other source flow these words we admire?[6]

Augustine does not insinuate that Monica's faith renders her achievements less authentic than those developed via more human channels. As his later writings suggest, Augustine was increasingly suspicious about the pedagogical possibilities of human teachers. Though these individuals play an important role in the journey of a student, Augustine (1995: 13.45.15) suggests that all education is ultimately the result of the inner workings of his God. Early traces of this conclusion can be found near the end of *De beata vita*. Augustine (1948a: 3.17) admits that he is not the proper host, the proper teacher, at Cassiciacum. The feast that the interlocutors have enjoyed, the lesson they have digested, has been provided by a higher being:

> It is, indeed, somebody else who continually offers all meals, especially such meals, for all. But we generally desist from eating, either because of feebleness or satiety or business. Unless I am mistaken, He is the one about whom we all piously and firmly agreed yesterday – that it is He, through His steady presence in men, who makes them happy.[7]

Consequently, Monica not only serves as a compelling answer to the question of the life of the student, the life of the individual who seeks 'the One'. She also functions as a precursor to an aspect of Augustine's philosophy of education that he will soon articulate more fully.

A Great Man

Augustine's depiction of his model student well reflects his theory of gender and the assumptions about women that subtend it. Though Monica's participation in Augustine's classroom would appear to be revolutionary, it also depends upon an act of feminine 'neutering'. This is clearest in Augustine's defence of his mother in yet another Cassiciacum dialogue – *On Order* [*De ordine*]. In an attempt to respond to the claim that Monica's femininity renders her

---

[6] 'Ubi cum omnes mirando exclamassent, me ipso etiam non mediocriter alacri atque laeto, quod ab ea potissimum dictum esset quod pro magno de philosophorum libris, atque ultimum proferre paraveram: Videtisne, inquam, aliud esse multas variasque doctrinas, aliud animum attentissimum in Deum? Nam unde ista quae miramur, nisi inde procedunt.'

[7] 'Alius est enim qui omnibus cum omnes, tum maxime tales epulas praebere non cessat: sed nos ab edendo, vel imbecillitate, vel saturitate, vel negotio plerumque cessamus: quem manentem in hominibus beatos eos facere, inter nos heri, ni fallor, pie constanterque convenerat.'

ill-suited to partake in philosophical debates, Augustine (1948b: 1.11.31) likens her gender to an article of clothing:

> I care but little about the judgments of proud and ignorant men, who rush to the reading of books in the same way they rush to greet men. They consider, not what kind of men these are, but what kind of clothes they wear and how conspicuously they shine in the pomp of worldly wealth.[8]

Augustine suggests that while Monica may wear the drudges of *femina* without, such external qualities are irrelevant when it comes to her presence at his school. What do matter are the spiritual/rational skills that make her an exceptional *homo* within. In particular, Augustine (1948b: 1.11.32) insists that Monica is more than welcome at his pedagogical feasts because of her love of wisdom:

> Then mother, so that you may not be uninformed, the Greek word from which the term, philosophy, is derived is in the Latin tongue called love of wisdom [. . .] Now if you had no love whatever for wisdom, I would utterly disregard you in my writings; if, however, you had just ordinary love for it, I would not entirely disregard you; and much less if you were to love wisdom as much as I love it. And now seeing that you love it even more than you love me.[9]

Augustine argues that Monica's love for wisdom is so strong that it compels a radical kind of separation from her *femina*. More specifically, the quality of Monica's insights alters the perception others have of her gender. Augustine (1948a: 2.10) shares: 'At these words, our mother exclaimed in such a way that we, entirely forgetting her sex, thought we had some great man in our midst, while in the meantime I became fully aware whence and from what divine source this flowed.'[10] Monica's philosophical prowess is so formidable that it causes her community to divide her from her body and, arguably, upgrade her to a new one – that is, the body of a male. The results of, what Kari Vogt (1995: 171) terms, this 'sex change' are pointed. Monica's transformation opens up important opportunities for her in the classroom, including positions of leadership. Augustine (1948b: 1.11.32) explains:

> And seeing that you have made such advance in [wisdom] that you are not frightened by the dread of any chance of discomfort or even death itself – a most difficult attainment for even the most learned, and a position which all acknowledge to be the stoutest stronghold of philosophy – in view of all of this, shall I not gladly entrust myself to you as a disciple?[11]

---

[8] 'Non valde curo, inquam, superborum imperitorumque iudicia, qui similiter in legendos libros atque in saluntandos homines irruunt. Non enim cogitant quales ipsi, sed qualibus induti vestibus sint et quanta pompa rerum fortunaeque praefulgeant.'

[9] 'Nam ne quid, mater, ignores, hoc graecum verbum quo philosophia nominatur, latine amor sapientiae dicitur [. . .] Contemnerem te igitur in his litteris meis, si sapientiam non amares; non autem contemnerem, si eam mediocriter amares; multo minus, si tantum quantum ego amares sapientiam. Nunc vero cum eam multo plus quam meipsum diligas.'

[10] 'In quibus verbis illa sic exclamabat, ut obliti penitus sexus eius, magnum aliquem virum considere nobiscum crederemus, me interim, quantum poteram, intellegente ex quo illa, et quam divino fonte manarent.'

[11] '[C]umque in ea tantum profeceris, ut iam nec cuiusvis incommodi fortuiti nec ipsius mortis, quod viris doctissimis difficillimum est, horror terrearis, quam summam philosophiae arcem omnes esse confitentur, egone me non libenter tibi etiam discipulum dabo?'

Monica's internal abilities prompt her son to offer her the role of teacher, to hand over his classroom and banquet. While the thrust of such remarks is surely tempered by the pedagogical authority Augustine gives to his God, this does not negate the exchange of power between mother and son itself. Monica emerges as the most fitting human host at Cassiciacum, regardless as to the presence of any divine one.

The Spectacle

At first glance, Augustine's depiction of his mother sheds a potentially positive light upon his understanding of gender and its practical implications. The figure of Monica suggests that, even in a world of bodies, there were some women for whom Augustine's theories had immediate concrete benefits. Monica's 'neutering' did not result in her inevitable marginalisation within the physical space of the classroom. Instead, it enabled her to participate, if not thrive, alongside the bodies of her male peers. By extension, Monica represents one possible moment where Augustine's ideas about women appear to be revolutionary both in terms of theory and in terms of practice.

Still, other lingering concerns remain. At the very least, one might well question the rhetorical motivation behind Augustine's account of his mother. As John H. D'Arms (1999: 301–19) explains, Roman banquets often placed as much of an emphasis on the 'spectacle' surrounding the meal as on the meal itself. Dinner was often accompanied by dancing or live performances. Hosts took great pleasure in the display of the food, often presenting one kind of dish in the form of another. Given this, one wonders if Monica and her transformation are simply a part of the show. Perhaps Augustine's portrayal of her as a model student/teacher, as a man, was simply his way of entertaining his guests – of presenting the fish in the guise of the fowl.

So, too, one wonders about those women who are 'neutered' in less encouraging ways within the dialogue. Monica may be the first student on Augustine's roster, but she is not the first woman he mentions. By way of introduction to *De beata vita*, Augustine (1948a: 1.4) states:

> I acknowledge that I did not fly quickly to the bosom of philosophy, because I was detained by woman's charm and the lure of honors, so that only after their attainment I finally, as occurs only to a few of the most fortunate, rushed with sails full set and all oars bent to that bosom where I found rest.[12]

Augustine opens his text by referencing his mistress of several years. As a part of his conversion to Christianity, Augustine left this unnamed woman – body and soul, *femina* and *homo* – behind. However, a decidedly 'spectacular' version of her remains. Augustine's mistress is present in the form of their male son, Adeodatus (Augustine 1948a:1.6). As the youngest student in Augustine's classroom, Adeodatus does not speak often. Yet, when he does it is clear that those present saw in him the seeds of a 'great man' – an upgraded version of the woman, the life, Augustine abandoned.

These textual possibilities suggest that the options for women in Augustine's classroom were by and large dependent upon him. Augustine is still running the show – doling out allowances to feminine experience as he sees fit. Some women get lucky. Others are all but

---

[12] 'Sed ne in philosophiae gremium celeriter advolarem, fateor, uxoris honorisque illecebra detinebar; ut cum haec essem consecutus, tum demum me, quod paucis felicissimis licuit, totis velis omnibusque remis in illum sinum raperem, ibique conquiescerem.'

'neutered' off the page. Thus, while Augustine's theory of gender may allow for some revolutionary wiggle room, its practical results are primarily dictated by those who already have the benefit of social/political power.

Abelard

The Weaker Sex

Peter Abelard's (1079–1142 CE)[13] conception of gender is largely rooted in his understanding of the divinely decreed 'natural order' (*ordine naturali*) of the world (Abelard and Heloise 1974: 101). Abelard (1974: 206) argues that, within this preordained arrangement, women exist as the 'weaker sex' (*sexus infirmior*), lacking the power granted to men. Such feminine impotence, he contends, is not only evident in the frailness of women's bodies – e.g., their susceptibility to physical violence and abuse (Abelard and Heloise 1974: 209–10); it is also clear in the fragility of their souls – for example, their vulnerability to the 'wiles' of the devil (Abelard and Heloise 1974: 206). Because of this, Abelard concludes that women are inherently suited to be submissive to their male counterparts. Drawing from his Christian scriptures, he explains:

> The weaker sex needs the help of the stronger, so much so that the Apostle lays down that the man must always be over the woman, as her head, and as a sign of this he orders her always to have her head covered. (Abelard and Heloise 1974: 101)[14]

Abelard's commitment to such feminine submission can be observed in the criticism he levies against those religious communities that allowed women to take on leadership roles. Abelard (1974: 101) argues that these 'unnatural' relationships give women an 'authority' that defies the best laid plans of his God:

> And so I am much surprised that the custom should have been long established in convents of putting abbesses in charge of women just as abbots are set over men, and of binding women by profession to the same Rule as men, for there is much in the Rule which cannot be carried out by women, whether in authority or not. In several places too, the natural order is overthrown to the extent that we see abbesses and nuns ruling the clergy who have authority over the people, with opportunities of leading them on to evil desires in proportion to their dominance, holding over them as they do a heavy yoke.[15]

---

[13] Translations noted in end-of-chapter references. I have used the following Latin edition: Abelard and Heloise (1974).

[14] 'Adeo namque sexus infirmior fortioris indiget auxilio, ut semper uirum mulieri quasi capud preesse Apostolus statuat; in cuius etiam rei signo ipsam semper uelatum habere capud precipit.'

[15] 'Vnde non mediocriter miror consuetudines has in monasteriis dudum inoleuisse, quod quemadmodum uiris abbates, ita et feminis abbatisse preponantur et eiusdem regule professione tam femine quam uiri se astringant, in qua tamen pleraque continentur que a feminis tam prelatis quam subiectis nullatenus possunt adimpleri. In plerisque etiam locis, ordine perturbato naturali, ipsas abbatissas atque moniales clericis quoque ipsis, quibus subest populus, dominari conspicimus, et tanto facilius eos ad praua desideria inducere posse quanto eis amplius habent preese, et iugum illud in eos grauissimum exercere.'

Abelard suggests that it is dangerous to permit women to rule in any capacity, including over the lives of other women. He contends that when the weaker sex is allowed to 'dominate', social and spiritual dysfunction inevitably follow.

Without denying the seemingly misogynistic aspects of Abelard's remarks, there are moments where he would appear to take a more critical approach to his own perspective about gender. For example, within his analysis of the most suitable dynamic between the monastery and the convent, Abelard (1974: 213) advocates for a surprising reversal of power. He insists that the monks who assist women religious must pledge themselves to the abbess:

> But so that the men, being stronger than the women, shall not make too heavy demands on them, we make it a rule that they shall impose nothing against the will of the abbess, but do everything at her bidding and, all alike, men and women, shall make profession to her and promise obedience.[16]

Abelard's advice garners women significant advantages. More pressingly, it toes the line when it comes to affirming the practicality of women's perceived weakness. While one might suppose that the fated hierarchy between men and women would translate well into the concrete realities of everyday life, Abelard (1974: 214) contends that it is often destabilising. If men and women want their communities to flourish, they must modify the assumed gap between the abbess's fragility and the monk's privilege:

> [F]or peace will be more soundly based and harmony better preserved the less freedom is allowed to the stronger, while the men will be less burdened by obedience to the weaker women the less they have to fear violence from them. The more a man has humbled himself before God, the higher he will certainly be exalted.[17]

Thus, like Augustine, Abelard's understanding of gender is perhaps best described as complicated. While the overall tone of his remarks would seem problematic, certain details are potentially redeeming.

Battle for the Mind

This entanglement is especially vivid in Abelard's *History of My Calamities* (*Historia calamitatum*) and the correspondences he exchanged with a female student by the name of Heloise (Mews 2005). Throughout these texts, readers are privy to the story of their romantic and, subsequently, religious relationship. Abelard explains that having risen in the ranks of his profession as a teacher, he succumbed to the temptations of 'lechery' (*libido*) and wooed his highly gifted student (Abelard and Heloise 1974: 65). These actions resulted in his eventual castration, decreed by Heloise's outraged uncle. In response, both teacher and student were compelled to take religious vows and transition from carnal lovers to spiritual siblings. As Barbara Newman (1999: 46) argues, the writings of Abelard and Heloise have generated a wide array

---

[16] 'Ne tamen uiri fortiores feminis in aliquo eas grauare presumant, statuimus eos quoque nichil presumere contra uoluntatem diaconisse, sed omnia ipsos etiam ad nutum eius peragere, et omnes pariter tam uiros quam feminas ei professionem facere, et obedientiam promittere.'

[17] '[U]t tanto pax firmior habeatur et melius seruetur concordia quanto fortioribus minus licebit, et tanto minus fortes debilibus obedire grauentur quanto earum uiolentiam minus uereantur. Et quanto amplius hic humiliauerit se apud Deum amplius exaltari certum sit.'

of scholarly interpretations. Abelard's dialectical skills (Abelard and Heloise 1974: 66) and Heloise's knowledge of 'letters' leave any number of rhetorical possibilities on the table (Heidenreich Findley 2005: 281–92). Still, while the hermeneutic play that surrounds these works is undeniable, their pedagogical context has remained generally uncontentious.

Abelard's own philosophy of education mirrors the military background of his family (Abelard and Heloise 1974: 57). He describes his vocation in teaching as a transition from one armed 'conflict' to another:

> For my part, the more rapid and easy my progress in my studies, the more eagerly I applied myself, until I was so carried away by my love of learning that I renounced the glory of the soldier's life, made over my inheritance and rights of the eldest son to my brothers, and withdrew from the court of Mars in order to kneel at the feet of Minerva. I preferred the weapons of dialectic to all the other teachings of philosophy, and armed with these I chose the conflicts of disputation instead of the trophies of war. (Abelard and Heloise 1974: 58)[18]

Abelard explains that the 'weapons of dialectic' offered him a more engaging 'war' that better suited his intellectual desires. Even after he committed himself to the study of Christianity, his skills in this regard rendered his (arguably male) students powerless to combat his aggressive advances (Grey 1992: 85):

> I applied myself mainly to study of the Scriptures as being more suitable to my present calling, but I did not wholly abandon the instruction in the profane arts in which I was better practiced and which was most expected of me. In fact I used it as a hook, baited with a taste of philosophy, to draw my listeners towards the study of true philosophy – the practice of the greatest of Christian philosophers. (Abelard and Heloise 1974: 77)[19]

Abelard implies that, like those his father met on the field, the students who worked with him were little more than prey, unable to fight off their teacher's 'hook' (*hamus*). So understood, Abelard suggests that his classroom was the site of a one-sided, if not inherently manipulative, battle.

Battle for the Heart

This militaristic approach to education only intensified in Abelard's interactions with his female student (Desmond 2006: 57–9). Abelard admits that Heloise is a worthy opponent. Her educational abilities are evident and well recognised. More importantly, he argues that Heloise's 'gift' is fully in keeping with her feminine nature (Abelard and Heloise 1974: 66). She is, in other words, exemplary of the female sex: 'In looks she did not rank lowest, while in the extent

---

[18] 'Ego uero quanto amplius et facilius in studio litterarum profeci tanto ardentius eis inhesi, et in tanto earum amore illectus sum ut militaris glorie pompam cum hereditate et prerogatiua primogenitorum meorum fratribus derelinquens, Martis curie penitus abdicarem ut Minerue gremio educarer; et quoniam dialecticarum rationum armaturam omnibus philosophie documentis pretuli, his armis alia commutaui et tropheis bellorum conflictus pretuli disputationum.'

[19] 'Vbi, quod professioni mee conuenientius erat, sacre plurimum lectioni studium intendens, secularium atrium disciplinam quibus amplius assuetus fueram et quas a me plurimum requirebant non penitus abieci; sed de his quasi hamum quendam fabricaui quo illos philosophico sapore inescatos ad uere philsophie lectionem attraherem, sicut et summum Christianorum philsophorum.'

of her learning she stood supreme. A gift for letters is so rare in women that it added greatly to her charm and had won her renown throughout the realm.' Abelard maintains that while Heloise's love of learning may have bent societal norms, it did not stand as an overt challenge to popular beliefs about the natural order of gender. Heloise is not held to be a monster. The quality of her mind only made her all the more irresistible.

By extension, Abelard's response to his student's gift well reflects his own assumptions about her gender. Rather than accepting Heloise's intellectual capacity as a strength, Abelard defines it as but another site of feminine impotence. He interprets Heloise's love of learning as a weakness that he might manipulate for the sake of his own erotic agenda:

> Knowing the girl's knowledge and love of letters I thought she would be all the more ready to consent, and that even when separated we could enjoy each other's presence by exchange of written messages in which we could speak more openly than in person, and so need never lack the pleasure of conversation. (Abelard and Heloise 1974: 66)[20]

Abelard suggests that Heloise's desire to know has left her susceptible to his sexual advances. Her love of letters functions as a liability that her teacher might 'hook' as he sees fit.

As a result, Abelard elects to enter into a decidedly sinister pedagogical battle with his young charge. Abelard fought with his male students in order to better structure the progression of their studies. With Heloise, Abelard wields the 'weapons of dialectic' to advance her progression towards him (Abelard and Heloise 1974: 66):

> I considered all the usual attractions for a lover and decided she was the one to bring to my bed, confident that I should have an easy success, for at that time I had youth and exceptional good looks as well as my great reputation to recommend me and feared no rebuff from any woman I might choose to honour with my love.[21]

Abelard's willingness to undertake such a significant transformation of Heloise's deepest longings speaks volumes. Instead of engaging in such 'conflicts of disputation' to impress her mind, the assumption of Heloise's weakness leads Abelard to manipulate her heart. Abelard suggests that what it meant for this woman to be a student in his classroom was to serve as the means to his own ends (Duran 2011: 41).

In many ways, Abelard won the battle (Abelard and Heloise 1974: 67):

> We were united, first under one roof, then in heart; and so with our lessons as a pretext we abandoned ourselves entirely to love. Her studies allowed us to withdraw in private, as love desired, and then with our books open before us, more words of love than of our reading passed between us, and more kissing than teaching.[22]

---

[20] 'Tanto autem facilius hanc mihi puellam consensuram credidi quanto amplius eam litterarum scientiam et habere et diligere noueram, nosque etiam absentes scriptis internuntiis inuicem licere presentare, et pleraque audacius scribere quam colloqui, et sic semper iocundis interesse colloquiis.'

[21] 'Hanc igitur, omnibus circumspectis que amantes allicere solent, commodiorem censui in amorem mihi copulare, et me id facillime credidi posse. Tanti quippe tunc nominis eram et iuuentutis et forme gratia preminebam, ut quamcunque feminarum nostro dignarer amore nullam uererer repulsam.'

[22] 'Primum domo una coniungimur, postmodum animo. Sub occasione itaque discipline, amori penitus uaccabamus, et secretos recessus, quos amor optabat, stadium lectionis offerebat. Apertis itaque libris, plura de amore quam de lectione uerba se ingerebant, plura erant oscula quam sententie.'

Years later, Abelard reiterates that Heloise's loss was primarily due to her natural weakness. He argues that her fragility was simply no match for the strength of his dialectical skills, especially when combined with the use of physical force (Abelard and Heloise 1974: 147): 'Even when you were unwilling, resisted to the utmost of your power and tried to dissuade me, as yours was the weaker nature I often forced you to consent with threats and blows.'[23] So too, Abelard describes the violent aftermath of their sexual encounter – that is, his castration – as the necessary consequence of their divinely established gender roles. He suggests that he was forced to pay a heftier price precisely because his God recognised Heloise's powerlessness (Abelard and Heloise 1974: 154): '[T]wo were guilty, one pays the penalty. That, too, was granted by divine mercy to your weaker nature and, in a way, with justice, for you were naturally weaker in sex and stronger in continence and so the less deserving of punishment.'[24]

Contradictions

And yet, despite the uniformity of Abelard's narrative, there is some indication that his theory of gender was, at the very least, met with a certain amount of resistance. At various points throughout their relationship, Heloise would seem to challenge the certainty of women's weakness. More specifically, Heloise battles back. One of the clearest examples of this is Abelard's account of Heloise's opposition to marriage (Kamuf 1982: 1–43; Nouvet 1990: 750–73). As Abelard explains, when her uncle discovered their affair, Abelard attempted to make amends by promising to wed his niece. Unfortunately, Heloise was not on board with the plan these two men laid out for her. In particular, Abelard states that Heloise found such a solution irreconcilable with Abelard's love of philosophy:

> What harmony can there be between pupils and nursemaids, desks and cradles, books or tablets and distaffs, pen or stylus and spindles? Who can concentrate on thoughts of Scripture or philosophy and be able to endure babies crying, nurses soothing them with lullabies, and all the noisy coming and going of men and women about the house? (Abelard and Heloise 1974: 71)[25]

Heloise argues that Abelard has forgotten that the life of philosophy is incompatible with the life of marriage. She contends that her teacher simply cannot have what he wants – Lady Wisdom and Lady Heloise. By pushing back in this regard, Heloise defies the expectation of feminine impotence. More pointedly, she does so in terms that echo her teacher's earlier manipulation of her. Heloise appeals both to the logical inconsistency of Abelard's position and to the longings of his heart. As Abelard used Heloise's love of learning to bring her to him, she now uses his love of philosophy to reclaim the terms of their relationship (Nye 1992).

---

[23] 'Sed et te nolentem et, prout poteras, reluctantem et dissuadentem, que natura infirmior eras, sepius minis ac flagellis ad consensum trahebam.'
[24] 'Duo in culpa, unus in pena. Id quoque tue infirmitati nature diuina indulgetur miseratione et quodam modo iuste. Quo enim naturaliter sexu infirmior eras et fortior continentia, pene minus eras obnoxia.'
[25] 'Que enim conuentio scolarium ad pedissequas, scriptoriorum ad cunabula, librorurm siue tabularum ad colos, stilorum siue calamorum ad fusos? Quis denique sacris uel philosophicis meditaionibus intentus, pueriles uagitus, nutricum que hoc mittigant nenias, tumultuosam familie tam in uiris quam in feminis turbam sustinere poterit?'

Silence

While Heloise ultimately loses this battle as well, her remarks would appear to have had an effect on her teacher. Abelard's later exchanges with his student suggest a general willingness to modify his militaristic philosophy of education. This change falls short of rebuking his allegiance to the 'natural order' of gender *per se*. However, it does present women like Heloise with new pedagogical possibilities – new educational 'power'. Evidence of this shift can be found in Abelard's advice about the application of the Rule of St Benedict within Heloise's convent. Abelard recommends that, above all, women religious should pledge themselves to a state of silence (Kramer 2000: 31). More specifically, Abelard encourages Heloise to 'study' silence (Abelard and Heloise 1974: 187):

> St. Benedict provides for this when he says that 'At all times monks ought to practice silence'. Evidently, to practice or study silence means more than to keep silence, for study is the intense concentration of the mind on doing something. We do many things carelessly or unwillingly, but nothing studiously unless we are willing and apply ourselves.[26]

Silence emerges, thereby, as a new form of learning – one that replaces the external battles of dialectic with the internal mindfulness of meditation. As such, Abelard's proposition urges Heloise to recommit herself to a much less violent pedagogical life.

Initially, Abelard's response may seem suspicious – that is, in keeping with his misgivings about the weakness of women. For instance, and drawing from his sacred scriptures, Abelard contends that silence is an especially valuable 'study' for women because of their susceptibility to the sins of words (Abelard and Heloise 1974: 188–9):

> The Apostle marks this vice especially in you [. . .] Again, in showing Timothy why he has ordered this, he explains that women are gossips and speak when they should not. So, to provide a remedy for so great a plague, let us subdue the tongue by perpetual silence, at least in these place and times.[27]

Abelard proposes that even, if not especially, within the convent walls, women remain frail – vulnerable to the linguistic abuses of others.

At the same time, it would also seem that there are practical benefits to this unique kind of learning. In particular, the turn to silence enables Heloise, enables women, to move from the position of 'prey' to that of teacher. Returning once again to his Christian Bible, Abelard explains that, though it is true that the Apostle expresses suspicions about women and their use of words, it is also true that the activity of teaching is far larger than the 'conflicts' of human speech alone. For example, Abelard maintains that the educational model one finds in the figure of Jesus highlights the importance of wordless teaching (Abelard and Heloise 1974: 201): '[A]s it is written of the Lord, he "set out to do and teach" . . . Let us pay careful heed to what abba Ipitius is recorded

---

[26] 'Quod beatus prouidens Benedictus: "Omni tempore", inquit, "silentium debent studere monachi". Plus quippe esse constat silentio studere quam silentium habere. Est enim studium uehemens applicatio animi ad aliquid gerendum. Multa uero negligenter agimus uel inuiti sed nulla studiose nisi uolentes uel intenti.'

[27] 'Quod in uobis precipue uicium Apostolus notans [. . .] Qui rursus eidem cur hoc preceperit innuens, uerbosas eas et loquentes cum nom oportet arguit. Huic igitur tante pesti remedium aliquod prouidentes, hiis saltem penitus locis uel temporibus linguam continua taciturnitate domemus.'

to have said: "He is truly wise who teaches others by deed, not by words."[28] Abelard argues that his God practised the pedagogy of the 'truly wise', a pedagogy of action. More pointedly, Abelard suggests that this divinely inspired approach to teaching falls under the distinct purview of the abbess, of Heloise. Regardless as to her formal experiences with 'letters', her expertise with words, the abbess is distinctly situated to teach through silent action:

> [B]y obedience she should be worthy of giving orders, and through practicing the Rule rather than hearing it she should have learned it and know it well. If she is not lettered let her know that she should accustom herself not to philosophic studies nor dialectical disputations but to teaching of life and performance of works. (Abelard and Heloise 1974: 201)[29]

It is, to be fair, a far cry from the position of privilege that Augustine would appear to give to Monica. Abelard does not offer Heloise any chance of becoming a teacher of men – 'great men' like himself. However, Abelard does suggest that there are ways in which the teaching and learning of silence nuances his initial equivocation between the 'weapons of dialectic' and the demonstration of (male) strength. He explains:

> To shame the wise, God has chosen what the world counts as weakness. God has chosen the base and contemptible things of the world so as to bring to nothing what is now in being; then no human pride may boast his presence. For the kingdom of God, as he says later, is not a matter of talk but of power. (Abelard and Heloise 1974: 201)[30]

Abelard contends that true 'power' is irreducible to the speeches of men, the war of words. More importantly, he argues that his God has chosen this broader notion of power – the power hidden in weakness – as His own. Such a conclusion hardly assuages the more troubling elements of Abelard's conception of gender. Still, it does leave individuals like Heloise in a far 'stronger' place.

Aquinas

Misbegotten Male

Aquinas's (1225–74CE)[31] understanding of gender was primarily influenced by the writings of Aristotle. As Kristin Popik (1979: 1) argues, the consistency with which Aquinas appeals to 'the Philosopher' gives his remarks a singularity of vision that is unmatched by other medieval

---

[28] '[S]icut de Domino scriptum est: "Qui cepit facere et docere" . . . Quod diligenter attendamus ut scriptum est: "Dixit abbas Ypitius: 'Ille est uere sapiens qui facto suo alios docet, non qui uerbis.'"'
[29] '[E]t que obediendo meruerit imperare, et operando magis quam audiendo Regulam didicerit, et firmius nouerit. Que si litterata non fuerit, sciat se non ad philosophicas scolas uel disputationes dialecticas sed ad doctrinam uite et operum exhibitione accomodari.'
[30] 'Que stulta sunt mundi elegit Deus ut confundat sapientes; et infirma elegit Deus ut confundat fortia. Et ignobilia mundi et contemptibilia elegit Deus ut ea que non sunt tamquam ea que sunt destrueret, ut non glorietur omnis caro in conspectus eius. Non enim, sicut ipse postmodum dicit, in sermone est regnum Dei, sed in uirtute.'
[31] Translations noted in end-of-chapter references. Latin editions of Aquinas's texts are from the Aquinas Institute's *Opera Omnia*. Available at <https://aquinas.institute> (last accessed 20 March 2019). Latin edition of Puer Jesus is from *Corpus Thomisticum*. Available at <https://corpusthomisticum.org> (last accessed 21 March 2019).

thinkers. While Aquinas did not produce a single text on gender, his ideas tempt of a unified whole. However, Aristotle's insights about women have been widely acknowledged as sexist (DeCrane 2004: 42–52). This has led many scholars to insist that the whole Aquinas offers is deeply flawed (Radcliff Richards 1982).

One of Aquinas's more problematic passages occurs within his *Summa Theologiae*. While attempting to account for the 'production' of human beings, Aquinas (1981:1.92.1) seemingly accepts Aristotle's claim that women exist as 'misbegotten males' (*mas occasionatus*) – that is, accidents. As Mary Daly (1968: 62–3) suggests, when combined with certain tenets of his theology, Aquinas's perpetuation of such language easily reinforces the social/political oppression of women: 'The idea of woman's special sinfulness, stemming from commonly held interpretations of the Bible, combined with a notion of her inferior "nature", affirmed in Aristotelian philosophy, thus made it seem that the sociological fact of women's subordination was inscribed in the heavens.' So understood, Aquinas's refusal to challenge the 'fathers' of the Western tradition did little to avert a growing trend of Christian misogyny.

Some scholars have proposed that a closer examination of the context that motivated Aquinas's conclusion might alleviate these concerns. As Michael Nolan (1994, 2000) argues, Aquinas's agreement with Aristotle would appear to have more to do with his grasp of procreation than politics. Aquinas (1.92.1) explains that during the process of human generation the male is by and large responsible for determining the particulars of the offspring, including its biological sex. Because it is more fitting for the male to produce a likeness of itself, Aquinas (1981:1.92.1) contends that the birth of a female implies that some aspect of the generative act must have gone awry:

> As regards the individual nature, woman is defective and misbegotten [*deficiens et occasionatum*], for the active force in the male seed tends to the production of a perfect likeness in the masculine sex; while the production of woman comes from a defect in the active force or from some material indisposition, or even from some external influence; such as that of a south wind, which is most, as the Philosopher observes.'[32]

Women would only seem to be 'misbegotten', in other words, from the standpoint of the 'male seed'. Aquinas (1981:1.92.1) maintains that when one considers the essence of women *per se*, their 'defectiveness' dissolves:

> On the other hand, as regards human nature in general, woman is not misbegotten, but is included in nature's intention as directed to the work of generation. Now the general intention of nature depends on God, Who is the universal Author of nature. Therefore, in producing nature, God formed not only the male but also the female.[33]

---

[32] 'Ad primum ergo dicendum quod per respectum ad naturam particularem, femina est aliquid deficiens et occasionatum. Quia virtus activa quae est in semine maris, intendit producere sibi simile perfectum, secundum masculinum sexum, sed quod femina generetur, hoc est propter virtutis activae debilitatem, vel propter aliquam materiae indispositionem, vel etiam propter aliquam transmutationem ab extrinseco, puta a ventis Australibus, qui sunt humidi, ut dicitur in libero de Generat. Animal.'

[33] 'Sed per comparationem ad naturam universalem, femina non est aliquid occaisionatum, sed est de intentione naturae ad opus generationis ordinata. Intentio autem naturae universalis dependet ex Deo, qui est universalis auctor naturae. Et ideo instituendo naturam, non solum marem, sed etiam feminam produxit.'

However, as Francisco J. Romero Carrasquillo and Hilaire K. Troyer de Romero (2013: 696–708) suggest, the potential nuance of this decidedly infamous passage fails to account for the glaring issues at work in a long list of others. For example, throughout his corpus, Aquinas (2012a:1.11.588) regularly upholds that women are the 'less perfect' sex, deficient in their bodies and their souls. Aquinas specifies that this shortcoming implies that women are 'weaker' in their rational capacities, both intellectually and morally. As a result, it signals that women are naturally suited to be subordinate to men in the private and public sphere:

> [A]nd this is the kind of subjection that existed before sin. For good order would have been wanting in the human family if some were not governed by others wiser than themselves. So by such a kind of subjection woman is naturally subject to man, because in man the discretion of reason predominates. (Aquinas 1981:1.92.1)[34]

Aquinas proposes that this process of 'subjection' is intended to be in the best interest of both genders. Men are expected to rule in such a way that serves their female counterparts well. However, he is also clear that this arrangement is only necessary because the majority of women lack the rational fortitude to govern in the first place.

Thus, while some of Aquinas's claims about gender may rightly be unhinged from the arena of politics, others indicate that he was only too happy to maintain women's position on the margins. It is, perhaps, a problem of the good doctor's own making. Aquinas's suspicions about women permeate his writings with the same systematic style, the same consistency, that has won him widespread acclaim.

Tyrants of the Commonwealth

The practical implications of such suspicions are evident in Aquinas's philosophy of education (Ozolins 2013). Many of these arise in conjunction with his commentaries on the Christian Bible, especially the letters of Paul. For instance, while unpacking Paul's first letter to the Corinthians, Aquinas argues that 'the Apostle' was correct to declare that women should not be allowed to teach. More specifically, Aquinas (2012a: 14.7.880) maintains that the notion of a female teacher defies women's proper 'function':

> [Paul] assigns the reason for this, saying: for it is not permitted them to speak, namely, by the authority of the Church, but their function (*officium*) is to be subject to men. Hence, since teaching implies prelacy and presiding, it is not suited to those who are subjects.[35]

Aquinas purports that teaching demands a posture of leadership, and women are obliged to serve as followers. Insofar as it would be unwise to be ruled by a 'subject', it is similarly unfitting to be taught by a woman.

---

[34] 'Et ista subiectio fuisset etiam ante peccatum, defuisset enim bonum ordinis in humana multitudine, si quidam per alios sapientiores gubernati non fuissent. Et sic ex tali subiectione naturaliter femina subiecta est viro, quia naturaliter in homine magis abundat discretio rationis.'

[35] 'Huius autem rationem assignat, dicens non enim permittitur eis loqui, scilicet ab Ecclesiae auctoritate, sed hoc est officium earum, ut sint subditae viris. Unde cum docere dicat praelationem et praesidentiam, non decet eas quae subditae sunt.'

Aquinas affirms that his allegiance to women's role as 'subjects' stems from his general belief in the imperfection of their rational souls. Returning to Aristotle, he explains:

> The reason they are subject and not in the forefront is that they are deficient in reasoning [*deficiunt ratione*], which is especially necessary for those who preside. Therefore, the Philosopher says in his *Politics* that corruption of rule occurs, when the rule comes to women. (Aquinas 2012a: 14.7.880)[36]

Aquinas argues that the 'deficiency' of women's reason not only indicates that female teachers would have little to offer their students intellectually; it further suggests that anything women might provide threatens the essence of 'rule' itself. More pointedly, Aquinas (2012b: 2.3.80) proposes that if women are permitted to teach, the delicate relationships that exist between human beings would deteriorate: '[T]hey are forbidden to use authority over the man: a woman, if she have superiority, is contrary to her husband (Sir 25:30). And the Philosopher says that the dominion of women is the death of a family, as tyrants (*tyranni*) of a commonwealth.'[37]

Given the severity of these consequences, it is no great surprise that Aquinas assents to Paul's final instructions regarding the question of women teachers. Rather than allowing women to speak as 'tyrants', Aquinas recommends that every effort should be made to compel their silence. In particular, Aquinas argues (2012a: 14.7.879) that such silence is especially important in public pedagogical venues like 'the church':

> [Paul] says, therefore: I will that men use the gift of prophecy in this manner, but I do not want women to speak in the church, so that women keep silence in the churches. 'I permit no woman to teach or to have authority over men' (1 Tim 2:12). And Chrysostom assigns the reason for this, saying: woman has spoken once and subverted the entire world.[38]

Aquinas defends 'the Apostle' by calling upon the Christian narrative of the Fall. When Eve spoke to Adam, when she 'taught' him to consume what the serpent offered, all of humankind suffered. Aquinas argues that this sin from the past is evidence enough to warrant the exclusion of women's voices in the present.

Shameful

This message of silent subjection further extends into Aquinas's analysis of the role of female students. At first, Aquinas's insights about women's ability to learn would seem to be more positive. He admits that, though it may be rare, some women are well suited to the life of learning. If anything, the rational shortcomings of women render them uniquely positioned for such an enterprise. Following Paul's first letter to Timothy, Aquinas (2012b: 2.3.79) explains that women should be allowed to learn 'because that is the proper function of one

---

[36] 'Ratio autem quare subditae sunt et non praesunt est quia deficiunt ratione, quae est maxime necessaria praesidenti. Et ideo dicit Philosophus, in Politica sua, quod corruptio regiminis est quando regimen pervenit ad mulieres.'

[37] '[I]nterdicitur eis dominium in virum. Eccle XXV, 30: mulier si primatum habeat, contraria est viro suo. Et Philosophus dicit, quod dominium mulierum est corruptio familiae, sicut tyranni in regno.'

[38] 'Dicit ergo: volo ut viri hoc modo utantur dono prophetiae, sed mulieres, in ecclesia, nolo loqui: sed taceant in ecclesiis, 1 Tim. II, 12: mulierem docere in ecclesia non permitto. Et rationem huius assignat Chrysostomus, dicens, quod semel est locuta mulier et totum mundum subvertit.'

who is weak in intellect [*deficiunt ratione*]'.[39] Aquinas's remarks imply a particularly top-down understanding of the pedagogical process. The notion that students enter the classroom mentally 'weak' has been challenged by much of contemporary philosophy of education (Freire 2000). Still, this does not negate the fact that such a methodology enabled Aquinas to locate an opening for the 'weakness' of the 'imperfect sex'.

However, the honeymoon does not last long. Aquinas is quick to distinguish between the weakness of female students and those of males. More specifically, here too, Aquinas argues that if women wish to learn they must do so not only as students. They must do so as 'subjects':

> [H]e recommends subjection, because it is natural for the soul to rule the body, and reason the lower powers. Therefore, as the Philosopher says, whenever any two things are related as the soul is to the body, and reason to sensuality, it is natural for the one with the greater amount of reason to rule and give orders, and for the other to be subject, since it is lacking in reason. (2012b: 2.3.79)[40]

Aquinas proposes that, even when it comes to learning, women are 'lower' than men – that is, ordered to them as the body is ordered to the soul. As the body depends upon the 'rule' of the soul, it is 'natural' for women to depend upon the 'rule' of their male peers.

The terms of this pedagogical 'rule' mirror Aquinas's conclusions about the gendered aspects of teaching. Aquinas maintains that female students must embrace a posture of silence. For example, and continuing his analysis of Corinthians, Aquinas suggests that what it means for a woman to learn is for her to resist the urge to ask questions: 'He says, therefore, "I say that let women keep silence in the churches, but if they would learn anything about which they doubt, let them ask their husbands at home: let women learn in silence"' (2012a: 14.7.881).[41] So understood, the female student as 'subject' is presented as doubly removed from her teacher. Like male students, she falls short of her teacher's mental acumen. However, she also lacks the means to enquire as a rational being in her own right. Aquinas argues that, as seekers of the truth, women should be compelled to use a mediator – a male go-between who can properly field the conditions of their education.

Aquinas stipulates that such double subjection is, in part, necessary because it is inappropriate for women to speak in any capacity within the public domain. He argues that in order to be an active learner one must stand at the centre of a discourse, and insert oneself into a wider conversation. Aquinas (2012a: 14.7.881) proposes that allowing women to take on such a central position would be fundamentally 'shameful':

> The reason for this is that it is a shame [*turpe est*] and not only unbecoming; for in women the natural feeling of shame is commended. A holy and shamefaced woman is grace upon grace (Sir 26:19). If therefore they ask and dispute in public, it would be a sign of shamelessness, and this is shameful to them. Hence it also follows that in law the office of advocate is forbidden to women.[42]

---

[39] '[U]t discant, quia eorum qui deficiunt ratione proprium est addiscere.'

[40] '[I]ndicit subiectionem, quia natural est quod anima dominetur corpori, et ratio viribus inferioribus. Et ideo, sicut Philosophus docet, quandocumque aliqua duo ad invicem sic se habent, sicut anima ad corpus, et ratio ad sensualitatem, naturale dominium est eius qui abundat ratione, et illud est principans, aliud autem est subditum, quod scilicet deficit ratione.'

[41] 'Dicit ergo: dico quod mulieres taceant in ecclesia, sed si aliqua, de quibus dubitant, addiscere volunt, interrogent viros suos domi: mulier in silentio discat cum omni.'

[42] 'Huius autem ratio est quia turpe est, non solum indecens: in mulieribus enim commendatur verecundia. Eccli. XXVI, 19: gratia super gratiam, et cetera. Si ergo in publico quaereret et disputaret, signum esset inverecundiae, et hoc ei turpe. Et inde est etiam quod in iure interdicitur mulieribus officium advocandi.'

Aquinas indicates that women's silence in learning complies both with the demands of the spiritual realm, dictated by 'holiness' and 'grace', and the political realm, where women's voices have already been denied. So understood, the silence proposed by Aquinas would appear to function in a radically different way than that advocated by Abelard. While Abelard's recommendation increased Heloise's standing in her community, Aquinas's depletes it.

Misbegotten Exceptions

Unlike Augustine and Abelard, Aquinas's ideas about gender lack obvious connection to his experiences with 'real' flesh and blood women. One wonders if his conclusions would have been different if he had been more open to the philosophical complexities raised by the lives of those who cohabited his world. Instead, Aquinas's writings leave readers with few opportunities for moments of interpretive generosity.

One possibility for such creative retrieval resides in Aquinas's assessment of the women who appear within his Christian Bible. These cases suggest that, in the context of his sacred scriptures, Aquinas did grant women some wiggle room – that is, options for surmounting their imperfection. For instance, in his sermon The Boy Jesus (*Puer Jesus*), Aquinas further elaborates on the nature of education. He argues, to an audience of young students, that the development of the intellect culminates in the mind's pursuit of wisdom: 'Likewise, we must be amazed that the truth advances in wisdom, because the progress of wisdom is knowledge of the truth, as Christ is himself the truth' (Aquinas 2010b: 2.02).[43] Interestingly enough, Aquinas (2010b: 3.4.1–3) intimates that a key example of this most important educative act can be found in the contemplative practice of Jesus's mother, Mary:

> We have an example in the blessed Virgin; she 'kept all these words with her in her heart' ... There is no doubt that someone who listens open-heartedly, responds prudently, inquires diligently, and meditates with attention will advance much in wisdom. This is the way to advance in wisdom.[44]

As such, Aquinas would seem to offer Mary as a model student who might inspire, if not lead, the pedagogical desires of others.

Aquinas supplements his account of Mary's wisdom with the suggestion that, in these cases, women's educative skills are typically due to forces outside themselves. He argues that Mary's growth in the truth, her ability to exceed the limits of her gender, was the result of the inner workings of his God. As Kristin Popik (1979: 32–3) explains, Aquinas considered even the imperfections of women to be no match for the redemptive power of grace:

> [G]race for St. Thomas is an equalizer which totally transcends and overcomes the inferiority-superiority of women and men on the natural level [. . .] [T]he inferiority of women is only in the natural sphere; it is overcome by grace, so that once grace enters the picture one cannot speak any longer of woman's inferiority to men.

---

[43] 'Item admirandum est quod veritas in sapientia proficiat, quia profectus sapientiae est cognitio veritatis, et Christus ipsa veritas est.'

[44] 'Exemplum habemus in beata Virgine: quae conservabat omnia verba haec conferens in corde suo [. . .] Non est dubium quin ille qui libenter audit, prudenter respondit, diligenter inquirit, et attente meditatur, quin multum proficiet in sapientia. Iste est modus proficiendi in sapientia.'

Thus, the exception one might find in the figure of Mary is an exception of the Christian God's own making. Aquinas posits that any alteration of the 'natural' infers the assistance of the supernatural.

While one may find such justification discouraging, Aquinas does give some indication that the imperfection of women can be overcome by more human means as well. For example, in his account of the Samaritan woman at the well, Aquinas attributes the extent of her learning to the pedagogical nature of her environment. He argues that her intellectual gift is hardly shocking:

> It is not surprising that she was taught about this, for it often happens in places where there are differences in beliefs that even the simple people are instructed about them. Because the Samaritans were continually arguing with the Jews over this, it came to the knowledge of the women and ordinary people. (Aquinas 2010a: 4.2.598)[45]

Aquinas contends that the setting within which an individual is raised can influence their rational abilities. The more a community embodies the life of learning, the easier it is for all of its members to grow.

As Popik (1979: 31) concludes, this does not change the fact that Aquinas saw women as secondary. However, it does suggest that he thought it conceivable for a woman to defy the odds through a combination of divine and human channels: '[T]heir inferiority is not so great as to be impossible of being overcome with a bit of practice, by cultural factors, and by education'. Thus, it is, perhaps, too generous to argue that Aquinas regarded these women as exceptions in the fullest sense of the word. Aquinas does not assume that their existence warrants any changes to his philosophies of gender or education. Instead, Aquinas presents these women as dangling anomalies that simply need to be brought back into the fold.

Conclusion

It would be inappropriate, not to mention ahistorical, to read the texts of Augustine, Abelard and Aquinas as a single overarching narrative. In the hundreds of years which transpired between Augustine's journey to the countryside and Aquinas's writing of the *Summa Theologiae*, a myriad of philosophical and political forces altered the intentions of their respective works. Likewise, it would seem ill-advised to assume that current concerns about the intersection of women and education match those held by many in the Christian medieval West. Still, such historical writings do remind us of the importance of engaging with our own ideas about gender. More pressingly, they highlight the value of philosophising about those gendered experiences that continue to be ignored.

In the United States, such philosophising would benefit greatly from a more intersectional approach (Crenshawe 1991). Like Augustine, Abelard and Aquinas, much of the talk about the 'feminisation' of education today has assumed the perspective of cis-gender white women. To argue that the pedagogical methods used in schools cater unequivocally to 'women' disregards recent reports (Inniss-Thompson 2017) suggesting that young black females are disproportionately more likely to be disciplined and suspended than white

---

[45] 'Nec est mirandum a quo docta fuerit, quia communiter contingit ut in terries in quibus diversa sunt dogmata, etiam simplices in eis sint instructi. Unde, quia Samaritani fuerant in continuo iurgio cum Iudaeis, ideo mulieres et simplices in materia ista edocti errant.'

females (Ricks 2014: 10–21; Morris 2016: 24–51). To argue that classroom curricula are overly focused on 'women's' interests denies those schools currently attempting to prohibit all formal pedagogical conversations about gender identity and gender expression (Jensen 2018). Whatever we might think about 'the era of the woman', it seems clear that this 'era' does not extend to everyone who identifies as such. All of this implies that modern-day applications of gender theory have, themselves, a long way to go. It is, perhaps, the most valuable insight our readings of the medieval past can offer teachers and students in the twenty-first century: It is easy to be critical of the ideas of those who have come before. It is imperative to remain critical of the limits of one's own.

References

Abelard and Heloise (1974). *The Letters*. Trans. Betty Radice. London and New York: Penguin Books.
Abelard and Heloise (2013). *The Letter Collection of Peter Abelard and Heloise*. Ed. and trans. David Luscombe and Betty Radice. Oxford: Clarendon Press.
Aquinas (1981). *Summa Theologiae*. Trans. Fathers of the English Dominican Province. Westminster, MD: Christian Classics.
Aquinas (2010a). *Commentary on the Gospel of John*. Trans. James A. Weisheipl and Fabian R. Larcher. Washington, DC: The Catholic University of American Press.
Aquinas (2010b). '*Puer Jesus*'. *The Academic Sermons*. Trans. Mark-Robin Hoogland. Washington, DC: The Catholic University of America Press.
Aquinas (2012a). *Commentary on the First Epistle of Saint Paul to the Corinthians*. Trans. Fabian R. Larcher, Beth Mortensen and Daniel Keating. Lander, WY: The Aquinas Institute.
Aquinas (2012b). *Commentary on the First Epistle of Saint Paul to Timothy*. Trans. Fabian R. Larcher. Lander, WY: The Aquinas Institute.
Aquinas Institute. *Opera Omnia*. <https://aquinas.institute> (last accessed 20 March 2019).
Augustine (1948a). *De beata vita*. Trans. Ludwig Schopp. Portsmouth: Bishop Litho, Inc. and Miller and Watson, Inc.
Augustine (1948b). *De ordine*. Trans. Robert P. Russell. Portsmouth: Bishop Litho, Inc. and Miller and Watson, Inc.
Augustine (1995). *De magistro*. Trans Peter King. Indianapolis and Cambridge: Hackett Publishing Company, 1995.
Augustine (2002). *De Trinitate*. Trans. Gareth B. Matthews. Cambridge and New York: Cambridge University Press.
Bauer-Wolf (2018). 'Student Wants to End Affirmative Action for Women'. *Inside Higher Education*, 21 May. <https://www.insidehighered.com/news/2018/05/21/yale-being investigated-discrimination-against-men-unusual-title-ix-complaint> (last accessed 15 December 2018).
Boersma, Gerald P. (2016). 'Monica as Mystagogue'. In *Wisdom and the Renewal of Catholic Theology*. Ed. Thomas P. Harmon and Roger W. Nutt. Eugene: Pickwick, pp. 104–25.
Borresen, Kari Elisabeth (1990). 'In Defense of Augustine: How *Femina* is *Homo*'. In *Collectanea Augustiniana*. Ed. B. Bruning, M. Lamberigts and J. Van. Houtem. Leuven: Leuven University Press, pp. 411–27.
Chavous, Tabbye and Courtney D. Cogburn (2007). 'Superinvisible Women: Black Girls and Women in Education'. *Black Women, Gender and Families*, 1/2: 24–51.
Chelius Stark, Judith (2007). 'Augustine on Women: In God's Image but Less So'. In *Feminist Interpretations of Augustine*. Ed. Judith Chelius Stark. University Park: The Pennsylvania State University Press, pp. 215–41.
Citta Nuova. *S. Aurelii Augustini Opera Omnia*. <www.augustinus.it.htm> (last accessed 20 March 2019).
Clark, Elizabeth (1999). 'Rewriting Early Christian History: Augustine's Representation of Monica'. In *Portraits of Spiritual Authority: Religious Power in Early Christianity, Byzantium, and the Christian Orient*. Ed. Jan Willem Drijvers and John Watt. Leiden: Brill, pp. 1–23.
Corpus Thomisticum. Available at <https://corpusthomisticum.org> (last accessed 21 March 2019).

Crenshaw, Kimberlé (1991). 'Mapping the Margins: Intersectionality, Identity Politics, and Violence Against Women of Color'. *Stanford Law Review*, 43/6: 1241–99.

Daly, Mary (1975 [1968]). *The Church and the Second Sex*. Boston, MA: Beacon Press.

D'Arms, John H. (1999). 'Performing Culture: Roman Spectacle and the Banquets of the Powerful'. *Studies in the History of Art*, 56: 301–19.

DeCrane, Susanne M. (2004). *Aquinas, Feminism, and the Common Good*. Washington, DC: Georgetown University Press.

Desmond, Marilynn (2006). *Ovid's Art and the Wife of Bath: The Ethics of Erotic Violence*. Ithaca: Cornell University Press.

DeVos, Betsy (2018). 'Title IX of the Education Amendments of 1972'. The Department of Education, November <https://www2.ed.gov/about/offices/list/ocr/docs/title-ixnprm.pdf> (last accessed 15 December 2018).

Dunbabin, Katherine M. D. (2003). *The Roman Banquet: Images of Conviviality*. Cambridge and New York: Cambridge University Press.

Duran, Jane (2011). 'Heloise: A Christian View on Ethics and Love'. *New Blackfriars*, 92/1037: 35–45.

Freire, Paolo (2000). *Pedagogy of the Oppressed*. Trans. Myra Bergman Ramos. New York and London: Bloomsbury.

Froese-Germain, Bernie (2005). 'Are Schools Shortchanging Boys'. *Canadian Teachers Federation*, November. <https://www.ctf-fce.ca/Research-Library/Are-Schools-Shortchanging-Boys_PD2003.pdf> (last accessed 15 December 2018).

Gargarin, Michael (2010). 'Roman Banquets'. *The Oxford Encyclopedia of Ancient Greece and Rome*. <http://www.oxfordreference.com.libdb.fairfield.edu/view/10.1093/acref/9780195170726 001.0001/acref-9780195170726-e-162?rskey=IUnj6J&result=162> (last accessed 1 December 2018).

Grey, Mary (1992). 'The Challenge of Heloise: Language, Truth, and Logic Revisited'. *New Blackfriars*, 73/857: 84–9.

Griffiths, Morwenna (2006). 'The Feminization of Teaching and the Practice of Teaching: Threat or Opportunity'. *Education Theory*, 56/4: 387–405.

Grumet, Madeleine (1981). 'Pedagogy for Patriarchy: The Feminization of Teaching'. *Interchange*, 12/2–3: 165–84.

Heidenreich Findley, Brooke (2005). 'Sincere Hypocrisy and the Authorial Persona in the Letters of Heloise'. *Romance Notes*, 45/3: 281–92.

Inniss-Thompson, Misha N. (2017). 'Summary of Discipline Data for Girls in U.S. Public Schools'. The Department of Education, September. <https://docs.wixstatic.com/ugd/0c71ee_e008841ccc434f08ac76d59199a0c2dc.pdf> (last accessed 15 November 2018).

Jensen, Phil (2018). 'Senate Bill No. 160'. Legislature of the State of South Dakota, January. <http://blogs.edweek.org/edweek/rulesforengagement/2018/02/in_a_first_a_state_may_n_its_schools_from_teaching_about_gender_identity.html> (last accessed 15 November 2018).

Kamuf, Peggy (1982). *Fictions of Feminine Desire: Disclosures of Heloise*. Lincoln and London: University of Nebraska Press.

Kevane, Eugene (2009 [1964]). *Augustine the Educator: A Study in the Fundamentals of Christian Formation*. Eugene: Wipf and Stock.

Kramer, Susan R. (2000). 'We Speak to God with Our Thoughts: Abelard and the Implications of Private Communication with God'. *Church History*, 69/1: 18–40.

Maher, Frances A. (2012), 'Feminization of Teaching'. In *Encyclopedia of Diversity in Education*. Ed. James A. Banks. Los Angeles and London: Sage Publishing, pp. 901–5.

Marcus, John (2017). 'Why Men Are the New College Minority'. *The Atlantic*, 28 August. <https://www.theatlantic.com/education/archive/2017/08/why-men-are-the-new-college-minority/536103/> (last accessed 15 December 2018).

Marrou, H. I. (1982). *History of Education in Antiquity*. Trans. G. Lamb. Madison: University of Wisconsin Press.

Matter, E. Ann. (2007). '*De cura feminarum*: Augustine the Bishop, North African Women, and the Development of a Theology of Female Nature'. In *Feminist Interpretations of Augustine*. Ed. Judith Chelius Stark. University Park: The Pennsylvania State University Press, pp. 203–14.

Mews, Constant J. (2005). *Abelard and Heloise*. Oxford: Oxford University Press.
Morris, Monique (2016). *Pushout: The Criminalization of Black Girls in Schools*. New York: The New Press.
Mulvey, Janet (2018). 'Feminization of Schools'. The Schools Superintendents Associations, November. <http://www.aasa.org/SchoolAdministratorArticle.aspx?id=5642> (last accessed 15 December 2018).
Newman, Barbara (1999). *From Virile Woman to Woman Christ*. University Park: University of Pennsylvania Press.
Nolan, Michael (1994). 'The Defective Male: What Aquinas Really Said'. *New Blackfriars* 75/880: 156–66.
Nolan, Michael (2000). 'The Aristotelian Background to Aquinas's Denial that "Woman is a Defective Male"'. *The Thomist*, 64/1: 21–69.
Nouvet, Claire (1990). 'The Discourse of the Whore: An Economy of Sacrifice'. *MLN*, 105/4: pp. 750–73.
Nye, Andrea (1992). 'A Woman's Thought or a Man's Discipline: The Letters of Abelard and Heloise'. *Hypatia*, 7/3: 1–22.
Osaat, S. D. and Ukoha Okenwa (2018). 'Feminization of Primary School Teaching: A Societal and Cultural Limitation to Boy-Child Education'. *International Journal of Education and Evaluation*, 4/2: 1–10.
Ozolins, Janis Talivaldis (2013). 'Aquinas and His Understanding of Teaching and Learning'. In *Aquinas, Education and the East*. Ed. T. B. Mooney and M. Nowacki (eds). New York: Springer, pp. 9–25.
Pollmann, Karla and Mark Vessey (eds) (2005). *Augustine and the Disciplines*. New York: Oxford University Press.
Popik, Kristin (1979). *The Philosophy of Woman of St. Thomas Aquinas*. Rome: Angelicum.
Power, Kim (1996). *Veiled Desire: Augustine on Women*. New York: Continuum.
Radcliff Richards, Janet (1982). *The Skeptical Feminist: A Philosophy of Inquiry*. Harmondsworth: Penguin Books.
Radford Ruether, Rosemary (2007). 'Augustine: Sexuality, Gender, and Women'. In *Feminist Interpretations of Augustine*. Ed. Judith Chelius Stark. University Park: The Pennsylvania State University Press, pp. 47–67.
Ricks, Shawn Arango (2014). 'Falling Through the Cracks: Black Girls and Education'. *Interdisciplinary Journal of Teaching and Learning*, 4/1: 10–21.
Romero Carrasquillo, Francisco J. and Hilaire K. Troyer de Romero (2013). 'Aquinas on the Inferiority of Woman'. *American Catholic Philosophical Quarterly*, 87/4: 685–710.
Sexton, Patricia Cayo (1965). 'Schools Are Emasculating our Boys'. *Sunday Review*, 48: 57.
Stephens, Bret (2017). 'The Dying Art of Disagreement'. *The New York Times*, 24 September. <https://www.nytimes.com/2017/09/24/opinion/dying-art-of-disagreement.html> (last accessed 15 December 2018).
Vogt, Kari (1995). 'Becoming Male: A Gnostic and Early Christian Metaphor'. In *The Image of God: Gender Models in Judeo-Christian Tradition*. Ed. Kari Elisabeth Borreson. Minneapolis: Fortress Press, pp. 170–86.

5

Shame: A Phenomenological Re-examination of Aquinas's Analysis

Daniel Dahlstrom

'Back to the matters themselves' (*Zurück zur Sache selbst*) – the slogan of early twentieth-century phenomenologists – effectively sets their new approach to philosophy off from that of contemporaries still committed to the late nineteenth-century refrain 'back to Kant'. Yet the slogan is easily misleading. Even Heidegger balks at it at times, worrying that it suggests returning to the subject matters already established by the various sciences and faculties in the academy, when in fact the import of the slogan is to return to matters in the way that they are originally given in experience, prior to any discipline-specific predetermination. The return to the matters themselves accordingly coincides with returning to the original experiences of them, and not merely ideas or concepts of them. So, too, phenomenology distances itself decisively from psychological studies of experience as something going on solely 'in the head' or in a subject. For phenomenologists, experiences are, to the contrary, the ways that we consciously find our bearings in the world – cognitively, instrumentally, affectively and ethically. Phenomenologists take upon themselves the task of attempting to determine the essential components, structure and process of such experiences. In just this sense, Husserl provides paradigmatic phenomenological analyses of imagination and perception, Heidegger of everydayness and Angst, and Scheler of empathy and shame.

Shame is a remarkably complex experience, the sort of experience that calls out for phenomenological analysis.[1] It is typically felt as very personal and intimate, yet at the same time

---

[1] Based upon writings by Augustine, Nemesius and John of Damascus in the Patristic period, shame was discussed by medieval thinkers who widely viewed it as part of the human post-lapsarian condition. In Book 14 of *The City of God* Augustine focuses attention on the human tendency to hide anything that is a matter of shame – especially the post-lapsarian shame of lacking control over sexual excitement (PL XIV, 16–24, esp. 17, p. 965, and 20, p. 971; *Confessiones* VIII). Peter Olivi's thirteenth-century commentary on Genesis picks up on the Augustinian reading of shame and, in his *Summa* of questions on Peter Lombard's *Sentences*, he lists 'shame and glory' as one of seven pairs of affects that testify to free will; see Olivi 1924, question 57, p. 317). A century earlier in Richard of St Victor's allegorical-tropological work, *Benjamin Minor* (chapters 45–59, PL CXCVI, 33–43), Dina (the daughter of Jacob's wife Leah) personifies a 'true and appropriate shame' (*veram et ordinatam verecundiam*). To feel shame at a single sin is to possess this good and appropriate shame (*solum peccatum erubescere, est bonam, est ordinatam verecundiam habere*). He contrasts this shame on God's account (*erubescere propter Deum*) with 'human shame', shame on our account (*propter seipsos*), i.e., the sort of shame due to damage to one's reputation. In his early fourteenth-century commentary on Boethius' *Consolation of Philosophy* (Book 3, chapter 11), William of Wheatley defines *erubescentia* as 'a reproach of disrepute caused by having performed some repulsive deed' (*crimen ingloriationis causatum ex aliquot turpi perpetrato*).

attesting to others and our distinctive, anxious relation to them. The experience makes abundantly clear that just as others are objects of a reproachful gaze or stare, so are we. That we are not only subjects but also objects in this sense is the painful ontological lesson of Sartre's famous analysis of the shame experienced by someone caught in the disgraceful act of a peeping Tom.[2] It is also apparently the lesson of the fall, as Adam and Eve fall from a naked existence without shame to the self-consciousness of being naked – further complicating the status of shame by placing it somewhere between a strictly natural and a cultural phenomenon.[3] We feel shame both when the reproach is deserved and when it is undeserved, when it is real and when it is imagined. All the while the experiences of shame have an unmistakably physical character, epitomised by the blushing that sometimes accompanies an equally involuntary sexual arousal. In all the foregoing ways, shame is, as noted, prime territory for phenomenological exploration and, in this regard, Scheler's trailblazing study, despite its incompleteness, does not disappoint, as he attempts to pin down what is essential to the experience.[4]

Although it would be blatantly anachronistic to characterise Aquinas's extensive reflections on shame as a phenomenological analysis, it bears many of the hallmarks of such an analysis. Indeed, it anticipates key aspects of Scheler's phenomenological study of shame in particular, even as it brings a different but no less illuminating perspective to bear on the analysis of shame. The aim of the present essay is to re-examine Aquinas's analysis with a view to demonstrating and evaluating both its proto-phenomenological character and its distinctive contribution to our understanding of shame. After the fall shame may be natural, as Augustine contends, and it may be quintessentially human, as Scheler insists,[5] but it is also culturally specific. Because Aquinas's understanding of shame, no less than that of Aristotle or that of Scheler, is dependent on the experience of shame within a distinctive cultural context, what is essential to it is in some regards historically specific.[6] Yet these dissimilarities, I hope to show, are no less instructive than the similarities, particularly when it comes to evaluating the strengths and weaknesses of the analysis for present-day study of shame.[7]

The first and more extensive part of the following chapter is concerned with reconstructing main themes of Aquinas's analysis of shame, while paying special attention to the analysis's proto-phenomenological character. The second and concluding part sketches critical questions regarding the analysis by way of comparison and contrast with Max Scheler's paradigmatic study of shame.

---

[2] Sartre (1943: 259): 'J'ai honte de ce que je *suis*. La honte réalise donc une relation intime de moi avec moi: j 'ai découvert par la honte un aspect de mon être.' Ibid.: 260: '. . . quelqu'un était là et m'a vu. Je réalise tout à coup toute la vulgarité de mon geste et j 'ai honte . . . j'ai honte de moi tel que j'apparais à autrui. Et, par l'apparition même d'autrui, je suis mis en mesure de porter un jugement sur moi-même comme sur un objet, car c'est comme objet que j'apparais à autrui.'

[3] Genesis 3:7; Augustine 1841, Book 13, chapter 3 and Book 14, chapters 17 and 20 in *Patrologia Latina*, Vol. 41, pp. 379, 428 and 430f.; I-II, q. 17, a. 9, ad 4; II-II, q. 164, a. 2; Velleman (2001: 27f.).

[4] Scheler (1957); see Dahlstrom (2017). Scheler's study of shame has proven to be a resource for several contemporary philosophers' studies of shame (Taylor 1985: 60f.; Williams 1993: 220; Nussbaum 2004: 174, 186).

[5] Scheler (1957: 69).

[6] Shame related to penitential practice and mendicant orders, for example, make up two distinctive elements of the context of Aquinas's treatment of shame; see Guindon (1969: 596–9, 606–11). Husserl himself develops the notion that what is essential to certain experiences is culturally specific in his remarks on art; see Dahlstrom (1998).

[7] For helpful criticism of earlier drafts of this chapter, I am indebted to Joseph Gamache, Rebeccah Leiby and Kevin White.

Reconstructing the Analysis

Proto-phenomenologist that he is,[8] Aquinas does not fail to describe the nature of the experience of shame, identifying it as a passion.[9] Shame is, more specifically, an irascible passion of fear. In keeping with the fact that fear is, in phenomenological terms, an intentional experience, he also unpacks the intentionality of the experience, i.e., its specific object and sense (an act insofar as it is disgraceful). In addition, Aquinas addresses the traditional distinction of two types of shame, while making clear how shame implicates others and how it figures into a virtuous life, and, as a result, how it differs from guilt, penitence and the like. The first part of this chapter accordingly reconstructs Aquinas's analysis along these lines, i.e., in terms of his account of (1) the phenomenology and (2) intentionality of shame, (3) the traditional types of shame, (4) the intersubjectivity of shame, (5) its moral relevance, and (6) its distinctiveness.

The Phenomenon of Shame

Aquinas identifies shame as a species of fear. Fear is itself a particular sort of passion, a motion of sensory appetites, situated midway between movements of the mind and those of the body – although he recognises the need to describe it metaphorically in terms of the latter (I-II, q. 37, a. 2). Sensory appetites are the human animal's natural tendencies, given its organic, bodily make-up, to move towards something good for it, motivated by a primarily sensory or imaginative apprehension (thus, from thirst and the sight of water as quenching the thirst, a movement towards the water ensues, with the aim of eliminating the thirst).[10] Passions are the corresponding movements of sensory appetites. The movement is, as Aquinas puts it (citing Aristotle), a moved moving (*movens motum*) that arises from an appetite's 'inclination or aptitude' for a certain kind of object and its activation, i.e., the process of being moved by the apprehension of an object of that sort (what Aquinas dubs *activa*) (I, q. 80, a. 2; I-II, q. 23, a. 4). Complicating human passions (in contrast to those of non-rational animals) is the fact that they are also subject to the input of reason and will – the apprehension of general goods and the ensuing intellectual appetite. Directly contesting the Stoic view of passions as evil, Aquinas follows Aristotle in deeming sensory appetites and passions generally to be distinct from but susceptible to reason and the will (I, q. 80, a. 1–2; q. 81, a. 3; I-II, q. 24, a. 1–3).[11] As Kevin White points out, Aquinas instructively invokes Aristotle's political

---

[8] The characterisation of Aquinas as a 'proto-phenomenologist' flags the obvious risk of applying a misleading anachronism to him. However, it also signals that his analysis of passions has some key earmarks of a phenomenological study in the contemporary sense, for example, a recognition that the analysis must return to the lived experience, that the experience is at once personal and internal yet charged with intersubjectivity, and – not least – that there is an intentionality (a directedness to objects) built into the content of an affective state.

[9] 'Passion' is a translation of Aquinas's *passio*. While 'passion' (as this translation) and 'emotion' may be anachronistically construed metonyms, Aquinas does not employ a direct equivalent of 'emotion' (although he does also speak of *affections*). How closely Aquinas's *passio* corresponds or coincides with modern conceptions of 'emotion' is a matter of debate. Floyd, for example, argues that *passio* should not be construed as an emotion since it lacks the latter's cognitive dimension (Floyd 1998: 161); Cates presents her interpretation as, in part, an attempt to rebut Floyd's interpretation (Cates 2009: 74f., 95f.). Miner argues that it is misleading to translate *passio* as an emotion since the terms have different histories, although the modern notion of emotion descends in his view from the medieval conception of passions (Miner 2009: 3–4).

[10] Or, as Aquinas also puts it, from inclination to movement to rest (I-II, q. 23, a. 4; q. 26, a. 2).

[11] I say 'generally' not 'universally' for two reasons important to the discussion below: (1) there is a difference between passions before and after the judgement of reason (I-II, q. 24, a. 3, ad 1) and (2) Aquinas deems shame (along with compassion) 'inherently good' and envy 'inherently evil' (I-II, q. 24, a. 4).

distinction between despotic and regal rule in this regard; while the body is completely subservient to the soul's despotic rule, sensory appetites have 'something of their own', enabling them to resist, even if unadvisedly, reason's command.[12]

Fear belongs to the class of irascible passions, the sort of passion that responds to a good that is difficult to achieve or an evil that is difficult to avoid. Building on and terminating in concupiscible passions (e.g., love for and experience of the delightful, hate for and experience of the painful), irascible passions arise from a comparison of one's powers with the difficulty of attaining or avoiding the relevant object (I, q. 81, a. 2; I-II, q. 23, a. 1, ad 1). Gripped by an irascible passion, we do not dwell in the present, as we might with concupiscible passions.[13] Thus we *hope* for a good that is hard to get and we *fear* an evil that is hard to avoid. To clarify, Aquinas cites Aristotle's observation in the *Rhetoric 2* (1382a22–23) that fear comes from imagining a future evil (*ex phantasia futuri mali corruptivi vel contristativi*: ἐκ φαντασίας μέλλοντος κακοῦ φθαρτικοῦ ἢ λυπηροῦ). In addition to being outside our control and will, the evil feared, he adds, must be neither too remote nor seemingly inevitable (I-II, q. 42, aa. 2–3).

Applying this account of fear to shame, we can construct the rudiments of a phenomenology of shame. It is a fearful and thus 'irascible' experience because it apprehends something potentially painful that is hard to avoid and outside our control, even choices that we might have to make. As a passion, it is a movement of our sensory appetites and, as such, an embodied experience (exemplified by blushing). Yet, in contrast to purely bodily movements like the flow of blood or the beating of the heart, it is activated in the first place by what we perceive or imagine. At the same time, it is capable of being affected by reason and will. By construing shame as fear and thus as an irascible passion, Aquinas accords it a status that is embedded in concupiscible passions (e.g., hate, pain) but irreducible to them and, as the political metaphors make clear, it has interests of its own that reason can only guide and not dominate.[14] Below I argue that this view of shame is in certain respects too restrictive, at least by contemporary standards. Yet there can be no doubt that Aquinas has put his finger on key aspects of certain typical experiences of shame by characterising it as an irascible passion of fear.

The Intentionality of Shame

Shame falls under the category of experiences that phenomenologists identify as intentional. Whereas all experiences are composed of conscious acts (e.g., acts of dreaming, perceiving, willing), what makes an experience intentional is the fact that the act is directed at a corresponding object (e.g., what is dreamt, perceived, willed) in a certain way or under a certain description. An intentional experience accordingly has three essential and essentially interconnected components: the act, the object of the act and the way the act intends the object. In the actual act of seeing a tree, I see the object as a tree, what we might call, somewhat expansively, the sense of the entire experience (since, in the actual experience itself, neither the object nor the act of seeing are independent of this sense).

---

[12] I, q. 81, a. 3, ad 2; I-II, q. 17, a. 7; White (2002: 103).

[13] Anger is the exception here in not being confined to the future; see White (2002: 110).

[14] Unlike Schopenhauer, Aquinas takes pleasure, not pain, to be primary. Whereas we begin with natural tendencies to fulfilment that are typically realised, issuing in pleasure, pain as the negation of pleasure, presupposes it. Pain involves the forcible removal of some good that is naturally enjoyed and desired (e.g., a pleasure or satisfaction). Aquinas characterises the experience as one of 'falling apart' to indicate that the disruption of a person's unity with that satisfaction that is proper to her (I-II, q. 36, aa. 1–4). While Aquinas thinks of pain primarily as a bodily sensation, he also acknowledges sorrow as an intellectual, potentially more powerful, passion (I-II, q. 31, aa. 3–5; q. 35, aa. 2, 7; q. 39, aa. 2–3; q. 49).

Aquinas addresses the intentionality of shame in this expansive sense – its specific object and the fearful way of intending it – at several junctures. As is the case generally for any object of any fear, there is something about the object of fear in the case of shame that exceeds the powers of the agent or at least is difficult to avoid. Aquinas follows the line of Aristotle, Damascene and Nemesius that the object is a base (disgraceful, ugly) deed, occurrent or past.[15] 'For this reason' (on account of this, *propter quid*) the agent shuns (*refugit*) the action. What is so feared is the disrepute or disgrace that does damage to a person's reputation (*turpitudo laedens opinionem*).[16] This characterisation may, to be sure, appear ambiguous if it makes sense to distinguish the ugliness itself from the ugliness insofar as it damages a reputation. Yet Aquinas promptly clears up some of the ambiguity by noting that it is not a sinful act itself but the ugliness and ignominy (*turpitudine et ignominia*) that follow from it, caused by something extrinsic (*causa extrinseca*) to the act (I-II, 42, 3, ad 4). This remark is telling. By identifying the cause of the ignominy with something extrinsic to the act in question and thus outside anything in our power to control, Aquinas underscores why shame is a species of the irascible passion of fear. But he also appears plainly to detach the ugliness and ignominy of the act from the act itself, treating them as matters of opinion extrinsic to the act itself.

Aquinas's view is more complicated, however, since he recognises a need to distinguish between two senses of 'disgracefulness' or 'ugliness' (*turpitudo*), that of the deformity inherent in a vice (*vitiosa*) and that of the quasi-penal disgrace (*quasi poenalis*) consisting in being censured for the vice (II-II, q. 144, a. 2). Insofar as an act is evil, an instance of a vice, it is, to be sure, disgraceful; that is to say, it consists in a 'deformity of the voluntary act'. However, it is also dependent upon our will and thus not something that exceeds our ability, the proper object of a fear (a point, Aquinas adds, already made by Aristotle in the *Rhetoric*). Hence, the deformity of a non-virtuous action in this sense is not, properly speaking, the object of shame.

What is, by contrast, an object of fear in the form of shame is the censure or blame (*vituperium seu opprobrium*) that vice deserves. Hence, the object of shame is not the vice as such – certainly not first and foremost (*primo et principaliter*) – but the disgrace or infamy (*ingloriatio*) warranted by the vice. The ugliness that is feared is not the ugliness of my choices but the ugliness that exposes my actions to censure. Aquinas may be mitigating this characterisation of shame's proper object when he adds that, since vice deserves to be censured (*vituperium proprie debetur vitio*), shame is directed, as a consequence, at the disgrace it warrants. Yet even with this qualification, the object of shame is not the vice but its disgracefulness.[17] To appreciate the real difference underlying the distinction that Aquinas is making here, consider the difference

---

[15] *NE*, iv, 9 (1128b11–12): φόβος τις ἀδοξίας; 1128b22–23; Damascence (1864: 932); Nemesius (1858: 687–92).

[16] See I-II, q. 41, art. 4, and art. 4, ad 2; also fear of dishonor (*timor dehonorationis*); see II-II, q. 75, a. 1, ad 1.

[17] II-II, q. 144, a. 2; my reading of Aquinas's views in this regard (that, as far as shame is concerned, the disgracefulness is a matter of external assessment of an act rather than something intrinsic to it) differs, I suspect, from those of Gilby, Cates and Ryan; see Gilby (1968: 55); Cates (2002: 324); and Ryan (2013: 81). Aquinas also notes that shame looks to, 'respects' (*respicit*) the estimation of human beings, not to be confused with being flummoxed (confusion as a kind of embarrassment) before God (*In Sent.* 4, d. 43, q. 1, a. 5, qc. 2, ad 4). However, as Guindon notes, in Aquinas's commentary on the Psalms he distinguishes turning red with shame (*erubescit*) in the eyes of human beings as the beginning (*principium*) of emendation from doing so in the end (*finis*) before the eye of a person's reason and 'God's eye'; see Guindon (1969: 601).

between the public censure a person experiences when his disgraceful act is exposed and the censure he knows that the act deserves, exposed or not.[18]

By characterising shame on these two levels, Aquinas underscores a difference parallel to that between shame and guilt, as understood in contemporary analyses.[19] The remorse that a person feels for committing some transgression is a feeling of guilt but, if Aquinas is right, it is not to be confused with the feeling of shame, the fear of the disgrace the transgression produces or should produce. At the same time, Aquinas may be acknowledging an ancient distinction between shame that merely follows public opinion and shame that, while shaped by the latter, is also a matter of personal conviction.[20]

It may be objected that this differentiation of the sorts of disgracefulness is too fine-tuned, particularly given the fact that people seem to be less ashamed of defects that are not the result of any fault on their part (a point made in Aristotle's *Rhetoric* and noted by Aquinas). In other words, our responsibility for the disgracefulness makes a difference to the force of the shame felt.[21] Aquinas handles this difficulty – somewhat peremptorily, I think – by drawing on observations in Aristotle and Scripture to the effect that a truly virtuous individual despises undeserved disgrace and is indifferent to the opinions of others generally. Aquinas thus cites Aristotle's telling remark: 'Shame is in the virtuous hypothetically.'[22]

Despite some hedging and mixed signals, Aquinas's position on the intentionality of shame is on the whole fairly clear. The object of shame is any action that we might perform; the sense of the object is that of something exposing us to censure or reproach by others. We are in fear of this object (*de turpe actu*) because, despite what we do, it is damaging to us yet lies outside our control. Precisely as an irascible passion, shame brings to light a tension in human existence on several levels: between our desires and their fulfilment, between our abilities and their exercise, between how we see ourselves and how others see us, and between movements centred in our bodies and events centred in the world – not least the world of public opinion. In all these ways, shame is, to be sure, humbling as a reminder of the limits of our powers but only because it also a reminder of their ennobling promise.

---

[18] See note 21 below.

[19] Taylor (1985: 85–92); Williams (1993: 88–95); Nussbaum (2004: 207–8).

[20] Williams (1993: 89): 'By the later fifth century the Greeks had their own distinction between a shame that merely followed public opinion and a shame that expressed inner personal conviction.' The difference is that between a servile shame and a healthy shame; see Calhoun (2004: 127–9) and Ryan (2017: 90).

[21] In this connection, two additional features of Aquinas's analysis are of note: (1) following Aristotle (*NE* IV, 9, 1128b21), he describes shame as a disposition such that if something base were done, the person with the disposition would be ashamed of it (I, q. 95, art. 3; *In Sent.* 3, d. 36, a. 2, ad 5); and (2) he acknowledges the difference between deserved and undeserved shame, shame based on true (*secundum veritatem*) moral deficiencies and shame based on what are merely thought to be so (*secundum opinionem*) (II-II, q. 144, a. 2, ad 3 and a. 4, ad 2; *In Ethicorum* IV, 17, p. 261).

[22] II-II, q. 144, a. 2 and a. 2, ad 1; see, too, n. 19 and his comment that neither shame nor erubescence are something that the holy experience (*In Sent* 4, d. 43, q. 1, a. 5, qc. 2, ad 3). Two other objections may be noted: (1) people are often ashamed of things other than evil actions (sins) but Aquinas regards this experience of shame as 'popular opinion's' extension of the proper sense of shame to any kind of defect; (2) the degree of shame is often out of proportion with the disgracefulness of the deed but this disproportion can be explained, Aquinas submits, by the fact that some vices (e.g., sins of the flesh) are more open to disgrace than others (e.g., spiritual sins) (II-II, q. 144, a. 2, ad 3 and ad 4).

Species of Shame and a Possible Discrepancy

Following a long tradition, Aquinas distinguishes two sorts of fear of disgrace: *erubescentia* and *verecundia* (here translated *erubescence* and *shame*).[23] Yet his accounts in the *Sentences* and *De veritate* differ markedly from the account in the *Summa*. In the *Sentences* he makes the distinction in terms of the precise evil feared. When the evil feared is the disgraceful act itself, the fear is shame; when it is fear of reproach (*convicio*), the fear is erubescence. The object of *verecundia*, Aquinas adds, is the disgracefulness of 'being at fault' (*turpitudo culpae*) while the object of *erubescentia* is that of the 'penalty' (*turpitudo poenae*). Here shame is the fear of the disgracefulness of an act for which I am responsible. Erubescence, by contrast, is fear of the social repercussions of the act, i.e., the fear of reproach.[24]

This difference between erubescence and shame – between shame at censurableness (*turpitudo poenalis*) and shame at disgracefulness of guilt (*turpitudo culpae*) – appears to anticipate Aquinas's distinction in the *Summa* (discussed above) between a quasi-penal disgracefulness and the disgracefulness inherent to vice. Yet, as argued above, Aquinas makes it clear that the object of shame is first and foremost the disgracefulness of a particular act or vice and, as a consequence, the disgrace due to it. It can be argued, moreover, that – in the wording of the relevant passages in the *Sentences* no less than those in the *Summa* – the object of shame is not the act itself but the disgracefulness, whether it be the actual disgrace or the disgrace that should attend such an act. So, an argument can be made that in this respect there is no discrepancy between the accounts in the *Sentences* and in the *Summa*.

In any case, Aquinas characterises the difference between erubescence and shame differently in the *Summa*, identifying it as a difference in the time of the action. If the deed that inspires the fear is being done (*in actu committendo*), then it is *erubescentia*, the passion with which blushing is typically associated; if it is already done, then it is a case of *verecundia* (I-II, q. 39, art. 1; q. 41, a. 4 and a. 4, ad 3; q. 42, a. 3, ad 4). This distinction seems roughly to parallel Nemesius's wording: 'Shame is fear in the disgraceful act or in the disgrace perpetrated [*timor in actu vel in turpi perpetrato*]' (II-II, q. 144, art. 2). Shame's future-directedness as a fear, Aquinas points out, is not incompatible with the fact that its object is a past act (*actu praeterito, turpi facto*) since 'future reproach and opprobrium can be feared in the case of a past deed' (I-II, q. 41, a. 4, ad 3).

Aquinas's gloss on the difference between erubescence and shame in the *Summa* makes it far less significant than the account in the *Sentences*. When it comes to the phenomena in question, he no longer appears to countenance an essential difference between fear of an action qua reproachful and fear of the reproach itself. (Indeed, he may be suggesting that it is an example of a distinction without a real difference.) By identifying the difference as merely a difference in the time of the disgraceful act, Aquinas appears in effect to be challenging the force of the

---

[23] Aquinas's six species of fear – including αἰδώς and αἰσκύνη, corresponding to *erubescentia* and *verecundia* respectively – duplicate those listed by Damascene and Nyssa. They define αἰδώς, an 'excellent passion', as a fear resulting from expectation of blame (φόβος ἐπὶ προσδοχίᾳ ψόγου; κάλλιστον . . . τὸ πάθος). They characterise αἰσκύνη as a fear resulting from having done something disgraceful (φόβος ἐπ' αἰσχρῷ πεπραβμένῳ); see Damascence (1864: 931–2); Nemesius (1858: 687–92); for discussion of related terms, *confusio* and *pudor*, see Guindon (1969: 597–8, 610).

[24] *In Sent* 3, dist. 26, q. 1, a. 3; in *De veritate*, Aquinas distinguishes shame as the fear of the action itself from fear of the sentiment provoked by others' blame (*De veritate*, q. 26, a. 4, ad 7). Müller sees this differentiation as tending to a distinction between moral and social shame, although in his view the social aspect increasingly occupies Aquinas's attention; Müller (2011: 65).

distinction (along with its ancient lineage). Whether I fear the disgrace that may be incurred by something I've already done (shame) or by something that I'm currently doing (erubescence), the essential object of the shame remains the same: an action insofar as it is disgraceful or subject to censure (in phenomenological terms, the action is the object under this description, i.e., intended/meant in this sense). There are, to be sure, several cognate differences that come into play here, e.g., between fearing/shunning an action because it is disgraceful and fearing that such an action, having been perpetrated, will come to light; between fearing disgrace and fearing that we'll do something disgraceful; or even between fearing disgrace deserved and fearing disgrace undeserved. Yet such differences, too, Aquinas seems to be suggesting, are not essential to the make-up of shame. In each case, shame remains a passion, the fear that my actions will be censured and sources of disgrace.

The Intersubjectivity of Shame

The foregoing gloss of Aquinas's study of shame underscores the intersubjectivity of shame. By identifying shame with the fear of the disgracefulness or censurability of an action, Aquinas ties shame to how we imagine others' view and judgement of the action. The fear that makes up shame presupposes a comparison of our abilities with the expectations of others. Shame is precisely the fear of others finding an action reproachful, indeed, whether it is or not. The thought that what matters to me is not what others think of my action but whether it is disgraceful or not is obviously self-defeating since the criteria of disgracefulness and censure are tied to what others think. So, too, as an integral part of temperance, shame figures centrally in the development of the virtuous character necessary for friendship, one of life's most indispensable goods.

Aquinas specifies the character and degrees of shame in explicitly intersubjective terms. The reproach that is the object of shameful fear must stem from someone who 'attests' (*importat testimonium*) to a person's shameful deficiencies ('principally', he adds, 'with respect to some guilt [*culpam*]'). After noting that the degree of shame corresponds to the weightiness of the reputation of the person 'attesting', Aquinas notes that this weightiness is based on either (1) the certitude of the truthfulness of the testimony or (2) its effectiveness with respect to some purpose or another. In the first case, the shame is greater, the more virtuous or knowledgeable the person is who is making the reproach (that is to say, when the reproach stems from those who are 'wise and virtuous' or from those more familiar with the matter in question and/or with us). Thus, a judge's censure of a person is typically considered weightier, more shame-inducing, than censure by a common criminal. In the second case, we are more liable to be ashamed by the reproach of those who can exact some advantage or do some harm to us by attesting to something shameful on our part. These individuals are more likely to be associated with us than strangers. Thus, a student may be more ashamed to give a wrong answer in front of his peers than in front of strangers.[25]

The Moral Relevance of Shame

Contemporary authors sometimes classify shame, along with pride and guilt, as moral emotions. In the course of addressing the question of good and evil in the 'passions of the soul', Aquinas claims that, while different passions are morally neutral insofar as they are species of

---

[25] Drawing on II-II, q. 144, a. 3, Ryan identifies three circles of relationships relevant to shame as a motivation; Ryan (2013: 82f.); for a valuable discussion of the non-epistemic, 'practical weight' attached to others' assessment with respect to shame, see Calhoun (2004: 139–46).

a natural genus, they can be distinguished as species of a moral genus insofar as (*prout*) they are subject to the rule of reason and the will, participating in some way in the will and judgement of reason (I-II, q. 24, aa. 1, 4). A passion is good to the extent that it 'tends' towards something truly good and 'recedes' from something truly evil (I-II, 24, 4, ad 2). As an example of such a passion the object of which is in keeping (*conveniens*) with reason, Aquinas mentions shame (*verecundia*). As fear of what is, under some description, morally base, unseemly, or ugly (*turpis timor*), shame is a 'laudable passion'.[26]

From the fact that shame is in some sense good and laudable, should we conclude that it is a virtue? The question is delicate and problematic, as the gloss in the last paragraph already suggests. In posing this question, Aquinas lists several reasons to think that shame is a virtue. Like virtue, it is a mean between two extremes;[27] what is laudable is either a virtue or part of a virtue (and shame is not a part of prudence, justice, fortitude or temperance); there is something honourable about shame (since it is a part of being honourable); it is opposed to vices (namely, shamelessness and inordinate disengagement: *inverecundia et inordinatus stupor*); and shame generates laudable habits.

In addition to underscoring the close connection between shame and virtue, these considerations explain why shame is commonly called a virtue. The term 'virtue' applies to shame, Aquinas concedes, insofar as it is used in a loose sense to designate whatever is good and laudable in human actions and passions. Nevertheless, he agrees with Aristotle that, strictly speaking, shame is not a virtue since it lacks the perfection implied by virtue. It is obvious that it lacks that perfection since it is a fear of some 'reproachable and base' (*exprobrabile et turpe*) action that no one who has perfected a virtuous habit would consider it possible to do or difficult to avoid (II-II, q. 144; *NE* iv.9, 1128b17–1129a1).[28]

Here again we see a reliance – perhaps an over-reliance – on the case of a perfected virtue. Still, the broad lines of Aquinas's position are clear: shame is a passion, temperance a virtue, and never the twain shall meet since no passion and only a virtue is an elective habit, a habit of choosing. Yet this reliance on a state of perfected virtue seems questionable, at least insofar as such a state is something seldom achieved. Moreover, as discussed below, shame figures into virtue in complex ways, as Aquinas himself notes, adding to the delicateness if not tenuousness of the distinction.

As for the reasons that Aquinas listed for classifying shame as a virtue, he appeals to its status as a passion to overrule them. Being a mean is necessary but insufficient for virtue; it is also necessary for it to be a chosen habit (*habitus electivus*), and shame – as a passion – is not. Shame is laudable and pertains to virtues – albeit pre-eminently temperance – but only as the fear of the vices that are their opposites. Similarly, while it fosters honourableness, as a passion it does so without attaining the complete significance of the latter. The fact that shame is at

---

[26] *In Sent.* 3, d. 33, q. 3, a. 4, qc. 4, ad 3; *In Sent.* 4, d. 50, q. 2, a. 4, qc. 3, ad 3.

[27] See Raymond (2017: 114); *NE* ii.5, 1106a5–6; *NE* ii.7, 1108a31–b1).

[28] In the *Sentences*, Aquinas distinguishes two senses of laudability, namely, what possesses the full significance (*ratio*) of virtue (what is virtuous in the full sense of the term) and what participates in something virtuous (what has some of the significance of virtue); by the latter he has in mind 'appropriate acts preceding virtue' (*actus virtutem praecedentes, si sint ordinati*) and as an example he mentions passions such as shame (*verecundia*) and mercy 'insofar as they follow from a good will, which shuns disgraceful deeds [*turpia*]' (*In Sent.* 3, dist. 23, q. 1, art. 3, qc. 2, ad 2). A good will, Aquinas adds, wills what is needed for virtue; also laudable insofar as they proceed from the requisite choice of the good (*In Sent.* 4, dist. 15, q. 2, art. 1, qc. 1, ad 4; d. 50, q. 2, a. 4, qc. 3, ad 3).

odds with vice does not qualify it as a virtue, since not everything opposed to vice is a virtue. Moreover, the laudable habits it engenders are, indeed, acquired virtues – but then no longer the same as the passion of shame.[29]

These considerations are compelling but the relationship of shame to virtue is more complex than they might suggest. As noted above, Aquinas does not consider shame a morally neutral passion. In fact, he considers it, along with honourability, an integral part of temperance. Shame is necessary because it shuns the ugliness (*turpitudo*) that is the contrary of the virtue (just as honorability is necessary because it loves the beauty of temperance). By an 'integral' part (in the next question he dubs shame and honourability 'quasi-integral'), Aquinas seems to have in mind a condition that must be met for the virtue.[30] It is an integral part, not in the sense of entering into temperance's essence, but in the sense of disposing someone to be temperate.[31]

Shame is thus a necessary but insufficient condition of the virtue of temperance and Aquinas's account rides on the difference but relatedness of the disposition (shame) and the virtue (temperance). In other words, shame in some sense disposes a person to being temperate yet that disposition falls short of a habit that is the result of choice. To the extent that I fear the reproach befitting gluttonous or inebriated behaviour (or their contraries), I consider such behaviour shameful and I would be ashamed of engaging in it. Inasmuch as this fear helps me identify and avoid such behaviour, it helps foster a disposition that accords with the virtue of temperance, i.e., with rationally chosen behaviour. But as long as the fear of disgrace alone moves me, I feel shame but am not virtuous. As a virtue, temperance requires, in addition to the disposition to act in the appropriate way, the character that comes from a habit of choosing to act in that manner.

The complexity of the relationship is by no means limited to the way that shame disposes a person to be temperate. It also extends to the way that the passion follows from choices made by a temperate (virtuous) person. Thus, after iterating that passions are not in our power like acts of the will, Aquinas notes that passions can sometimes be meritorious by virtue of anticipating and even arousing a meritorious volitional act. They can also be said to be meritorious insofar as they are willed or aroused by the will. As an example of the latter, where a higher power overflows (*redundat*) into a lower, he gives the example of the 'inferior appetite for shame' being affected by someone who wilfully detests the ugliness of sin. In general, passions are thus meritorious insofar as they are the effects and indices of a good will – a point, Aquinas adds, that is especially clear in the case of shame 'which indicates the will of a human being to resist [*repugnare*] the disgracefulness of sin'.[32]

The take-away here is clearly the complexity of the relation of shame to virtue. As a passion, shame is not, in the strict sense, a matter of choice, let alone the iterated choice that makes

---

[29] II-II, q. 144, a. 1; a. 1, ad 1 and ad 5; a. 2, ad 1; a. 4, ad 3; *In Ethicorum*, IV, 17.

[30] On the difference between integral, subjective and potential parts, see II-II, q. 48, a. 1 and q. 143, a. 1; 'quasi-integral' parts are required (*exiguntur, requiruntur*) for the virtue or its perfection (II-II, q. 49, a. 5 and q. 53, a. 2), 'subjective' parts are the species of the virtue, 'potential' parts are adjunct virtues or dispositions.

[31] II-II, q. 144, a. 4, ad 4: 'Verecundia non est pars temperantiae quasi intrans essentiam eius, sed quasi dispositive se habens ad ipsam.' In addition to deeming corporal sins more disgraceful but hardly more grievous than spiritual sins (II-II, q. 141, a. 2, ad 4; a. 4; q. 151, a. 4, ad 2), Aquinas also observes that vices of intemperance have the greatest disgracefulness (*turpitudinem*) (II-II, q. 143).

[32] *De veritate*, q. 26, a. 6, ad 16; see note 17 above for Aquinas's characterisation of *erubescentia* as *principium et finis emendationis* in his commentary on the Psalms.

for a virtue. Yet since intemperate behaviour is disgraceful, the fear of it (i.e., shame) disposes a person to be temperate (to be moderate), a disposition that is in turn reinforced by virtuous choices.

The Distinctiveness of Shame

The distinctiveness of shame, on Aquinas's account, consists in its status as a passion with social ramifications. It is a socially determinate fear that, while not itself a virtue, plays a formative role in disposing us to virtue as well as a constitutive role in virtue. That is to say, shame disposes us to be temperate and to be temperate is – among other things – to have the disposition of being ashamed of acting a certain way. While the principal virtue in this respect is temperance, shame is relevant to every virtue since every vice is disgraceful. Yet in Aquinas's view, shame, as a passion, is clearly different from guilt.[33] It is concerned with something extrinsic to the sin itself, indeed, the ignominy not so much of the act itself as the public response to it. It is entirely appropriate, to be sure, to speak of moral shame, i.e., shame that is morally fitting; but in that case it is precisely the shame – the fear of reproach – that comes with being culpable. 'Shame in the proper sense concerns the scorn that guilt [*culpa*] deserves insofar as this is a defect of the will [*defectus voluntaris*]' (II-II, q. 144, a. 2, ad 1 and a. 3).[34]

This moral shame is not the same as penitence. Like Scheler, Aquinas recognises that feelings of remorse, i.e., penitent feelings, come close to feelings of shame but remain fundamentally different from them. As for their similarities Aquinas notes that both kinds of feeling are dispositions of someone less than perfect, that they are related to temperance, and that they concern some disgraceful act (*turpe factum*). Despite these similarities, however, shame is in his view a passion whereas penitence is caused not only by passion but more by choice (*electio*); hence, in contrast to shame, penitence is 'properly speaking' a virtue (*In Sent.* 4, d. 14, q. 1, a. 1, qc. 2; III, q. 85, a. 2). Their temporal orientations point to a further difference. Inasmuch as shame, as a fear, indicates a disposition towards the possibility of future reproach for a disgraceful action, it implies an imperfection; by contrast, penitence is about something disgraceful in the past, which does not rule out perfection in the present (III, q. 85, a. 1, ad 2). Last but not least is the difference in their respective genera (indicating different phenomenologies respectively). Thus, Aquinas observes that shame is in a different genus from penitence, inasmuch as shame is a fear and penitence a sadness (*dolor*).[35]

---

[33] In a different way, contemporary thinkers also often distinguish shame (pertaining to a loss of self-respect) and guilt (pertaining to a transgression); see Taylor (1985: 89–92, 134); for a different differentiation of shame and guilt, see Card (2002: 206); Stump (2010: 142–7).

[34] So, too, he distinguishes shame from modesty (*modestia*) and decency (*pudor*); see *In Sent.* 3, dist. 33, q. 3, art. 2. Given the intentional character of the experience, we may characterise 'moral shame' proper as a morally fitting disposition towards certain actions, i.e., actions that are immoral. A person who lacks moral shame is someone who would not experience – or, by Aquinas's account, would not fear – the disgracefulness of acting immorally.

[35] *In Sent.* 4, d. 14, q. 1, a. 1, qc. 5, ad 4. While Aquinas distinguishes shame from penitence in both the commentary on the *Sentences* and the *Summa*, his manner of doing so in the latter complicates the account of shame that he gives there. He stresses that shame is a passion but, in contrasting it with penitence, he notes that while the latter is about 'something done basely' as past, shame is about 'something done basely as present' (*turpe factum ut praesens*). Also, in the course of discussing the mode of someone penitent, Aquinas notes that shame can be an impediment to a confession (*In Sent.* 4, d. 17, q. 3, art 2, qc. 3, ad 2) – a note that further underscores the complexity of the relation between the passion and the virtue.

Critical Observations

Deliberately hazarding an obvious anachronism, I have attempted in the foregoing to demonstrate the proto-phenomenological character of Aquinas's analysis of shame. By embedding that account in his conception of irascible passions and shame's role in temperance and other virtues, he provides penetrating insights into the nature of the experience in ways that hardly seem confined to the thirteenth century. If my interpretation is right, he unflinchingly puts his finger on both the essentially intentional character of the experience of shame and its object. Whether imagined or real, internalised or not, the object of shame is an action's disgracefulness (*turpitudo*).

Yet Aquinas's analysis of shame, for all its phenomenological prowess, is by no means flawless. The analysis is vulnerable in particular to two lines of criticism. At the risk of additional anachronism, I develop these critical observations in part by comparison and contrast with Scheler's study of shame. The comparison and contrast are made only for the sake of setting similarities and differences into relief, without any presumption of the correctness of Scheler's study. These observations about Aquinas's analysis are critical, not in the sense of identifying considerations that are debilitating for Aquinas's analysis, but in the sense of raising questions and challenges that someone convinced in the present of the basic correctness of the direction of the analysis should want to resolve. The first group centres on the question: What is the feeling of shame? Or if there is a range of different experiences that we label 'shame', what qualifies them as experiences of shame rather than something else (e.g., embarrassment, crimes)? Does Aquinas have it right when he classifies shame as a fear? The second group addresses the thicket of issues centreing on the question: What is the morality of shame? How do or should experiences of shame figure into a moral life? How does Aquinas's view of shame as an integral part of virtue square with his claim that it is not itself a virtue? My aim here is not to answer these questions but merely to show how they present reasonable challenges to the understanding of shame entailed by Aquinas's analysis.

What is the Feeling of Shame?

Fear in Aquinas's view is, it bears recalling, an intentional experience, directed at a future evil that is difficult or impossible to avoid, i.e., something that is, to a significant degree, beyond our control. Aquinas's characterisation of shame as a species of the irascible passion of fear brings to light the fact that it is the experience of the possibility of a disharmony between what is hoped for (approval) and what ensues (disapproval). As such, it is the experience of our impotence.[36] In other words, shame is the fear of others' reproach of our actions, precisely because their assessment is not in our power. In this way, shame entails (1) the recognition of

---

[36] In Bernard Williams, shame is experienced as a loss of power, a view akin to that of Augustine for whom shame constitutes the post-lapsarian inversion of the natural order of the spirit over the flesh. Thus, a male's shame at his lack of control moves him to cover his genitals to conceal that they are not subject to his will is the punishment for disobeying God; see the Augustine references in note 3 above. Echoing the Augustinian conception, Scheler observes that because we're more than our bodies, we *can* feel shame; but because we are bodies we *must* feel shame (Scheler 1957: 69, 148). Both Aquinas's characterisation of shame as an irascible passion and Scheler's characterisation of it as a disharmony rooted in a certain self-regard can be seen as attempts to do justice to this contentiousness and struggle within us. Drawing on Aristophanes, Scheler and others, Nussbaum also construes shame in terms of a self-regard and the disappointment of lack of control or impotence; Nussbaum (2004: 182–9).

the clear difference between those actions and others' view of them, not least in terms of what we can control, (2) a reflection on (a turning back to) his/her actions and abilities in the light of others' view of them ('the looking glass self'), and (3) the further recognition that the difference can rise to the level of a conflict. This conflict, moreover, can take place regardless of my view of those actions and regardless, too, of whether they are voluntary or involuntary – hence, the fearfulness. More broadly, to live in shame is to live in constant fear that one's abilities do not meet expectations.

In this respect, Aquinas puts his finger on the very 'sphere' in which, according to Scheler, shame occurs, namely, the sphere of a 'conflict' (*Widerstreit*) between the concrete existence of an act and its essential meaning – in Aquinas's idiom, its disgracefulness (*turpitudo*). In the case of shame, this conflict typically corresponds to a 'disharmony' between what is and what ought to be the case, between bodily neediness and claims not confined to bodily neediness. This lack of harmony, Scheler submits, is the basic condition from which the feeling of shame originates (Scheler 1957: 69). A person's experience of this disharmony coincides with her turning her attention back to herself (*Rückwendung*). While the parallel between the two analyses is stark, it deserves to be noted that Scheler alone emphasises how the feeling of shame is a feeling of the need to protect the self (*Selbstschutz*) from notoriety.[37]

Yet, despite these similarities in their understanding of the phenomenology of shame,[38] Aquinas and Scheler seem to differ precisely in their classification of the experience. I say 'seem to differ' since it is possible that they use the operative term (here translated 'fear') in different ways. Nonetheless, while Aquinas in his terminology clearly identifies shame as a fear, Scheler explicitly takes issue with the idea of construing it as a fear. Fear (*Furcht*) is, in Scheler's view, the force, co-extensive with life, of feeling dangers in advance and presenting the sentient creature with dangerous things and processes, before they actually do harm to the organism. Yet whereas fear is always directed at the sorts of things already experienced, shame need not be and, indeed, in this respect, Scheler adds, it is more akin to anxiety (*Angst*) than to fear (Scheler 1957: 88). Scheler stresses, furthermore, that shame is a feeling of oneself or, more precisely, of a self in general being held accountable (since we can feel shame for others) and, indeed, a protective feeling that overcomes us (*Überkommenwerden*) (Scheler 1957: 81). However, instead of further specifying the quality of the feeling, he tries to get at its character by contrasting it with several related feelings (for example, sadness, humility, disgust and fear). If shame is, indeed, a *sui generis* feeling, then Scheler's approach, if not his exact analysis, recommends itself.[39] More importantly, for our purposes, the difference between this sort of approach and Aquinas's classification of shame as a fear is as patent as it is striking.

---

[37] Scheler (1957: 90); note, however, that Ryan reads shame in Aquinas view as a 'sentinel', protecting 'us in our deepest convictions' (Ryan 2013: 79).

[38] The two analyses also converge in construing shame as a mean between two extremes. Aquinas cites Aristotle on this score (II-II, q. 144, a. 1, ad 1; *NE* ii.7, 1108a31–b1; *EE* iii.7, 1233b25–28). Scheler situates shame between prudishness (*Prüderie*) on one extreme and cynicism, exhibitionism or obscenity on the other. While essentially connected with shame, these extremes largely arise, in Scheler's view, from a conflict between what is objectively taken to be shameful and feelings of shame (Scheler 1957: 93ff.). Gilby suggests a parallel account in Aquinas to the effect that shame's close relationship to a sense of sin (guilt) makes it more 'personal and agonizing than the fear of earning a bad name' (Gilby 1968: 55).

[39] Psychologists differ on listing shame among basic emotions; Ekman and Scheff list shame as a basic emotion (Ekman 1999: 55; Scheff 2015); Izard and Zinck and Newen do not (Izard 2007: 261, 266; Zinck and Newen 2008: 11f.).

Whether or not one shares Scheler's view of the matter (his views on fear or shame), Aquinas's classification of shame as a fear – despite its Aristotelian pedigree – seems, at least *prima facie*, fairly problematic. Do we not experience shame in the present, precisely in being caught in an act (recalling Sartre's example) that we know others regard as disgraceful? Shame in this sense is certainly something that we fear but it is hardly itself a fear. So, too, to live in shame is not necessarily to fear that something disgraceful that we are doing or have done will be viewed as such; it is instead to live with this view, in the present, of what we are doing or have done – to live in its shadows, as it were.[40] In other words, insofar as fear is essentially future-directed and shame may be present-directed, shame is not essentially or unqualifiedly a species of fear. These considerations do not undermine the accuracy and level of nuance that Aquinas achieves in his analysis of the experience of fearing that others will censure what I have done or am doing. The richness of this analysis, particular as an irascible passion, is undeniable. But, based at the very least on contemporary use of the term, it seems overly restrictive and in a certain sense misleading to restrict the meaning of 'shame' to that experience.

What is the Morality of Shame?

As noted above, contemporary philosophers typically distinguish between feelings of embarrassment, shame and guilt. On this score, at least when it comes to shame and guilt, Aquinas seems to be in close agreement, if his views of penitence, glossed above, are indicative of his conception of guilt. However, while Scheler agrees that feelings of shame and of penitence can be distinguished, he contends that only penitent feelings are necessarily about something of negative value. When a person's advantageous or desirable qualities are demonstrated to others or even to oneself, that manifestation of them can awaken a 'deeper and purer shame than the shame of a mistake' (Scheler 1957: 82). Scheler's view of shame is thus clearly more expansive than Aquinas's view in this respect (although the difference is perhaps attributable to a more figurative use of the term by Scheler and/or to a difference in their eras and cultures).

More importantly for our purposes, their views on the morality of shame diverge considerably. Scheler identifies shame precisely with a 'feeling of culpability' (*Schuldgefühl*); he also acknowledges that the feeling of remorse (a penitent feeling) and shame can coincide when someone first appreciates the wrongness of their behaviour by experiencing someone else's reproach and sharing in the feeling of (*nachfühlen*) that reproach. Having to confess a lie, Scheler submits, is a prime example of this feeling of remorse coinciding with the feeling of being ashamed of oneself (Scheler 1957: 81, 83). So, in short, Scheler is not prepared, as Aquinas is, to distinguish feelings of shame cleanly from feelings of guilt.

However, as flagged above, the question of the morality of shame in Aquinas is complex. Although he insists on the Aristotelian line that it is a passion and thus not a virtue, he also follows Aristotle in considering it a good and laudable passion. He goes a step further by identifying it as an integral part of temperance. As a disposition, shame is not a mere passing episode; it is integral to the acquisition and maintenance of temperance precisely because it disposes us to shun disgraceful acts.

---

[40] Aquinas does discuss shame in the context of discussing the fact that sadness on account of a present evil is good. The discussion seems to imply that shame, as this sort of good, is in fact an experience of pain or sorrow; see I-II, q. 39, art. 1. However, he gives no indication of how this solitary comment relates to his predominant view of shame as a fear. Zinck and Newen characterise shame as a 'secondary cognitive emotion unfolded out of fear' (Zinck and Newen 2008: 18). After acknowledging that prospective shame in Greek narratives can be seen as a form of fear, Williams adds that 'fear is there, but . . . it is not the whole story' (Williams 1993: 80).

The viability of Aquinas's account turns in large measure on giving an adequate account of the relationship between the passion and the elective habit, that is to say, between shame as a disposition and temperance or some other virtue as it relates to that disposition. Through the use of reason, a person can instigate or mitigate a fear (I, q. 81, a. 3) but fears are by no means always responses to reason. This distinction – between what Claudia Murphy dubs 'reason-dependent' and 'reason-independent' passions – applies, as noted above, in like measure to shame.[41]

This distinction helps frame two stubborn difficulties with Aquinas's account of the morality of shame. The first concerns the sense in which shame disposes a person to virtue, an elective habit (particularly when shame is not caused by a reasoned judgement) without amounting to a virtue itself. When I act in a measured way, avoiding extremes, how do I know that I am virtuously choosing this path and not simply acting out of shame (as Aquinas understands the latter)? Bad faith is surely possible here and an answer, if it is forthcoming at all, can perhaps only be given on a case-by-case basis. If, however, this soul-searching scruple is not overwrought, that is to say, if it cannot be reasonably dismissed, it presents a challenge to Aquinas's differentiation of the passion (shame) from the virtue (temperance).

The second difficulty concerns the sense in which a person is responsible for the disposition (both when shame is a response to reason and when it is responsive to reason).[42] While the first difficulty calls into question the distinction between the disposition and the virtue on the basis of the disposition's import for the virtue, the second difficulty calls the distinction into question on the basis of the virtue's import for the disposition. Insofar as a virtuous person 'instigates and arouses' shame (to use Aquinas's terms), s/he is responsible for the shame. By the same token, that shame is the work of reason and the will. But in that case, why is this passion, the fear that takes the form of shame, not itself a virtue?[43]

Both difficulties concern questions of the bilateral determination or responsibility posited by Aquinas with respect to shame and virtue. They highlight the fact that any difference between shame and virtue is often clouded in experience. Even if on some level shame and virtue were clearly distinguishable in a person's moral development, their effect on one another is often so encompassing that the differentiation often seems to fade. Aquinas's characterisation of shame as an integral or quasi-integral part of temperance is perhaps an acknowledgement of this ambiguity.

Still, while the difficulty of sorting out the difference between shame and virtue in experience is real, Aquinas remains on firm ground when he insists on their difference. Indeed, he is on firm phenomenological ground when due consideration is given to their differing intentionalities, that is to say, to the difference in their objects. Thus, it is one thing to be motivated solely by fear of possible disgrace; quite another to choose to do what is right because it is morally becoming. The distinction holds given the existence of situations where a person chooses to act virtuously, even at the risk of being disgraced – and worse – for doing so (a Berliner sheltering Jews in 1938; a Caucasian Tuscaloosa citizen, in the same year, sitting down in a restaurant with someone of African-American descent).

With these sorts of examples in mind, one might object that the difference between shame and virtue is even less clear, particularly insofar as the right action coincides, in the

---

[41] Murphy (1999: 177).

[42] On the difference between being responsive to reason and being a response to reason or the will, see Murphy (1999: 174f.).

[43] For a parallel argument that Aristotle, on these grounds, should have recognised *aidos* as a virtue, see Raymond (2017: 158f.).

agent's mind, with the sort of action that is becoming and, thus, the antithesis of what his/her upbringing has taught him/her is subject to condemnation and disgrace. The intersubjectivity of shame, it may be objected, runs accordingly deep, figuring into the internalisation of standards of what is and is not appropriate or permissible. Yet Aquinas, following Aristotle, recognises that the approval of others or at least some others – even if necessary on some level, certainly the level of actual moral development – is insufficient to determine what is right or morally becoming. We can always ask why they approve such an action and it begs the question to give, as the reason for the approbation, yet another approbation. The object of virtue is what reason tells us is the right thing to do and, while it is also the reason for approbation or disapprobation, it is not to be confused with the latter. Accordingly, while the object of shame is a disgraceful action, the object of virtue is the sort of action that provides the reason for such disgracefulness. Experience can continue to be ambiguous, to be sure. Yet sorting out the motivations for our experience (was I acting out of shame or was I acting virtuously?) remains a challenge precisely because the difference that Aquinas holds fast to – the difference between shame and virtue – holds.

What does Aquinas's study of shame tell us about him as a philosopher? Perhaps above all it reveals Aquinas to be a philosopher keenly attuned to the profound tensions that define the human condition. His classification of shame as fear may be off target, as I have suggested, but his penetrating analysis of it as a passion with a complexity all its own is nonetheless at odds with an overly rational conception of human nature. His analysis of shame's distinctive object (disgracefulness) also underscores this passion's intersubjective character, anticipating contemporary views of it as a social emotion. Thus, his analysis exposes the way our sense of ourselves – or, better, how we feel about ourselves – entails not only how others view us but just as much our sense of how they do. Yet if Aquinas's analysis of shame is deeply sensitive to this affective, intersubjective dimension of human life, it is also clear that he is sensitive, as a philosopher, to this dimension because, in his view, a genuine philosophical analysis of human existence can only be conducted with a view to what is good for a human life as a whole. This concern for the good of human life is evident in his way of negotiating the moral implications of shame. Thus, while shame for him is not, strictly speaking, a virtue, it is, from a moral point of view, a 'laudable passion'. In sum, Aquinas's analysis of shame reveals him to be a philosopher who does not shy away from coming to terms with the emotional tensions and complexities of a shared life lived to the fullest.

Bibliography

Aquinas, Thomas (1888–1906 [1265–73]). *Summa Theologiae.* In *Opera Omnia,* Leonine edition, Vols 4–12. Rome: Typographia poliglotta S. C. de Propaganda Fide. (Abbreviations: 'I' for the first part, 'I-II' for the first part of the second part, 'II-II' for the second part of the second part, 'III' for the third part.)

Aquinas, Thomas (1929–47 [1252–6]). *Scriptum super libros Sententiarum.* Ed. P. Mandonnet and M. Moos, 4 vols. Paris: Lethielleux. (Abbreviation: *In Sent.*)

Aquinas, Thomas (1969 [1271–2]). *Sententia libri Ethicorum, Opera Omnia.* Leonine edition, Vol. 47. Rome: Ad Sanctae Sabinae. (Abbreviation: *In Ethicorum.*)

Aquinas, Thomas (1972–6 [1256–9]). *Quaestiones disputatae de veritate.* In *Opera Omnia,* Leonine edition, Vol. 22. Rome: Editori di san Tommaso. (Abbreviation: *De veritate.*)

Augustine (1841 [413–27]). *De civitate Dei.* In *Patrologia Latina,* Vol. XLI. Ed. J. P. Migne. Paris: Migne.

Calhoun, Cheshire (2004). 'An Apology for Moral Shame'. *The Journal of Political Philosophy,* 12/2: 127–46.

Card, Claudia (2002). *The Atrocity Paradigm: A Theory of Evil.* Oxford: Oxford University Press.

Cates, Diana Fritz (2002). 'The Virtue of Temperance (IIa IIae, qq. 141–70). In *The Ethics of Aquinas*. Ed. S. Pope. Washington, DC: Georgetown University Press, pp. 321–39.
Cates, Diana Fritz (2009). *Aquinas on the Emotions: A Religious-Ethical Inquiry*. Washington, DC: Georgetown University Press.
Dahlstrom, Daniel (1998). 'Edmund Husserl'. In *Encyclopedia of Aesthetics*, Vol. 2, pp. 433–9. Ed. Michael Kelly.
Dahlstrom, Daniel (2017). 'Scheler on Shame: A Critical Review'. *Metodo. International Studies in Phenomenology and Philosophy*, 5/1: 239–62.
Damascence, John (1864 [c. 725]). *Expositio accurata fidei orthodoxae*. In *Patrologiae Cursus Completus, Series Graeca*, Vol. XCIV. Ed. J. P. Migne. Paris: Migne, pp. 789–1228.
Ekman, Paul (1999). 'Basic Emotions'. In *Handbook of Cognition and Emotion*. Ed. Tim Daigleish and Mick Power. New York: John Wiley & Sons, pp. 45–60.
Floyd, Shawn D. (1998). 'Aquinas on Emotion: A Response to Some Recent Interpretations'. *History of Philosophy Quarterly*, 15/2: 161–75.
Gilby, Thomas, OP (1968). 'Introduction and Notes'. In Thomas Aquinas, *Summa Theologiae (2a.2ae, qq. 141–154)*, Vol. 43. London: Eyre and Spottiswoode.
Green, Keith (2007). 'Aquinas's Argument against Self-hatred'. *Journal of Religious Ethics*, 35/1: 113–39.
Guindon, André (1969). 'La "crainte honteuse" selon Thomas d'Aquin'. *Revue Thomiste*, 127, LXIX/4: 589–623.
Izard, Carroll E. (2007). 'Basic Emotions, Natural Kinds, Emotions Schemas, and a New Paradigm'. *Perspectives on Psychological Science*, 2/3: 260–80.
Knuuttila, Simo (2004). *The Emotions in Medieval and Ancient Philosophy*. Oxford: Clarendon.
Knuuttila, Simo (2012). 'The Emotion of Shame in Medieval Philosophy'. *SpazioFilosofico*, 5: 243–9.
Miner, Robert (2009). *Thomas Aquinas on the Passions, Summa Theologiae, 1a2ae, 22–48*. Cambridge: Cambridge University Press.
Müller, Jörn (2011). 'Scham und menschliche Natur bei Augustinus und Thomas von Aquin'. In *Zur Kulturgeschichte der Scham, Archiv für Begriffsgeschichte*, Sonderheft 9. Ed. M. Bauks and M.F. Meyer. Hamburg: Meiner, pp. 55–72.
Murphy, Claudia Eisen (1999). 'Aquinas on our Responsibility for our Emotions'. *Medieval Philosophy and Theology*, 8/2: 163–205.
Nemesius Episcopus Emeseni (1858 [c. 400]). *De natura hominis*. In *Patrologiae Cursus Completus, Series Graeca*, Vol. XL. Ed. J. P. Migne. Paris: Migne, pp. 503–844.
Nussbaum, Martha (2004). *Hiding from Humanity: Disgust, Shame, and the Law*. Princeton: Princeton University Press.
Olivi, Peter of John (1924). *Quaestiones in secundum librum Sententiarum* (Bibliotheca Franciscana Scholastica 5). Vol. II. Ed. B. Jansen. Quaracchi: Collegium S. Bonaventurae.
Olivi, Peter of John (2007). *On Genesis*. Ed. David Flood. St. Bonaventure, NY: Franciscan Institute Publications.
Raymond, Christopher C. (2017). 'Shame and Virtue in Aristotle'. In *Oxford Studies in Ancient Philosophy*. Ed. Victor Caston. Oxford: Oxford University Press, pp. 111–61.
Richard of St. Victor (1979). *The Twelve Patriarchs*. Trans. and introduced by Grover A. Zinn. New York: Paulist Press.
Ryan, Thomas (2013). 'Aquinas on Shame: A Contemporary Interchange'. In *Aquinas, Education and the East*, ed.T. B. Mooney and M.Nowacki. New York: Springer, pp. 73–100.
Ryan, Thomas (2017). 'The Positive Function of Shame: Moral and Spiritual Perspectives'. In *The Value of Shame*. Ed. E. Vanderheide and C.-H. Mayer. New York: Springer, pp. 87–105.
Sartre, Jean-Paul (1943). *L'être et le néant*. Paris: Gallimard.
Scheff, Thomas (2015). 'Toward Defining Basic Emotions'. *Qualitative Inquiry*, 21/2: 111–21.
Scheler, Max (1957). 'Uber Scham und Schamgefühl'. In *Gesammelte Werke*, Band 10. Bern: Francke, pp. 67–154.
Stump, Elenore (2010). *Wandering in Darkness: Narrative and the Problem of Suffering*. Oxford: Clarendon Press.

Taylor, Gabrielle (1985). *Pride, Shame, and Guilt: Emotions of Self-assessment*. Oxford: Clarendon Press.
Velleman, J. David (2001). 'The Genesis of Shame'. *Philosophy and Public Affairs*, 30/1: 27–52.
Wheatley, William (1980). *Expositio in Boethii De consolatione Philosophiae*. In *Opera Omnia Sanctae Thomae Aquinatis*, Vol. 7. Ed. Robert Busa, S. J. Stuttgart-Cannstatt: Frommann-Holzboog.
White, Kevin (2002). 'The Passions of the Soul (Ia IIae, qq. 22–48)'. In *The Ethics of Aquinas*. Ed. S. Pope. Washington, DC: Georgetown University Press, pp. 103–15.
Williams, Bernard (1993). *Shame and Necessity*. Los Angeles: University of California Press.
Zinck, Alexandra and Albert Newen (2008). 'Classifying Emotion: A Developmental Account'. *Synthese*, 161/1: 1–25.

Part II

Soul and the World/Soul Beyond the World: Experience, Thought and Language

6

Experience in Monastic Theology and Philosophy in the Eleventh and Twelfth Centuries[1]

Emmanuel Falque
Translated by Ian Alexander Moore

Reading Experience

'Today we read in the book of experience' – *Hodie legimus in libro experientiae*. This phrase, which can be found in Book III of Bernard of Clairvaux's *Sermons on the Song of Songs* (Bernard 1981),[2] marks a turning point, or rather a new beginning, in the history of philosophy. Indeed, within the framework of the monastic theology of the eleventh and twelfth centuries, something new comes about that had never before seen the light of day. It certainly was not necessary to wait for medieval philosophy to establish a connection between 'spiritual exercises and ancient philosophy', in support of Seneca, Cicero or Marcus Aurelius, for example.[3] Nor was it necessary for us to wait for it to base a philosophy, nay a spirituality, on the story of an experience, and this in a fashion that has been paradigmatic ever since Saint Augustine's *Confessions*.[4] Experience is not new to the turn of the new millennium, nor is its story. But because it is necessary to pass from one millennium to the next in a precise fashion – and this links up with the situation of our own *Dasein* perfectly and brings us so close to this medieval period – one will not be content with demanding an *askesis* (Greek wisdom) or with basing a discourse on the story of an experience (Saint Augustine). Rather one will be forced to point out, describe and analyse what 'having an experience' means. The conceptualisation of experience suddenly belongs to experience itself.

Starting in the eleventh century with Anselm of Canterbury, and in the twelfth with Hugh and Richard of Saint-Victor, or with Aelred of Rievaulx and Bernard of Clairvaux, to '*parler de l'expérience*', as the expression goes in French, means not only to speak *from* experience but also to speak *about* experience. One can certainly speak *from* experience (in the sense of the subjective genitive of *parler d'expérience*) insofar as one undergoes it, is familiar with it, and passes through it. *Parler d'expérience* here refers to oneself, to one's own lived experience and

---

[1] Here, with great strides, we take up again the course of experience as we have described and analysed it in our work: *Le livre de l'éxperience: D'Anselme de Cantorbéry à Bernard de Clairvaux* (Falque 2017), translation forthcoming from University of Notre Dame Press. The text here was given as a lecture on 28 November 2017 at the University of Notre Dame (USA) within the framework of the Medieval Institute. We acknowledge Alexander Moore as the translator of the chapter.

[2] This text will be referred to as Sermon and paragraph numbers: 3, 1.

[3] See Hadot (2004: ch. 7, 'The Hellenistic Schools').

[4] Saint Augustine, *Confessions*, Book VII.

to one's past, through which one enriches one's present. But one can also speak *of* experience (in the sense of the objective genitive of *parler d'expérience*) insofar as experience itself becomes the site of a discourse, of a reflection, indeed of a theorisation. *Parler d'expérience* then amounts less to a turn towards oneself than to an investigation of the objective laws through which an experience is constructed and manages to be articulated. There is in fact a danger in restricting experience to what is lived through, indeed even to the story of what one has lived through. Experience is always essentially ephemeral, and it must be conceptualised in order to abide. This is like 'affective charity' and 'effective charity' in Bernard of Clairvaux. It is not enough to wait for the affect; one must also have recourse to reason, or to the rule by which what is given once (God as sensible to the heart) can also be given many times (by reason, which remembers it, refers to it and sometimes also allows one to return to it). There is a 'command to love', which, paradoxically, allows one to discover in oneself 'an affection that is governed by reason [. . .], which "consents to the law of God because it is simply good"'.[5]

The phrase 'Today we *read* in the book of experience' thus means that experience is to be *read* (*legere*) and not only to be *lived* (*vivere*), or rather that it is *to be lived* only to the extent that it is *to be read*: 'Therefore read and love [*legite ergo atque diligite*], and whatever you read by love, read it in order to love [*et quod propter dilectionem legitis, ad joc legite ut diligatis*]', as Hugh of Saint-Victor recommends to his brothers so magnificently in *On Praise of Charity* (Hugues de Saint-Victor 1997: 183).[6] There is not experience on the one side (phenomenology) and its reading on the other (hermeneutics), but the reading of experience (hermeneutics) is itself a mode of experience (phenomenology). Phenomenology *is* hermeneutics, and hermeneutics *is* phenomenology – whence the formulation of a 'reading' (hermeneutics) of 'experience' (phenomenology). Far from merely 'grafting' hermeneutics onto phenomenology (Ricoeur), today one will recognise that they belong together and mutually penetrate one another, to the point of no longer separating, nor even grafting, the *discourse on experience* on the one side (hermeneutics) and the *lived character of experience* on the other (phenomenology). The discourse on experience (hermeneutics) is itself a mode of experience (phenomenology). To interpret is to live, and to live is to interpret. In the circle, not only of faith and reason (Ricoeur), but of hermeneutics and phenomenology, it becomes necessary today to 'read' and not only to 'live' experience.[7]

The Today of Experience

Such a detour through an experience that is not only 'to be lived' (*vivere*) but also 'to be read' (*legere*) – or the requirement to speak not solely 'from' experience but also 'on' experience when one is speaking '*d*'expérience' – thus of course refers to an experience of 'yesterday' (*ieri*), but it also refers to an experience of 'today' (*hodie*). The 'today of experience' goes back first of all to the experience of the monks of the eleventh and twelfth centuries at the turn of the new millennium. But – and this is what is new – it also opens on to the 'today' of our today, where we ourselves would not even know how to remain indifferent, i.e., to the twenty-first century, to that which is said and done as we for our part are passing towards another millennium. The

---

[5] (Bernard 1981: 50, 4). Cited and analysed in Falque (2017: 340–2). Henceforth, this text will be cited as LLE followed by page numbers. See also LLE 339–42: 'Lire pour aimer'.

[6] See LLE 154–7: 'Lire pour aimer'.

[7] This perspective is also developed in (Romano 2010, 2015: chapter XXII, 'La phénoménologie *en tant qu*'herméneutique'.

here and the now, or the *hic et nunc*, of monastic theology is certainly not or no longer that of today, but we can learn to live from one another, or rather to think what living means, as soon as thought has itself become a mode of life.

At issue for the 'today of yesterday', that is to say for the today of the monastic period – if, namely, it is a *philosophical* contribution of monastic theology – is not only being able or having to experience God there (in communities that have secluded themselves in order to dedicate themselves to him), but also returning to this period of medieval philosophy in order to develop 'laws' according to which what was done in the past can still be done, or redone, today, even if differently or in another modality: 'the voice of the word is to be understood in the present as the flesh was at that time [*hic intelligenda est vox Verbi quod ibi caro Dei*]', as Hugh of Saint-Victor says, thereby underlining that the today of the 'voice of God', and thus his spoken word incarnated in a body, does not replace the yesterday of his 'flesh', but is anchored fully in it and acts in service of it. To build on the Victorine's analogy: just as the disciples of the apostolic era saw him through his 'flesh', so we in the post-apostolic era hear him through his 'voice' (Hugues de Saint-Victor n.d./1969: 63).[8] Thus, in this monastic period, the *today* of experience designates first of all the possibility of reiterating it – whether in different places (e.g., Le Bec-Helloin, the monastery of Saint-Victor, or the abbey of Clairvaux instead of Jerusalem) or in different times (e.g., in this monastic period rather than during apostolic times). It is because experience is read, and therefore understood, that the conditions, if not of its reproduction, then at least of its production, are reunited in an actual monastery where it can be lived and once again deciphered.

But there is something else, something better, in the today of experience when it is described from the perspective of our 'today of today', that is to say from the perspective of the twenty-first century. To be sure – and we have not ceased to emphasise this in what we have called a 'phenomenological practice of medieval philosophy' – there is a great danger that we will project what we ourselves are in the process of looking for on the authors of the past. The Medievals will not respond to the questions we ask ourselves; they already have enough to do when it comes to their own. But the way in which we *ourselves* respond to our own questions depends on the way in which they *themselves* responded to theirs.[9] In other words, if the experience of the past can explain the experience of the present, it is not because there is an 'identity of experience' (which is threatened by the danger of anachronism and which we would in any case look for in vain), but because the 'quest *de l'expérience*' in monastic theology *yesterday* links up in many respects with the requirements of a so-called experiential (and not exclusively conceptual) phenomenology *today*.[10]

It is at this point that we will return to monastic theology and reread it directly as well as historically through Martin Heidegger on the basis of Bernard of Clairvaux. To be exact, there is only one note that the philosopher from Freiburg took from the Cistercian monk. This note is indicated in a letter and can be found later in a manuscript notebook. It reads: *Hodie legimus in libro experientiae* – 'Today we read in the book of experience'. Heidegger offers a difficult and strange translation of it as 'Today we want to move apprehendingly (descriptively) in the

---

[8] See LLE 172–7: 'Le grand sacrement', and 177–81: 'La chair et la voix'. A formulation which will serve as a basis for the 'Catholic hermeneutics of the body and voice', in contrast to the 'Jewish hermeneutics of the body of the letter' (Levinas) and the 'Protestant hermeneutics of the sense of the text' (Ricoeur). See (Falque 2013: chapter II, pp. 61–85, 'Pour une herméneutique du corps et de la voix').

[9] See (Falque 2008: §4, 'L'arbre à ses fruits' [in particular p. 26]).

[10] See Falque (2008: Introduction, pp. 13–40, '*Fons signatus*: la source scellée').

field of personal experience' (Heidegger 1995: 334–7, 2004: 252–4). Heidegger's translation attempt aligns the reading of the *'liber experientiae'* with the hermeneutics of facticity rather than with the hermeneutics of the text. Irrespective of this, we should note that monastic theology and phenomenology have been connected ever since the birth of the phenomenological approach and method – this reference dates from 1920, at a time when the young Heidegger had not yet chosen the corpus on which he would work (medieval theology or Aristotle [the latter choice will lead to *Being and Time*]), nor the place at which he would make his career (Freiburg or Marburg).

Will monastic experience thus tend towards *Erlebnis* (internal lived experience) or rather towards *Erfahrung* (the passage and modification of the self)? Is there not, including within the framework of French phenomenology, a sort of 'swerve of *Erlebnis* to the detriment of *Erfahrung*', concomitant with what we have elsewhere called the 'swerve of the flesh to the detriment of the body'?[11] If in phenomenology there is indeed a thinking of the 'event' (*Ereignis*) as a radical incursion into and modification of the self by that which is not the self, and not solely as an auto-affection of the self, it is safe to bet that the monastic theology of the eleventh and twelfth centuries is at this point in time one of the most important wellsprings for this; the God who comes to visit me is not only there in order to comfort me, but also to encounter me and even to transform me. *Experto crede* – 'believe in my experience' – writes Bernard of Clairvaux to his brother Henry Murdach, as though to indicate thereby that the passage through another – who is himself thereby passed through – will assure me that I too can pass by there, without wasting away or the fear of letting myself change.[12]

Fields for Experience

But experience is not only read or conceptualised in the eleventh and twelfth centuries. Nor does it stop at making sense just for 'today' (whether it be a that of monastic theology or of phenomenology). It breaks down into different *fields* in which it becomes not only diversified, but also exemplified. For, 'everything *is* experience' in the nascent Middle Ages, not because one is aware of it, but because all the sectors and all the modes of the human being become places for 'experiencing God': 'the experience in thought' for Anselm of Canterbury; the 'experience of the world' for Hugh and Richard of Saint-Victor; and the 'experience in affects' for Aelred of Rievaulx and Bernard of Clairvaux. Because God can 'come to mind' and even 'manifest himself as a concept in thought', as Anselm will teach us in his *Proslogion* through his famous ontological argument, which we will call 'theophanic' here; because an 'art of reading' or a *Didascalicon* can serve as the basis for the entire culture and thus consecrate interpretation itself as a mode of life, as Hugh will confirm for us in the adequation of gesture and speech in the *Formation of Novices*; because the aim of the *Commentary on the Song of Songs* is nothing other than to give us the 'experience of God in affects', to the point of 'feeling oneself alive' in the *Dialogue on the Soul*, Bernard and Aelred give us the possibility of reading this in treatises that are less explications than descriptions of the way in which the divine comes to encounter us phenomenologically and mystically.

The 'experience in thought', the 'experience of the world' and the 'experience in affects' thus mark the three moments of a veritable 'conceptualisation' of the concept of experience in

---

[11] See Falque (2011: 23–38, 'L'embardée de la chair' [*Triduum philosophique*, 377–80]).

[12] Bernard of Clairvaux, Letter 106 (to Henry Murdach) (LLE 321–8: 'Crois en mon expérience').

the monastic theology of the eleventh and twelfth centuries. They do so not only in the guise of certain brothers who are singularised in their mode of thinking, but also in the expression of monks who are rooted in a community to which they address themselves and from which they are given the opportunity to write or teach: the Benedictine vision at Bec-Hellouin for Anselm the abbot, the Victorine perspective at the porch of Paris in the Abbey of Saint-Victor for Hugh and Richard, the Cistercian entrenchment at the Rievaulx Abbey for Aelred and at the Clairvaux Abbey for Bernard. So many manners of living that do not just give voice to 'a way of viewing the world' or develop 'a self-contained image of the world', but also mark 'the spirit of an age' (*Zeitgeist*) – namely 'the mode of thinking and conceiving on the part of those who are not philosophers, indeed who do not even read the works of the creative philosophers, but who are reached only through various mediations of their effects', to take up Edith Stein's formulation here (Stein 1962: 4).[13]

At Saint-Victor, the abbot Guildin prescribed in his *Liber ordinis* the following to his brothers, including those who did not know how to read: 'No one is to be seen without a book in his hand.'[14] To be sure, this did not mean that all the monks had to *read the book* – we know how few there were who were able to read at this time and the important number of lay brothers in a monastic community of the eleventh and twelfth centuries – but that everyone had to hold the *book open*, even if they needed illustrations or illuminations in order to know what was going on. For under the 'signs' of the letters there is always the 'meaning' of the presence of God, or behind the 'order of the reading' (*ordo legendi*) there is always the 'order of life' (*ordo vivendi*). Indeed, what is true for the theologian monk or for the copyist in order to decipher manuscripts in the scriptorium is true for the peasant monk in the fields for the harvest, for the cowherd monk at the stable dealing with the animals, for the cook monk at the stove preparing the meal, or for the innkeeper monk accommodating the pilgrims.

Everything 'speaks of God', we have said, because 'everything becomes experience' in the wake of the first millennium: philosophy, theology and mathematics, of course, but also the fabrication of wool, armament, navigation, agriculture, hunting, medicine and the theatre, which, according to the *Didascalicon* of Hugh of Saint-Victor, are explicitly so many activities in which God gives himself to be read as well as to be interpreted (Hugues de Saint-Victor 1991).[15] Monastic theology in the eleventh and twelfth centuries therefore trains itself to think, and even to conceptualise. What a lesson is for this burgeoning *culture of reading* in the monastic schools is, in reality, a lesson also for the whole of this changing society. With the copying of manuscripts yesterday, everything could be read on the 'page' (parchment), just as with the development of the internet today, everything can be discovered on the 'web'. No one will expect that everyone knows how to read the pages, no more than that everyone knows how to surf the net. But everyone will understand that the act of browsing the lines, like that of networking, defines a new mode of being whose past may well be able to teach us something today. Within the framework of monastic communities in the Middle Ages, people don't just read books; *by way of reading*, they interpret the totality of the world, or even their own lives. From page to web, the result is good, less in what is to be deciphered than in the new way of thinking, or even experiencing, that comes about.[16]

---

[13] Translation is that of the translator.
[14] Guilduin (second abbot of the order under whose jurisdiction Hugh taught), *Liber ordinis*, quoted in Baron (1961: 13). See also LLE 169–71: 'Le sens de la lecture'.
[15] This work is divided into theoretical, practical, mechanical and logical philosophy.
[16] See Grafton and Chartier (2012).

The Theophanic Argument or the 'Experience in Thought' (Anselm of Canterbury)

It is possible to have an experience of God 'in thought'. Better: nothing would be more false, as we have said, than to separate thought and life, indeed the conceptualisation of experience and the lived character of experience. The conceptualisation of experience is itself an experience and a mode of the lived character of experience. Only in forgetting this was it possible to separate *theoria* on the one side and *praxis* on the other. 'The Spirit itself beareth witness with our spirit.' With this formula from Saint Paul's Epistle to the Romans (8:16), people will take literally the idea that God can manifest Himself in our own thought, including by means of concepts in which He comes to reveal himself. To be sure, the theologian is not a prophet, and the philosopher even less of one. Yet it remains the case that no one will forbid God from addressing Himself to thought (Anselm of Canterbury) in the same way He speaks forth in the world (Hugh of Saint-Victor) or at the heart of affects (Bernard of Clairvaux). Such is the originality of the abbot of Bec, whose so-called ontological proof – which everyone knows is neither a 'proof' nor 'ontological' – has in our view a *liturgical* or *theophanic* sense, rather than a simply mystical or exclusively logical one.

It would be wrong to place Anselm of Canterbury's argument in the *Proslogion* either on the side of the Fathers as a simple commentary on Scripture (Barth, Corbin), or on the side of the scholastics as a sort of pure dialectical reasoning (R. Roques, P. Vignaux). Anselm, as a monk, is first of all and exclusively a monk, that is to say in search of the unity in himself between the abbey and the scriptorium, between the Highest as sung in the Psalms (*Kyrie Eleison*) and 'that of which nothing greater can be thought' as formulated in the argument (*aliquid quo nihil majus cogitari possit*). It is therefore at the heart of this monastic and religious life that one must read it, whether or not one is a monk or a religious person. For, one understands oneself in order to enter into the light of the other, at the risk, conversely, of remaining forever encapsulated in one's own thought, looking only for what one has in reality already found oneself:

> In any attempt to define his position in the sequence of major European figures, the old saw about his being the 'last of the Fathers and the first of the Scholastics' has a certain fascination. It stimulates by vexing: he is neither the one nor the other. He is a *representative of that intermediate period* between the Patristic and scholastic centuries, which may best be called the '*Benedictine centuries*'. (Southern 1990: 441; emphasis added)[17]

A Sensible Sense of the Senseless One

When, to use the lovely title of Emmanuel Levinas's work, 'God comes to mind', what exactly is going on? God manifests himself not only as a 'concept', but also as 'the life of God'.[18] The life of God that does not consist, according to what we are saying here, in opposing the concept, but in accepting that the concept itself, or the apparition of God as 'idea', belongs also to his life or his manifestation. Paradoxically, and this is the 'theophanic' sense of the argument, 'God as that than which nothing greater can be thought' (*aliquid quo nihil majus cogitari possit*),

---

[17] See also LLE 42–5: 'Liturgie et théophanie'.
[18] 'Yet this is also – with the placing in me of the idea of the Infinite – a prophetic event beyond its psychological particularity: it is the beating of the primordial time in which, for itself or of itself, the idea of the Infinite – deformalized – signifies. God-coming-to-the-idea, as the life of God' (Levinas 1998: xv).

which can be found in chapter 2 of the *Proslogion*, holds good as an experience not just for the believer, but also for the senseless one. There is a 'sensible sense of the senseless one'. People forget this too readily when they repeatedly condemn him. Indeed, when the senseless one says in his heart, like the psalmist (Psalm 13:1 and 52:1), that 'there is no God' (*non est Deus*), he is not against God, and perhaps not without God either, even though nothing would serve to baptise him without him realising it, and still less to impose on him an experience of the heart when he claims for himself the sole experience in thought.

But what, then, does this experience *in thought*, which the senseless one has, signify? It signifies much – for the senseless one, as the abbot of Bec emphasises quite precisely, 'hears' (*audit*), 'understands' what he hears (*intelligit*), and knows where the place of this comprehension is situated (*ubi*), that is to say, at least in the intelligence: 'Certainly, this same senseless one, when he hears me say "something of which nothing greater can be thought", understands what he hears [*intelligit quod audit*], and what he understands is in his intelligence [*et quod intelligit in intellectu ejus est*], even if he does not understand what this is.'[19] In other words, the senseless one is neither a 'sinner' incapable of understanding who God is because he had denied or blasphemed against him (Barth), nor a bad 'dialectician' who made a logical mistake by not recognising his necessary existence (Roques). Rather he points to the search for a place 'in common' by which men could gather together on a shared basis of humanity.

Anselm's true and great discovery, upstream from Thomas Aquinas, was, we contend, that humans have and ought to find each other, or find similarity and unity before next producing dissimilarity or differing. Not, to be sure, negatively, by virtue of a common unbelief (which is of course not the case for the senseless one in the eleventh century), but positively, around a common piece of evidence: the hearing of the other when he speaks to me of God (he hears), the common comprehension of what he hears (the formulation of the argument) and the place of this understanding (in the intelligence). That is a lot, and not nothing. 'Reason', which, yesterday, was the place of the in-common, is today called 'finitude' – whence the contemporary imperative of a *Métamorphose de la finitude*.[20] The aims remain the same (the search for an in-common), although the contexts and the issues are largely different (the pagans or the infidels on the one side, the atheists or the agnostics on the other). At this point in time, as at all points, it is not the 'for' or the 'against' God that will dominate the debates. Rather it is the search for a 'commonality of nature' or a 'human as such', without which there would be no possible encounter, even if we might have forgotten this due to our affirmation of a separate identity. On the one hand, there is, of course, the 'negative certainty' that exposes one to the evidence of an apophatic absolute that surpasses one. But, on the other hand, there is also the 'positive uncertainty' by which a community of understanding or a research community (*quaero*), even if it is just for the reason alone, traces the horizon in which Anselm and the senseless one – those who believe and those who do not believe or who believe differently – can nevertheless together engage in dialogue. As Anselm puts it in a magisterial formulation from *Cur Deus homo*, 'The infidels [*infidelium*] are seeking a reason because they do not believe [*quia non credunt*]; we on the other hand are doing so because we believe [*quia credimus*]: what we are seeking is nevertheless [*tamen est quod quaerimus*] one and the same [*unum idemque*].'[21]

It is certainly necessary 'to believe in order to understand' and 'to understand in order to believe', as the abbot of Bec will reply to Augustine at the beginning of his *Proslogion* with his

---

[19] Anselm, *Proslogion*, chapter 2.
[20] See Falque (2004: in particular, chapter III, 'Y a-t-il un drame de l'humanisme athée?').
[21] Book I, chapter III. See LLE 84–9: 'Le sens sensé de l'insensé'.

famous adage of *fides quaerens intellectum* or 'faith seeking understanding'.[22] The end of chapter I of the 'Address' moreover testifies to this by placing belief at the beginning of understanding, or faith at the source of all reflection: 'And I do not seek to understand in order to believe [*neque enim quaero ut intelligere, ut credam*], but I believe in order to understand [*sed credo ut intelligam*]. For, I believe also that I could not understand if I did not believe [*nisi credidero, non intelligam*].'[23] But, if we were to stop there, the senseless one would remain either a 'sinner' or a 'fool', lacking either grace (sin) or reason (logical flaw) to make use of what is given first, and uniquely, through faith.

And yet, the end of chapter 4, which is precisely what closes the passage on the senseless one as Anselm's privileged interlocutor, opens a breach in what Saint Augustine would never have said, or even thought, himself. This is the idea that it is also possible to 'understand *without* believing', not because one is 'against' belief, but because the in-common of comprehension remains always and first of all what unites the senseless one and Anselm in an 'identity of nature' in which the difference of the 'confessing belief' will be able to take on flesh and also be incarnated: 'Even if I do not want to believe that you are [*si te esse nolim credere*]', confesses Anselm, after having let himself be transformed by the senseless one, 'I wouldn't be able *not* to understand [*non possim non intelligere*]'.[24] As we have indicated elsewhere, one is able to be 'always believing', not in the sense that it is necessary to require everyone to confess, at the risk of understanding nothing, neither oneself nor the world, but rather in the sense that an original belief in others or in the world is characteristic of everyone, and it is on this belief that religious belief is grafted or takes place. The senseless one perhaps does not believe 'everything' or 'in everything', but his belief as comprehension constitutes the common foundation on which confession is spoken.[25]

The Theophany of the Argument

But the fact that one, including both the senseless one and Anselm, 'hears' (*audit*) what the formula 'God is that than which nothing greater can be thought' signifies; the fact that one 'comprehends' what one hears (*intelligit quod audit*); and the fact that that one comprehends 'where' one understands (*ubi*), i.e., 'in the intelligence' (*in intellectu*) – does not mean that this is the case in reality, or rather that 'it is': 'even if one does not understand that it is' (*etiam si non intelligat illud esse*).[26] Such is the reef, or rather the difference, separating the protagonists of the debate: the author of the *Proslogion* on the one side (the abbot of Bec) and the methodological fiction created by the author (the senseless one) on the other.

The classical, and moreover exact, explication of the argument as it is spelled out by Saint Anselm is well known: 'And certainly that of which one cannot conceive something greater cannot be in the intellect alone [*non potest esse in solo intellectu*]. Indeed, if it were only in the intellect, one would be able to think that it is also in reality [*et in re*], which is greater [*quod majus est*].'[27] Far from taking it up in terms of essence and existence (Thomas Aquinas), far from casting it in terms of a proof by infinity (Descartes) and far from rejecting it by reason of a definition of existence as the 'position of something' (Kant), the so-called ontological

---

[22] *Proslogion*, Preface (*Prooemium*).
[23] *Proslogion*, chapter 1 (end).
[24] *Proslogion*, chapter 4 (end) (LLE 70–89: 'L'expérience en commun' [not believing and understanding]).
[25] See Falque (2013: 89–120, 'Toujours croyant').
[26] *Proslogion*, chapter 2.
[27] *Proslogion*, chapter 2.

argument can in reality be understood here only on the basis of a unique mode of comprehension: 'the greater' (*majus*). And Anselm knows this: a little later, he distinguishes the comparative without complement from comparison ('that which is more') and the act of signifying the thing according to its word in the intelligence from signifying the thing '*in re*' – in reality, to be sure, but also 'as such': 'One does not think a thing [*res*] in the same way [*aliquid*]', the *Proslogion* points out, 'when one thinks the word that signifies it [*vox eam significans*], and when one thinks the thing itself [*idipsum quod res est intelligitur*]'.[28]

In other words, if the sense of the argument, as everyone knows or at least apprehends and comprehends it, amounts to affirming that the God who is at once in the intelligence (*in intellectu*) and in reality (*in re*) is 'greater' (*majus*) than a God who would be only in the intelligence and thus would lack reality or being – and that therefore 'God is' – everything depends in reality on the sense that one attributes to the 'thing' (*res*) or to the said 'reality' that is. If one maintains that the '*in re*' or 'in the thing' remains the presence and existence of a God outside of oneself, a God who is objectively independent of myself and almost without me, the argument thereby certainly falls into the terms of ontology, and not those of theophany, phenomenology or liturgy. But, conversely, if one grants that what is at issue in all of this is not the objective existence of God outside of me – which, properly speaking, would be something nonsensical in an epoch in which no one ever doubted God is not – but the subjective experience of the divine in me – not in such a way that He is reduced to me but rather in such a way that Christian experience, and that of the monk in particular, is first of all able to encounter Him – then one understands that the 'thing' (*res*) or the 'in the thing' (*in re*) designates less the ontological independence of God in relation to the human than God's theophanic dependence on the human in order to manifest Godself in them.

I am far from holding, or supporting, the idea that the 'greater' would be a sort of apophatic or ineffable God, in a pseudo-reference to the mystical theology of Dionysius the Areopagite, which the abbot of Bec probably never held in his hands or read. I am instead affirming the opposite: the argument lets us see the 'limit' of the one who receives God (subjectively in the intellect, even in not reality), rather than letting us see the 'grandeur' of God who surpasses him. Better: God is never as great as when He gives himself to faith in the limit of His *kenosis* and in the smallness of the humility to which every monk is called. This is probably the meaning of that 'greater than can be thought', inasmuch as it is thought in me and from me: 'The intelligence of God imposes a path by way of the negation of thought, a *negative path via limitation* [. . .] There is nothing ordinary about the *aliquid*; it therefore differs completely from [empirical] experience, and we affirm it only in this difference' (Gilbert 1990: 68).[29]

What about the aforementioned reality, then, or rather the discovery of God 'in the thing' (*in re*) and not 'in the intellect alone' (*in intellectu*)? It designates nothing other, at least in our eyes and according to an interpretation that only follows the text, than the *thrust of the manifest*, which makes it such that God, who has already manifested himself in the intelligence – according to what Anselm and the senseless one hold in common wants this time to also make himself seen or show himself in that which he himself is: not only an 'object of thought' or a concept of which one also has a communal experience, but 'someone' whom one encounters and who is able to transform us. 'And this being [of which nothing greater can be thought] is you, our God [*et hoc es tu, Domine Deus noster*]',[30] confesses the abbot of Bec, as though crying out, relying this time and definitively on him, the God thought in the scriptorium and the God prayed to

---

[28] *Proslogion*, chapter 4. LLE 93–5: 'Du comparatif à l'acte de signifier'.
[29] See LLE 89–109: 'La limite et le manifeste'.
[30] *Proslogion*, chapter 3.

in the abbey. The *thrust of the manifest*, and thus the 'theophany', is in reality what determines the entirety of Anselm's objective; it makes the God, of whom one could think it possible for him not to exist and therefore to remain in the intelligence alone, be unable *not* to be in reality; it makes him manifest himself, for he also wants to give himself in himself, in the reality of that which he is – *in re*, in the 'thing', even in the 'thing itself' (*Sache selbst*), as the phenomenologist would say. God is in reality (*in re*) insofar as God concerns me and calls me, awaits me and wants to transform me, provided that what is first of all a common experience in thought can also become the proper experience of an encounter.

But the lived character of experience 'in the heart' here neither opposes itself, nor imposes itself as superior, to the lived character of experience 'in thought'. It is quite simply *other*, and strictly designates an *other* mode and an *other* type of experience. Numerous believers agree, perhaps wrongly, that one can experience God in the 'heart' without conceptualising him in 'thought'. Inversely, what the senseless one shows us is that one can experience God in 'thought' without making it an experience of the 'heart' or in the 'heart'; believers would do well to recognise or at least accept this as well. Without being incomplete, but only different, the experience of the manifestation of God in thought or *in intellectu* (the senseless one) is something that is common to each of us, even though its aim *in re* (Anselm) would only affect those who lend themselves to this strange game of an encounter that could also, and in addition, 'upset' the concept of God. The structure is not one of insufficiency, nor one of fulfilment, as though there were no experience of God in thought, or as though this would have no other goal than to be completed in affectivity or another mode of alleged reality. It is simply one of *difference* and of *respect for alterity*, according to a new dialogical situation that Anselm of Canterbury begins to initiate, perhaps for the first time and even without his knowledge.

Hence the necessary and proper translation of the title of chapter 2 of St Anselm's *Proslogion*: *Quod vere sit Deus* – that '*God is truly*' – in the sense that 'God is *truly* God', and not in the sense that 'God is as *true being*', as though he had to be in some reality exterior to himself without having first of all been, as such and under the thrust of the manifest, already present 'as God' in thought.[31]

Proof of this can be found in what follows in the text, which does not cease to speak of manifestation, of exhibition or theophany, precisely where one has falsely seen existence and ontology. God in fact *is* 'so truly' (*sic vere*) that 'one cannot even think that he is not', as chapter 3 insists. He is 'in such a true way' (*si ergo vere*), and 'you are in such a true way' (*sic ergo vere es*), that 'you cannot be thought not to be'. The *quomodo* [how] of manifestation takes precedence here over the *quid* [what] of existence, as is also the case in the phenomenological reduction. This is why, in Anselm, God is strictly said to possess 'being in the truest way' (*solus igitur verissime omnium*), and thus also 'being in the highest way' (*et ideo maxime omnium habet esse*).[32] The *aliquid quo nihil majus cogitari possit* – or the 'that than which nothing greater can be thought' – is what lends itself the best, or at its best, to the *thrust* of the divine that is seeking to manifest itself.

Se obtulit – 'and "*suddenly*" what I had despaired of finding "*presented itself to me*".'[33] This prayer, as preface, of the *Proslogion* – which is taken back up in chapter 2 at the end of a long battle for an argument that is said to have first been written on tablets that were lost, then rewritten on tablets that were themselves broken, and finally recopied definitively on a parchment in order to be conserved (Eadmer 1976: 270–1)[34] – gives us a glimpse into the fact that

---

[31] *Proslogion*, chapter 2.
[32] *Proslogion*, chapter 3. (LLE 95–104: 'Expérience et manifestation'.)
[33] *Proslogion*, Preface. (LLE 50–3: '*Se obtulit*'.)
[34] See LLE 53–4: 'Le nom de la rose'.

the experience in thought is not something one decides, it arrives (*advient*). Whether it be for the senseless one in the event of understanding the argument, or for the monk Anselm in the advent of the encounter, something 'appears', 'comes over us, overwhelms and transforms us' (Heidegger 1971: 57, 1985: 149). It is in order to change us that thought must also work on us. This is the sense of the 'final joy' that the abbot of Bec, in his *Proslogion*, does not cease to bear witness to: 'True God [. . .] may I receive [*accipiam*] what your truth promises us, so that my joy may be complete [*ut gaudium meum plenum*]. May my mind meditate on it [*meditetur*], may my tongue speak of it [*loquatur*], may heart love it [*amet*], and may my mouth preach it [*sermoncinetur*].'[35]

The Figure of the Proud One

Whence, then, comes, and very often comes, the false understanding or misinterpretation of Anselm's argument? Whence comes the approach of making the senseless one either a 'sinner' (Barth) or a 'faulty logician' (Roques), such that the scriptural argument and the dialectical argument end up duelling it out, without seeing that Anselm's aim is, first of all, contained within a liturgical and theophanic prism – and thus directly rooted in the monastic world?

A trace of this can probably be found in the fact that people have not known, or have not seen, that there is a 'third man' lurking behind the argument, who has often been confused with the senseless one due to a lack of ability to unlock his specificity. As we have said, there is nothing unwarranted or prideful in the figure of the senseless one; rather, in him there is a search for community. The 'Highest' of 'that than which nothing greater can be thought' is not one to whom it is necessary to elevate oneself, but one in whom one will recognise an in-common in the 'experience in thought', even if it is not, even if it is different from, a 'confessional experience' or a 'confession of belief'.

There is thus someone – a 'certain other', a 'third man', or 'some mind' (*aliqua mens*) – between Anselm and the senseless one who precisely unites them in their common comprehension, so as to better distinguish himself and withdraw from them into his own pride. Far from looking for the 'symbol' or the 'union' (*sun-bolon*), he plays the game of the 'devil' (*dia-bolon*) or of disunion. He, and he alone, has no other ambition than precisely to elevate himself, to compete with this God 'than whom nothing greater can be thought', which he wants to attain and even surpass – something which was obviously never the case for the senseless one: 'If in fact *some mind* [*si enim aliqua mens*] could conceive something better than you [*aliquid melius te*], the creature *would elevate itself* beyond the creator [*super creatorem*], and would judge its creator [*judicaret de creatore*], which is perfectly absurd [*quod valde est absurdum*].'[36] The absurdity of the figure of the prideful one shares nothing here with the nonsense of the senseless one, which would consist only in his 'experience in thought' not being converted into an 'experience in affects', according to a complete trajectory that will effectively have to wait for the Cistercians and Bernard of Clairvaux to be precisely and definitively carried out. Anselm does, however, recognise this from the beginning of the treatise, which does not accuse the senseless one but does not seek to elevate itself either. Although he would have dreamed of heights as a grandchild of the Aosta Valley, to climb towards such summits is not to attain God; it is a matter of letting oneself be invited, in that the divine gives itself in its revelation or its *shekhina*, rather than a matter of man penetrating the secrets of the mysteries that are unfathomable for him. As the abbot of Bec confesses with complete monastic humility, and in conformity with the Rule

---

[35] *Proslogion*, chapter 26 (end).
[36] *Proslogion*, chapter 3. (LLE 106–9: 'L'hypothèse du troisième homme'.)

of Saint Benedict: 'I do not try, Lord, to penetrate your Height [*non tento Domine penetrare altitudinem tuam*], for I in no way compare my intelligence to it, but I do desire to glimpse your truth, which my heart believes and loves.'[37]

Here the 'experience in thought' is achieved, not in order to surpass it but in order to orient oneself otherwise. The *phenomenology* of the appearing God – both in the intellect (*in intellectu*), and in the thing itself or reality (*in re*) (Anselm of Canterbury) – gives way to the *hermeneutics* of the God to be interpreted, from the spoken word to the book, from the legible to the visible, such that 'living one's body' becomes, in the last instance, the proper way for man to express himself (Hugh of Saint-Victor).

The Art of Interpreting or the 'Experience of the World' (Hugh of Saint-Victor)

The Art of Reading and the Art of Living

There is an 'art of reading' (*ordo legendi*), but this is also an 'art of living' (*ordo vivendi*). From the quasi-*phenomenological* manifestation of God appearing in thought (Anselm), we turn now to the *hermeneutic* necessity of a world to be interpreted (Hugh). But everything depends on which interpretation we are dealing with. We have a tendency to reduce every form of hermeneutics to the hermeneutics of texts, not that such a priority should be disputed, but because it has developed in this way – within the framework of theology in particular.

This is what Hugh of Saint-Victor's 'Art of Reading' or *Didascalicon* also teaches us today, in different times, at different places and according to a different perspective. As we emphasised in the introduction, the *ordo legendi* does not require that everyone know how to read; quite the contrary: it requires that the necessity of 'deciphering' the meaning under the signs be extended to the whole of reality. The canon of Saint-Victor does not require reading in such a way as to make it obligatory in the schools, whether they be monastic and not yet scholastic, royal or republican. It makes reading the new paradigm of thought, and thus of life. The *ordo legendi* moves within an *ordo vivendi*.

But what does reading mean in the *ordo legendi*? It does not, or not only, as one might wrongly believe, mean books or parchments, but the meaning of the art of the blacksmith, the baker, the stonemason or the graphic designer. 'Everything is an object of experience' in the monastic world of the eleventh and twelfth centuries, not in the sense that it would be necessary to experience 'everything', but in the sense that a reflection on experience ought to guide, and be drawn from, every experience. 'To know how to live' (*ordo vivendi*) is thus also 'to know how to read' (*ordo legendi*), not that life is reading or vice versa, but in the sense that the order of reading delivers the keys to the order of life. It is therefore advisable for one to search for 'what one ought to read' (*quid legere debeat*), 'in what order one ought to read' (*quo ordine legere debeat*) and finally 'in what manner one ought to read' (*quomodo legere debeat*) – in order to define *what* one ought to live, *in what order* one ought to live and *how* one ought to live (to strictly apply the lesson) (Hugh of Saint-Victor1968: 44). Here it is not books which direct one's life, but it is the case that the art of living follows on the art of reading. The 'web' today, as we have indicated, has taken the place of the 'page' (parchment). We must not rely on the internet today any more than we could once trust libraries alone or copies of parchments. But the model of 'navigating the net' has now become a mode, even *the* mode, of life, as that of 'deciphering the text' was the mode of life in the nascent, even re-nascent Middle Ages.

---

[37] *Proslogion*, chapter 1. (LLE 49–50: 'Le val d'Aoste'.)

Since 'reading' teaches me how to 'live', and since therefore 'the book of Scripture' (*liber Scripturae*) has no meaning apart from 'the book of life' (*liber vitae*), or even apart from the 'book of the world' (*liber mundi*), we will need to distinguish three sorts of reading (*ordo legendi*) as we also distinguish three sorts of lives (*ordo vivendi*).

> Reading consists [. . .] of three types, the teacher's [*docentis*], the student's [*discentis*], and the individual reader's or the beginner's [*per se incipientes*]. For we say, 'I am reading a book *to* this man [*lego librum illi* (the teacher)]', 'I am reading a book *under* this man [*lego librum ab illo* (the student)]', and 'I am reading a book [*lego librum* (the beginner)]'. The order [*ordo*] and the manner [*modo*] are what especially deserve attention in the matter of reading. (Hugh of Saint-Victor 1968: 51–2; translation modified)

What to say here about the book, and thus about hermeneutics? Not that it is the book that counts first of all, but rather the *manner* of reading and *to whom* the reading is addressed. The spoken word or the teaching, and thus the exchange, guides the act of reading, and not the other way around. Reading, or in French '*lecture*' – in Latin *lectio*, according to a homonymy that is also in play in English (a 'lecture' in the sense of giving a talk) but not in French (reading as an activity that is first of all private and silent) – is an 'address to' (*illi*) if one is teaching, a book 'under' (*ab illo*) if one is studying, 'a book as such' (*librum*) if one is beginning. Reading is therefore not egoity, but alterity, not a relation to the text but a relation to the other. Everything therefore tends and moves towards the spoken word rather than towards what is written. For what matters is that God speaks and not only that man reads. And God does not speak only 'through himself' (*per se*), Hugh explains, but 'through humans' (*per homines*): 'multiple words through humans [*multos sermones*]; through himself only one [*unum*]' (Hugues de Saint-Victor n.d./1969: 61). Thus, the spoken word becomes a 'great sacrament' (*magnum sacramentum*) (Hugues de Saint-Victor n.d./1969: 61) at a moment when the sevenfold list of sacraments is not yet fixed. This speaks to the efficacy of reading, which in the Middle Ages, as in the Anglo-Saxon tradition, is therefore a way of life rather than a simple way of thinking; it is an experience of life as a privileged mode of life or of the unfolding of experience. The world is 'to be read' because it is to be deciphered. God does not only appear in thought (Anselm), he gives himself to be deciphered in the world (Hugh). Hence, as we emphasised in the introduction, the importance of the voice, which today and for us steps in and takes over from the flesh – since there is no voice without the body, just as there is no 'writing table' without the 'table of the Eucharist': 'the Word of God, clothed in human flesh [*humana carne vestitum*], appeared once in visible form [*semel visibile apparuit*]', as the Victorine explains in his treatise on *The Word of God*, 'and now, everyday [*quotidie*], this same Word itself comes to us under the guise of a human voice [*humana voce conditum*]' (Hugues de Saint-Victor n.d./1969: 61–3).[38]

A Definition of Gesture

It is therefore through the voice that one passes from speech to the body, or rather roots speech in the body, insofar as the voice cannot be 'without the body' – whether it be issued from a 'hidden' body (behind a door for example) or from a 'remote body' (the 'tele-phoned' voice[39]). But if there is no speech without the voice, no more is there voice without body. Whereas *The*

---

[38] See LLE 177–81: 'La chair et la voix'.
[39] For this 'phenomenology of the voice', which is necessarily attached to the body, see Falque (2013: 69–72, 'De la voix nue à la voix crue').

Art of Reading anticipates hermeneutics (the hermeneutics of the text and the hermeneutics of facticity), *The Formation of Novices* makes ready the great discoveries of phenomenology (constitution of space from the body): 'the gesture is a measure and a posture of the members of the body for every way of acting and comporting oneself' (Hugues de Saint-Victor 1997: 59).[40]

(1) Being a measure, or rather a 'mode' (*modus*), the gesture is therefore, first of all, a 'manner of being' or rather a 'way of acting'. Like the 'mode of love without mode' (rather than the 'measure of love without measure') in Bernard of Clairvaux, which we will come back to, the mode 'makes' the thing rather than being a manner of being of the thing. I do not accomplish gestures, gestures accomplish *me* – which means that I am identified and even singularised by them: the being of my life is expressed by the mode of my body. (2) The 'posture' of the gesture or rather its 'figuration' (*figuratio*) does not designate a simple position in space, but also creates space, inasmuch as the gesture not only 'assumes a figure' *within* the world, but 'configures' *a* world. By my gestures, or by the whole of my kinestheses, it is the world that turns around me rather than I who turn around the world. (3) The 'way of acting and comporting oneself' (*agendi et habendi modum*) thus has no relation here with any sort of behaviourism, as though it were a matter of observing a comportment in its relation to an environment. The 'mode of acting' ought rather to be understood here, first of all, in the sense of a '*praxis*' (Aristotle), where the gestured being of the body is its own end unto itself, in that it expresses itself; and then in the sense of a 'style' (Merleau-Ponty), to the extent that the way of being also sometimes makes being, this time in the paradoxical sense that 'the habit sometimes makes the monk'.

L'habit fait le moine

Since the gesture makes the body rather than the body making gestures, the appearance of the gesture takes precedence as much as, nay more than, the supposed hidden interiority. Since the master of novices must know about his young monks, he will watch them live before asking what they think. For, as is well known, the tongue is quick to lie, whereas the body never does (the redness of shame, for example). From the 'categories of the gesture' there follows the 'definition of the gesture', before the 'categories of speech' take over. Everything in man is indeed, first of all, made for being in relation, and the very constitution of his body testifies to this, according to a nice adjustment of creation:

> in the human body, the *eyes* are placed appropriately, in the front, in order for one to be able to see and contemplate the works of God in the world. But the *ears* are also placed appropriately: situated on the side, so as to make us understand that our intention should be directed toward what is nearest only secondarily, but toward God first of all.[41]

The unity of the interior and the exterior – of the *intus* and the *foris* – is what constitutes that heart of Victorine inspiration and its deepest meaning. As the master of Saint-Victor warns, in opposition to novices who are too scattered: 'Whoever loses the seat of the mind then slips outward [*foras*] toward a fickle agitation, and through this external mobility [*exteriori mobilitate*] prevents anything from maintaining him inwardly [*interius subsistat*].'[42] The move from being to appearing is good for the Victorines. It no longer suffices to see in appearance the double

---

[40] *Gestus est modus et figuratio membrorum corporis ad omnem agendi et habendi modum.*
[41] Hugues de Saint-Victor, 'In Ecclesiasten Homeliae', 141D–143A.
[42] Hugues de Saint-Victor, *La formation des novices*, §10, p. 49.

deception of a hidden interiority; rather, one must see the manifestation of what is interior in it: 'discipline [*disciplina*], is a manner of living [*conversatio*] [. . .] that makes sure to appear [*apparere*] irreprehensible in all things'.[43] It is a matter of teaching the young novice to 'link the members of his body with the outside [*foris*], so that the seat of the mind can be consolidated inwardly [*intrinsecus*]'.[44]

The famous French expression '*l'habit ne fait pas le moine*' (the habit doesn't make the monk) must therefore be reversed; for the book of experience is not only what is read in the heart, but also what is seen on the body. At the abbey of Saint-Victor, against all expectation and in opposition to the proverb, we can say that 'l'habit *fait le moine*', the habit *makes the monk*. To be sure, it is not enough just to wear a habit if one is to be a monk (whence the expression *l'habit ne fait pas le moine*). But the *way* of wearing the habit will say *who* the monk is – whence the necessity to reverse the expression: '*l'habit fait le moine*'.[45] Like an echo, and almost in anticipation, the master of Saint-Victor points out that 'We know a man by his looks [*ex visu*]; we know the man of sense by his face [*ab occursu faciei*]. The habit of body, the laughter of the teeth, and the gait of the man speak of him [*enutiant de illo*].'[46] Since the habit makes the monk, one will need to be mindful of the way the monk, and, in particular, the young novice, wears the habit.

Since, as we have said, what manifests itself speaks to the being of the manifestation, or since what shows itself is '*that which shows itself in itself*, the manifest' (Heidegger 1962: 51), the master of novices will be *phenomenologically* attentive to what shows itself in the young monk's mode of being, and to the way in which it shows itself. Attention to 'discipline' (*disciplina*) is not solely the observance of a coercive ethic, but the implementation of a monstrative phenomenology. The habit makes the monk because the way of wearing the habit also says something about the one wearing the habit, or because 'fashion [*la* mode]' first says what 'the mode [*le* mode]' or 'way of wearing' (*modum portandi*) is. As brother Hugh emphasises, and not without a touch of humor:

> Certain fools who wish to please the fool deck themselves out somewhat artificially. Others, by a still greater buffoonery, distort their clothing in a ridiculous way; others, to make people speak about them, open it up and spread it out as widely as they can. Others gather it together into tight folds; others wisp it down into twists and creases. Others, squeezing into it with all their strength and splitting it, expose, by the most shameful of turpitudes, all the contours of their bodies, the details of which can be seen by spectators. Others, waving their furbelows in the wind, show the flippancy of their minds by the very feverishness of their constancy. Others, as they walk, sweep the floor with the meandering of their long frocks, and erase the traces of their footsteps with their trailing fringes, or rather, like foxes, with their tail following behind them.[47]

---

[43] Ibid.

[44] Ibid.

[45] Maurice Merleau-Ponty knew this, or rather rediscovered it in *The Phenomenology of Perception*. Others are recognised by their silhouettes, by their styles or gaits, rather than by the negative image of what is without movement, insofar as their 'own body' (Leib) is manifested there: 'we do not recognize our own hand in a photograph [. . .] but [. . .] everyone recognizes his own silhouette or a filmed version of his own gait' (Merleau-Ponty 2013: 150).

[46] Hugues de Saint-Victor, *La formation des novices*, §12, p. 73.

[47] Hugues de Saint-Victor, *La formation des novices*, §11, pp. 51–3.

One therefore teaches 'by speech and by example' – *docere verbo et exemplo* – in canonical life, which joins the word to the body, or the rule to its observance. 'Categories of gesture' and 'categories of speech' therefore define the places and the times. One does not ontically act in space with one's body; rather one ontologically constitutes space through one's body. One does not ontically enunciate phrases through speech; rather, one ontologically determines a mode of relation to the other by speaking. *From the point of view of the gesture*, the human, or rather the superior of the novices, ought to consider 'with diligence and discernment', as Hugh emphasises very precisely, 'what is allowed and what is not . . . in every act [*in omni actu*], in every place [*in omni loco*], at every time [*in omni tempore*], with regard to every person [*erga omnem personem*]'.[48] Others are therefore spaces not because they are extended or are 'empty blocks' that would need to be inhabited; others are spaces because the manner of living through the body ought to determine them: 'one way is [*alius est modus*] holding oneself in a place where one adores God', the Victorine master cautions his novices; 'another [*alius*] is in a place where one restores one's body; another [*alius*] in a place intended for conversation; another [*alius*] in a place where silence is kept; another [*alius*], finally, inside, another [*alius*] outside, another [*alius*] in private, another [*alius*] in public'.[49]

It is not the places that are named here, but the manner of 'gesturing' them that makes their alterity (*alius*). With respect to the canonical rule, the monk discovers that he is less objectively constituted *in* space than subjectively constitutive *of* space. The manner of being of his body determines what bodies or rooms of the monastery are around him: the Church for 'holding oneself where one adores God', the refectory where one 'restores one's body', the parlor where being-with is 'intended to converse', the dormitory where 'silence is kept', the enclosure 'within' and the world 'without', the cell 'in private' and the chapter house 'in public'. There are no places (*topoi*); rather, places *make themselves* or *are made* by being acted.

What is true of the body and space thus also becomes true of speech and one's relation to others. As we have said, the categories of the gesture, which determine places, are followed by categories of speech, which also make the being of the community. There is not only the visible discipline (*disciplina*) in the gesture, but also 'the discipline to be kept in speech' (*de disciplina in locutione servanda*): 'what to say? [*quid loquendum*], to whom to speak? [*cui loquendum*], where to speak? [*ubi loquendum*], when to be silent and when to speak? [*quando tacendum et quando loquendum*], how to speak? [*quomodo loquendum*]'; these are thus the modes of being that define 'who speaks' (*qui loquendum*) – which is not named in the list of categories precisely because it is always already there in the act of speech.[50] In monastic life, the quantity or the flux of our spoken words will therefore be opposed to the 'quality [or the parsimony] of our spoken words [*nostri sermonis qualitate*]' depending on 'the one *to whom* they are to be said' (*cui dicendum*).[51] The pertinence of a discourse will thus be measured less by 'what one says' (*quid loquendum*) than by the 'manner in which one says it' (*quomodo loquere*). As the Victorine insists: 'the quality of a discourse, that is to say the manner of speaking [*modus loquendi*], has three components, namely: the gesture [*gestu*], the tone [*sono*], and the sense [*significatio*]'.[52] And because the word does not go without the body, or speech without space, there will be 'places for speaking' and 'places for keeping silent', 'times for speaking' and 'times for keeping silent': 'silence' in the

---

[48] Hugues de Saint-Victor, *La formation des novices*, §1, p. 23.
[49] Hugues de Saint-Victor, *La formation des novices*, §3, p. 25.
[50] Hugues de Saint-Victor, *La formation des novices*, §13, p. 75.
[51] Hugues de Saint-Victor, *La formation des novices*, §14, p. 81.
[52] Hugues de Saint-Victor, *La formation des novices*, §17, p. 89.

dormitory or at the abbey church, 'disputing' at the cloistral school or 'conviviality' in the canonical cloister.

After the experience of God *in our thought*, including in the appearing of God's theophany as a concept in Anselm of Canterbury, we also spoke about the experience of God *in the world* – which is to be deciphered everywhere and at all times, even when one cannot read (*Didascalicon*), and to be lived through the body and speech in the maintenance of a discipline that is less coercive than demonstrative of what one is (*De Institutione novitiorum*). It now remains for Bernard of Clairvaux to translate the experience into affects, so that the 'book of experience' (*liber experientiae*) may this time be of a God who is capable of moving us to the very depths of our being, and of engaging at the level of the heart (Bernard) what was first discovered in thought (Anselm) and in the world (Hugh).

'Believe in my Experience' or 'Experience in Affects' (Bernard de Clairvaux)

The phrase 'book of experience' (*liber scripturae*) is, first of all, Bernard de Clairvaux's. It comes up in the third *Sermon on the Song of Songs*, where one reads, in the whole formulation: 'Today we read in the book of experience [*hodie legimus in libro experientiae*]. Make a return to yourselves [*convertimini ad vos ipsos*], and each should examine his own consciousness [*et attendat unusquisque conscientiam suam*] with respect to what we have to say' (Bernard 1981: 3, 1) Experience, as we see here, marks a return towards oneself, or better towards one's own consciousness. Everything thus depends on how we understand 'consciousness' (*conscientia*) here, and especially for the Cistercian master. No doubt, we will need to avoid every sort of Cartesian *cogitatio*, as though consciousness were anticipating some sort of certitude belonging to self-knowledge. For, if it is indeed necessary to know *oneself* for Bernard, such knowledge belongs, first of all, to affect and does not allow one to presuppose any sort of introspection on the order of reflection alone.

Noverim te, noverim me

'That I may know *you* and that I may know *myself*.' Such is the movement that Bernard of Clairvaux thinks properly constitutes the book of experience, to the point of drawing from it the 'true philosophy'. As Bernard recounts in a recently discovered sermon: 'a saint prayed thus: God, he said, may I know *you* [*noverim te*] and may I know *myself* [*noverim me*]. A short, but faithful prayer. Such is indeed the true philosophy [*vera philosophia*]' (Bernard de Clairvaux 1970: 104).[53] Paradoxically, the philosopher here is not one who knows himself, but one who gains access to oneself by means of another – making the relation to the other (*noverim te* [mysticism]) the condition for the relation to oneself (*noverim me* [philosophy]). In a surprising inversion of Saint Augustine's *Soliloquies* – 'God is always the same [*Deus semper idem*]; may I know *myself* [*noverim me*] and may I know *you* [*noverim te*]' (II, 1, 1) – this sermon, *De diversis*, by Bernard of Clairvaux, definitively excludes all access to oneself that is not first of all access to the other and access to oneself by means of the other.

To be sure, one will of course find the same movement in the Doctor of Hippo, even though the formula would be reversed here. Nevertheless, what is at issue with respect to 'consciousness' in Bernard of Clairvaux is, this time, less the act of knowing oneself than that of sensing

---

[53] This text was rediscovered and added by J. Leclercq in his critical apparatus for this new Latin edition.

oneself – or rather of knowing oneself only in the very thing one senses. Affect takes precedence over knowing, or rather affect is the veritable mode of knowing; this is probably the greatest contribution the Cistercian master made to his predecessor's thought and to that of all the Augustinians: 'I could master my tears [on the day of the funeral]', confesses Bernard in the twenty-sixth sermon on the Song of Songs at the time of his brother (by blood) Gérard's death, 'but not my sadness [. . .] Now, I confess, I am vanquished [*fateor, victus sum*]. It is necessary that *everything I suffer inwardly come out* [*exeat . . . foras quod intus patior*]. Yes, *that it come out* before the eyes of my sons; knowing my misfortune, they will judge my lamentations with more indulgence, and will console me with more tenderness.'[54]

Exeat – 'it is necessary that this come out!' Bernard of Clairvaux's exclamation does not just ask, as Hugh of Saint-Victor did above, that what occurs 'inwardly' (*intus*) also conforms to what is at play 'outwardly' (*foris*). He requires that the outward and the inward be one, not in the order of discipline, but, as it were, in that of indiscipline. A pioneer in, perhaps, the entire history of philosophy, the Cistercian master makes our passions, even our urges, the basis of the human being, and even of God's in-dwelling in man. Far from wanting to distance us from our affects, or even imposing on us the task of mastering them, he designates affect (*affectus*) as the very place in which God first of all reveals himself, not in a manner contrary to understanding (*intellectus*), but insofar as God makes us accede to another mode of understanding – neither that which conceives (Anselm) nor that which comprehends or deciphers (Hugh), but that which only loves and makes of love its own language: 'it is affect which speaks, not the understanding [*ita est affectus locutus est, non intellectus*]; this is why it does not address itself to understanding [*et ideo non ad intellectum*]'.[55]

The Language of Affect

'Its beginning [i.e., that of the descriptive theory of consciousness] is the pure – and, so to speak, still mute (Husserl 1999: 38–39)[56] – psychological experience, which now must be made to utter its own sense with no adulteration.' If it is therefore a 'book of experience' (*liber experientiae*), in medieval philosophy as in phenomenology, this will inscribe itself less in the text than in the world, less in speech than in the body – or rather does not require speech except insofar as it inscribes itself in a body by the 'voice'. In this sense, if 'affect speaks' (*affectus locutus*), or if 'affections have their language or their own voice' (*habent suas voces affectus*), it is not in this that they speak, but rather that they do not speak, or better, that they speak *otherwise*: 'the bride does not speak in order to express what she feels [*neque quod sensit ut exprimeret*], but in order not to keep quiet [*sed ne taceret*]. The mouth has spoken out of the abundance of the heart [*ex abundantia cordis*]. The affections have their language [*habent suas voces affectus*] by which they uncover themselves, even despite themselves [*etiam cum nolunt*].'[57]

---

[54] Bernard de Clairvaux, *Sermon on the Song of Songs*, 26, 2.

[55] Bernard de Clairvaux, *Sermons on the Song of Songs*, 67, 3.

[56] This expression probably provides the basis for everything that is to be looked for today within the framework of phenomenology. An 'ontology of the sensible' or an 'ontology of the visible', to speak with Maurice Merleau-Ponty, is still to be developed, and it is in search of this that philosophy is employed, not just today, but in all times, provided that it is always only read and deciphered from this time (Merleau-Ponty 1964: 166–7): 'It is imperative that we recognize that this description also overturns our idea of the thing and the world, and that it results in an ontological rehabilitation of the sensible.' As well as (Merleau-Ponty 1968: 140): 'ontology of the visible'.

[57] Bernard de Clairvaux, *Sermons on the Song of Songs*, 67, 3.

There is indeed something quite specific in affect, which makes its speech be comprised, not of the verb but of the cry, not of words but of groans, not of reflection but of impulsion. Affects, like flesh, have '*their* language' (*suas voces*), in that they let themselves overflow by means of themselves, and say, in the manner of an *index sui* – like the 'belching of an overfull stomach' (*seu etiam saturatorum ructus*) – what words, on the contrary, must hide. The language of affect in some way affects language itself – not in such a way as to disqualify it, but in such a way as to show how little verbal consciousness would know how to say the whole of experience, and even less the strongest aspect of our existence. Better: it is in letting affect speak that the human, even God himself, speaks. For the language of the bridegroom vis-à-vis his bride is neither that of reason nor of consciousness, nor of 'consciousness' (*conscientia*) understood here as affect (*affectus*), that is to say the act of turning back towards oneself; for it is there, first of all, that the self that I do not know, or only know little of, is held, but that nevertheless determines me: 'these expressions [the wails of those who feel pain, the groans of the afflicted, the sudden cries of those who are struck or frightened] are not reflected [*non nutu prodire animi*], but come from a sudden and unexpected movement [*sed erumpere motu*]', as Bernard of Clairvaux describes in the *Sermon on the Song of Songs* with a rare psychological and affective finesse. 'Thus burning and passionate love [*sic flagrans ac vehemens amor*] [. . .] is not worried about the order and sequence of the words [*nec verba*], provided it does not lose any of its vigor. Sometimes it does not even need to have recourse to words [*nec verba*] or language [*nec voces*], but is satisfied to sigh [*solis ad hoc contentus suspiritis*].'[58]

We are always 'affected' in the passive voice; this is what the 'affect' or *affectus* proper to man comes to teach us, insofar as he is not free to experience it (or not to experience it) in his 'interior passion'. But God is 'affection' or *affectio* in the active voice, because in God's 'deliberate compassion' God makes the choice to affect and be affected. There is a long road from 'passion' to 'compassion', not because God does not himself suffer his passion, but insofar as he lives *by choice* what we for our parts would know how to experience only *by way of undergoing it*. 'God is not affected, he is affection' (*non est affectus Deus, affectio est*), as Bernard emphasises with precision in *De consideratione*, which we will not translate falsely and too quickly as 'God is not affected, he is love.'[59] Here this means that God is 'not affected' insofar as the affect of man (*affectus*) is almost always exterior or received from without (we receive our affects without choosing them or deciding to be subjected to them); but he is nevertheless 'affection' (*Deus affectio est*) insofar as the active love he demonstrates (*affectio*) is always interior and intentional (he makes the choice to sympathise with what we ourselves suffer). A certain mode of empathy therefore ties man to man and man to God. For if we are first 'affects' (*affectus*), and if God gives us his 'love' or his 'affection' (*affectio*), it is insofar as we are also ourselves capable of deliberately loving, according to a measure of love that is itself without measure, or a mode that is itself without mode.

The Mode of Love Without Mode

'The measure of loving God is loving without measure' (*modus diligendi Deum, sine modo diligere*).[60] This famous sentence taken from the *Treatise on the Love of God* by Bernard of Clairvaux is most often interpreted in the sense of a quantitative excess, as though we were to

---

[58] Ibid.
[59] Bernard of Clairvaux, *De consideratione*, V, VII, 17. Translated as 'il n'est pas affecté, il est amour' in Clairvaux (2012: 133).
[60] Bernard of Clairvaux, *De diligendo Deo*, Preface.

love God 'outside' of every measure because his love is itself infinite and 'without measure'. This, in our eyes, is to profoundly misunderstand the meaning of the 'book of experience' in monastic and Cistercian theology, since affect is precisely what is at issue. The question posed by Aimeric, a brother of Bernard's, concerning the 'reasons of love' opens on to another path, one that is more qualitative or modal than quantitative or quodditative: 'why and how is it necessary to love God' (*quare et quomodo diligendus sit Deus*)?[61] 'Why?' (*quare*) and 'how?' (*quomodo*), but not 'what?' (*quid*) or 'how much?' (*quanto*); this decision is clear. To love God and to be loved by him is not a matter of definition or quantity, but of *raison d'être* and quality.

The four degrees of the love of God – 'the love of the self for oneself', 'the love of God for oneself', 'the love of God for God', and 'the love of the self for God' – will thus designate a *specific way* of loving, that by which God certainly invites us to the 'love of no return', but also and above all makes us love 'in him' everything that is he and everything that is not he. The degrees consist not only in elevating us, but in 'incorporating' us – not in wanting an excess (of love) but in letting oneself be transformed (by love).

(1) With the 'first degree' (*primo gradu*) of love, by which 'man loves himself for himself' (*quo diligit homo se propter se*), the Cistercian master paradoxically opens the path by which one loves God by loving oneself.[62] For, as the abbot of Clairvaux aptly cites Saint Paul, 'the animal comes first [*prius quod animale*], and then the spiritual [*deinde quod spirituale*]' (1 Corinthians 15:46). Far from interpreting carnal love as a 'sickness of nature and of natural affection' (Delfgaauw 1953: 238), here, and for the Cistercian master, it designates rather 'the first step of a normal evolution' (Blanpain 1974: 232–3). The love of God begins by way of the love of self, not only insofar as it is necessary to 'love one's neighbor *as oneself*', but because the self that is to be loved is first the 'oneself' or the 'for oneself' (*propter se*) that is designated and discovered as an 'animal' without for all that being 'bestial'. This is probably one of Bernard of Clairvaux's great discoveries, even his greatest moment of originality – namely, the distinction he draws between the humility of truth (ontological humility or the return to the nothing of the humus) and the humility of severity (the humility of humiliation). Everything does not come from sin, and recognition of this fact does not deny the 'flesh' (*sarx, caro*) in the manner of 'turning away from God' or 'living without the flesh' (Romans 8:13), but consecrates it as a fact of our humanity as well, one that is constitutive of our nature and in which we are rooted: 'carnal love [*amor carnalis*] is that by which man first of all loves himself for himself [*propter ipsum*]', as one reads clearly and incisively in the *Treatise on the Love of God*. 'It is not a commandment that is given [*non praecepto indicitur*], but a fact inherent to our nature [*se naturae inseritur*].'[63]

In loving himself for himself, man certainly does not deny God nor love himself without God. For what is at stake in the four degrees of the love of God is not solely loving oneself, nor exclusively loving God, but loving God and one's neighbor 'in God'. 'He who does not love God [*Deum*] cannot love in God [*in Deo*]', as Bernard explains cautiously in this first degree of the love of God ('the love of the self for oneself'); 'he must therefore first [*prius*] love God in order to be able to love his neighbor [*et proximus*] in God [*in Deo*] as well'.[64] Better, and this is the end point or the greatest suggestion of this initial moment: I will love the other not only 'as myself' or 'as yourself [*sicut ipsum*]' (Matthew 19:9), but I will love him as I myself love, or rather as I am loved (according to God) – either 'because he loves'

---

[61] Ibid.
[62] Ibid., VIII, 23.
[63] Bernard of Clairvaux, *De diligendo Deo*, VIII, 23.
[64] Ibid., VIII, 24.

(*quia diligit*) or 'in order that he love' (*ut diligat*) the God whom I love: 'a man loves his enemy because he will perhaps [*forsitan*] love God one day', as the *Sermon on the Song of Songs* emphasises magnificently.[65]

The triangulation is perfect here, and this from the first degree of the love of God. I 'love myself for myself' *because* and *so that* I love my neighbor – the *socius* or the one who is closet to me – 'in' (*in*) the God whom I love. The love of self is never for Bernard disconnected from the love of the other, and still less from the love of God, but it is rooted 'in' God with the other, in order that what is first in me and in us – 'the animal' or the 'psychic' (*animale* in Latin) – be first of all integrated in God. The experience of affect in the Middle Ages makes us recognise ourselves as affected, and even as dependent on our animality (*psuchê*), so long as the separation between *mens* and *anima* (Descartes) has not yet come about.[66]

(2) But 'the love of the self for oneself' cannot suffice, even if one loves oneself and one's neighbor in God, even if it is in order that he love God with me and like I do. It is still necessary also 'to love God for oneself', i.e., the second degree of love. For the love of self for oneself could still have made us believe that we could love God or our neighbor 'by ourselves'. The supernatural character of the love of God makes it such that 'there is a sort of wisdom in distinguishing what one is capable of by oneself [*quid ex te*] and what one is capable of with the help of God [*quid ex Dei adiutorio*], and in guarding ourselves from opposing the one who always guards us', as *De diligendo Deo* explains.[67]

Be on guard, however. In order to 'love God for oneself' (second degree) and not only 'oneself for oneself' (first degree), it does not suffice to have recourse to the supernatural, even if it was necessary in order to not make the love of God depend *only* on oneself. For, as Bernard of Clairvaux explains, in man there are limits of the human that are never to be surpassed, such that the *appeal to the supernatural* is held within the *limits of the natural*, or that the *recognition of dependence* is discovered in the *failure of independence*: '*if trials* strike and multiply' (*si frequens ingruerit tribulatio*), underlines the saint with a conditional that we must also underline, they can 'provoke a frequent return to God' (*frequens ad Deum conversio fiat*) and make sure that man 'obtains from him as frequent a liberation' (*et a Deo aeque frequens liberatio consequatur*).[68] In other words, 'recourse to God' requires his 'succour', even though tribulation would not be something to be desired as a necessary path towards one's liberation. The 'mode' (*modus*) of our love for God is thus a love 'without mode' (*sine modo*) in the already *negative* sense that he refuses the mode of being sinful or proud, according to Bernard, in a false independence of man in relation to God.

(3) With the 'love of God for God', i.e., the third degree of love, something absolutely new is in the process of being born and articulated. What was *negatively* a mode of love as the refusal of its contrary (pride) becomes *positively* a mode of love in order to turn towards what the very substance of love is (goodness): 'he gives thanks [*rend grâce*] to the Lord not because it is good for him [*non quoniam sibi bonus est*], but because it is good [as such] [*sed quoniam bonus est*]; he truly loves God for God and not for himself'.[69]

---

[65] Bernard de Clairvaux, *Sermon on the Song of Songs*, 50, 8.
[66] Descartes (2006: 15): 'I am therefore precisely nothing but a thinking thing [*res cogitans*], that is, a mind [*mens*], or intellect, or understanding [*animus*], or reason [*intellectus*].'
[67] IX, 26 (for the whole second degree).
[68] Ibid.
[69] Ibid. (The second and the third degree are in the same §26 of the *Treatise on the Love of God*, as though to show thereby their deep unity and generativity, and not juxtaposition.)

One will, to be sure, find here the famous distinction between the action of giving thanks [*grâce*] (loving God for what he gives me) and that of praise (loving God for what he is). But there is more, even a lot more. For the mode of divine love 'without the mode' (*sine modo*) of the sinner's self-interested love (second degree of the love of God) becomes the mode of divine love 'with the mode' (*cum mode*) of the saint's disinterested love: 'the love of God is full of interest [*amor est merito gratus*]', the text emphasises paradoxically and literally, 'because it is "disinterested" [*quia gratuitus*]'.[70] In Bernard of Clairvaux, pure love (*amor purus*) is gratuitous love (*amor gratuitus*), not only in the sense that it breaks man of his perverse inclinations or of his curving inwards, but in that he learns and receives from Him, who lives love in this mode (of disinterest), what it's like to live without the mode (of profit-sharing [*intéressement*]). The modality of love here comprises his being, even more than his excess or his simple overflowing.

The third degree of love – the 'love of God for God' – makes us thus see qualitatively *how* [*comment*] God loves us (*quomodo*) so that we ourselves can love *as* [*comme*] he loves us (*sic amat*), that is to say in a disinterested fashion (*gratuitus*) – and not solely quantitatively how much (*quantum*) or how far (*usque*); he loves us in order to make us see the immoderation of his love:

> someone who loves God truly [*veraciter*] loves as a consequence everything that belongs to God [. . .] His love is just because *as* one receives it [*qualis suscipitur*] *so* one returns it [*talis et redditur*]. Indeed, whoever loves God *in this way* (*sic amat*) loves *in the same way* he is loved [*quam amatus est, amat*] [. . .] – with a love full of interest [*merito gratus*] because it is 'dis-interested' [*gratuitus*].[71]

(4) The fourth degree of love – 'the love of the self for God' – thus completes the task of *rendering love to love*; or, in other words, of making the mode of the love of man for God ('no longer loving oneself except for God') pass into the mode of the love of God for man ('the charity [*caritas*] that retains nothing of what it possesses for itself').[72] In this last degree, man 'no longer loves himself *except* for God' (*nec seipsum diligat homo nisi propter Deum*).[73]

This must be recognised, though, and we have already emphasised this with respect to 'affective charity' and 'effective charity' at the beginning of this chapter. Such an experience of total and disinterested union of man with God does not come about, or does so only rarely, 'in this mortal life' (*in hac mortali vita*), either 'at rare moments' (*raro interdum*) or even 'only once' (*vel semel*), even 'in passing' (*raptim*) or 'barely within the space of an instant' (*unius vix momenti spatio*).[74] In short, what serves as the summit of love is probably not of the order of those conquests that are so easy to accomplish here below (*in via*).

Better, such an accomplishment of 'the love of self for oneself' (first degree) in the 'love of the self for God' (fourth degree) might well end up making us believe that there is a strict analogy here between the Cistercian path and Rhenish mysticism. The Cistercian abbot does in fact conclude that 'no longer loving oneself *except* for God' amounts to 'losing oneself *in such a way as though* one did not exist' (*perdere tamquam qui non sis*), to 'no longer having any self-awareness' (*et omnino non sentire teipsum*), even 'being almost reduced to nothing'

---

[70] Ibid.
[71] Ibid.
[72] Ibid., X, 27.
[73] Ibid.
[74] Ibid.

(*et paene annullari*)⁷⁵ – which, it will be recognised, in many ways resembles the 'Detachment' or *Abgeschiedenheit* of Meister Eckhart.⁷⁶ And yet this is not the case. For, far from requiring that his brothers no longer exist in losing their personality, that they forget themselves to the point of detaching themselves from everything – namely from themselves as from God – the abbot of Clairvaux recommends they do the contrary, namely what we just mentioned: to act 'in such a way *as though* [*tamquam*] one did not exist'. He thereby underlines that in this supreme state, man will be 'almost [*paene*] reduced to nothing', and therefore *not totally* or *entirely* dissolved into the divinity. As the medievalist Étienne Gilson indicates rightly and brilliantly, 'to eliminate from oneself everything that impedes one from truly being oneself is *not for man to lose himself*, but for him *to find himself*' (Gilson 1941: 151; emphasis added). We have insisted elsewhere that 'The resurrection is *not annihilation* but *transformation*.'⁷⁷ This is, in reality, but now transposed into the contemporary framework of the *Metamorphosis of Finitude*, only the translation of what Bernard of Clairvaux, as a thinker of the 'limit', had also already pursued. Man's empathy for God (*Einfühlung*) is never an affective fusion of man and God (*Einsfühlung*). The strongest aspect of the debate between Edith Stein (empathy) and Theodor Lipps (affective fusion)⁷⁸ at the beginning of the twentieth century actually finds, in the monastic theology of the twelfth century, if not its first lineaments, then at least a way of thinking identity as not fully able to dissolve into alterity. As the abbot of Clairvaux insists on and explains at the end of the fourth degree of the love of God, 'human nature will indeed persist [*manebit quidem substantia*], but under another form [*sed in alia forma*], in another glory [*alia gloria*] and another power [*alia potentia*]'.⁷⁹

* * *

Feeling Oneself Alive

At the end of this voyage or rather of this unity – that which makes it such that the speculative and the affective are never separate in the monastic theology of the eleventh and twelfth centuries – one will say of the 'book of experience', and one will read in the 'book of experience', that nothing of man or the world or God is received if it is not lived, but also is not thought if it is not deciphered. Far from every anti-rationalism and every fideism, the monastic theology teaches us that experience 'traverses us and transforms us' – in the world, in speech and in the body, to be sure (Hugh of Saint-Victor), but also in our feelings and our affects (Bernard of Clairvaux), and in our thought and our concepts (Anselm of Canterbury). To 'make' an experience of God is to 'let oneself be made' by it, and there are thus many habits of 'unmaking'; and it is therefore necessary to unmake 'oneself', if not in order to arrive at the stage of 'experiencing', then at least in order to not count on one's own powers to arrive at it.

In the *Dialogue on the Soul*, Aelred of Rievaulx, brother and contemporary of Bernard of Clairvaux, gives the following lesson, or at least raises the following question: 'to begin', asks Aelred's disciple Jean, who opens the disquisition, 'I would like you to tell me *whether you feel*

---

⁷⁵ Ibid.
⁷⁶ Meister Eckhart (2010: 567): 'detachment [*Abgeschiedenheit*] is quite free of all creatures [. . .] Now detachment comes so close to nothing, that between perfect detachment and nothing no thing can exist.'
⁷⁷ See Falque (2004: 111–40) and Falque (2015: 253–76): 'La résurrection change tout.'
⁷⁸ See Stein (1989).
⁷⁹ Bernard of Clairvaux, *Treatise on the Love of God*, X, 28.

yourself alive (si te sentis vivere).'[80] And then the response of the Cistercian master uncovers within him a 'sort of secret force' that grants the 'feeling of existing', even before Jean-Jacques Rousseau and many others made it the place of a full and complete conceptuality: 'A *hidden force [vim aliquam occultam]*', corroborates Aelred,

> without being sensibility, presently unfolds within the latter – and, by its intermediary, the soul stands in the body [. . .] See if perhaps you can also think that, by this *very force* or intermediary power, there is *another* more powerful and subtler *force* coming not from a carnal union, but from an '*élan of affection*' [*sed affectu procedens*], and residing invisibly and immaterially in this seed – a force that, even without being the rational soul, nevertheless constitutes the cause and occasion of its creation.[81]

The question and response are so incisive as to require being remarked upon, even emphasised. The *Cistercian cogito*, and probably that of all monastic theology, is not one of reason or *cogitatio* at first, but one of the *affectus* or affect by which nothing appears or is discovered except what belongs to thought (Anselm), to the world (Hugh) or to affectivity (Bernard). It is *in order to hold together the faculties* – whether those of the barely nascent universities that are not yet totally separated, or that in us that makes us a unified being – that monastic theology will work for us today as a model, with the confidence that borders will make sense only when they do not erect barriers. As Aelred, a bit distraught, confides to his brothers and to the whole of his community: 'I fear I won't have any way to explain to you what I feel [*quid inde sentiam*]. But I will nevertheless speak, as far as I am able, so that you can at least *conceive* [*concipere*] what you yourselves have perhaps *experienced* [*experti*].'[82]

References

Baron, R. (1961). *Hugues et Richard de Saint-Victor*. Brussels: Bloud et Gay.
Bernard de Clairvaux (1970). 'Sermo de diversis'. *Sermones*, Sancti Bernardi Opera, Vols 1–8, Vol. VI.1. Rome: Éditions cisterciennes.
Bernard of Clairvaux, Kilian Walsh and M. Corneille (1981). *The Works of Bernard of Clairvaux*. Trans. K. Walsh, OCSO. Cistercian Fathers Series, Reprint edition, Vol. 2. Kalamazoo: Cistercian Publications, Inc.
Blanpain, J. (1974). 'Langage mystique, expression du désir dans les Sermons sur le Cantique des cantiques de Bernard de Clairvaux'. *Collectanea Cisterciensia*, 36: 226–47.
Clairvaux, S. B. de. (2012). *De la considération: Suivi de L'architecture de saint Bernard*. Trans. P. Dalloz. Paris: Cerf.
Delfgaauw, P. (1953). 'La nature et les degrés de l'amour selon saint Bernard'. *Analecta Sacri ordinis Cisterciensis*, fascicles 3–4: 234–52.
Descartes, R. (2006). *Meditations on First Philosophy*. Trans. D. A. Cress and R. Ariew. Indianapolis: Hackett Publishing Company.
Eadmer, and Anselme (1976). *l'oeuvre de s. anselme de cantorbery*, Vol. 9. Paris: Cerf.

---

[80] *Dialogus de anima*, Book I, §53 (CCCM I, 701).
[81] Ibid., Book I, §§54–7 (CCCM I, 702–3).
[82] Aelred of Rievaulx, *Sermon for the Purification of the Virgin Mary*, Sermon 34, 24 (CCCM II A, 284). One will find these sentences translated and commented on in Nouzille (1999: 247). A book at the source of the entirety of the essay that has been transformed here (*Le livre de l'expérience*), for which we deeply thank the author and our friend for having initiated.

Falque, E. (2004). *Métamorphose de la finitude: Essai philosophique sur la naissance et la résurrection*. Paris: Cerf.
Falque, E. (2008). *Dieu, la chair et l'autre: D'Irénée à Duns Scot*. Paris: Presses Universitaires de France.
Falque, E. (2011). *Les noces de l'agneau: Essai philosophique sur le corps et l'eucharistie*, CERF edition. Paris: Cerf.
Falque, E. (2013). *Passer le rubicon: Philosophie et théologie: essai sur les frontières*. Bruxelles: Editions Lessius.
Falque, E. (2015). *Triduum philosophique*, édition revue et augmentée. Paris: Cerf.
Falque, E. (2017). *Le livre de l'expérience: d'Anselme de Cantorbéry à Bernard de Clairvaux*. Paris: Cerf.
Gilbert, P. (1990). *Le Proslogion De S. Anselme: Silence De Dieu Et Joir De L'homme*, Orphelins Apprentis D Auteuil edition. Roma: Pontifical Gregorian University.
Gilson, E. (1941). *La théologie mystique de saint Bernard*. Paris: Vrin.
Grafton, A. and R. Chartier (2012). 'De la page à la toile: une rupture essentielle?' *Critique*, 785: 854–65.
Hadot, P. (2004). *What is Ancient Philosophy?* Trans. M. Chase. Cambridge, MA: Belknap Press of Harvard University Press.
Heidegger, M. (1962). *Being and Time*. Trans. J. Macquarrie and E. Robinson. New York: Harper and Row Publishers.
Heidegger, M. (1971). *On the Way to Language*. Trans. P. D. Hertz. New York: Harper and Row.
Heidegger, M. (1985). *Unterwegs Zur Sprache*. Ed. F.-W. V. Herrmann. Gesamtausgabe, Vol. 12. Frankfurt am Main: Verlag Vittorio Klosterman.
Heidegger, M. (1995). *Phänomenologie des religiösen Lebens*. Ed. C. Strube. Gesamtausgabe, Vol. 60. Frankfurt: Vittorio Klostermann.
Heidegger, M. (2004) *The Phenomenology of Religious Life*. Trans. Matthias Fritsch and Jennifer Anna Gosetti-Ferencei. Studies in Continental Thought. Indianapolis: Indiana University Press.
Hugh of Saint-Victor (1968). *The didascalion of Hugh of St. Victor, a Medieval Guide to the Arts*. Trans. J. Taylor. New York: Columbia University Press.
Hugues de Saint-Victor (n.d./1969). 'de verbo Dei'. *Six Opuscules Spirituels*. Sources chrétiennes. Paris.
Hugues, de Saint-Victor. (1991). *L'art de lire, Didascalicon*. Trans. M. Lemoine. Paris: Cerf.
Hugues de Saint-Victor (1997). *L'oeuvre de Hugues de Saint-Victor*. Trans. D. Poirel and H. Rochais. Turnhout: Brepols.
Husserl, E. (1999). *Cartesian Meditations: An Introduction to Phenomenology*. Trans. D. Cairns. Dordrecht: Kluwer.
Lévinas, E. (1998). *Of God who Comes to Mind*. Trans. B. Bergo. Stanford: Stanford University Press.
Meister Eckhart (2010). 'On Detachment'. In *The Complete Mystical Works of Meister Eckhart*. Ed. M. O. Walshe. New York: The Crossroad Publishing Company.
Merleau-Ponty, M. (1964). 'The Philosopher and His Shadow'. Trans. R. C. McCleary. In *Signs*, pp. 159–81. Evanston: Northwestern University Press.
Merleau-Ponty, M. (1968). *The Visible and the Invisible*. Trans. A. Lingis. Evanston: Northwestern University Press.
Merleau-Ponty, M. (2013). *Phenomenology of Perception*. Trans. D. Landes. New York: Routledge.
Nouzille, P. (1999). *Expérience de Dieu et théologie monastique au XIIe siècle: étude sur les sermons d'Aelred de Rievaulx*. Paris: Cerf.
Romano, C. (2010). *Au coeur de la raison, la phénoménologie*. Paris: Folio-Essais.
Romano, C. (2015). *At the Heart of Reason*. Trans. M. B. Smith. Evanston: Northwestern University Press.
Southern, R. W. (1990). *St. Anselm: A Portrait in a Landscape*. Cambridge and New York: Cambridge University Press.
Stein, E. (1962). *Welt und Person: Beitrag zum christlichen Wahrheitsstreben*. Ed. L. Romaeus and L. Gelber. Edith Steins Werke, Vol. 6. Louvain: Nauwelaerts.
Stein, E. (1989). *On the Problem of Empathy*. The Collected Works of Edith Stein, Vol. 3. Washington, DC: Springer.

7

Medieval Neoplatonism and the Dialectics of Being and Non-being

Dermot Moran

In memory of Werner Beierwaltes (1931–2019)

Introduction: Neoplatonism in the Medieval Period

In this chapter, I propose to introduce medieval Neoplatonism by focusing in particular on the pivotal figure of John Scottus Eriugena. Eriugena is pivotal because he had access not just to the Latin Christian Neoplatonism of Augustine, Marius Victorinus, Boethius and others, but because he could read Greek and was able to translate and interpret the works of Greek Christian Neoplatonists, including Gregory of Nyssa, Dionysius the Areopagite and Maximus Confessor. This meant that Eriugena has the most expansive vision of the Neoplatonic tradition in the medieval period, up to the rediscovery of the Greek manuscripts of Plotinus and Proclus by Renaissance humanists such as Ficino and others.

The term 'Neoplatonism' was developed by nineteenth-century German historians of philosophy to refer to those philosophers in the later Roman period who sought to synthesise the views of Plato, as presented in the various dialogues, into a single coherent system, especially focusing on the need to place some order on the Forms discussed by Plato. Plotinus (201–70), who wrote in Greek, is normally considered the founder of Neoplatonism (although he himself was influenced by those now called the 'Middle Platonists' (see Dillon 1977). In his *Enneads* (Gerson 2017) Plotinus expounds a complex system that claims that all things depend upon and receive their being from the One which is 'beyond being' and 'unnameable' (Corrigan 2004). Neoplatonism, broadly speaking, prioritises the transcendent, unnameable One as the source of all things. All other things flow in an 'outgoing' (*proodos, exitus*) from the One in a way that makes all these things derivative of and secondary to the One. According to Plotinus, the highest principle, the One, proceeds into *nous* (intellect), which is a unity of thinking and thought, and hence the first Dyad. *Nous* then proceeds into soul (*psyche*, see Emilsson 2007). This outflowing reaches its limit when the outgoing exhausts itself into nothingness or unformed matter. There is then a 'return' (ἐπιστροφή, *epistrophe, reditus*) of all things to the One.

Porphyry (c. 234–c. 305), Plotinus's student and editor, who also wrote in Greek, attempted further to reconcile the thought of Plato with that of Aristotle. Both Plotinus and Porphyry were pagans but many of their works were translated and synopsised by late Latin Christian writers, such as Marius Victorinus. Proclus (c. 412–85) is often seen as the last of the pagan Neoplatonic philosophers, and his literary remains are the most extensive. Proclus, head of the Platonic Academy in Athens, had extensive but subterranean influence in the Middle Ages (primarily through his Christian follower, Pseudo-Dionysius the Areopagite). Plotinus's works, on the other hand, were mostly unavailable in the Latin West during the Middle Ages until the fifteenth century when they were translated into Latin and commented on by Marsilio Ficino (Gersh 2014).

Plotinus, Porphyry and Proclus represented a late pagan resistance to Christianity, but Christian thinkers (St Gregory of Nyssa, St Ambrose, St Augustine) turned to Neoplatonism precisely to articulate, in an intellectually coherent and systematic way, the truths of their revealed religion, particularly about the nature of the deity as a transcendent unity and the total dependence of all created reality on the divine One (Beierwaltes 1969; Sheldon-Williams 1970a). Plato was considered to have anticipated the Christian account of creation with his account, in the *Timaeus*, of a divine artificer who made the world (and the *Timaeus* was known through the partial Latin translation of Calcidius). According to his autobiographical *Confessions* (Chadwick 2009), Augustine tells us he was convinced of the truth of Christianity by his reading of what he called the 'books of the Platonists' (*libri platonicorum*, *Confessions* Book VII.20.26) – now thought most probably to be the Roman rhetor Marius Victorinus's translations of Plotinus and Porphyry – texts which convinced Augustine that truth was incorporeal, that God was eternal, unchanging, the cause of all things – paralleling the truths revealed in St Paul's epistles. In his early *De vera religione* (*On True Religion*) IV. 7, Augustine claimed one need only change a few words to see how closely Plato resembled Christianity. But even in his much later work, *De civitate Dei* (*The City of God*), Plato is portrayed as the philosopher closest to Christianity (*City of God* Book VIII, chapter 11). Augustine frequently refers positively to Plato and to the Platonists ('*Platonici*', see Gersh and Hoenen 2002). In his *De Trinitate* (*On the Trinity*), furthermore, Augustine uses many of the Neoplatonic triads, for example, being-intellect-will, as images of the divine Trinity. St Augustine found in the books of the Neoplatonists an account of the divine as an infinite, immaterial, omniscient and transcendent One that helped him to overcome a Manichean-inspired view that God was some kind of refined substance like light.[1] In his *On Diverse Questions* (*De diversis quaestionibus*, Q. LXXXIII), for instance, St Augustine presented and defended a version, which he had found in Cicero, of Plato's Forms as eternal archetypes. St Augustine also regarded the Neoplatonic account of non-being as an absence or privation as a decisive argument against the Manichean position that evil is a really existent being in the world. According to Augustine, the Manicheans maintained that two equal and opposite principles of light and darkness governed the universe. He calls this the theory of 'two substances' (*opinio duarum substantiarum*, *Confessions* Book VII.14, Chadwick 2009). Augustine embraced the Neoplatonic conception that all beings derive their being from one source – the infinite transcendent divinity – and, strictly speaking, evil is not something existent but rather the absence of goodness. This diagnosis of evil as privation and lack continues in the later Neoplatonists, including Pseudo-Dionysius. In *Divine Names*, Dionysius removes evil from the realm of being and *non-being:* 'Evil is not a being . . . nor is it a non-being; for nothing is completely a non-being, unless it is said to be in the Good in the sense of beyond being . . . It has a greater nonexistence and otherness from the Good than non-being has' (*Divine Names* IV.19 716d, Lúibhéid 1987, p. 85). At *Divine Names* IV.32.732d, Dionysius says that evil is 'unfounded, uncaused, indeterminate, unborn, inert, powerless, disordered. It is errant, indefinite, dark, insubstantial, never in itself possessed of any existence' (Lúibhéid 1987: 94).

---

[1] See Chapter 1 in this volume by Karmen MacKendrick and Chapter 17 by Wayne Hankey.

Despite his admiration for Plato (Augustine had even suggested that Plato had studied with the prophet Jeremiah), Augustine, however, had many issues with Neoplatonism including the doctrine of the transmigration of souls, and the claim that the return of all things to the One happened as a matter of necessity rather than through freely given divine grace. Augustine also considered the doctrine of the incarnation to be a challenge to the Neoplatonist view that body descends from soul and returns thereto.

In thinking about the nature of the divine, Augustine places a great emphasis on the saying from Exodus 3:14 that God is He Who Is, pure being, eternal being, fullness of being. The Neo-Thomist revival of the late nineteenth and early twentieth centuries (figures such as Étienne Gilson [1952, 1954] and Jacques Maritain [1931]) sought to emphasise that medieval Christian philosophy began from the recognition of God as absolute being, as pure *esse*, or act of existence. According to this interpretation, Christian metaphysics focuses on the infinite *being* of the divine understood as pure unlimited act and also on the limited and dependent being of created natures. Thomas Aquinas, as a radical Aristotelian, came to be regarded as the pinnacle of Christian metaphysics in the Middle Ages and the Neo-Thomists elevated Aristotelian substance metaphysics as the most appropriate tradition to articulate the truths of Christian faith. This Neo-Thomist version of the history of philosophy, however, greatly downplayed the influence of Neoplatonism in the Christian Middle Ages, downplaying even the impact of the Pseudo-Dionysius on Thomas's own thought. Thomas Aquinas cites Dionysius more frequently than he does Aristotle, for example.

In fact, contrary to the interpretation of Neo-Thomism, the Neoplatonic tradition is the most dominant philosophical tradition in medieval Latin philosophy, from the writings of St Augustine to Albertus Magnus, at which point the rediscovery and Latin translation of Aristotle's texts led to an Aristotelian revival. But the Platonist tradition continued especially in the faculties of theology in the new universities of Paris, Bologna and Oxford, as witnessed by the writings of St Bonaventure and Meister Eckhart (himself a Dominican and thus a follower of St Thomas Aquinas).

John Scottus Eriugena: Pivotal Christian Neoplatonist

In the remainder of this chapter, I shall investigate the importance of the Neoplatonic contribution to medieval philosophy, focusing in particular on the writings of the medieval Irish Christian philosopher, John Scottus Eriugena (c. 800–c. 877), specifically his great dialogue in five books, *Periphyseon* or *On Natures*.[2] Eriugena occupies a pivotal position in the history of

---

[2] The main edition of Eriugena's *Periphyseon* for many years was the Patrologia Latina edition by H.-J. Floss, *Johannis Scoti Opera quae supersunt Omnia, Patrologia Latina* (hereafter 'PL') vol. 122 (Paris, 1853). The current critical edition is Édouard Jeauneau, *Iohannis Scotti seu Eriugenae Periphyseon curavit Eduardus A. Jeauneau*, 5 vols, Corpus Christianorum Continuation Mediaevalis (= CCCM) nos. 161, 162, 163, 164 and 165 (Turnhout: Brepols, 1996–2003). The *Periphyseon* (hereafter '*Peri.*') is cited according to the following translations: I. P. Sheldon-Williams (ed.), *Iohannis Scotti Eriugenae Periphyseon (De Divisione Naturae)* Book One (Dublin: Dublin Institute for Advanced Studies, 1968); Book Two (Dublin: Dublin Institute for Advanced Studies, 1970b); Book Three, with John O'Meara (Dublin: Dublin Institute for Advanced Studies, 1981); Book Four. Ed. E. Jeauneau (Dublin: Dublin Institute for Advanced Studies, 1995). There is a complete English translation by I. P. Sheldon-Williams and J. J. O'Meara, published in John J. O'Meara (ed.), *Eriugena. Periphyseon* (Dumbarton Oaks/Montréal: Bellarmin, 1987). For more on Eriugena's life and writings, see the classic study by Dom Maïul Cappuyns, *Jean Scot Erigène: sa vie, son oeuvre, sa pensée* (Louvain: Abbaye du Mont César and Paris: Desclée de Brouwer, 1933) and see Dermot Moran, *The Philosophy of John Scottus Eriugena. A Study of Idealism in the Middle Ages* (Cambridge and New York: Cambridge University Press, 1989).

medieval Neoplatonism, as he was one of the few scholars of his day who could read Greek. Eriugena's uniqueness in part stems from his harmonious synthesis of the Greek, Eastern Christian authorities (chiefly Dionysius, Gregory of Nyssa and Maximus Confessor), on the one hand, and Latin, Roman Christian authorities, especially Augustine, Boethius, Macrobius, on the other (Koch 1969; Carabine 1995). He translated and commented on the works of Pseudo-Dionysius and Maximus Confessor (see Jeauneau 1988; Laga and Steel 1990) and also translated some works by Gregory of Nyssa (Cappuyns 1965) and possibly others. Eriugena also had familiarity with Rufinus's Latin translation of Origen's *On First Principles* (see Moran 1992a) and was often linked with Origen in the Middle Ages (his *Homily on the Prologue to John* circulated under the name of Origen; Jeauneau 1969). Eriugena shows extensive knowledge of Plato's *Timaeus* in the Latin translation of Calcidius and also in his Commentary on Martianus Capella (whom he sees as a Platonist; Gersh and Hoenen 2002: 75). For Eriugena, Plato is the 'highest' (*summus*) of all philosophers (*Peri*. I.476c) and the one who looked beyond created things to discover the Creator (*Peri*. III.724a).

Eriugena always declares a preference for the Greeks and was especially influenced by the negative theology of Dionysius (McGinn 1975). One could say that Eriugena was awoken from his dogmatic, Augustinian slumbers by reading the *Corpus Dionysii*, contained in one manuscript given to him by the Carolingian king, Charles the Bald. His encounter with Dionysius transformed his life and gave him a passion for negative theology framed around the idea of the not-being of the divine.

As a convinced Neoplatonist, Eriugena sees God as the unnameable, transcendent One, who may properly be called 'non-being' because He is 'above being'. Eriugena not only offers the term 'Nothing' (*nihil*) as a name for God but also claims that God is 'beyond essence' (*superessentialis*) and 'beyond being' (*super esse*). Eriugena is, in many ways, the most consistent and also the most systematic Christian Neoplatonist of the Middle Ages prior to Albertus or Cusanus. In this chapter, therefore, I shall focus on Eriugena's account of 'nothingness', or, to borrow a term from Schelling, his *meontology* (from μή, *me* and ὄν, *on*). I shall claim that Eriugena offers the most elaborate discussion of the meanings of 'non-being' (*non esse, quae non sunt*) in medieval Latin philosophy, far outstripping what was available from Augustine, Boethius or even Marius Victorinus (who had translated Plotinus and was familiar with Porphyry). Furthermore, Eriugena reads Augustine as also recognising the transcendence and unknowability of God. Indeed, Eriugena argues that Augustine actually has a version of the *via negativa*, when he proclaims in *De Ordine*, for example, that God is better known by not knowing (*qui melius nesciendi scitur, cuius ignorantia vera est sapientia*; *Peri*. I.510b).

Eriugena highlights Augustine's determination to go beyond being in the description of the divine nature. Augustine recognises that the term 'substance' (Greek: οὐσία, *ousia*) does not fully capture the nature of the divine. The divine transcends all the categories of Aristotle.

Both Augustine and Boethius had insisted that God transcends all the Aristotelian categories (and Maximus Confessor also claimed the categories apply only to the created world and not to the divine being that transcends them). Thus Boethius, in his *On the Trinity* (*De Trinitate*), chapter IV (with which Eriugena was familiar), proclaims that God is not substance in the normal sense of the categories:

> There are in all ten categories which can be universally predicated of all things, namely, substance, quality, quantity . . . But when anyone turns these to predication of God, all the things that can be predicated (*quae praedicari*) are changed . . . For when we say 'God' (*deus*) we seem indeed to denote a substance; but it is such as is supersubstantial (*quae sit ultra substantiam*). (Stewart et al. 1918: 16–18)

There is then, already in the Latin Neoplatonic tradition of Augustine and Boethius the move away from the simple identification of God with '*ousia*' or '*to on*' (being) and the recognition that God's nature transcends being. The Neoplatonic tradition had similarly described the One as 'beyond being' and 'beyond intellect'. But this tradition of divine transcendence is carried much further by Dionysius the Areopagite (Pseudo-Dionysius), who was, most probably, based on textual evidence, a Christian follower of Proclus (Dillon and Klitenic 2007). Indeed, it is through Dionysius (and also through the anonymous *Liber de causis*; Sezgin 2000) that Proclus's thought influenced the Latin West until Proclus's own texts emerged in the Renaissance and were studied intensively by Nicholas of Cusa (1401–64; see Moran 2008), among others.

There is a strong tradition – stemming from Augustine but greatly amplified by Dionysius the Areopagite – that God, in God's inexpressible infinity, transcends being, and is better said as 'not to be'. Dionysius's *De divinis nominibus* (*On The Divine Names*; Lúibhéid 1987), especially, examines Scriptural and philosophical appellations for the divine and argues that they all fail to fully express the nature of the highest being, who is nameless and beyond all names. Names are really processions from the divinity or 'divine appearances' (theophanies) and do not 'properly' pick out the divinity itself in its own nature, because its nature transcends all names and all concepts. Negations, for Dionysius, express the nature of the divine more accurately than affirmations. This theme is expressed even more radically in Dionysius's *Mystical Theology*, which had enormous influence on the later medieval mystical tradition, transmitting to the Latin West the Platonism of the *Parmenides* in the form of negative theology. Dionysius is the source of the idea of the divine transcendence above all creation so that God cannot be called by any of the names of created things except by a kind of metaphor.

Neoplatonic Christian writers from John Scottus Eriugena to Nicholas of Cusa followed Dionysius in describing God as both transcendent beyond being or essence (*superessentialis*) and yet present in all creation. God is not essence but is 'more than essence' (*plus quam essentia*), or beyond essence, 'superessential' (*superessentialis*). But God is also the cause of all things and hence is the 'form of all created beings' (*forma omnium*). Eriugena even described God as the 'form of forms' (*forma formarum*). But God is also formless and beyond form. God is the cause, as Eriugena puts it, not only of things like God but also of the unlike. God is the cause of all opposites. God, for Eriugena, is the 'opposite of opposites' (*oppositio oppositorum*). Nicholas of Cusa, especially his *De docta ignorantia* (Hoffmann and Klibansky 1932; *On Learned Ignorance*, Hopkins 1985), developed a strongly Neoplatonic account of the nature of the divine being who so transcends and reconciles all oppositions as to be called the 'coincidence of opposites' (*coincidentia oppositorum*), echoing Eriugena's view of God as 'the opposite of opposites' (*oppositio oppositorum*; see Moran 1990).

Eriugena even speaks of God as the 'essence beyond essence' (*superessentialis essentia*) and as the 'divine superessentiality' (*divina superessentialitas*; *Peri*. III.634b), and, quoting from Dionysius's *Divine Names* I 1–2 (PG 588b-c), the 'superessential and hidden divinity' (*superessentialis et occulta divinitas*; *Peri*. I.510b). Composite terms such as 'superessential' (*superessentialis*) bring together the two kinds of theology – positive and negative. The term outwardly appears to be affirmative in meaning, Eriugena says, but, actually, the Latin prefix '*super*' (Greek: *hyper*), meaning 'above', has a negative or 'abdicative' force (*virtus abdicativae*; *Peri*. I.462c). For Eriugena, superlative terms ('more than') really have a negative connotation. He writes:

> For when it is said: 'It is superessential', this can be understood by me as nothing else but a negation of essence (*negatio essentiae*). For he who says 'It is superessential', openly denies (*aperte negat*) that it is essential, and therefore although the negative is not expressed in the words pronounced, yet the hidden meaning of it is not hidden from those who consider them well. (*Peri*. I.462a-b)

God is not 'essence' (*ousia, essentia*) but is more than *ousia* and the cause of all *ousiai* (*Peri.* I.464a). The Aristotelian categories are not predicated *proprie* but *metaphorice* of God. Indeed, there was a long Neoplatonic tradition that argued that the Aristotelian categories (substance, quantity, quality, relation, place, time, position, etc.) circumscribe the created universe but cannot be applied literally to the Creator who is beyond essence, who has no quantity, has no relations, and so on (see Moran 1992b).

The Claim that God is 'Not Being' (*Nihil*)

The context of Eriugena's discussion of nothing is the meaning of creation from nothing. Medieval Christian philosophers struggled to explicate the idea of the divine creation of the world from nothing (*ex nihilo*). What is that 'nothing' from which God created the universe?

In his dialogue *Periphyseon* (c. 867 AD), a dialogue between a Master (Nutritor) and a disciple (Alumnus), which offers an entire cosmology of 'universal nature', Eriugena makes the radical and shocking claim that God can be understood as 'Not-being' (*Nihilum*, glossing the Greek *ouden*). He is translating the neuter pronoun and adverb οὐδέν (*ouden*) meaning 'in no way', 'not at all', 'nothing' as *nihil*. Forms of *ouden* appear frequently in the New Testament but are never applied directly to God. Yet Eriugena writes in *Periphyseon* Book Three that God is 'often' called 'nothing' in Scripture:

> For according to the rules of theology the power of negation is stronger than that of affirmation [*plus negationis quam affirmationis uirtus ualet*] for investigating the sublimity and incomprehensibility of the Divine Nature; and anyone who looks into it closely will not be surprised that often in the Scriptures God Himself is called by the name Nothing [*eo uocabulo, quod est nihilum, saepe in scripturis ipsum deum uocari*]. (*Peri.* 684d–685a; Jeauneau 1999: 93)

Especially in *Periphyseon* Book Three (III.634a–690b), Eriugena discusses various ways in which being and non-being can be understood in what amounts to a mini-treatise on nothing (*de nihilo*). There is a chapter entitled '*de nihilo*' commencing at *Periphyseon* III.634a. I.-P. Sheldon-Williams calls it a 'little treatise' on the *quaestio de nihilo* (Sheldon-Williams 1981: 5, note 1), following Gustavo Piemonte (Piemonte 1968). Jeauneau agrees and singles out Eriugena's concept of '*le Néant divin*' (Jeauneau 1999: ix; see also Jeauneau 1997b). Indeed, Eriugena will go so far as to argue that all things can be thought of as 'nothingness' in one form or another: God, the primary causes, corporeal things, matter, are all species of non-being. It would later influence Nicholas of Cusa,[3] in particular, and his concept of God as '*non aliud*' or 'not other' (Hopkins 1987).

The Superessential Goodness of the Divine is 'Beyond Being'

The Neoplatonists thought of the One and the Good as 'beyond being' (a notion already found in Plato, *Republic* 509b, the Good is *epekeina tes ousias*). The Christian Neoplatonists – Augustine, Eriugena and Dionysius – all see God as the *summum bonum* and therefore as preceding being in some sense. Eriugena could read in Pseudo-Dionysius of the priority of goodness over being. Dionysius writes in *The Celestial Hierarchy*:

> One truth must be affirmed above all else. It is that the transcendent deity has out of goodness established the existence of everything and brought it into being. It is characteristic

---

[3] See Chapter 10 in this volume by Peter Casarella.

of the universal cause, of this goodness beyond all, to summon everything to communion with him to the extent that this is possible. Hence everything in some way partakes of the providence flowing out of this transcendent Deity which is the originator of all that is. Indeed, nothing could exist without some share in the being and source of everything. Even the things which have no life participate in this, for it is the transcendent deity which is the existence of every being. (Lúibhéid 1987: 156)

Eriugena follows Dionysius in thinking of the Good as that which is responsible for the movement from non-being to being. It is because of the outpouring of divine goodness that things move from non-existence to existence. Goodness is then prior to being. Eriugena makes this clear in *Periphyseon*, Book Three:

For the Cause of all things, the creative Goodness which is God, created that cause which is called goodness-through-itself first of all for this purpose: that through it all things that are should be brought from non-existents to essences. For it is a property of the divine Goodness to call (*uocare*) the things that were not into existence. For the Divine Goodness and More-than-Goodness is both the essential and superessential cause of the universe that it has established and brought to essence. Therefore if the creator through his goodness brought all things out of nothing so that they might be, the aspect of goodness-in-itself must necessarily precede the aspect of being through itself. For goodness does not come through essence but essence comes through goodness [*Non enim per essentiam introducta est bonitas set per bonitatem introducta est essentia*]. (*Peri.* III. 627c-d)

Eriugena cites the typical Neoplatonic slogan to the effect that 'all things that are, are in so far as they are good' (echoing Augustine's *De Doctrina Christiana* Book 1, 32.35). If goodness is withdrawn, Eriugena says, then things cannot come to essence (*Peri.* III.628a). Goodness, then, precedes essence (*ousia*) in the meontological scheme.

The Fives Modes of Being and Non-Being as 'Contemplations'

Right from the opening of his *Periphyseon*, the 'universal nature' (*universalis natura, physis*), that is, the subject of the dialogue, is defined as 'the general name for those things that are and are not' (*generale nomen . . . omnium quae sunt et quae non sunt*; *Peri.* I.441a). Eriugena then outlines the four 'divisions' or 'forms' of nature: nature that creates and is not created; nature that creates and is created; nature that is created and does not create; and nature that neither creates nor is created. The first three divisions correspond to God, the Primary Causes and the Created Effects, but the fourth is puzzling. It seems to refer to 'nothing' at all.

Eriugena immediately embarks on a discussion of the meaning of being and non-being in relation to 'five modes of interpretation' (*quinque modi interpretationis*; *Peri.* I.443a). He often returns to discuss the various ways under which things can be approached and interpreted – various '*theoriae*' or '*contemplationes*'. We can think about nothingness from different standpoints. Eriugena builds his cosmological and ontological framework on the idea that the same entity can be understood in different ways depending on how it is viewed. This, of course is exemplified most especially in the fourfold division of nature into that which creates and is not created; that which is created and creates; that which is created and does not create; and, finally, that which neither creates nor is created. The one God is all of these divisions or 'forms' or 'species' and is each one depending on how God is approached – as Creator, as incarnate in the Son, or as transcendent hiddenness and darkness.

Eriugena usually takes a twofold, dialectical approach to the meaning of nothing: *Nihil* means either *nihil per privationem* or *nihil per excellentiam*. Eriugena frequently speaks of this as '*duplex theoria*', a twofold way of viewing (Beierwaltes 1990). Of course, St Paul and Augustine are also his sources for this twofold mode of viewing – St Paul claims we can approach matters *carnaliter* and *spiritualiter* (Romans 8:6) and Augustine distinguishes the *homo inferior* from *homo superior*. Augustine, for instance in *The City of God* (*De Civitate Dei*) Book Eight (Viii.3), states that only purified minds – and not minds tarnished by earthly desires – could grasp the 'causes of all things' (see Eriugena; *Peri*. III.688b-c).

Eriugena similarly explains the twofold approach to 'nothingness' several times. In Book Three, the student in the dialogue Alumnus asks:

> But when I hear or say that the divine Goodness [*diuinam bonitatem*] created all things out of nothing [*omnia de nihilo creasse*] I do not understand what is signified by that name, 'Nothing' [*eo nomine, quod est nihil*], whether the privation of all essence or substance [*priuatio totius essentiae uel substantia*] or accident, or the excellence of the divine super-essentiality [*diuinae superessentialitatis excellentia*]. (*Peri*. III.634a-b; Jeauneau 1999: 244)

God is legitimately called 'nothing' because God is 'more than being' (*plus quam esse*; *Peri*. III.634b). God's 'ineffable excellence and incomprehensive infinity' (*Peri*. III.634b) means that God can be said not to be, but it does not follow that God is 'nothing at all' (*omnino nihil*), mere nothing, nothing understood through the stripping away of all predicates. Obviously, this discussion of nothingness has a long history in philosophy since Plato's *Parmenides* and the *Enneads* of Plotinus, but Eriugena can also discover it in his Latin sources (Duclow 1977). Again, Eriugena's original hermeneutical achievement consists in his ability to identify this radical *meontology* in both his Greek and his Latin sources.

'Nothing' in Eriugena's Latin Sources: Augustine, Boethius and Marius Victorinus

Eriugena first discussed the meaning of 'non-being' in his treatise *De praedestinatione* (395a ff.; Brennan 1998: 66–9), where he argued, drawing on Augustine, that evil is not to be understood as substance but as non-being ('for all that lacks, matter, form and species is, without doubt, nothing'; Brennan 1998: 69) and, therefore, as neither created by God nor known to Him. He develops this argument further in the *Periphyseon* Book Two, for example, where he argues that God's nature is simple and, therefore, God cannot be said to know evil (*Peri*. II.596a-b); and in Book Five, at *Periphyseon* V.926a, where Eriugena says that God cannot be said to know the wickedness of angels or humans. Of course, the Latin source of this assessment of evil is undoubtedly Augustinian, especially his *Confessions*, which Eriugena knew, but Eriugena also cites Augustine's *De civitate Dei* XII 7, *De natura boni* 38.38, *De Trinitate* VII.5.10, and his *Contra Epistulamcquae uocant Fundamenti* (Brennan 1998: 67).

Eriugena often quotes a powerful passage from St Augustine's *De Ordine* (*On Order*, Burroso 2007; Green 1970), where Augustine praises the liberal arts for helping theology understand such issues as the nature of nothingness and formless matter:

> ... yet, if he does not know what nothingness is, what formless matter is [*quid sit nihil, quid informis materia*], what an inanimate unformed being is, what a body is, what species in a body is, what place and time are ... and what are beyond time and forever, anyone ignorant of these matters who nonetheless seeks to inquire and to dispute concerning his own soul,

not to speak of that supreme God Who is better known by not knowing [*qui scitur melius nesciendo*], he indeed will fall into error, to the greatest extent that error is possible. (*De Ordine* 2.16.44; Green 1970: 131)

Eriugena, who loves to cite the line that God is better known by not knowing, was deeply inspired by *De Ordine*. Augustine also discusses nothing in *De Magistro*. For Augustine it is not a sign of something extra-mental but something in the mind. It perhaps indicates the state of mind of not finding what one is looking for (*De magistro* 7).

Augustine also regards creatures in their being as creatures as mere nothingness, as Eriugena and later Eckhart also hold (Lanzetta 1992; Brunn 1993). Thus, Eriugena says in *Periphyseon* Book Three (at *Peri*. III.646b) that every creature considered in itself is nothing, and he cites a passage from St Augustine's *Confessions* Book Seven, which states that creatures are neither entirely being *(nec omnino esse)* nor entirely non-being *(nec omnino non esse)*. In general, Augustine sees the corruptibility of all creatures as due to their genesis from nothing, and he believes all creatures have an innate 'desire' to return to nothing, unless they are sustained by their Creator. Thus, in the *Confessions* Book Twelve, he says that bodies may get small but will never fall away into nothingness, on their own. It is not hard to find other references to non-being in the work of Augustine. For example, in *De magistro*, chapter 7, Augustine discusses the meaning of *nihil* and is uncertain as to whether it signifies something or nothing. He wants to say that all signs signify objective realities, but that nothing does not signify an objective reality.

Eriugena may also have had contact with other Latin discussions of non-being – notably, Boethius's *Opuscula sacra*. Eriugena had read Boethius's *Contra Eutychen et Nestorium* and had found there a discussion of nature in which it is remarked that 'nothing' signifies something, but it does not stand for a nature. Boethius distinguishes *nihil* from *natura*. For Boethius, *nihil* signifies 'something' (*aliquid*) but not a nature. *Aliquid* here designates a concept.

Marius Victorinus's theological works (especially *Ad Candidum Arrianum* and *Adversus Arium*; Hadot 1960; Clark 2001) were known in the Carolingian era and are referenced by Alcuin, for instance, and by Hincmar of Reims (Hadot 1954). Eriugena does not mention him specifically, but at least one scholar, Gustavo Piemonte, is convinced Eriugena has access to the text of Marius Victorinus (Piemonte, in Allard 1986). There is one particular passage in *Periphyseon* Book Three (III.634b-c) where Eriugena debates whether God can be called '*non esse*' as some theologians do. Eriugena says he will not allow that God can be called non-being on the basis of a privation; God is *plus quam esse*. Possibly he is referring her to Marius Victorinus, Piemonte believes (see Allard 1986: 108).

For Marius, God is 'above all things, all existents and all non-existents' (*Ad Cand.* 3.1; Clark 2001: 61). God is the cause of being (*esse*) and non-being (*non esse*). God is *ON*. At *Ad Cand*. 3.2.4, he gives his four modes of non-existence. Victorinus posits non-being (*id quod non est*) as divided according to four modes: 'according to negation' (*iuxta negationem*); 'according to being different from another nature' (*iuxta alterius ad aliud naturam*); 'according to "to be" which is not yet and can be', as futural or potential being (*iuxta nondum esse, quod futurum est et potest esse*); and as transcendent non-being, 'to be which is above all the things that are (*iuxta quod supra omnia quae sunt, est esse*) (*Ad Cand.* 3, 1–2, Clark 2001: 63–4; 4, 1–5; CSEL LXXXIII (Vienna, 1971)). Piemonte sees these four divisions as reminiscent of the first three of Eriugena's *quinque modi* (Allard 1986: 92). Victorinus uses the same argument as Eriugena that privation indicates a prior possession and it is a fantasy to imagine the privation of all being as the cause of being. Generally speaking, there are remarkable parallels between Marius and Eriugena, but Marius does not use Eriugena's distinctive formulation '*per excellentiam*' (Allard 1986: 106). Rather, Marius uses '*per praelationem et per eminentiam*' (*Adv Ar.* IV, 19, 11), but the intention is the same. Marius's idea of the non-being above being ('*me on hyper to on*') has its source in Porphyry and, in fact, Marius is the conduit of Porphyrian ideas of the principle beyond the One into medieval Neoplatonism. Marius Victorinus operates with a fourfold division (also found in Augustine) between *quae vere sunt* (*ontos onta*), *quae sunt* (*onta*), *quae non vere non sunt* (*me ontos me onta*) and *quae non sunt* (*me onta*) (*Ad Cand.* 5, 6–7).

With regard to the Carolingian authors who were Eriugena's immediate predecessors (Marenbon 1981), it is possible that Eriugena knew the work of Fredegisus entitled *Epistola de nihilo et tenebris* (Gennaro 1963), which argued that the term 'nothing' must actually stand for something, since all meaningful terms signify something, as we know Augustine also believed. Fredegisus was an Anglo-Saxon disciple of Alcuin and a member of the Carolingian court, tutor to Charlemagne's sister. He asked a basic question: 'Whether nothing is anything, or not?' (*Nihilne aliquid sit, an non*, Colish 1984). What kind of 'thing' is nihil? He begins with an argument drawn from grammar. Fredegisus argues that all finite nouns signify something. Therefore '*nihil*' must signify something, for example, a human, a stone, a tree (*Omne nomen finitum aliquid significat, ut 'homo', 'lapis', lignum'*). Therefore, it is something; and something that is existent (*Nihil autem aliquid significat. Igitur nihil eius significatio est quod est, id est rei existentis*). Fredegisus then turns to Scripture and the meaning of creation *ex nihilo*. *Nihil* is not *materia informis*, he says (as Eriugena will also later affirm). Nothing, Fregedisus concludes, must be something great (*magnum quiddam ac praeclarum*). God knows the nature of this *nihil* even if humans do not. Fredegisus then turns to discuss the meaning of '*tenebrae*' – the darkness that lay over the waters in Genesis. This, too, is something created. If the words '*dies*' and '*lux*' signify something, then so must their opposites *nox* and *tenebrae*. Fredegisus concludes his letter without actually identifying this 'great' non-being with God, as Eriugena would explicitly do, but there is no doubt that his work is pointing in that direction. It is clear from this text from Alcuin's Circle that the problem of non-being was a living issue in Carolingian philosophical and theological debates. But Eriugena takes it to new heights. Eriugena will transform these Latin discussions by integrating them into the even more radical speculations of the Eastern Christian Neoplatonists and especially Dionysius the Areopagite, to whom we now turn.

'Nothing' in Eriugena's Greek Sources: Dionysius the Areopagite

Eriugena found the idea of divine nothingness primarily in Dionysius the Areopagite. In *Periphyseon* Book Five, Eriugena says he was inspired by Dionysius's *Divine Names* to name God as non-being: 'for it shall return into Him, who, because He transcends being, is called Not-Being' (*In ipsum enim, qui propter superessentialitatem suae naturae nihil dicitur, reversus est*, *Peri.* V.897d). God is 'above being' (*Peri.* V.898b-c). Earlier in *Periphyseon* Book Three, furthermore, Eriugena quotes a long section from Dionysius's *Divine Names* (*De divinis nominibus*) Book Five chapters 4–5 (PG III 817c–820a; Suchla 1990: 182, l.17–183, l.17) and chapter 8 (V.8. 821d–824b; Suchla 1990: 182, l.14–187, l.12), where Dionysius speaks about 'being' and describes God as ON (ων) and also as the 'ante ων' (III.682b) or the 'pre-existent' (*ante existens*). Eriugena translates Dionysius as saying: 'He is before all things and has constituted all things in himself' (. . . *ipse est ante omnia et omnia in se constituit*, *Peri.* III.682c). Eriugena goes on to quote Dionysius, who identifies ON with God (*sic enim uocat deum*, *Peri.* III.682a, l. 2596 or 'so Dionysius calls God' as Sheldon-Williams translates):

> But being itself [*Esse autem ipsum*] is never bereft [*deseritur*] of all things that exist. Being itself, indeed, is from the Pre-Existent; and from it is being; and ων (is) the beginning and measure before essence and is not itself being; and being possesses it; and ων is the

substantiating beginning and middle and end both of that which exists and of age and all things; and therefore by the Oracles He Who is in truth Pre-ων is multiplied in every notion of the things that exist, and in Him is properly celebrated what was and what is and what shall be and what has become and what becomes and what shall become. (*Peri.* III.682c-d – translating *Divine Names* V.8.821d–824b; Suchla 1990: 182, l.14–187, l.12; Lúibhéid 1987: 101)

The divine being possesses an ineffable, infinite nature that transcends all things and is in some sense prior to or 'before' (*ante*) all things. Going further, Eriugena finds a Scriptural basis in what he calls the 'sacred oracles' (*sacri eloquii*) or 'sacred theology' (*sacra theologia*) for his application of the term 'non-being' to God. And the theologians that Eriugena is invoking here are Dionysus, Gregory of Nyssa and Maximus – the Greek Christian authorities.

Eriugena, of course, thought of Dionysius[4] as the convert of St Paul and hence as an authority equivalent to scripture. For Dionysius, the Godhead (θεότης, *theotes*, *deitas*) is transcendent 'oneness' (ἑνότης, *henotes*, *unitas*), 'a henad unifying all henads'. As Dionysius puts it in his *Divine Names*, the divine is 'Oneness beyond mind' (*he hyper noun henotes, Divine Names* 588B; Lúibhéid 1987: 50). This Oneness is beyond being and can better be said not to be than to be.

Very early in the *Periphyseon*, at I.443b, Eriugena quotes Dionysius's *Celestial Hierarchy* iv.1 (PG III.177d1–2; Heil 1986: 20, ll.16–17): 'For, he says, the being of all things is the Divinity Who is above being' (*Esse enim, inquit, omnium est super esse diuinitas, Peri.* I.443b; Jeauneau 1996: 5). Eriugena will repeat this phrase from Dionysius very often (for example, at *Peri.* I.516c, III.664b and *Peri.* V.903c; as well as in his *Homily on the Prologue to the Gospel of St John* often called *Homilia*, or *Vox spiritualis* [Jeauneau 1969]). As God is *in se* comprehended by no intellect, God is equally incomprehensible from the point of view of the creature that subsists in God (*Peri.* I.443b-c). Later at Book One I.481c, Eriugena cites 'Gregory the theologian' (*Gregorius theologus*) and Maximus Confessor's I *Ambigua* vi. 38 (PG XCI. 1180b8–13) saying that 'God alone properly subsists above being itself' (*qui solus super ipsum esse proprie subsistit*) – everything else is located in time and space or can be circumscribed within the categories. God is incomprehensible by reason of His transcendence above all beings.

Eriugena on Creation as Making Eternally 'from Nothing'

In *Periphyseon* Book Three 680c-d, Eriugena says that God is called *Nihilum* in the Bible. Alumnus asks Nutritor at Book III.680c: 'But I beg you to explain what Holy Theology means by that name of "Nothing"' (*Quid autem eo nomine quod est nihilum sancta significat theologia explanari a te peto*). What motivates Eriugena to speak of the divine nothingness, what Jeauneau terms '*le néant divin*'?

Book Three as a whole is meant to focus on the third division of nature, namely, that which is created and does not create (*Peri.* III. 619d–620a). Eriugena's concern for the meaning of 'nothing' is largely motivated by his attempt to understand the meaning of the Christian doctrine of divine creation as 'creation from nothing'. Eriugena frequently says that creation consists in making things 'from nothing' (*ex nihilo, de nihilo*), as for instance in his *Expositiones* 4:73–82 (Barbet 1975: 67, *credimus enim ipsum de nihilo omnia fecisse*). But Eriugena also has

---

[4] See Chapter 3 in this volume by Lisa Mahoney.

to make sense of Dionysius the Areopagite, who proclaimed that God makes all things and *is made* in all things. God is somehow not just the creator but also is in some sense 'created'. This appears shocking and scandalous. In the *Periphyseon*, Eriugena has Alumnus express the novelty of this claim:

> Alumnus: . . . I thought that only God is *anarchos* (ἄναρχος), that is, without beginning – for He is the Beginning and the End which arises out of no beginning and concludes to no end – whereas all other things begin and tend each to its proper end, and therefore are not eternal *but* made. And incomparably more profound and wonderful than all this seems to be the assertion you made on the authority of St. Dionysius the Areopagite, namely, that God Himself is both the Maker of all things and is made in all things [*deum et omnium factorum esse et in omnibus factum*]; for this was never heard or known [*inauditum et incognitum*] before either by me [*non solum mihi*] or by many [*et multis*], or by nearly all [*ac paene omnibus*]. For if this is the case, who will not at once break out and exclaim in these words: God is in all things and all things God? (*Deus itaque omnia est et omnia deus*, *Peri*. III.650c-d)

Alumnus has never heard that God is in all things and made in all things. In order to discuss this Dionysian claim further, Eriugena turns not to theology but to the liberal arts. The teacher in the dialogue, Nutritor, replies to the student, Alumnus, by asking about his knowledge of the art of arithmetic (*ars arithmeticae*). All numbers are one in the Monad. The numbers are infinite, and these infinite numbers are eternal in the Monad (*Peri*. III.654a), which itself must be infinite. The One contains all numbers potentially. After a long discourse on numbers, which explains how they can be both eternal and also created, Nutritor says it is time to consider again how things can be eternal and made. Eriugena regularly speaks of creation as things coming from the non-existent things into the existent ones (*ex non esse in esse*; *ex non existentibus in existentia*; see Rorem 2005: 107). He often describes creation as a '*motus*' or 'movement' – a 'motion': see, for instance, *Periphyseon* Book One I.470a:

> . . . for all things move through the process of generation from the state of non-existence into the state of existence, for the divine Goodness summons all things out of not-being into being so that they are [created] out of nothing [*ex non existentibus in existentia per generationem moventus ex non esse in esse divina bonitate omnia vocante ut sint de nihilo*] and each one of the things that are is moved by a natural desire [*appetitus*] toward its own essence and genus and species and individuality. (*Peri*. I.470a; Jeauneau 1996: 41, ll.1188–95)

There is a general movement of all things from non-existence to existence. Things that do not subsist in themselves but have their being in something else are said to be in motion (*Peri*. I.470a). Eriugena finds this thought in the *De Imagine* (*De hominis opificio*) of Gregory of Nyssa, which he quotes using his own translation of Gregory of Nyssa (PG 44.184c; Cappuyns 1965). This whole discussion of the manner the categories apply to God is in part inspired by the Pseudo-Augustinian *Categoriae decem*. God is not situated in place (*locus*) or time (*tempus*), or quantity, or position, etc. Similarly, Eriugena argues that *ousia*, which subsists by itself is not contained in any place (I.470c).

But there is a puzzle here because normally a cause contains everything that it produces in the effect. If creatures literally came from nothing understood as the absence or privation of being, then this law of causation would be violated.

In this 'treatise' on Nothing, Eriugena first considers the traditional view that God is not being but the privation of created being – the absolute privation of all being (III.634c):

> Alumnus: By the name 'nothing' [*nomine quod est nihilum*], then, is meant the negation and absence [*atque absentia*] of all essence or substance, indeed of all things that are created in nature [*in natura rerum creata*]. (*Peri.* III.635a – 'absence' [*absentia*] is added in the text of Rheims – marked in bold in the Jeauneau edition, 1999: 248, ll.1169–73)

Nutritor agrees – saying almost all the commentators on Holy Scripture agree on this. God made everything not out of something but out of nothing at all (*non de aliquo set de omnino nihil*, III.635a). However, Alumnus expresses worries – he is surrounded by 'dark clouds' (*nebulis tenebrosis*, l.1180). Alumnus is concerned about the status of the Primordial Causes (*causae primordiales*, III.635c). It had earlier been agreed that these had been made in the Word by the Father – in His Wisdom, all gathered together as one. The concept of the artificer precedes the concept of his art.

> Alumnus: For if all things that are, are eternal in the Creative Wisdom, how are they made out of nothing [*quomodo de nihilo sunt facta*]? (*Peri.* III.636a)

The artist [*Artifex*] makes things out of his own art [*ars*] and that art precedes the things that are made in it (*Peri.* III.636a). Nutritor is really at a loss to explain why people think the world was made from unformed matter or from nothing understood as privation. He writes in Book Three:

> But concerning those who think that the world was made from that nothing which means the privation or absence of the whole of essence [*de eo nihilo quod totius essentiae priuationem significat*] I do not know what to say. For I do not see why they do not bethink them of the nature of opposites [*oppositorum naturam*]. For it is impossible that there should be privation where there is not possession of essence. For privation is the privation of possession and therefore where possession does not precede privation does not follow. How, then, do they say that the world was made from privation? (*Peri.* III.686a)

Eriugena thinks the only answer (if one does not accept privation or absence) is to recognise this nothing as God:

> But if one should say that neither deprivation of possession nor the absence of some presence is meant by the name 'Nothing' [*nihili nomine significari*], but the total negation of possession and essence or of substance or of accident or, in a word, of all things that can be said or understood, the conclusion will be this: So that is the name by which it is necessary to call God, Who alone is what is properly meant by the negation of all the things that are, because He is exalted above everything that is said or understood, Who is none of the things that are and are not [*qui nullum eorum quae sunt et quae non sunt*], Who by not knowing is the better known [*qui melius nesciendo scitur*]. (*Peri.* III.686c–687a)

Note that again Eriugena invokes Augustine's *De Ordine* II.44.

Eriugena embarks on a long discussion about the location and status of the 'Primordial Causes' that produce the visible effects of this created order and he locates them in the divine Word (*Verbum*, *Logos*). God then already contained all the causes – but they are in him as a seamless unity – as the infinite radii belong to the circle and radiate from the central point. God then causes the world to come to be not from nothing understood as privation but from the superessential nothingness of his own being. *Ex nihilo* means *ex deo*. Creation then is really the self-manifestation of the divine, a divine theophany, an *exitus* or *proodos* from its own nature. The transcendent God is unknown and unknowable but can be known through his theophanies or divine manifestations. God radiates outwards from God's transcendent darkness into the manifest light of creation. In this eternal outpouring, God at once eternally creates Himself and all other things. God's self-creation is a form of self-manifestation (*Peri*. I.455b), that is, God manifests Himself in an infinite series of revelations or theophanies. Furthermore, Eriugena defines theophany as divine manifestation *theophania, hoc est dei apparitio*, *Peri*. I.446d). This self-creation is understood by Eriugena as a self-expression, a 'speaking of the Word' a 'divine cry' (*clamor dei*) which, at the same timeless moment in the process, brings about the creation of all other things, since, according to Scripture, all things are contained in the Word. Eriugena summarises creation as *manifestatio in aliquo*. God's act of self-manifestation is at the same time the creation of all things, *Periphyseon* I.455b:

> For when it is said that it creates itself [*se ipsam creare*] the true meaning is nothing else but that it is establishing [*condere*] the natures of things. For the creation of itself, that is, the manifestation of itself in something [*hoc est in aliquo manifestatio*], is surely that by which all things subsist [*substitutio*]? (*Peri*. I.455b; Jeauneau 1996: 22, ll.553–7)

Eriugena says at *Periphyseon* Book Three 633a-b, in a section that is entitled 'on theophanies' (*de theophaniis*):

> For everything that is understood and sensed [*quod intelligitur et sensitur*] is nothing other but [*nihil aliud est*] the appearance of what is not apparent, the manifestation of the hidden [*occulti manifestatio*], the affirmation of the negated, the comprehension of the incomprehensible, [the utterance of the unutterable, the access to the inaccessible], the understanding of the unintelligible [*inintelligibilis intellectus*], the body of the bodiless, the essence of the superessential [*superessentialis essentia*], the form of the formless . . . . (*Peri*. III.633a-b; Jeauneau 1999: 238–40, ll.1057–73)

At Book Three 633d Eriugena speaks of the 'ineffable diffusion' (*ineffabilis diffusion*) of divine goodness into all things that is responsible for the creation of all things: '. . . this ineffable diffusion both makes all things and is made in all things and is all things' (*Peri*. III.634a). Eriugena describes this creative motion paradoxically as 'mobile stability and stable motion' (*status mobilis et motus stabilis*; *Peri*. III.633d). This motion is described in almost Hegelian fashion as 'from itself in itself back to itself' (*a se ipsa in se ipsa ad se ipsam*) [in an addition added in the text of Rheims in Eriugena's supposed autograph]:

> For the motion of the supreme and threefold and only true Goodness, which in Itself is immutable [*immutabilis motus*], and the multiplication of its simplicity [*simplex multiplicatio*], and Its inexhaustible diffusion from Itself in Itself back to Itself [*et inexhausta a se ipsa in se ipsa ad se ipsam diffusio*], is the cause of all things, indeed *is* [*est*] all things. (*Peri*. III.632d; Jeauneau 1999: 238, ll.1035–40)

Outside it there is nothing and it possesses and circumscribes all things.

In *Periphyseon* Book Three 688a, Eriugena returns again to give a recapitulation (*recapitulatio, anakephalaiosis*) as to why the fourfold division (*quadripertita totius naturae discretio*) applies to God. Eriugena says the intellect is moved in one way when it contemplates God as beginning, and in another way when it sees God as medium, and in another way as end (*Peri.* III.688b). Eriugena is clearly endorsing a perspectivist account of being and non-being – which is in line with his recognition that there are an infinite number of revelations of theophanies of the divine One. Furthermore, Eriugena thinks that all things shall be unified in God – just as the stars are converted into light when the sun rises (*Peri.* III.689a). Eriugena's fifth book of the *Periphyseon* deals with this return of all things to the One, when, in the end, God shall be 'all in all' (*omnia in omnibus*).

Conclusion

The Neoplatonic tradition is the dominant intellectual tradition for the whole of the Middle Ages from St Augustine to Ficino and Nicholas of Cusa, especially useful for expressing the transcendence and infinity of the divine nature and the total dependence of created nature on its divine source. No more fitting encapsulation of these concerns can be found than in the work of John Scottus Eriugena, who, I have argued, is a pivotal figure for medieval Neoplatonism. His fourfold division of nature is a kind of anagram for thinking the nature of the divine as both being and non-being under different modes of contemplation, as we have seen. But, furthermore, Eriugena offers an extraordinary and original account of the divine nature as a transcendent 'nothing' (*nihil*). The concept of 'nothingness' has a long and still under-explored history in Western philosophy beginning with Parmenides and reaching a high point in Greek-Roman pagan philosophy with Plotinus, Porphyry and Proclus. But the study of 'nothing' received a further boost from Christian philosophy seeking to accommodate the notion of creation from 'nothing' and to repudiate the Manichees and others who maintained that creation took place from a pre-existent matter. Augustine and others sought to distinguish '*nihil*', '*tenebrae*' (darkness) and *materia informis*. Eriugena inherits this discussion – extended in Carolingian times by Fredegisus and others. But the relatively Aristotelian categorial and grammatical context (*materia informis*) is completely disrupted by Eriugena's discovery of Dionysius, whom he quotes extensively. Eriugena is rightly seen as developing the first true *summa* of the Middle Ages, paving the way for scholasticism, by offering a systematic meontological account of 'nature' according to four divisions which deals with the central topics of being and non-being, and shows the consistency between the Greek and Latin authorities, while strongly articulating a Neoplatonic vision. Eriugena's account of the divine nothingness inspired mystical thinkers in the later medieval period, especially Meister Eckhart and Nicholas of Cusa, and has attracted the interest of Japanese Buddhist scholars in recent decades.

Bibliography

Allard, Guy (ed.) (1986). *Jean Scot écrivain*. Montréal: Bellarmin.
Barbet, Jeanne (1975). *Iohannis Scoti Eriugenae Expositiones in Ierarchiam coelestem*. Corpus Christianorum. Continuatio Mediaevalis XXI. Turnhout: Brepols.
Beierwaltes, Werner (1969). *Platonismus in der Philosophie des Mittelalters*. Darmstadt: Wissenschaftliche Buchgesellschaft.
Beierwaltes, Werner (1990). '*Duplex Theoria*. Zu einer Denkform Eriugenas'. In *Begriff und Metapher. Sprachform des Denkens bei Eriugena*. Ed. W. Beierwaltes. Heidelberg: Carl Winter Verlag, pp. 37–64.

Beierwaltes, Werner (1994). 'Eriugena und Cusanus'. In *Eriugena. Grundzüge seines Denkens*. Ed. W. Beierwaltes. Frankfurt: Klostermann, pp. 266–312.
Brennan, Mary (1998). *John Scottus Eriugena. Treatise on Divine Predestination*. Trans. Mary Brennan with an Introduction by Avital Wohlman. Notre Dame: University of Notre Dame Press.
Brunn, E. (1993). 'God as Non-Being from Meister Eckhart'. *Revue des Sciences Religieuses*, 67/4: 11–22.
Burroso, Silvano (2007). St Augustine *On Order [De Ordine]*. Trans. Silvano Burroso. South Bend, IN: St. Augustine's Press.
Cappuyns, Dom Maïul (1933). *Jean Scot Erigène: sa vie, son oeuvre, sa pensée*. Louvain: Abbaye du Mont César. Paris: Desclée de Brouwer.
Cappuyns, Dom Maïul (1965). 'Le *De imagine* de Grégoire de Nysse traduit par Jean Scot Erigène'. *Recherches de théologie ancienne et médiévale*, 32: 205–62.
Carabine, Deirdre (1995). *The Unknown God: Negative Theology in the Platonic Tradition: Plato to Eriugena*. Louvain: Peeters.
Chadwick, Henry (2009). St. Augustine, *Confessions*. Trans. H. Chadwick. Oxford: Oxford University Press.
Clark, Mary T. (2001). *Theological Treatises on the Trinity. Marius Victorinus*. Trans. Mary T. Clark. Washington, DC: Catholic University of America Press.
Colish, Marcia L. (1984). 'Carolingian Debates over *Nihil* and *Tenebrae*: A Study in Theological Method'. *Speculum*, 59/4: 757–95.
Corrigan, Kevin (2004). *Plotinus: A Practical Introduction to Neoplatonism*. West Lafayette, IN: Purdue University Press.
Dillon, John (1977). *The Middle Platonists*. Ithaca: Cornell University Press.
Dillon, J. M. and S. Klitenic (2007). *Dionysius the Areopagite and the Neoplatonist Tradition: Despoiling the Hellenes*. Ashgate Studies in Philosophy and Theology in late Antiquity. Aldershot: Ashgate.
Duclow, Donald F. (1977). 'Divine Nothingness and Self-Creation in John Scotus Eriugena'. *The Journal of Religion*, 57/2: 109–23.
Emilsson, Eyjólfur Kjalar (2007). *Plotinus on Intellect*. Oxford: Oxford University Press.
Floss, H.-J. (1853). *Johannis Scoti Opera quae supersunt Omnia*. Patrologia Latina CXXII. Paris.
Gennaro, Concettina (1963). *Fridugiso di Tours e il 'De substantia nihili et tenebrarum'*. Edizione critica e studio introduttivo. Pubblicazioni dell'Istituto universario di magis- tero di Catania, serie filosofica, saggi e monografie 46. Padua.
Gersh, Stephen (1978). *From Iamblichus to Eriugena*. Leiden: Brill.
Gersh, Stephen (2014). *Interpreting Proclus. From Antiquity to the Renaissance*. Cambridge: Cambridge University Press.
Gersh, Stephen and Martin J. F. M. Hoenen (eds) (2002). *The Platonic Tradition in the Middle Ages*. Berlin: Walter de Gruyter.
Gerson, L. (ed.) (2017). *Plotinus: The Enneads*. Trans. G. Boys-Stones, J. Dillon, R. King, A. Smith and J. Wilberding. Cambridge: Cambridge University Press.
Gilson, Étienne (1952). *Being and Some Philosophers*, 2nd edn. Toronto: Pontical Institute of Mediaeval Studies.
Gilson, Étienne (1954). *History of Christian Philosophy in the Middle Ages*. New York: Random House.
Green, W. M. (1970). St. Augustine, *De ordine*. Ed. W. M. Green. CCSL 29. Turnhout: Brepols.
Hadot, Pierre (1954). 'Marius Victorinus et Alcuin'. *Archives d'Histoire Doctrinale et Litteraire du Moyen Age* [AHDLMA] XXI: 5–19.
Hadot, Pierre (1960). Marius Victorinus, *Traités théologiques sur la Trinité*, 2 vols. Paris: Les Éditions du CERF.
Hankey, Wayne J. (1998). 'From Metaphysics to History, from Exodus to Neoplatonism, from Scholasticism to Pluralism: The Fate of Gilsonian Thomism in English-Speaking North America'. *Dionysius*, 16: 157–88.
Harrington, L. Michael (ed. and trans.) (2004). *A Thirteenth-Century Textbook of Mystical Theology at the University of Paris: The 'Mystical Theology' of Dionysius the Areopagite in Eriugena's Latin Translation with the Scholia translated by Anastasius the Librarian and Excerpts from Eriugena's 'Periphyseon'*. Leuven: Peeters.

Hedley, Douglas and Sarah Hutton (2008). *Platonism at the Origins of Modernity. Studies on Platonism and Early Modern Philosophy.* Dordrecht: Springer.

Heil, G. (1986). *Pseudo-Dionysius Areopagita. Uber die himmlische Hierarchie. Uber die Kirchliche Hierarchie.* Trans. G. Heil. Stuttgart: Hiersemann.

Hoffmann E and R. Klibansky (1932). Nicholas of Cusa *De docta ignorantia.* Ed. E. Hoffmann and R. Klibansky. Hamburg: Felix Meiner.

Hopkins, Jasper (1985). *Nicholas of Cusa on Learned Ignorance. A Translation and Appraisal of De Docta Ignorantia.* Minneapolis: Arthur J. Banning Press, 2nd edition.

Hopkins, Jasper (1987). *Nicholas of Cusa on God as Not Other: A Translation and an Appraisal of De Li Non Aliud.* Minneapolis: Arthur J. Banning Press, 3rd edition.

Jeauneau, Édouard (1969). *Jean Scot: L'Homélie sur le Prologue de Jean.* Sources Chrétiennes 151. Paris: Editions du Cerf.

Jeauneau, Édouard (1972). *Commentaire sur l'Evangile de Jean.* Sources Chrétiennes 180. Paris: Cerf.

Jeauneau, Édouard (1987). *Études érigéniennes.* Paris: Études Augustiniennes.

Jeauneau, Édouard (ed.) (1988). *Maximi Confessoris Ambigua ad Iohannem iuxta Iohannis Scotti Eriugenae latinam interpretationem.* Corpus Christianorum Series Graeca, 18. Turnout: Brepols. Leuven: Leuven University Press.

Jeauneau, Édouard, with the assistance of Mark A. Zier (eds) (1995). *Iohannis Scotti EriugenaePeriphyseon (De Divisione Naturae) Liber Quartus.* Trans. John J. O'Meara and I. P. Sheldon-Williams. Scriptores Latini Hiberniae Vol. XIII. Dublin: Dublin Institute for Advanced Studies.

Jeauneau, Édouard (ed.) (1996). *Iohannis Scotti seu Eriugenae Periphyseon,* liber primus, Corpus Christianorum Continuatio Medievalis 161. Turnhout: Brepols.

Jeauneau, Édouard (ed.) (1997a). *Iohannis Scotti seu Eriugenae Periphyseon,* liber secundus, Corpus Christianorum Continuatio Medievalis 162. Turnhout: Brepols.

Jeauneau, Édouard (1997b). 'Néant divin et théophanie'. In *Langages et philosophie: Hommage à Jean Jolivet.* Ed. Alain de Libera, Abdelali Elamrani-Jamal and Alain Galonnier. Paris: Vrin, pp. 331–7.

Jeauneau, Édouard (ed.) (1999). *Iohannis Scotti seu Eriugenae Periphyseon,* liber tertius, Corpus Christianorum Continuatio Medievalis 162. Turnhout: Brepols.

Jeauneau, Édouard (ed.) (2000). *Iohannis Scotti seu Eriugenae Periphyseon,* liber quartus, Corpus Christianorum Continuatio Medievalis 164. Turnhout: Brepols.

Jeauneau, Édouard (ed.) (2003). *Iohannis Scotti seu Eriugenae Periphyseon,* liber quintus, Corpus Christianorum Continuatio Medievalis 165. Turnhout: Brepols.

Koch, Joseph J. (1969). 'Augustinischer und Dionysischer Neuplatonismus und das Mittelalter'. In *Platonismus in der Philosophie des Mittelalters.* Ed. W. Beierwaltes. Darmstadt: Wissenschaftliche Buchgesellschaft, pp. 317–42.

Laga, Carl and Carlos Steel (eds) (1990). *Maximi Confessoris Quaestiones ad Thalassium II. Q. LVI-LXV una cum latina interpretatione Iohannies Scotti Eriugenae.* Corpus Christianorum Series Graeca, 22. Turnhout: Brepols. Leuven: Leuven University Press.

Lanzetta, Beverly J. (1992). 'Three Categories of Nothingness in Eckhart'. *The Journal of Religion,* 72/2: 248–68.

Lúibhéid, Colm (ed.) (1987). *Pseudo-Dionysius, The Complete Works.* Trans. Colm Luibheid. Foreword etc. by Paul Rorem. New York: Paulist Press.

McGinn, Bernard J. (1975). 'Negative Theology in John the Scot'. *Studia Patristica,* 13: 232–8.

Marenbon, John (1981). *From the Circle of Alcuin to the School of Auxerre: Logic, Theology and Philosophy in the Early Middle Ages.* Cambridge. Cambridge University Press.

Maritain, Jacques (1931). *St. Thomas Aquinas.* Trans. F. J. Scanlan. London: Sheed and Ward.

Moran, Dermot (1989). *The Philosophy of John Scottus Eriugena. A Study of Idealism in the Middle Ages.* Cambridge: Cambridge University Press.

Moran, Dermot (1990). 'Pantheism from John Scottus Eriugena to Nicholas of Cusa'. *American Catholic Philosophical Quarterly,* LXIV/1: 131–52.

Moran, Dermot (1992a). 'Origen and Eriugena: Aspects of Christian Gnosis'. In *The Relationship Between Neoplatonism and Christianity.* Ed. T. Finan and V. Twomey. Dublin: Four Courts Press.

Moran, Dermot (1992b). 'Time, Space and Matter in the *Periphyseon*: An Examination of Eriugena's Understanding of the Physical World'. In *At the Heart of the Real*. Ed. F. O'Rourke. Dublin: Irish Academic Press.

Moran, Dermot (1996). 'Eriugena's Theory of Language in the *Periphyseon*: Explorations in the Neoplatonic Tradition'. In *Ireland and Europe in the Early Middle Ages IV. Language and Learning*. Ed. Próinséas Ní Chatháin and Michael Richter. Frankfurt: Klett-Cotta, pp. 240–60.

Moran, Dermot (1999). 'Idealism in Medieval Philosophy: The Case of Johannes Scottus Eriugena'. *Medieval Philosophy and Theology*, 8: 3–82.

Moran, Dermot (2008). 'Nicholas of Cusa (1401–1464): Platonism at the Dawn of Modernity'. In *Platonism at the Origins of Modernity: Studies on Platonism and Early Modern Philosophy*. Ed. Douglas Hedley and Sarah Hutton. Dordrecht: Springer, pp. 9–29.

Moulin, Isabelle (2016). *Théologie et Philosophie Chez Jean Scot Erigène*. Paris: Vrin.

O'Meara, John J. (1969). *Eriugena*. Cork: Mercier Press.

O'Meara, John J. (1988). *Eriugena*. Oxford: Clarendon Press.

Otten, Willemien (1991). *The Anthropology of Johannes Scottus Eriugena*. Leiden: Brill.

Piemonte, Gustavo A. (1968). 'Notas sobre la *Creatio de Nihilo* en Juan Escoto Eriúgena'. *Sapientia*, 23/87: 37–58.

Piemonte, Gustao A. (1986). 'L'expression *quae sunt et quae non sunt*: Jean Scot et Marius Victorinus'. In *Jean Scot Ecrivain*. Ed. G.-H. Allard. Paris and Montreal: Vrin and Bellarmin, pp. 81–113.

Rorem, Paul (2005). *Eriugena's Commentary on the Dionysian Celestial Hierarchy*. Toronto: Pontifical Institute of Advanced Studies.

Sezgin, Fuat (2000). *Proclus Arabus and the Liber de Causis (Burûklûs 'inda l-'Arab wa-kitâb al-îdâh fî l-khayr al-mahd)*. Frankfurt am Main: Institute for the History of Arabic-Islamic Science at the Johann Wolfgang Goethe University.

Sheldon-Williams, I.-P. (ed.) (1968). *Iohannis Scotti Eriugenae Periphyseon (De Divisione Naturae)* Book One. Dublin: Dublin Institute for Advanced Studies.

Sheldon-Williams, I.-P. (1970a). 'The Greek Platonist Tradition from the Cappadocians to Maximus and Eriugena'. In *The Cambridge History of Later Greek and Early Medieval Thought*. Ed. A. H. Armstrong. Cambridge: Cambridge University Press.

Sheldon-Williams, I.-P. (ed.) (1970b). *Iohannis Scotti Eriugenae Periphyseon (De Divisione Naturae)* Book Two. Dublin: Dublin Institute for Advanced Studies.

Sheldon-Williams, I.-P. (ed.) (1981). *Iohannis Scotti Eriugenae Periphyseon (De Divisione Naturae)* Book Three. Dublin: Dublin Institute for Advanced Studies.

Sheldon-Williams, I.-P. and O'Meara, J. J. (trans) (1987). *Eriugena. Periphyseon (The Division of Nature)*. Montreal and Paris: Bellarmin.

Sheldon-Williams, I.-P. (ed.), with Mark Zier (1995). *Iohannis Scotti Eriugenae Periphyseon (De Divisione Naturae)* Book Four. Dublin: Dublin Institute for Advanced Studies.

Stewart, H. F., E. K. Rand and S. J. Tester (1918). Boethius, *Tractates, De Consolatione Philosophiae*. Trans. H. F. Stewart, E. K. Rand, S. J. Tester. Loeb Classical Library Harvard: Heinemann.

Suchla, Beate (1990). Pseudo-Dionysius Areopagita. *De Divinis Nominibus*. Ed. Beate Suchla. Regina Series: Patristische Texte und Studien 33. Berlin: De Gruyter.

8

Medieval Semiotics and Philosophy of Language (Ninth to Fourteenth Centuries)

Costantino Marmo

Introduction

The Middle Ages represent a rich period of explicit theories about signs and language, worked out not only in the field of the *trivium*[1] (above all grammar and logic), but also in that of theology and natural philosophy. There are many theoretical starting points: for the definition of sign and its classification, the main authority is undoubtedly Augustine of Hippo's *De doctrina christiana* (and to a lesser extent his *De Dialectica* and *De magistro*); for the theories of language, on the one hand, we can point to Aristotle's *De interpretatione* in the translation and interpretation, strongly influenced by Porphyry and imbued with Neoplatonism, proposed by Manlius Severinus Boethius (sixth century), and on the other hand to the Latin grammatical treatises by Donatus and Priscian. The reflections on signs and language are strictly intertwined, starting from these texts, producing a mass of diverse and original theories. In what follows, given the limits of space, we will be able to give a full account neither of all the medieval contributions, nor of the numerous studies that have made them known to scholars, limiting ourselves to touching upon the main authors and currents between the ninth and the fourteenth centuries, starting with a theologian who, in the ninth century, was decisive for the imposition of the Augustinian model in semiotics.

1. Discussions of the Eucharist and Signs (Ninth–Eleventh Centuries)

The first debate on the Eucharist takes place in the abbey of Corbie, in the north of France, and begins with a work by the monk Paschasius Radbertus (later abbot of Corbie), who in his treatise *De corpore et sanguine Domini* (831–3), proposes a genuine novelty in theology: the theory of the substantial transformation of bread and wine into the body and blood of Christ during the celebration of the Eucharistic rite. Around the year 843, Paschasius produces a copy of this treatise dedicating it to King Charles the Bald who (perhaps on the occasion of a visit to the abbey in that same year) addresses to another monk, Ratramnus, some questions related

---

[1] In medieval culture *trivium* indicated, as a whole, the disciplines that dealt with language, namely grammar, logic and rhetoric, as opposed to the mathematical disciplines of the *quadrivium* (arithmetic, geometry, music and astronomy).

to the thesis of his abbot: he asks if 'the body and blood of Christ who, in church, the mouth of the faithful assumes . . . is realized through a mystery (*in mysterio*), or in truth (*in veritate*)'.[2] The opposition around which the discussion revolves is that between *figura* and *veritas*; the difference between the two monks lies in the fact that according to Paschasius this opposition, precisely in the Eucharistic sacrament, is reconciled, whereas according to Ratramnus it does not find any conciliation and what happens in the sacrament takes place *in figura* (or *in mysterio*) and not *in veritate*.

The opposition between the two points of view is not only theological but also semiotic in nature. If Ratramnus, on one side, proposes a rather traditional conception of the sign, inspired by Augustine (but without quoting his definition[3]), in which the sign is also ontologically distinct from its meaning (it is an *aliquid aliud*), and a notion of *figura* as allegorical discourse, true in the sense translated but false in the literal sense (following the tradition of biblical exegesis), Paschasius consciously proposes a notion of sign that is anomalous with respect to the Augustinian tradition and manages to reconcile through it the opposition between *figura* and *veritas*. However, this conciliation is based on the polysemy of the term *figura*, which, according to Paschasius, 'is not only shadow or falsity' (1969: IV, 29: 'Non enim omnis figura umbra uel falsitas'). In fact, this term is not only used in exegetical context to interpret the events and persons of the Old Testament as anticipations of those of the New Testament, but also in grammatical milieus, where it indicates a feature of language that takes the name of *character*. This is the property of the *littera* (elementary linguistic sound or phoneme, as we would say nowadays) that allows the transcription, that is its visualisation through a (alphabetic) graphic device. It is in this sense that the *figura* or *character* assumes a particular semiotic value in Paschasius's interpretation: 'This species [of sign] is very famous among the Grammarians, so that saying "sign" one indicates something that now does not mean anything beyond itself.'[4]

The relationship between the graphic device and its vocal correlate (between grapheme and phoneme, as we would say nowadays), which was traditionally acknowledged from Aristotle onwards as a signification relation holding between two distinct entities, is almost nullified since the sign means nothing other than itself. The novelty with respect to the Augustinian conception of the sign is evident, and it is functional to the theological novelty introduced by Paschasius: in the Eucharist, the substantial transformation of the bread into Christ's body and of the wine into His blood makes the sign and the meaning coexistent in the same thing, thus making them (almost) identical, just as the Son and the Father are identical in the Trinity or the *character* or *figura* and the *littera* in our language. The figures of the letters, or their graphic expressions or characters – explains Paschasius – serve to make visible what in our pronunciation are the aspiration and the value (vocalic or consonantal) of the elementary linguistic sounds. Paschasius attributes to the grammarians the idea that between alphabetic letters and the elementary sounds of a language there exists a biunivocal relation, so narrow as to reduce the mutual distinction, similarly to what happens between

---

[2] 'Quod in ecclesia ore fidelium sumitur corpus et sanguis christi quaerit vestrae magnitudinis excelentia in misterio fiat, an in veritate' (Ratramnus of Corbie 1954: 44).
[3] 'Signum est res, praeter speciem quam ingerit sensibus, aliquid aliud ex se faciens in cogitationem venire' (A sign is a thing that of itself causes something else to enter into thought beyond the appearance it presents to the senses) (Augustine of Hippo 1962: II.1.1).
[4] 'Quae speciaes [sic] apud Gramaticos notissima est ut dicatur signum res quae iam nihil ultra de se signat sed quia signi formam olim praemissam in se repraesentat' (Paschasius Radbertus 1984: 793).

the Son and the Father in the Trinity or between Christ's human and divine nature. In all these cases, there is a relationship of unity so close as to 'narcotise', almost to cancel, the distinction between signifier and signified. It seems to me that we can speak, therefore, of an (almost) identity between signifier and significance that brings Paschasius's semiotics much beyond the Augustinian theory of signs (to which Ratramnus of Corbie essentially adheres in his critiques).

The case of Eucharistic bread and wine is analogous to those mentioned above: what is perceived, that is, the sensitive features of bread and wine, is a figure or *character* of Christ's body and blood that are really present after the consecration and from which the believer is nourished, not only spiritually, but also physically. The incarnation of Christ and the preservation of the sensitive appearances of bread and wine in the Eucharist would have a purely pedagogical meaning according to Paschasius, analogous to the function of the letters of the alphabet: as we children learn the relationship between letters and sounds we come slowly to reading and then gradually ascend to the spiritual understanding of the Scriptures, so – thanks to the unity of human and divine substances in Christ – we can pass from the humanity of Christ to the divinity of the Father, and from the species of bread and wine to the truth of Christ's body and blood. On the other hand, the (almost) identity between signifier and signified thing, due to the real and physical presence of Christ's body and blood under the Eucharistic species, is what makes possible the temporary unveiling of the mystery in the miracles narrated by Paschasius (1969: XIV, 85–92): miracles that show what would be normal after the Eucharistic consecration, if this did not run the risk of producing horror in believers – as suggested in an Epistle sent to one of his own disciples some years later – and execration and condemnation by the pagans. Like that of Ratramnus of Corbie, the first reactions by contemporary theologians, like Rabanus Maurus or like John Eriugena, were not favourable. Two centuries later, the balance would have completely overturned in favour of Paschasius's thesis (Marmo 2005, 2008).

The protagonists of the revival of the debate in the eleventh century are Berengar of Tours, who takes up and deepens the positions of Ratramnus (whose book, by the way, is attributed to John Eriugena) and Lanfranc of Pavia, who defends the position of Paschasius Radbertus, now considered as the orthodox position by the Roman Curia (Berengar is in fact condemned twice to abjuration). Berengar of Tours, in a letter to his friend Adelman of Liège (before 1059), specifies the untenability of Paschasius's thesis. Berengar rejects them with arguments of a physical, linguistic and, more generally, semiotic nature.

The former are based on the impossibility, in the framework of the Aristotelian ontology, that there can be accidents without a substratum, or that a substance can be destroyed while its accidents continue to exist, and that the body of Christ could be created from nothing at each consecration, when – on the contrary – He sits instead *ab aeterno* to the right of the Father. The only possible conversion for bread and wine is their transformation into signs (or sacraments) that signify Christ in his integrity: a conversion that is not material or sensible, but intellectual and spiritual (see Rosier-Catach 1996: 51).

In the arguments of linguistic nature, Berengar advances semantic reflections on the value of the copula (analogous to those that will be discussed in the following century in the glosses on Prisciano and by Abelard) and on the literal or figurative value to be attributed to the terms at play in the consecration formulas. According to Berengar, none of the propositions proposed for his abjuration by the Roman Curia is sustainable: the first ('the bread and wine after the consecration are *only* sacraments') because, if bread and wine are sacraments and therefore signs, they are signs of something and therefore they cannot be *only* sacraments; the second (reformulated by Berengar as 'the bread and the wine of the altar is *only* the true body and blood of Christ') is simply false.[5] In both propositions, Berengar emphasises, referring to a logical rule, that it is assumed that bread and wine maintain their existence: according to this rule it is not possible that an affirmation be true if one of its parts (subject or predicate) is missing (that is, it has no existing referent). If you say 'Socrates is', this implies that Socrates exists; if you says 'Socrates is right', you assume that Socrates exists, otherwise you could not even attribute to him the property in question (Berengar of Tours 1988: I, 61 and 66). Both propositions contained in Berengar's recanting formula (even the one that corresponds to the most extreme Eucharistic realism) cannot help but presuppose the existence of bread and wine (in their substance) even after their consecration. In addition to these propositions, the classical formula of consecration (*Hoc est corpus meum*) is subjected to a similar linguistic analysis: the demonstrative pronoun *hoc* should be interpreted as equivalent to *hic panis* (this bread), and the term *panis* should not be taken in a figurative sense (as Lanfranc claims) but in its proper sense; what is to be understood metaphorically is rather the predicate *corpus*, just as the predicates of propositions such as 'Christ is the cornerstone' (1988: I, 73; II, 173) should be interpreted figuratively.

The arguments of semiotic nature have at their centre the explicit resumption of Augustine's definition of sign and rely on Ratramnus's positions according to which Christ is present *in figura* and not *in veritate*, and for which the Eucharistic sacrament is a sign, an image, a similitude of Christ, not as physically present, but as spiritually attainable for the believer through the sacrament. Berengar compares the Eucharist to baptism and argues that as in the first case water does not change into something substantially different, but becomes a sign of Christ's death, thus assuming a spiritual meaning, so in the Eucharist bread and wine are not substantially transformed but only converted into signs. In support of his thesis, Berengar collects a dossier of Augustinian quotations, among which is the definition of sign of his *De doctrina christiana* (II.1.1). As pointed out by Irène Rosier-Catach (1996: 52), for Berengar every word of this definition is crucial: 'the sensitive nature of the sign, the idea that, starting from what it is (*ex se*), something else is produced (this implies that the sign cannot be the body of Christ), and finally that all this is realized for the mind (*cogitatio*)'. Berengar, in fact, glosses Augustine's definition in this way: 'he does not say: [the sign is a thing that, beyond its sensitive features, starting from itself puts something else] in the hand, in the mouth, on the teeth or in the womb, but in mind'.[6] The body of Christ is not the sacrament', but rather the *res sacramenti*, its invisible meaning, only intellectually or spiritually attainable. Berengar also emphasises the relational nature of the sacrament (and of the sign): it has a sensitive pole, the bread and the wine, which subsist as such after the consecration and are essentially distinct from their meaning, namely Christ's body and blood.

Lanfranc of Pavia, unlike Berengar, does not seem fully aware of what is at stake on a semiotic level, and in fact he does not offer any reply on this front, but simply accepts Augustine's definition of sign without grasping its possible incompatibility with Paschasius's positions. On the contrary, one of the main protagonists of the second debate on the Eucharist seems to be well aware of it. Among the most eminent characters in the ecclesial hierarchy who contributed to the condemnations of Berengar of Tours, we find Humbert of Silva Candida, cardinal of

---

[5] 'Ego Berengarius . . . anathematizo omnem haeresim, praecipue eam . . . quae astruere conatur panem et vinum, quae in altare ponuntur, post consecrationem solummodo sacramenta esse, et non verum corpus Christi et sanguinem' (Berengar of Tours, *Rescriptum* 1988: I, 64).

[6] '(. . .) non ait: in manum, in os, in dentem, in ventrem, sed in cogitationem' (*Epist. ad Adelmannum*, in Montclos 1971: 532).

Ostia. In one of his works against the simoniacs, he takes on Paschasius's conceptions and, when he opposes the sacraments of the heretics to those of the Catholics, proposes a notion of sign that corresponds exactly to that recalled by Paschasius in his treatise and is exemplified in his texts by notion of *character*. The sacraments for Humbert 'are signs so as to be things too . . . [i]n fact they mean what they are and have in themselves' (*ita signa sunt ut sint etiam res. Nam quod sunt et in se habent, significant*). Such sacraments, he adds, 'are signs in such a way as to be things in a true and essential sense' (*sic signa sunt ut res quoque essentialiter et vere sint*.) (*Adversus simoniacos*, 188–9). Precisely this identity between sign and meaning, *signum* and *res*, justifies, on the one hand, the heated opposition of Humbert against the positions that are considered valid and not replicating the sacraments imparted by heretics and, on the other, the text of the abjuration imposed to Berengar at the Council of Rome in 1059.

The dossier of Augustinian quotations elaborated by Berengar, as underlined by Montclos (1971), was resumed at the end of the eleventh century and at the beginning of the next by Ivo of Chartres and Gratian (the fathers of canon law), by Abelard (in his *Sic et non*), until it reached Peter Lombard, whose definition of sacrament, in the fourth book of his *Sententiae*, would represent the basis of discussions on the sacraments over the following centuries (see Marmo 2007). Re-established paradoxically by the heretic Berengar, the Augustinian definition of sign becomes a point of obligatory reference and the starting point of the subsequent sacramental theology.

2. Anselm of Canterbury: Language and Signs

Anselm of Canterbury (1033/4–1109) merges the Augustinian and the Aristotelian-Boethian theories of meaning and will have a certain following between the thirteenth and fourteenth centuries (Panaccio 1999a). On the one hand, from Augustine's *De trinitate* he takes up the idea that three levels of language exist: the spoken one, the mental one (which is reproduction or image of the spoken language), and the one that cannot be referred to any historical language (*nullius linguae*) and that is made up of inner words or concepts. On the other hand, from Aristotle's *De interpretatione* and Boethius's commentaries on it he takes up the idea that the concepts are natural similitudes or images of things, the same for everyone and therefore universal (Anselm 1968d: 10): the words of the spoken languages were established to signify the inner ones, the concepts, which reflect the universal essences of things and are all the more true the more they resemble the signified things. In inner mental language, words constitute propositional complexes, which are the meanings of spoken propositions, whose truth is discussed – together with the more general problem of the truth of signs – in a dialogue *On the truth* (Anselm 1968b: 2). Anselm argues that the truth of an assertion can be understood in two very different ways: in a first sense (which we might call 'logical'), it is identical with its truth conditions, that is, the state of things that makes it true; in another sense (a 'semiotic' one), it is not at all identical with its conditions of truth (see King 2004a: 102) since these are changeable, but it rather consists in signifying what it must mean by the force of its institution, or in what Anselm calls its 'correctness' (*rectitudo*). The truth of an affirmative sentence, in this sense, consists in meaning something existing that exists (*significat esse quod est*), and also of a negative one in meaning something non-existing that does not exist (*significat non esse quod non est*). The truth or correctness of a proposition, in this sense, is therefore immutable, natural and independent of its use (in every circumstance of enunciation, an assertion always means that which has been instituted to mean, regardless of its truth value); in the first sense, however, it is changeable, accidental and dependent on its use (under certain circumstances of enunciation, an assertion is true because there exists or does not exist what it claims to exist or not exist, and it is false otherwise). In the case of necessary (or always true) propositions, such as 'man is a rational animal' or 'man is not a stone' – as Anselm underlines – the two senses of truth and correctness coincide. In other cases, the correctness of signification is presupposed by the truth, in its logical sense, of the assertion.

Anselm's appeal to the linguistic usage (*usus loquendi*) is rather frequent in his works, in particular in his *De grammatico*, the only dialogue by Anselm explicitly about logical and semantic arguments. It deals with a specific problem, namely whether one should classify, according to the Aristotelian categories, the term *grammaticus* (or its meaning) among the substances or the qualities, on the example of other paronym words, such as 'white' (*album*), which derives from another term ('whiteness', *albedo*); they differ in their terminations (*Categories* 1). The problem is that the term 'whiteness' (or its meaning) falls into the category of quality, while the individual in which it exists (or inheres) falls into the category of substance. The question is therefore whether *grammaticus* means the literate person, who has competence in the written language (that is, what the grammarians call 'substance'), or the competence itself (that is, the 'quality' of the grammarians), regardless of the one who owns it. Anselm's answer (through the teacher's lines) is that the term *grammaticus* signifies directly, or by itself (*per se*), the grammar and signifies only indirectly (*per aliud*) the person who is endowed with it. Anselm calls the secondary signification of the concrete terms (1968a: 12) *appellatio* – the term will have its own particular story in the subsequent centuries. The term *grammaticus* (or rather its meaning), for this reason, should be classified among the qualities and not among the substances, unlike terms such as 'man' or 'stone' which, being nouns, signify both principally and secondarily (that is, they mean and 'appeal' to) some substances.

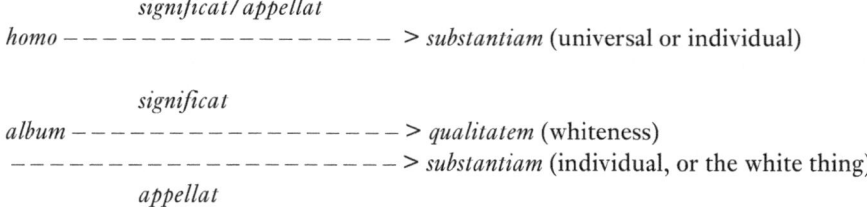

Fig. 8.1 Significatio and appellatio

Some scholars tried to interpret this distinction between signification and appellation in the light of that introduced by John S. Mill (1843) between connotation and denotation, or that proposed by Frege (1892) between *Sinn* (sense) and *Bedeutung* (reference), but in both cases the comparison does not work. Even if appellation for the concrete accidental terms (*grammaticus* or *album*) indicates the substratum of the quality (the person who possesses the grammar or that which is white), and therefore a concrete individual (though undetermined), in the case of the names of substance (such as *homo*) appellation is identical with its own signification and is essentially addressed to the universal (humanity, which in turn is individualised in every single human being). Given the connections that *appellatio* shows with *usus* in Anselm's texts, McCord Adams (2000) proposed to interpret it in the light of the contemporary pragmatic notion of reference, as an act of referring to something or someone through language. In his *De grammatico*, in fact, Anselm makes use of various examples to show how a concrete accidental term like 'white' – which in itself would mean nothing else than the quality of whiteness – can be used in particular contexts and circumstances to indicate a particular substance, like a horse. Let us say, for instance, that in a house there is a white horse and you do not know it; if someone tells you 'there's something white in the house' (*in domo est album vel albus*), do you think you know that it is actually a horse? The answer cannot be but negative, according to the theory of signification *per se* of concrete accidental names described above: if the term *albus* also meant its bearer (the substance), its knowledge should at least be inferred; if, instead, this is not possible, then the term will not signify the substance. At this point, the circumstances of enunciation and the knowledge derived from previous experiences or shared between the interlocutors, which can be taken for granted when an act of reference is realised, come into play. If, finding yourself in a stable with two horses, a white and a black one, someone tells you 'Give a blow to the horse' without making any explanatory sign, you would not be able to execute the order because you would not know which one to strike; but if he/she adds 'To the white one', you would immediately understand it, not because white means its bearer *per se*, but because it means it indirectly (*per aliud*), because you know that there is a white horse in the stable (Anselm 1968a: 14).

The knowledge provided by the environment (or the circumstances of enunciation) becomes crucial in order to implement a reference act (and correctly execute the order to give the horse a blow). Referring to the horse, in the above described situation, using only the name 'white' would be incorrect from the strictly semantic point of view (*per se* meaning), but it is correct from the pragmatic point of view or linguistic usage, since it effectively discriminates the white horse from the black and allows the interlocutor to recognise it. Anselm says that paronym words work in a similar way: if from them, from a strictly semantic point of view, it is not possible to infer the named object (what we call white or literate, or the object to which one can refer with these terms), from a pragmatic point of view this becomes possible; if from a semantic point of view one cannot infer 'if x is literate, then it is a human' (and we know very well that no other animal can be), this is plausible from a pragmatic point of view or from the point of view of its use. Anselm's reluctance to recognise the legitimacy of certain inferences, based on the knowledge of the natural course of events, and the need to make semantic analysis more stringent, are probably justified by the needs of the theological discourse (Eucharistic and Trinitarian questions, mainly, on which it would be too long to dwell here), but the interesting aspect of the question is that Anselm does not throw the baby out with the bathwater: the reference to the *appellatio* and the *usus loquendi*, far from being derogatory, paves the way for a broader consideration of the analysis of linguistic meaning, which will produce considerable fruit in the subsequent centuries (see Marmo 2011, 2016).

3. Abelard: Universals and Individuals

The philosophy of Peter Abelard (1079–1142) represents one of the cornerstones of medieval philosophy, in all fields, including that of logic and philosophy of language (see Marenbon 1997; Brower and Guilfoy 2004). Abelard develops his own theory of universals, in particular, opposing the two extremes of vocalism, advocated by his master Roscelin of Compiègne, and of realism, in the different forms proposed by another of his masters, William of Champeaux. In a nutshell, Roscelin supports two related theses, which can be summarised as follows: (1) a whole is not really made up of parts: these do not exist, because only the whole exists; (2) the universal is only a *flatus vocis* (a bare utterance). The first thesis has the consequence that the words denoting a complex object (like a house) no longer designate the same reality if it misses one of its parts (the roof, for instance): in this case it will be necessary to call it an incomplete-house (Jolivet 1992: 126–7). The second thesis, on the other hand, should be interpreted as a metalinguistic assertion: universal terms (like Porphyry's predicables, such as *genus* and *species*) do not refer to any really existing entity, but apply to other names (cf. de Libera 1996: 155):

this implies that universal terms, such as *homo* (human being) or *canis* (dog), refer to individual human beings (Socrates, Plato, etc.) or to individual dogs (Fido, Bailey, Duke, etc.), but not to any common essence that individuals could actually share. Roscelin's positions on the nature of universals attracted the condemnation of Anselm of Canterbury, who reproached him for impeding himself from understanding the relations between the persons of the Trinity: 'If you do not understand how a plurality of man, how will you understand how, in that secret and highest nature, a plurality of persons, of whom each is perfectly God, are one and the same God?'[7] Abelard, while sharing the position that denies the existence of universals and only admits that of individuals, does not accept both the reduction of universals to *flatus vocis* and the rigidity of Roscelin's theory of whole and its parts (mereology). According to Abelard, in fact, the separation of a part from its whole does not change the essence of the whole: a man without a hand is still a man (1987: III.20.6).

The realist theory of universals on the other hand, developed from the observations of Porphyry and Boethius's commentaries, bears strong links with the theory of linguistic signification and predication. It generally maintains that: (1) genera and species are really existing things (*res*); consequently, (2) there is something beyond the individual and perceivable entities; and, therefore, (3) in predication, not only words, but also things, come into play as meanings of those predicates. Abelard repeatedly attacks William of Champeaux, even causing him to change his mind and to move from a theory of universals as material essences to that of their indifference (de Libera 1996: 150). If the first theory recognises in the universal thing an identical material essence that is contracted in its individuals thanks to some accidental forms or properties (King 2004b: 66–7), for the second the individual things are not identical because of a common essence but because of the indifference that the universal has with respect to its individuals: Socrates is identical to the species of man as he is indifferently equal to any other men (de Libera 1996: 150–1; King 2004b: 71). After examining the paradoxes that both theories imply, Abelard works out his own theory that, keeping only the real existence of individuals, maintains that the universal is a meaningful word (*sermo* or *nomen*) and that only names and not the signified things enter predication (de Libera 1996: 152). In his theory of signification, Abelard argues that a universal term primarily means an act of understanding that is aimed at an image that resembles equally all the individuals that are named by that term (Martin 2009: 196). Names (and verbs) have in fact a double signification: they can signify the concepts (*significatio de intellectibus*), which are their meanings, and can signify the individual things (*significatio de rebus*) that they name or refer to. A universal term such as *homo* names individual men with respect to a common cause, that is, that they have in common their being-human (*esse hominem*): this being-human is also called *status hominis* (*human condition*); it is not a property falling under one of the Aristotelian categories, but is simply the cause of the imposition of that name on human individuals (Abelard 1919: 19–20).

A similar ontological statute is also reserved by Abelard to the meanings of propositions (on which, see Guilfoy 2004; Marenbon 2004; Rosier-Catach 2004a). The *propositiones*, that is to say the expressions vocally expressed (propositional sentences, as John Marenbon translates – see Marenbon 2004: 59, note 2), like names and verbs, have a double signification: one is directed to the concepts, and one is directed to the things about which they speak (Abelard 1970: II, 154; *Log. Ingredientibus, Sup. Peri Herm.*, 367). The general concept of a proposition derives

---

[7] 'Qui enim nondum intelligit quomodo plures homines in specie sint unus homo: qualiter in illa secretissima et altissima natura comprehendet quomodo plures personae, quarum singula quaeque perfectus est deus, sint unus deus?' (Anselm of Canterbury 1968c: 1, 10).

from a triple action of our mind: with the first two our mind turns its attention (*attentio*, a concept of Augustinian origin, see Rosier-Catach 2004a: 19–23) to the concepts of its parts (names and verbs, or subject and predicate); with its third action, our mind focuses on the syntactic-semantic connection between subject and predicate (*iunctura*), a connection conveyed by the *copula* (it is with Abelard that we begin to use this term with reference to verb *est*, third person singular, present, indicative of the verb *esse*, to be, see Rosier-Catach 2003: 187) or by a conjunction (Abelard 2010: 330; cf. Rosier-Catach 2004a: 23). However, when one evaluates the truth value of an assertion, such as *homo currit* (a human being is running), one does not refer to any concepts or their union, but to the fact that in reality things are as asserted by the proposition. Here certain problems arise: what does the proposition mean in its second kind of signification, that is, that directed to things? Does the proposition designate or refer to the things (which are only individuals in Abelard's ontology) to which its categorical parts refer? Or does it refer to something different? Abelard's answers to these questions are different in his two main logical works, his *Dialectica* and his *Glosses on the Peri hermeneias*. In the first one, he holds that assertive statements, verbally expressed, do not designate things in the same way names denote things but rather indicate how these things relate to each other, so that a proposition is called 'true' when it indicates things as they are in reality (*in re*), without designating any individual thing in particular. What an assertive statement (affirmative or negative) proposes or expresses is not a thing, but it is 'almost a way of relating things' (*quasi quidam rerum modus habendi se*) (Abelard 1970: II, 160). In his second work, probably a later one, Abelard gives the name of *dicta* (plural of *dictum*) to these propositional meanings and also stresses that these are not things (*res*), but they are indeed nothing (*nullae penitus essentiae sint*): they must be considered in the same way as things related to the utterance (*sunt quasi res propositionum*) (2010: 367–70). It is not so important, in my view, how we translate the word *dictum* – some translated and interpreted them as 'facts', others as 'contents of thought', 'propositions' or 'states of things' – or whether we consider them as the starting point or the point of arrival of an evolution of Abelard's thought: these 'realities' enjoy a particular ontological status, similar to that attributed to the images that populate our dreams (2010: 314–15; cf. Rosier-Catach 2004a: 18).

4. Theological Language and Ordinary Language in the Porretan School

Gilbert of Poitiers, a theologian active in Paris in the 1130s and 1140s, inaugurates a fruitful reflection on the semantic potentials of human language, inspired by texts from the Platonic tradition (especially Boethius's theological treatises, *De trinitate* and *De hebdomadibus*). The premises, accepted by Gilbert and his followers, are substantially two: (1) what exists, from the point of view of natural science and philosophy, derives from some form and comes into being by participating in it; (2) (ordinary) language reflects this ontological derivation in the phenomenon of *denominatio* (paronymy), according to which the qualifications attributed to existing objects signify, first, the forms from which they derive (*id quo est*) and, second, the objects that play the role of substrata of those forms (*id quod est*) (see de Rijk 1988, 1989; Spruyt 2000; Valente 2008: 123–49). From these premises Gilbert draws some conclusions on the language of theology. In the first place, when we speak of God, our language, established to refer to existing objects, composed of substratum and form, is transferred from its proper sense to an improper, since God is absolutely simple: when we say *homo est iustus* (A human being is just) and *Deus est iustus* (God is just) there is a difference in the use of the predicate: talking about human beings, *iustus* means justice (namely the form or quality from which participation a human being can be called 'just') and the human being as two distinct entities, whereas in the case of God the same adjective means the divine essence as a whole, since the divine essence coincides with justice in itself. From this a second conclusion is derived (in apparent contradiction with the previous one), namely that from a theological point of view some words (such as 'being', 'good' or 'just') speak more properly of God than of creatures: these in fact exist and are good and just only because of the divine Goodness and Justice from which their qualifications derive. The contradiction between the two statements is only apparent because the points of view adopted can be different: that of the philosopher in the first case, and that of the theologian in the second. In theology, things are good because they derive from the *primum bonum* and are called 'good' through a multiple process: denominative translation, morphological derivation and, finally, metaphorical transposition (which Gilbert, following the anonymous *Rhetorica to Herennium*, calls 'metonymy'). Despite the recognition of the inadequacy of language to deal with the divine sphere – with its illustrious neoplatonic precedents – the attitude of Gilbert towards the possibility of speaking and knowing the divine through human language is positive, unlike other contemporaries such as Theodoric of Chartres (see Valente 2008: 150–7).

Among Gilbert's followers, exponents of the so-called 'Porretan school', Simon of Tournai and Alan of Lille develop the reflections of their teacher, showing that he shares his basic semantic platonism ('every word is [. . .] established starting from a form', in Valente 2008: 198) and his theory of *denominatio*; they appear however to be more influenced by the Pseudo-Dionysian negative theology, which leads them to underline the radical inadequacy of human language to express the divine truths, and therefore the fundamental impropriety of the theological language. As Alan of Lille claims: 'All the affirmative statements about God are improper, and all the negative ones are true' (1981: XVIII).

5. Simon of Tournai's General Semiotics

The sections of the theological works dedicated to the sacraments, as hinted at above, in the second half of the twelfth century become the classical place in which Augustine's definition and classification of signs is revived.[8] Also Simone of Tournai – in his *Institutiones in sacram paginam* (c. 1165–1170, still unpublished),[9] a work, articulated in eight parts or *distinctiones*, which aims to introduce the study of theology and of the Holy Scriptures – follows this tradition (in *d*. 8, dedicated to the sacraments), but precedes the entire work with an introduction centred on the discussion of the different modes of signification that shows an interesting interweaving of sources and themes (from Augustine to Aristotle's so called *nova logica*) and can be considered the first explicit treatise of general semiotics.

The introductory part of Simon's *Institutiones* opens with the distinction, traditional in theology, between two ways of signifying, that of the voice (or of human language) and that of things. Besides the signification of words 'there is also another kind of signification, that of a thing compared to another thing, when one thing is signified by another thing [. . .] For the vulgar, in fact, the circle [of a wine cask] means the wine for sale' (*Est et alia significatio rei ad rem, quando res significatur alia re . . . Vulgo etiam significat circulus vinum venale*) (*d*. 1, § 2, in Marmo 1997a: 95). Simon, however, goes much further than the tradition, building below this simple distinction a complex classification of the different ways of signifying (see Marmo 1997b), which on the side of the signification of words includes the tripartition of the types of discourse proposed by Cicero in his *De inventione* (I.19), between *fabula*, *argumentum* and *historia*, while on the other side, that of the signification of things, he proposes a more complex articulation.

---

[8] On the relations between theology and logic in the twelfth century, cf. Valente (2008).
[9] A critical edition was prepared by Francesco Siri (2011, PhD dissertation with a provisional critical edition of Simon's text). On the dating of the *Institutiones*, cf. Siri (2011: 33–6).

In the first place, Simon proposes the different ways in which things signify, which was traditional in biblical exegesis: on the basis of the characters of the things mentioned in the Scriptures, these things can take the place of other things (material and spiritual), thus conveying further meanings: for example, King David is interpreted as an anticipation and a figure of Christ both because of the meaning of his name in Hebrew and because of the characters and behaviour of his person. It is under this type of signification that some of the traditional senses attributed to Scripture fall (three or four depending on the author, see Valente 1995). Alongside these modes of signification, Simon lists and illustrates others that are used in all disciplines (*in omni facultate*), and not only in theology (d. 1, § 4.2.1, in Marmo 1997a: 101). These are the meanings 'in a thing' (*in re*) and 'from a thing' (*ex re*), as when we understand, for instance, the concept of animal in that of human being, or when we understand something starting from one thing (*ex re*), and this can happen either according to a relation of opposition (*ratione oppositionis*) or according to a relation of consequentiality (*ratione consecutionis*).

In the first case, inspired by *Categories* 10, it is possible to signify something from the opposite (black from white), a privation from the corresponding disposition or habit (blindness from sight), and the term of a relationship from the correlated term (the son from his father). The second type of *ex re* signification is further subdivided into two subtypes that correspond to two categories of natural signs indicated in d. 8 (as said above, dedicated to the sacraments): for instance, when starting from something earlier (*antecedens* is used here in a temporal and not logical sense) you understand something that is next (from the set table you can infer that probably someone is going to eat), or vice versa (if you see someone who clears a table you can infer that probably someone has eaten). As Simon explains, these are examples of probable inference; there are also necessary inferences such as 'the sun goes to the west, then it will set' (*sol tendit ad occasum*) (from the antecedent to the consequent) or 'this woman has given birth, so she has had intercourse with a man' (*aliqua peperit . . . quia cum viro concubuit*) (from the consequent to the antecedent) (*ibidem*).

Starting from these and other examples, from the parallel passages in his *Disputationes*, and from some explicit sources, it is possible to reconstruct the range of sources underlying this complex classification: first of all, the traditional theory of the four senses of Scriptures which, starting from an analysis of the scriptural language, ends up projecting onto the world a complex web of signification relationships; second, the classical Latin rhetorical tradition that from Cicero to Quintilian has always dedicated a certain attention to the use of signs in various fields of oratory; finally, the first evidence of the assimilation of the Aristotelian *Posterior Analytics* can be noticed here (accompanied in the twelfth and thirteenth centuries by the pseudo-Alexander of Aphrodisias's lost commentary on it). As will be seen, in the system elaborated by Roger Bacon (§ 8) the inferential signs will find an explicit collocation in the context of natural signs, and the modes of signification classified as *in re* and *ex re* will be interpreted as examples of connotation, a semantic concept that Bacon explicitly takes from theology.

6. The Semantics of *Suppositio* Between the Twelfth and Thirteenth Centuries

The theory of *suppositio* probably represents the most original contribution given by medieval philosophy to the history of semantics (Ebbesen 1981: 36; see Marmo 2010: chapter 2). It provides medieval logic with a very articulated theory of reference (extensional semantics), capable of producing the development of a theory of truth for assertive statements or propositions. There are two distinct traditions or currents in thirteenth-century supposition theory: an English (Oxonian) tradition, which includes some anonymous treatises (*Logica 'Cum sit nostra'*, in de Rijk 1967: II.2) and authors such as William of Sherwood and Roger Bacon; and a continental (Parisian) tradition, which is represented by the anonymous *Summulae antiquorum* (in de Rijk 1968) and by authors such as Johannes Pagus, Peter of Spain and Lambert of Lagny. Both semantic traditions identify in *suppositio* and *significatio* (together with other properties of terms) their basic concepts; the main differences are played out in terms of the relationships between these two properties. The English tradition defines *suppositio*, in syntactic terms, as the subordination of the concept (or of the corresponding thing) expressed by the subject to the concept (or thing) expressed by the predicate. Signification is the reference to a form (a common one in case of universal terms) and is a permanent property of the term, whether it occurs in a proposition or not. The supposition, on the other hand, is a property which belongs to the term only when it occurs in a proposition and thus brings into the discourse the form signified by it (de Rijk 1967: II.2: 447; William of Sherwood 1995: 132). Opposed to what has been called a 'contextual approach', typical of the English tradition, the continental approach considers supposition as a distinct property but not directly dependent on signification. As for the English tradition, a name derives its signification from its original imposition to a thing; for the continental logicians, however, supposition is the acceptation of a term for something individual. Thus, in the proposition 'some human-being runs' (*homo currit*) the term 'human-being' stands for Socrates or Plato or another individual and signifies the general form of humanity. The difference, if one compares this to the Oxonian tradition, is that the term can stand for individuals even outside the proposition. The continental treatises generally distinguish between a natural supposition, which a term also has outside the propositional context and which extends to all the individuals who participate (in the Platonic sense) in the signified form, and an accidental supposition, which a term has only as it occurs into a propositional context. If we take the case of the term 'human-being', in *suppositio naturalis* it will stand for all human individuals that exist in the present (at the moment of its utterance), existed in the past, will exist in the future, or simply could exist; the scope of the reference of the same term taken in *suppositio accidentalis* is instead determined by the time of the verb (or of the predicate): so that 'human-being' in 'there is a human-being' (*homo est*) will refer to a present human-being, in 'there will be a human-being' to a future human-being, and so on (de Rijk 1968: 9, 1972: 81).

Both approaches also make use of the notion of *appellatio*, indicating the reference of a term to individuals present at the time of its utterance; they diverge, however, by the fact that the English tradition identifies it with the standard scope of *suppositio* (that which derives from the imposition of the name), while the continental tradition considers it a restriction of the original scope of reference of the term, which, as we have seen, includes all the past, present, future or even only possible individuals of which the term is or can be said (de Rijk 1967: II.2: 49). The options that open up to the two traditions are therefore simmetrically opposed: on the one hand, the continental semantics gives more room to the restriction (*restrictio*) that determines the modes of accidental supposition (see de Libera 1981), while the English semantics focuses on the enlargement (*ampliatio*) of the scope of reference of the subject term determined by the tense or by modal verbs. Both elaborate complex classifications of the types of *suppositio* that reflect these fundamental differences and that would be too long to recall here (but see Marmo 2010: 37–45).

7. Theological Language in the Thirteenth Century: The Theory of Analogy

The thirteenth-century theological reflection deepened the insights offered by the Neoplatonic tradition on theological language itself conceived as a way of knowing and accessing the divine sphere (Marmo 2010: chapter 7). Thomas Aquinas is certainly the best known of medieval theologians to have faced the problem of the knowledge of God that one can derive from the names the Scriptures and theology used to speak about Him (Porro 2012). The starting point of his reflection is the relationship between names and concepts posed by Aristotle in the first chapter of his *De interpretatione* and handed down in Boethius's translation: as we know God imperfectly through created things, so – imperfectly – we name God, 'almost stuttering' (Aquinas 1929–47: d. 22, q. 1, a. 1, sol.). But, one might ask, how is it possible to signify God, who is a simple essence, through names, which – as was stated by the grammarians – mean a composition of substance and quality? And how can God be understood through verbs (and participles) if these – according to the Aristotelian definition (*De int.* 3 16b6) and according to the grammarians – consignify time, which is incompatible with divine eternity? To reply to these objections, Aquinas recalls some fundamental, albeit standard, distinctions of the grammatical theory of his time. In the first place, he recalls the distinction between *significatum* and *modus significandi* (Rosier 1995), which allows him to solve the first objection: substance and quality – he clarifies – are not to be understood in the ontological sense as two of the ten Aristotelian categories, but in the way in which the grammarians take them. According to the grammarians, they are only modes of signifying (that is, grammatical accidents, see below) and not what is signified by names. These modes of signifying correspond not only to the way in which our intellect understands things (and God among them), but also to the way in which meaning is found in creatures (imperfect, as compared to the perfection it has in God; Rosier 1995: 151). The relationship (of identity or diversity) between these modes of signifying and meaning does not affect the fact that God is still nameable; as we can signify an abstract quality with a name such as whiteness (*albedo*), although this is not a substance (in the Aristotelian sense), so we can name God, although there is no distinction between substance and quality in God, but God's properties are all identical to His essence or substance. Similarly, God can be signified by a verb, even if this consignifies time, without implying that God exists in time. In all these cases, what is defective does not lie in the meaning but in the mode of signifying, that is, in the representation that each word offers of its meaning through its grammatical features. According to Aquinas, with the name we express the thing as we understand it with our intellect (1918–30: I.30). Let's take the names 'goodness' or 'good'. For Thomas Aquinas as well as for Gilbert of Poitiers, they mean a property that is at its highest level in God (and is identical with the divine essence); creatures participate in this property only as effects of the highest Good. Since we know God only from God's effects (the creatures, precisely) and creatures participate in it in a 'degraded' way (according to a rather widespread Neoplatonic scheme), this name 'good' has divine perfection as its proper meaning, and as mode of signifying the limited way in which it is understood by our intellect through the creatures that participate in that property (Aquinas 1929–47: d. 22, q. 1, a. 2, sol.). The divine names, however, are not only of this kind. In his works, Aquinas distinguishes at least four types of divine names: (1) negative names (such as 'immense' or 'infinite'); (2) names that signify a relationship with creatures (such as 'lord' or 'creator'); (3) names that express the persons of the Trinity ('Father', 'Son', 'Holy Spirit') and their constitutive relationships ('Paternity', 'Sonhood', etc.); and (4) names of divine properties (such as 'Goodness' or 'Wisdom', as seen above). These names are said of God and of creatures according to analogy or proportion, according to two models: that of the term 'healthy' (*sanum*) in that it is predicated of medicine and of urine, which are a cause and a sign of health in an animated being (which is its main meaning); and that of the term 'being' (*ens*) in that it is predicated of substance (its main meaning) and of accidents. Consequently, the divine names are analogical and are predicated neither in a univocal nor in an equivocal way of God and creatures. Moreover, these terms, from the point of view of their meaning, are principally predicated of God and secondarily of creatures, contrary to terms metaphorically said of God (Aquinas 1927: I, q. 13, a. 6).

8. Roger Bacon: The Sign and its Interpreter

Roger Bacon (c. 1214–92) also gives room to discussing these issues, but to adopting theoretical solutions that distance themselves far from the mainstream, both in the theological and in the semantic fields. His positions are framed in a precise theory of sign and in a complex classification of signs that has its roots in the theological tradition of Augustinian inspiration and in the tradition of Aristotelian logic.[10] The main work in which Bacon addresses these issues is his *De signis*.[11] The starting point of his semiotics is the affirmation that 'a sign stands in the (Aristotelian) category of Relation' (*Signum est in praedicamento relationis*) (I, § 1, in Fredborg et al. 1978: 81). The sign, however, is not a simple relation (which connects two terms or related objects) but a double relation: the first connects the signifying object (*signum*) to someone for whom it means (which we might call 'interpreter', in a very broad sense), and the second connects the sign to its meaning. According to Bacon both these relationships are necessary for there to be a sign, but the first is 'more essential' than the second. This implies that in the absence of someone who receives the sign as such (that is, understands it by interpreting it), what remains is only an object, endowed with its own essence, or a substance devoid of relationships, and therefore nothing that can be taken as a sign. Just as a man is a father (that is, characterised by the paternity relationship) when his child is alive, but remains a simple man, a father in potency and not in act, when the child no longer exists, even the sign ceases to be such (becoming a sign in potency, but not in act) when the interpreter who receives it as a sign is missing. The previous theological tradition (Richard Fishacre and Bonaventura of Bagnoregio, in particular), in tune with the logical tradition (theory of *suppositio*, see above § 6), supported expressly or implicitly the opposite position, that is, that the relation to meaning makes of a sign what it is. Both Bacon's definition of sign and his classification of signs are based on these assumptions. Criticising in fact a widespread definition of sign that focuses (just like the Augustinian one) on the perceptibility of signs, Bacon proposes a definition according to which not only the sensible things are signs, but also the concepts (which by definition do not offer themselves to perception): 'The sign is something that, once presented to a sensory faculty or an intellect, designates something to that intellect' (*Signum autem est illud quod oblatum sensui vel intellectui aliquid designat ipsi intellectui*) (Bacon 1978: *De signis* I, § 2). The definition expresses the two relations that make up a sign: the one which connects the signifier to the signified object (*aliquid*) and that which puts it in relation to the interpreter's mind (*intellectui*). Moreover, its classification shows, as said above, the convergence of the two lines of reflection, the Augustinian and the Aristotelian, widely diffused and adopted respectively in the theological and logical fields. Signs are divided by Bacon into two general classes: the natural ones and those constituted by the soul according to an intention to signify; the first are signs by virtue of their essence, while the latter receive their ability to signify from an underlying intentionality (ibid.: I, § 3–9).

The natural signs, in turn, are divided into two classes: those that are related to their meaning by a relation of inference and those that are linked to it by resemblance or natural conformity (a third class of signs, based on the relationship of causality is reduced to the first in a subsequent work, the *Compendium studii theologiae* [1292]). The inference that characterises the

---

[10] The bibliography on these issues is enormous: see Marmo (2010: chapter 2) for an overview; for a definitive analysis and further bibliographical references see Cesalli and Rosier-Catach (2018).

[11] This portion of the text was only rediscovered in 1978. It was a part of one of Bacon's works, the *Opus majus* (1267), addressed to Pope Clement IV. It was aimed at presenting his vision of the world and how best to reform Catholic education.

signs of the first type may be necessary or probable and temporally determined with respect to a present, past or future object/event. What differentiates Bacon's approach, compared to that of other authors who had proposed a classification of signs (such as the grammarian known as pseudo-Kilwardby, cf. Marmo 2010: chapter 4), is a clearer awareness of the role of the interpreter in the process of lexicalisation and understanding of the natural relationships that underlie these sign relations (causality, contemporaneity, conformity or similarity), as already seen in the definition of 'sign'. The difference between a causal relation and a sign relation lies precisely in the essential reference of the latter to the interpreter; a causal relation, on the other hand, exists in act even in the absence of any mind understanding it. The second type of natural signs is when an object acquires a function of vicarious representation of another, by virtue of the relationship of similarity that binds them. An example is the footprint of a foot on the snow, which means the animal that has impressed it, or the image of a person with respect to the person him-/herself and, in general, all the artificial objects with respect to their creator or the idea that their designer wanted to achieve through them.

Signs constituted by the soul represent the second large group of signs. They are in turn divided into two classes: the voluntary signs, which follow a deliberation, and the involuntary signs, which instead constitute a spontaneous and immediate reaction to an external stimulus. Of the first type are the words of human language, the insignia of shops or artisan workshops (circles to signal that wine is sold, arms and armour, saddles, and so on) and the objects placed in the windows as samples of goods for sale. Of the second type are instead the inarticulate sounds that animals emit, the moans of the sick, and everything that is expressed by an animated organism able to emit sounds to communicate, albeit without the intervention of any voluntary deliberation. These signs are also called 'naturally signifying', but in a different sense from the way in which natural signs signify: if in describing these, in fact, Bacon means by 'nature' the essence of an object that has a relation of concomitance, causality or conformity to another object, in this context he interprets 'nature' as the faculty of giving signifying capacity without deliberation, a faculty that may also coincide with the essence that is common to an entire species of brute animals and by virtue of which they operate constantly in the same way. It is by virtue of this common nature that animals of the same species can communicate to each other. Halfway between these naturally signifying sounds and those of human language are the interjections that participate in both the immediate reaction to an emotion, and the conventionality typical of the other parts of the speech.

A further character of Bacon semiotics depends on the features of the notion of sign seen above. If his contemporary logicians and grammarians, in fact, completely ignore linguistic change, Bacon not only recognises it, but proposes an explanation which leans, on the one hand, on the freedom of the speaker and, on the other, on the centrality of the sign-interpreter relationship at the expense of that between sign and meaning. If his contemporaries, in fact, solve the question of the stability of meanings regardless of the mutability of the world and its objects, appealing to the permanence of concepts (which were therefore considered the first meanings of words), Bacon accepts until its last consequences his own positions: on the one hand, we are able to change at will the meaning of the words we use, imposing them on new objects compared to those to which they were connected by the original imposition; on the other hand, words cease to be meaningful when the things to which they have been imposed no longer exist. This implies that it depends on the will of those who use them to maintain their significations, renewing the imposition explicitly (on the model of baptism), but more often implicitly and without a full awareness of the operation: this is what happens to us when we name a person who is alive with a certain word and cry his/her death using the same name; this is only possible thanks to a new imposition of this name on an object (the dead person) that now no longer has anything in common with the one who previously was alive (Bacon 1978: IV.2–3, §§ 149–61).

9. The Modists: Lexical Signification, Ambiguity and Grammatical Signification

When we talk about the Modists, we usually think of the complex task of speculative grammar, neglecting the fact that as Masters of Arts at medieval European universities, as well as holding grammar courses, they taught logic and worked out their own semantic theories (Pinborg 1967). This applies not only to the most famous masters of the 1260s and 1270s, such as Martin or Boethius of Dacia, but also to those less known, such as Gentilis of Cingoli (teaching at Bologna University between the late thirteenth and early fourteenth centuries) or Radulphus Brito, 'the last of the great arts masters' in Paris, at the end of thirteenth century (see Ebbesen 2000). In the debate on lexical signification (what is sometimes called 'denotation'), the Modists hold to rather traditional positions. The first-generation Modists faithfully propose the 'semantic triangle' of the Aristotelian-Boethian tradition: (1) *dictiones* (words) immediately signify (2) concepts, and only mediately (that is, through them) (3) things. In the 1290s some of them (like Gentilis, Radulphus and John Duns Scotus) discuss, according to a scheme then in vogue, whether words first mean the concepts and then things or rather directly signify things, and opt for the direct signification of things (albeit with some distinction).[12] Even from the early Modists, however, the signified things (of general terms) were conceived of as 'common natures', universals *in re* that constitute the essence of individuals who belong to one and the same species. Despite these discussions on lexical signification, in a grammatical context the basic scheme remains that of a correspondence between linguistic items, concepts and things.

Aristotle's *Sophistical refutations* are the starting point for the Modists' reflections on linguistic ambiguity, and in particular on homonyms and on analogical terms. Homonymy, or 'strong' lexical equivocation, is characterised as the signification of a plurality of mutually independent objects which, in turn, derives from a plurality of *impositiones*, the original acts that have instituted a relationship between phonic expressions (*voces*) and signified things (*res*). A homonym, such as *canis* (which can signify both the barking animal, the constellation and a marine animal) is a unique name only apparently, hiding in reality as many linguistic signs (or *dictiones*) as original impositions it underwent. In fact, for the Modists, the *dictio* is a linguistic item deriving from the composition of a phonic expression (*vox*) and relation of signification (*ratio significandi*) (see Marmo 1994: 112–16). We will soon return to the theoretical consequences of this conception. The second type of equivocation, analogy, is a weaker one, based as it is on a single act of imposition; at a later time, a new relation of signification is added to it following its use. This new signification is addressed to objects that are different from the first one but are nevertheless linked to it in some way. Thus, for example, the adjective 'healthy' (*sanum*) refers, in the first place (that is, thanks to the original imposition), to the health of an animated living being; thanks to an extension of its semantic scope, it also becomes applicable to other objects, such as a diet (which preserves health), a medicine (which restores health) or a sample of urine (which signifies it as a symptom). As seen above, this is a classic example of an analogous term, derived from Aristotle's *Metaphysics* and also used by Thomas Aquinas. Characteristic of these names is that their signification does not depend on several acts of

---

[12] They discuss this problem in their commentaries on Aristotle's *De interpretatione*. Only Duns Scotus's are edited in his *Opera omnia*. On this discussion, see Mora-Márquez (2015).

imposition: one is enough, the one addressed to their principal meaning; the other meanings derive from the use of the term and the relationships their main meaning entertains with other objects or properties. The fundamental difference between equivocal terms in the strong sense and analogous terms lies, therefore, in their different origin and has consequences on the way in which they react to their occurrence in a linguistic context. If for us today, at least from a pragmatic point of view, the (linguistic or enunciative) context plays the role of a disambiguating factor, for the Modists things went differently. The equivocal terms of the first type, in fact, almost do not interact with their 'linguistic surroundings': when an equivocal term is directly linked, for instance, to a qualifier connected to one of its meanings, then it is determined to signify only that meaning (as in 'the barking dog', *canis latrabilis*); when instead the term is only indirectly connected to the same qualifier (as in 'the dog can bark', *canis est latrabilis*), here the same term maintains its lexical ambiguity, transferring it to the sentence in which it occurs. This depends on a peculiar conception of the imposition, which, for the term, plays a role equivalent to that of nature for natural objects; the occurrence of the term in a linguistic context is seen only as an accidental fact that does not affect what is essential (that is, its imposition). The addition of a determination to the equivocal term does not change its nature, that is, its homonymy, which derives from the multiplicity of its impositions. The equivocal term, whose ambiguity is not eliminated by its occurrence in a linguistic context, therefore maintains the whole spectrum of the meanings originally assigned to it, and that are at the interpreters' disposal; each of the listeners, however, because of human cognitive limits, can only grasp one meaning at a time. The English logicians of the Oxonian tradition of *suppositio*, as we have seen, argued the exact opposite, namely that the equivocal terms are determined or disambiguated by their predicative context. Modists of the second generation, such as Simon of Faversham or the Anonymous of Prague (1280s), and of the third, such as Radulphus Brito or John Duns Scotus (1290s), admit this eventuality, but only from a particular point of view, that is, that of the interpreter (see Marmo 2006). They deny, however, that, from the point of view of the objective properties of language (*de virtute sermonis*), an equivocal term is determinable or can be made univocal by its linguistic context; they argue instead that the univocal determination of the meaning of an ambiguous term by its context can be accepted from the point of view of 'the goodness of those who understand' (*de bonitate intelligentis*), thus making room for pragmatic considerations (Marmo 1995, 2014). Analogous terms, for the Modists up to the second generation, work in the opposite direction to equivocal terms. The analogical terms, which, as we said, have a principal meaning and one or more derivatives, if taken alone (that is, outside of any context or without determinations of sorts) only convey their first meaning. The linguistic context can lead them to also mean one or more of the secondary meanings, making them ambiguous together with the sentence in which they occur. For example, if taken alone, the term 'healthy' means only health, as the quality of an animal; when it is instead associated with a predicate semantically connected to one of its derivative meanings, the word becomes ambiguous, since it also preserves its main meaning. The interest of this last position also lies in the fact that the reflection on how analogous terms function becomes the occasion to rethink in a radically different way the original imposition with respect to tradition. If the imposition was traditionally presented as an act of simple labelling of the objects (or their essences), Simon of Faversham, at least for analogous terms, conceives it as a complex act or as the stipulation of instructions for their insertion in a linguistic context. The third-generation Modists, however, reject, together with the analogous terms, also this representation of the original imposition. For Radulphus Brito and the young John Duns Scotus, there are no analogous terms. What their predecessors call 'analogous term' should be traced back either to univocal or to homonymous terms (Marmo 1994: chapter 5).

What the Modists are best known for, however, is their grammatical theory. This offers a considerable complexity and numerous aspects that are difficult to understand, even for modern linguists. I will therefore try to concentrate on the more general features and the way in which they are integrated into the semantic framework outlined above. Grammatical signification (resulting in the *modi significandi*) is expressly conceived by Modist grammarians as a secondary level of signification that is superimposed on the first level, the lexical one. For them, the original act of imposition does not therefore consist of a single act of labelling, but of (at least) two subsequent steps: one addressed to objects or their essences (the level of primary signification), the other addressed to their modes of being or properties of objects, which constitutes the secondary or grammatical signification level, also called 'consignification'. The Modists talk about a *prima articulatio* and a *secunda articulatio* of the imposition. The *dictio* (word) is the product of the first step; the part of speech (*pars orationis*) – distinguished in name, pronoun, verb, participle and the four indeclinable parts – is the product of the second step, so that a part of speech is the result of the composition of a *dictio* with some *modi significandi* (grammatical signification and grammatical properties, as we will see). If on the first level, the signification is clearly the result of convention (*ad placitum imponentis*), according to the dictates of the Aristotelian-Boethian tradition, at the second level, some constraints are introduced that make consignification motivated rather than arbitrary: the *impositor* cannot ascribe to a word, endowed with a certain meaning, modes of signifying (*modi significandi*) that are in contrast with the thing itself. Thus, the noun *homo* cannot have the comparative degree, nor the proper noun *Socrates* the plural number, nor *vir* the feminine gender. This incompatibility (*repugnantia*), as explained by Boethius of Dacia, does not concern the linguistic item as a phonic expression (*vox*), but rather its meaning and the properties that go with the signified thing.

The conception of the imposition as a process of successive addition of semantic traits to a predetermined phonic material appears to be extremely widespread: many Modistic texts, both of grammatical and logical nature, present the sequence *vox-signum-dictio-pars orationis*, in which each stage adds a form to the previous one, in a systematic application of the notions of matter and form (intended in a functional and non-substantial sense) to the different levels of the linguistic phenomenon, according to a precise stratification scheme. The *vox* (phonic expression) is thus constituted of a matter (the exhaled air) and of a form that is its pronunciation (*prolatio* or *modus proferendi*); the *dictio* (word) adds to the *vox*, as its matter, the form of signification; the *dictio*, in turn, becomes the material part of the part of speech (*pars orationis*) thanks to the addition of a new essential form that is the mode of signifying, the object of the second articulation of the original imposition (Marmo 1994: chapter 3). This theoretical construction serves purposefully to illustrate the two functions of the modes of signifying: (1) that of defining the traditional eight parts of speech, and (2) that of specifying the conditions for syntactically well-formed complex expressions, explaining the phenomena of regency and combination. The main function of the modes of signifying remains, however, the definition of the parts of speech. This takes place through the indication of the essential, general and specific, modes of signifying of the various parts: the noun and the pronoun share the general mode of signifying of permanence and repose (*m.s. habitus et quietis*) and are differentiated by the modes of determined vs. indeterminate understanding (name vs. pronoun); the verb and the participle, on the other hand, share the general mode of signifying of flowing or becoming (*m.s. fluxus vel fieri*) and are distinguished by the modes of distance from the subject (the verb as predicate is a syntactic constituent distinct from the subject-noun) or of the proximity to it (the participle constitutes in fact a single syntactical element with the noun with which it is linked). With regard to the indeclinable parts, it is debated whether for them the modes of signifying coincide with their signification, which is equivalent to asking if the meaning of syncategorems (adverbs, conjunctions, prepositions and interjections, linguistic items with no independent signification) coincides or not with the their function, that is, their ability to modify the meaning of categorems (linguistic units endowed with an independent meaning) with which they are syntactically constructed (Pinborg 1967). The expression which the grammarians use to define the parts of speech follows this pattern: the noun signifies its own (lexical) meaning through the mode of permanence or repose and that of determined understanding; or the verb signifies its own (lexical) meaning through the mode of flowing or becoming and of distance from the subject, thus producing the traditional typology of the eight parts of the discourse.[13]

Finally, the modes of signifying have the purpose of allowing the formulation of rules for the well-formedness of a sentence (*congruitas*), on which necessarily depends the *perfectio* of the sentence itself, that is, its communicative efficacy (at least for the decidedly anti-pragmatic first-generation Modists). The criterion for defining a congruous *constructio* (that is, a pair of words) is the correspondence between their respective modes of signifying, which may consist either in the proportion between the general meanings of the words in question (as between *homo* and *currit* in the sentence *homo currit* – 'a human being runs' – in which the mode of permanence corresponds to that of flowing) or in the similarity between their accidental modes of signifying (or grammatical categories, as in the case of *homo* and *albus* in *homo albus* – 'a white human being' – in which the two terms have the same number, gender and case). In the first case we will have the regency between one element of the syntagm and the other (the verb requires a name or a pronoun as its own subject); in the second we will have instead an explanation of the agreement that regulates different types of syntactic construction (and that concerns case, gender, number and person, also considered among the modes of signifying) (Marmo 1994: chapter 6). The theories of first-generation Modists are well represented by the treatise on the *Modi significandi* by Martin of Dacia (1260s); those of the third-generation Modists by the *Novi modi significandi* (New modes of signifying) or *Speculative Grammar* by Thomas of Erfurt (first decade of the fourteenth century, but for a long time attributed to John Duns Scotus).

10. The Linguistic Turn: William of Ockham and John Buridan

William of Ockham (c. 1288–1347) is undoubtedly the most influential philosopher and logician of late scholasticism. With his semantic and cognitive conceptions, he can be said to have started a true linguistic turn in fourteenth-century philosophy. This change goes hand in hand with a clear position in ontology: only individuals of substance and quality exist, nothing else; no universal entity and no relation, in particular, are admitted in his world. As a consequence, the Aristotelian categories become more a classification of terms than a classification of the objects that furnish our extramental reality. Taking up radically some positions already expressed in the previous century by Roger Bacon and the last Modists, Ockham argues that words directly signify things, but in his view these things are only individuals and not universal

---

[13] Cf. Martin of Dacia, *Modi significandi*. Ed. H. Roos, Copenhagen: G. E. C. Gad, 1961; Boethius of Dacia, *Modi significandi sive Quaestiones super Priscianum maiorem*. Ed. J. Pinborg, Copenhagen: G. E. C: Gad, 1969; Radulphus Brito, *Quaestiones super Priscianum minorem*. Ed. J. Pinborg, Stuttgart: Frommann-Holzboog, 1980; Thomas of Erfurt, *Grammatica speculativa*, in G. L. Bursill-Hall, *Grammatica speculativa of Thomas of Erfurt. An Edition with Translation and Commentary*, London: Longman, 1972 (see also Marmo 1994: chapter 4).

essences. This semantic theory brings with it a precise explanation of how language works in relation to thought and world. At the centre of his philosophical system lies *thought*, understood as a mental language, a universal language (see above § 2 on Anselm of Aosta) which, in a natural way, signifies (that is, refers to) the individuals that inhabit our world, and consists of mental concepts or terms as acts of simple (intuitive or abstractive) knowledge of these individuals (Panaccio 1999a, 1999b, 2004). Expelled from our extramental world, universals are first and foremost concepts or natural signs giving us the knowledge of a plurality of individuals; only secondarily can the oral and written terms, corresponding to those concepts, be considered as universals. Starting from simple knowledge, according to Ockham, a propositional language is constructed and articulated. This is nothing other than a complex knowledge of the world and represents the hinge between the traditional fields of logic and semantics, on the one hand, and the theory of knowledge and of science, on the other. Mental language, constituted as it is of natural signs, does not coincide with any of the historical conventional languages and is not affected by their defects, such as synonymy and homonymy (Chalmers 1999). It is a universal language, common to all humans who use it to know and to think. In common with historical languages is the ability that the mental terms have to stand for individuals in forms that resume positions of the English tradition of *suppositio* (see above, § 6): 'signifying', for a categorematic term, means first and foremost standing for (*supponere pro*) individual things that exist or can exist; second, it means connoting or indirectly referring to other things (other substances, qualities, or parts of substances); for a syncategorematic term, 'signifying' consists in the ability to modify the supposition of categorematic terms (*Summa logicae* I.33). The play between these different ways of signifying makes it possible to refer to and describe, even scientifically, our world. Ockham can thus effectively oppose the philosophies of realistic-style language, which make their ontological distinctions too closely related to linguistic distinctions (Panaccio 1991; Klima 1999). Those who adhere to these conceptions end up explaining how language works by making appeal to more entities than necessary. The rigorous application of the principle of economy (Ockham's razor) implies for Ockham, first of all, the elimination of every universal or common entity, really participated or shared by several individuals who are different in number; it also implies the elimination of relations, understood as bridge entities that actually unite individuals and add to them as enumerable properties; and, finally, the elimination of discrete or continuous quantities, and of other alleged entities such as time or movement. All this is made possible by a systematic use of the notion of connotation and ends up transforming even natural philosophy in a 'metalinguistic analysis' (cf. Murdoch 1981). Things and the world are radically contingent for Ockham, in the sense that they depend on God's free choice to give the universe a certain order and regularity (it is always possible for God to violate these natural laws, producing miracles: in these cases, Ockham speaks of *potentia dei absoluta*, as opposed to the ordered one). The appeal to divine omnipotence, in the hands of Ockham, becomes a methodological tool that contributes to freeing philosophical reflection and the investigation of nature from the ballast of useless reification and contingent phenomena, to raise humans to the knowledge of the essence of things. Denying, therefore, that there are relationships or quantities, as autonomous entities, is not equivalent to denying the existence of a natural order and to holding that the existing objects offer themselves to the experience in a chaotic and fundamentally unknowable way (there is no room for scepticism in Ockham's epistemology). Talking about the order of the world or of the causal relationships that can exist between things implies the systematic use of connotative concepts or terms: the notion of cause is exactly one of these concepts, and denotes a certain number of individuals connoting other individuals whose existence derives from the first ones, regardless of whether there exists any intellect that can form this concept in itself.

John Buridan (c. 1290–1361) was one of the most important philosophers and arts masters at the University of Paris in the fourteenth century. Within logic and philosophy of language, his positions are very close to Ockham's, although it is not clear whether there is any direct dependency. Both identify three levels of language – written, spoken and mental – and place in the last level the fulcrum of their respective logico-semantic and epistemological conceptions. For Buridan, spoken words derive their ability to signify from an arbitrary original imposition, which is not however directly exercised on things, as it was for Ockham, but on mental concepts or terms. Things also in Buridan's ontology are individual but are signified by spoken (or written) words only through the corresponding concepts, the only ones that can be designated as 'universal'. Concepts are therefore the immediate meanings of spoken words, while things constitute the ultimate meanings, the object of the property of the *suppositio* that characterises mental language terms and those subordinate to them. The three levels of language are not perfectly parallel, in the sense that there is no one-to-one correspondence between elements of spoken language and elements of mental language. What at the verbal level appears as a single word (for example, 'empty', *vacuum*), and the grammarians analyse as a single linguistic unit (*dictio*), actually corresponds to a plurality of concepts, or rather to a complex concept that constitutes a sort of mental discourse ('emptiness' for example is defined as 'the place not occupied by any body'). At this level comes an additional semantic property of words, with respect to signification and *suppositio*, the property of *appellatio*, which is sometimes assimilated to connotation or secondary signification. Not all terms have both *suppositio* and *appellatio*, though. Some supposit without appealing anything, as the concrete terms of the category of substance or the abstract terms of quality (they correspond to Ockham's absolute terms); others supposit and appeal, that is, they refer to a habit or a property of the principal referent, such as, for example, the term 'white' (*album*), which stands for every white thing, connoting the fact that these things possess the quality of whiteness; other terms, finally, do not supposit, but only appeal, referring to incompatible habits (as in 'chimaera') or to 'things' that in fact do not exist (as in 'empty') or that cannot exist together with the substance for which a part of the expression in question stands (as in *homo hinnibilis*, 'human being able to neigh'). The theory of *suppositio* represents, for Buridan as well as for Ockham, the semantic theory on which one can ground the theory of truth of propositions and in particular of the propositions of science (Klima 2009).

11. Conclusions

Some conclusions can be drawn from what precedes. First, the debates on transubstantiation show that the identification of the sign with the thing signified, in the Eucharist, as proposed by Paschasius, appears to question one of the basic tenets of semiotics, namely the distinction between signifier (expression plane) and significate (content plane): as we saw, the reception and success of Paschasius' positions in the Eucharistic debate did not go together with the reception of this semiotic features, so that in the following centuries the distinction between the two planes remains unquestioned. Second, the role played by Berengar of Tours is crucial in explicitly introducing into the debate on sacraments the Augustinian definition of sign and in obliging all his opponents to discuss it in order to give a sound theory of sacraments: together with St Paul, the historian of semiotics has to acknowledge that 'it was necessary to have some heretics' (*oportet et haerese esse*, I Corinthians 11,19) after all. Third, while there is a general agreement upon the original contribution of the medieval supposition theory to the history of semantics, it is only in recent times that the medieval contribution to the history of pragmatics – such as that of Anselm of Canterbury or of the third-generation Modists – has been acknowledged (cf. Marma 2011, 2015). There is not enough space in this chapter to underline the importance of the thirteenth-century debates on how sacraments work to the development of a pragmatic approach to language analysis, as Irène Rosier-Catach (2004b) has shown. Fourth, while general reflections on signs from the ninth to the twelfth centuries are worked out in theology, from the mid-thirteenth century on they find space also in the arts of trivium (see Roger Bacon, pseudo-Kilwardby and William of Ockham), where they are combined and integrated with a grammatical or a logico-semantic approach to language: in particular, it is in the pseudo-Kilwardby's commentary on Priscian where one finds the first explicit discussion about the possibility of a *scientia de signis*. Fifth, medieval thought was going to exert a great impact on Charles S. Peirce's semiotics: not only would he collect ancient editions of medieval authors, but he would develop many of his own reflections from medieval texts, so that, for instance, he would name a part of his semiotics *Grammatica speculativa* with reference to the Modistic approach to language (cf. Bellucci 2018), and would begin his reflection on relations from the medieval one (cf. Marmo 2015). Finally, the development of a Peircean semiotics by Umberto Eco from the 1970s onwards, based as it is on a solid medieval scholarship (cf. Marmo 2017), confirms the idea that studying medieval semiotics is worth the effort.

References

Abelard, Peter (1919). *Logica Ingredientibus. Die Glossen zu Porphyrius*. In *Philosophischen Schriften*, I. Ed. B. Geyer. Münster: Aschendorff.
Abelard, Peter (1970). *Dialectica*, 2nd revised edn. Ed. L. M. de Rijk. Assen: van Gorcum.
Abelard, Peter (1987). *Theologia summi boni*. In *Opera theologica*, III. Ed. E. M. Buytaert and C. J. Mews. Turnhout: Brepols.
Abelard, Peter (2010). *Petri Abaelardi Glossae super Peri hermeneias*. Ed. K. Jacobi and Ch. Strub. Turnhout: Brepols.
Alain of Lille (1981). *Regulae caelestis iuris*. Ed. N. M. Häring. Archives d'Histoire Doctrinale et Littéraire du Moyen Age, 48: 97–226.
Anselm of Canterbury (1968a). *De grammatico*. In *S. Anselmi Cantuariensis Opera omnia*, I. Ed. F. S. Schmitt. Seckau-Rom-Edinburgh, 1938 (anast. repr. Stuttgart-Bad Cannstatt: Frommann Holzboog, pp. 145–68).
Anselm of Canterbury (1968b). *De veritate*. In *S. Anselmi Cantuariensis Opera omnia*, I. Ed. F. S. Schmitt. Seckau-Rom-Edinburgh, 1938 (anast. repr. Stuttgart-Bad Cannstatt: F. Frommann (G. Holzboog), pp. 173–99).
Anselm of Canterbury (1968c). *Epistola de incarnatione Verbi* (posterior recensio). In *S. Anselmi Cantuariensis Opera omnia*, II. Ed. F. S. Schmitt. Seckau-Rom-Edinburgh, 1938 (anast. repr. Stuttgart-Bad Cannstatt: F. Frommann (G. Holzboog), pp. 3–35).
Anselm of Canterbury (1968d). *Monologion*. In *S. Anselmi Cantuariensis Opera omnia*, I. Ed. F. S. Schmitt. Seckau-Rom-Edinburgh, 1938 (anast. repr. Stuttgart-Bad Cannstatt: F. Frommann (G. Holzboog), pp. 5–87).
Aquinas, Thomas (1918–30). *Summa contra gentiles*. Ed. Commissio Leonina, Rome.
Aquinas, Thomas (1927). *Summa Theologiae, I pars*. Ed. Commissio Leonina, Rome.
Aquinas, Thomas (1929–47). *Scriptum super libros Sententiarum Petri Lombardi*, I–IV. Ed. P. Mandonnet and F. Moos. Paris: Lethielleux.
Bacon, Roger (1978). *De signis*. In K. M. Fredborg, Lauge Nielsen and Jan Pinborg, 'An Unedited Part of Roger Bacon's *Opus Maius*: "De Signis"'. Traditio, 34: 75–136.
Bellucci, F. (2018). *Peirce's Speculative Grammar: Logic as Semiotics*. New York and London: Routledge.
Berengar of Tours (Beringerius Turonensis) (1988). *Rescriptum contra Lanfrannum*. Ed. R. B. C. Huygens. Turnhout: Brepols.
Brower J. E. and K. Guilfoy (eds) (2004). *The Cambridge Companion to Abelard*. Cambridge: Cambridge University Press.

Cesalli, L. and I. Rosier-Catach. (2018). '"Signum est in praedicamento relationis". Roger Bacon's Semantics Revisited in the Light of His Relational Theory of Signs'. *Oxford Studies in Medieval Philosophy*, 6: 62–99.
Chalmers, D. (1999). 'Is there Synonymy in Ockham's Mental Language?' In *The Cambridge Companion to Ockham*. Ed. P. V. Spade. Cambridge: Cambridge University Press, pp. 76–99.
de Libera, A. (1996). *La querelle des universaux: de Platon à la fin du Moyen Âge*. Paris: Seuil.
de Libera, A. (1981). 'Supposition naturelle et appellation. Aspects de la sémantique parisienne au XIIIe siècle'. *Histoire Epistémologie Langage*, 3/1: 63–77.
de Rijk, L. M. (1967). *Logica Modernorum. A Contribution to the History of Early Terminist logic*, Vol. II/1: The Origin and Early Development of the Theory of Supposition; Vol. II/2: Texts and Indices. Assen: van Gorcum.
de Rijk, L. M. (1968). 'On the Genuine Text of Peter of Spain's Summule logicales, I: General Problems Concerning Possible Interpolations in the Manuscripts'. *Vivarium*, 6/1: 1–34.
de Rijk, L. M. (1972). *Peter of Spain, Tractatus, called afterwards Summulae logicales*. First Critical Edition from the Manuscripts. Assen: van Gorcum.
de Rijk, L. M. (1988). 'Semantics and Metaphysics in Gilbert of Poitiers. A Chapter of Twelfth Century Platonism (1)'. *Vivarium*, 26/2: 73–112.
de Rijk, L. M. (1989). 'Semantics and Metaphysics in Gilbert of Poitiers. A Chapter of Twelfth Century Platonism (1)'. *Vivarium*, 27/1: 1–35.
Ebbesen, S. (1981). 'Early Supposition Theory'. *Histoire Epistémologie Langage*, 3/1: 35–48.
Ebbesen, S. (2000). 'Radulphus Brito: The Last of the Great Arts Masters'. In *Geistesleben im 13. Jahrhundert*. Ed. J. A. Aertsen and A. Speer. Berlin: De Gruyter, pp. 231–51 (Miscellanea Mediaevalia, 27). (Reprinted in S. Ebbesen, *Topics in Latin Philosophy from the 12th–14th Centuries: Collected Essays*, Farnham: Ashgate, 2009, vol. 2, pp. 179–96.)
Fredborg, M., L. O. Nielsen and J. Pinborg (1978). 'An Unedited Part of Roger Bacon's "Opus maius": "De signis"'. *Traditio*, 34: 75–136.
Frege, G. (1892). 'Über Sinn und Bedeutung'. *Zeitschrift für Philosophie und philosophische Kritik*, 100: 25–50. (Translated as 'On Sense and Reference' by M. Black, in P. Geach and M. Black (eds), *Translations from the Philosophical Writings of Gottlob Frege*. Oxford: Blackwell, 1980.)
Guilfoy, K. (2004). 'Peter Abelard's Two Theories of the Proposition'. In *Medieval Theories on Assertive and Non-Assertive Language*. Ed. A. Maierù and L. Valente. Firenze: Olschki, pp. 35–57.
Jolivet, J. (1992). 'Trois variations médiévales sur l'universel et l'individu: Roscelin, Abélard, Gilbert de la Porrée'. *Revue de Métaphysique et de Morale*, 1: 111–55.
King, P. (2004a). 'Anselm's Philosophy of Language'. In *The Cambridge Companion to Anselm*. Ed. B. Davies and B. Leftow. Cambridge: Cambridge University Press, pp. 84–110.
King, P. (2004b). 'Metaphysics'. In *The Cambridge Companion to Abelard*. Ed. J. E. Brower and K. Guilfoy. Cambridge: Cambridge University Press, pp. 65–125.
Klima, G. (1999). 'Ockham's Semantics and Ontology of the Categories'. In *The Cambridge Companion to Ockham*. Ed. P. V. Spade. Cambridge: Cambridge University Press, pp. 118–42.
Klima, G. (2009). *John Buridan*, Oxford and New York: Oxford University Press.
McCord, Adams M. (2000). 'Re-reading "De Grammatico" or Anselm's Introduction to Aristotle's "Categories"'. *Documenti e Studi sulla Tradizione Filosofica Medievale*, 11: 83–112.
Marenbon, J. (1997). *The Philosophy of Peter Abelard*. Cambridge: Cambridge University Press.
Marenbon, J. (2004). 'Dicta, Assertion and Speech Acts: Abelard and some Modern Interpretations'. In *Medieval Theories on Assertive and Non-Assertive Language*. Ed. A. Maierù and L. Valente. Firenze: Olschki, pp. 59–80.
Marmo, C. (1994). *Semiotica e linguaggio nella Scolastica: Parigi, Bologna, Erfurt 1270–1330. La semiotica dei Modisti*. Roma: Istituto Storico Italiano per il Medio Evo (Nuovi Studi Storici, 26).
Marmo, C. (1995). 'A Pragmatic Approach to Language in Modism'. In *Sprachtheorien in Spätantike und Mittelalter*. Ed. S. Ebbesen. Tübingen: Gunter Narr Verlag, pp. 169–83 (Geschichte der Sprachtheorie, 3).

Marmo, C. (1997a). 'Simon of Tournai's *Institutiones in sacram paginam*. An Edition of His Introduction about Signification'. *Cahiers de l'Institut du Moyen Âge Grec et Latin*, 67: 93–103. (Errata corrige in *CIMAGL* 73 (2002), p. 259.)

Marmo, C. (1997b). 'Inferential Signs and Simon of Tournai's General Theory of Signification'. In *Vestigia, Imagines, Verba. Semiotics and Logic in Medieval Theological Texts (XII–XIV Century)*. Proceedings of the XI Symposium on Medieval Logic and Semantics, University of San Marino, 24–8 May 1994. Ed. C. Marmo. Turnhout: Brepols, pp. 61–82.

Marmo, C. (2005). 'Il *simbolismo* altomedievale: tra controversie eucaristiche e conflitti di potere'. In *Comunicare e significare nell'Alto Medioevo*, Atti della LII Settimana di Studio del Centro Italiano di Studi sull'Alto Medioevo, 15–20 aprile 2004. Spoleto: Centro Italiano di Studi sull'Alto Medioevo, pp. 765–819.

Marmo, C. (2006). 'La funzione del contesto: teorie "continentali" e "inglesi" a confronto sull'eliminazione dell'equivocità tra fine XIII e inizio XIV secolo'. In *"Ad Ingenii Acuitionem". Studies in Honor of Alfonso Maierù*. Ed. S. Caroti, R. Imbach, Z. Kaluza, G. Stabile and L. Sturlese. Louvain-La-Neuve: FIDEM, pp. 249–80.

Marmo, C. (2007). 'Segno e immagini nella teologia di Pietro Lombardo'. In *Pietro Lombardo*, Atti del convegno internazionale, Todi, 8–10 ottobre 2006. Spoleto: Centro Italiano di Studi sull'Alto Medioevo, pp. 51–88.

Marmo, C. (2008). 'Semiotica della presenza: l'emergere della transustanziazione nel IX secolo e le sue implicazioni semiotiche'. In *Destini del sacro. Discorso religioso e semiotica della cultura*. Ed. G. Marrone and N. Dusi, atti del XXXV Congresso dell'Associazione Italiana di Studi Semiotici. Roma: Meltemi, pp. 59–71.

Marmo, C. (2010). *La semiotica del XIII secolo tra teologia e arti liberali*, Bompiani, Milano.

Marmo, C. (ed.) (2011). *Usus loquendi, discretio audientis, intentio proferentis. Pragmatic Approaches to Language During the Middle Ages*. Special Issue of *Vivarium*, 49/1–3.

Marmo, C. (2014). '*De virtute sermonis/verborum*: l'autonomie du texte dans le traitement des expressions figurées ou multiples'. In *Le pouvoir des mots*. Ed. N. Bériou, J.-P. Boudet and I. Rosier-Catach. Turnhout: Brepols, pp. 49–69.

Marmo, C. (2015). 'Peirce e la teoria medievale delle relazioni'. In *VS. Versus. Quaderni di Studi Semiotici*, 120/1: 15–29.

Marmo, C. (2016). 'Anselmo de Aosta: una filosofía del lenguaje con impronta pragmática'. *deSignis*, 25: 67–75.

Marmo, C. (2017). 'Eco's Semiotics and Medieval Philosophy'. In *The Philosophy of Umberto Eco*. Ed. S. C. Beardsworth and R. E Auxier. Chicago: Open Court, pp. 103–31.

Martin, C. J. (2009). 'Imposition and Essence: What's New in Abaelard's Theory of Meaning?' In *The Word in Medieval Logic, Theology and Psychology*. Ed. T. Shimizu and Ch. Burnett. Turnhout: Brepols, pp. 173–214.

Mill, J. S. (1974 [1843]). *A System of Logic Ratiocinative and Inductive*, 2 vols. Ed. J. M. Robson. Toronto and London: University of Toronto Press and Routledge & Kegan Paul.

Montclos, Jean de (1971). *Lanfranc et Bérenger. La controverse eucharistique du XIe siècle*. Leuven, Spicilegium sacrum lovaniense.

Mora-Márquez, A. M. (2015). *The Thirteenth-Century Notion of Signification. The Discussions and Their Origin and Development*. Investigating Medieval Philosophy, 10. Leiden and Boston: Brill.

Murdoch, J. E. (1981). '*Scientia mediantibus vocibus*. Metalinguistic Analysis in the Late Medieval Natural Philosophy'. In *Sprache und Erkenntnis im Mittelalter*. Ed. W. Kluxen. Miscellanea mediaevalia, 13/1–2. Berlin and New York: De Gruyter, pp. 73–106.

Panaccio, C. (1991). *Les mots, les concepts et les choses. La sémantique de Guillaume d'Occam et le nominalisme d'aujourd'hui*. Montréal and Paris: Bellarmin and Vrin.

Panaccio, C. (1999a). *Le discours intérieur de Platon à Guillaume d'Ockham*. Paris: Seuil.

Panaccio, C. (1999b). 'Semantics and Mental Language'. In *The Cambridge Companion to Ockham*. Ed. P. V. Spade. Cambridge: Cambridge University Press, pp. 53–75.

Panaccio, C. (2004). *Ockham on Concepts*. Aldershot: Ashgate.

Paschasius Radbertus (1969). *De corpore et sanguine domini*. Ed. B. Paulus. Corpus Christianorum, Continuatio Mediaevalis, 16. Turnhout: Brepols.
Paschasius Radbertus (1984). *Expositio in Matheo libri 12*. Corpus Christianorum, Continuatio Mediaevalis, 56–56A–B. Ed. B. Paulus. Turnhout: Brepols.
Pinborg, J. (1967). *Die Entwicklung der Sprachtheorie im Mittelalter*. Münster: Aschendorff.
Porro, P. (2012). *Tommaso d'Aquino: un profilo storico-filosofico*. Roma: Carocci.
Ratramnus of Corbie (1954). *De corpore et sanguine domini*. Ed. B. van den Brink. Amsterdam: North Holland.
Rosier, I. (1995). Res significata et modus significandi: Les implications d'une distinction médiévale. In *Sprachtheorien in Spätantike und Mittelalter*. Ed. S. Ebbesen. Tübingen: Gunter Narr Verlag, pp. 135–68 (Geschichte der Sprachtheorie, 3).
Rosier-Catach, I. (1996). 'Langage et signe dans la discussion eucharistique'. In *Histoire et grammaire du sens. Hommage à Jean-Claude Chevalier*. Ed. S. Auroux, S. Delesalle and H. Meschonnic. Paris: Colin, pp. 42–58.
Rosier-Catach, I. (2003). 'Abélard et les grammairiens: sur le verbe substantif et la prédication'. *Vivarium*, 41/2: 175–248.
Rosier-Catach, I. (2004a). 'Les discussions sur le signifié des propositions chez Abélard et ses contemporaines'. In *Medieval Theories on Assertive and Non-Assertive Language*. Ed. A. Maierù and L. Valente. Firenze: Olschki, pp. 1–34.
Rosier-Catach, I. (2004b). *La parole efficace. Signe, rituel, sacré*. Paris: Seuil.
Siri, F. (2011). Le Institutiones in sacram paginam *di Simone di Tournai. Contributo alla storia delle scuole teologiche a Parigi nel XII secolo*. PhD dissertation, University of Rome.
Spruyt, J. (2000). 'Gilbert of Poitiers on the Application of Language to the Transcendent and Sublunary Domains'. In *The Winged Charriot. Collected Essays on Plato and Platonism in Honour of L. M. de Rijk*. Ed. M. Kardaun and J. Spruyt. Leiden: Brill, pp. 205–36.
Valente, L. (1995). 'Une sémantique particulière: la pluralité des sens dans les Ecritures Saintes (XIIe siècle)'. In *Sprachtheorien in Spätantike und Mittelalter*. Ed. S. Ebbesen. Tübingen: Gunter Narr Verlag, pp. 12–32 (Geschichte der Sprachtheorie, 3).
Valente, L. (2008). *Logique et théologie. Les écoles parisiennes entre 1150 et 1220*. Paris: Vrin.
William of Sherwood (1995). *Introductiones in logicam*. Ed. H. Brands and Ch. Kann. Hamburg: Meiner.

9

A Path to Identity: Meister Eckhart's Ascesis of the Soul

Alberto Martinengo

Meister Eckhart's thought has been presented in innumerable forms during the course of the history of philosophy. All great thinkers of the Western tradition have been subject to such multiplication of images. It is indeed a *sine qua non*: an author becomes a classic only if he or she reaches us through a mirror broken into countless fragments, each of which bears an image that is slightly different from the others. This is true of the great Greek philosophers and of the most important modern thinkers. But as far as medieval philosophy is concerned, Meister Eckhart is the author for whom this description is most apt, and probably the only one it fits so fundamentally.

Disseminating Meister Eckhart

The picture of interpretations of Meister Eckhart's thought is therefore multifaceted and resists any attempt at an unequivocal reconstruction. How to reconcile the Meister Eckhart considered as the harbinger of German idealism with the one that Alfred Rosenberg tragically associated with the blood and soil of Nazi pseudo-mysticism? How to reconcile Arthur Schopenhauer's or theosophy's appropriation of him with the line taken, in quite another direction, by Erich Fromm or by Carl Gustav Jung?

On the other hand, this fragmentation is not limited to being a question of reception: it is not only Eckhart's interpreters who have split the mirror into various fragments, sometimes faithful, sometimes completely arbitrary. Meister Eckhart himself is at one and the same time many different things. At least three, according to Kurt Ruh (1985), one of the most authoritative contemporary scholars: Meister Eckhart was in fact principally a theologian, preacher and mystic. Each of these labels refers to spheres that only partly overlap; for example, Eckhart's theology is not only mystical, nor is his mysticism only theological – indeed it is a mysticism that goes far beyond theology. But the situation is even more complex with regard to his preaching – or, rather, preachings. As most of his interpreters observe, Meister Eckhart's sermons differ fundamentally depending on his audience, according to a pattern that is easily traced: the German sermons are addressed to the laity, while the Latin sermons are meant for his religious brothers.

The history of interpretation of Eckhart takes different and often irreconcilable directions, depending on whether the focus is his theological research, mystical reflection or teaching – and indeed according to the different kinds of teaching directed towards a religious or lay audience. It is, moreover, a history that branches out into ever more bumpy paths according to the way in which the links or contradictions between these different aspects of Meister Eckhart's *corpus* are reconstructed. On the whole, however, the prevailing interpretations follow the pattern established by Franz Pfeiffer, to whom we owe the first modern edition of Eckhart's German works (1857). Pfeiffer draws a very clear distinction between the German and Latin works. Pfeiffer draws the distinction on philological grounds, but most interpreters also see it in terms of subject matter. So although 'images of Meister Eckhart' have proliferated during the course of modern and contemporary history (Degenhardt 1967) there is also a prevailing line of thought, based on two principles: (1) recognising the specificity of the doctrinal content of the German works and (2) reserving the possibility of reading Meister Eckhart from various points of view, not only under the three labels of theologian, preacher and mystic, but also as philosopher or anti-philosopher, metaphysician or anti-metaphysician, as orthodox or heretical, and so on.

This interpretative scheme is the result of a process that began long ago, at least as far back as the so-called romantic rediscovery of Meister Eckhart, the main exponent of which was Franz von Baader, and then continued in the opposing directions of idealism on the one hand and Schopenhaurean anti-idealism on the other. The Eckhartian revival continued throughout the nineteenth century, including in the field of philology, first with the publication by Pfeiffer of the German works, followed by a similar undertaking by Heinrich Denifle for the Latin *corpus* (1886). The twentieth century, considered broadly, was characterised by the continuation of this philological effort, that manifests itself in the critical edition published by Kohlhammer, from 1936 on. But it was also the century in which Eckhart was widely appropriated, in the ways I outlined above: in fields ranging from philosophy to Nazi ideology, from psychoanalysis to the history of religions.

In such a broad and fragmented scenario, in which considerations of a philological nature have completed the critical work, it is now up to philosophy to navigate the various 'images of Meister Eckhart', to distinguish on a case-by-case basis those in which the figure of Meister Eckhart emerges from those in which it gives way to the interpreter alone, and often to his arbitrary judgement. It is a task that is all the more difficult insofar as one tries not to reduce Meister Eckhart to the role of an authority used to support or oppose other people's theories – or even worse, to justify them and disappear inside them, as in some readings of an eclectic nature, especially the field of comparative religion. To resort to a commonplace phrase, the task today, if anything, is to think with Meister Eckhart: to really understand him, and profoundly so, as a classic thinker.

Twentieth-century philosophy has made more than one attempt at this. The most substantial, both in depth and breadth, is without doubt to be found in the constellation of thought linked to Martin Heidegger. Not so much in Heidegger himself, whose attention with respect to Meister Eckhart is limited both to a certain time and in terms of depth (Heidegger 1959), but rather in some of his interpreters. The most important name in this regard is without doubt that of Reiner Schürmann.

Within the vast literature on Martin Heidegger, Schürmann's contributions hold a very distinctive position. Schürmann (1941–93) is one of the authors who most clearly posed the problem of how to construct a connection that is not merely coincidental between the end of Western metaphysics and the crisis of scholasticism. In taking this path, Schürmann's thesis is that Heidegger retraced Meister Eckhart's *Denkweg* and in so doing clarified its philosophical significance. Schürmann's first book, *Wandering Joy*, published in French in 1972, is the primary reference in this regard. The volume consists of the translation of some of Meister Eckhart's German sermons, accompanied by generous sections of analysis and commentary, focusing on the soul's ascent to God.[1] But, beyond the strong theological tenor dictated by the subject matter, Schürmann's entire discourse moves in another direction: the aim is to show that the spiritual and theological considerations of the sermons presuppose a specific understanding of being, a sort of undeclared ontology which goes beyond the Thomistic metaphysics of *analogia entis*, prefiguring what Heidegger will later call ontology of the event. For Schürmann the claim to a non-cognitive dimension as a presupposition for thinking suggests a decisive analogy between Heidegger and Rhineland mysticism, according to which the ascetic road of detachment is the practical condition for access to truth.

According to Schürmann, Meister Eckhart is the most important voice of this strand of Western thought. As he states: 'Thinking is a consequent [of acting] inasmuch as it does not arise without preparation. On this crucial point – still more than on the two topics of *Gelassenheit*, "releasement," and of *Anwesen* understood as a verb, as "presencing" – Heidegger belongs to the tradition initiated by Meister Eckhart' (Schürmann 1982: 235) Thus even before he is the master of the mystical path to God, Eckhart is first and foremost the author of the priority of 'acting'. As he teaches in the sermon *Beati pauperes spiritu*: 'So long as you do not equal this truth of which we now want to speak, you cannot understand me' (Schürmann 1972: 210).

Thinking with Meister Eckhart: Reiner Schürmann

Wandering Joy essentially focuses on the theme of the mind's detachment from the world (the *abegescheidenheit*, in Eckhart's Middle High German). The severing of the ties with beings is the key to explaining the birth of the *Logos* in the ground of the soul, the beginning of that unity with God's ground that is the endpoint of the ascetic's path. The book is a collection of eight German sermons, translated into English and accompanied by a detailed commentary: *Intravit Iesus*; *Qui odit animam suam*; *Mulier, venit hora*; *Quasi vas auri solidum ornatum*; *Surrexit autem Saulus de terra*; *Videte qualem caritatem*; *Praedica verbum*; and *Beati pauperes spiritu*. Schürmann's choice of the German sermons is not accidental, as his hypothesis is that they are written in the context of Eckhart's activity of promoting a spiritual journey and are, therefore, completely free of the doctrinal requirements characteristic of the Latin works. *Wandering Joy* further develops this idea, presenting a veritable watershed between Eckhart's institutional teachings (which are academic, and therefore in Latin) and the pastoral teaching (in the vernacular, for the most part at the Rhineland monasteries). Yet, apart from questions of historiography – on which the literature on Eckhart is still divided – Schürmann's discussion is doubtless mainly philosophical: Eckhart's reflections on the *abegescheidenheit* constitute, to all intents and purposes, a description of the ways in which the soul is initiated into the understanding of God; and this initiation is accomplished thanks to the union of the ground of the soul with the ground of God.

The path taken by Schürmann's reading starts at exactly this point. The ascetic's process is tellingly outlined in the sermon *Intravit Iesus*, where Eckhart comments on Luke 10:38, the

---

[1] Of course, Meister Eckhart's sermons pose a primary problem of translation, as they are entirely grounded on non-philological interpretations of the New Testament. As far as possible, Schürmann follows Eckhart's Middle High German, from Quint's edition (Eckhart 1936–). The present chapter follows Schürmann's translation (Schürmann 1972), so as to emphasise Eckhart's contemporary presence in Heideggerian debate.

incipit of the episode of Martha and Mary. In the sermon, the verse reads as follows: 'Our Lord Jesus Christ went up into a little castle and was received by a virgin who was a wife' (Schürmann 1972: 3).[2] As Schürmann explains, the entire sermon centres on three figures: the virgin, the fertile woman and the castle. In order to embrace the Word, one must be free and unburdened by any intellectual image: this condition is the virginity of the soul. One can have such great wisdom as to embrace the essential images of all things that are in God, but as long as one is attached to them, one cannot enter God's essence. In order to know God, the soul must be virgin, as it was before it was born. At the same time, however, if the soul always remained virgin, it would not bear the fruits required before God; in order to bear fruit, it must become a 'fertile woman'. A virgin spirit, which is detached from things, but 'at the same time' fertile, is close to God and is able to bear fruit, in the same way that God the Father gave birth to the Son. Thus, Eckhart can affirm that one who combines virginity with regard to the world and fertility with regard to God will experience a power that engenders the Word directly within their soul. The site of God's action is the *castellum* evoked in the verse of the gospel, a kind of citadel in which is enshrined the profound essence of man: the ground of the soul. The castle is a region that is untouched by either time or flesh (Schürmann 1972: 5). It is a kind of immaterial spark, devoid of any objective and formal determination. This separation is so deep – Eckhart concludes – that not even God can live in the ground of the soul, at least not until he divests himself of his attributes.

Of the three components (virginity, fertility, God's intervention in the *castellum*), Schürmann places emphasis on a methodical assumption, which he sums up as the 'wandering understanding of virginity' (Schürmann 1972: 13). In Schürmann's view, the sermon, which draws in a negative sense on the Platonic and Aristotelian doctrine of the *psyché*, connotes virginity as the possibility of erasing all trace of things from the soul. Yet, in spite of the explicit references to traditional theories, virginal freedom is not understood as an essential dimension, granted to humans *ab origine*, but as a condition that must be regained. As Schürmann writes:

> Meister Eckhart integrates both traditions, the Platonic and the Aristotelian, into a new context by blending the theory of the preexistence of the soul and that of the receptive intellect. From this amalgam results the Eckhartian dictum that one become 'devoid of all foreign images, as void as he was when he was not yet'. (Schürmann 1972: 13)

This is the practical and paraenetic dimension of Eckhart's reflections, which Schürmann deals with at length: 'Man has been virgin, ledic, in his preexistence, he is always thus in his intellect, and he must become so again in his entire being' (Schürmann 1972: 13). Therefore 'both elements of doctrine are thus recast not in a theoretical dogma of what man is, but as a practical guide to what he must become' (Schürmann 1972: 13). This is very significant with regard to the way Eckhart treats traditional doctrines: although it makes use of traditional categories, his preaching endows them with a significance that is for the most part novel. These categories no longer take as their subject the essence of the human spirit but are enlisted in the exhortative endeavour of the sermon. As Schürmann states: the language of the German sermons 'is opposed to the language of metaphysics as an exhortation is opposed to verification: Meister Eckhart's words never state facts; rather, they open our eyes to new possibilities and, in

---

[2] The whole sermon plays around the sentence 'Und wart enpfangen von einer juncvrouwen, diu ein wip was', which Eckhart translates with the Latin phrase 'Et mulier quaedam, Martha nomine, excepit illum in domum suam' (Luke 10:38).

making us see, they engage our existence on a new road' (Schürmann 1972: 27). To make us see and to engage existence on the path of detachment: these are the elements of what Schürmann calls the wandering understanding of existence, which he considers to be the fundamental intention of the German sermons. Not so much a metaphysical analysis of the mind, then, but a preaching that points to detachment as a path to reach man's deepest freedom.

If 'exhortation' is the most characteristic feature of the sermons, Meister Eckhart's teaching seems above all aimed at clarifying a misunderstanding, which Schürmann points out in a very clear way. Virginity should not be read as an attribute of the soul, but as the reassessment of the relationships that the soul establishes with the world. *Intravit Iesus* deals with this complex reorientation of the notion of virginity – and with the theme of the *abegescheidenheit*, which is related to it. This reorientation has nothing to do with the necessity for privation. To detach oneself from the world, in Eckhart's teaching, does not mean to escape from it, but to open up the possibility of a totally renewed relationship with things: indeed, what impedes the virginity of the soul is not so much the possession of images but attachment to them. Through a transition that reminds Schürmann of the Hymn to Charity from the First Letter to the Corinthians, the sermon shifts the focus from 'what one has' to 'what one is'; that is, from property to modality. To quote the sermon:

> I could have so vast an intelligence that all the images that all human beings have ever received and those that are in God himself were comprehended in my intellect; however, if I were in no way attached to them, to the point that everything I do or neglect to do, I did not cling to any of them with attachment [. . .] then I should indeed be a virgin. (Schürmann 1972: 3–4)

The movement towards virginity, then, is not a matter of objective contents but the distinction between two different inner-worldly behaviours. Freedom from images has nothing to do with things possessed or abandoned, but rather with something radically different. According to Schürmann, it is the distinction between two opposite temporal modalities: one bound to things lives in a temporality that stretches between the before and the after, while one is liberated in what Eckhart defines as the 'gegenwertigen nû', the present moment that circumscribes detachment. In its turn, the present moment does not result in a total exit from the world and from time, because to all effects and purposes it establishes another way of operating in daily life: detachment teaches us to be 'among things, without restraint' (Schürmann 1972: 15), producing an existential change that leads man to a new, radically different, temporality.

Temporality, then, is the context in which any commerce with things takes place. In this sense, the sermon is very explicit in speaking of the possibility of a 'fertile virginity', that is, a virginity that nevertheless stretches along a temporal course. To detach oneself from things, as we have seen, means above all opening oneself up to something that occurs from outside (in this case, the birth of the *Logos*): authentic detachment does not halt before God, but proceeds ready and willing to cooperate with divine intervention. This cooperation takes place at two different levels of radicalness. First, the soul embraces the birth of the Word, becoming one with it. At the same time, however, in embracing and generating the Son, the soul becomes co-responsible for this generation and is thereby united with the Father: one liberated from things becomes (like) the Son but, at the same time, allows oneself to be generated as Son and joins the Father in this creation. It is through a single movement that the soul opens itself to the intervention of the Father and generates within itself the Son.

However, it remains to be seen in real terms in what sense the process of detachment produces a 'wandering' understanding of virginity. The generation of the Son and the union of creature and Creator certainly imply an interpretation of identity in terms of a development. This means that any reference to identity must be understood as a sort of 'generative unity', that Schürmann resorts to in order to dispel all possible misunderstandings. The two possible forms of identity between soul and God are excluded *a priori*: soul is not God, either by virtue of an identity of substance or in the sense of instant rapture. It is always the process of generation that mediates unity, a progressive identification that leads the two entities to produce the conditions for a simultaneous birth. In this sense Schürmann prefers to speak of 'operative identity' and considers it the best rendition of Eckhart's *'einheit im gewürke'*, dealt with in the sermon *Justi vivent in aeternum*: 'God and I are one in this work [*Got und ich wir sint ein in disem gewürke*]: he acts and I become. Fire transforms all things it touches into its own nature' (Schürmann 1972: 101). The detached soul and the Father are but one thing, but only within the process by which the Son is generated little by little.

According to Schürmann, then, the unity between human and God – or, better, between the ground of the soul and the ground of God – cannot be confused with an indistinct and static identity, but is rather a simultaneous working in the same direction: the human who converts to detachment is able to take the same path as that taken by the Father when he generates the Son. As in the Aristotelian theory of knowledge – where the knower and the known are different but are assimilated in the act of knowing – so God and the soul become one in the act of generation.

From this point of view, Meister Eckhart's statements certainly have a heterodox significance. It is precisely the most radical implications of Eckhart's theory that drew the attention of the ecclesiastical hierarchy. This, according to Schürmann, is no coincidence. In the Avignon trial, what is at stake is the correct interpretation of the identity between creature and Creator. What issued from the inquiry is one of the possible solutions to the question of the fertility of mind. For Schürmann it is based on the misunderstanding mentioned above: the identity of the ground of mind and the ground of God is interpreted in a substantive and indicative way, which is the exact opposite of Schürmann's reading.

Conversely, if Eckhart's arguments had been read in the sense of the wandering understanding of virginity (or identity), a completely different side of Eckhart's thought would have emerged, which the ecclesiastical authorities were unable to grasp. According to Schürmann, this alternative interpretation is not only possible but more reliable than the other, as it places Eckhart's arguments on identity within their context: when Eckhart speaks of a fertile virginity, he is speaking above all as a preacher, rather than a philosopher. And, as we have seen, this is not a coincidental difference, if the sermons are studied for what they are, as homiletic texts addressed to the Rhineland religious communities.[3] Meister Eckhart 'speaks less of what man is prior to the itinerary of his existence, than of what he is destined to become' (Schürmann 1972: 27). In this sense, Eckhart's conviction for heresy is the inevitable result of the Avignon inquiry, since 'a form of "wandering" thought, concerned with showing a way, is subject to the judgement of the "thetic" thought of late Scholasticism and is rejected as heterodox' (Schürmann 1972: 28). In language that is not Schürmann's, one could say that the arguments of the sermons have, first of all, a 'performative' value: union is produced only if the exhortation to detachment is taken literally and if the creature agrees to follow the path of the Father

---

[3] As mentioned above, the assumption that Meister Eckhart is, first and foremost, a preacher and that he should be read as such is anything but foregone for contemporary interpreters. Among those who do not share this conviction, one should at least mention Alain de Libera's emphasis on the theological side of Eckhart's model (de Libera 1999). On the other side, see for example (Ruh 1985).

who creates the Word. Identity is not a fact but a conquest: because it stands at the end of a journey, it is in every sense a wandering identity.

Deconstructing Teleology

The question of the wandering identity and of its ontological premises is the subject of another important sermon, *Mulier, venit hora*, in which Meister Eckhart comments on the episode of the Good Samaritan. (John 4:23) The sermon strives to show that the soul of the true worshipper is the one that has completed the path of the *abegescheidenheit*. At the end of this path, the true worshipper attains a reality that Eckhart outlines as follows: the human detached from things places themselves in that separate 'other' temporality, which is perfect eternity, insofar as eternal life is the only appropriate condition for adoration in spirit and truth. But there is a more fundamental element distinguishing the ascetic's economy from that of daily life. In detachment, ordinary commerce with things is suspended starting from its most characteristic element, that is, its teleological orientation. All things in ordinary time have a reason: man makes use of them for his own purposes and includes them in a system governed by the law of the *telos*. Conversely, the soul of the true worshipper renounces this system and opens itself up to an anti-teleological attitude towards the world. Only when it agrees to renounce teleology, can the soul open out to God, and this is so because the Father asks to be sought as such by the Son, beyond any reason. As the sermon states: 'All things that are in time have a why. Thus, when someone asks a man: "Why are you eating?" – "In order to gain strength." – "Why are you sleeping?" – 'For the same reason.' And so with everything that is in time'. To the contrary, 'if someone asked a good man: "Why do you love God?" – "I do not know, because of God." – "Why do you love the truth?" – "Because of the truth." – [. . .] "Why are you living?" – "My word, I do not know! But I am happy to be alive"' (Schürmann 1972: 54).

From the spiritual point of view, Eckhart's argument is clear: we cannot seek God in the same way that we look for things in the world, that is, with a concern for their usage – or, to use Heidegger's term, their readiness-to-hand. Renouncing the inner-worldly economy means, first of all, giving up the law that holds together all worldly things and that is based on the relationship between intention and end. From the philosophical point of view, however, this passage has far more important consequences: God is no longer sought as the bearer of names and attributes but for his nobility that exceeds that of any Person (of the Trinity). This means that the human detached from things enters into a particular relationship with the Creator, that enables him/her to discover in the dimension where there is no reason the most authentic existential dimension. As the sermon *Omne datum bonum* puts it: 'Know this: as long as in one way or another you seek your own advantage, you will never find God, for you do not seek God exclusively' (Schürmann 1972: 61). Thus, continues Eckhart, in doing so 'you behave as if you transformed God into a candle, in order to find something; and when one has found what one looked for, one throws away the candle' (Schürmann 1972: 61). So, those who live ruled by concern for purposes are unable to adore the Father in spirit and truth, because they seek God only with a view to their own ends. The true worshipper is required to learn detachment, taking the 'without a why' as the cipher of their daily existence.

This confirms that Eckhart's *abegescheidenheit* does not entail a flight from the world, but rather a particular behaviour 'in the midst of the world': this behaviour revives inner-worldly commerce with things and steers it towards God. This radical understanding of detachment, already explicit in the notion of the wandering identity between the creature and the Creator, allows Schürmann however to take a further step towards arriving at one of the most significant features of his interpretation. In fact, we can infer that the shift to the economy of the 'without a why' implies, as its precondition, a notion of inner-worldliness, which can be defined as 'wandering existence'. As detachment is primarily a way of leading one's own life among inner-worldly things, it is detached existence itself that is characterised by the condition of wandering. This is why, in the sermon *Mulier, venit hora*, Schürmann chooses the notion of *itinerancy* as the most appropriate key for interpreting Eckhart's model (Schürmann 1972: 57–8). Itinerancy first appears in the form of the wandering understanding, in explaining the identity between creature and Creator. Later, it undergoes a first ontological radicalisation, in order to characterise the dimension of detachment; finally, it becomes itinerancy of existence more generally when the issue is to make sense of the call towards ascesis.

Schürmann resorts to this model in order to distinguish Meister Eckhart's argument from the *itinerarium in Deum*, typical of medieval theology from Bernard of Clairvaux to Bonaventure: if the *itinerarium mentis* is essentially the *iter*, the path of the soul towards God, Eckhart's itinerancy, on the other hand, is the way in which the condition of wandering becomes absolute and – if the anachronism be allowed – a sort of existential category. On this reading, the interpretation of detachment in terms of process is structured around four figures, in Eckhart's terms: '*unglîcheit*' (dissimilarity), '*gelîcheit*' (similarity), '*einheit*' (identity), '*ûzbruch*' (or '*ûzvluz*', dehiscence). These concepts should not be interpreted as four stages in a progressive journey (as in the *itinerarium*), but rather as the ontological 'coordinates' of the detached soul. The creature differs from and resembles God at the same time (*unglîcheit* and *gelîcheit*); but only at the moment in which one is identical to the Creator does one make space for the generation of the Word (*einheit* and *ûzbruch*). These, in other words, are the four directions through which the creature and the Creator enter into contact: ascesis is and continues to be a journey (and, undoubtedly, in ascetic practice a progressive one); this, from the ontological point of view, however, is entirely irrelevant, because when ascesis is reached, the soul still remains oriented to those four cardinal points that make relationship with God possible. Dissimilarity, similarity, identity and dehiscence draw 'the horizon within which God encounters man' (Schürmann 1972: 82).

In these passages Schürmann's reading is very detailed, but it is necessary to follow it, albeit briefly, in order to understand its ontological implications. The first three levels of the analysis are as follows: 'Under Dissimilarity, God and man appear as radically foreign to one another. With Similarity, the latter discovers himself to be a reflection of the former. Identity brings to the fore the unique nobleness of the ground of man' (Schürmann 1972: 82). Something rather different takes place at the fourth level that Schürmann denotes with the term *dehiscence*: 'Finally, "Dehiscence," the last road sign, points in the direction of itinerancy where there is no longer God or man, but only the desert' (Schürmann 1972: 82). Let us try to clarify the terms of the question. The dissimilarity between human and God manifests itself through the absolute opposition between being and nothing:[4] before the Father – says the sermon *Omne datum bonum* – all creatures are 'mere nothingness' ('*ein lûter niht*') (Schürmann 1972: 62). The creature is nothing compared to God: its being wholly resides in the Creator, from whom it receives at all times. In this case, a radical dualism is at play between the spark of the soul and creaturality: in the former, the human is one with God, while in the latter he or she is pure non-being. Nonetheless, once again, the discussion on dissimilarity does not derive from a merely descriptive perspective but is rather the condition for the exhortation to ascesis: in the mind there are not two different substances – a human nature and a divine one – but rather a

---

[4] For another perspective on the opposition between and relation of being and non-being, see Chapter 7 in this volume by Dermot Moran.

constant conflict that pulls the mind in two directions. And it is on the basis of this conflict that Eckhart addresses one to exhort oneself to ascesis. This is all the more evident in the transition from difference to similarity, the second term of the *abegescheidenheit*. The discussion on the *gelîcheit* largely clarifies what, for Schürmann, is the operative unity between creature and Creator: 'similarity' does not describe a static condition of sameness, but the dynamism of the 'becoming one', the drawing together of two dissimilar entities. In this gradual assimilation, creature and Creator are like the wood and the burning flames: originally two different substances, gradually, however, they fuse into one event, the fire.

The metaphor of fire clarifies in what sense the first two levels of the *abegescheidenheit* are unified in the third term: the actual identity between God and human. Since identity manifests itself in the event (*im gewürke*), it cannot be referred to the category of *ousia*, but to that of *energeia*. Identity becomes a unitary and productive flow in which essences have become wholly indistinct. And in this indistinctiveness, one feature stands out above all others: the impossibility of distinguishing an active and a passive component of the relationship. Schürmann recalls here the image of a musical performance: when the performance is perfect, the listener and the interpreter disappear as such, and only the event in which the two parts merge remains. In this fusion, distinguishing the different elements is no longer possible: the action of the interpreter and the reception of the listener are replaced by a unique and sole act in which dissimilarity approaches identity. Thus, the Father and the creature are embraced in one single event, in which God acts on the soul and the soul acquiesces.

This relationship, however, conceals something else, which is dealt with in the last part of the argument of *Wandering Joy*. If ascesis is not the mere abandonment of the world, but the beginning of a different economy with it, the identity of creature and Creator takes on a new meaning, which necessarily includes the horizon of the world. This is what Schürmann describes when he speaks of the rooting of all things in a more originary dimension – the *ûzbruch*, the fourth level of the *abegescheidenheit* – where their plurality is lost in the flowing together towards a unitary and indistinct condition. Therefore, the *einheit im gewürke* is not only the operative identity of God and man, but also the identity of all things. Where the detached soul comes to rest, things lose their otherness because, once the teleological context has been abandoned, they are rendered to the world in their pure and simple presence. Through ascesis, entities are recovered as part of a more inclusive horizon, the event in which everything that is originally rises to being.

Being Without Reason Why

It is clear that Reiner Schürmann's aim is to assert the possibility of reading Eckhart's ontology in Heideggerian terms – and this attempt is certainly the most engaging purpose of *Wandering Joy*, one that touches one of the most controversial aspects of Eckhart's doctrine, that of the continuous 'generation of the Word' in the ground of the soul. This is the most openly anti-Christological presupposition of the sermons, as the bull 'In agro dominico', which sentenced Eckhart, points out (sentences XII–XIII):[5] for Eckhart, the incarnation is less an historical

---

[5] 'The twelfth article. Whatever holy scripture says of Christ, all that is also true of every good and divine man. The thirteenth article. Whatever is proper to the divine nature, all that is proper to the just and divine man. Because of that, this man performs whatever God performs, and he created heaven and earth together with God, and he is the begetter of the Eternal Word, and God would not know how to do anything without such a man' ('In agro dominico', sentences XII–XIII).

event which is realised in Jesus of Nazareth the man, than an event involving every human at the apex of detachment. In this perspective, Schürmann prefers to stress how the generation of the Word takes place in practice in the detached soul; in the sermons, this process is placed in the category of the *ûzbruch*.

In botanic terms, dehiscence is the process by which some types of fruit, when rotting, open up and release their inner seeds. For Schürmann, Eckhart's *ûzbruch* coincides exactly with this death and opening of the soul, by which the Word is created: when the soul has reached absolute detachment and thus its unity with God, there is no longer any trace of a distinction; soul and God have become one thing and exist in the most essential divine dimension, the Deity. But in its energetic (and not substantive) dimension, this identity is unstable and able to 'release' the seeds that, fertilising the soul, generate the Word. The generation of the *Logos* is thus the teleological dimension of dehiscence. Because the Word is that by means of which everything is created (John 1:1–3), the production of the Word is the firstling of the emergence of being in its totality. Dehiscence, then, is the event in which the Son and, with Him, being in its entirety are produced in the ground of the soul. As the sermon *Praedica verbum* says: 'Here, in the innermost and the most sublime part of the mind, into which time has never penetrated and into which no image has ever cast its reflection, God creates the entire universe.' And, further: 'All that God created six thousand years ago, and all that God will create six thousand years from now, if the world exists that long, he creates in the innermost and the most sublime part of the mind' (Schürmann 1972: 179).

Thus, the dehiscence of the Word, apex of the *abegescheidenheit*, is not only a theological determination, but the epiphenomenon of a more general ontological structure. The abyss from which dehiscence occurs is the pre-original place for all coming into being, the place where being, as yet undifferentiated between eternity and creation, starts being structured in a world. Schürmann correctly describes the abyss of dehiscence as absolute nothingness, the empty and sterile desert from which, suddenly, being springs. But beyond the spiritual meanings, which are certainly relevant in Eckhart's reflection, we must not forget that the call to the *abegescheidenheit* implies a very powerful assumption that, for Schürmann, is precisely an ontological one.

In order to explain the understanding of being that underlies Eckhart's teaching on detachment, Schürmann starts from a very broad principle. Undoubtedly, the most fundamental presupposition of the *abegescheidenheit* is that of the so called *contemptus mundi*. Contempt for the world is of course a central element of all mystical theologies, but in Eckhart's sermons it takes on a theoretical meaning that goes far beyond any moral considerations. In this case, the different steps of the *abegescheidenheit* explain the sense of the *contemptus*, as the 'existential attitude' required of the believer. The last stage of detachment is particularly telling in this regard. In fact, the operative identity with the Deity reveals God's ground – and the soul's – to be the source from which everything draws its being. This sort of insight into the 'pre-original' ground of everything lays the framework within which the call to detachment receives its most authentic sense: it is only when the soul grasps in the Deity the origin of all that is, that it understands the meaning of the path it has taken. This new economy, issuing from the rejection of things, demonstrates in a tangible way what spiritual exhortations have always preached: things are nothing in themselves because they owe their being to a more originary donation. In this sense, the imperative to interrupt ordinary commerce with the world rests on nothing if not an *a posteriori* acquisition: if the authentic essence of things is not self-determined, nor grounded on the telic continuity of human *praxis*, what is truly relevant in things is not their temporal, causal or final coordinates, but their rooting in the Deity. The reality of the ground of God is the only one to which being truly belongs: everything else has only an indirect value, a value which depends on what its origin is. In this regard, the presupposition upon which the *abegescheidenheit* is based is easily identified: being is a sort of 'ontological loan', which is attributed to things thanks to a contingent act, or, better, to an event. As Schürmann explains: 'Creatures receive being as a loan, not as their own. Their being resides in God, it is a gift; but he who gives can also take back. Their being is precarious, it comes to them from another' (Schürmann 1972: 60).

Upon a closer look, then, the real issue in this radical negation of the creature's being is not so much the legitimacy of the contempt that the ascetic should nurture towards the world, as the theoretical sustainability of the model associated with it. Entities owe their being to the *ûzbruch* that happens in the ground of God. Nevertheless, in a more radical sense, this means not only that entities are called into being, but also that the generative act never exhausts itself, that things are sustained by a dynamic of continuous assistance. For this reason, Eckhart can state that things, in themselves, are *ein lûter niht*: everything that is owes its being to an attribution that is continuously repeated and unstable; God lifts things from nothingness not only at the first instant in which they come into being, but at every instant of their continuing presence. In this sense, ascesis definitively shifts the focus of the problem from the world to that which, moment after moment, makes it exist: the ascetic realises that behind the finite being, there is always the sustaining presence of God, without which everything would go back to nothingness.

Schürmann coins the expression 'ontology of the loan' based on a terminology that does not appear in the sermons but in *Daz bouch der götlichen troestunge*: Meister Eckhart's problem is not that things do not deserve attention in themselves but that, within them, that from which they draw their being is worthy of attention: everything that is created is not attributable to itself but to the Creator; should the Creator, for one moment, move its gaze away, things would cease to be. There is undoubtedly in these ideas an underestimation, which should not be overlooked, of the gap between the notion of generation and the concept of creation, a gap that Schürmann himself in *Wandering Joy* tends to leave unexplored. Instead, in this case the focus shifts above all to the dynamics of the loan, a concept that can be clarified starting from two sermons in particular.

Schürmann recalls first of all *Videte qualem caritatem*, in which Eckhart comments on the passage from I John 3:1: 'See what love the Father has given us: we are called Sons of God and we are' (Schürmann 1972: 129). In this sermon, Meister Eckhart deals again with the identity structure linking the creature to the Creator, but with greater attention to the *analogon* of the knowing act, already found in the sermon *Iusti vivent in aeternum*: one knows God, only to the extent that God lets himself be known; and because, in God, knowledge, nature and essence coincide, when one reaches knowledge of the Father, one receives from God God's own essence. Yet, given that the nature of God is unlike anything else, the soul must necessarily erase all images in order to embrace its Creator with the intellect. This is an extremely important point for Schürmann. Eckhart's recourse to a gnoseological theory as a metaphor for the *einheit im gewürke* is certainly based on the revival of some elements of Aristotelian doctrine. However, Eckhart applies significant amendments to the idea that the knower and the known are united in the intellectual act, amendments inspired by Platonic metaphysics: the accidental relationship between the knower and the known is replaced by a necessary relationship, similar to that between the original and the copy in the Platonic theory of ideas. Thus, on the one hand, the sermons refer to the Aristotelian tradition in order to show that the soul–God union takes place *in actu* (and therefore is not substantial in nature); but, on the other, they restate that this relationship, inasmuch as it is necessary, requires the constant sustaining presence of God to the soul's ground.

The relationship between the creature and the Creator, then, requires a particularly complex explanation that Schürmann simplifies by reducing it to a structure based on the model of 'participation by perfect appropriation' (Schürmann 1972: 173–7). According to this principle, the soul united to God in the generation of the *Logos* has no autonomous attributes but partakes in God's perfections. At the same time, however, as the soul is rooted in the continuing and necessary relationship with the Father, it does not have a lower ontological status and, through the birth of the Word, wholly appropriates the very ground of God. In *Videte qualem caritatem*, the relationship that occurs in the ground of God is very clear, but paradoxical, as is, moreover, the expression 'participation by perfect appropriation': 'What someone possesses in the beyond, another possesses equally – not as acquired from him or taken from him, but as dwelling in me as my proper good' (Schürmann 1972: 131). This ambiguity is closely linked to the kind of relationship established: 'Therefore I say that in the sense of which I have spoken there will be no similarity and no difference, but rather, without any difference, we shall be the identical being and the identical substance and nature that [the Son] is himself' (Schürmann 1972: 131). The creature's perfect and whole participation in God's being is, at the same time, the complete union of the two: even if it is a created thing, which absolutely and continuously depends on the Creator, the human mind wholly identifies with God and accommodates itself inside him.

The decision to introduce a relationship that can be explained as participation by perfect appropriation makes it particularly difficult to place the sermons within the Scholastic paradigm. In schematic terms, the classical model of the *analogia entis* is built on the constitutive multivocity of the term 'being', a multivocity that rests on the relationship *pros hen*: being can be said in many ways, but always with reference to a definite unity. Therefore, there are multiple meanings for the term *to on*; all of them, however, contain a reference to a fundamental modality, which is the *ousia*. In Aristotle's works, the analogical relationship remains for the most part a logical question. Broadly put, only in the Middle Ages does the discussion on the subject–predicate relationship flow over into the affirmation of a universal and real *primum*. In this framework, analogy becomes the way in which the relationships between un-created substance and created things are regulated: the very structure determining the link between God and created entities is grounded on analogy. This depends on two things: any determination weaker than analogy would entail a complete split between creature and Creator, making it impossible to speak of the creature's autonomous being and precluding the very possibility of knowing the Creator; conversely, any structure stronger than analogy would lead to suppressing one of the two terms, descending into pantheism or atheism. Aquinas definitively clarifies the analogical nature of the relationship between the predicates of the creature and those of the Creator: God fully and infinitely owns the attributes that the creature has only through participation. The perfections characterising creature and Creator are the same, but the way in which they are predicated is different.

In Eckhartian mysticism, this relationship is fundamentally transformed: participation by perfect attribution implies that the tension between analogy and identity clearly leans towards the latter. In turn, because identity is established between two such different realities, it requires an act of continuing participation and, therefore, annuls all autonomy of the created entity. An attribute is shared perfectly by the finite individual only thanks to its always renewed identity with the corresponding eternal essence. This means, for example, that one is good only if one partakes perfectly and without mediation in the divine goodness. As *Daz Buoch der götlichen troustunge* states: 'The good man and Goodness are but one thing, absolutely one goodness, with the difference that one generates, while the other is generated.' God, then, is the perfection of all divine attributes: a human has a given perfection if and only if they live off (or in) the divine essence. Therefore, Schürmann can conclude that 'a just man, considered as just, is nothing: he is just only in Justice. A good man, as good, is nothing: he is good only in Goodness. A true man, as truthful, is nothing: he is true only in the Truth' (Schürmann 1972: 63).

Naturally, what applies to attributes also applies *a fortiori* to being. The creature is 'hungry' for God: it is something only to the extent that it feeds on the divine being. This is the most authentic meaning of the ontology of the loan. If Aquinas relates the entity's being to God's being, against which it is measured, for Eckhart the two terms perfectly coincide, for the simple reason that the entity depends on what God is. In Thomism, things are partly similar to and partly different from God; in Eckhartian mysticism, on the other hand, any type of analogy is erased and replaced by a pure and absolute identity. If being is God's possession alone, the being of the creature not only comes directly and continuously from the Creator, it also totally identifies with it: in practice, there can be nothing outside the relationship of identity (Schürmann 1972: 62–5).

According to Schürmann, then, we can argue that the predicative act (the creature is good, is just, is true . . .) does not at all represent a mode of being, but simply the modality through which God is present in His creatures. It remains to be understood, however, exactly what ontology is implied by the principle of participation by perfect appropriation. The *analogon* of knowledge that appears in *Videte qualem caritatem* allows us to grasp another fundamental element. The analogy chosen by Eckhart emphasises a dimension that can be easily related to an ontology of the event; it is this ontology that takes away and effectively replaces the Thomistic analogy. Clearly, for Eckhart, knowledge cannot develop according to a polar or dual scheme: as has been mentioned, what makes a difference in the process of knowing is the act of learning itself, and not the subject's and object's standing before each other. In other words, knowledge is fed through an overlap whereby the two extremes are in a particular relationship: in the act of knowing, the knower and the known do not own each other, but rather are at the service of a more originary dimension that embraces both. This dimension is simply the event of knowledge, the identity *im gewürke* of the two sides. Similarly, also in the generation of the Word, the ground of the soul and of the Father are joined starting from one and the same activity, which proceeds beyond them: operative identity realises the coincidence between the two entities and excludes any other relationship.

The metaphysics of analogy is summarised in whole and rebutted in the other text that, according to Schürmann, is fundamental to clarify Eckhart's ontology. This is the sermon *Praedica verbum*, which comments on a passage of the Second Letter to Timothy: 'Proclaim the word, pronounce it, produce it, and beget the word!' (Schürmann 1972: 178). In Eckhart's commentary, the announcement of the Word becomes *tout court* an ontological act: the act of pronouncing is no longer human speech, but the manifestation of God's generative act, the surfacing of things from nothingness. The originary *praedicatio* is the event by which God creates the Son, the Spirit and the world. The goal of the sermon is to remind us that this act not only takes place at the beginning of time but is repeated every time that something comes to being: God continuously recreates things and He does this in a chosen site that is neither the world, nor time, but the intimacy of the detached soul. If the world and the flow of things are simply a derived reality, in the *castellum* placed at the bottom of the soul God pronounces in each moment all that is.

The (proto-)event(u)al concept of being, therefore, consists in this, at least according to Schürmann: 'something is' means that it is called to being and this occurs in the form of the *praedicatio*, the event in which the seeds of being are released. Terminologically, this concept is expressed through a language that Eckhart's *Mittelhochdeutsch* for the most part coins or freely modifies. According to Schürmann, one of the most interesting aspects of the language of the sermons is the use of the term '*wesene*' (or '*wesen*'), which connotes being generically but, in particular, reflects the idea that what manifests itself does so through an essential deployment. Eckhart uses different terms to say 'being': '*iht*', that is, 'something in general' (*entitas*); '*isticheit*', that is, 'intimate presence'; and '*wesene*'. Of these, '*wesene*' is certainly the most interesting because, on the one hand, it relates to what Scholasticism defines as *ens commune* and, on the other, it closely relates to what we could call 'essence'. 'We therefore', Schürmann concludes,

> translate '*wesen*' either by essence or, according to the context, by 'essential coming forth.' *Wesen* is the word for the totality of what shows itself, from the point of view of its coming forth. The being of beings is thought of as coming continually to the light. Being is thought of as the daybreak over beings. (Schürmann 1972: 83)

The meaning of the word '*wesene*', then, is related to the (medieval and modern) German term '*bleiben*', to the notion of remaining and inhabiting: being conceived as *wesene* suggests a coming-to-being that lasts and places itself in a stable context of entities (Schürmann 1972: 184). From this point of view, the staying unfolded of a region of beings, the maintenance of an opening of being, is *wesene*. As such, it refers to a further dimension, indicated by the other important word used by Eckhart: '*isticheit*'. The unfolding that occurs in the *praedicatio* maintains itself in presence thanks to the fact that being makes itself present for beings, continuously pulling them away from nothingness: if *wesene* indicates the state of openness, *isticheit* indicates the intimate presence in things that is able to preserve them.[6]

This terminological inventiveness is one of the aspects most clearly emphasised not only by Schürmann, but in the critical literature on Eckhart generally; as we can see, Schürmann does not hesitate to associate it with the terminology of Heidegger. Certainly, much of Eckhart's originality rests on the relation that the German works establish with a language that, in the fourteenth century, is still developing. Beyond this, however, the linguistic distinction between *wesene* and *isticheit* is clearly functional to the idea of generation followed in the sermons: the creature is nothing in itself, because through the *wesene* it is pulled away from non-being; this, however, would be impossible without a principle of proximity (*isticheit*). Presence, from the point of view of the created being, is the essential unfolding, while from the point of view of the uncreated being it is its being intimately present in created beings. The important element in these linguistic variations is the potential for transformation of the analogy paradigm. The *wesene* and the *isticheit* are in no way attributes of the created being, even if they are intimately concerned with it. The event of the *wesene* is unique, because it is the only condition of possibility of what is (and does not allow for any analogical consideration). In the same way, the proximity of the *isticheit* indicates the presence of the uncreated to the created being: the created being is in presence as unfolded, but not as *istic*.

This profound revolution of scholastic metaphysics, then, goes to the heart of Meister Eckhart's German works. On the one hand, metaphysical theology is necessarily a foundational doctrine: by moving the analogy from the linguistic to the ontological level, it uses the relationship *pros hen* in order to place the temporal entity in relation to the eternal substance. The

---

[6] Concerning the *isticheit*, Schürmann refers to a noteworthy version of the sermon *Iusti vivent in aeternum*, reproduced by Quint: 'If God's nature is my nature, then the divine being is my being. Thus God is more intimately present to all creatures [Do ist got istiger allen creaturen] than the creature is to itself' (Schürmann 1972: 185; see Eckhart 1936–: I, 97).

hierarchy linking the substance to the predicates works analogically in the perfect and infinite modality of God and in the imperfect and finite modalities of created entities, enabling to ground existing things on the divine foundation. On the other hand, the teaching of Eckhart's sermons moves wholly beyond this scheme: the divine word evokes and pronounces the world, but in such a way that, in the *praedicatio*, it is impossible to find any trace of the foundation.

Better still, for Schürmann there is a subterraneous river that runs beneath the whole of Western philosophy and that in Meister Eckhart blows apart the scholastic foundationalism. Eckhart's thought is structured in an ontology of the event that, emerging at the other end of Western thought, was to become once again central in Heidegger. Yet – what counts the most – this is not a coincidence or an anachronistic echo from one thinker to another almost 700 years apart. It is the focusing of the fundamental question of philosophical modernity – a question with which we continue to come to terms.[7]

References

Degenhardt, Ingeborg (1967). *Studien zum Wandel des Eckhart–bildes*. Leiden: Brill.
de Libera, Alain (1999). *Maître Eckhart et la mystique rhénane*. Paris: Cerf.
Denifle, Heinrich (1886). 'Meister Eckharts lateinische Schriften und die Grundanschauung seiner Lehre'. In *Archiv für Litteratur– und Kirchengeschichte des Mittelalters* (ALKG), vol. 2. Freiburg: Herder.
(Meister) Eckhart (1936–). *Die deutschen und lateinischen Werke*, vols 1–4. In *Die deutschen Werke*. Ed. Joseph Quint and Georg Steer. Stuttgart: Kohlhammer.
Heidegger, Martin (1959). *Gelassenheit*. Pfullingen: Neske. (English translation: *Discourse on Thinking*. New York: Harper & Row, 1966.)
'In agro dominico', *Archiv für Litteratur– und Kirchengeschichte des Mittelalters* (ALKG), vol. 2. (English translation: *Meister Eckhart – The Essential Sermons, Commentaries, Treatises, and Defense*. Mahwah, NJ: Paulist Press, 1981, pp. 77ff.)
Pfeiffer, Franz (1857). *Die deutschen Mystiker des 14. Jahrhunderts, vol. 1, Meister Eckhart*. Leipzig: Göschen.
Ruh, Kurt (1985). *Meister Eckhart: Theologe, Prediger, Mystiker*. München: Beck.
Schürmann, Reiner (1972). *Maître Eckhart ou la joie errante. Sermons allemands traduits et commentés*. Paris: Planète. (English translation: *Wandering Joy: Meister Eckhart's Mystical Philosophy*, Great Barrington: Lindisfarne Books, 2001.)
Schürmann, Reiner (1982). *Le principe d'anarchie. Heidegger et la question de l'agir*. Paris: Seuil. (English translation: *Heidegger on Being and Acting. From Principles to Anarchy*. Bloomington: Indiana University Press.)

---

[7] The author wishes to thank Hero and Brunello Lotti for their thoughtful suggestions during the revision process.

10

The Enigma of God and Dialogue in the Midst of an Epochal Threshold: The Case of Nicholas of Cusa (1401–1464)[1]

Peter Casarella

The *Longue Durée* of Cusan 'Modernity'

No sooner had Nicholas of Cusa been championed as a forerunner of the type of modernity envisaged by Neo-Kantians like Hermann Cohen than he was deemed to have eclipsed the modern paradigm itself. In this chapter, we will consider the legacy of the fifteenth-century philosopher, theologian and cardinal Nicholas of Cusa. In particular, we will scrutinise his thinking about the power of language and the interpersonal challenge of dialogue. He stands at the edge of what was once considered a wholly novel epochal shift from the Middle Ages to the modern era.[2] But epochal beginnings and endings coincide in their fading novelty. Elsewhere I have written about the fact that multiple agendas were at stake when scholars pinned the idea of an end of the Middle Ages on the novel thinking of the cardinal from Kues (Casarella 2013). There I argued that I think that Cusanus did inaugurate a new way of thinking, but I am not convinced that he set out to do this. In this chapter I would like to examine the positionalities involved in trying to pin the end of modern thought on the polymorphous figure of Cusanus. Here too affinities can be named even though the actual thought of the philosopher from the fifteenth century remains something of a puzzle.

I argue here that an enigmatic theory of dialogue arises from his unique speculation about the divine Absolute precisely when the reader is freed from the narrow straitjacket of a hastily proclaimed epochal change. In this way, the real contours of what Cusanus said in the fifteenth century can come into view while also keeping in view the concerns of the present to interrogate the excesses of modern rationalism and its own archaeology of belief. This is not so much a claim to return to the historically verified origins of his thought as it is part of an ongoing process to make sense of what he unwittingly and with great perspicacity bequeathed to the generations of seekers who followed a path that he called learned ignorance. Nicholas of Cusa's necessary unlearnedness about our present position thus makes it possible that we adopt true learned ignorance with

---

[1] This chapter owes much to the many and varied suggestions made by colleagues at the American Cusanus Society session dedicated to philosophy of language at the 51st International Congress on Medieval Studies, Kalamazoo, 12–15 May 2016 and to the participants at the VII Jungcusaner Tagung in Chieti on 21–3 September 2016.
[2] For more on this issue, see 'Editors' Introduction'.

respect to the relevance to our day of what he wrote. With such learned ignorance in view (ours and his), we can then approach a fresh new narrative about what his speculative thought might signify for a reader immersed in the philosophical problems of our day.

We begin with the latter stages of the advent of the 'modern' Cusanus (Cubillos 2012). When Karl Jaspers published his *Nicolaus Cusanus* in 1964, there was already a resurgence of interest across Europe in the philosophy of the Catholic cardinal from the fifteenth century. That year was the quincentenary of his death in Todi, and jubilee conferences on his thought took place in Trier, in Brixen-Bressanone in South Tirol and in Madrid (Casarella 2006a: xi–xxv). The speakers at these events included pivotal figures like Paul Oskar Kristeller and Hans-Georg Gadamer. The former was the most important editor of Cusanus's works of the first half of the twentieth century, and the latter played an equally decisive leadership role in bringing the critical edition by the Heidelberg Academy of Sciences to completion. The spirit of the times was evident in the papers that were read. The still unfinished Second Vatican Council, for example, made apposite Cusanus's medieval appeals to his openness to dialogue with other religions, a point highlighted by the brilliant Egyptian Dominican, George Anawati. The Western philosophical interpretations were dominated by two strands of thought. Cusanus's speculation about infinite worlds was placed into the context of early modern cosmology and confirmed his role in the eyes of the participants as a forerunner of modern science. Hans Georg-Gadamer must have harboured some doubts about this label. He properly noted the proto-modern legacy of the Neo-Kantians that had been extended brilliantly one generation earlier by Ernest Cassirer but added that Cusanus still managed to bring 'to light an ontological truth that surpasses the most exaggerated expressions of the modern age (*die äußerste Zuspitzung der Moderne*)' (Santinello 1970: 48). That Heideggerian formulation sounded slightly daring in 1964. Retrospectively, we could now say definitively that Gadamer was damning Cusanus's 'modernity' with his faint praise for that already well-worn label.

In reality, the book by Jaspers entertained very little of these post-Kantian preoccupations. Jaspers was much more concerned about Cusanus's philosophy of life and existence. He noted that few noteworthy philosophers during the entirety of the Middle Ages had led a life as active as that of the cardinal from Kues. In terms of Jaspers's central preoccupation, the birth of the modern experience of individual freedom, Cusanus leaned too heavily on the declarations of the Catholic Church to count as an unblemished forerunner of a new paradigm of authentic existentialism. But his speculative thought still yielded an original synthesis of the *vita contemplativa* and the *vita activa* that intrigued the mid-twentieth-century philosopher of life. In terms of his own modernist project, Cusanus remained an enigma, a figure still trapped in the vestiges of medieval hierarchies waiting to be freed by the new epoch at whose threshold he stood.

Unwittingly, Jasper had opened the door to an investigation of late medieval thought that sought to find a form of life in the philosophical speculations of Christian thinkers. This synthetic view of the history of ideas and the phenomenology of life can now absorb the wealth of information codified in the critical editions of voluminous *Acta Cusana* and the, as of 2005, officially completed *Opera Omnia*. More importantly for the purposes of this chapter, the new approach only adumbrated by Jaspers needs to be interrogated in terms of what Giorgio Agamben labels the philosophical archaeology of the relationship between the forms of life in the life and thought of Nicholas of Cusa and his place in the history of Being and its forgetfulness (Agamben 2013). Here it is not a question of trying to Heideggerianise the thinker from the Mosel River Valley of the fifteenth century, a temptation of which Gadamer was aware and to which I myself have succumbed (Casarella 1990, 2006b). It is a question rather of situating the enigmatic Cusanus and his much-misunderstood milieu into a narrative that highlights the inner unity of the emergence of new life and the ontological insight suggested by Gadamer.

Cusanus moreover foresaw the age of the printed book inasmuch as he was an avid collector of manuscripts and incunabula. Moreover, there is a vellum copy of the *Catholicon* (a ponderous but influential scholastic grammar) in the library established by Cusanus in Bernkastel-Kues, and the printing of this work was part of the ecclesial reform envisaged by Johannes Gutenberg in his choice of the earliest books to put into print. Lotte Hellinger interprets this fact as a conjectural sign that Cusanus himself encouraged the printing of books as part of a programme of Church reform (Hellinger 2018: 194–200). But Cusanus neither lived at nor touted the advent of an epochal threshold like the age of the printing press; however, the difficulty of classifying his thought at the interstices of what we and others have demarcated as late medieval and early modern makes possible a revealing philosophical archaeology of this unique moment in Western thought.

Several other scholars have already trodden this path, for example Hans Blumenberg, Louis Dupré, Ernesto Grassi and João Maria André. Blumenberg's monumental *The Legitimacy of the Modern Age* questioned Cusanus's ability to reconcile 'the theological furor of the Middle Ages' with the will of 'perplexed man (sic) to secure his own right over against transcendence' (Blumenberg 1983: 547). Blumenberg blamed Augustine for a theological absolutism that not even the flexibly Augustinian Cusanus could overcome. Dupré, by contrast, evinced genuine hermeneutical sophistication in placing the Cusan project of reconciliation precisely at the juncture at which early modern thinkers chose to separate too squarely the order of nature from the order of grace (Dupré 1993: 192–4; Casarella 1994). Cusanus, writes Dupré, was not at fault for this epochal shift towards modern secularism, but his brilliant and idiosyncratic synthesis failed to inspire a new path for Western thought that could have averted the ensuing spiritual crisis. Grassi was an Italian student of Heidegger who faced the breakdown in the Idealist tradition between the two World Wars in Italy by returning to the rhetorical tradition of the *quattrocentro* (Grassi 1980). Grassi was the first, to my knowledge, to place *quattrocento* literary and metaphysical problems about language, rhetoric and symbol in conversation with the post-World War II claim for the end of philosophy. He initiated an important conversation that this chapter aims to continue without his flawed Heideggerian yearning for a bygone linguistic primordiality.

André is a Portuguese Cusanus scholar whose Cusanus Lecture in Trier in 2006 dealt with the power of the word in Cusanus's thought (André 2006). He is the first one to fulfil a promise that was already contained in the decision of the editors of the critical edition to include all of the known sermons with the philosophical and theological works, a decision that was much easier to fulfil in the case of Meister Eckhart. In other words, André culled the power of the proclaimed word from the sermons as a power that pertains to *both* evangelisation *and* the Cusan speculative determination of the definitional power of a word. Cusanus ties this semantic force to dialogue and the attainment of peace in such a way as to bind the interlocutors from distinct religious and cultural standpoints into a relationship of love. This insight is not separate from the illocutionary force of the biblical message but also has wider ramifications for a dialogical theory of language, implications not limited to the Christian recipient of the proclaimed Word. Cusanus binds his interlocutors together by virtue of a shared linguisticality (Gadamer 1972: 361–82; Casarella 2006b).

My interest in the distinctively Cusan form of dialogue has been for some time piqued by the reference to it in Jacques Derrida's 1964 essay 'Violence and Metaphysics: An Essay on the Thought of Emmanuel Levinas' (Derrida 2005). The reference in the context of that year and of that interchange is not accidental nor without its own genealogical implications. As just noted, Gadamer and others opined about Cusanus's significance for a new, more linguistically oriented theory of modernity at precisely that juncture in the Western European appraisal of its relationship to the philosophical past. The reference to the layman in Derrida's essay, no doubt mediated by the translation of Cusanus made possible by Derrida's friend, Maurice de Gandillac, is not in passing (Derrida labels the translation no less than *une admirable meditation*). The relationship between the two was long-standing, for de Gandillac had supervised Derrida's thesis on Husserl's *Origin of Geometry*. The marshalling of a Cusan trope in this context helps to sustain the dialogue that the thirty-four-year-old Derrida hoped to undertake with the elder Levinas. The latter's ground-breaking *Totality and Infinity* had been published just three years earlier. Like Derrida, I recognise the peculiarity of the question of God in the dialogue *Idiota de sapientia* to be the imbedding of the very metaphysics of God in the question of God and vice versa (Derrida 2005: 223). There is no questioning of God (or God's nature, existence, reality, etc.) without the presupposing of the question of God, according to Derrida. God as 'questionable' is imbedded in the dialogue about God and in the nature of dialogue itself. We will return to this intriguing point after examining the Cusan theory and theology of dialogue in more detail.

Theo-logy: God as the Absolute Presupposition of all Dialogue

What evidence is there for a new theory of language in Nicholas of Cusa? Might this dialogical approach just mentioned too be tainted with personalist baggage derived from twentieth-century thinkers like Franz Rosenzweig, Martin Buber, Ferdinand Ebner, and the like? Cusanus was, as Jaspers noted, thoroughly enmeshed in the practical affairs of the fifteenth century, and that milieu carries with it very different expectations for dialogue. The Cusan practice of dialogue does not map easily onto the map of inter-religious encounters of late modernity.

Cusan language is, however, distinctive and distinctively aiming for a new approach to dialogue. One need only examine the peculiarities of the Cusan lexicon to become aware of a form of thinking in the major works that grows out of medieval sources even while offering radically new insights into them. *Theologia sermocinalis*, for example, is a key term in the Cusan vocabulary even though it is used explicitly in just one work. It has been translated in many ways, and none is completely satisfying. The term is meant to show the speculative convergence of all dialogue and dialogue about God but also has close connections with the kerygmatic dimensions of language just noted. In my dissertation, which was rewritten as a book entitled *Word as Bread*, I investigated in two separate chapters the meaning and sources of the notion of a *theologia sermocinalis* in the Cusan dialogue *Idiota de sapientia* (Casarella 2017b: 89–164). These sources were varied and tended to confirm the homiletic and medieval roots of the concept even though similarities with some forms of the Italian humanism of the *quattrocento* were also evident. I did not, in that place, attempt to explain either the dialogical genre of the writing nor its dialogical mode of theology. As a result, I will now examine these two pivotal questions: (1) What form of dialogue did Cusanus adopt in this work? and (2) In what way, if at all, does Cusanus adopt a dialogical theology? The two questions, it turns out, are closely intertwined.

Cusanus's approach to dialogue is therefore epitomised by an exchange about the relationship of theology and language in *Idiota de sapientia*.[3] The orator, a symbol of Roman humanist eloquence, states:

> I now understand what you wish to say. In the *theologia sermocinalis*, that is, where we allow statements concerning God and where the meaning of words is not altogether excluded, you have transformed the fitness of the difficult ways [*sufficientia difficilium*] of forming more true propositions about God to the ready accessibility of the one way.

---

[3] This section is a lightly edited reworking of what I have already published in *Word as Bread*.

To which the layman responds:

> You have caught on well. For if I must disclose to you my own concept of God and if what I am to say is to be useful to you, then it is necessary that the words which I speak are meaningful. In this manner, I can lead you to what you have been searching for in the meaning of the word [*vis vocabuli*], a meaning which is commonly recognized by both of us. Hence, by means of the *theologia sermocinalis*, I strive to lead you through the meaning of the word to God in whatever way in which I can do so more easily and more truly. (Cusa [1450] 1983: 66)[4]

Although the term *theologia sermocinalis* is brought into the discussion by the orator, the wisdom of the layman determines its ultimate meaning. It is a term of art that had never been used in exactly this way in the previous literature on the arts of the *trivium* (grammar, rhetoric and logic), the so-called *artes sermonicales*. Cusanus is fashioning a neologism about the very fashioning of neologisms. The newly minted term is even a rhetorical figure, but only inasmuch as it is intended to lay bare the uselessness of the merely eloquent rhetorical figures commonly associated with the orator.

There are important precedents for *theologia sermocinalis* among both the medieval theologians whom Cusanus studied and the Italian humanists *with* whom he studied. Moreover, it is decisive for understanding the term that the definition is made by the layman and in the layman's own terms. For Cusanus, the layman represents Christian piety, the practical wisdom of the marketplace, and *docta ignorantia* (learned ignorance). Unlike the orator, he is not encumbered by the weighty learning that comes from having read many books. In sum, all three of the principal sources for Cusanus's thought converge in *theologia sermocinalis*: the rigour of medieval theology, the rhetorical eloquence of *quattrocento* humanism and the newly discovered learned ignorance of the layman. Cusanus's *theologia sermocinalis* is offered as a critique and an expression of *quattrocento* humanism. The orator displays his erudition by introducing *sermocinalis*, a term that had been employed by medieval theologians from the eleventh century onwards and even enjoyed a favourable reception among humanist orators. The orator claims to have understood the layman's at times perplexing logic. He paraphrases in his own learned words what he has understood. *Sermocinalis* describes a theology that admits utterances concerning God (in contrast to the undialectical way of negation that Cusanus sometimes practised in his meditative works) and in which the meaning of words can in fact be applied to God. *Theologia sermocinalis*, at first glance, can be read as a *via positiva* that stands in opposition to a *via negativa*. But unlike the treatment of that opposition in *On Learned Ignorance*, Book I, chapters 24–6, there is no mention of a scholastic *via eminentiae* nor of the typically Cusan resolutions of this opposition through a retracing of one's path to God as an absolute maximum. Instead, the term seems to be a reconciliation of the oppositions found in the forms of discourse of positive theology itself. Difficulty and ease are the poles of opposition to reaching

---

[4] 'Orator: Intelligo nunc te dicere velle, quod in theologia sermocinali, scilicet ubi de deo locutiones admittimus et vis vocabuli penitus non excluditur, ibi sufficientiam difficilium in facilitatem modi de deo propositiones veriores formandi redegisti. Idiota: Bene cepisti. Nam si tibi de deo conceptum, quem habeo, pandere debeo, necesse est, quod locutio mea, si tibi servire debet, talis sit, cuius vocabula sint significativa, ut sic te ducere queam in vi vocabuli quae est nobis communiter nota, ad quaesitum. Deus est autem qui quaeritur. Unde haec est sermocinalis theologia, qua nitor te ad deum per vim vocabuli ducere modo quo possum faciliori et veriori.'

an agreement through *theologia sermocinalis*, not speech and silence. *Theologia sermocinalis* thus transforms the unavoidable difficulty of the three separate ways (medieval scholasticism, Italian humanism and learned ignorance) to the ready accessibility (*facilitas*) of the one way of forming propositions about God.

The ready accessibility of the layman's theology not only relativises the eager display of erudition on the part of the orator but also reveals the ardent desire of the *idiota* for a participation in the divine life. Both concepts, *sufficientia nostra* and *facilitas difficilium*, refer to the layman's capacity to demonstrate a 'simple' path to learned ignorance. At least it appears simple in its divergence from the formal methods of the scholastics and from the neoclassical eloquence of the humanist orators. The orator's admission that in *theologia sermocinalis* the *sufficientia difficilium* will be reduced to the ready accessibility of the one way of forming propositions about God is a concession by the orator to the layman's superior wisdom.

The layman responds approvingly to the orator's introduction of the term and then turns his attention to the ready accessibility of *theologia sermocinalis*. His explanation presupposes that the notion of God that he wishes to convey might be fundamentally different from that of his interlocutor. The layman's response sets, in effect, conditions for the possibility of a meaningful dialogue about God. He first states that if his locution is to be of use, then the mere words that he uses must carry meaning (*significativus*). What is meant by meaningfulness? Words are meaningful, Cusanus states, if their meaning is intelligibly recognised by both interlocutors. Meaning, in other words, is shared by a community of interpreters. Finally, if these conditions have been met, then the layman can 'lead' his interlocutor to what is being sought after. He concludes by saying that whoever asks what God is, since this question presupposes being, will respond that God is absolute being itself. The layman draws the conclusion that God is the absolute presupposition of all things, just as in every effect one presupposes the existence of a cause. In fact, the speech of the *idiota* about God as the absolute presupposition of all things concludes with a characteristically paradoxical remark: '*Vide igitur, orator, quam facilis est theologica difficultas*' (Look, orator, at how easy theological difficulty is) (Cusa [1450] 1983: 61). Therefore, when the layman states in paragraph 33 that he will lead us through the meaning of the word (*per vim vocabuli*) to what is sought after, he is not claiming to unveil knowledge that is only accessible through particular words or concepts. Rather, like Socrates, he can only bring to light whatever 'preunderstanding' (*Vorurteil*) his interlocutor presupposes.

On the basis of this exchange, we can develop a working definition of the layman's *theologia sermocinalis*. Namely, it is the theology in which he can disclose his interlocutor's already presupposed concept of God through dialogue, and, more specifically, through the meaning of words that are mutually agreed upon. The historical novelty of Cusanus's use of the term *sermocinalis* is the connection with the theology of the layman. The term is introduced by the orator and, to my knowledge, does not reappear in Cusanus's works. Consequently, one may conclude that Cusanus introduces the term in order to allow the layman to define very concisely his position over and against the traditions of the 'learned' theologians and orators. Nonetheless, the unique placement of the term in the middle of a debate about knowledge of God also calls for a look at the sources.

The exchange about the question of God as an absolute presupposition of all things is a good example of this oratorical dissonance. It is not a static claim, but its rhythms are not that of *eloquentia*. It comes as the crescendo of a series of absolutes in the dialogue: truth, goodness, precision, etc. Cusanus is acutely aware of the problem of the vicious circle in his reasoning and for that reason has the orator raise the question in this unusual and paradoxical manner, noting the dialogical coincidence of ease and difficulty, question and answer. Here the *idiota* asks whether the question as to whether something exists presupposes being, and the response of the orator concerns the *facilitas* not only in the layman's speech but also in God:

> *Layman:* So when you are asked whether God exists, reply by stating what is presupposed, that is, that He exists, for *being* is presupposed by the question. Likewise, if someone asks what God is, then since this question presupposes that there is quiddity, you will reply that God is Absolute Quiddity. A similar point holds true in all cases. And there is no doubt about this point. For God is the Absolute Presupposition of all things that are in any way presupposed – even as in the case of every effect a cause is presupposed. See, then, O Orator, how easy [a difficulty] a theological difficulty is.
>
> *Orator:* Assuredly, this easiness is maximal and stupendous.
>
> *Layman:* Indeed, I tell you that God is infinite facility and that it does not at all befit God to be infinite difficulty. For it is necessary – as you will hear a bit later regarding a curve and a straight line – that difficulty pass over into facility if difficulty is to befit the infinite God. (Hopkins 1996: 512)

Several points are worth making about this key moment in the dialogue. First, the dialogue begins with a question about the existence of being and ends with an enquiry into the being of the question. Being is not rejected, but it becomes something puzzling in the process of introducing a new mode of enquiry. Second, the relationship between the layman and the orator is not just maieutic or Socratic, for the one posing the question and the one answering the question posed are affectively fused by an almost musical relationship into a single search for the Absolute. Renate Steiger points to the affinity to a medieval tradition that runs from the bride-bridegroom mysticism of Bernard of Clairvaux to the fourteenth-century text, *The History of the Life of the Reverend Doktor John Tauler* (Steiger 1988: xxi–xxii). In this latter text, a layman rich in God's grace teaches the Master of Holy Scripture to preach friendship with God to both clergy and laity.

Second, the dialogue brings together into a new form of unity the form and the content of questioning:

> *Layman:* Every question (*quaestio*) about God presupposes what is being asked about (*quaesitum*); and, in regard to every question about God, that which the posing of the question (*quaesitio, die Fragestellung*) presupposes is that which is to be given as the answer. (Hopkins 1996: 511)

The question does not come to an end with the answer that one had sought at the outset (*quaesitum*). The movement of intellect and desire began with a 'fore-taste' (*praegustatio*) of wisdom and continues with the dialectic of posing a question and giving an answer. Medieval mysticism and humanist theologies of language had gestured towards this paradoxical logic of seeking and finding, but none had achieved it in exactly the same way.

Derrida's Ironically Cusan Questioning of Levinas's Platonism

Let us return now to the young Derrida's struggle with the elder Levinas. This is a struggle about the very nature of transcendence in the contemporary age. Both thinkers have proud Jewish roots, and both accept aspects of Heidegger's critique of modern subjectivistic humanism. But their diverse positions on the validity of the reference to the Absolute come into play in this debate. Derrida deconstructs the fundamental starting point of the Levinasian anti-system and maintains that Levinas's anti-system is akin to the anti-Platonism of Kierkegaard. In the process of this reflection, he deploys Cusanus's absolute thinking about questioning as a rewriting of the still largely Platonic and oral encounter with the transcendent face of the Other in Levinas. This is quite ironic, and the irony is no doubt intentional. Derrida claims to make Cusanus a forerunner of the idea that the question of being, the Levinasian overcoming of metaphysics through ethics, and a new deconstructive empiricism all implicate one another. It is highly questionable that he is being fair to either Levinas or to Cusanus, but that is not really the point of his essay. Derrida's misprision is itself an object of wonder since the invocation of the ancient authority is hardly dismissive or an act of reproach. Derrida was invoking an authority on dialogue from the so-called 'onto-theological' tradition precisely in order to make that tradition unravel before the eyes of his reader. Whether he succeeds in this deconstruction depends upon whether he has correctly applied the Cusan innovation to the Levinasian scaffold.

Let us first listen to Derrida's narrative. He begins with what he considers a fact, namely, the fact of the death of philosophy heralded by Nietzsche and Heidegger. What does Derrida applaud in Levinas's new path for thinking after the death of philosophy? Levinas's difference from the Greek tradition is that his new way of thinking arises in the wake of the definitive but unending death of philosophy: 'At the heart of the desert, in the growing wasteland, this thought, which fundamentally no longer seeks to be a thought of Being and phenomenality, makes us dream of an inconceivable process of dismantling and dispossession' (Derrida 2005: 99).

Levinas, Derrida claims, posits the face of the other that remains unbound by its phenomenality. Levinas's thought, he continues, is concerned with ethics, understood as 'otherwise than being'. The other is always different from the thought of being for Levinas. Like Cusanus, Levinas attends to the saying of what is said as well as the questioning of what is questioned. The thought of the other includes that of the saying that is always adding to the said. Thus, in Derrida's version, Levinas's thought is 'the other of the Greek'. It is, in the words of James Joyce, ineluctably hybrid, that is, 'Jewgreek'. Levinas's thought, so states Derrida, 'seeks to liberate itself from the Greek domination of the Same and the One (other names for the light of Being and of the phenomenon) as if from oppression itself' (Derrida 2005: 102). Beyond a metaphysics of both presence and phenomenon, Levinas and Cusanus belong together according to Derrida in

> a community of the question, therefore, within that fragile moment when the question is not yet determined enough for the hypocrisy of an answer to have already initiated itself beneath the mask of the question, and not yet determined enough for its voice to have been already and fraudulently articulated within the very syntax of the question. (Derrida 2005: 98)

Derrida wants to show that Levinas is utilising a more mixed genre of Platonic philosophy and new thinking than he is willing to admit. At the heart of Derrida's struggle is the desire to show in his *Essai* the fact that Levinas has written himself into a tradition of prioritising orality that extends from Plato to Kierkegaard to Nicholas of Cusa. In that process, the reference by Derrida to Cusanus's notion that every question about God presupposes the thing questioned is the pivot to Derrida's own deconstructive move from orality to writing. Cusanus's *idiota* (layman) in the dialogue of 1450 bests the Roman rhetorician by inscribing the question of God into the dialogue about God in such a way that questioning becomes both infinite and infinitely God-oriented. Cusanus's rhetoric against Roman rhetoric allows Derrida to develop an ethical standpoint regarding the virtue of writing that complicates the Levinasian path to ethics as first philosophy. Derrida writes:

A classical schema here complicated by a metaphysics of dialogue and instruction, of a demonstration which contradicts what is demonstrated by the very rigor and truth of its development. The thousand-times-denounced circle of historicism, psychologism, relativism, etc. But the true name of this inclination of thought to the Other, of this resigned acceptance of incoherent incoherence inspired by a truth more profound than the 'logic' of philosophical discourse, the true name of this renunciation of the concept, of the a priori and transcendental horizons of language, is empiricism. For the latter, at bottom, has ever committed but one fault: the fault of presenting itself as a philosophy. And the profundity of the empiricist intention must be recognized beneath the naïveté of certain of its historical expressions. It is the dream of a purely heterological thought at its source. A pure thought of pure difference. Empiricism is its philosophical name, its metaphysical pretention or modesty. (Derrida 2005: 189)

Derrida wants to implicate Levinas in what he considers the necessary 'complicity between metaphysics and empiricism' (Derrida 2005: 190). This involves heightening the metaphysics of presence in Levinas by associating him with Cusan Platonism and questioning the sharp distinction that Levinas will make between empiricism and positivism. The empirical claim in the *Idiota de sapientia* that is decisive for Derrida is the fact of a path of thinking extending back to Cusanus about a form of questioning that is infinitely presuppositioned.

In the light of this rather sharp criticism, one could legitimately question whether the Cusan dialogue is in fact a dialogue about dialogue. It is more properly a dialogue about the Absolute that calls into question the absoluteness of the question of the Absolute. The figure of the *orator* is neither a standard trope as used in fifteenth-century circles nor does it represent a single living person. In light of the foregoing, one might also ask about the remains of a metaphysics of presence in the *Idiota de sapientia*. Cusanus does not deconstruct presence. The light of being radiates throughout the dialogue as a source of wisdom. The question of being is dialogically refracted through the theology of the Word. This point is no less valid in this dialogue. Cusanus constructs a theology of dialogue to the degree that the wisdom of the incarnate Word is present in all questions about the nature of discourse. At the same time the distinctiveness of the Cusan dialogue is that it uncovers what the great Catalan thinker Eusebio Colomer calls *die Fraglosigkeit Gottes* ('Our inability to pose a question to God', Colomer 1975: 212). If God is presupposed in every question, then God cannot be posed as a question alongside other questions. The question of God remains a question, but not a question that can be posed without itself being subjected to the question of its very being as a question. The question of God cannot be posed in its absoluteness without also questioning how this question relates to all other questions. In this sense, there is a coincidence of opposites between die *Fraglosigkeit Gottes* and die *Fragwürdigkeit Gottes* ('the worthiness of questioning God'). Derrida's questioning of Levinas's implicitly metaphysical mode brought this paradox to light even though there is no reason to believe that Derrida and Colomer are making the same point. Colomer has found traces of both modern rationalism and postmodern questioning in the fifteenth century, an ambiguity that seems to elude Derrida, a thinker who is otherwise famous for his vigilance of undetected ambiguities.

This standpoint on the question of God raised by Colomer also raises interesting issues regarding human certainty vis-à-vis knowledge of God. In Cusanus's own words, the *theologia sermocinalis* yields the conclusion that '[God is] undoubtable by any doubting [*in omni dubitatione indubitabilis*]' (Hopkins 1996: 501). Colomer thinks that Cusanus's method here is not altogether different from that of Descartes and that his approach to the self-evidence of God's knowability is in line with the logic of proof in the Augustinian St Bonaventure. In contrasting the method of Thomas and Bonaventure, Colomer states: '*Nicht das* an sit Deus, *sondern das utrum sit Deus cognoscibilis*' ('Not the question of whether or not God exists but rather the question of whether God is a knowable'; Colomer 1975: 214). The certainty that arises here is different in kind from the certainty that many associated with a successful proof for the existence of God. It is rather the certainty that discourse about God, by virtue of its very object, has a theo-logical character. The speculative character of the discourse is deceiving. This principle of theo-logical questioning holds whether one is interrogating the Absolute as the inaccessible source of all dialogical expression or whether one is interrogating a rhetorician milling about near the Temple of Eternity in Rome. Cusanus has one great achievement in this regard, which is detailed in other writings such as *On the Search for Wisdom*, chapter 33, namely, he thinks the presence of Word as a *vis vocabuli* and thereby interrogates the double meaning of the word *vis* (Hopkins 2001: 1339–40). In other words, the trace of the Absolute in God and in the interlocutor arises as both shared meaning *and* a force or impetus to respond to an already meaningful foretaste of wisdom and engage the other as other. It is in this sense that Cusanus breaks new ground in the development of a theology of dialogue.

Vis vocabuli: Semantic Force and its Relation to the Life-World

The idea that a word is a force appears to break the bounds of the medieval worldview. For Cusanus, language is clearly an expressive force that plays itself out beyond the confines of an isolated proposition and within the world of everyday life. Is that move actually the breaking through of an epochal barrier? We need to consider this question carefully in terms that correspond to his own milieu. In general, Cusanus defended the *via negativa* in contrast to the more empirical view of language championed by what he labelled, in the 'Defense of Learned Ignorance', the *secta Aristotelica* (Hopkins 1988: 46). Derrida's attempt to pin down the latently empiricist strain in Levinas's overcoming of metaphysics via Cusanus ignored this anti-empirical vector in Cusanus's speculative thought. Cusanus unveils a mystical force to language that is neither undialectically hidden behind the veil of the unknown God nor in the plain sight of everyday discourse. Rather than carrying forward the anti-essentialism of late medieval nominalism, this view of language has deeper affinities with the pre-Reformation Epicurean approach to *theologia sermocinalis* in his companion Lorenzo Valla as well as *La fabula di Orfeo* that Angelo Ambrogini (known popularly as Poliziano) wrote in 1490 (Dupré 1993: 192–4; Mazzotta 2001: 5–23). Before the advent of a modern, post-Reformation theology of the Word (with its problematic uprooting from the metaphysics of creation) as well as the modern idea that language is power that begins to develop in the wake of Giambattista Vico (1688–1744), the late fifteenth-century humanists had developed a fabular theology of *cosmopoiesis* that extends the Cusan play of language into a more explicitly secular domain. Writing about Poliziano and his beloved mentor Petrarch together, Giuseppe Mazzotta states: 'Poliziano writes a text in which history and imagination overlap: Each reaches into the other, each is the dream and truth of the other' (Mazzotta 2001: 23). Cusanus is no modern Epicurean, for his ethical standpoint is still teleological in an Aristotelian and Christian sense. But he has, in his speculation about language, opened the door to artistry and worldmaking in a fashion that is unlike that of any other medieval thinker (Casarella 2017b: 165–274). His texts are not themselves fabular, but his defence of a ludic principle in thinking about God lends itself to the current highlighted by Mazzotta and Dupré.

Nicholas of Cusa was by trade a bishop and artisan of canon law. As a practising canon lawyer, Cusanus was actually not at all naïve with respect to the fact-based study of history. A great deal of his hunting for manuscripts was motivated by this very cause. To say that he endeavoured to think about historical facts and the power of imagination at once is no exaggeration, since his very life points to this intersection. Whether he carried out that integration in his philosophy is a different question. In our examination of the *theologia sermocinalis*, we do not find a strict humanist convergence of two separate disciplines, but we do discover the presence of the overlap in thought to which Mazzotta alluded. The Epicureans still do not capture the Eckhartian mystical impulse in the Cusan theology of language. The later Lutheran mystic Jakob Boehme (1575-1624) in his (to quote Cyril O'Regan) 'coagulated cyclone of language, a form or unform of linguistic implosion that repels and excludes' perhaps best captures this dimension of the radical ingenuity of Cusanus in an early modern and decidedly more heterodox key (O'Regan 2002: 3). The Boehmian 'signature' of God in all things is a hidden power not wholly unlike the everyday apophatic path of *theologia sermocinalis* (Boehme [1621] 1981: 88). The Epicureans do not see the dialectical hiddenness of the Trinitarian grammar of creation to the same degree as Eckhart, Cusanus and Boehme. The Cusan genealogy therefore partakes of a history of effects drawn equally from a Rhineland, and later, nature mysticism that codetermines Cusanus's humanist vintage.

Not one of the standard narratives of the passage to modernity allows the enigmatic figure of Nicholas of Cusa to find a ready-made place. Unlike Erasmus and Luther, his uniqueness is not so much due to a spirit of rebelliousness against traditional forms as to the unprecedented reconfiguration of prior traditions of philosophy, theology and rhetoric. A new angle is needed for capturing the novelty we have been attempting to name. As a result, I would like to conclude this reflection by investigating Cusan worldmaking from two converging standpoints: the overcoming of the priority of actuality to possibility in the later works of Nicholas of Cusa, and the similar attempt to rethink the facticity of everyday experience in the work of Giorgio Agamben. Let us begin with the Cusan point of departure, a point that I have elsewhere treated at length (Casarella 1990). In sum, Cusanus raises a critical question about the divine name 'pure act' (*actus purus*). The idea that God is pure act devoid of all potentiality is open to question. Instead he postulates a new approach by means of the divine signifier *possest*, an amalgam composed of *posse* ('to be able to') and *est* ('is') (Hopkins 1986: 926–7). In surveying the meaning of *possest*, Cusanus clarifies that it is not the reduction of infinite, eternal *posse* to the temporal finitude of *est*. Nor is he projecting the 'being-there' (*Dasein*) of *est* into an a-temporal indeterminacy of unrealised divine ideas. There exists a mystery of actuality in *posse* just as there is a hitherto unimagined potentiality to the being-there of *est*. The latter exceeds the dialectic of presence and absence of what is possible to be (*posse esse et non posse esse*) as well as a dialectic from within possibility itself (*posse esse et posse non esse*) (Hopkins 1986). The power of language derives from this novel overturning of the relationship of possibility to actuality. What is possible is not just a deficient actualisation waiting to come to fruition. Without focusing on the abstraction of an unrealised possible, Cusanus plumbs the depth of possibilising as a mode equal to or (possibly) higher than actualising.

Possest is not unrelated to the Cusan innovation with regard to the power of language. The enigma of the *vis vocabuli* proves that there is a connection between possibilising and discourse. *Vis*, in Cusanus's usage, can signify meaning in the Fregean referential sense of *Bedeutung*, or it can mean 'force' in the Augustinian rhetorical sense of how the expression of the word has an impact on the hearer that goes beyond the mere assimilation of its meaning into one's mental interiority (André 2006: 16–22). By alluding to the simultaneous presence of *Bedeutung* and a new form of Augustinian semiotics, Cusanus uncovers a new way to grasp the performance of speech. With respect to the actualised possibility of the word, the *Bedeutung* corresponds to its *actualitas* (what has been said), and the semiotic force to its *posse ipsum* (possibility itself). Cusanus is suggesting that there is a force within the meaning of the word that is not fully actualised by a seeming transformation of a signifier into a mental concept. Likewise, there is an actuality to the rhetorical possibilities that invest the rhetorician (or in Nicholas's case, the preacher of the Word) with the task of reinventing language such that it reaches its fullest potential in everyday life. The kind of *cosmopoiesis* highlighted by Mazzotta tended to play off the fabularity of *posse* as a language unto itself, an a-cosmic possibilising. From this imaginary realm comes both Machiavelli's politics and the invention of the novel in that narrative. The Cusan possibilising is not hampered or held back by the real order of things but seeks to 'see' within the actual world the emergence of a new order. The power of language is thus a power to visualise reality in a new, more dynamic fashion. It is not mechanism for the *homo faber* to invent a reality that does not already exist. Cusanus was known for his prodigious linguistic gifts and his genuine humility in the face of the soaring, elaborate and ornate eloquence of his humanist companions (O'Malley 1997). Both of these qualities cohere with this everyday reading of the *possest* of language. The Cusan power of language invests the hearer and speaker of the Word with a second naiveté with respect to the possibilities of moral and political activity in the world.

How does *possest* of language relate to Agamben's archaeology of factical life? Agamben, like Cusanus, is a thinker of the limits of language. Agamben even daringly suggests the replacement of the Platonic idea with the religiously determined mediation of language itself. As he formulates this revision: 'What unites human beings among themselves is not a nature, a voice, or a common imprisonment in signifying language; it is the vision of language itself and, therefore, the experience of language's limits, its *end*' (Agamben 1999: 39–47, here at 47). Another central thesis of Agamben's archaeology is the questioning of the Aristotelian priority of actuality over possibility alongside the revival of what he calls the 'passion of facticity' (Agamben 1999: 185–204). Let us first situate his concept of facticity in the context of what we have just discussed. Agamben notes that the publication of Heidegger's lecture courses from the 1920s allows for a reconsideration of the overwhelming importance of the category of facticity in the early Heidegger. Facticity was not derived from the Husserlian *Tatsächlichkeit*, which refers to a static relationship to the objects of experience (Agamben 1999: 188). Rather, Agamben argues, the origins of Heideggerian facticity are to be found in a phrase that comes from Augustine, namely, *facticia est anima*, the human soul as something 'made' by God. The form of human being that Heidegger elicits from Augustine (which is very much an invention of Heidegger) is a dialectic of concealment and unconcealment (Agamben 1999: 190). The hermeneutics of facticity is not an addendum to *Dasein* for the early Heidegger. It is inscribed in *Dasein*'s structure of being (Agamben 1999: 195). Agamben writes:

> If Heidegger can simultaneously pose the question of the meaning of Being anew and distance himself from ontology, it is because the Being at issue in *Being and Time* has the character of facticity from the beginning. This is why for Dasein, quality, *Sosein*, is not a 'property' but solely a 'possible guise' (*mögliche Weise*) to be (a formula that must be heard with the same ontological contraction that is expressed in Nicholas of Cusa's *possest*). (Agamben 1999: 194)

This listening to the contraction of the hermeneutics of being from within the dynamics of *possest* opens the door to our analysis.

Agamben then formulates his notion of potentiality in terms of an aporia of im-possibility within the Aristotelian corpus (Agamben 1999: 244–5, 250–3). To be able to be is also a capacity to be able not to be. Agamben explores the theological and mystical ideas interlaced with the potential not to be or not to do. This analysis points to a form of potentiality that is neither an analogue to God's absolute potency nor an analogue to God's ordained potency (Agamben 1999: 255). Herein lies another point of intersection with the Cusan *possest*. *Dasein*, according to Agamben, makes itself possible through the releasement of the will to an infinity of possibilities and impossibilities and without the ordinance of a quasi-divine command. This is not far from Cusan possibilising. Agamben also notes the curious convergence in Heidegger's *Letter on Humanism* between possibilising (*mögen*) and loving (Heidegger 1977: 196; Agamben 1999: 199–202). If, for Heidegger, *mögen* (to be able) is *lieben* (to love), then for Agamben freedom is above all passion (Agamben 1999: 202). This passion is not determined by a dialectic of desire in which *Dasein* struggles to bring into the clearing of everyday life all that has been repressed as mere affect. It is rather a passion of facticity that guards and appropriates both non-belonging and darkness: '*In love, the lover and the beloved come to light in their concealment, in an eternal facticity beyond Being*' (Agamben 1999: 204; original emphasis). The Cusan mystery of learned ignorance and concealed being is here reappropriated in a secular mode as the passion of facticity. Agamben retains Cusanus's reticence to divorce the imagination from the real world as it appears to the image-maker, but both thinkers are engaged in a poetic revision of the relationship of actuality to possibility.

Cusanus at the End of Modernity

This chapter represents a first attempt to situate the thought of Nicholas of Cusa within the discourse of the end of modernity. No pretense was made to baptise Cusan archaeology with the waters of postmodernism. Nicholas of Cusa assembled a plethora of works that he wished to be read in his beautiful codices by generations of scholars in the future. He was waiting for a future reader to help to solve the puzzle of enigmas in his writing that he himself presented as struggles for thought. One cannot claim that the postmodern Cusanus is the final liberation of his thought from the strictures of his day any more than one can claim that Cusanus's aim in his writing was the definitive liberation of the medieval Christian for a modern self-understanding. But this hermeneutical exercise in situating Cusanus at a new, late modern epochal shift is nonetheless highly instructive.

This reading bears some similarity to a recent essay by the Argentine semiotician Valentín Cricco on the semio-linguistic 'ultrametaphysics' of Nicholas of Cusa (Cricco 2015: 137–8). The Cusan dynamics of knowing are dubbed by Cricco 'pluridimensional' in such a way that that nature of knowing is revealed to betray non-being of Cusanus as an 'ontology of the unconscious' (Cricco 2015: 132). Instead of Agamben's archaeology of linguistic potentiality through a hermeneutics of facticity, Cricco favours the reading of the pluridimensional creativity of the mind in Nicholas of Cusa in terms of the veiling of difference as deferral in the deconstructive strategies of Jacques Derrida (Cricco 2015: 137). In Cusanus, he maintains, *archi-écriture* is hiddenly one with 'ultrametaphysics'. The traces of the unconsciously hidden Absolute in the writings of Cusanus therefore need to be read recursively in their Augustinian and Plotinian contexts and subtexts to discover the enfolding therein of the impossible signification of 'the Other of the Not other' (Cricco 2015: 142).

Cricco may go too far in his rhetorical embrace of a postmodern Cusanus, but he does thematise squarely the same issue that I attempted to lay bare in this chapter. If the twentieth century witnessed the rise of a rigorously modernising paradigm for allowing for the thought of this thinker from the fifteenth century to enter into our consciousness, then the present milieu is no doubt one in which the strictures of that hermeneutic will become more obvious. But the point of this exercise is not simply to revise the modern reappropriation and replace it with a new straitjacket of thought. The purpose is rather to explore with Derrida, Agamben,

Cricco and others the path of learned ignorance as a path in which the loving-possibility of the Absolute leaves its traces in our midst. Agamben ends his essay on the passion of facticity by citing a phrase of Jean-Luc Nancy that 'love is that of which we are not masters, that which we never reach but which is always happening to us' (Agamben 1999: 204). One day in the future, Cusanus's love for the hunt for wisdom is likely to find new adherents who rewrite the emerging postmodern hermeneutic, and for that possibility I am also grateful.

Bibliography

Agamben, Giorgio (1998). *Homo Sacer: Sovereign Power and Bare Life*. Trans. Daniel Heller-Roazen. Stanford: Stanford University Press.
Agamben, Giorgio (1999). *Potentialities: Collected Essays in Philosophy*. Stanford: Stanford University Press.
Agamben, Giorgio (2011). *The Sacrament of Language: An Archaeology of the Oath*. Trans. Adam Kotsko. Stanford: Stanford University Press.
Agamben, Giorgio (2013). *The Highest Poverty: Monastic Rules and Form-of-Life*. Trans. Adam Kotsko. Stanford: Stanford University Press.
André, João María (2006). *Nikolaus von Kues und die Kraft des Wortes*. Trier: Cusanus-Institut.
Blumenberg, Hans (1983). *The Legitimacy of the Modern Age*. Cambridge, MA: MIT Press.
Boehme, Jacob (1981 [1621]). *The Signature of All Things*. Cambridge: James Clark & Co.
Casarella, Peter (1990). 'Nicholas of Cusa on the Power of the Possible'. *American Catholic Philosophical Quarterly*, 64/1: 7–34.
Casarella, Peter (1991). 'Neues zu den Quellen der cusanischen Mauer-Symbolik'. In *Mitteilungen und Forschungsbeiträge der Cusanus-Gesellschaft*, vol. 19. Trier: Paulinus Verlag, pp. 273–86.
Casarella, Peter (1994). 'On Dupré's Passage to Modernity'. *Communio: International Catholic Review*, 21: 551–61.
Casarella, Peter (1996). '"His Name is Jesus": Negative Theology and Christology in Two Writings of Nicholas of Cusa from 1440'. In *Nicholas of Cusa on Christ and the Church: Essays in Honor of Chandler M. Brooks*. Ed. Gerald Christianson and Thomas Izbicki. Leiden: Brill, pp. 281–307.
Casarella, Peter (2002). 'Sacra ignorantia: Sobre la doxología filosófica del Cusano'. In *Concidencia Dos Opostos e Concordia: Caminhos do Pensamiento em Nicolau de Cusa*. Ed. João Maria André and Mariano Alvarez Gómez. Coimbra: Faculdade de Letras, pp. 51–65.
Casarella, Peter (2003). 'Nicholas of Cusa (1401–1464), On Learned Ignorance: Byzantine Light en route to a Distant Shore'. In *The Classics of Western Philosophy*. Ed. Jorge J.E. Gracia, Gregory M. Reichberg and Bernard N. Schumacher. Basil Blackwell: Oxford, pp. 183–9.
Casarella, Peter (2005). 'La productividad de la imagen en San Buenaventura y Nicolás de Cusa'. In *El problema del conocimiento en Nicolás de Cusa: genealogía y proyección*. Ed. Jorge M. Machetta and Claudia D'Amico. Buenos Aires: Editorial Biblos, pp. 49–65.
Casarella, Peter (ed.) (2006a). *Cusanus: The Legacy of Learned Ignorance*. Washington, DC: The Catholic University of America Press.
Casarella, Peter (2006b). 'Selbstgestaltung des Menschen nach Nikolaus von Kues und modernes Verständnis des Menschen: aufgezeigt an Hans-Georg Gadamer'. In *Mitteilungen und Forschungsbeiträge der Cusanus-Gesellschaft*, Vol. 31. Trier: Paulinus Verlag, pp. 29–50.
Casarella, Peter (2009). 'Cusanus on Dionysius: The Turn to Speculative Theology'. In *Re-Thinking Dionysius the Areopagite*. Ed. Sarah Coakley and Charles M. Stang. Oxford: Wiley-Blackwell, pp. 137–48.
Casarella, Peter (2012). 'Naturae Desiderium: The Desire of Nature between History and Theology'. In *Christianity and Secular Reason: Classical Themes and Modern Developments*. Ed. Jeffrey Bloechl. Notre Dame: University of Notre Dame Press, pp. 33–63.
Casarella, Peter (2013). 'Nicholas of Cusa and the Ends of Medieval Mysticism'. In *Wiley-Blackwell Companion to Christian Mysticism*. Ed. Julia Lamm. Oxford: Wiley-Blackwell Publishing, pp. 388–403.
Casarella, Peter (2017a). 'Nicholas of Cusa' In *The Internet Encyclopedia of Philosophy*. ISSN 2161–0002 <https://www.iep.utm.edu/nicholas>.

Casarella, Peter (2017b). *Word as Bread: Language and Theology in Nicholas of Cusa*. Münster: Aschendorff.

Colomer, Eusebio (1975). 'Die Erkenntnismetaphysik des Nikolaus von Kues im Hinblick auf die Möglichkeit der Gotteserkenntnis'. *Mitteilungen und Forschungsbeiträge der Cusanus-Gesellschaft*, 11: 211–13.

Cricco, Valentín (2015). 'Nicolás de Cusa: diferencia y recursividad'. In *Revista de la Facultad de Filosofía, Ciencias del a Educación y Humanidades*, Universidad de Morón, 21–2: 123–45.

Cubillos, Catalina (2012). 'Nicholas of Cusa Between the Middle Ages and Modernity'. In *American Catholic Philosophical Quarterly*, 86: 237–49.

Cusa, Nicholas (1983 [1450]). *Idiota de sapientia*, Book II. In *Nicolai de Cusa Opera Omnia* [=h]. Hamburg: Felix Meiner, V, N. 33.

Derrida, Jacques (2005). 'Violence and Metaphysics: An Essay on the Thought of Emmanuel Levinas'. In *Writing and Difference*. London: Routledge, pp. 97–192.

Dupré, Louis (1993). *The Passage to Modernity: An Essay in the Hermeneutics of Nature and Culture*. New Haven, CT: Yale University Press.

Gadamer, Hans-Georg (1972). *Wahrheit und Methode. Grundzüge einer Philosophischen Hermeneutik*. Tübingen: J. C. B. Mohr.

Grassi, Ernesto (1980). 'Italian Humanism and Heidegger's Thesis of the End of Philosophy'. *Philosophy & Rhetoric*, 13/2: 79–98.

Heidegger, Martin (1977). *Basic Writings*. New York: Harper & Row.

Hellinger, Lotte (2018). *Incubula in Transit: People and Trade*. Leiden: Brill.

Hopkins, Jasper (1986). *Introduction to the Philosophy of Nicholas of Cusa*. Minneapolis: Banning Press.

Hopkins, Jasper (1988). *Nicholas of Cusa's Debate with John Wenck*, 3rd edn. Minneapolis: Banning Press.

Hopkins, Jasper (1996). *Nicholas of Cusa on Wisdom and Knowledge*. Minneapolis: Banning Press.

Hopkins, Jasper (2001). *Complete Philosophical and Theological Treatises of Nicholas of Cusa: Volume Two*. Minneapolis: Banning Press.

Jaspers, Karl (1966). *Anselm and Nicholas of Cusa*. New York: Harcourt, Brace, Jovanovich.

Mazzotta, Giuseppe (2001). *Cosmopoiesis: The Renaissance Experiment*. Toronto: University of Toronto Press.

O'Malley, John W. (1997). *Praise and Blame in Renaissance Rome: Rhetoric, Doctrine, and Reform in the Sacred Orators of the Papal Court, c. 1450–1521*. Durham, NC: Duke University Press.

O'Regan, Cyril (2002). *Gnostic Apokalypse: Jacob Boehme's Haunted Narrative*. Albany: State University of New York.

Santinello, Giovanni (ed.) (1970). *Niccolò Cusano agli inizi del mondo modern*. Florence: Sansoni.

Steiger, Renate (1988). 'Einleitung'. In Nicolai de Cusa, *Idiota de sapientia*, Philosophische Bibliothek. Hamburg: Felix Meiner.

Part III

Politics/Community: Justice, Injustice and Power

11

Cosmopolitanism in the Medieval Arabic and Islamic World

Josh Hayes

Introduction

Whither cosmopolitanism? How are we to speak and much less write of cosmopolitanism today? In our global age marked by the seemingly interminable crises of the immigrant and refugee, we are consistently confronted with the spectre of cosmopolitanism. Indeed, cosmopolitanism has come to haunt those governments that still embody the institutional practices of the modern nation-state defined by the determination of perpetual sovereignty. Throughout the twentieth century and into the twenty-first century, the refugee and the immigrant have remained a constant source of political deliberation. Since Hannah Arendt's own reflections upon the role of the refugee in her landmark essay, 'The Decline of the Nation-State and the End of the Rights of Man', the Western world has witnessed a disturbing rise in nationalism and the decline of cosmopolitanism amidst the alleged demise of the nation-state (Arendt 1967: 267–302). If we are to investigate the ethical foundations of cosmopolitanism as a political principle, perhaps we might turn to the twentieth-century French philosopher of deconstruction, Jacques Derrida, who argues that cosmopolitanism is first and foremost to be grounded in an ethics of hospitality:

> Hospitality is culture itself and not simply one ethic amongst others. Insofar as it has to do with the *ethos*, that is, the residence, one's home, the familiar place of dwelling, inasmuch as it is a manner of being there, the manner in which we relate to ourselves and to others, to others as our own or as foreigners, *ethics is hospitality*; ethics is so thoroughly coextensive with the experience of hospitality. (Derrida 2001: 16–17)

However, the concept of cosmopolitanism bears within itself a contradictory logic. Although cosmopolitanism by its own nature calls for an unconditional hospitality by welcoming the foreigner, the immigrant and the stranger, how can we speak of such an unconditional hospitality as the absolute limit of ethics in light of the concrete political and juridical difficulties limiting its own enactment among current debates regarding rights of residency and citizenship? Derrida's own deconstruction of the contradictory logic of cosmopolitanism begins with the Stoic and Pauline tradition before culminating with Immanuel Kant's essay, 'Perpetual Peace'. However, the legacy of cosmopolitanism may also be traced to Plato's *Timaeus*, which ranks among the most widely translated works throughout the Middle Ages. Although medieval commentators possessed only the beginning of the *Timaeus*, the conception of the cosmos presented therein has long-standing ethical and political implications for the medieval Arabic and Islamic tradition.[1] Most importantly, the connection between the soul, the city and cosmos as governed by the principle of oneness and unity (*al-ṭawḥīd*) remains essential to the political topography of Islam. If God (*Allāh*) as a divine principle is one, then consequently the city and the cosmos are one reality. The Islamic doctrine of the oneness and unity of all things is first presented in the Qur'ānic profession of faith (*shahāda*), 'there is no divinity but the Divine' (*lā ilāha illā Allāh*).[2] The path to realising this unity is to be found in reason as the instrument to understand the intelligibility of the world and hence the unity of the divine. As a reflection of the divine intellect, human reason seeks this unity by overcoming the passions that impede it. The ethical and political doctrines of Islam follow directly from this principle of unity insofar as the human good strives to be in accordance with the divine good.

Beginning with Galen's summary of the *Timaeus*, lost in Greek but preserved in Arabic translation, Arabic readers had access to both Galen's paraphrase and Proclus's extensive commentaries. Given the degree of harmonisation of Plato and Aristotle that occurred throughout Late Antiquity, Plato's divine demiurge was often read in conjunction with the rational theology propounded by Aristotle in Book Lambda of his *Metaphysics*. As Cristina D'Ancona (2003: 211) notes, the translation of the *Metaphysics* was among the first translations of ancient Greek philosophy to be produced in the middle of the ninth century within the circle of al-Kindī in Baghdad. Al-Kindī's circle produced translations of both Plotinus's *Enneads* and Proclus's *Elements of Theology* that were to remain influential for subsequent Arabic and Islamic commentators.[3] This synthesis of cosmology and metaphysics also extended into the ethico-political domain. Aristotle's *Nicomachean Ethics* was read as a culmination of his *Metaphysics* insofar as the intellectual virtues decisively orient our investigation into first principles as the condition for all metaphysical enquiry.[4] Once the rationale for the unity between ethics and metaphysics had been established, it became possible for Aristotle's account of virtue

---

[1] Plato's *Timaeus* describes the cosmos that impels one to imitate the beautiful order of the heavenly bodies, 'God devised and bestowed on us vision to the end that we might behold the revolutions of Reason in the Heaven and use them for the revolvings of the reasoning that is within us, these being akin to those, the perturbable and imperturbable; and that through learning and sharing in calculations which are correct by their nature, by imitation of the absolutely unvarying revolutions of the God we might stabilize the variable revolutions within ourselves' (28C). Citing Simplicius's third argument that physics has moral pertinence, Remi Brague argues that what makes the cosmological physics of the *Timaeus* interesting from a moral and political perspective is 'in a word: we should imitate nature; more precisely, what is the most highly worthy of our imitation, which is the majestic order of the army of the skies, so as to put order into our lives' (Brague 2009: 84).

[2] See Nasr's presentation of the microcosm-macrocosm analogy in Islamic cosmological doctrines, 'It is quite significant that the phenomena of Nature, the events taking place within the soul of man, and the verses of the Quran are called *āyāt*, the human soul and Nature, being respectively the microcosmic and macrocosmic counterparts of the celestial archetypes contained in the Divine Word' (Nasr 1993: 6).

[3] Another later example of the syncretic reading of antiquity is al-Fārābī's harmonisation of Plato and Aristotle in his interpretation of Plato's *Timaeus*: '[Aristotle] explained there [i.e., in the *Physics*] the question of causes and how many they are; he established the existence of the efficient cause and also explained there the question of the generating principle and of the moving one, and that it is different from what is generated and moved. And in the same vein, Plato explained in his book known as *Timaeus*, that every generated reality necessarily comes into being through a cause generating it, as well as that the generated reality cannot be the cause of its own generation' (D'Ancona 2003: 212).

[4] On the intellectual virtues, see Chapter 12, this volume.

to be understood on a global and even cosmic scale. At stake, then, was nothing less than a reconceptualisation of the cosmos for the sake of producing a uniquely Arabic conception of cosmopolitanism. Although neither Plato nor Aristotle explicitly address the alleged value of ethics and politics as domains of enquiry that transcend the historical and cultural boundaries of the city-state (*polis*), the medieval Arabic commentary tradition extends their enquiry in the direction of a global political community (*cosmopolis*).

It is not surprising that a *cosmopolis* could be imagined given that the philosophers who were present in al-Kindī's circle in ninth-century Baghdad originated from all parts of the Islamic world and were constantly travelling from one court to another, thereby allowing for a wider conception of friendship and solidarity. Since philosophers by nature are 'citizens of the world' as Socrates has proclaimed, a primary challenge confronted by philosophers during the Būyid Age (945–1055) was the pressure to conform to the religious standards of Sunnī and Shiite Islam while confidentially espousing radical views. A strategy of prudent dissimulation (*taqiyya*) became commonplace for the sake of self-preservation. In order to avoid the claim of heresy, Islamic philosophers adopted both exoteric and esoteric techniques of hermeneutical exegesis reflecting the dialectical interplay between the outward (*ẓāhir*) and the inward (*bāṭin*) (Strauss 1945 and 1973). Among the first proponents of cosmopolitanism include Abū Naṣr al-Fārābī (870–950). Al-Fārābī's political writings have been highlighted for their contributions to a uniquely Muslim nation-state (*umma*) (Orwin 2017). However, al-Fārābī is less known for his utopian tendencies portending the existence of a political community extending across the entire inhabited world (*oikoumenē*).[5] By retrieving the ethical and political dimensions of Platonic, Aristotelian and Neoplatonic cosmology, al-Fārābī's ambitious introduction of an ecumenical society has long-standing consequences for understanding the possibility of global political association (*maʿmūra*) today. In what follows, I shall aim to demonstrate how these cosmopolitan ideals of the *oikoumenē* and the *maʿmūra* are presented throughout al-Fārābī's political treatises ranging from his *Attainment of Happiness* (*Taḥṣīl al-Saʿāda*) and *Selected Aphorisms* (*Fuṣūl al-Muntazaʿa*) to the *Political Regime* (*Kitāb al-Siyāsa al-Madaniyya*) and the *Opinions of the Inhabitants of the Virtuous City* (*Mabādiʾ Ārāʾ Ahl al-Madīna al-Fāḍila*). Al-Fārābī's cosmopolitanism inaugurates a conception of a political association oriented by the realisation of friendship, solidarity, equality and justice on a global scale. After investigating al-Fārābī's appropriation of these cosmopolitan themes adopted from his harmonisation of Plato and Aristotle, the chapter concludes by considering the historical legacy of al-Fārābī's cosmopolitanism upon subsequent medieval Arabic and Islamic commentators, including Miskawayh (932–1030), al-Ghazālī (1058–1111), Ibn Rushd (1126–1198), al-Ṭūsī (1201–1274) and Ibn Khaldūn (1332–1406).

Al-Fārābī

Al-Fārābī's *Attainment of Happiness* (*Taḥṣīl al-Saʿāda*) remains the most explicit example of his appropriation of the Platonic analogy between the city and the cosmos. The principle aim of *Taḥṣīl al-Saʿāda* concerns the achievement of human happiness by citizens of cities and nations. Beginning with Aristotle's *Organon* and proceeding to the natural sciences, al-Fārābī is keen to apply the first principles of metaphysics to his own account of human happiness to justify their long-standing unity. Al-Fārābī adumbrates the limits of metaphysics and the need for ethics to complement metaphysics if only to emphasise the partial and limited

---

[5] For a further discussion of utopian political thought in the period, see Chapter 14, this volume.

character of metaphysical enquiry. Contemplation alone cannot accomplish the perfection of the human being,

> Furthermore, it will become evident to him in this science that each man achieves only a portion of that perfection, and what he achieves of this portion varies in its extent, for an isolated individual cannot achieve all the perfections by himself and without the aid of many other individuals. (Al-Fārābī 1981: 14.6–8)

Therefore, to arrive at the ultimate perfection that deems one to be truly substantial requires the existence of others. Al-Fārābī is adamant to claim that the practice of metaphysics aspires towards the fundamental communality of ethics and political science. It is only by way of this 'innate disposition of every man to join another human being or other men in the labour he ought to perform' (al-Fārābī 1981: 14.9–10) that human perfection can be attained. Since Aristotle retains a fundamental ambivalence towards the role of the philosopher in political life by privileging the *vita contemplativa*, al-Fārābī rightly interrogates the theoretical perfection achieved by contemplation as always infused by the practical labour of the political. The practice of philosophy, especially the contemplation of the first principle, the divine being, does not occur outside of political community. Metaphysics begins and ends with ethics.[6] Al-Fārābī's own account of political association therefore assumes an intimate correspondence between the metaphysical and ethico-political domains. The association of citizens in cities and nations reflect the association of physical bodies constituting the totality of the world.[7] Following Aristotle's division of the parts of the animal, every citizen fulfils a function within the city and the nation. By the realisation and perfection of this function, one comes to see the likeness between the order of cities and nations *and* the order of the cosmos.[8]

With his consistent reference to the entire inhabited world (*oikoumenē*) as the condition for global political community (*ma'mūra*), al-Fārābī presupposes a certain solidarity ('*aṣabiyya*) of all humanity to include three kinds of perfect societies: great, medium, and small. The great society encompasses all the societies of the world, 'The great one [being] the union of all the societies in the inhabited world [*oikoumenē*]' (al-Fārābī 1895: 53.12). Human solidarity can only manifest itself through individuals belonging to a larger political community, that is, a city-state, nation-state and world-state. Al-Fārābī envisions a great society encompassing all the societies of the world oriented towards the realisation of

---

[6] Al-Fārābī illustrates how the four metaphysical principles – *what* and *by what* the thing is, *from what* it is, *for what* it is – are essential to the task of political science. 'Then he should investigate all the things by which man achieves this perfection or that are useful to him in achieving it . . . He should make known *what* and *how* every one of them is, and *from what* and *for what* it is, until all of them become known, intelligible, and distinguished from each other. This is political science' (al-Fārābī 1981: 15.3–16.2–4).

[7] 'It will become evident to him that political association and the totality that results from the association of citizens in cities correspond to the association of the bodies that constitute the totality of the world. He will come to see in what are included in the totality constituted by the city and the nation the likenesses of what are included in the total world' (al-Fārābī 1981: 16.6–7).

[8] Aristotle compares the constitution of an animal to a well-governed city-state: 'For when order is once established in a city, there is no need of *a special ruler* with arbitrary powers to be present at every activity, but each individual performs his own task as he is ordered' (*De motu animalium* 703a29). This is a rather common analogy throughout antiquity. However, Aristotle characteristically provides a further complication to prove that there is no need for a soul in each part of the animal. The analogy extends to *Metaphysics* 1075a19 where the same order that prevails in a household between the freeman, wives and sons, and slaves is postulated for the whole cosmos.

eudaimonia, 'the excellent universal state will arise only when all the nations in it cooperate for the purpose of reaching felicity' (al-Fārābī 1895: 54.10). Since *eudaimonia* (*sa'āda*) requires leisure, the attainment of *eudaimonia* is framed by the condition of war (*jihād*) to achieve its end.[9] Without war, the parts constituting the universal state might not possibly act in unison with one another and perfect order cannot be achieved. Such a cooperation demands 'a sovereign over whom no other human being has any sovereignty whatsoever; he is the *Imām*; he is the first sovereign of the excellent city, he is the sovereign of the excellent nation, and the sovereign of the inhabited world' (Al-Fārābī 1895: 59.5–7).[10]

Despite adopting a hierarchical scheme of emanation between the whole and the parts, al-Fārābī does not hesitate to privilege the role of friendship, equality, justice and solidarity at the level of tribes, nations and societies.[11]

Among those things that remain useful for citizens in achieving perfection in the civic and cosmic order is friendship (*ṣadāqa*). By allusion to Aristotle's cosmopolitan claim that 'friendship seems to be innate in a parent for offspring and in an offspring for a parent . . . it is innate too in those that are alike in kind to one another', al-Fārābī distinguishes between love (*mawadda*) that arises from a spontaneous innate disposition and love (*maḥabba*) that arises from a volition guided by virtue, utility and pleasure.[12] As Aristotle claims in his *Nicomachean Ethics*, friendship classified by utility includes political friendship (*homonoia*) aimed at ensuring that the *polis* remains intact.[13] Beginning with the *Selected Aphorisms* (*Fuṣūl al-Muntaza'a*)

---

[9] 'Happiness, moreover, is held to reside in leisure; for we are occupied or are without leisure so that we may be at leisure, and we wage war so we may be at peace' (NE 1177b4–6).

[10] To speak of a universal state as al-Fārābī does here may appear rather strange and unthinkable without the Hellenising influence of Alexander the Great. While any attempt to attribute a world-state to Aristotle will most likely be met with incredulity (see Stern [1968] for the debate about the authenticity of a letter to Alexander discovered by the twelfth-century Jewish philosopher, Abraham Ibn Ezra), we can at least entertain this possibility for the subsequent generation of Arabic philosophers who adopted his cosmopolitan views.

[11] Hence, al-Fārābī's respect for singularity, diversity and variability extends from political enquiry to his own epistemology with the intellection of both natural and voluntary intelligibles, 'The accidents and states of these intelligibles vary whenever certain events occur in the inhabited part of the earth [*oikoumenê*], events common to all of it, to a certain nation or city, or to a certain group within a city, or pertaining to a single man' (al-Fārābī 1981: 20.1–3).

[12] NE 1155a19–22: 'which is why we praise people who are "lovers of humankind" (*philanthropoi*). One might see in one's travels too that every human being is akin (*oikeios*) to every other human being and a friend to him.' See also Aristotle's student, Theophrastus, cited in Porphyry's *De Abstinentia*, 'But Theophrastus has made use of an argument like the following: We say that those with the same progenitors (I mean, the same father and mother) are by nature kin (*oikeious*) to one another. And for this reason we think that those who are descended from the same distant ancestors are kin to one another, as are fellow citizens since they have in common their land and mutual relations. For we do not judge such people to be kin to each other on the grounds that they are descended from the same people, unless the very founders of the clan are the first forebears. For just as we think that a Greek is kin and family to a Greek, and a barbarian to a barbarian, so we can say that every human being is kin and family to every other. We say this for one of two reasons: First, all people have the same forebears. Second, all people have in common their food, culture, and membership in the same kind . . .' (*De abstinentia* 3, 25). Note Theophrastus's consistent use of *oikeios* or kin to refer to a common humanity contra Plato's claim that Greeks and barbarians are not kin.

[13] 'It appears that *poleis* are held together by friendship, and that the lawgivers study this more than they do justice; for *homonoia* appears to resemble friendship, and this they desire most, while *stasis*, because it is enmity, is what they want most to banish' (NE 1155a22–3).

al-Fārābī highlights the role of neighbourly love (*maḥabba*) as akin to Aristotle's account of political friendship:

> They are bound by love [*maḥabba*], and they hold together and stay preserved through justice and actions of justice. Love may come about by nature, like the love of parents for the child. And it may come about by volition in that its starting point is voluntary things followed by love. That which is by volition is threefold: one is by sharing in virtue, the second is for the sake of the useful; and the third is for the sake of pleasure. (Al-Fārābī 1971: 70.3–5)

Al-Fārābī demonstrates a clear familiarity with Aristotle's ethical corpus by distinguishing between the virtuous, the useful and the pleasant corresponding to objects of volition.[14] Political friendship (*homonoia*) is needed to hold political community together in contrast to familial love that arises naturally and spontaneously. Therefore, political friendship is a matter of choice determined by a range of certain dispositions that need to be cultivated in order for volition to be guided in the most rational manner.

Al-Fārābī's account of neighbourly love also extends to the role of equality (*musāwāt*) and justice (*'adl*) within the political community.[15] Equality or fairness is a mode of justice responsible for assessing individual citizens depending upon merit or what is deserved.[16] Both equality and justice arise from a love (*maḥabba*) that involves the mutual sharing of goods, 'Justice first has to do with dividing the shared goods that belong to the inhabitants of the city among them all. Then, after that, [it has to do] with preserving what has been divided among them' (al-FFārābī 1971: 71.14–15). Following Aristotle, al-Fārābī applies a specific kind of legal justice to inhabitants of the city and a more general kind of political justice to 'the people' and 'all people' as if to discern the equal status of all persons beyond both civic and national boundaries: 'When that is set down as a right of the inhabitants of the city or of all people, no account is taken of excusing by the one to whom the injustice has occurred' (Al-Fārābī 1971: 74.10).[17] His assessment of the value of equality and justice also extends to the existence of virtuous communities within the democratic city.[18] The

---

[14] '[F]or since there are three things that lead to choices and three that lead to avoidance, the former being what is beautiful, what is advantageous, and what is pleasant' (NE 1104b30–1).

[15] Following Aristotle's account of the equality (*isonomia*) of both distributive and corrective justice: 'Since the unjust person is unequal and what is unjust in unequal, it is clear that there is also a certain middle term associated with what is unequal. And this is the equal, for in whatever sort of action in which there are degrees, the more and the less, there is also the equal. If then, the unjust is unequal, the just is equal, which is in fact what is held to by the case by everyone, even without argument' (NE 1131a10–15).

[16] As Baracchi notes, 'We notice here, once more, Aristotle's reluctance to consider human beings in terms of numerical equality, that is, of presuming homogeneous rights simply in virtue of being a human being, of counting as one. On the contrary, he suggests, in each case human beings must be subjected to an axiological assessment. Only thus may interactions be regulated in a fair way' (Baracchi 2008: 154).

[17] This more general kind of justice is to be exercised in such a way without regard to the individual parts of the city according to rank or even if they are kin to us, see Goldin (2011: 270).

[18] Retrieving Aristotle's account of political justice, al-Fārābī privileges the justice 'of which one exploits the acts of the virtues possessed by all others, whether they are nations, cities within a nation, groups within a city, or parts within each group' (al-Fārābī 1981: 24.18–19). Political justice considers citizens of the polis to be equal, free and pursuing a self-sufficient life, 'For these are in accordance with law, and among people for whom it is natural for there to be law, and these are people among whom there is an equality of ruling and being ruled' (NE 1134 b15–16).

democratic city ensures that equality is measured at the individual level of human character. The relationship between virtuous individuals and virtuous communities consists of free associations between individuals.

By returning to Plato's *Republic* where the democratic city is portrayed as an imperfect city, al-Fārābī nevertheless concludes that it is the best of the imperfect cities, 'this is the most admirable and happy city [*al-madīnah al-mu'jabah wal-madīnah al-sa'īdah*]' (al-Fārābī 1964: 70.11). Despite its apparent imperfections, virtue and happiness are inextricably conjoined in the democratic city if only to indicate how the health of a democracy composed of virtuous men (*al-afāḍil*) of many kinds reflects the diversity of the entire inhabited world, 'the countless similar and dissimilar groups [*ṭawā'if*]' (al-Fārābī 1964: 69.11–12). The democratic city 'develops into many cities, distinct yet intertwined [*dākhilah ba'ḍuha fī ba'ḍ*] with the parts of each scattered throughout the parts of the others' (al-Fārābī 1964: 70.16–18). The multicultural and multi-ethnic character of the democratic city clearly warrants al-Fārābī's attention, 'the nations emigrate to it and reside there, and it grows beyond measure. People of every race multiply in it . . .' (al-Fārābī 1964: 70.14–15). To further demonstrate the cosmopolitan character of the democratic city, the *ethos* of hospitality remains pervasive, 'Strangers cannot be distinguished from the residents' (al-Fārābī 1964: 70.18). In contrast to Plato's prohibition against intermarriage, al-Fārābī suggests the value of intermarriage between diverse ethnic groups for the sake of strengthening the bond of cooperative association. The increased unison of the democratic city effectively establishes and promotes happiness, 'Everybody loves it and loves to reside in it, because there is no human wish or desire that this city does not satisfy [*kull insān lahu hawā aw shahwah fī shay'in mā qadara 'alā nayliha min hādhihi al-madīnah*]' (al-Fārābī 1964: 70.13–14). Contesting Socrates's account of the democratic city, al-Fārābī's democratic city composed of philosophers, rhetoricians and poets retains the possibility of becoming a virtuous paradigm for more defective cities to emulate and follow. Such a multifarious community of free individuals mutually cooperating in the pursuit of happiness may therefore be imagined on a global scale beginning with the seminal contributions of the tenth-century Muslim historian and philosopher, Miskawayh (932–1030).

Al- Fārābī's Cosmopolitan Legacy: Miskawayh

As a patron of the Būyid sovereigns of tenth- and eleventh-century Baghdad, Miskawayh and his philosophical circle contributed widely to the cosmopolitan ethos of the age. His ethical treatise, the *Refinement of Character* (*Tahdhīb al-Akhlāq*) inspired by both Aristotle's *Nicomachean Ethics* and Islamic religious law (*sharī'a*) remains an important contribution to the history of Islamic ethics (Miskawayh 2002: xvii; see also Khadduri 1984: 110–13). In his composition of the *Tahdhīb al-Akhlāq*, Miskawayh was also influenced by Ibn al-Khammār, the Muslim disciple of the Jacobite Christian, Yaḥyā ibn 'Adī, a translator and commentator of Plato and Aristotle, and student of al-Fārābī. Miskawayh's cosmopolitanism indeed echoes Ibn 'Adī's claim that 'our highest perfection lies in the universal love of humankind as a single race, united by humanity itself. The core of that humanity, our crowning glory, is the divinely imparted rational soul, which all men share, and by which, indeed, all men are one' (Yaḥyā ibn 'Adī 1946: 517–18).

Miskawayh's belief in the unity of humanity is expressed in a natural sociability (*uns*) that extends even to strangers. In his *Tahdhīb al-Akhlāq*, Miskawayh remains in agreement with Arab grammarians that the word for 'man' (*insān*) is derived from the same stem '-*n*-*s* ('to be sociable') (Kraemer 1986: 233). Miskawayh thus shares al-Fārābī's aspiration for a great society to attain human happiness:

> Since these human goods and the corresponding aptitudes in the soul are many in number, and since it is not within the power of one man to achieve them all, it is necessary that a large group associate in this total achievement. This is why the number of individual human beings should be large, and they should get together at the same time for the achievement of these common kinds of happiness, so that each one among them may attain this perfection through the cooperation of the others. (Miskawayh 1966: 14.18–15.2)[19]

Like al-Fārābī, Miskawayh privileges the disposition of benevolence (*khayr*) aimed at ensuring that justice is equally distributed throughout such a society. The benevolent person exercises circumspection by their capacity to identify justice as the mean, 'Benevolence, then, does not violate the conditions of justice, but is rather circumspect in it. For this reason, it has been said that the benevolent man is nobler than the just' (Miskawayh 1966: 130.12). Since benevolence functions as a kind of excessive attention to the singular individual beyond the universal law, 'benevolence is exercised in the kind of justice which pertains to man himself' (Miskawayh 1966: 131.21). Reflecting Aristotle's suggestion that 'benevolence seems to be the beginning of friendship' (Aristotle 1167a4), Miskawayh importantly retrieves al-Fārābī's own account of neighbourly love (*maḥabba*) to attain individual perfection:

> To this end, people must love one another, for each finds his own perfection in someone else, and the latter's happiness is incomplete without the former. Each one thus becomes like an organ of the same body; and man's constitution depends upon the totality of organs forming his body. (Miskawayh 1966: 15.6–9)

Neighbourly love thus extends to the love of humanity (*philanthropy*) as a guiding source for both ethical and political perfection.

Al-Ghazālī

In contrast to the progressive cosmopolitanism of al-Fārābī and Miskawayh, al-Ghazālī (1058–1111) retrieves the pietist and mystic traditions of Islam. Through his apprenticeship with al-Julwaynī (1028–1085), a renowned Muslim cleric known for promoting the authority of the Imām, al-Ghazālī came to resolutely defend the established Sunnī orthodoxy in Baghdad against the rival Ismāʿīlī dynasty of the Fāṭimids. After embarking on his own intense experience of conversion by wandering for a decade as an Islamic mystic (*ṣūfī*), al-Ghazālī argues in his *Incoherence of the Philosophers* (*Tahāfut al-Falāsifa*) that reason and therefore *falsafa* must ultimately remain subordinate to revelation:

> Rather, in the treasury of things that are enacted by [God's] power there are wondrous and strange things that one has not come across. These are denied by someone who thinks that only those things exist that he experiences similar to people who deny magic, sorcery, the talismanic arts, [prophetic] miracles, and the wondrous deeds [done by saints]. (Al-Ghazālī 1997: 226. 20–4)

---

[19] Kraemer notes that the great society (*tamaddun*) is presented in his lesser known treatise, *al-Fawz al-Aṣghar*, as occupying a range of geographical places from deserts, to towns, to mountain tops (Kraemer 1986: 232, note 67).

Al-Ghazālī's defence of the intuitive knowledge of the mystic over the rational knowledge of the philosopher has long-standing consequences for redefining the mainstream view of Sunnī political authority. Al-Ghazālī assumes a natural hierarchy between religious and political authority.[20] Although *The Balance of Actions* (*Mīzān al-'Amal*) is clearly indebted to Aristotle's account of the Golden Mean by retrieving his concept of equality (*musāwāt*) to effect a harmonious relationship between individual persons and hence parts of society, al-Ghazālī ultimately defends religious monarchy whereby religion (*din*) and kingship (*mulk*) remain inseparable. Al-Ghazālī importantly downplays the role of solidarity (*'aṣabiyya*) and the possibility of democracy for the sake of preserving sovereignty through force:

> Sovereignty nowadays is possible only through force [*shawka*]. The caliph is the person to whom the possessor of force [*ṣāḥib al-shawka*] pays allegiance. Anyone who seizes power by force and is obedient to the caliph . . . is a sultan wielding valid jurisdiction [*ḥukm*] and judgement [*qaḍā'*] in the different regions of the earth. (Al-Ghazālī 1967: 179)

By privileging the role of the sultan as the holder of juridical power, al-Ghazālī presents a perspective of political power that is overwhelmingly concerned with its consolidation. He thus proposes a new relationship between religious and political authority grounded in a literalist interpretation of *sharī'a*. Therefore, al-Ghazālī may be viewed as a proponent of the fusion of theological and political authority predating Thomas Hobbes and Carl Schmitt. The tenets of cosmopolitan humanism, namely solidarity, equality and justice, illustrated in al-Fārābī and Miskawayh are effectively erased in favour of the preservation of theological and political sovereignty. In opposition to Ibn Rushd, al-Ghazālī rejects legal constitutional restraint that would effectively limit the power of the ruler. Absolute power rules absolutely. Al-Ghazālī's traditionalist approach to legal authority has long-standing historical consequences for Islamic politics by reinforcing Sunnī political orthodoxy for generations of Muslims to come.

Ibn Rushd

The decrees of al-Ghazālī were not to fall upon deaf ears. Beginning with *The Incoherence of the Incoherence* (*Tahāfut al-Tahāfut*), Ibn Rushd (Averroes, 1126–98) defends the cosmopolitan humanism of al-Fārābī and Miskawayh. As a prolific author, Ibn Rushd commented extensively on Aristotle's corpus, ranging from short epitomes to great commentaries. His *Middle Commentary on the Nicomachean Ethics*, lost in Arabic but surviving in Hebrew and Latin translations, even demonstrates an intimate familiarity with al-Fārābī's lost commentary on the *Nicomachean Ethics*. Given his innate propensity towards jurisprudence (*fiqh*), Ibn Rushd's account of political association in both Plato and Aristotle is oriented by a reverence for *sharī'a*.[21] Although Ibn Rushd did not have access to Aristotle's *Politics*, his *Commentary on Plato's Republic*, lost in Arabic but preserved in Hebrew in the early fourteenth century by Samuel ben Judah of Provence, presents an Aristotelian reading of Plato clearly indebted to

---

[20] 'We sent Our Messengers with the clear signs, and We sent down with them the Book and the Balance so that men might uphold justice. And We sent down iron, wherein is great might . . . so that God might know who helps him, and his messengers, in the unseen' (Qur'ān 57:25).
[21] Rosenthal contends that Ibn Rushd was a Muslim philosopher first and a disciple of Plato, Aristotle and their commentators second (Rosenthal 1958: 177).

the influence of al-Fārābī.[22] However, Ibn Rushd also departs from Aristotle in some key ways, especially with regard to his treatment of women:

> The competence of women is unknown, however, in these cities since they are placed at the service of their husbands and confined to procreation, upbringing, and suckling. This nullifies their [other] activities. Since women in these cities are not prepared with respect to any of the human virtues, they frequently resemble plants in these cities. Their being a burden upon the men in these cities is one of the causes of the poverty of these cities. (Ibn Rushd 1956: 54.5–11)

Ibn Rushd's belief that women ought to share in the same end as men is considered controversial for his day and importantly reflects al-Fārābī's own claim that in the democratic city all are equal and hence 'no one has a better claim than anyone else to a position of authority' (al-Fārābī 1964: 71.9). Like al-Fārābī, Ibn Rushd addresses the lack of virtue and honour in the democratic city. If not strengthened by virtue and honour, the democratic city risks its own demise. Therefore, the wise leaders of the democratic city chosen by chance bear the responsibility to ensure that the democratic city becomes virtuous. By addressing the general size of cities, Ibn Rushd echoes al-Fārābī by advocating for the possibility of the democratic city becoming a global political community (*ma'mūra*), 'Out of this [democratic] State will grow the Ideal State and other States of these [various] kinds, because they exist in it potentially' (Ibn Rushd 1956: 93.20–1). Despite the desirability of having cities determined according to their geographical locality, Ibn Rushd also acknowledges the possibility of having cities large enough to be coterminous with entire climate zones if not the entire inhabited world (*oikoumenē*):

> Yet if these communities be of a determined number intended to limit them, then the truth of this ought to be shown by the conformity of this opinion to the natural climates or all the natural people. This is alluded to in the saying of the Lawgiver: 'I have been sent to the Red and the Black.' If this be the [correct] opinion, Plato does not favor it; but it is Aristotle's opinion, and it is the indubitable truth. (Ibn Rushd 1956: 46.17–19)

In an admission to the possibility of the *oikoumenē*, Ibn Rushd cites the Prophet Muḥammad indicating the universal significance of his mission to promote the spread of Islam by the practice of philosophy which remains paramount to global flourishing.[23] Assent to the divine law by the three methods of demonstration, dialectic or rhetoric is available to every human being, 'That is because, when this Divine Law of ours called to people by means of these three methods, assent to it was extended to every human being . . . Therefore, he [that is, the Prophet] (peace upon him) was selected to be sent to "the red and black"' (Ibn Rushd 1859: 7.2–3). Ibn

---

[22] Ibn Rushd describes Aristotle's *Politics* as 'the book in which (is contained) the perfection of wisdom' since 'that which is (contained in Plato's *Politea* is not complete)'. As Ibn Rushd states at the beginning of his commentary on the *Republic*, 'The first part of his art (of Politics) is contained in Aristotle's . . . *Nicomachea* and the second part in his . . . *Politica*, and in Plato's book also upon which we intend to comment. For Aristotle's *Politica* has not yet come into our hands. But before we begin with a detailed commentary on these treatises, it is fitting that we should mention what was explained in the first part and may be laid down as a root principle for what we should first like to say here . . .' (Rosenthal 1958: 187).
[23] As Urvoy claims, 'The process by which philosophy is carried out is . . . the concern of humanity as a whole. Both are eternal, and philosophy must always be being enacted in one part of the world or another' (Urvoy 1991: 110).

Rushd's allusion to the 'red and black' extends the universal mission of Islam to all human beings and thus decisively promotes a cosmopolitan vision of global political community.[24]

Al-Ṭūsī

Alongside Miskawayh's *Tahdhīb al-Akhlāq*, al-Ṭūsī's *Nasirean Ethics* (*Akhlāq-i Nāṣirī*) was widely known among ethical treatises throughout medieval Persia.[25] Al-Ṭūsī (1201–74) who lived during the demise of 'Abbāsid rule was also influenced by the Peripatetic tradition. Following in the tradition of al-Fārābī and Miskawayh, al-Ṭūsī focuses on two fundamental concepts that reflect his own cosmopolitan background as counsellor to the Mongol conqueror, Hūlāgū Khan (1218–65) and the Ismā'īlī governor of Quhistān. The first concept of equality (*musāwāt*) remains pivotal to his account of justice ('*adl*), 'none is more perfect than the virtue of justice, as is obvious in the discipline of ethics [*ṣinā'at-i akhlāq*] for the true midpoint is justice ['*adl*], all else being peripheral to it and taking its reference therefrom' (al-Ṭūsī 2011: 95). Al-Ṭūsī's account of equality importantly reflects Aristotle's own influence, 'the best man is not he who exercises his virtue toward himself but he who exercises its towards another' (NE 1130a6). In tandem with the notion of equality (*musāwāt*) is the concept of oneness (*waḥda*). Al-Ṭūsī's ethical writings are indebted to the Islamic tradition of *ḥadīth* beginning with an account of what the Muslim believer owes to *Allāh* as the One. Reverence for *Allāh* is expressed primarily by the virtue of justice as the most perfect virtue and secondarily by the virtue of generosity: 'It is for this reason, that people love the liberal man more than the just, notwithstanding the fact that the order of the universe depends more on justice than liberality' (al-Ṭūsī 2011: 105). Al-Ṭūsī also relates justice to favour (*tafāḍul*) by addressing justice as the mean between favour and disdain, 'favour is praiseworthy, but it has no part in justice, for justice is equivalence, while favour is augmentation' (al-Ṭūsī 2011: 106). To reject the conclusion that favour must therefore be blameworthy, al-Ṭūsī contends that favour performs the role of circumspection (*ihtiyāṭ*) in justice. Just as Miskawayh privileges the role of benevolence in justice, al-Ṭūsī argues that 'favour cannot be realized without prior observance of the conditions for justice, which first fulfils the obligation of merit [*istiḥqāq*] and then, out of circumspection [*ihtiyāṭ*], adjoins an augmentation thereto' (al-Ṭūsī 2011: 106). Circumspection as a capacity that enables one to discern the given circumstances of a situation prior to the application of justice is requisite for attaining order within the city. However, circumspection may be superseded by love in its comprehensive attention to nobility, virtue and perfection.

Al-Ṭūsī devotes the third discourse of the *Nasirean Ethics* to developing the themes of love and friendship. The generality of love is contrasted with the singularity of friendship, 'love is more general than friendship; for love is conceivable amid a swarming throng, but friendship does not reach this degree of comprehensiveness' (al-Ṭūsī 2011: 197). The Neoplatonic commentary tradition dedicated to the *Symposium* also becomes apparent with al-Ṭūsī's renewed

---

[24] Ibn Rushd's reference to pursuing the universal mission of Islam, the 'red and black', even extends to his discussion of the afterlife: 'It seems that the learned person who commits an error with respect to the question is to be excused and the one who hits the mark is to be thanked or rewarded. With respect to this [question] denying its existence is what is unbelief, because it is one of the roots of the Law and something to which assent comes about by the three methods shared by the red and black' (Ibn Rushd 1859: 17.8–10).

[25] Al-Ṭūsī's *Nasirean Ethics* is widely considered to be the 'best known ethical digest to be composed in medieval Persia, if not all of Islam' (Khadduri 1984: 122).

focus upon the dialectic of multiplicity and unity, 'but division into halves is one of the consequences of multiplicity, whereas love is one of the causes of union' (al-Ṭūsī 2011: 196). The perfection of both civic and global political association is attained by a synthesis congruent with the organs of the body cooperating with one another. Love functions as the expression of this natural yearning for synthesis and perfection.[26] Al-Ṭūsī's description of love as the erotic consummation between desire and its object may be applied to society in the case of divine love guided by *sharī'a*. The possessor of *sharī'a* is granted the duty of 'performing his observance and ceremonies [to] impose respect and veneration for the Religious Law in men's hearts producing a speedy response and obedience to the calls of goodness' (al-Ṭūsī 2011: 200–1). *Sharī'a* works to ensure happiness within the city by promoting the social bond through devotion to the divine good. Al-Ṭūsī claims that this act of religious devotion is most concretely realised by pilgrimage (*ḥajj*) to Mecca:

> all the inhabitants of the world have been put under the obligation of combining together, once in a life-time, in one location . . . the intention was, rather, that by making matters easy the inhabitants of distant lands might come together, acquiring some share of that felicity to which the inhabitants of cities and localities have been made receptive, and making a display of that natural fellowship to be found in their innate disposition. (Al-Ṭūsī 2011: 200)

The pilgrimage sustains al-Ṭūsī's vision of cosmopolitanism as capable of bringing citizens together in global fellowship. The solidarity ('*aṣabiyya*) achieved by such an event also anticipates the cosmopolitan contributions of fourteenth-century judge, historian and philosopher, Ibn Khaldūn (1332–1406).

Ibn Khaldūn

Ibn Khaldūn's *Introduction to History*, also known as the *Prolegomena* (*Muqadimma*), remains foundational to the study of the history and culture of the Islamic world. Reflecting the inductive sensibility of Aristotle in his attention to the empirical development of both religious and secular concepts, the *Muqadimma* is at once sociological and historical in its direction and thus serves as the first attempt in the Islamic world to document what we might call the 'Great Society' in its multifaceted geographical and cultural complexity. Following al-Fārābī, Ibn Khaldūn contends that the basic unit of society is the state. Hence, the task of the sociologist and historian is to genealogically trace the rise and demise of the state. Ibn Khaldūn distinguishes between three kinds of states: the first derived from revelation or divine order; the second derived from human or secular order; and the third derived from their combination. In his analysis of the three kinds of states, Ibn Khaldūn identifies two major social forces responsible for the rise of the state: solidarity ('*aṣabiyya*) and religion. If religion is understood 'as a spiritual feeling of brotherhood'

---

[26] '[F]or no individual can reach perfection in isolation, as has been explained. This being so, there is an inescapable need for a synthesis, which will render all individuals, cooperating together, comparable to the organs of one individual. Again, since Man has been created with a natural direction towards perfection, he has a natural yearning for the synthesis in question. This yearning for the synthesis is called Love' (al-Ṭūsī 2011: 195).

most likely found in cities, then *'aṣabiyya* is found in nomadic societies and thus gives rise to the birth of cities.[27] Throughout the *Muqadimma*, Ibn Khaldūn documents how the natural geography of the harsh desert environment prompts the innate Arab disposition to seek human culture and society. Beginning with the family nucleus and extending to tribal affiliation, there arises the filial bond of *'aṣabiyya* oriented by concentric spheres of obligation.[28]

Even after the demise of the 'Abbāsid Caliphate (750–1258), *'aṣabiyya* remained a potent secular force as an expression of the natural instinct of caring for the 'other'. In addition to family members and close relatives, *'aṣabiyya* may be applied to those who are physically far apart by virtue of the imagination. Therefore, a cosmopolitan conception of political association becomes possible as an 'imagined community' (Anderson 1983).[29] Reflecting al-Fārābī's own account of the rise of human culture and political institutions in his *Book of Letters* (*Kitāb al-Ḥurūf*), Ibn Khaldūn at least indicates how *'aṣabiyya* may be applied to the role of justice on a global scale. The intersection between *'aṣabiyya* and justice becomes pertinent to how justice can be imagined as something that develops out of *'aṣabiyya*.[30] As a natural outgrowth of *'aṣabiyya*, justice would entail an innate recognition of reciprocity between citizens as equals. The justice arising from *'aṣabiyya* is thereby grounded in an altruism that values the sacrifice of one's own self-interest for the sake of preserving the interests of another.[31] Although Ibn Khaldūn does not provide a normative account of either justice or political association, his extensive description of the merits of *'aṣabiyya* among the rise and demise of states presents the possibility of re-imagining a form of justice reflecting the cosmopolitan ideals established by his predecessors.

---

[27] Reflecting al-Fārābī's cosmopolitan account of neighbourly love (*maḥabba*), *'aṣabiyya* as a distinctive Arab social type arises from the geographical and climatic conditions of the city-state, that is, the association and cooperation conditioned by life in a harsh desert environment. '*Aṣabiyya* implies the most elementary form of social solidarity and may be said to originate 'in a natural desire to be compassionate toward and help and defend one's immediate relations' (Mahdi 1957: 196).

[28] Ibn Khaldūn's account of *'aṣabiyya* clearly demonstrates both Stoic and Ptolemaic influence, informed by both Hierocles's account of *oikeiosis* and Ptolemaic astronomy. As Goldin notes in his account of the Stoic cosmopolitanism of Hierocles, 'our place within the human community is described as being like the center or a number of concentric circles on which lie other human beings. The circles closest to us contain immediate family and loved ones, those farther include those of the same tribe or community, and the farthest include strangers' (Goldin 2011: 279).

[29] Ibn Khaldūn appropriates the importance of the imagination from al-Fārābī who emphasises its role in the proliferation of a multiplicity of religions; see al-Fārābī (1970).

[30] As Nusseibeh states, 'For Ibn Khaldūn, on the other hand, the basic glue binding a polity is this instinct, and it is significantly a glue in which "the other" – even though it is a specific other at its basis, a blood relative, the object of one's affection, or a loved one – counts at least as much as oneself, if not more' (Nusseibeh 2015: 186).

[31] The justice developing from *'aṣabiyya* and anticipating Rousseau's *amour de soi* might be said to originate in the Stoic account of *oikeiosis*. 'If the direct relationship between persons who help each other is very close, so that it leads to close contact and unity, the ties are obvious and clearly require the (existence of a feeling of solidarity) without any outside (prodding). If, however, the relationship is somewhat distant, it is often forgotten in part. However, some knowledge of it remains and this causes a person to help his relatives for the known motive, in order to escape the shame he would feel in his soul were a person to whom he is somehow related be treated unjustly' (Ibn Khaldūn 2005: 235.10–15).

Conclusion

If we are to return to Jacques Derrida's essay, 'On Cosmopolitanism', the ethics of hospitality clearly remains a pervasive presence throughout the medieval Arabic and Islamic cosmopolitan tradition. Hospitality and the attendant virtue of solidarity might even be said to constitute our own cosmopolitan paradigm of globalisation. However, with the contemporary resurgence of sovereignty in the Western world, we are now confronted with the danger of a renewal of more virulent forms of nationalism and tribalism which undoubtedly occlude the non-Western 'other'. The occlusion of the barbarian, the stranger, the immigrant and the refugee are indeed endemic to the 'grand narrative' of the West. Beginning with the Greco-Roman heritage of Stoicism, cosmopolitanism is all too often conceived as reaching a kind of denouement in Renaissance humanism. The Latin Renaissance of fourteenth-century Florence continues to overshadow the Arabic Renaissance of ninth-century Baghdad. However, the inception of the Latin Renaissance remains indebted to the Arabic transmission of the Aristotelian corpus into the Western world. Just as Thomas Aquinas could not have composed his *Summa* without the influence of Averroes as a primary interlocutor, Dante Aligheiri could not pen his *De monarchia* without recourse to al-Fārābī. Indeed, Dante's own ecumenical account of world government combining the universality of 'common law' that applies to all nations with the 'particularity' of local laws is indebted to al-Fārābī's description of the excellent universal state and the prudence of the *Imām*-philosopher-ruler who must strike a balance between global universality and cultural specificity (Stone 2006: 124).[32] Al-Fārābī's application of Aristotle's distinction between the universality of reason and the particularity of sense perception, namely imagination, also proves to be central to the content and structure of Dante's *Purgatio*:

> And your imagination [*imagine*] will quickly
> Come to see how, at first, I saw the sun
> again which was now setting
> So matching mine to the trusty steps
> of my master [*maestro*], I came forth from such a fog
> to the rays which were already dead on low shores
> (*Purg.* XVII. 1–12)

Contra Plato's dismissal of the poets from the *kallipolis* in Book X of the *Republic*, both al-Fārābī and Dante extend the role of the imagination into the global political domain as a necessary condition for the accomplishment of *eudaimonia*.[33] Perhaps al-Fārābī's decision to privilege the imagination in its hermeneutical traversal of cultural and geographical boundaries remains his most enduring contribution to the political topography of Arabic and Islamic cosmopolitanism.

---

[32] 'Therefore, he (the supreme ruler) has to secure certain groups of men or individuals who are to be instructed in what causes the happiness of particular nations, who will preserve what can form the character of a particular nation alone, and who will learn the persuasive methods that should be involved in forming the character of that nation' (al-Fārābī 1981: 35.9–11).

[33] 'He (i.e. the philosopher) is the man who knows every action by which felicity can be reached. This is the first condition for being a ruler. Moreover, he should be a good orator and be able to rouse other people's imagination by well-chosen words' (al-Fārābī 1895: 59.1–3).

Although this brief survey of the medieval Arabic and Islamic cosmopolitan tradition cannot possibly capture the historical transmission and appropriation of the Greco-Roman cosmopolitan tradition in its entirety, it may suggest at least a new direction for approaching the intersection between both cultures that strives to revive their cosmopolitan integrity. The Arabic Renaissance of ninth-century Baghdad retains a Socratic spirit of free thinking aimed at questioning the core assumptions of any historically specific orientation be it religious or secular. For example, we are told by Ibn Bājja that al-Fārābī's lost commentary on the *Nicomachean Ethics* was said to have been incendiary enough to harm the faith of the simple man as made evident by his claim that 'religious belief in an afterlife was nothing but tales for old women' (Strauss 1973: 14). Of course, this was not lost on al-Ghazālī who in his famous work, *the Incoherence of the Philosophers* (*Tahāfut al-Falāsifa*), condemns al-Fārābī and those who follow his opinions as unbelievers (al-Ghazālī 1997: 2–4). This probing spirit of robust debate between Arabic and Islamic thinkers across generations is quite remarkable and poignantly anticipates Kant's own Enlightenment dictum, *'sapere aude!'* If we are to return to al-Fārābī's rationalist claim that philosophical truths can and should be known with certainty, we might conclude by reflecting upon the words of his predecessor, al-Kindī, the founder of the ninth-century Baghdad circle. In his treatise, *On First Philosophy* (*fī al-Falsafa al-Ūlā*), al-Kindī calls a Muslim, 'he who is not to be ashamed of appreciating the truth and acquiring it wherever it comes from, even if it comes from races distant and nations different from us' (al-Kindī 1950–3: 103.3–7). One may only hope that al-Kindī's invitation to appreciate and acquire the truth no matter how strange the source might prompt us to retrieve the ecumenical origins of this rich and enduring tradition for the sake of promoting the renewal of cosmopolitanism today.

Bibliography

al-Fārābī, Abū Naṣr (1895). *Mabādi' Ārā' Ahl al-Madīna al-Fāḍila*. Ed. F. Dieterici. Leiden: Brill.
al-Fārābī, Abū Naṣr (1964). *Al-Siyāsa al-Madanīyya*. Ed. Fauzi M.Najjar. Bayrūt: al-Maṭba 'ah al Kāthūlīkīyyah.
al-Fārābī, Abū Naṣr (1970). *Kitāb al-Ḥurūf*. Ed. Muhsin Mahdī. Bayrūt: Dār al-Mashriq.
al-Fārābī, Abū Naṣr (1971). *Fuṣūl al-Muntaza'a*. Ed. Fauzi M.Najjar. Bayrūt: Dār al-Mashriq.
al-Fārābī, Abū Naṣr (1981). *Taḥṣīl al-Sa'āda*. Ed. Jafar al-Yasin. Bayrūt: al-Andaloss.
al-Fārābī, Abū Naṣr (1998). *On the Perfect State*. Trans. Richard Walzer. Chicago: Great Books of the Islamic World, Inc.
al-Fārābī, Abū Naṣr (2001a). *Philosophy of Plato and Aristotle*. Trans. Muhsin S. Mahdi, Ithaca: Cornell University Press.
al-Fārābī, Abū Naṣr (2001b). *The Political Writings: 'Selected Aphorisms' and Other Texts*. Trans. Charles Butterworth. Ithaca: Cornell University Press.
al-Ghazālī, Abū Hāmid (1967). *Iḥyā' 'Ulūm al-Dīn*, II, Cairo.
al-Ghazālī, Abū Hāmid (1997). *The Incoherence of the Philosophers* (*Tahāfut al-Falāsifa*). Trans. Michael E. Marmura. Provo, UT: Brigham Young University Press.
al-Kindī, Ya'qūb ibn 'Isḥāq aṣ-Ṣabbāḥ (1950–3). *Rasā'il' al-Kindī al falsafiyya*. Ed. M. A. Abū Rīda. Cairo: Dār al-Fikr al-'Arabī.
al-Kindī, Ya'qūb ibn 'Isḥāq aṣ-Ṣabbāḥ (1974). *Al-Kindi's Metaphysics: A Translation of Ya'qub ibn Ishaq al-Kindi's 'On First Philosophy'*. Trans. Alfred Ivry. Albany: State University of New York Press.
al-Ṭūsī, Naṣīr al-Dīn (2011). *The Nasirean Ethics*. Trans. G. M. Wickens. London: George Allen & Unwin Ltd.
Alighieri, Dante (1996). *Monarchy*. Ed. and trans. Prue Shaw. Cambridge: Cambridge University Press.
Alighieri, Dante (2003). *Purgatio*. Trans. Jean Hollander and Robert Hollander. New York: Doubleday.

Anderson, Benedict (1983). *Imagined Communities: Reflections on the Origins and Spread of Nationalism*. New York: Verso Publications.
Arendt, Hannah (1967). 'The Decline of the Nation-State and the End of the Rights of Man'. In *The Origins of Totalitarianism*. London: George Allen and Unwin Ltd, pp. 267–302.
Baracchi, Claudia (2008). *Aristotle's Ethics as First Philosophy*. Cambridge: Cambridge University Press.
Black, Antony (2011). *The History of Islamic Political Thought: From the Prophet to the Present*. Edinburgh: Edinburgh University Press.
Brague, Remi (2009). *The Legend of the Middle Ages: Philosophical Explorations of Medieval Christianity, Judaism, and Islam*. Trans. Lydia G. Cochrane. Chicago: University of Chicago Press.
D'Ancona, Cristina (2003). 'The *Timaeus* Model for Creation and Providence: An Example of Continuity and Adaptation in Early Arabic Philosophical Literature'. In *Plato's Timaeus as Cultural Icon*. Ed. Gretchen J. Reydams-Schils. Notre Dame: University of Notre Dame Press, pp. 206–37.
Derrida, Jacques (2001). *On Cosmopolitanism and Forgiveness*. Trans. Mark Dooley. New York: Routledge.
Goldin, Owen (2011). 'Conflict and Cosmopolitanism in Plato and the Stoics'. *Apeiron* 44/3: 264–86.
Goodman, Lenn E. (2003). *Islamic Humanism*. Oxford: Oxford University Press.
Hillenbrand, Carole (1988). 'Islamic Orthodoxy or Realpolitik? Al-Ghazālī's Views on Government'. *Iran: Journal of Persian Studies*, 26: 81–94.
Ibn Khaldūn, Walī al-Dīn 'Abd al-Rahmān (1967). *The Muqaddimah: An Introduction to History*. Trans. Franz Rosenthal. Princeton: Princeton University Press.
Ibn Khaldūn, Walī al-Dīn 'Abd al-Rahmān (2005). *al-Muqaddima*. Al-Dār al-Bayḍā': Khizānat Ibn Khaldūn, Bayt al-Funūn wa-al'Ulūm wa-al-Ādāb.
Ibn Rushd, Abu l-Walīd (Averroes) (1859). *Kitāb faṣl al-maqāl* in *Philosophie und Theologie von Averroes*. Ed. M. J. Müller. Munich: Commission bei G. Franz.
Ibn Rushd, Abu l-Walīd (Averroes) (1956). *Averroes' Commentary on Plato's Republic*. Ed. E. I. J. Rosenthal. University of Cambridge Oriental Publications, No.1. Cambridge: Cambridge University Press.
Ibn Rushd, Abu l-Walīd (Averroes) (1974). *Averroes on Plato's Republic*. Trans. Ralph Lerner. Ithaca: Cornell University Press.
Ibn Rushd, Abu l-Walīd (Averroes) (2011). *The Decisive Treatise*. Trans. Charles Butterworth. In *Medieval Political Philosophy: A Sourcebook*. Ed. Joshua Parens and Joseph C. Macfarland. Ithaca: Cornell University Press.
Khadduri, Majid (1984). *The Islamic Conception of Justice*. Baltimore: Johns Hopkins University Press.
Khalidi, Muhammad Ali (2003). 'Al-Fārābī on the Democratic City'. *British Journal for the History of Philosophy*, 11/3: 379–94.
Kraemer, Joel L. (1986). *Humanism in the Renaissance of Islam: The Cultural Revival during the Buyid Age*. Leiden: Brill.
Lameer, Joep (2015). *The Arabic Version of al-Ṭūsī's Nasirean Ethics*. Leiden: Brill.
Mahdi, Muhsin S. (1957). *Ibn Khaldūn's Philosophy of History: A Study in the Philosophic Foundation of the Science of Culture*. London: George Allen & Unwin Ltd.
Miskawayah, Abū 'Alī (1966). *Tahdhīb al-Akhlāq*. Ed. Constantine K. Zurayk. Beirut: American University of Beirut Centennial Publications.
Miskawayah, Abū 'Alī (2002). *Refinement of Character (Tahdhīb al-Akhlāq)*. Trans. Constantine K. Zurayk. Chicago: Great Books of the Islamic World, Inc.
Nasr, Seyyed Hossein (1993). *An Introduction to Islamic Cosmological Doctrines*. Albany: State University of New York Press.
Nusseibeh, Sari (2015). 'To Justice with Love'. In *Comparative Philosophy without Borders*. Ed. Arindam Chakrabarti and Ralph Weber. London: Bloomsbury Press, pp. 175–204.
Orwin, Alexander (2017). *Redefining the Muslim Community: Ethnicity, Religion, and Politics in the Thought of Alfarabi*. Philadelphia: University of Pennsylvania Press.
Porphyry (2000). *Porphyry: On Abstinence from Killing Animals*. Trans. G. Clark. Ithaca: Cornell University Press.
Rosenthal, E. I. J. (1958). *Political Thought in Medieval Islam: An Introductory Outline*. Cambridge: Cambridge University Press.

Stern, S. M. (1968). *Aristotle and the World State*. Columbia: University of South Carolina Press.
Stone, Gregory B. (2006). *Dante's Pluralism and the Islamic Philosophy of Religion*. New York: Palgrave Macmillan.
Strauss, Leo (1945). 'Farabi's Plato'. In *Louis Ginzberg: Jubilee Volume*. New York: The American Academy for Jewish Research, pp. 357–93.
Strauss, Leo (1973). *Persecution and the Art of Writing*. Westport, CT: Greenwood Press.
Urvoy, Dominique (1991). *Ibn Rushd (Averroes)*. London: Routledge.
Yaḥyā ibn 'Adī, Abū Zakariyyā' (1946). *Tahdhīb al-Akhlāq*. In *Rasa'il al-Bulagha'*, 3rd edn. Ed. M. Kurd 'Ali. Cairo.

12

Intellectual Virtues and the Attention to *Kairos* in Maimonides and Dante

Jason Aleksander

Aristotle stipulates in *Nicomachean Ethics* 6.3 that there are five habits of true thinking: *technê*, *epistêmê*, *phronêsis*, *sophia* and *nous* (artistic knowledge, scientific knowledge, practical judgement, wisdom and intellect). Of these five, Aristotle devotes particular attention to the respective importance of *phronêsis* and *sophia* in the development of human excellence (*arête*) and the possibility of happiness (*eudaimonia*). This discussion, in turn, was taken up through various lines of transmission and transformation by the philosophical traditions of the Middle Ages and Renaissance. This chapter focuses on Maimonides and Dante Alighieri in order to illustrate how this period's distinctive perspectives on the intellectual virtues mobilise and transform a common Aristotelian heritage to respond to unique concerns that arise from diverse political and religious considerations.

In the first part of this chapter, I will focus on two main questions: (1) how Maimonides departs from Aristotle in maintaining a difference of kind rather than degree in identifying prophecy rather than wisdom as the ultimate human perfection; and (2) why Maimonides does not explicitly identify a virtue of practical reasoning that corresponds to Aristotle's understanding of *phronêsis*. In the second part of the chapter, I will discuss why Dante, contrary to Maimonides, emphasises the significance of practical judgement in his redeployment of Aristotelian ethical theory. I will also discuss how the didactic and protreptic purposes of his poetic discourse are shaped by the same underlying psychological theory that grounds his emphasis on this intellectual virtue.

The modest aim of this chapter is to treat these two engagements with Peripatetic philosophy as case studies that reward attention to the inextricable links between politics/religion and philosophical enquiry, even against the grain of seemingly common lineages sharing similar concerns. Connected with this modest aim, this chapter will also discuss how Maimonides's and Dante's attention to didactic and protreptic concerns impacts their treatment of philosophical questions and therefore indicates how attention to the *kairos* of their writings exposes and helps appreciate their philosophical rigour.

Maimonides on Wisdom, Prophecy and the Law

Although the *Guide of the Perplexed* will come into the discussion below, Maimonides's explicit consideration of the intellectual virtues is most fully elaborated in the *Eight Chapters* (the introduction to the commentary on *Pirqei Avot* in his *Commentary on the Mishnah*). In this context, two main objectives shape Maimonides's discussion. First, according to Maimonides

(1975: 60), the *Eight Chapters* articulates the basic principles of ethics that will help readers understand his subsequent commentary on *Avot*. Second, Maimonides seems intent on interpreting rabbinic discussions of the significance of Mosaic law and divine providence through the lens of Aristotelian ethical philosophy and of reconciling these two sources when they appear to be in tension with each other. Indeed, Maimonides (1975: 61–2) encourages this assessment in his introduction to the *Eight Chapters* with the protreptic directive to 'hear the truth from whoever says it' before immediately going on to state that he intends to suppress citations of the Aristotelian source material in order to avoid raising the suspicions of those who lack philosophical experience.

The irony of the way in which Maimonides situates this protreptic remark in conjunction with an acknowledgement of his reticence to trust his readers to follow his advice deserves discussion, and I will return to its importance later. However, at the outset, we should note that, in both the *Guide of the Perplexed* and the *Eight Chapters*, Maimonides does not merely discuss and interpret the same topics in two different idioms. Rather, his effort to reconcile his philosophical and religious sources deploys Aristotelian ethical theory in a manner that engages it with problems it was not originally designed to handle. In other words, these two works do more than provide a philosophical reinterpretation of religious doctrines; they also transform Maimonides's philosophical resources by bringing them to bear on questions that arise specifically in this context and are shaped by his particular didactic and protreptic concerns.

By engaging with religious tradition in this manner, these texts offer two specific transformations of Aristotelian ethical theory that I will discuss in this chapter. First, the fifth and seventh chapters of the *Eight Chapters* and several key chapters of the *Guide of the Perplexed* discuss the importance of the unity of the virtues in a way that responds to and transforms Aristotle's discussion of *phronêsis* and *theôria* in Books Six and Ten of the *Nicomachean Ethics*. Second, the *Eight Chapters* also offers reflections on the significance of the relationship between continence and virtue that intersect with Aristotle's treatment of the phenomenon of *akrasia* in Books Three and Seven of the *Nicomachean Ethics*.

In the *Eight Chapters*, following Aristotle, Maimonides distinguishes between two varieties of virtue that correspond with two powers of the soul: ethical virtues, which correspond to the appetitive power, and intellectual virtues, which correspond to the intellectual power. Also following Aristotle, Maimonides (1975: 67) defines ethical virtue (*faḍīlah*) as a habit of the soul that is 'balanced in the mean between two bad states, one of which is excessive and the other deficient'. Although there are important differences of emphasis and focus between Aristotle and Maimonides regarding the identification and analysis of the ethical virtues,[1] the basic conceptual structure is similar, and the discussion in chapter four of the *Eight Chapters* basically follows the paradigm established by Book Two of the *Nicomachean Ethics*.

Similarly, Maimonides (1975: 63) is roughly consistent with Aristotle in defining the intellectual power as that by which the human being 'deliberates, acquires the sciences, and distinguishes between base and noble actions'. Like Aristotle, he subdivides these activities into varieties that are theoretical – concerned with 'the essence of the unchanging beings' (Maimonides 1975: 63) – and those that are practical. Concerning the latter, Maimonides also follows Aristotle in distinguishing between productive activities (the arts) and reflective ones (the species of deliberation). However, whereas Aristotle identifies wisdom (*sophia*) and practical judgement (*phronêsis*) as the virtues that correspond with theoretical and practical intellectual activities, Maimonides identifies and defines the intellectual virtues differently.

---

[1] For a discussion, see, for instance, Weiss (1987: 281–7) and Jacobs (1997).

In the first place, even though Maimonides defines wisdom (*ḥikma*) as the intellectual virtue concerned with knowledge of remote and proximate causes of things, as I will discuss below, he accords this virtue a different role than Aristotle with respect to the ultimate aims of human life. Second, although *ḥikma*'s connotations may include an intellectual capacity that is similar to *phronêsis*,[2] Maimonides does not explicitly identify a virtue that would be a direct and exclusive correlative of the Aristotelian virtue. This is peculiar, especially since al-Fārābī, for instance, explicitly aligns *ta'aqqul* with the Aristotelian identification of this virtue. Nevertheless, neither the *Eight Chapters* nor the *Guide of the Perplexed* offers any explicit indication that Maimonides recognises a distinct virtue for practical judgement (see Weiss 1987: 283–6). Rather, Maimonides (1975: 65) shifts away from Aristotle by identifying intellect (*al-'aql*) as the second intellectual virtue – one which does not explicitly involve deliberation about practical activities.

In the *Eight Chapters*, the significance of this departure from Aristotle is most apparent when we attend to the discussion, in chapters five and seven, of the ultimate ends of human conduct. Concerning the relationship between ethical and intellectual virtues, for example, Maimonides (1975: 75) states explicitly that 'man needs to subordinate all his soul's powers to thought . . . and to set his sight on a single goal; the perception of God . . . insofar as that lies within man's power'. Superficially, this understanding of the ultimate possibility of perfection of the human being – knowledge of God insofar as is possible – seems to resemble Aristotle's emphasis on the activity (*energeia*) of contemplation (*theôria*) as the one most intimately associated with happiness (*eudaimonia*). Moreover, if *sophia*, as a virtue, consists of both scientific knowledge (*epistêmê*) and intellect (*nous*) 'directed at things that are most honorable in their nature' (Aristotle 2002: 1141b2–3), then there does seem to be a resemblance between it and Maimonides's understanding.

Despite these superficial similarities, there are important differences that emerge from the consideration of Maimonides's treatment of prophecy as well as his explicit statements regarding the fundamental unity of the virtues in a complete life. In the first place, there is no obvious indication that Maimonides intends to imply that the intellectual perfection that is mentioned in the fifth chapter is a philosophical perfection strictly speaking. Indeed, the *Eight Chapters* suggest that philosophical perfection may be instrumental for achieving this aim without exhausting the effort required to develop the ethical and intellectual orientations required for its fulfilment. For instance, in the introduction to the *Eight Chapters*, Maimonides asserts that 'following the discipline described in this tractate [*Pirqei Avot*] leads to prophecy' (Maimonides 1975: 60). More tellingly, chapter seven of the *Eight Chapters* explicitly focuses on the relationship between ethical virtue and prophecy (rather than wisdom) but has little to say about intellectual perfection itself.

In other words, what is missing from the account offered in *Eight Chapters* that helps see why prophecy is fundamentally different from *sophia* is an explicit discussion of the relationship between prophecy and the Law. Thus, we must look to *Guide of the Perplexed* to see why Maimonides maintains that prophecy involves perfections of human capacities over and above

---

[2] Dobbs-Weinstein notes that that the term *ḥikma* 'is used in the medieval Islamicate and Jewish philosophical traditions to designate knowledge of the various sciences in a manner similar to the Latin use of *scientia*, in contradistinction to *sapientia*. The same term is used generally in Hebrew to designate wisdom. It can also be used to designate phronesis' (Dobbs-Weinstein 1995: 238, note 433). But, in both *Eight Chapters* and in the discussions of intellectual perfections in the *Guide of the Perplexed*, the term seems to resonate primarily with Aristotle's definitions of *sophia* and *epistêmê*.

those that Aristotle has in mind for *sophia*. In the *Guide*, Maimonides's core discussion of the conditions that give rise to prophecy occupies II.32–8 and establishes the basis for Maimonides's discussion in II.39–40 of the capacities of different varieties of laws to stimulate ethical and intellectual development.[3] In these chapters, consistent with the *Eight Chapters*, the *Guide of the Perplexed* emphasises that prophecy requires perfection of both ethical and intellectual capacities. However, II.36 elaborates on this discussion by insisting that

> the true reality and quiddity of prophecy consist in its being an overflow overflowing from God ... through the intermediation of the Active Intellect, toward the rational faculty in the first place and thereafter toward the imaginative faculty ... And it is not something that may be attained solely through perfection in the speculative sciences and through improvement of the moral habits. (Maimonides 1963: 369)

In the subsequent chapters of the *Guide*, Maimonides goes on to catalogue three classes of human perfection in terms of relationships between the imaginative faculty and the intellectual virtues. At the lowest level are those who possess perfection of imagination but lack genuine intellectual perfection. In this category, Maimonides includes legislators, soothsayers, augurs and dreamers of veridical dreams. At best, this rank is capable of promulgating laws that 'are directed exclusively toward the ordering of the city and of its circumstances and the abolition in it of injustice and oppression', but do not direct any attention 'toward speculative matters' or 'to the perfecting of the rational faculty' (Maimonides 1963: 383). At the middle rank are those who are perfect in intellect but not in imagination. These Maimonides might have called 'academics' or even 'philosophers' (he calls them 'men of science engaged in speculation'; 1963: 374). In any case, according to Maimonides, one of the consequences of the lack of imaginative perfection in this class is that it deprives them of the capacity to guide others fully to develop ethical and intellectual perfections – that is, they may be able to teach, but they cannot legislate. Only at the highest level of perfection are those whom Maimonides calls prophets, and these are not only intellectually perfect in their own right but through their imaginative perfection are most able to stimulate the development of ethical and rational perfection in others through both legislation and instruction.[4] Thus, the ultimate perfection of the human being is in the capacity for prophecy over and above any of the natural perfections that Aristotle emphasises.

This distinction between intellectual perfection *per se* and intellectual perfection accompanied by the perfection of imagination also underlies Maimonides's allegorical description of the degrees of human perfection in *The Guide of the Perplexed* III.51 as well as his explicit discussion of varieties of human perfection in III.54. In III.51, for instance, Maimonides (1963: 619) likens those who have achieved the highest degrees of intellectual perfection and have understood both natural things and divine science to those who 'have entered in the ruler's place *into the inner court* and are with him in one habitation'. However, there are different

---

[3] See especially Dobbs-Weinstein (1995) and Ravven (2001) for sustained discussions of Maimonides's treatment of prophecy.
[4] To this extent, Maimonides's view resembles but also departs from al-Fārābī's notion that the true philosopher is also the most perfect imam and legislator (see, for instance, al-Fārābī's *On the Perfect State* [1998: chapter 15] and *The Attainment of Happiness* [2001: chapter 4]). For sustained discussions of al-Fārābī's influence on Maimonides, see Berman (1988) and Macy (1986). For discussion of Maimonides's understanding of the nature and function of law, see Galston (1978).

grades of perfection even within these ranks, and among them, only the prophets 'turn wholly to God ... renounce what is other than He, and direct all the acts of their intellect toward an examination of the beings with a view to drawing from them proof with regard to Him, so as to know his governance of them in whatever way it is possible' (Maimonides 1963: 620).

This allegorical description is reinforced in III.54. After having first outlined four different senses in which the Sages use the Hebrew term ḥokhmah ('wisdom', spelled the same as the Judeo-Arabic ḥikma), Maimonides goes on to discuss four species of human perfection according to ancient and contemporary philosophers. There is only a partial correspondence between these two taxonomies. On the one hand, whereas ḥokhmah applies in various contexts to either ethical perfection or aptitude for apprehending true realities, it also applies in other contexts to the amoral perfections of the aptitude for stratagems and ruses or to excellence in the arts. According to Maimonides, the philosophers, on the other hand, include wealth, health, ethical virtues and intellectual virtues among the perfections. In both taxonomies, Maimonides asserts that the truest perfection is intellectual perfection and that the other varieties of wisdom or perfection are, at best, instrumental preparations for the sake of the highest human perfection. But even where there is an apparent consistency between the Sages and the philosophers regarding the notion that the highest human perfection involves intellectual virtues, Maimonides (1963: 636–8) still emphasises the difference between philosophical perfection and prophetic attention by insisting that ḥokhmah, 'used in an unrestricted sense', involves an imitation of loving-kindness (ḥesed), righteousness (ṣedaqah) and judgement (mishpaṭ) in the glorification of divine providence.[5]

These passages make clear that the difference between Maimonides's understanding of prophecy and Aristotle's understanding of *sophia* is not so much one of degree but of kind. However, the significance of this difference – and the way in which it implicates Maimonides's reticence explicitly to include practical judgement among the intellectual virtues – requires further elaboration. In the first place, it is important to keep in mind the respective roles of prophecy and philosophy within the community. In *Guide of the Perplexed* II.39–40, Maimonides implies that, properly speaking, there can be only one Law that is truly aimed both at the abolition of injustice and oppression as well as the perfection of intellect. The reasons underlying this view have to do with Maimonides's stipulation that, whereas a system of Law aimed exclusively at the production of ethical behaviour requires no more than a recognition of the expediency of conventions that reward or punish behaviours insofar as they are conducive to a well-ordered society, the Law, which is directed simultaneously to ethical and intellectual perfection, necessarily originates in and is patterned after a comprehensive understanding of the natural world and of the human being's ability to understand this world through intellectual apprehension. For this reason, the Law is not fundamentally oriented around the question of the expediency of particular forms of behaviour but, instead, expresses a comprehensive understanding of the human potential to embrace and emulate a providential natural order.

Chapter six of the *Eight Chapters* highlights the significance of this understanding of the law for Maimonides's distinction between philosophical perfection and prophecy. Maimonides (1975: 78) correctly states that according to a strictly philosophical (Aristotelian) view, 'the continent man does good things while craving and strongly desiring to perform bad actions', but the virtuous man, 'who is better and more perfect than the continent man', does not experience this inner conflict. However, Maimonides (1975: 79) notes that this view appears to contradict the

---

[5] See Seeman (2013: 325–7) and Dobbs-Weinstein (1995: 153–4 and 180–2) for further discussion of why prophetic perfection differs in kind from philosophical wisdom.

view of the Sages, who maintain that 'someone who craves and strongly desires transgressions' but does not perform them 'is more virtuous and perfect than someone who does not crave them and suffers no pain in abstaining from them'. On the surface, Maimonides appears to try to reconcile these views by pointing to an equivocation in the term transgression. He explains that the Sages consider the continent person superior only with regard to desires for transgression against traditional laws – desires to act towards ends 'which, if it were not for the Law . . . would not be bad at all' (Maimonides 1975: 80) – but agree with the philosophers that virtue is superior to continence with regard to desires to do things that are 'generally accepted by all people as bad, such as murder, theft, robbery, fraud, harming an innocent man, repaying a benefactor with evil, degrading parents, and things like these' (Maimonides 1975: 80).[6]

This superficial reconciliation acknowledges that, with respect solely to the intrinsic faculties of the individual human being, the virtuous person would indeed always be superior to the continent person, and for the same reasons that Aristotle offers in his discussion of the problem of *akrasia* in *Nicomachean Ethics* 7.[7] However, with respect to the law, there are two overriding considerations – one that concerns the question of obedience to the law in relationship to the appetitive power and one that concerns the intellectual orientation required for prophecy. The subtlety of Maimonides's (1975: 80) discussion at this point obscures the fact that there is no philosophical discussion (in Aristotle, at any rate) that corresponds to his interpretation of the Sages' views regarding statutes prohibiting actions that, 'if it were not for the Law . . . would not be bad at all'. Simply put, although it is true that Aristotle would likely allow that the Sages are correct to say that an impulse to disobey conventional laws does not in and of itself indicate a deficiency of character, the question of the ethical value of obedience to social or legal conventions simply is not a salient question for Aristotle in the context of his discussion of the problem of *akrasia*. Moreover, whatever Aristotle might have to say about the relationship between ethical virtue, *sôphrosunê*, and obedience to legal statutes or social conventions, it is not at all clear what he would have made of Maimonides's peculiar claim that, with regard to the question of obedience, the continent person is in fact superior to the virtuous person. In fact, there are good reasons to doubt that Aristotle would accept that obedience to the law could be equivalent to the enkratic condition that interests him in *Nicomachean Ethics* 7. For Aristotle, the temperate person is, by definition, not enkratic. But the enkratic person in this account is self-restrained with respect to desires that conflict with ends that s/he has identified for her-/himself as good actions. In other words, for Aristotle the enkratic person's inner conflict is between wishing to act in two contrary ways – one that is in harmony with right reason and one that is not. Hence, whereas Maimonides is concerned with the question of one's motivation to obey – a motivation that may or may not be accompanied by some corresponding intellectual perfection – Aristotle is concerned strictly with the intrinsic motivations of an agent who has properly identified a fine and good end of action.

---

[6] Dobbs-Weinstein (1995: 148–9) approvingly cites Stern (1986) for the argument that these two varieties of commandment discussed in the *Eight Chapters* correspond, respectively, to the *mishpatim* (judgements) and the *ḥuqqim* (statutes) as discussed in *Guide of the Perplexed* III.26.
[7] Especially pertinent is the following passage: 'the self-restrained person [*enkratís*] is of such a kind as to do nothing contrary to a rational understanding on account of bodily pleasures, and so is the temperate person [*sophron*], but the former has base desires while the latter does not, and the latter is the sort of person who does not feel pleasure contrary to reason, while the former is the sort who feels it but is not led by it' (Aristotle 2002: 1151b34–1152a3).

With respect to the question of obedience, Maimonides therefore transforms the Aristotelian foundations for his view by agreeing with the Sages that, with respect to actions that are bad only because they are prohibited by the Law, the continent person is, indeed, superior to the person who obeys the Law without any difficulty. This is partly because the law's claim on its adherents is not exclusively a function of the ways in which obedience to it would lead to individual perfection. The Law demands obedience even regarding actions that have no direct bearing on the question of one's personal perfection. With respect to appetitive ends, then, the law seems to stand in as a substitute for *phronêsis* for the purposes of directing individual conduct (see Jacobs 1997: 446–52), but is not keyed to the relationship between temperance, practical judgement and the appetites in the same manner as Aristotle describes. In short, while deliberative ability is undoubtedly essential to the prophet's role in the community, Maimonides is nevertheless silent on the possibility that this deliberative ability rests in an intellectual virtue that may arise independently of the more general intellectual perfection associated with apprehension of the principles of nature and divine science.[8]

But, this answer is not sufficient for addressing the purpose of the Law with respect to the question of intellectual guidance – nor, for that matter, does it explain why continence would be superior to ethical virtue with regard to the cultivation of intellectual virtue. To see why, we must note that, for Maimonides, the Law is not merely a reliable and expedient tool for orienting people to the proper moral or ethical goods. Rather, the Law is itself the most appropriate expression and focus of the prophet's intellectual orientation. Thus, when dealing with aspects of the Law that have no obvious instrumental value in the cultivation of ethical habits, the *Guide of the Perplexed* suggests that the relationship that is required for ultimate human perfection would be a devotional orientation to the Law as an intrinsic personal aim for the purposes of stimulating and guiding contemplation of the divine. Consequently, unlike Aristotle, Maimonides's understanding of the intellectual virtues does not have to confront the possibility of tensions between *phronêsis* and *sophia* – epitomised especially in the case of Anaxagoras and Thales, who 'seem to know things that are exceptional and wondrous and difficult and miraculous, but useless, because they do not inquire about human goods' (Aristotle 2002: 1141b4–8). And finally, because the Law requires obedience even regarding matters that are neither good nor bad by nature, the fact that the Law permits the recognition that the obedience that it demands is instrumental, the cultivation of social harmony or intellectual development simultaneously inoculates its adherents against an idolatrous relationship to it. That is, by encouraging continent obedience rather than blind devotion, the Law indicates that its capacity to guide intellectual development, not its instrumental value for promoting social harmony, is its true source of uniqueness as divine Law.

Especially in light of Maimonides's protreptic and didactic aims and his attention to the needs of his audience(s), it is now possible to understand Maimonides's reticence to include practical judgement among the intellectual virtues. Indeed, this reticence is also, arguably, analogous to Maimonides's reticence to discuss the possibility of personal immortality (see Ivry 1990) as well as his reticence to mention Aristotle by name in the *Eight Chapters*. Moreover, as Dobbs-Weinstein (1995: 123) has noted, 'the possession of a faculty able to distinguish good from evil is the punishment imposed upon Adam or human beings as a consequence of disobedience, a punishment reducing human beings to a status closer to beasts and further from intellects'. In this light, perhaps Maimonides regards even a well-developed capacity for practical reasoning to be not so much a perfection as it is a compensation for a fallen condition.

---

[8] See Novak (1993) for a sustained discussion of the prophet's reliance on a variety of practical reasoning that is derived from theoretical reason.

Were it possible to extricate these texts from his particular didactic concerns, it might be worth asking whether Maimonides would allow that there is a virtue akin to *phronêsis* that would be necessary in contexts other than those governed by divine Law. But we should be hesitant to speculate on the matter, and not merely because the primary audience of the *Eight Chapters* and the *Guide of the Perplexed* understands itself to be bound by the Law.[9] Rather, on Maimonides's terms, if prophecy is possible, then so is the Law. Consequently, to ask why Maimonides does not follow Aristotle in articulating a robust role for practical judgement as an intellectual perfection would simply call for a recapitulation of his views regarding the distinction between prophecy and intellectual perfection *per se*.

There are, in any case, other indications that suggest that Maimonides's didactic concerns cannot be divorced from his specific understanding of the relationship between Law and prophecy and that, therefore, we should be sceptical of the possibility of extricating from his views a clear conception of practical judgement as an intellectual virtue. Dobbs-Weinstein (1990: 34) spells out these other indications succinctly:

> While it can be argued that Maimonides could have had recourse to a theoretically informed prudence as the virtue which instructs the moral virtues, and hence can both promulgate laws and determine the threshold of assent in all moral matters, such a formulation necessarily assumes the temporal priority of the theoretical virtues, a possibility that could not be accepted by Maimonides for three reasons. First, it would permit a morally corrupt individual both to contemplate and apprehend Divine matters. Second, it could render the Law superfluous. Third, a prudent man, informed by reason alone, would judge metaphysical contemplation to be the only worthy activity and hence would neglect other activities necessary for ultimate perfection, the utility of which is inaccessible to unaided reason. If the apprehension of the whole of being is required in order to render love an intrinsic principle of action, and if love of God is necessary for ultimate human perfection, then not only is reason insufficient for ultimate perfection, but also this perfection becomes unattainable for the philosopher.

Given Maimonides's explicit endorsement of the view that the most perfect expression of human intellectual capacity participates with the Law in embracing *ḥesed*, *ṣedaqah* and *mishpaṭ*, Dobbs-Weinstein's analysis is more than plausible. But even if one does not wish to interpret Maimonides's reticence as an explicit rejection of a virtue associated with practical judgement, this analysis provides sufficient indications that the prudent reader should be cautious to draw any distinct conclusions about the matter. In short, Maimonides's views on the intellectual virtues certainly respond to Aristotle's, but his emphasis on prophecy and the role of law integrates practical and theoretical activities in a way that Aristotle could not have envisioned. Maimonides's view leaves open, however, the question of whether there might be resources other than the Law to which philosophy can appeal for such an integration.

---

[9] Raymond Weiss raises the interesting point that Maimonides's commentary on Sanhedrin (also from the *Commentary on the Mishnah*) emphasises the role of law by calling attention to the unique situation of the Diaspora. 'Maimonides does not speak of the Exile in the strictly ethical sections of the [*Eight Chapters*], but toward the end of the work he refers to its severity, to "our being strangers and cut off" [chapter 8, p. 92] from the land of Israel ... Elsewhere in [the *Commentary on the Mishnah*] the Exile is evaluated from the standpoint of how it comports with human virtue: it "hinders us from acquiring all of the virtues" (*Commentary on Sanhedrin*, 10.1)' (Weiss 1987: 272–3).

Regal Prudenza and Philosophical Rigour in Dante's *Divine Comedy*

Like Maimonides, Dante is indebted to Aristotle for the basic features of his understanding of human psychology and ethics. Like Maimonides, Dante follows Aristotle in identifying two main powers of the soul to which virtues may correspond.[10] Also like Maimonides, Dante's mature writings – especially the *Divine Comedy* – espouse philosophical views that cannot be divorced from his protreptic aims. However, whereas Maimonides's emphasis on the relationship between prophecy and law displaces the Aristotelian concern with *phronêsis* and subordinates *sophia* to prophecy, Dante, on the other hand, emphasises the significance of *phronêsis* and displaces, instead, Aristotle's concern with the relationship between *theôria* and happiness.

One key indication of Dante's departure from Aristotle occurs in Thomas Aquinas's descriptions in *Paradiso* 10 of the twelve lights that encircle Beatrice in the sphere of the Sun. In that context, Dante has Thomas describe King Solomon in lines 109–14 as follows:

> The fifth light, the loveliest among
> us, breathes from such love that the whole
> world down there is greedy to have news of it:
> within it is the lofty mind [*mente*] where
> such deep wisdom [*senno*] was placed that, if truth
> is true, no second ever rose to see so much.[11]

A few cantos later, however, recognising that the pilgrim had been perplexed by this praise of Solomon, Thomas acknowledges in *Paradiso* 13.106–11 that human nature was never so perfect as in Adam and Christ.[12] Yet, when describing Solomon's wisdom in superlative terms, Dante, through Thomas, makes clear that it is not the same variety of wisdom – whatever its source – that Adam and Christ may have possessed, but 'regal prudence'. Accordingly, in *Paradiso* 13.95–105, Thomas emphasises that this kind of wisdom differs from Aristotle's *sophia* by providing the ironic explanation that Solomon was unconcerned with the sorts of scholastic topics discussed at length in Thomas's own writings:

> I have not spoken in such a way that you
> cannot see clearly that he was a king who
> asked for the wisdom [*senno*] to be a worthy king,
>   not in order to know the number of the Movers
> up here, or if *necesse* with contingent ever made
> *necesse*, not *si est dare primum motum esse*, or

---

[10] For a more detailed discussion, see Aleksander (2011a).

[11] Some commentators have asserted that the reason for Dante's attention to the world's curiosity about Solomon's fate is tied to his reputation for licentiousness. It is possible that the pilgrim's perplexity is partly related to this attitude towards Solomon, but Thomas's focus on Solomon's wisdom in *Paradiso* 13 suggests that the pilgrim's perplexity mainly concerns the nature of that wisdom rather than Solomon's ethical character.

[12] Dante does not provide Thomas very many lines of poetry to explain the nature of Adam's and Christ's wisdom, but if it is based on the supposition that these two intellectual capacities differ from that of other creatures because of their supernatural geneses, then it would not conform to Thomas's actual discussion of the question of the limitations of Christ's knowledge in *Summa Theologiae* III, q. 10.

> whether in a semicircle one can make a triangle
> that lacks a right angle.
> Thus, if you consider this and what I have said,
> the prudence of a king [*regal prudenza*] is that unequalled seeing
> at which the arrow of my intention strikes.

It is debateable whether the *Divine Comedy* is meant to illustrate settled opinions about the sorts of philosophical quandaries to which Thomas alludes in his discussion of Solomon's regal prudence.[13] Of course, simply by setting the poem in the afterlife, Dante does at least encourage readers to imagine the sorts of perfections that would only be possible by entertaining a conception of human nature that would make the pilgrim's experience in the poem credible. However, rather than harness the power of poetic language to generate assent to any specific conception of human nature, Dante instead continually draws attention to the difficulties in maintaining a coherent understanding of the very principles that would govern such a reality. As Jacoff (2007: 119, 123) rightly remarks on the culminating canticle of the *Divine Comedy*, 'paradox, in fact, is constitutive of the *Paradiso* both theologically and poetically . . . The *Paradiso* oscillates between statements of its daring originality and confessions of its impossibility, of the ineffability of its vision and of the inadequacies of language to render it.'

Consequently, even if Dante's emphasis on his own pilgrim-persona's intellectual confusion tacitly reinforces the illusion of the poem,[14] his tactical choices do not warrant the conclusion that the primary purpose of the *Divine Comedy* is to employ poetic language to produce assent to the doctrinal underpinnings that constitute the scaffolding for its narrative. Instead, the prudent reader will also resist the temptation to assume that the *Divine Comedy* provides a poetic path to satisfy a desire to understand something that cannot be fully grasped through overtly philosophical discourse. That is, even if the *Divine Comedy* suggests that poetic imagination might successfully overcome the material limitations that undermine our capacities for intellectual apprehension of the divine, it also consistently emphasises the significance of these material limitations to the human condition. In other words, the *Divine Comedy* neither endorses nor rejects mystical theology, but, instead, poetically mobilises an overtly mystical language to refocus our attention on the temporal world and on the possibilities of ethical and intellectual development within the constraints that our embodied natures impose upon us. Moreover, this project does not regard poetic discourse as an alternative to philosophical discourse but as its partner in attuning desire to the proper intellectual orientations that develop the ethical and intellectual dispositions. In this way, the *Divine Comedy* recognises the limitations of our intellectual scope and then takes this recognition as justification for a project that reinvests the desire to exceed the limits of our capacities back into a project that is oriented irreducibly to the project of temporal ethical perfection and the cultivation of practical judgement. The paradoxes and the insights of Christian theology are thus rendered into a philosophical project that emphasises not only human frailty – especially as understood through the theological trope of human fallenness – but also a means for responding to these.[15]

---

[13] Ironically, several of the specific topics that Thomas mentions are implicated in the depiction of theophantic moment depicted in *Paradiso* 33. For further discussion see Aleksander (2011b).
[14] See Barolini (1992) for a sustained discussion of the *Divine Comedy*'s formal techniques for securing its readers' suspension of disbelief.
[15] Whereas my remarks in this chapter focus on a few key moments in *Paradiso*, Stern (2018) emphasises this theme throughout his recent commentary on *Purgatorio*.

These interpretive conclusions about the *Divine Comedy* require a more detailed defence than I am able to provide in this context. However, the plausibility of this interpretation can be established by a reflection on the opening twelve lines of *Paradiso* 4, where Dante's narrator reports that his conversation with Piccarda in the previous canto had left him paralysed by conflicting desires:

> Between two foods, equally distant and
> attractive, a free man would die of hunger
> before he brought either to his teeth;
>   so a lamb would stand between two hungers
> of fierce wolves, fearing both equally, so a
> hound between two does:
>   therefore if I was silent, urged in equal measure
> by my two doubts, I do not reproach myself,
> since it was necessary, nor do I commend myself.
>   I was silent, but my desire was depicted on
> my face and my questions with it, much more
> warmly than if articulated in speech.

Dante is, of course, drawing on the famous thought experiment that since the mid-fourteenth century has been referred to as Buridan's Ass.[16] In the version offered in *Paradiso* 4, Dante's depiction of the pilgrim's paralysis is squarely in the intellectualist tradition regarding the will's determination by the intellect, since the second line of the canto insists that a human placed in such a predicament would indeed die of hunger. In short, Dante invokes the thought experiment in a way that implies that he regards the so-called freedom of the will in the voluntarist sense as an illusion and instead understands genuine freedom of choice as a form of autonomy or self-rule that requires the cultivation of a capacity for exercising good judgement in rightly choosing between desired goods.[17] However, that Beatrice's intercession subsequently delivers the pilgrim from his state of mental paralysis also suggests a pessimistic view about the power of human intellection in unredeemed human beings. What follows on this view, then, is that, because the intellect is weak, the will to act in one way or another, no matter how decisive the action may seem in its irrevocability, is an expression of this weakness. Thus, unlike others in the intellectualist tradition (e.g., Averroes and Thomas Aquinas), Dante uses this occasion to emphasise that the intrinsic weakness of human intellect necessitates the intervention of divine grace in the rectification and liberation of the will – and in this regard, the closest analogue to Dante's view might be that of Augustine in *Confessions* VIII.12, where Augustine's conversion seems directly abetted by God's grace. In other words, philosophically, this is intellectualism, but Dante's version, by emphasising the weakness of both the intellect and the will, arrives at a theology that also resonates with aspects of views held by some voluntarists.

---

[16] Dante was probably familiar with Thomas's version in *Summa Theologiae* I-II, q. 13, a. 6. For a discussion of a version of this thought experiment that may have been relevant to Maimonides, see Stern (1986: 105–8).

[17] It is beyond the scope of this essay to discuss whether this understanding of practical judgement is consistent with all of the details of Aristotle's treatment of *phronêsis*. Suffice it to note here that it is debatable whether or not Aristotle holds that *phronêsis* deliberates about ends of action or only about the means of accomplishing good ends. For further discussion of this quandary in interpreting the *Nicomachean Ethics*, see for instance, Irwin (2007: 53–197).

In any case, even from this brief discussion, I think it should be clear that this moment in *Paradiso* suggests that, from Dante's view, we learn more about moral accountability by focusing on how deliberation occurs in contexts that involve doubt than we do by focusing on the kinds of voluntary choices that are possible in cases in which the intellect's grasp on the praiseworthiness of a single object of desire is unassailable (especially since desire is frequently impervious to correction when it is ethically compromised). Specifically, because of the ways in which desires arise in us and because the power of imagination is so great that it 'sometimes so steals us from the world outside that we do not hear [even] though a thousand trumpets sound around us' (*Purgatorio* 17.13–15), we are often faced with difficult quandaries in sorting out competing ends that we nevertheless represent to ourselves as good under different circumstances. Moreover, when the chips are down and we find ourselves in desperate situations, our capacities for judgement are often compromised so that the acts that result from our choices reflect the kinds of intellectual confusions to which we are prone. Thus, whether or not it is stimulated by one's personal faith in divine grace, often only interpretive humility can save us from deceiving ourselves into accepting a superficial analysis of our complex moral situations. It is therefore not surprising to find that, once Dante's pilgrim has acquired an insight into the phenomenon of willing, he summarises Beatrice's lesson in *Paradiso* 4 by reporting to her in lines 124–32:

> I see well how our intellect is never satisfied
> unless illumined by that Truth outside of which
> no truth can range . . .
> Thus doubt is born like a burgeoning at the
> foot of truth, and it is our nature that drives us
> toward the summit from peak to peak.

Finally, this point receives additional confirmation in the protreptic speech that Dante assigns to Thomas Aquinas in summarising the lesson we are to take away from Solomon's presence in the circle of the Sun. There Thomas concludes the canto with an extended exhortation to cultivate the relationship between practical judgement and humility, including the following lines (112–20, 130–8):

> And let this ever be lead upon your feet, to
> make you move slowly, like a weary man, to both
> the yes and the no that you do not see:
> for surely he is low among the fools who
> affirms and denies without distinction in either case,
> for it often happens that a hasty opinion turns
> in a wrong direction, and then affect binds the intellect.
> [. . .]
> And let not people be too sure to judge, like
> one who appraises the oats in the field before
> they are ripe:
> for I have seen all the previous winter long the
> thornbush appear rigid and fierce, but later bear
> the rose upon its tip,
> and I have seen a ship run straight and swift
> across the sea for all its course, only to perish at
> last when entering the port.

In light of these exhortations, it should be clear that, for Dante, because of the fragility of our intellectual capabilities, often only interpretive humility can save us from self-deception. However, if this is true, then it may seem that the *Divine Comedy* will always thwart the humble reader's ability to derive any conclusions regarding the poem's philosophical content. In fact, Dante encourages this hesitancy insofar as the speeches that explicitly articulate philosophical views are offered within the framework of a poem that frequently challenges us to consider the implications of its own treatment of the issue of truth and falsity in poetic representation. Consequently, no matter how rigorous and coherent the philosophical discourse may seem to be in the *Divine Comedy*, the depiction of this mode of discourse always points to something beyond the explicit content of the arguments, and so the reader is consistently encouraged to engage with the possibility that the apparent rigour of these arguments may be both genuine and yet subordinate in importance to their status as poetic devices.

One should be careful, however, not to overestimate the degree to which the poem resists efforts to identify its underlying philosophical commitments. In the first place, the very ways in which the *Divine Comedy* defies efforts to reach easy conclusions about these commitments exposes aspects of Dante's distinct understanding of human psychology – above all, his concern with the capacity for practical judgement. Moreover, the *Divine Comedy* draws attention to the experience of reading and writing as a way of cultivating our capacities for judgement. This is because making interpretive choices about texts – particularly about highly difficult, deliberately ambiguous texts – models the way that the peculiar species of willing that we call free choice works, precisely because meaning only emerges from a work of literature when the text engages the intellect of the reader who is the text's pilgrim by introducing a tension between its apparent meaning and the reader's intuitions about the same subject and, in so doing, generates doubts about the meaning of the text. Or, to be more precise, the *Divine Comedy* suggests that the role of practical judgement as the species of willing that constitutes voluntary choice in the morally significant sense is most important in contexts in which our knowledge and beliefs are experienced as insufficient for the determination of the course of action that one ought to take.

The *Divine Comedy* thus confronts us with the question of the value and purpose of philosophical argumentation itself, especially when it frustrates our inescapable desire for knowledge. In particular, even though the *Divine Comedy* explicitly defends the superiority of an intellectual path to salvation, the poem sacrifices the question of the veracity of its doctrinal content in order to generate an intellectual tension for its readers that redirects the desire for knowledge towards a variety of thinking that is practical rather than theoretical in orientation. Dante does not, however, abandon philosophy in favour of poetry. Rather, he puts rigorous philosophical thinking to use in a poetic project whose aim is to stimulate its readers' capacities for practical judgement.

Conclusion

Irrespective of the obvious differences between Maimonides and Dante concerning the intellectual virtues that can be discerned from my discussion above, there is a fundamental similarity that I would like to highlight by way of a conclusion. In order to introduce the significance of this similarity, I would like to illustrate my point by recounting my experience at a recent conference devoted to medieval philosophy in which attendees of a plenary round-table discussion were encouraged to debate Thomas Aquinas's contributions to philosophy by entertaining the question 'Where Would Medieval Philosophy Have Been (or: Where Would it Be) without Thomas Aquinas?'

I have no wish to disparage either the conference organisers or the participants in this discussion. As a matter of fact, I enjoyed it immensely and found that the question provoked interesting responses that helped appreciate the significance of the subtending presuppositions that shape the ways in which historians of philosophy try to render meaning from the subjects of their enquiries. Nevertheless, the predominant view expressed in that venue rests upon a view of philosophy's proper methods and scope of activity that would have been alien to many (perhaps all) thinkers whose legacies were significantly affected by Thomas's influence in the philosophical canon. In particular, I cannot imagine either Dante or Maimonides subscribing to the view endorsed by at least some of the participants (though not necessarily as a matter of serious conviction or importance) that Scotus was (or is?) superior to Thomas as a philosopher because Thomas was generally conservative in his efforts to reconcile disparate points of view while Scotus pursued his objectives with extreme (abstract) rigour and without being compromised by any undue concern for didactic or pedagogical accessibility.

On the one hand, even leaving room for the probability that my own biases and imperfect attention to the *kairos* of the discussion have distorted my characterisation of the professed attitude towards philosophy's proper methods and scope of concerns, it should not come as a surprise that I grant that, if Scotus is taken as the most appropriate measure, Dante ought not rate very highly in the contemporary canon of the history of early fourteenth-century philosophy. But regardless of what contemporary professional philosophers may think of the merits of Dante's philosophical rigour (or Thomas's for that matter), the fact that Dante abandoned the *Convivio* to write the *Divine Comedy* indicates at least in general terms where he chose to stand in what Plato made Socrates call the 'ancient quarrel' between philosophy and poetry (*Republic* 607b). Moreover, given Dante's overall standing in the canon of world literature, one imagines that he would have few complaints about his status in the pantheon of poets, at any rate. Maimonides, on the other hand, continues to speak in a language that is more accommodated to the secular concerns of the contemporary professional practice of philosophy, though I have given reasons above for keeping in mind the way in which his philosophical concerns are embedded in a didactic context that rejects entirely the notion that the highest form of intellectual perfection can occur independently of the Law's concerns with ḥesed, ṣedaqah and mishpaṭ.

In any case, the point at which I am driving is not whether these standards are useful for interpreting Maimonides or Dante. Rather, I would simply insist that both thinkers offer philosophically significant considerations for writing in the ways that they do for the audiences they have chosen. In Maimonides's case, both of the texts I have discussed in this chapter involve an explicit defence of prophecy as the highest human perfection while also exhibiting reticence to discuss philosophical views that are not strictly subordinated to his concerns to emulate and encourage the sort of perfection that prophecy would require. In Dante's case, too, the choice to capture his readers' imaginations through poetic discourse is the result of his deep philosophical considerations about human nature. The evident fact that these texts provide endless possibilities of continued re-engagement and reflection – both by professional philosophers as well as in other contexts – ultimately attests to the philosophical significance of those considerations, whether or not one adopts the same presuppositions that shape their responses to the *kairoi* of their inceptions. At the same time, the ability of these texts to continue to provide these possibilities depends upon a process of historical transmission that will always cloud our appreciation of their timeliness. Nevertheless, the prudent reader will acknowledge that failing to attend to the historical circumstances of their authors at the very least poses the risk of depriving oneself of some of the possible benefits of engaging with their writings.

References

Aleksander, Jason (2011a). 'Dante's Understanding of the Two Ends of Human Desire and the Relationship Between Philosophy and Theology'. *Journal of ReligionI*, 91: 158–87.
Aleksander, Jason (2011b). 'The Problem of Theophany in *Paradiso* 33'. *Essays in Medieval Studies*, 27: 61–78.
al-Fārābī, Abū Naṣr (1998). *On the Perfect State (Mabādi' ārā' ahl al-madīnat al-fāḍilah)*. Ed. and trans. Richard Walzer. Chicago: Great Books of the Islamic World.
al-Fārābī, Abū Naṣr (2001). The *Attainment of Happiness*. In *Philosophy of Plato and Aristotle*, rev. Ed. and trans. Muhsin Mahdi. Ithaca: Cornell University Press, pp. 13–50.
Aristotle (2002). *Nicomachean Ethics*. Trans. Joe Sachs. Newburyport, MA: Focus Publishing.
Barolini, Teodolinda (1992). *The Undivine Comedy: Detheologizing Dante*. Princeton: Princeton University Press.
Berman, Lawrence (1988). 'Maimonides, the Disciple of Alfarabi'. In *Maimonides: A Collection of Critical Essays*. Ed. Joseph A. Buijs. Notre Dame: University of Notre Dame Press, pp. 195–214.
Dante [Alighieri] (1996–2011). *The Divine Comedy of Dante Alighieri* (bilingual edition), 3 vols. Ed. and trans. Robert Durling. Oxford: Oxford University Press.
Dobbs-Weinstein, Idit (1990). 'Is the Philosopher a Perfect Man? Man's Natural Capacity for Perfection'. In *The Thought of Moses Maimonides: Philosophical and Legal Studies*. Ed. Ira Robinson, Lawrence Kaplan and Julien Bauer. Lewiston, NY: The Edwin Mellen Press, pp. 26–41.
Dobbs-Weinstein, Idit (1995). *Maimonides and St. Thomas on the Limits of Reason*. Albany: State University of New York Press.
Galston, Miriam (1978). 'The Purpose of the Law According to Maimonides'. *The Jewish Quarterly Review*, 69: 27–51.
Irwin, Terrence (2007). *The Development of Ethics*, Vol. 1. Oxford: Oxford University Press.
Ivry, Alfred (1990). 'The Problematics of the Ideal of Human Perfection for Maimonides'. In *The Thought of Moses Maimonides: Philosophical and Legal Studies*. Ed. Ira Robinson, Lawrence Kaplan and Julien Bauer. Lewiston, NY: The Edwin Mellen Press, pp. 16–25.
Jacobs, Jonathan (1997). 'Plasticity and Perfection Maimonides and Aristotle on Character'. *Religious Studies*, 33: 443–54.
Jacoff, Rachel (2007). 'Introduction to *Paradiso*'. In *Cambridge Companion to Dante*, 2nd edn. Ed. Rachel Jacoff. Cambridge: Cambridge University Press, pp. 107–24.
Macy, Jeffrey (1986). 'Prophecy in Alfarabi and Maimonides: The Imaginative and Rational Faculties', In *Maimonides and Philosophy: Papers Presented at the Sixth Jerusalem Encounter, May 1985*. Ed. Shlomo Pines and Yirmiyahu Yovel. Dordrecht: Martinua Nijhoff, pp. 185–201.
Maimonides, Moses (1963). *Guide of the Perplexed*. Trans. Shlomo Pines, 2 vols. Chicago: The University of Chicago Press.
Maimonides, Moses (1975). *Eight Chapters*. In *Ethical Writings of Maimonides*. Ed. and trans. Raymond L. Weiss and Charles E. Butterworth. New York: Dover Publications, pp. 59–104.
Novak, David (1993). 'Maimonides' Concept of Practical Reason'. In *Rashi 1040–1990: hommage á Ephraim E. Urbach: congress europeen des etudes juives*. Ed. Gabrielle Sed-Rajna. Paris: Les Editions du Cerf, pp. 615–29.
Ravven, Heidi (2001). 'Some Thoughts on What Spinoza Learned from Maimonides about the Prophetic Imagination Part 1. Maimonides on Prophecy and the Imagination'. *Journal of the History of Philosophy*, 39: 193–214.
Seeman, Don (2013). 'Reasons for the Commandments as Contemplative Practice in Maimonides'. *The Jewish Quarterly Review*, 103: 298–327.
Stern, Josef (1986). 'The Idea of *Hoq* in Maimonides' Explanation of the Law'. In *Maimonides and Philosophy: Papers Presented at the Sixth Jerusalem Encounter, May 1985*. Ed. Shlomo Pines and Yirmiyahu Yovel. Dordrecht: Martinua Nijhoff, pp. 92–130.
Stern, Paul (2018). *Dante's Philosophical Life: Politics and Human Wisdom in* Purgatorio. Philadelphia: University of Pennsylvania Press.
Weiss, Raymond (1987). 'The Adaptation of Philosophic Ethics to a Religious Community: Maimonides' *Eight Chapters*'. *Proceedings of the American Academy for Jewish Research*, 54: 261–87.

13

Ethics of Property, Ethics of Poverty[1]

Pascal Massie

For most contemporaries, private property is so unquestionable a principle that the idea of probing its validity or enquiring into its foundation seems sacrilegious. As for the possibility of voluntarily renouncing it, it is barely imaginable. Yet, although it is difficult to imagine life without private property, it is surprisingly difficult to justify it. It is often assumed that property is natural and necessary for the well-being of individuals and the maintenance of social order. This alleged naturalness would turn it into an inalienable right while its alleged necessity would turn its effects into social goods. Without it, would we not feel deprived? Would we not lose any motivation to act or work? Would society not cease to function? Yet, the urgency with which we run to the defence of property and proclaim it an undeniable requirement, a just institution and a moral good betrays some uneasiness.

This issue reached an unprecedented importance during the twelfth and thirteenth centuries as a new moral ideal appeared, an ethics of dispossession – *paupertas altissima*. It is often said that the late medieval period saw the birth of claims to individual private rights (Pierson 2013: 96).[2] While this is probably true, we must also observe that it occurred in a context of profound questioning and contestation. What is more, this was not a purely speculative debate; at least for some, it became a form of life. Finally, the issue had a political impact: it entailed a critique of the clergy's lavish lifestyle and the tendency of the Church, arguably the first international corporation, to amass riches.[3]

The debate engages two different questions, which, for being interwoven, are nevertheless distinct: (1) metaphysical and juridical questions concerning the nature and justification of property, and (2) an ethical question concerning wealth and our attitude towards it. At stake are notions such as 'dominion', 'possession', 'use', 'proper', 'common' and 'poverty' which, *prima facie*, are quite ordinary and readily understood, yet prove particularly difficult to delineate with precision. Some contemporary legal scholars have argued that the transition from the traditional sense of property as involving *materials* to the modern conception that

---

[1] A previous version of this chapter appeared in *The Saint Anselm Journal*, 12/1 (2016): 38–62. I thank the editors for their permission to republish.
[2] Pierson's work is essential to the study of this question and the present chapter is indebted to it.
[3] Marsilius of Padua offers a strong support to the 'perfection of poverty' championed by the Franciscan order and a very explicit condemnation of clerical and papal abuses. According to Marsilius, the members of the episcopate 'have a burning desire for pleasures, vanities, temporal possessions, and secular rulership, and they pursue and attain these objectives with all their energies not by rightful means, but by wrongdoing both secret and open' (Marsilius of Padua 1956: 185).

sees property as a '*bundle of rights*' that includes intangibles (for instance, intellectual property, copyrights and promissory notes) has led to the disintegration of the notion. Thomas Grey (1980: 81), who defends the so-called 'eliminative position', declares that, ultimately, property 'ceases to be an important category in legal and political theory'. The notion would now be replaced by a multiplicity of specialised conceptions that do not overlap and even conflict in some cases. Depending on the circumstances, rights and obligations vary greatly: for instance, one who possesses intellectual property does not have the same rights as one who owns a house.

To make sense of the medieval debate, it is important to first understand its theoretical background. Despite their divergence, medieval thinkers share a conceptual vocabulary that articulates a vast set of ideas, distinctions and assumptions that forms a common framework. I will begin this chapter by tracing the parameters within which the debate occurred, focusing on three authoritative sources: Scripture, Roman law, and the ancient philosophical tradition. In the second part, I will analyse the justification of property as it is articulated in particular by Augustine and Aquinas. Their thought ended up being the dominant and 'official' doctrine – although it is not devoid of ambiguities and uneasiness. Finally, I will conclude with the challenge raised by the Franciscan controversy on the status of the mendicant orders and the debate on poverty in which Bonaventure played a key role. My hope is that by rediscovering the arguments in favor of *paupertas altissima* contemporary readers will, at the least, notice the strangeness of our ordinary relation to the world and the entities that constitute it.

Authorities and Foundational Narratives

Medieval philosophy operates within a circle of recognised authorities and authoritative texts the command of which was essential to the training of a university Master. Medieval legal theory is no exception. On the issue of property, medieval thinkers appealed to three major sources: Scripture, Roman legal theory, and the ancient pagan philosophers (the knowledge of whom varied greatly depending on what was available to scholars at different times). These authorities, however, do not offer an unambiguous teaching nor are they necessarily in agreement with each other. In this matter, too, philosophy is inseparable from hermeneutics and innovation does not occur without interpretation.

Scripture

The primary task of the Church Fathers during the first five centuries of the Common Era was to define Christianity by determining what is *canonical* (what counts as Scripture) and what is *orthodox* (what Scripture means). What then, according to Scripture, should be the proper relation of a Christian to property? As Pierson (2013: 59) puts it 'among those texts which were seen as more or less unproblematically of divine inspiration (those works which became a part of the New Testament canon), the message on property seemed troublingly ambiguous'. In multiple occurrences, Jesus expresses contempt for riches while the poor are promised the kingdom of God (Luke 6:20). Three Gospels (Mark, Matthew and Luke) recount the story of a young and wealthy man anxious to know how he may receive eternal life. Obedience to the Old Law is not sufficient; rather, Jesus commands him to 'sell whatsoever thou hast, and give to the poor, and thou shall have treasure in heaven'. Then, in response to the astonishment of his disciples, Jesus, famously, declares: 'How hard it will be for rich people to enter the Kingdom of God [. . .] It is much harder for a rich person to enter the Kingdom of God than for a camel to go through the eye of a needle' (Mark 10:23, 25).[4] This claim goes much further than promoting an ethics of giving; this is an exhortation to *abandon* wealth and shed earthly goods as one would an unnecessary burden. The story can also be read along with Luke 14:26: 'Those who come to me cannot be my disciples unless they love me more than they love father and mother, wife and children, brothers and sisters, and themselves as well.' On this account, property is associated with sinfulness and is irreconcilable with a godly life; salvation and wealth are simply incompatible. In a striking formula, James declares: 'Your riches have rotted away, and your clothes have been eaten by moths. Your gold and silver are covered with rust, and this rust will be a witness against you and will eat up your flesh like fire. You have piled up riches in these last days' (James 5.2–3). Greed is not just morally reprehensible; according to Tertullian (1987: 41), it has its source in the sin of covetousness which is the 'root of all evil'.

Those who embrace an apocalyptic narrative are keen to stress these passages that agree with Jesus's claim according to which the end of the world will come within his generation (Luke 21:32). If the end of times is imminent, it is pointless to cling to impermanent possessions. This abnegation of wealth expresses a general resentment against the world – a profane world of sin – which separates us from the promised kingdom of God. Thus, Augustine (2003: 191) mentions that 'Cain, whose name means "possession", is the founder of the earthy city. This indicates that this city has its beginning and end on this earth, where there is no hope of anything beyond what can be seen in this world.' Even Augustine, however, did not hold this interpretation throughout his career and, at times, expressed a more conciliatory position.[5]

Another essential Scriptural text on the question of property, the Acts of the Apostles, indicates that the early Church at Jerusalem held property in common:

> A multitude of them that believed who were of one heart and of one soul; neither said any of them that aught of the things which he possessed was his own, but they had all things in common. Neither was there any among them that lacked: for as many as were possessors of lands or houses sold them and brought the prices of the things that were sold and laid them down at the apostles' feet; and distribution was made unto every man according as he had need. (Acts 4:32, 34)

This practice of communal property contributed to the transformation of a 'multitude' into a community of 'one heart and of one soul'.

The positive relation one has to what one owns presupposes a foundational act of appropriation which, by definition, excludes others. When property becomes private, others must be deprived. Even common property, by granting right of use to the members of a specific community, wards members of other communities off it. To own is *ipso facto* to exclude and to exclude even those who have a greater need. Without this act of exclusion property could not occur. One possible way of reconciling the rejection of wealth advocated in the Gospels with the practices of ordinary life or the material owned by the Church is to argue that in order

---

[4] Bible references are from the New Revised Standard Version, Philadelphia: American Bible Society.

[5] In *Letter 157* (dated 414) Augustine reinterprets Mark 10:25 to simply mean that with God all things are possible – thus, with God's help, camels can, presumably, go through the eye of a needle. 'Let the rich hearken to this: "what is impossible for man is easy for God", and whether they retain their riches and do good work by means of them, or enter the kingdom of heaven by selling them and distributing them to provide for the needs of the poor, let them attribute their good work to the grace of God, not to their own strength' (Augustine 1953).

to flee from the approaching ruin of this world, a rich man should give up his wealth to the 'celestial treasury' since God is the only true possessor of all wealth (see Ganz 1995). While the ultimate goal is the City of God, we live in the earthly city and in this world to endow the Church is to give back to God.

Roman Legal Theory

If medieval thinking on property operates within the framework of Scriptural teachings, its juridical apparatus, however, is mostly derived from Roman law, particularly the *Corpus Juris Civilis*, a legal compendium composed in the sixth century under the rule of the Eastern Roman Emperor Justinian. The basic distinction between *ius civilis* (which governs citizens), *ius gentium* (the law of nations or people that governs foreigners and citizen alike) and *ius naturale* (natural law, the source of the other two) is at the heart of the ancient Roman thinking about property.[6] This distinction articulates the legal apparatus in terms of spontaneous and conventional, untaught and taught, universal and particular, but also, and importantly, in terms of original and derivative. The *Institutes of Justinian* declares that 'natural law is clearly the older, having been instituted by nature at the first origin of mankind, whereas civil laws came into existence when states began to be founded, magistrates to be created, and laws to be written' (Moynes 1906, *Institutes*: 37, II, 1, 11). Accordingly, the task of the jurist is to bring the civil law in agreement with the natural law. At what point then does property arise for the first time? Can it be traced back to the root of all laws? Does it belong to the natural order of things? Does it occur through rational nature (*iuris gentium*)? Or is it merely the result of a particular civil agreement (*iuris civilis*)? In accord with the genealogical order that derives civil from natural, the *Digest* (Watson 2009: 16) defends a version of the natural origin of property thesis:

> The younger Nerva says that the ownership of things originated in *natural possession* and that a relic thereof survives in the attitude to those things which are taken on land, sea, or in the air; for such things forthwith become the property of those who first take possession of them. In like manner, things captured in war, islands arising in the sea, germs, stones, pearls found on the seashore become the property of him who first takes possession of them.

Property is 'natural' not because people have an innate right to own things, but in the sense that whatever nature produces has no *initial* owner. In the state of nature, all land is no man's land, and it is this *absence* of original property that justifies the initial act of acquisition; it is because it belongs to no one that one can justly claim that a thing is one's own. Nature provides; to take from it is to receive its gifts. Surprisingly perhaps, the *Digest* places in the same category things found on the ground and 'things captured in war' even though, in the second case, whatever is captured is taken by force from someone who, presumably, was entitled to it. The two instances were nevertheless assimilated on the ground that war cancels civil laws and thus returns things to a state of nature.[7]

---

[6] While Gaius and Ulpian were near contemporaries (second century CE), Gaius drew a twofold distinction between *civile* and *gentium*. It is Ulpian who made the above-mentioned tripartite distinction, defining *iuris naturale* as 'that which nature has taught to all animals; for it is not a law specific to mankind but common to all animals'. It includes self-defence against aggression, sexual union, procreation and rearing of the young (see Pierson 2013: 80–1). *Naturale* and *gentium*, however, were often used interchangeably.

[7] During Roman history, there was some uncertainty as to whether the booty goes to the individual who captured it or to the state; see Watson (1968: 64).

The basic form of appropriation is *occupatio*, the acquisition of ownership of a *res nullius* (nobody's property) by taking physical control of it. This, as we saw, assumes that things are originally available to all and anyone. Some medieval thinkers, however, doubted that this initial *occupatio* is enough to justify dominion. Thus, in *Ordinatio* IV, Scotus declares that, although 'in the natural state he who first finds a thing necessarily might use it as far as he needed it', this does not show that in the natural state there is distinct dominium. 'Occupancy referred only to common use' (Mäkinen 2001: 137). A secondary mode of acquiring property is by *traditio*, that is, through the delivery of possession with the intention of passing ownership by giving, bequeathing, selling, and the like. The main difference between *occupatio* and *traditio* is that, in the second case, the thing already had the status of a property; it is the owner who changes. Thus, what is passed on is not simply a (movable or immovable) object but a *legal title*. To signify the transfer of this incorporeal title, a ceremony was often required (at least in cases of *res mancipi* or things held as particularly valuable) in order to mark symbolically that it is *ownership* itself, and not simply the object, that is transmitted.[8]

To own something entails having *dominium* over it; the converse, however, is not necessarily true. In general, the notion of *dominium* connotes the power that a dominant entity exercises over a subjugated being. But the meaning of *dominium* varies according to the kind of things it applies to and, despite its name, it was probably never taken to be truly 'absolute' (Birks 1985).[9] The Justinian Code, for instance, not only never advocated the *ius utendi et abutendi* (the so-called 'right to use and abuse') but on the contrary declares that it is in the interest of the commonwealth that no one shall make ill use of their property (Moynes 1906, *Institutes*: 1.8.2). Thus, Ockham (William of Ockham 2001: 70) defined *dominium* in the narrow sense as signifying that the holder 'may treat it [a good] in any way not forbidden by natural law'.

As J. Coleman (1983: 212) observes:

> in the twelfth and thirteenth century there was a blurring of a distinction that had been crucial to the Romans between holding office and owning property. This confusion of office and ownership paralleled a comparable development in secular political life and is reflected in their use of the single word *dominium* to denote both proprietary right and governmental authority.

While a Roman jurist would have used '*dominium*' to denote property rights alone, as Coleman observes, it is significant that modern English speakers understand 'dominion' as denoting governmental authority.

According to Roman law, *possessio* occurs when two conditions are met: a person must have (1) *corpus*, that is, sufficient control over a thing and (2) *animus*, that is, the requisite intention or manifest will to treat something as one's own. Thus, in principle, infants and the insane

---

[8] Watson mentions that classical law required five witnesses, all Roman citizens of full age, who held a bronze scale. The transferee grasped with his hand the thing to be mancipated (unless land), struck the scale with a bronze ingot, and gave it to the transferor as a symbolic price (Watson 1968: 17).

[9] The idea of limiting something absolute is, literally, a contradiction: whatever is absolute does not admit of degrees. 'Absolute' should therefore be understood in a looser sense. It is possible to argue that one's right to own something is absolute in the sense that, so long as rightful ownership can be established, it is not to be challenged. However, the *use* one makes of what is rightfully one's own remains bound by social norms. Max Radin talks of *dominium* as a 'complex of privileges rather than claims' (Radin 1925: 211).

(*furiosi*) are excluded.[10] The second requirement (*animus* or intention to own) will be of great importance in the mendicant dispute. Thus, in the fourteenth century, Marsilius of Padua insists that to have dominion requires the *will* to exercise and defend dominion. Likewise, appealing to the Roman law, Bonaventure (Marsilius 1956: 311) declares: 'it is stipulated in the law that liberty cannot be acquired for he who does not wish it and that a benefit is not given to an unwilling person'. But how, from this state of affairs, does a right emerge? At what point and through what process does a fact (*detentio*) become a right (*possessio*)? To answer this difficult question the Roman jurists appealed to the notion of *usucaptio*, which is best defined as the acquisition of a thing through possessing it without interruption for a certain period of time. Thus, so long as it had a 'valid beginning' (*bonum initium*) – that is, the good was not stolen, had been obtained in good faith and with 'just cause' – the passage of time is all it takes to turn having into owning. This doctrine responded to a practical concern: land-grabbers taking possession of a land as soon as the previous owner had been evicted had an interest in establishing lawful title as quickly as possible (Pierson 2013: 57).[11] Thus, to require *usucaptio* (two years for land and one for chattels) was a way of preventing uncertainty over titles and to answer a practical problem. But *usucaptio* is not just an *ad hoc* solution; it also articulates the belief that prolonged possession of a good generates a right, that a *de jure* claim can, in some sense, be derived from a *de facto* state of affairs.

Ancient Pagan Philosophy

Finally, two main sources from pagan thought had a great impact on medieval jurists and philosophers: Aristotle and the Stoics. Classical Greek thought regards property as a matter of *oikonomia*, that is, as belonging to the sphere of activities concerned with the handling and management of assets and material goods. To situate the issue at this level is already to indicate that it is an ancillary skill and that it cannot count as an end in itself. The value of economy resides entirely in the fact that it provides the necessary conditions that make possible something else, something infinitely more important, namely: an active and virtuous life.

Initially, Aristotle (II, chapter 5) focuses on the distinction between public and private. Theoretically, various permutations are possible; for instance, we could eliminate common property altogether and place everything in the hands of private interests. This, however, would be absurd and dangerous; it would be the end of the political community. To treat everything as a commodity, to place every aspect of life in the hands of private entities would tear apart the social fabric. Politics is about coexistence and there is no coexistence where there is no *common*-wealth. But then, where should we draw the line? What should be private? What should be held in common? Should we, as Plato suggested, give it a maximal extension so that what is held in common includes almost everything (even women and children)?

This is both impractical and undesirable. Consequently, Aristotle's discussion of property is primarily about land. Appealing to a distinction between ownership and use, Aristotle

---

[10] It has been observed that, at least during the last century of the Republic, even an infant could acquire possession without the authority of his tutor (Watson 1968: 83). At that point, the intention of the acquirer would have had little weight. Even so, *animus* must have been at least assumed in order to uphold the distinction between detention and possession since, as we saw, the proper legal sense of *possessio* does not designate a thing (a property) nor even the factual act of detaining something, but a right.

[11] As Pierson mentions, this is not unlike the process of primitive accumulation analysed by Marx in *Capital* whereby a violent expropriation is followed by a claim to the 'sanctity of property'.

(II, chapter 5: 1263a27–32) eventually declares that private ownership with common use is preferable on the ground that private property has the added advantage of preventing disputes about the distribution of goods whereas to share without clear rules of allocation is to open the door to endless disputes.

> When each attends to his own property, men will not complain against one another, and they will produce more since each will be paying special attention himself to what he regards as being his own; while on the other hand, because of virtue, the *use* of property will agree with the proverb according to which 'common are the possessions of friends'.

Assuming optimal conditions, private property has the advantage of quelling feuds as people agree on recognising each other's spheres of rights. Furthermore, private property provides the satisfaction associated with what is one's own and the result of one's own achievement; as Aristotle (II, chapter 5: 1263a42–1263b1) puts it: 'to regard property as one's own gives a man immense pleasure; for it is indeed natural and not in vain for each man to love himself'. It also improves the care devoted to what is one's own.[12] Finally, some virtues, for instance generosity, could not be exercised without private ownership and personal resources. Thus, for all the above-mentioned reasons and for the sake of political stability, the state should guarantee some minimum level of property.[13] During the scholastic era, Albert and Aquinas will follow these arguments very closely.

Faithfully or not, Aristotle's defence of private property has been rehashed for centuries. Yet, before praising or disparaging it, we should observe Aristotle's ambivalence. Private property is at the service of *common use*, which is conducive to virtue and friendship. 'In these [well administered states] each has his own property; yet, he makes available a part of it to his friends and another part for common use' (Aristotle II, chapter 5: 1263a34–5).[14] By itself, the art of acquisition is certainly not where the good life can be found; quite to the contrary, the relentless yearning for accumulation (*pleonexia*) is a recipe for a life of constant frustration. For all his idiosyncrasy, Epicurus (1994: 39) expressed a view shared by many ancient philosophers when he declares that 'nothing is enough to someone for whom what is enough is little'. Augustine (1951: 262) likewise acknowledges the danger of *pleonexia*, albeit for theological reasons: 'Fear is all the more increased and covetousness is all the more unloosened according as there is an increase of those things which are called riches . . . Riches, more than anything else, engender pride.'

Ancient philosophers, however, did not limit themselves to discussing the relative merits of private versus common property. In fact, this debate does not say anything about the ontological status and the justification of property. For this, we need first to turn our attention to the human psyche. The first thing I can truly call 'mine' is myself; the self appears simultaneously as owner and owned. To be is not just to be alive but to live one's *own* life. The human psyche

---

[12] 'Each man pays more attention to what is his own, and less attention to what is common . . . for each man . . . pays less to it on the ground that someone else will take care of the matter' (Aristotle, II, chapter 5: 1261b35–9).

[13] 'Measures should be adopted then to make possible a lasting prosperity. And since this is beneficial to the prosperous also, the proceeds of the special revenues should be accumulated and distributed to the needed in sums, as far as possible, to enable them to save enough to buy a piece of land, or else to start a trade or become a farmer' (Aristotle, VI, chapter 5: 1320a–35b4).

[14] Accordingly, Aristotle praises the Cretan practice of communal meals. The Cretans used to reserve a part of the harvest from publicly owned and rented land to replenish the provisions of common meals.

presents a remarkable feature: it can master itself (albeit with various degrees of success and occasional failures). Without this, temperance (the virtue that deals with the appetites) would not be possible since to be temperate is to control oneself.[15] This means that I (acting) and 'me' (object acted upon) must, somehow, be different; otherwise, as Plato (IV: 431a) observed, the soul could not be in conflict with itself. Yet, obviously there is only one 'me'; therefore, this difference must be internal. Plato portrays the human psyche as an inner political arena; it is not only a seat of plurality but of conflicts and struggles, authority and obedience. *Psyche* relates to itself as observer and observed, ruler and ruled; it is a self-relation that allows human beings to be responsible for themselves, caring for themselves and controlling themselves, all traits that make what we call 'personhood' possible. Thus, we can describe the accomplished act of being human as an act whereby one owns oneself. It is precisely for this reason that, according to Aquinas (I, q. 96, a. 2), *dominium* is inscribed in human nature: 'Man in a certain sense contains all things; and so just as he has dominion over what is within himself, in the same way he can have dominion over other things . . . [I]n man reason has the position of a master and not of a subject.' However, Aquinas adds that this dominion is not a matter of commanding but of *using*. In order to claim property rights over a natural thing outside me, I must treat that aspect of myself which resembles most a natural thing as something I own.

To appeal to the soul is, in some sense, to naturalise property. Even defenders of the mendicants will acknowledge the point. Thus, Marsilius of Padua (1956: 193) declares:

> This term 'ownership' is used to refer to the human will or freedom in itself with its organic executive or motive power unimpeded. For it is through this that we are capable of certain acts and their opposite. It is for this reason too that man alone among the animals is said to have ownership or control of his acts: this control belongs to him by nature, it is not acquired through an act of will or choice.

But of course, as Marsilius will argue, if the ability to have ownership or control of oneself is part of our nature by virtue of the faculty of willing (*velle*), then not willing (*nolle*) to own an external object is also exercising our natural capacities.

Any defence of property rights that embraces this view should recognise, at least implicitly, the peril it harbours. The very properties that can objectify my virtue can also be my downfall. If the *rightful* possession of something is grounded in the condition that I own myself, that I exercise self-control, then those who become ensnarled by the very things they possess lose control of themselves. The moral danger is that as one accumulates goods, one can end up not simply *obsessed* by the relentless desire to acquire more but literally *possessed* by it. A life lived for the sake of having or for the sake of self-gratification would be a corruption of the very thing that justifies property in the first place. Thus, if I must be free *in order to* own, I must also be free *from* what I own. This moral ambiguity didn't escape the attention of medieval thinkers.

The Stoics pursued the exploration of this metaphysical hypothesis, and their observations had a significant impact on medieval thought, too. While Stoic ethics places wealth among the indifferents (i.e., wealth, by itself, is neither conducive to virtue nor to vice), property can nevertheless be traced back to a phenomenon observable in animals no less than in humans: '*oikeiōsis*' (variably translated as 'disposition', 'appropriation', 'familiarity', 'affinity'

---

[15] Self-mastery is itself a prerequisite for other virtues such as courage, for instance.

or 'endearment'). The term designates the appropriation to oneself, the perception of oneself as well as of something else as one's own;[16] it is related to *oikeiotes*, which denotes the sense of belonging, of being at home. Thus, *oikeiōsis* designates a care for oneself that also extends beyond the self. On this view, all human beings (indeed, all sentient beings) are the rightful owners of themselves.

Insofar as some things (but not all) possess the intangible property of being owned, a theory of property needs a metaphysical account. But insofar as a theory of property seeks a beginning in some original act of appropriation, it also needs a foundational myth, an '*in illo tempore*' story of a primordial age of innocence that ignored lack and want and is now lost. This loss is supposed to explain the sinfulness and scarcity of our times. In 'Letter 90', Seneca (1920: 397) declares that 'the first men and those who sprang from them, still unspoiled, followed nature'. Primeval life was ruled by a fellowship which 'remained unspoiled for a long time, until avarice tore the community asunder and became the cause of poverty, even in the case of those whom she herself had most enriched'. Avarice introduces evil and with it the rise of a second age of humanity.[17]

Christian thinkers will likewise conclude from the similar myth of Genesis that private property can only be a sign of our fallen condition. Thus, in the pre-lapsarian state of mankind, common property had pre-eminence over private property: the goods of creation are destined for the whole human race, and although the fall alters the human condition, it does not erase this original divine dispensation for all.[18] In a post-lapsarian condition, however, appropriation is a legitimate means to satisfy human needs and maintain well-being. Thus, the universal destination of goods remains primordial. As Augustine notes, private property depends on civil law, for the earth was given by God to all mankind. As Bonaventure (2010: 252) puts it: 'we should understand that private property resulted from the iniquity of the first parents, because if they [Adam and Eve] had not sinned, there would have been no appropriation of this kind'. For the medieval thinkers, however, it is fundamental to distinguish between what *results from sin* and what constitutes an *actual sin*. Private property may result from sin without being intrinsically sinful. In the original condition, God entrusts the earth and its fruits to the *common* stewardship of humanity.

If it is so, it becomes difficult to avoid the conclusion that at bottom private property results from an act which, although it could not have been a theft since things did not have a prior owner, was nevertheless a violent appropriation that deprived others. A possible consequence one could draw from the foundational myth is that, in a sense, property cannot be fully justified. At best, we have only guardianship. As Seneca (1920: 355–7) puts it, if one complains

---

[16] 'Chrysippus affirms in the first book of his work *On Ends* that the dearest thing to every animal is its own constitution and its consciousness thereof; for it was not likely that nature should estrange the living thing from itself or that she should leave the creature she has made without either estrangement from or affection for its own constitution. We are forced then to conclude that nature in constituting the animal made it near and dear to itself' (Diogenes 1925: 193).

[17] 'But avarice broke in upon a condition so happily ordained, and, by its eagerness to lay something away and to turn it to its own private use, made all things the property of others, and reduced itself from boundless wealth to straitened need. It was avarice that introduced poverty and, by craving much, lost all' (Seneca 1920: 425).

[18] This at least was the dominant narrative. John XXII's *Quia Vir Reprobus* constitutes an important deviation from this view since it argues that property was *originally* private. See the section entitled '*Paupertas Altissima*' below.

that he is being driven from the farm that his father and grandfather owned, it can always be answered:

> Well? Who owned the land before your grandfather? Can you explain what people (I will not say what person) held it originally? You did not enter upon it as a master, but merely as a tenant. And whose tenant are you? If your claim is successful, you are tenant of the heir. The lawyers say that public property cannot be acquired privately by possession; what you hold and call your own is public property – indeed, it belongs to mankind at large.

Yet, in fact, many thinkers (including Seneca himself) shrunk away from this position that seems to condemn all social civil order as unjust and unjustifiable.[19] As a consequence, it will be an important task for medieval thinkers to ward off this idea and determine the condition of a just property in accord with religious dogma and rational analysis. Their effort will result in the establishment of what could be called an 'official doctrine', but even it will not be without contestation.

Just Ownership: Augustine and Aquinas

Most medieval thinkers who discussed the status of property ownership asked three questions: (1) What is the source of property? (2) Under what condition is acquiring property rightful? (3) What constitutes its right use? Even those who justified private property admitted that the institution is fundamentally a human device rather than a divine institution. From that standpoint, property can be seen as a subset of the more general question concerning the purpose and justification of social organisation. To this, the general answer is that, in the present condition of fallenness, it is necessary to impose restraints on human sinfulness; in a similar manner, ownership rights are necessary in order to restrain violent accumulation and theft. But in order to be just, human institutions must also agree with divine dispensation. Thus, virtually all defences of the right to property see it as a necessary institution but also as one that must be restricted.

Augustine

In the Christian West, Augustine and Aquinas, more than anyone else, contributed to shaping the core principles that guide reasoning in this matter. Concerning the origin of property, Augustine (1994: 248–9) makes the following observation:

> Look, there are villas! By what right do you protect those villas? By divine or human right? Let them reply: 'Divine right we have in the Scriptures; human rights in the laws of kings'. On what basis does anyone possess what he possesses? Is it not by human right? By divine right 'the earth and its fullness belong to the Lord' (Ps. 24. 1). God made the poor and the rich from one clay and the one earth supports both the poor and the rich. Nevertheless, by human right one says 'this villa is mine; this house is mine; this slave is mine'. Thus, by human right, by right of emperors. Why? Because God has distributed these same human rights to the human race through the emperors and kings of the world.

---

[19] A remarkable exception is the Pseudo-Pelagius's *De divitiis*. The anonymous author argues that wealth cannot be just and that the few who are rich are the reason for the many who are poor. See Anonynomus (2002: 15–33) and Morris (1965: 69–71).

In its basic form, human property is relative. Despite social agreements and customs, we do not truly own what we possess. All that is not by divine institution expresses an impermanent order. The *human* laws in the name of which I claim that this thing is mine cannot supersede the ultimate divine ownership of all things. In fact, it is not unusual to see the laws of emperors and kings protecting the interests of those who unjustly acquired their wealth. Nevertheless, from the fact that private property was not contained in the original Edenic state, it does not follow that it must be condemned altogether. This imperfect arrangement whereby mine and thine are distinguished may contribute to a more peaceful social order, and while a human invention it is not thereby *averse* to divine disposition.

It would, however, be incorrect to conclude from the remark in the *Tractates on John* that Augustine abandons the jurisdiction of private property to the relativism of the law of the land. Laws have a remedial purpose (the restraint of violence), and, ultimately, earthly authority remains accountable to divine authority. Finally, although the temporal law, *by itself*, cannot be the source of right possession, it may be so insofar as 'God has distributed these same human rights to the human race *through the emperors and kings of the world*.'[20] What is ordained by the will of human rulers is distributed by divine law; God's providence works through the tribulations of history.

What interests Augustine most is not the juridical claims or the legal apparatus that property rights require but the nature of our relation to things that the very existence of property presupposes. Property is a determinate mode of our attachment to things. To own is to absolutise this attachment by warding off the possibility of losing what we covet. The fear of destitution is never far away from the desire to own. The broadest term for this attachment, perhaps, is 'love'. Love attaches an object to a subject, but since the term 'love' is so broad a term, it is of great importance to clarify its form and the nature of its object. At an initial level, Augustine poses a basic distinction between *cupiditas* (love directed at earthly things) and *caritas* (love of the *summum bonum*). Thus, the earthly city is ruled by *cupiditas* while the heavenly one is governed by *caritas*. Although both are forms of love, the movements that animate each one go in opposite directions. *Caritas* loves the object for the object's sake, not for the lover's sake. *Caritas*'s movement aims at an other; it longs for what it cannot possess and keeps it at a distance; it is love that adores and worships. For this reason, *caritas*'s ultimate object is unlike anything in the world and cannot be owned. *Caritas*'s desire never appropriates its object. By contrast, *cupiditas* attaches itself to 'one of those things that can be lost'; it seeks fulfilment in the possession of transitory things of all sorts. Insofar as *cupiditas* attempts to order the beings it covets to its *own* private good, it ultimately has only one object: itself. *Cupiditas*'s love is *amor sui*; it makes its object subservient to the self. What it seeks in the object is not the object itself but one's own *jouissance*. Human love, qua *cupiditas*, is fundamentally acquisitive and the value of the object it seeks is a function of the gratification it promises. From that standpoint, property is an expression of *cupiditas* since to claim ownership is to appropriate, to turn an object into something self-centred (*privatus*).

The opposition of *caritas* and *cupiditas* is the foundation of the two cities. 'Two societies have issued from two kinds of love . . . [W]orldly society has flowered from a selfish love which dares to despise even God, whereas the communion of saints is rooted in the love of God that is ready to trample on self' (Augustine 2003: 593). Should we stop at this stark dichotomy, it would seem that no earthly goods could be the object of *caritas* and that the only path to the heavenly city requires transcending or suppressing the self. Yet, the demand to sacrifice one's

---

[20] '*Quia ipsa iura humana per imperatores et reges saeculi Deus distribuit generi humano.*'

own happiness seems not only psychologically, but also logically, impossible. We cannot simply oppose term to term *caritas* and *cupiditas* in such a way that the affirmation of one term entails the negation of the other. While *cupiditas* excludes *caritas*, the converse is not necessarily true. The very turn towards the heavenly city and God could not occur if the lover did not assume that it is there that her or his *own* true good and felicity resides. If acquisitiveness is in the nature of human love, then self-love not only cannot be eliminated but it is a component of loving God. S/he who is willing to 'trample on self', as Augustine says, is still doing so because s/he is seeking a good and, as we learned from Plato, that which is intrinsically good is also necessarily beneficent. There is no such thing as a good that would not be good for me.

Thus, a new structure must be proposed: a hierarchy of measured or proportioned loves must mediate the initial dichotomy of *caritas* and *cupiditas*. The possibility of some justice within the city of man (and consequently of some just property) demands that the two orders be more than mutually exclusive. Privately owned goods, which are the objects of *cupiditas*, can nevertheless be rightly governed when they are directed to the common good. Instead of demeaning self-love, one must consider how self-love can be oriented to the final end. Legitimate property may be a human device that follows from the post-lapsarian condition; it may depend on rights granted by secular proclamations, but, through the decrees of emperors and kings, God has distributed these rights to humanity.[21] Thus, God neither commands nor prohibits but rather permits all to proclaim this right in the earthly city.

The divide between the eternal city of God and the temporal city of man leads to a dual approach to property and wealth. Insofar as they depend on the relative and temporal decrees, adjudications of claims are better left to human jurists. As a consequence, the question concerning the most equitable distribution of wealth among citizens is of little concern for Augustine. Alms are primarily necessary for salvation, rather than social justice. But insofar as we must prepare for the city of God, our present *disposition* towards wealth and our *use* of it are of crucial importance. One who clings to those things that can be taken from them against their will,

> becomes subject to those things which ought to be subject to him and creates for himself goods whose right and proper use require that he himself be good. But the man who uses these rightly proves that they are indeed goods, though not for him (for they do not make him good or better) but become better because of him. (Augustine 1985: 32)

While neither the owned property nor ownership itself can be said to be righteous, the righteousness of the agent grants some goodness to one's property and one's use thereof. Thereby, morality and property can be reconciled.

Aquinas

In medieval Europe, Augustine's views on matters of property will rarely be challenged. They will, however, be adapted to changing circumstances. Many scholars have observed that a shift of attitude occurred around 1200, when the claim that wealth is inherently sinful began to erode.[22] In that regard, Aquinas plays an exemplary role insofar as he managed to maintain a tradition of moral suspicion towards private property and acquisition in general while simultaneously accommodating important new social developments. To do so without contradiction

---

[21] *Pace* Dougherty (2003: 482).
[22] See (among others) McGovern (1972) and Gordon (1975).

depends on distinguishing carefully the case of the laity and that of religious communities. Contemplative life requires the stricter standard of religious perfection, a demand that cannot be imposed upon the laity. Depending on the audience, Aquinas upholds the anti-wealth stand of the Church Fathers or a more tolerant attitude towards accumulation.[23] It is contrary to contemplative life to possess anything in private because, by definition, such a self-oriented practice induces a sinful self-love. In accord with Augustine, Aquinas (II-II, q. 188, art. 7) declares that

> the care that one takes of one's own wealth pertains to love of self, whereby a man loves himself in temporal matters, whereas the care that is given to things held in common pertains to the love of *caritas* which 'seeketh not her own', but looks to the common good.

But even the approval of common property among members of a religious order remains cautious: 'the care that is given to common goods *may* pertain to *caritas*, although it *may prove an obstacle* to some higher act of *caritas* such as divine contemplation or the instructing of one's neighbor' (II-II, q. 188, art. 7). These last two are, of course, the very activities that constitute contemplative life. At best, the care for common goods in monasteries and convents can be an expression of *caritas* if it remains subservient to the activities that properly constitute contemplative life. The laity, however, cannot be held to the same demands; there, private property, the search for profit, commerce and even some (limited) form of usury all have a justified place.[24]

Turning to the question of the naturalness of property, Aquinas posits a conceptual distinction between the *nature* of an external thing and its *use*. In general, property means dominion and 'dominion' denotes power. But clearly, we have no power over the *nature* of external things; they are what they are independently of our will, and 'we can work no change in their nature' (II-II, q. 66, art. 1, ob. 3); consequently, their nature does not fall under our dominion. As regards their use, however, 'man has a natural dominion over natural things, because by his reason and will he is able to use them for his own profit, as they are made on his account' (II-II, q. 66, art. 1, ob. 3). In linking this 'natural dominion' to the use of things, Aquinas appeals to the authority of Aristotle and Genesis 1:26 ('let him have dominion over the fish of the sea, and over the fowl of the air, and over the cattle, and over all the earth . . .'). Human dominion has, therefore, a divine origin, but it is limited to *use* and should not be confused with sovereignty.

As such, the argument leaves many things unclarified. It is not clear, in particular, whether the distinction between the 'nature' of a thing and its 'use' leaves any room for human property in the full sense of the term. Thus, in his response to the objection according to which 'no man should ascribe to himself that which is God's', Aquinas appeals to a 'natural dominion over things *as* regards the power to *make use* of them'. Yet, man's 'natural dominion' and his 'power to make use' of them cannot be identical (for from the fact that I use something, it does not follow that I own it). Even if *sovereign* dominion can only belong to God (since his power extends to the nature of things), there still remains a distinction in human matters between use and property.

In this respect, article 2 of question 66 provides an important development. First, Aquinas argues that 'use' calls for *common* possession. Second, because the acts of procuring and

---

[23] This interpretation is defended by Worden (2010: 71–93).

[24] In general, to take usury for money lent is unjust in itself, because 'this is to sell what does not exist, and this evidently leads to inequality which is contrary to justice'. Nevertheless, Aquinas claims that 'a lender may without sin enter in agreement with the borrower for compensation for the loss he incurs of something he ought to have for this is not to sell the use of money but to avoid a loss' (II-II, q. 78, a. 2, ad 1).

dispensing external things are, as Aquinas puts it, 'competent to man' (i.e., they agree with human nature) this makes property lawful. In addition, property is necessary for the reasons already articulated by Aristotle. Thus, there can be personal use of common property (as one person at a time may read a book which nevertheless belongs to the library). In such a case, use and property remain distinct. Furthermore, while community of goods is ascribed to natural law, it does not follow that

> all things should be possessed in common and that nothing should be possessed as one's own: but because the division of possession is not according to natural law but rather arose from human agreement which belongs to positive law . . . the ownership of possession is not contrary to the natural law, but an addition thereto devised by human reason. (II-II, q. 66, art. 2)

It is a matter not only of what the natural law commands but of what it tacitly permits. Since private property is neither a part of natural law nor opposed to it, humans seem free to practise the private ownership of goods. Yet, Aquinas alters this apparent neutrality of the natural law by an appeal to the authority of Aristotle and the Old Law in terms of the effects of private property: 'a more peaceful state is ensured to man if each one is contented with his own'. Thus, while the division of possessions is neither a divine command nor according to natural law, it is nevertheless *rationally* and *practically* preferable.

The difficulty in ascertaining the legal place of property is linked to the fact that Aquinas inherits the Roman notion of *ius gentium* as a juridical sphere distinct from natural and civil law.[25] Thus, Gaius understood natural law as the source of all laws and *ius gentium* as its application. Insofar as it is established by natural reason, *ius gentium* applies to *all* people while civil law bears upon Roman citizens alone. Jurists would also appeal to this distinction in order to adjudicate in matters that involved people from different nations when their respective civil laws did not agree. In that sense, *ius gentium* may be better understood as a specification of natural law rather than as a legal sphere distinct from it. Aquinas (I-II, q. 94, art. 2) defines *lex naturalis* as it applies specifically to humans as

> an inclination to good according to the nature of man's reason, which nature is proper to him . . . [W]hatever pertains to this inclination belongs to the natural law; for instance to shun ignorance, to avoid offending those among whom one has to live, and other such things regarding the above inclination.

Although *ius gentium* is not strictly identical with the first and second forms of natural law (that is, self-preservation and the 'inclinations that belong to human beings according to that nature which is common to all animals') insofar as it is the product of rational deliberation that draws consequences from true premises about human nature, it is distinct from local conventions. Chroust and Affeldt (1950–1: 178) conclude from this that: '*ius gentium* understood in this sense is not really the consequence of the fall of man . . . Hence, private property is not so much an institution which has become necessary through the fall of man, than an institution of intelligent social co-existence based on ratiocination.' Aquinas's appeal to Aristotle at this

---

[25] As Chroust and Affeldt (1950–1: 177) write: 'The Roman concept of *ius gentium* has succeeded in becoming one of the most nebulous terms in Thomistic jurisprudence, a constant source of confusion to scholastic philosophy.'

precise junction provides a justification to turn private property into a decree of *ius gentium* and makes it, if not a precept of natural law, at least an acceptable consequence thereof. This does not remove the temporal and imperfect character of this institution, but it makes it '*conditionally* justifiable on the basis of the *ius gentium*, while at the same time . . . the community of all property and possessions is *absolutely* justified through the *lex naturalis*' (Chroust and Affeldt 1950–1: 181; original emphasis).

The lawfulness and goodness of private property is not an absolute and immutable characteristic; it depends on its ability to contribute to the common good. An indication of this conditional status can be seen in the fact that, in general, material goods are to meet human needs and purposes (that is, the perpetuation of life and the development of virtues). Should private property fail to serve this purpose (or should a more urgent need occur), the institution could be cancelled. Thus in article 7 of question 66, Aquinas famously declares that 'it is lawful for a man to succor his own need by means of another's property, by taking it either openly or secretly, nor is it properly speaking theft or robbery'. Further, 'in the case of a like need, a man may also take secretly another's property in order to succor his neighbor in need' (ad 3). It should be noted that the argument depends on a specific condition: the need in question must be 'so manifest and urgent that it is evident that [it] must be remedied by whatever means be at hand (for instance when a person is in some imminent danger and there is no other possible remedy)'. Any other appropriation of another's possessions would be a theft and therefore a sin. Further, this permissibility derived from natural right does not signify a return to a prior state of common property; it is simply a limited and temporary suspension of the law. The same is true with respect to superabundance. Natural law prescribes that what one owns in superabundance is owed to the poor for their sustenance; but Aquinas (II-II, q. 66, ad 3) adds that the 'stewardship of his own goods is left to the judgment of each so that from these he may meet the need of those suffering it'. Thus, short of dire necessity, superabundant goods become disposable for the welfare of others according to the judgement of the original owner, but not by virtue of a common property right.[26] In these matters the act remains discretionary not supererogatory and the determination of what is necessary and what is superfluous is left to individual judgement.

Paupertas Altissima

The anonymous Italian author of the burlesque *Canzone del fi' Aldobrandino* (late twelfth or early thirteenth century) talks of his allegorical marriage to the cadaverous Lady Poverty whose relatives are Sorrow, Beggary, Longing and Distress (see Havely 2004: 9–10). Poverty brings suffering, disgrace and shame. Dante, in contrast, portrays poverty as an unrecognised gift. For all the repugnance it elicits, poverty may be a means of spiritual renewal, and those who can overcome their initial revulsion may receive from her a great reward. The distance that separates the repulsive Lady Poverty of the *Canzone* from her allegorical Dantean counterpart (in *Canto* XI she is Christ's wife and Francis's lover) is huge and it is not, as it has been suggested, a matter of a 'variety of coexisting attitudes and doctrines' or of historical 'transformation of values'

---

[26] Weithman (1993: 171) puts it: 'Aquinas does *not* say that property held in superabundance is common in the sense that it is owned by society corporately, or that it is owned by the poor corporately, or that it is owned by some specifiable poor person or persons singly. The weak sense of "common property" to which Aquinas commits himself is not, therefore, the sort of common property which is a prerequisite for governmental redistribution.'

(Havely 2004: 8–9); rather, it is first of all a matter of *will*. The poverty that is proclaimed (if not deified) as an ideal is *voluntary*. This alone separates it from the involuntary poverty which remains an ignoble calamity.

With the emergence of mendicant orders in the thirteenth century, the concept of property undergoes an unprecedented scrutiny. Between the 1279 bull *Exiit qui seminat* in which Nicholas III acknowledges that the Franciscans have abdicated every *right* of ownership while maintaining the simple *de facto use* over things and the 1322 bull *Ad conditorem canonum* in which John XXII abrogates Nicholas's decision, a theological, legal and philosophical debate raged over the nature of property and, by extension, the meaning of 'rights'. Although the debate deploys the conceptual arsenal of scholasticism and although the Franciscan claim is defended on legal grounds, it is evangelical perfection as a preparation for a new and final era that is sought. As the revised Franciscan rule of 1221 declares: 'The rule and life of the friars is to live in obedience, in chastity, and without property . . . remembering that of the whole world we must own nothing' (quoted in Pierson 2013: 99). Poverty is pursued because contemplative perfection requires the greatest simplicity. The mendicants thought of their order as instrumental in 'hastening the dawn of a new contemplative era in the life of the Church'.[27] No doubt, claims of evangelical perfection and demands of humility and subjection of the self are open to ambiguity and paradoxes. How can one *publicly* advocate humility without perjury? Thus, objection 14 in Bonaventure's (quoted in Hughes 2014: 516) *Disputed Questions on Evangelical Perfection* raises this dilemma:

> You who present humility in appearance, either you consider yourself humble or you do not. If you do, you thus attribute yourself a noble virtue, and so you are proud. If you do not, then when external habit shows you to be humble, you bear one habit in your soul and another in your appearance and so you are a hypocrite.

Bonaventure responds by arguing that the mendicants' humility is not a sign of *acquired* humility but a *desire to strive to acquire humility*. This may resolve the double-bind dilemma, but of course it leaves unanswered the further question of whether humility can ever be acquired without contradiction and, if not, whether it makes sense even to strive to acquire it.

The rule of poverty that is essential to the Franciscan identity states: 'Let the friars appropriate nothing for themselves, neither a house, nor a place, nor anything else' (Franciscan Rule, chapter 6). In terms of its concrete application, it meant that the friars renounced private and common property but were allowed to use movable and immovable goods that belonged to the Church. In the *Defense of the Mendicants* (*Apologia Pauperum*) of 1269 (that is to say, in the wake of the polemics between secular and mendicant masters at the University of Paris), Bonaventure provided a sustained justification of this claim. The starting point is the distinction of four possible relations one can have to temporal things: ownership, possession, usufruct and simple use. Since the last one is absolutely necessary to human life, it is not based on secular laws and, as such, it is unrenounceable. 'The life of mortals is possible without the first three but necessity requires the fourth, no profession may ever be made that renounces entirely the use of all kinds of temporal goods' (Bonaventure 2010: 307). More importantly, since use is simply a matter of fact, it does not require establishing a *right*.

---

[27] According to Hughes (2014: 521): 'he [Bonaventure] is quite sure that he is living in the last days; he is quite sure that Francis and Dominic and his followers have a singular and decisive role to play in this final act in the evangelical stance against avarice'.

The source of the difference between the first three cases and the last one (use) can be traced back to the will. Following the principles of Roman law, Bonaventure insists that there cannot be ownership where there is no will to own. This entails that property and ownership primarily depend on psychological and procedural conditions. The rule of poverty is thus not a matter of forsaking *things*; it is a matter of freeing oneself from *the will to possess* things. What is at stake in this debate, in Agamben's words (2013: 110), is the

> '*abdicatio omnis juris*' (abdication of every right) that is the possibility of a human existence beyond the law . . . Franciscanism can be defined – and in this consists its novelty, even today unthought, and in the present conditions of society totally unthinkable – as *the attempt to realize a human life and practice absolutely outside the determinations of the law*.

This is possible only if the basic concepts of *ius*, *dominium*, *proprietas*, *possessio* and *usus* become objects of sustained critical analysis that puts their limits to the test. What remains beyond (or below) them, untouched by the legalistic apparatus, is nothing more than mere life.

Thus, the mendicant orders were seeking a *forma vivendi* (*habitus*). Such a life does not violate the law for the simple reason that it places itself outside its jurisdiction. The legal terminology in which it is embedded tends to mask the nature of the debate. As we saw earlier, the Latin term '*dominium*' does not simply refer to ownership (*proprietas*) but also connotes power and authority. Bonaventure distinguishes *dominium* proper from *proprietas*, that is the right (*ius*) of dominion by which someone is said to own something. The third case, usufruct, seems *prima facie* less evident since usufruct is defined as a 'right of enjoyment' that allows the holder to derive some profit or benefit from a property that is owned by another or is held is common ownership. Thus, by definition, those who enjoy the benefits of usufruct do not claim to have a property right on the good (for instance, a parcel of land offered for lease) from which the usufruct is derived. However, although the beneficiaries do not own the property, they still have a *right* over the profit derived from it; the harvest from a field or the fruits from an orchard are rightly 'theirs'. For this reason, usufruct too must be abandoned. Finally, the friars also renounce money, since it is not possible to engage in commercial transactions, to handle coins and valuables, without having *dominium* over them.[28]

Even a modern labour theory of property – that is, the claim according to which property is a natural right that comes about as the result of the application of labour over natural resources – is circumvented. The assumption that in the labour process some of it, somehow, enters 'into' the object and is irremediably mixed with the material on which labour is exerted would still not be sufficient to make it 'mine'. Something else must be assumed. The fact that Bonaventure places usufruct alongside *dominium* and *proprietas* indicates that the mendicant project seeks not to renounce things, but to renounce a certain ethos towards things. In Richard of Conington's terms (quoted in Tierney 1997: 147): 'no one has dominion without desire and will'. It is this *animus acquirendi* or will to acquire that is regarded as the source of property rights, and consequently it is such a will that the

---

[28] In the event of practical necessity, the friars could make use of money (or other valuables) on reserve, but it was kept and spent on their behalf by a money-agent (*nuntius*) who operated outside the order and could receive donations (see Mäkinen 2001: 63–4).

friars must renounce (see Tierney 1997: 147). Bonaventure (2010: XI, 9, 311): insists on this point:

> Since a sum total of things, for example an inheritance, is acquired through the sole acquiescing of the will, so also nothing more is required for its rejection than a contrary intention. And just as, by means of a mere act of the will, a stranger becomes an heir, so too by means of the opposite disposition he is immediately cut off from the inheritance.

Life requires no more than a relation of 'simple use' (*simplex usus*) towards things. But what does it mean to simply 'have' something? Appealing to the authority of 1 Timothy 6:17–19,[29] Bonaventure (2010: XII, 20, 343) claims that 'he [Paul] uses the word "having" not in the sense of the power of *dominium*, but of the ability to use [*ad facultatem utendi*], as we say that we have anything we use, even though it doesn't belong to us but was provided without cost by someone else'.[30] Thus, the Franciscan rule of poverty does not deny the legitimacy of property; it does not have the revolutionary purpose of abolishing property, since it actually depends on it; instead, it simply attempts to live without it and to demonstrate this possibility through its performance. *Dominium* is placed in the hands of the Church without which the Franciscan experience would be impossible. The mendicant project does not advocate renouncing private property in order to return to a presumed original form of *common* property; it proposes – and this is its true originality – to do away with property altogether. If we imagine common property as the zero degree in relation to which private property is super-added, then the Franciscans can be understood as seeking an *infra*-property form of life.

As we saw, the argument depends on the premise that the will to own is the source of property. Bonaventure (2010: XII, 29, 353), however, does not propose to do away with the will but appeals to *another kind* of volition that can be stronger than the desire to acquire.

> A person would be unwise to prefer the compulsion of necessity to the spontaneity of the will in the works of supererogation. This is as absurd as if a person were to prefer the hanging of robbers to the suffering of martyrs, since martyrs suffer voluntarily whereas robbers suffer necessarily.

The renunciation of property is an affirmation of the will; it is a wilful renunciation of the will to acquire. The suffering it causes is self-inflicted and, in that sense, the order attempts to carry the abnegation of the martyrs in everyday life. 'Supererogation' refers to the 'counsels of perfection' (that is, those counsels that concern acts performed beyond what God requires) and therefore indicate that the vows of poverty are not meant to be a universal precept. For this reason, the Franciscan contention is not and should not be confused with a critique of property. Not all forms of private property are sinful. As Bonaventure (2010: IX, 3, 251–2) carefully

---

[29] 'As for those who in the present age are rich, command them not to be haughty, or to set their hopes on the uncertainty of riches, but rather on God who richly provides us with everything for our enjoyment. They are to do good, to be rich in good works, generous, and ready to share, thus storing up for themselves the treasure of a good foundation for the future, so that they may take hold of the life that really is life.'

[30] Vinck (Bonaventure 2010) translates *ad facultatem utendi* as 'of the opportunity to use'. Opportunities, however, depend on external conditions, situations or contexts in which the agent happens to find her-/himself. The Latin term '*facultas*' designates, on the contrary, an ability that belongs to the agent, not to her/his context. What matters is that this ability can be exercised without a will to own.

observes: 'it is certain that Clement's dictum, "because of inequity one person says that this object is his, and another says it is his" should not be taken as a universal statement but merely as one that applies in many cases'.

Yet, the argument is ambiguous. If it admits that renouncing property is not for everyone, it also intimates that those who can live without property are spiritually above those who depend on it. It is impossible to use the language of perfection and imperfection without conveying this connotation.

> Although riches, both private and common, can be possessed without sin, relinquishing them is a matter of perfection, because just as imperfection by itself is not sinful . . . so too perfection is not only the rectitude of justice but also a liberation. Since they are alluring and dangerous, riches prevent this liberation. (Bonaventure 2010: IX, 4, 252)

Thus, not only is this self-inflicted suffering liberation, but the renunciation it implies, while placing its practitioners outside the law, also perfects the law (what Bonaventure calls 'rectitude of justice').

In 1279, Pope Nicholas III in the bull *Exiit qui seminat* adopted, for the most part, Bonaventure's argument but proposed to distinguish five kinds of relations to things, making a further distinction between the right of use (*ius utendi*) and simple factual use (*simplex usus facti*), the last one constituting the only relation to temporal things that is necessary for sustenance of life (Mäkinen 2001: 96). To enjoy *ius utendi* is to use a temporal good as one's own but such a use is still the exercise of a right established by some human covenant. By contrast, simple *de facto* use is mere employment.

> By [the fact] that they [the Franciscans] seem to have abdicated the ownership, use, and *dominium* of any thing, it is not proved that they have renounced simple use of everything. That is, a use which, I say, having the name not of the *use of right*, but only *of fact*, being only factual, offers users in using only what is fact, nothing of right. (Mäkinen 2001: 97)

Nicholas's appeal to the *de facto/de jure* distinction to differentiate between two forms of use stresses that simple use occurs outside the realm of jurisdiction.

Yet, is this distinction tenable? Among the secular masters who first opposed the Franciscan argument, Gerard of Abbeville (died 1272) occupies a pre-eminent position. First, it is greed, argues Gerard, not possession, that perverts our relation to temporal things. Greed is unlimited and unsatisfied want. Appealing to Aristotle, Gerard (as well as his fellow master at the Sorbonne, William of Saint-Amour) argues that the Franciscans do not opt for the virtuous choice (which would be the proper mean between greed and poverty) but simply select one extreme (Hughes 2014: 530–1). Further, in his *Contra adversarium* Gerard (cited in Mäkinen 2001: 47) adds a central argument that focuses on the use/*dominium* distinction: in the case of consumable things, ownership cannot be separable from use.

> To say that you have only the use of them, and that the *dominium* pertains to those who have given them, until they are consumed by age, or until the food is taken into the stomach, will appear ridiculous to all, especially since among men *usus* is not distinguished from *dominium* in things that are utterly consumed by use.[31]

---

[31] The same argument appears in John XXII's *Quia Vir Reprobus* (Pierson 2013: 111–12).

The assumption that guides the objection is that we can properly 'use' something only if the substance of the thing in question retains its integrity. Whatever I use I can return or restitute. If I reside in your house or borrow your horse, use and property can clearly be distinguished. However, in consumption the thing ceases to exist (to use it is to *use* it *up*). Thus, in this instance at least, no matter how 'simple' use is, it cannot happen without the exercise of *dominium*. Even an adamant defender of the Franciscan position such as Marsilius of Padua (1956: 193) acknowledges that his claim goes against linguistic conventions since the term 'possession' commonly conveys both the incorporeal ownership and the corporeal 'handling of the thing or of its use or usufruct in the present or in the future'.

In answer, Bonaventure (2010: 310) argues that the situation is similar to the case of a son-in-power's proprietary personal fund where the son-in-power has the use without having dominion over this fund for a single instant.[32] What the son-in-power (*filius familias*) enjoys is the use of a possession that he can neither retain nor proclaim; 'rather, it is sought through the son-in-power for his father. So also in the case of these poor it should be understood that the *dominium* over the things they receive for their sustenance is delegated to the Father of the Poor, while their use is conceded to them' (idem.).

John XXII's intervention in the poverty controversy adds an important doctrinal revision to the debate. In *Quia Vir Reprobus* (a vitriolic refutation of Michael of Cesena, the Minister General of the Franciscan Order), John argues that property was *originally* private (in the sense of exclusive ownership).[33] Appealing to Genesis 1:28 ('Be fruitful and multiply, and fill the earth and subdue it; and have dominion over the fish of the sea and over the birds of the air and over every living thing that moves upon the earth'), John concludes that property was God's gift to Adam rather than the result of human fallen nature.

Ockham and Marsilius of Padua (among others) will strongly oppose this view. Ockham, in particular, leads the charge by returning to the conceptual analysis of *dominium*. In the *Work of Ninety Days* written in 1332, Ockham (William of Ockham 2001: 67) claims that, in a broad sense, *dominium* refers to 'a principle human power of laying claim to and defending some temporal things in a human court'. In a narrower sense, *dominium* (William of Ockham 2001: 70) adds the following specification: 'the [property] holder may treat it in any way not forbidden by natural law'. In either case, Ockham understands *dominium* as a right that arises from agreement and is a matter of civil law. A right allows one to litigate in court for the use of things, should this use be obstructed by someone else. This, however, is precisely what the mendicants have renounced. As for the dominion mentioned in Genesis, it is best understood as a power of use over temporal things. 'Thus it must be conceded that in the state of innocence our parents had lordship, in some sense, over temporal things, nevertheless it should not be conceded that they had ownership of temporal things' (William of Ockham 2001: 309).

Focusing on the impossibility to separate use and dominion in consumable goods, Marsilius of Padua (1956: 303), for his part, maintains that 'one who is perfect could catch a fish and eat it, but nevertheless with the express vow of never contentiously claiming the said fish (or any

---

[32] This point is borrowed from Roman law. A *peculium* is a sum of money given by the *paterfamilias* to a son (or a slave) for their own use, usually in the context of a commercial transaction. Any obligation (right, duty or debt) arising from the use of the *peculium* is directly acquired by the *paterfamilias*. See Evan-Jones and MacCormack (1998: 171).

[33] Available at <http://www.mq.edu.au/about_us/faculties_and_departments/faculty_of_arts/mhpir/staff/staff-politics_and_international_relations/john_kilcullen/john_xxii_quia_vir_reprobus/> (last accessed 12 June 2017).

temporal thing) in the presence of a coercive judge', thus stressing that where there is no legal claim there cannot be ownership. Finally, Wyclif argues that the crucial act in God's dominion is one of *lending*, so that men can only have a temporary share of whatever is on loan. In other words, human dominium over the world is, as it were, borrowed (see Lahey 2003: 97–9).

Conclusion

These examples suffice to demonstrate that the dispute between the defenders of *paupertas altissima* and their opponents concerns the limit of the law. Gerard and John XXII find a contradiction in the idea of a *right to use* that would exclude ownership and this may well be the case; yet, what the Franciscans were seeking was something else, it was *use without right*. Thus, Gerard's arguments appeal to civil law, where property is attached to usufruct, while Bonaventure (2010: 11.7), on the contrary, places poverty as a practice beyond the law:

> If perchance someone tries to oppose our reasoning by claiming that there is a warning in civil law that use cannot be separated perpetually from dominion, we will answer that this principle of civil law has no application here, since the law pronounces such a decree lest dominion becomes useless, and hence be nothing but an empty word.

One of John's most trenchant objections consists in arguing that use without a right to use cannot belong to a state of perfection since it is to act unjustly. This objection goes to the heart of the issue, for, if John is right, it follows that nothing can occur outside the juridical sphere. Every act whatsoever is either just or unjust – it may be so in varying degrees, but it cannot be extra-juridical. In response, the mendicants argue that simple use is *licit* although it is not *legal*. This is why Ockham appeals to a 'licit power' that is acquired by a mere revocable permission or grace and as such is not a right (see Van Duffel and Robinson 2010: 14–15). If a rich man invites poor people and places food and drinks before them, the poor have the *licit power* to eat and drink, but they have not for that reason acquired a *right* since the host could, if he pleases, take the food away and the guest could not appeal to any right. 'When the permission obtained cannot be revoked at will, a right is acquired; but when it can be revoked at will and the one having permission cannot by virtue of the permission litigate in court, no right is acquired' (William of Ockham 2001: 433). Only a permission that cannot be revoked constitutes a right; short of this, there is no right.

The question, as Agamben (2013: 144) puts it, is: 'how can use – that is, a relation to the world *insofar as it is inappropriable* – be translated into an ethos and a form of life?' Even nature depends on grace in order to exist and persist, and although the mendicant renunciation does not entail disdain for temporal goods and the natural world, it is a precarious existence that requires a blind trust in providence. By renouncing dominion and the right to earthly goods, the mendicants find themselves entirely sustained by what is not their own. What the opponents of the Franciscan experience were most worried about is thus the possibility of a form of life that is nothing more than this: life pure and simple, life beyond the law. Peter John Olivi (Flood 1972: 119), among others, stresses how the *rule* (by contrast with the *law*) requires to be lived:

> it makes more sense to say 'living in obedience' than to say 'observing obedience' or 'obeying': one says, in fact, that someone lives in a certain state or in a certain work only if his whole life has been applied to it, in which case he is rightly said to be and live and dwell in it.

Such a rule does not dictate the acts of a subject; rather, it constitutes the agent her-/himself. It does not establish common property but creates a cenoby (a '*koinos bios*', a life that is both unique and common). The rule does not apply *to* life the way a universal precept applies to a particular case; instead, it produces a form of life and produces itself in it.[34] Rules of this kind (by contrast with deontic or governing ones), function as 'constitutive norms'; they institute what they command. Use designates, then, a space outside the law, a void that the law can neither institute nor govern. Insofar as use entails a temporal process, insofar as it is a *habitus*, it cannot be appropriated.

To relate to the world as something that is essentially inappropriable is to seek a form of life that is prior to the order of the law and that the law (despite all its coercive power) cannot erase. In this condition, the self is not constituted by an act of appropriation but by its activity of dwelling. Centuries after the medieval debate, the possibility of such a relation to the world remains to be discovered.

References

Agamben, Giorgio (2013). *Highest Poverty, Monastic Rules and Forms-of-Life*. Stanford: Stanford University Press.
Anonynmous (2002). '*De divitiis* (On Riches)'. In *Radical Christian Writings*. Ed. A. Bradstock and C. Rowland. Oxford: Blackwell.
Aquinas, Thomas. *Summa Theologiae*, I, q. 96, a. 2. Available at <http://www.newadvent.org/summa/1096.htm#article2> (last accessed 12 June 2017).
Aristotle. *Politics* Book II, chapter 5, author's translation.
Augustine (1951). *Commentary on the Lord's Sermon on the Mount*. Trans. D. Kavanaugh. New York: Fathers of the Church, Vol. 11.
Augustine (1953). *Letters*, Vol. III (131–164). Trans. W. Parsons. Washington, DC: Catholic University of America Press.
Augustine (1985). *On Free Choice of the Will*. Trans. Anna Benjamin and L. Hackstaff. New York: Macmillan.
Augustine (1994). *Tractates on John VI*, 25. In *Augustine: Political Writings*. Ed. E. Fortin and D. Kries. Trans. M. Tkacz and D. Kries. Indianapolis: Hackett Publishing.
Augustine (2003). *City of God, Against the Pagans* (XV, 17). Trans. Henry Bettenson. London: Penguin Random House.
Birks, Peter (1985). 'The Roman Law Concept of Dominium and the idea of Absolute Ownership'. *Acta Juridica*, 1: 1–37.
Bonaventure (2010). *Defense of the Mendicants* (Works of Bonaventure, Vol. 15). Trans. José de Vinck and Robert J. Karris. Saint Bonaventure, NY: Franciscan Institute Publications.
Chroust, Anton H. and Robert J. Affeldt (1950–1). 'The Problem of Private Property According to St. Thomas Aquinas'. *Marquette Law Review*, 34: 3.
Coleman, Janet (1983). 'Medieval Discussions of Property'. *History of Political Thought*, 4: 2.
Diogenes Laertius (1925). *Lives of Eminent Philosophers*, Vol. II, Book 7. 85. LOEB Classical Library. Trans. R. D. Hicks. Cambridge, MA: Harvard University Press.
Dougherty, Richard J. (2003). 'Catholicism and the Economy: Augustine and Aquinas on Property Ownership'. *Journal of Markets and Morality*, 6: 2.
Epicurus (1994). *Vatican Sayings* 68. In *The Epicurus Reader*. Trans. Lloyd P. Gerson and Brad Inwood. Indianapolis: Hackett Publishing.

---

[34] It has been noted that Francis and his followers frequently use the phrase '*regula et vita*' in the sense of one single phenomenon or that they use '*vita*' in sentences where one would expect '*regula*': for instance, 'If anyone desiring to accept this life . . .' (Agamben 2013: 100).

Evan-Jones, Robin and Geoffrey MacCormack (1998). 'Obligations'. In *A Companion to Justinian's Institutes*. Ed. Ernest Metzger. Ithaca: Cornell University Press.
'*Expedit enim rei publicae nequis re sua male utatur*'. *Institutes* 1.8.2. Latin text. Available at <http://www.thelatinlibrary.com/justinian/institutes1.shtml#i:viii> (last accessed 12 June 2017).
Flood, David (ed. and trans.) (1972). *Olivi's Rule Commentary*. Wiesbaden: Steiner.
Franciscan Rule of 1223 chapter 6. Available at <https://www.ewtn.com/library/PRIESTS/OFM1223.TXT> (last accessed 23 February 2019).
Ganz, David (1995). 'The Ideology of Sharing: Apostolic Community and Ecclesiastical Property in the Early Middle Ages'. In *Property and Power in the Early Middle Ages*. Ed. Wendy Davies and Paul Fouracle. Cambridge: Cambridge University Press, pp. 17–30.
Gordon, Barry (1975). *Economic Analysis before Adam Smith*. New York: Macmillan.
Grey, Thomas (1980). 'The Disintegration of Property'. In *Nomos XXII: Property*. Ed. J. Roland Pennock and J. Chapman. New York: New York University Press.
Havely, Nick (2004). *Dante and the Franciscans*. Cambridge: Cambridge University Press.
Holy Bible (1997). New Revised Standard Version. Philadelphia: American Bible Society.
Hughes, Kevin (2014). 'Bonaventure's Defense of Mendicancy'. In *A Companion to Bonaventure*. Ed. Jay Hammond, J. A. Wayne-Hellmann and Jarred Goff. Leiden: Brill.
Lahey, S. E. (2003). *Philosophy and Politics in the Thought of John Wyclif*. Cambridge: Cambridge University Press.
McGovern, John F. (1972). 'The Rise of New Economic Attitudes in Canon and Civil Law, AD 1200–1550'. *The Jurist*, 32: 39–50.
Mäkinen, Virpi (2001). *Property Rights in the Late Medieval Discussion on Franciscan Poverty*. Leuven: Peeters.
Marsilius of Padua (1956). *The Defender of the Peace (Defensor Pacis)*. Trans. A. Gewirth. New York: Harper.
Morris, J. (1965). 'Pelagian Literature'. *Journal of Theological Studies*, 26/1: 26–60.
Moynes, J. B. (trans.) (1906). *The Institute of Justinian*, 4th edn. Oxford: Clarendon Press.
Pierson, Christopher (2013). *Just Property, A History in the Latin West, Vol. 1: Wealth, Virtue, and the Law*. Oxford: Oxford University Press.
Plato. *Republic*, author's translation.
Radin, Max (1925). 'Fundamental Concepts of the Roman Law'. *California Law Review*, 13: 3.
Seneca (1920). *Moral Epistles*, Vol. II. Trans. R. M. Gummere. LOEB Classical Library. Cambridge, MA: Harvard University Press.
Tertullian (1987). *De idolatria, Critical Text, Translation, and Commentary*. By J. H. Waszink and J. C. M. van Winden. Leiden: Brill.
Tierney, Brian (1997). *The Idea of Natural Rights, Studies on Natural Rights, Natural Laws and Church Laws 1150–1625*. Grand Rapids: Eerdmans Publishing.
Van Duffel, Siegfried and Jonathan Robinson (2010). *Ockham's Theory of Natural Rights*. Available at <http://individual.utoronto.ca/jwrobinson/articles/vanduffel-robinson_ockhams-theory-of-natural-rights.pdf> (last accessed 12 June 2017).
Watson, Alan (1968). *The Law of Property in the Later Roman Republic*. Oxford: Oxford University Press.
Watson, Alan (ed. and trans.) (2009). *The Digest of Justinian*, Vol. IV. Philadelphia: University of Pennsylvania Press.
Weithman, Paul (1993). 'Natural Law, Property, and Redistribution'. *The Journal of Religious Ethics*, 21: 1.
William of Ockham (2001). *The Work of Ninety Days*, Vol. I. Trans. J. Kilcullen and J. Scott. Lampeter: Edwin Mellen Press.
Worden, Skip (2010). *Godliness and Greed: Shifting Christian Thought on Profit and Wealth*. Lanham, MD: Lexington Books.

14

Humanity, Nature, Science and Politics in Renaissance Utopias

Georgios Steiris

During the European Renaissance, scholars and members of the *bourgeoisie* showed a strong interest in practical philosophy, namely ethics and politics. This shift was expressed in works that described ideal societies, also known as utopias. Meanwhile, the Renaissance philosophy of nature, influenced by Late Ancient philosophy and mysticism, imposed a new worldview, according to which nature was seen as a living entity. Renaissance political thinkers attempted to imbue their socio-political visions with a sense of natural philosophy. A principal idea in utopian literature is the strong presence of science, a key factor in the transformation of nature. In its search for the ideal political order, humanity was not content with maximising nature's benefits but envisioned creating a new nature, one that better served the socio-political ideals of the Renaissance and the early modern era. I would like to argue that the prominent role of technocracy in sixteenth- and seventeenth-century utopias led gradually to the disruption and perversion of nature. Despite of the intentions of the utopian thinkers, their views on nature – which range from the unconditional respect to nature to its advancement through science – encouraged finally the mastery of nature, because they connected the socio-political progress with the exploitation of nature and the control of natural forces.

In particular, a discussion on the relationship between humanity, nature and science in Renaissance utopian thought can shed some light on how early technocracy progressively led to the ravaging of nature. Departing from the major Renaissance philosophers' all-encompassing perspective, political philosophers of the time, especially those who contributed to utopian literature, predominantly viewed nature as an instrument at the disposal of humanity and its science – a playground for human inventiveness and resourcefulness. With their works, they provided a new rationale, non-religious this time that defended humanity's full exploitation of nature (for an earlier, less detailed, discussion of the thematic, see Steiris 2012: 181–94).

Renaissance Philosophy of Nature as an Inspiration for Political Thinkers

During the Renaissance, philosophy in Europe changed course, along with the conception of nature. Several philosophers, who turned to new sources and interpretations, challenged the widely popular Aristotelian view of nature. Aristotle and his medieval commentators had set the conceptual apparatus for the examination of core issues, like causation, motion, place, time, generation and perishing. Their main concern was the understanding and interpretation of nature. As a result, hylomorphism and teleology were the dominant concepts of medieval natural philosophy. In Aristotelian physics there is little or no room for evolution and improvement in nature. During the Renaissance, despite the centrality of the Aristotelian paradigm, philosophy of nature was enriched by further approaches. New translations appeared and scholars had the opportunity to read Aristotelian natural philosophy through the lenses of Neoplatonism. Moreover, the revival of Stoicism and Epicureanism offered alternative natural philosophies and opened new paths to the study of nature (see Freeland 1987: 392–407; Blair 1992: 541–51; Copenhaver 1992: 387–407; Joy 1992: 573–83; Stavrineas 2015: 46–65). As a result, sixteenth-century philosophers aimed towards the transformation and amelioration of nature.

Under Petrarch's influence, a new-found worship of nature emerges, not only as a religious but also as an aesthetic concept. Philosophers of the Renaissance were not content only with observing and comprehending the world; they were looking for ways to exploit nature and even transform it for humanity's benefit. This stance towards nature would be adopted by non-scholastic philosophers of the time due to their broader worldview. Under the influence of Stoicism, Neoplatonism and the Christian philosophy of Pseudo-Dionysus the Areopagite, the universe was perceived as a single, large, living entity, whose soul permeates all things and breathes life into them. Just as in the human body the organs function and affect one another, living creatures of the universe affect one another too. The idea that things share similarities was widely accepted in the Middle Ages too; however, these common traits were only exterior ones. But Renaissance philosophers, fascinated by the microcosm-macrocosm analogy, delve into astrology and magic, which they see as instruments for achieving their goals. Going beyond ancient Greek and Roman philosophy and science, inquisitive minds of the time are haunted by the quest for the *prisca theologia*, pure, primeval and complete knowledge. The new study of nature aimed to restore the knowledge God once bestowed to humanity, but that traditional, established philosophy perverted and plunged into obscurity. The pursuit of the occult, especially alchemy and magic, also encouraged a shift towards experience, observation and early laboratory experimentation. Philosophy, science and mysticism are inevitably interlinked, or the spirit of this age would be inevitably perverted (see Debus 1978: 16–53; Ingegno 1988: 236–63; Copenhaver and Schmitt 1992: 288–9; Zambelli 2007: 13–34; Harman 2013: 6–10).

Unsurprisingly, under these influences, nature was conceived as a living entity. All metals were believed to be products of astral insemination, coming from processes similar to those that result in the creation of a human foetus. Air was naturally associated with *spiritus mundi*. The study of nature and its secrets also had practical applications, as it was tied to medicine. The closer observation of the animal and plant worlds led to the discovery and classification of thousands of species, which were either unknown or overlooked in the Middle Ages (see Debus 1978: 34–73; Hirai 2011: 1–7). Humanity realised that the available knowledge on nature was not sufficient and a vibrant research field was waiting to be conquered. This conviction was reinforced by the then recent overseas discoveries that introduced Europeans to aspects of nature they had previously overlooked. The feeling that the world was different and that it could become even more different, led numerous thinkers to author detailed descriptions of their visions of new worlds in utopian narratives.

Utopianism is not a phenomenon of the sixteenth century. In many ancient cultures and religions there are narratives about ideal societies, where humanity flourishes. Even Genesis would be read as a utopian story. Moreover, Hesiod, Plato, Plutarch, Tao Yuanming and Augustine, among others, composed utopian works so as to persuade people that a better society was achievable (see Sargent 2010: 10–32, 66–101). It is worth noting that in the utopias before the sixteenth century there were no references to science as a socio-political tool. Even in the cases where the inhabitants of the utopian societies were uncivilised savages, in a stage of primitive innocence, science was not perceived as a cornerstone of evolution. Citizens enjoyed the beneficial outcomes of science, which was sometimes the gods' gift and not humanity's achievement. Although magic and alchemy were well known, the authors of utopias did not encompass occult arts in their socio-political vision. People in antiquity and the Middle Ages did not hold occult arts in high regard. Furthermore, science was equated to crafts. Consequently, political thinkers did not regard them as factors of socio-political evolution (see Classen 2017: 1–108).

Nature and Politics

In the sixteenth century, Thomas More (1478–1535) boldly reinstates the concept of the ideal society in the philosophical and political stage. Although his work is interpreted in multiple ways, it certainly paved the way for several similar works in which scholars present ideal societies (see More 1999: 43–8; and also Goldie 1983: 727–46; Vieira 1996: 3–27; Houston 2016: 15–40). However, all human societies work with assumptions of a nexus of relationships, not only among humans but also between humanity and nature. These get further complicated with the introduction of the factor of science, which will play an increasingly important role in the relationship nexus within each ideal society. Although the use of the word science before the nineteenth century is an anachronism, empirical investigation of the natural world and scientific method were employed in the sixteenth century. In addition, early modern science was characterised by its focus on biological sciences and chemistry. Far from advocating the superiority of science, More does not attack the philosophy of nature but sees it as humanity's duty towards God, in order to achieve social progress (see More 1999: 75, 87–8; and Adams 1949: 377).

In *De optimo rei publicae statu deque nova insula Utopia* (1516), More paints a rather bleak picture of the state of the animal and plant kingdoms in England, aiming to highlight the need for a comprehensive reform that would save it from its wretched socio-political condition. Starting with a description of the avaricious, rapacious attitude of noblemen and some church officials, More criticises the uncontrolled increase of pasture, which had led to the decrease of crop production, because crop growing grounds were used as grazing grounds. Focusing on the trade of wool rather than the trade of agricultural products led to a food shortage. Human intervention in nature, according to More, brings imbalance in the environment and is responsible for several socio-political issues (see More 1999: 21–6; and Baker-Smith 2000: 107–8; Wilde 2016: 56). More's criticism inspired many subsequent polemics against private property, Marx included, which found footing in his points (see Balasopoulos 2006: 136–8). However, More does not condemn human intervention in nature; he only attacks practices that put profit over life and nature, which creates a political and moral problem. More's counter proposal, put into Hythlodaeus's mouth, is the balanced development of farming and stockbreeding (see Flesher 1973: 47). But the emergence of protoscience, rather than serving the alchemical ideal of promoting and facilitating nature's own work,[1] corrupts nature's ways. A fascinated More describes the hatching of spring chickens with the use of heat, so when they break out they follow around the people who feed them, not other chickens (see More 1999: 51–2; and Healy 2011: 26, 38). More was clearly not as fervent an advocate of science as his subsequent fellow authors. In our time he is considered the forefather of modern science fiction.

---

[1] According to the majority of the Renaissance alchemists, nature has hidden fixed causes. Nature aspires to its perfection. The alchemist's duty was to reveal these causes, to understand the physical procedures, and to facilitate and promote them, in other words, to expedite nature in order to let humans enjoy its perfection.

However, More's conception of nature remains strictly conservative. Humanity has absolute dominion over nature, which may be used as humanity sees fit in securing its survival, which necessarily requires self-sufficiency, even from an Aristotelean perspective, although More's work has been labelled as Platonising (see Weisgerber 1940: 14–75; White 1976: 641–2; Olin 1989: 20–5; Starnes 1990: 9–10, 91–3; Boesky 1996: 47–9). At the same time, More proposes that humanity's goal is to live by nature, which is inseparable from the pursuit of pleasure. The pleasure derived from living in harmony with nature is what constitutes a virtuous life. Maximising pleasure becomes the motivation of a moral life (see More 1999: 76–9; and Wegemer 1996: 135). More, much like his close friend, Desiderius Erasmus, was obviously influenced by Stoic philosophy, which was revived in the Renaissance, although some scholars have attempted to draw connections with an Epicurean-inspired hedonism (see Nichols 1976: 181–5; Engeman 1982: 142; Marius 1999: 174–5), or with Platonic and Aristotelian moral philosophy (see White 1976: 651; Logan 2014: 169–71). Nevertheless, for More, nature assumes proportions that unmistakably resemble its Platonic notion, as even virtue, in Utopia, is defined as an arrangement of elements that accord with nature (see Nelson 2001: 895).

Indicative of More's conservative approach is the contention that only slaves should be allowed to slaughter animals, so that free citizens can maintain their natural, noble instincts. He is not interested in the practice itself, only in its impact on the morality of citizens who have a broader socio-political role (see More 1999: 64, 76–7; and Shannon 2013: 23). While slaughtering and skinning animals for the purpose of eating are not criticised by More, the practices of animal hunting are condemned. More sharply criticises anyone who seeks and finds pleasure in the agony and bloodshed of animals, claiming that in Utopia hunting is an activity reserved for slaves. Only beasts draw pleasure from hunting (see More 1999: 80–1; and Gaffney 1998: 109–10; Wolloch 2006: 70–4; Raber 2013: 177–8; Wilde 2016: 79–80). Furthermore, More (1999: 118) posits that animal sacrifice is forbidden in Utopia as it is unthinkable for a merciful God to take pleasure in the offering of blood or to condone the slaughtering of His creatures. Erasmus held similar views on this and was unable to perceive what kind of pleasure anyone could draw by the slaughtering of animals (see Spencer 1995: 185–6; Preece 2008: 154; Yoran 2010: 159–85). More's attitude is clearly a philosophical one, influenced by the study of the classics and Renaissance humanism.

According to More, nature is a caring, indulgent mother, offering an abundance of gifts to her children for the delight of the senses. However, it cannot ensure the self-sufficiency of utopians, who do not resort to science but engage in trade to cover their needs (see More 1999: 69; and Shephard 1995: 845–6). In fact, only humanity has the capacity to enjoy nature's gifts, as only humanity can have a higher nature. Therefore, disregarding or rejecting the natural gifts in the name of so-called virtues or higher purposes is ingratitude towards nature. More (1999: 84–5, 111) describes the epitome of living according to nature as practical philosophy. Science, as the study of nature, for utopians is a way of paying gratitude to God, and God loves and accepts humanity's enquiries, as they are the only creatures capable of contemplating His work. Moreover, science, according to More (1999: 87–8), not only has a practical dimension but also offers pleasure to its practitioners. More's choice to create this contrast between Utopia and his contemporary Europe is an obvious way to make a case for the need to promote a politics of natural science and reason – in other words, he makes a plea for new politics (see Adams 1949: 374–98).

Another interesting part of More's work is his stance regarding animals' souls. Utopians reject any opinion that questions the afterlife of the human soul, as that would degrade its noble nature to the level of the beasts. On the other hand, More admits that some thinkers have reasonably claimed that animals' souls, although inferior to those of humans, are also immortal and eternal. However, they are not capable of achieving the highest degree of happiness (see More 1999: 109–11). More's claims are in direct contradiction to the traditional Christian dogma, as expressed in Aristotelian Thomism, according to which animals' souls cannot be immortal (see Aquinas 1888–9: 1, q. 75, a. 3; Sorabji 1993: 201; Badham 1998: 181–9; Hall 2011: 70). Although More's exact sources are disputed, he seems inspired by ancient Greek and Latin sources, as well as by the Neoplatonists Plotinus, Iamblichus, Damascius, Numenius the Neopythagorean, Plutarch, Arnobius of Sicca, and Lactantius. These authors addressed the same issue but their stance towards it remained unclear (see Sorabji 1993: 201–3).

Another important work within the utopian tradition is *La città felice* (1553) by Francesco Patrizi (1529–97), although it is not fully aligned with most works of literature, lacking the usual description of a fictional city or community, it stands as a philosophical exercise, where the notion of history is removed from its narrative 'for the sake of the truth of the theory itself' (Blum 2000: 72). Patrizi claims that the land alone cannot provide humanity with everything needed for its survival. Therefore, it is humanity's resourcefulness, in other words science and human labour, that allows us to unlock and exploit nature's hidden, untapped potential (see Patrizi 1553: IV; Castelli 2002: 3–30; Hough 2002: 31–47). In Patrizi's work, there is no detailed description of nature and its creatures, nor of their relationship with humanity, as in other utopian works. However, overall Patrizi maintains that humanity needs to carefully consider natural priorities and qualities, as well as nature's riches, to achieve prosperity. It is important for humanity to be in harmony with nature, for instance in the case of the selection of a suitable place for building a city.

Science in Utopias

Reipublicae christianopolitanae descriptio (1619) by Johannes Valentinus Andreae (1586–1654) is a typical work in the utopian tradition. The author was familiar not only with Francis Bacon's but also with Campanella's broader work, which has led many scholars to investigate the similarities in their utopian texts (see Held 1914: 16–40; Dickson 1996: 777). The ideal community is again located on an island. The author is impressed by how efficiently every bit of land in Christianopolis is used, either for farming or for any other activity that brings a practical benefit to the community – of course, with the aid of science (see Andreae 1999: 156). This island essentially serves as a model of the entire world, another Noah's ark, where all known animal and plant species could be found. The study of nature is crucial, as humanity has a duty to unlock nature's mysteries and use them for its benefit. Plants and animals are studied and experimented on in special laboratories. In fact, Andreae (1999: 209–10) criticises whoever refused to practice research or condemned scientists. Plants and their substances' properties are studied, and animals are dissected in dedicated laboratories – experimentation on animals is not considered cruel or inhumane but a contribution to knowledge (see Andreae 1999: 210–13; and Manuel and Manuel 1979: 304). Nature's gifts have been given to humanity to be used towards its happiness. For these wonders of creation, humanity owes gratitude to God (see Andreae 1999: 240). In Christianopolis, chemistry has a principal role, as the branch of science used for the comprehensive study of nature and the betterment of human life, the transformation of human life (see Pepper 1996: 206). Olson (1983: 278) aptly supports that in

> *Christianopolis* one can see the modern scientific vision – the 'better living through chemistry' mentality – being born out of the merger of humanistic emphases on service to mankind, the mathematicization of Renaissance art and architecture, the dreams of Paracelsan alchemists, and the substance (but not necessarily the spirit) of classical natural philosophy, mathematics and astronomy.

But the most important theme in Christianopolis is that science is not separated from society, as in Bacon's work, but is integrated in society and is widely available. It does not reside in a closed, secluded laboratory; it stands at the heart of the city (see Bierman 1963: 496–7; Dickson 1996: 780). In Christianopolis, science becomes a *de facto* socio-political institution.

Similarly disposed towards science, Tommaso Campanella (1568–1639) authored *La Città del Sole* (1602), one of the most popular utopian texts. The City of the Sun is located again on an island, Taprovane, probably on modern Sri Lanka. The city's circular design with its seven concentric walls stands as proof of the prominence given to natural science, as natural law also governs public and private life (Ernst 2010a: 95–104). The entirety of human knowledge is depicted on the interior and the exterior of each wall; specifically, between the second and the fifth circuit of the city each wall is adorned with illustrations and samples of rocks, minerals, liquids, as well as information on lakes, seas, geographical formations, weather conditions, herbs and plants and their properties, as well as birds and animals – everything is on display and all citizens learn by walking around all their life, experiencing an ongoing natural education (see Campanella 1995: 24–5, 27–9). It is noteworthy that in the City of the Sun, no new knowledge is produced. Research activity, as presented in Bacon's and Andreae's works, is nowhere to be found – although not known how, all knowledge has been conquered and the only remaining goal is to use it for the good of the commonwealth. I would suppose that, under the influence of Hermeticism, they accepted the view that an almighty God transferred all knowledge to humanity in the beginning of this world and the duty of a selected elite was the preservation of this body of knowledge. The walls are not meant to be expanded with illustrations of new discoveries or newly explored knowledge (see Bierman 1963: 495–6). At the very centre of the circular City of the Sun stands the temple, its most important building. Placing the temple at the end of the natural path of human knowledge suggests the natural conclusion and the fulfilment of natural philosophy in Campanella's design: the city is not open to the outside, to new knowledge, but its citizens are drawn inwards – from the material world, to the pure intellect – towards the temple and metaphysics (see Reiss 1973: 87–9).

Conversely to More, Campanella (1995: 38, 43–4) accepts the value and usefulness of animal hunting, which keeps the citizens prepared for emergencies. Yet the explanation provided by Campanella about the citizens' attitude towards hunting is quite interesting. In the early years of the City, people avoided hunting, because killing animals seemed cruel. However, later on, destroying herbs also seemed cruel to them, because plants have feelings too. As they were at risk of perishing from hunger, they decided it was justifiable to kill animals for their meat, with the argument that humble creatures were born to help sustain the omnivorous, nobler ones. Nevertheless, their worldview makes them unwilling to slaughter useful animals, such as horses and oxen. For the benefit of their health, Solarians follow a moderate diet alternating flesh and fish to ensure the natural balance and preserve natural resources (see Campanella 1995: 45). Respect for animals prevents them from using them even for sacrifices, as they do not use unwilling creatures for this purpose. Instead, Solarians prefer sacrificing humans who volunteer for the highest offering to God; although the selected ones endure much suffering, they do not die in the end (see Campanella 1995: 49–50). Campanella holds animals in high regard and elsewhere praises their skills (see Ernst 2010a: 263–5).

Regarding the land, and specifically agriculture and the collection of the fruits of the earth, Solarians rely on ancestral knowledge, surviving in books. For the prosperity of the plant and animal species under their care the stars play a crucial role, and farmers seriously consider astrology. However, farming in the City of the Sun is based on science, more than it is in previous utopian societies (see Campanella 1995: 42–4; and Thorndike 1958: 293; Camporesi 1988: 275; Pohl 2010: 58–9). Near the end of Campanella's work there is a reference of particular importance, which describes the world as a large animal and humanity living within it like worms, under God's sovereign rule (see Campanella 2011: 123, 195). In this metaphor, humanity is relegated from its traditional, privileged place in creation and reaches the level of the animal; nevertheless, Campanella does not attach a negative connotation to this, as, in the Renaissance philosopher's worldview, the universal soul pervades all creatures.

Francis Bacon's perspective (1561–1626) is rather different. In his work *Nova Atlantis* (1624), science clearly has the principal role (see Rossi 1996: 25–46). His ideal society is again located on an island, Bensalem. The new science is in urgent need of a new world, as the old one is unable to support it (see Albanese 1990: 506). On this island, there is Solomon's House, a prototypical research centre, whose mission is 'the knowledge of causes and the secret motions of things; and the enlarging of the bounds of Human Empire, to the effecting of all things possible' (Bacon 1999: 177). It is noteworthy that this type of institution did not exist in Bacon's time (see Zilsel 1945: 345). According to Bacon, nature not only offers resources and means of prosperity but also it is a field of expression for human inventiveness. Humanity is encouraged to produce imitations of natural minerals and create new metals by using natural resources. Humanity also uses nature's forces combined with engines and instruments in order to multiply or interact with them, and even produce new animal and plant species (see Bacon 1999: 177–85; McCullough et al. 2008: 155–7). Everything taking place inside Solomon's House does not just advance nature while expressing the alchemical ideal but, in many cases, causes a rupture of the existing natural order. Nature becomes merely another instrument in humanity's hands for creating power through knowledge. Some scholars have claimed that Bacon's ideal is the restoration of nature to its perfect pre-lapsarian state through the help of science (see LaFreniere 2008: 140–1). But as this work leaves no room for religious interpretation and the pre-lapsarian nature is nowhere praised, it follows that Bacon is probably envisioning a new, completely different nature. Bacon's vision was a complete overhaul of society, an *instauratio magna*, which was also the title of his last, unfinished work. Prerequisite of this major reform was the correct and unprejudiced interpretation of nature. The lack of any mention of education in *Nova Atlantis* raises questions about how the knowledge produced in Solomon's House would be used and how the institution's new personnel would be recruited (see Prior 1954: 368–9; Bierman 1963: 499). Conversely, in other utopian societies, the educational system is an essential pillar. Indicative of the novel, predatory attitude advocated by Bacon is the portrayal of nature as female, which human inventiveness is meant to dominate and violate (see Aughterson 2002: 156–79; Gimelli 2005: 69–88; Schönpflug 2008: 43–4). Human intervention in nature has a dominating, violent character: humanity and science 'impregnate' it, which results in the creation of a new nature. As *Nova Atlantis* is a work of Bacon's maturity, we could say it represents the epitome of his scientific thought (see Dickinson-Blodgett 1931: 763–4).

As a last addition in this utopian literature review, we could also include *The Isle of Pines* (1668) by Henry Neville (1620–1694). Although this work was not written during the Renaissance and it lacks the depth of the previously discussed utopias, it obviously emerges from the same tradition. In *The Isle of Pines*, there is no single hint at some form of scientific development or of human intervention in nature. The islanders, descendants of an Englishman, George Pine, live in almost primitive conditions. Despite their civilised origins, the island conditions led the inhabitants to a way of living that shows nature's negative impact on human behaviour, as it leads to injustice and moral degeneration. The theme of the 'noble savage', although popular during the Enlightenment, has no place in this work (see Neville 1999: 190–212; Sim and Walker 2003: 87–96).

Conclusions

As expected, seminal works of political philosophy would inevitably touch on the topic of organic and inorganic nature. Nature has a crucial political function and cannot be cast aside. The utopian literature reflects Renaissance humanism, and the frequent references to animal rights do not derive from a personal worldview or religious sensibility but are proof of a humanist spirit, which commanded dignity as a natural virtue. Meanwhile, humanity is not just part of nature. Throughout the utopian literature, with only few exceptions, the general idea is that humanity has the right to exploit nature. The new factor is the alchemical ideal, which claims its place in natural research, albeit not as a mere expectation but as a scientific ideal. Humanity has the capacity and the duty to transform and advance nature, even by creating new species. This research is conducted in laboratories, like Solomon's House, with the invaluable aid of chemistry, which during the seventeenth century will become the principle science that drives civilisation's progress. Humanity does not settle for merely admiring nature but seeks to explore and exploit its secrets. The relationship between humanity and nature (universe), seen as a counterpart of the paired concept of microcosm-macrocosm in the Renaissance, is present in Campanella's work but is missing from other utopian works. Andreae's, and most importantly Bacon's, vision of uncontrollable scientific intervention, with the aim to advance nature through its transformation, would define human society ever since. Humanity, unshackled from any lingering inhibitions – philosophical, moral or religious – assaults nature, not just to exploit it, but aiming to transform it, create another nature and perhaps a new humanity. Renaissance utopian literature bequeathed to the modern era the belief in perpetual progress. Contrary to Darwin's views about the evolution of natural species, utopian authors proposed that humanity is able to transcend any natural limit and create a new order so as to serve its goals: longevity, eternal youth and prosperity. Bacon envisioned the homo-deus, who will succeed the homo-faber: a new stage in the evolution of humans, a creature who would be able to change his nature and create his own universe. Consequently, politics was no longer a matter of distributing power and governing people. In the new, utopian, era of humanity, politics will serve science and the basic role of politicians will be the distribution of knowledge and wealth among people. Besides the devastation of nature, utopian visions contributed to modern political dystopias. In most of them people do not have the right to shape the future of their political societies. Scientists take all the strategic decisions and people are obliged to follow so as to safeguard a luxurious life. In addition, sex and birth control in the utopian texts – predominantly Campanella's – signify another dystopic aspect of early modern utopias.

References

Adams, R. (1949). 'The Social Responsibilities of Science in Utopia, New Atlantis and after'. *Journal of the History of Ideas*, 10/3: 374–98.
Andreae, J. V. (1999). *Christianopolis*. Dordrecht: Kluwer.
Albanese, D. (1990). 'The New Atlantis and the Uses of Utopia'. *ELH*, 57/3: 503–28.
Aquinas, T. (1888–9). *Opera omnia iussu impensaque Leonis XIII P. M. edita, t. 4-5: Pars prima Summae theologiae*. Romae: Ex Typographia Polyglotta S. C. de Propaganda Fide.
Aughterson, K. (2002). '"Strange thing so probably told": Gender, Sexual Difference and Knowledge in Bacon's New Atlantis'. In *Francis Bacon's New Atlantis: New Interdisciplinary Essays*. Ed. B. Price. Manchester: Manchester University Press, pp. 156–79.
Bacon, F. (1999). 'New Atlantis'. In *Three Early Modern Utopias: Utopia, New Atlantis, The Isle of Pines*. Ed. S. Bruce. Oxford: Oxford University Press, pp. 149–86.

Badham, P. (1998). 'Do Animals Have Immortal Souls?' In *Animals on the Agenda: Questions about Animals for Theology and Ethics*. Ed. A Lizney and D. Yamamoto. London: Illini Books, pp. 181–9.

Baker-Smith, D. (2000). *More's Utopia*. Toronto: University of Toronto Press.

Balasopoulos, A. (2006). '"Suffer a Sea Change": Spatial Crisis, Maritime Modernity, and the Politics of Utopia'. *Cultural Critique*, 63: 122–56.

Bierman, J. (1963). 'Science and Society in the New Atlantis and Other Renaissance Utopias'. *PMLA*, 78/5: 492–500.

Blair, A. (1992). 'Humanist Methods in Natural Philosophy: The Commonplace Book'. *Journal of the History of Ideas*, 53: 541–51.

Blum, P. R. (2000). 'Francesco Patrizi in the "Time-Sack": History and Rhetorical Philosophy'. *Journal of the History of Ideas*, 61/1: 59–74.

Boesky, A. (1996). *Founding Fictions: Utopias in Early Modern England*. Athens and London: University of Georgia Press.

Campanella, T. (1995). *La citta del Sole*. Roma: Edizione Integrale.

Campanella, T. (2011). *Selected Philosophical Poems of Tomasso Campanella*. Ed. and trans. S. Roush. Chicago: The University of Chicago Press.

Camporesi, P. (1988). *The Incorruptible Flesh: Bodily Mutation and Mortification in Religion and Folklore*. Cambridge: Cambridge University Press.

Castelli, P. (2002). 'Le Fonti de "La Città Felice"'. In *Francesco Patrizi filosofo platonico nel crepuscolo del Rinascimento*. Ed. P. Castelli. Florence: Olschki, pp. 3–30.

Classen, A. (2017). 'Magic in the Middle Ages and the Early Modern Age – Literature, Science, Religion, Philosophy, Music and Art. An Introduction'. In *Magic and Magicians in the Middle Ages and the Early Modern Time: The Occult in Pre-Modern Sciences, Medicine, Literature, Religion, and Astrology*. Ed. A. Classen. Berlin and Boston: De Gruyter, pp. 1–108.

Copenhaver, B. (1992). 'Did Science Have a Renaissance?' *Isis*, 83: 387–407.

Copenhaver, B. and C. Schmitt (1992). *Renaissance Philosophy*. Oxford: Oxford University Press.

Debus, A. (1978). *Man and Nature in the Renaissance*. Cambridge: Cambridge University Press.

Dickinson-Blodgett, E. (1931). 'Bacon's New Atlantis and Campanella's Civitas Solis: A Study in Relationships'. *PMLA*, 46/3:763–80.

Dickson, D. (1996). 'Johann Valentin Andreae's Utopian Brotherhoods'. *Renaissance Quarterly*, 49/4: 760–802.

Engeman, T. (1982). 'Hythloday's Utopia and More's England: An Interpretation of Thomas More's Utopia'. *The Journal of Politics*, 44/1: 131–49.

Ernst, G. (2010a). *Tommaso Campanella: The Book and the Body of Nature*. Dordrecht: Springer.

Ernst, G. (2010b). 'Tommaso Campanella (1568–1939): The Revolution of Knowledge from the Prison'. In *Philosophers of the Renaissance*. Ed. P. R. Blum. Washington: The Catholic University of America Press, pp. 256–74.

Flesher, M. (1973). *Radical Reform and Political Persuasion in the Life and Writings of Thomas More*. Geneve: Librairie Droz.

Freeland, C. (1987). 'Aristotle on Bodies, Matter, and Potentiality'. In *Philosophical Issues in Aristotle's Biology*. Ed. A. Gotthelf and J. Lennox. Cambridge: Cambridge University Press, pp. 392–407.

Gaffney, J. (1998). 'Can Catholic Morality Make Room for Animals?' In *Animals on the Agenda: Questions about Animals for Theology and Ethics*. Ed. A. Lizney and D. Yamamoto. London: Illini Books, pp. 100–12.

Gimelli Martin, C. (2005). 'The Feminine Birth of the Mind: Regendering the Empirical Subject in Bacon and His Followers'. In *Francis Bacon and the Refiguring of Early Modern Thought: Essays to Commemorate the Advancement of Learning (1605)2005)*. Ed. J. Solomon and C. Gimelli Martin. Aldershot: Ashgate.

Goldie, M. (1983). 'Obligations, Utopias, and Their Historical Context'. *The Historical Journal*, 26/3: 727–46.

Hall, M. (2011). *Plants as Persons: A Philosophical Botany*. New York: State University of New York Press.

Harman, P. (2013). *The Scientific Revolution*. Abingdon: Routledge.

Healy, M. (2011). *Shakespeare, Alchemy and the Creative Imagination: The Sonnets and A Lover's Complaint*. Cambridge: Cambridge University Press.

Held, F. E. (1914). *Johann Valentin Andreae's Christianopolis, An Ideal State of the Seventeenth Century*. Chicago: The Graduate School of the University of Illinois.

Hirai, H. (2011). *Medical Humanism and Natural Philosophy: Renaissance Debates on Matter, Life and the Soul*. Leiden: Brill.

Hough, L. E. (2002). '"La Città Felice": A Renaissance Utopia'. In *Francesco Patrizi filosofo platonico nel crepuscolo del Rinascimento*. Ed. P. Castelli. Florence: Olschki, pp. 31–47.

Houston, C. (2016). *The Renaissance Utopia: Dialogue, Travel and the Ideal Society*. Abingdon: Routledge.

Ingegno, A. (1988). 'The new philosophy of nature'. In *The Cambridge History of Renaissance Philosophy*. Ed. C. B. Schmitt, Q. Skinner, E. Kessler and K. Krave. Cambridge: Cambridge University Press, pp. 236–63.

Joy, L. S. (1992). 'Epicureanism in Renaissance Moral and Natural Philosophy'. *Journal of the History of Ideas*, 53: 573–83.

LaFreniere, G. (2008). *The Decline of Nature: Environmental History and the Western Worldview*. Palo Alto: Academica Press.

Logan, G. (2014). *The Meaning of More's Utopia*. Princeton: Princeton University Press.

McCullough, L., J. Caskey, T. Cole and A. Wear (2008). 'Scientific and Medical Concepts of Nature in the Modern Period in Europe and North Africa'. In *Altering Nature: Concepts of 'Nature' and 'the Natural' in Biotechnology Debates*. Ed. B. Lustig, B. Brody and G. McKenny. Dordrecth: Springer, pp. 137–96.

Manuel, F. and F. Manuel (1979). *Utopian Thought in the Western World*. Cambridge, MA: Harvard University Press.

Marius, R. (1999). *Thomas More: A Biography*. Cambridge, MA: Harvard University Press.

More, T. (1999). 'Utopia'. In *Three Early Modern Utopias: Utopia, New Atlantis, The Isle of Pines*. Ed. S. Bruce. Oxford University Press: Oxford, pp. 1–148.

Nelson, E. (2001). 'Greek Nonsense in More's "Utopia"'. *The Historical Journal*, 44/4: 889–917.

Neville, H. (1999). 'The Isle of Pines'. In *Three Early Modern Utopias: Utopia, New Atlantis, The Isle of Pines*. Ed. S. Bruce. Oxford: Oxford University Press, pp. 187–212.

Nichols, J. H. (1976). *Epicurean Political Philosophy*. New York: Cornell University Press.

Olin, J. (1989). *Interpreting Thomas More's Utopia*. New York: Fordham University Press.

Olson, R. (1983). *Science Deified & Science Defied: The Historical Significance of Science in Western Culture*. Berkeley, Los Angeles, London: University of California Press.

Patrizi, F. (1553). *La città felice*. Venice: G. Griffio.

Paul, J. (2017). *Thomas More*. Cambridge: Polity Press.

Pepper, D. (1996). *Modern Environmentalism: An Introduction*. London: Routledge.

Pohl, N. (2010). 'Utopianism after More: The Renaissance and Enlightenment'. In *The Cambridge Companion to Utopian Literature*. Ed. G. Claeys. Cambridge: Cambridge University Press.

Preece, R. (2008). *Sins of the Flesh: A History of Ethical Vegetarian Thought*. Vancouver: UBC Press.

Prior, M. (1954). 'Bacon's Man of Science'. *Journal of the History of Ideas*, 15/3: 348–70.

Raber, K. (2013). *Animal Bodies, Renaissance Culture*. Philadelphia: University of Pennsylvania Press.

Reiss, T. (1973). 'Structure and Mind in Two Seventeenth-Century Utopias: Campanella and Bacon'. *Yale French Studies*, 49: 82–95.

Rossi, P. (1996). 'Bacon's Idea of Science'. In *The Cambridge Companion to Bacon*. Ed. M. Pletonen. Cambridge: Cambridge University Press.

Sargent, L. T. (2010). *Utopianism: A Very Short Introduction*. Oxford: Oxford University Press.

Schönpflug, K. (2008). *Feminism, Economics and Utopia: Time Travelling through Paradigms*. Abingdon: Routledge.

Shannon, L. (2013). *The Accommodated Animal: Cosmopolity in Shakespearean Locales*. Chicago: University of Chicago Press.

Shephard, R. (1995). 'Utopia, Utopia's Neighbors, Utopia, and Europe'. *The Sixteenth Century Journal*, 26/4: 843–56.

Sim, S. and D. Walker (2003). *The Discourse of Sovereignty, Hobbes to Fielding: The State of Nature and the Nature of the State*. Aldershot: Ashgate.
Sorabji, R. (1993). *Animal Minds and Human Morals: The Origins of the Western Debate*. New York: Cornell University Press.
Spencer, C. (1995). *The Heretic's Feast: A History of Vegetarianism*. Lebanon, NH: University Press of New England.
Starnes, C. (1990). *The New Republic: A Commentary on Book I of More's Utopia Showing its Relation to Plato's Republic*. Waterloo: Wilfrid Laurier University Press.
Stavrineas, S. (2015). 'Nature as a Principle of Change'. In *Aristotle's Physics: A Critical Guide*. Ed. M. Leunissen. Cambridge: Cambridge University Press, pp. 46–65.
Steiris, G. (2012). 'Anthropos, Fise, Episteme ston utopiko stochasmo tes Anagenises'. In *Perivalontiki Ethiki: Prokliseis kai Prooptikes gia ton 21o aiona*. Ed. E. Manolas and E. Protopapadakis. Orestiada: Demokritio Panepsitimio Thrakis, pp. 181–94.
Thorndike, L. (1958). *History of Magic and Experimental Science Part 4*. New York: Columbia University Press.
Vieira, F. (1996). 'The Concept of Utopia'. In *The Cambridge Companion to Utopian Literature*. Ed. G. Claeys. Cambridge: Cambridge University Press, pp. 3–27.
Wegemer, G. (1996). *Thomas More on Statemanship*. Washington, DC: The Catholic University of America Press.
Weisgerber, C. A. (1940). *Two Utopias: A Comparison of the Republic of Plato and St. Thomas More's Utopia*. Chicago: Loyola University of Chicago.
White, T. (1976). 'Aristotle and Utopia'. *Renaissance Quarterly*, 29/4: 635–75.
Wilde, L. (2016). *Thomas More's Utopia: Arguing for Social Justice*. London: Routledge.
Wolloch, N. (2006). *Subjugated Animals: Animals and Anthropocentrism in Early Modern European Culture*. Amherst, NY: Humanity Books/Prometheus Books.
Yoran, H. (2010). *Between Utopia and Dystopia: Erasmus, Thomas More and the Humanist Republic of Letters*. Lanham, MD: Lexington Books.
Zambelli, P. (2007). *White Magic, Black Magic in the European Renaissance*. Leiden: Brill.
Zilsel, E. (1945). 'The Genesis of the Concept of Scientific Progress'. *Journal of the History of Ideas*, 6/3: 325–49.

15

Religion and Just War in the Conquest of America: Sepúlveda, Las Casas and Vitoria

Felipe Castañeda

I said I would 'combat' the other man, but wouldn't I give him *reasons*? Certainly; but how far do they go? At the end of reasons comes *persuasion*. (Think what happens when missionaries convert natives.) (Ludwig Wittgenstein, *On Certainty*, #612)

The Duty of Evangelism and the Right to Propaganda

The notion of 'religious' or 'holy war' covers a broad spectrum of types of conflict that took place in the sixteenth century. On the one hand, there are the wars that defend Christianity in general against the Turkish threat (see Luther 1983 and Sepúlveda 2003). On the other, there are the wars waged between members of the Christian faith who became polarised and divided into many factions, leading to different distinctions between the orthodox and the heretics (see Gotthard 2014).

Without purporting to be exhaustive, there was a third type of religious war, exemplified in the Christian Catholic evangelisation of the 'New World'. In this version, war is motivated and justified as something that can ultimately favour the mission or moral obligation to convert unbelievers (see Maier 2008 for an overview of this topic). The purpose of this type of war is, therefore, to turn the other into an equal as far as one's own beliefs are concerned; to extend the republic of believers, so to speak. Thus, in the pursuit of making the other an equal in religious terms, it identifies the adversary's belief system, and any other obstacle that impedes unbelievers from abandoning their ancestral values, as the enemy. The violence of war emerges as an integral aspect of a process of persuasion: how to make others want and accept one's own worldview, how to make them share the same idea of what is reasonable, when they resist and stubbornly cling onto an ancestral tradition? From this perspective, the study of such conflicts transcends the strictly religious. Rather, these conflicts emerge when we assume that we possess ultimate political and social truths that must not only be defended but also accepted by others, whatever the price (see Schmitt 1966: 129).[1]

---

[1] 'New forms of absolute enmity must emerge in a world in which opponents push each other towards the abyss of total disregard before physical annihilation [. . .] [Destriction] no longer targets an enemy, rather, it will serve the so-called objective imposition of higher values, and these, as is known, are priceless.'

Towards the middle of the sixteenth century, Spain was witness to the debate regarding the different positions in relation to the justification of the conquest of America which would have set the bases of the modern law of nations and, accordingly, of part of current international law. And the issue of the relationship between religion and the takeover of the Indies was not alien to this debate.

From a philosophical perspective, these discussions involved the justification, based on the principles of natural law and law of nations, of obligations pertaining to the religious sphere itself; in particular, of divine law, according to the Roman Catholic interpretation of Christianity. And therein lies its main interest: if we understand the duty to evangelise as a specific case of the exercise of ideological propaganda, how is it – towards the middle of the sixteenth century and based on the development of natural law that, in principle, should be valid for any human being – that the imposition of a specific system of values and beliefs on peoples from markedly different cultures and traditions was justified?

I will begin by presenting the position of Juan Ginés de Sepúlveda who served as a reference for Bartolomé de las Casas in articulating his criticism and qualms regarding the way in which the Conquest was progressing. I will then examine the proposal offered by Las Casas in an attempt to show a reading of his ideas that is, so to speak, 'realistic' or pragmatic. Finally, I will touch upon the considerations of Francisco de Vitoria in which the freedom to spread the Christian faith is linked to the freedom of movement and trade.

Domination and Fear are Persuasive: Sepúlveda

In general terms, we can say that Juan Ginés de Sepúlveda based his notion of natural law on the scholastic tradition (see Aquinas 1989: q. 90–7), which, fundamentally, assumes that there is a series of precepts that show people what is considered good or evil, and that respond to the following characteristics. First, they are correlated to human nature. That is, following them will allow the human being to become fully realised as such, according to the characteristics of being human. Thus, the violation of natural law would result in some kind of degradation or dehumanisation of the offender. Second, they deal with standards that do not require special learning, as they would be etched into the rational soul of all human beings (Sepúlveda 1996: 63).[2] Finally, natural law is the same for all human beings, regardless of their history or culture.[3] This is explained as it is assumed that it is supported by the presumption of human nature as universal and necessary. As a consequence, natural law would not be subject to the constraints of the differences of time and place. If this is so, natural law cannot be different for different peoples, but it also means that no nation is exempt forom fulfilling such law. In the words of Sepúlveda:

> This light of right reason, which is what one understands by natural law; this is what declares, in the conscience of good men, what is good and just (. . .) and this, not only among Christians, but all those who have not corrupted right nature with bad habits . . . . (Sepúlveda [1780] 1996: 67)[4]

---

[2] Citing Graciano: '. . . no one lacks the knowledge to discern good from evil, nor the power to do good and flee from evil'.

[3] 'Philosophers call natural law that which everywhere has the same force and does not exist by people's thinking this or that' (Sepúlveda [1780] 1996: 67).

[4] 'Nam hoc est rectae rationis lumen quae lex naturalis intelligitur. Haec enim quid bonum sit atque justum (. . .) in bonis viris declarant, non christianis solum, sed in cunctis qui rectam naturam pravis moribus non corruperunt . . .' (Sepúlveda 1996: 66).

That said, there is a close connection between natural law and just war. In fact, natural law is broken down into particular laws, such as those mentioned in the Decalogue, and into a series of regulations and conventions that, in principle, have been valid for all peoples. As these regulations constitute an obligation, their infringement, in turn, constitutes an offence. Punishment for these offences could lead to a corrective war; that is, a warlike endeavour aimed at re-establishing the violated rights, when politically organised societies are involved in the problem, and when the conduct of some may be understood as greatly damaging to others. Sepúlveda examines the three fundamental reasons for waging a just war as devised by Augustine of Hippo and systematised – if I may say so – by Thomas Aquinas (1989: q. 40) in his *Summa Theologiae*: a defensive war, whereby a community is defended through the use of military power against a foreign force, which by attacking damages the attacked. Defensive wars would thereby be just. Wars of aggression, which constitute the restitution of goods unlawfully seized. And, finally, a reason especially important in the context of the relationship between war and religion: the use of force against certain communities in which there is tolerance for impunity for crimes which, in one way or another, affect another community, which, in this case, would be the offended. By the sixteenth century, it was already appreciable that there was a clear extension of the scope of impunity for crimes against humanity and against the Christian Catholic God, as we will see below.

Sepúlveda proposes an addendum to the causes mentioned above, and, in the first place, mentions the possibility of engaging in just wars due to natural slavery:

> There are other causes of just wars less clear and less frequent, but not, therefore, less just or based any less on natural and divine law, and one of them is to subdue through the use of arms, if no other way is possible, those who by natural condition must obey others and refuse their rule. (Sepúlveda 1996: 81)[5]

It is not the case, here, to delve into a disclosure of natural slavery as a cause of war and its role in the conquest of America (see Pagden 1992). However, a few brief words, I find, are pertinent, as it is an issue closely linked to the possibility of engaging in war for reasons of evangelisation.

According to Sepúlveda, taking up the ideas of Aristotle,[6] there are peoples who, by nature, are not particularly apt for an adequate and full development of rational capacity. This is revealed by at least two main characteristics: they are not able to create, by themselves, the knowledge typical of a rational being, be it technical, cultural or scientific. They are, however, able to recognise that others can do so. Second, they are not particularly prudent, in the sense of having the rational capacity, in their practical lives, to adjust the means to the ends; that is, to ponder a reasonable path to follow in order to reach what is considered to be good, and that, that which is considered to be good is, in truth, good. In this sense, they can present particularly marked shortcomings, for example, in the way in which they embark on their religious rituals, in which God is confused with material things, and divine worship with human sacrifice and even with anthropophagy. But just as these nations exist, so do those that do, in fact,

---

[5] 'Sunt et aliae justi belli causae, quae minus quidem late patent minusque saepe accident, justissimae tamen habentur, nitunturque jure naturali et divino: quarum una est, si non potest alia via in ditionem redigantur hi quorum ea conditio naturalis est, ut aliis parere debeant, si eorum imperio recusant . . .' (Sepúlveda 1996: 80).
[6] On this subject, consult the Latin translation of Book 1 of *Politics* by Aristotle, in particular chapters 1, 3, 4, 5 and 8 (Aristotle 2015).

reach an adequate level of rational development both in terms of knowledge and in the business of everyday life. These nations include – in the eyes of Sepúlveda – the Spanish.

Given that the latter are apt to reflect appropriately, in the sense that they are able to correctly determine the ends they must aim for, and the means to achieve such ends, they would be apt to rule by nature, justifying that, by nature, it is advisable that some should dominate others, enabling a differentiation between 'masters and slaves by nature'. Consequently, some people would be predisposed by nature to rule and others to obey.[7] Be that as it may, if natural slaves refuse to serve natural masters, this would lead to a natural offence and, thus, a reason for just war.

Sepúlveda considered that the dominion of the natural master over his slave would be in the interest of the latter. The slave's ignorance could be remedied through the transfer of knowledge from the master; his imprudence could be corrected under the guidance of his virtuous lord. Given the above, Sepúlveda has no problem in asserting:

> . . . and the end of this [the war against the barbarians] is to fulfil natural law for the great good of the defeated, so that they can learn humanity from the Christians, so that they become used to virtue, so that with their doctrine and pious teachings they can prepare their spirits to gladly receive the Christian religion . . . . (Sepúlveda 1996: 93)[8]

The second reason is related to idolatry. First, it is important to note that for Sepúlveda, the mere difference of faith cannot constitute, in itself, a cause for just war (see Sepúlveda 1996: 117). In fact, the unbelievers' rejection of the faith could be due to many factors such as, for example, the impossibility of their having had any prior knowledge of Christianity. In such cases, given that the ignorance is involuntary, it should not be considered an infraction. Accordingly, it cannot be considered an offence. On the other hand, Sepúlveda also accepts that belief must correspond to a voluntary act, in the sense that it should not be motivated directly by violence. As such, it would also lack any sense to consider a war whose immediate end is the forced conversion of the defeated, as this would vitiate the unbelievers' act of conversion and a religious war of this type could never be considered just. However: '. . . we have not yet spoken of their godless religion and of the heinous sacrifices through which they venerate the devil as God, to whom they did not believe in offering a better tribute that human hearts' (Sepúlveda 1996: 111s).[9]

As we can see, although it would not be considered correct to wage war against unbelievers for the mere fact that they do not believe, the type of belief they have is not irrelevant. In fact, Sepúlveda seems to accept two types of infidelity. First, those which constitute beliefs that do not violate the precepts of natural law and which, by extension, imply no offence. These would include those which postulate the existence of a single, immaterial, just and good God, even if they do not accept or include specific content from biblical texts. Second, faiths which are considered idolatrous. In this case, we are talking about religions which confuse the divine with material things, or with a multiplicity of gods, and which apply, as the precepts of the faith,

---

[7] Aristotle had no problem in considering the Persians and other non-Greeks as the natural slaves of the Greeks (*Politics* 1252b).

[8] '. . . hoc [barbarorum bellum] lege naturae in magnam eorum qui vincuntur commoditatem ut a christianis humanitatem discant, virtutibus assuescant, sana doctrina, piisque monitiis praeparent animos ad religionem christianam . . .' (Sepúlveda 1996: 92) (translation: T. Laudato).

[9] '. . . necdum tamen impia ipsorum religione verba fecimus, et nefariis sacrificiis; qui cum daemonem pro Deo colerent, hunc nullis sacrificiis aeque placari putabant ac cordibus humanis' (Sepúlveda 1996: 110s) (translation: T. Laudato).

commandments that, in some way, oppose the content of natural law. In this case, the possibility of a just war given by a difference of religion would be acceptable, and could be applied to the barbarian American Indians (Sepúlveda 1996: 129).

That said, this type of war is not only religious due to its revenge for offences against the 'true' God, but also because it seems to fall under the power of the Pope:

> It is not in the power of the High Priest to oblige the pagans through Christian and evangelical laws, but their work included attempting, by any means that are not too difficult, to banish the pagans from their inhuman and barbarous customs, and bring them to good and human customs and to the true faith . . . . (Sepúlveda 1996: 125)[10]

And with this, we would already have the foundation from which to move, directly, to the issue of the propagation of the Christian faith and its relationship with war. On the one hand, there is the obligation of banishing the unbelievers from their idolisms, especially when their rituals in themselves imply grave breaches of natural law. Thus, if this cannot be carried out by peaceful means, then it could through war. Nevertheless, and on the other hand, it is also the obligation of every Christian, by natural and divine law, to do everything possible to convert the unbeliever. In fact, if it is proper to natural law to 'Love your neighbour as thyself', it would not be moral to foster the eternal damnation of entire communities of recently discovered unbelievers by not converting them to Christianity in order to save them. The good Christian has to do everything possible to bring all lost and confused sheep to the flock, even if the sheep in question do not consider this the best option for their lives.[11] Thus, to the extent that a war is justified to combat idolatry, it is, at the same time, closely linked with the obligation to convert the infidel:

> . . . I believe that the barbarians can be conquered within the same right which makes them compelled to hear the words of the Gospels . . . because he who demands for something to be done legitimately, by the same law asks for all the means to that end to be licit, and that which is preached to the infidels is [. . .] required by natural law and human charity . . . . (Sepúlveda 1996: 139)[12]

A new factor is added to the argument: a principle of natural law. If the law requires the fulfilment of a specific end, then it has to legitimise the use of the means necessary and convenient to carry out the task. The end is evangelisation. The context is that of a war of conquest justified by natural slavery, but also by the idolatry associated to the commission of crimes such as human sacrifice and anthropophagy. However, it is accepted, at the same time, that conversion must not be forced but voluntary. The question then would be: how to persuade people of the goodness of the saving message of Christianity in such a circumstance?

---

[10] 'Non est potestatis summi Sacerdotis christianis et evangelicis legibus paganos obligare, tamen ejus officii est, dare operam si qua non admodum difficilis ratio iniri possit, ut paganos a criminibus et inhumanis flagitiis [. . .] ad probos et humanos mores veramque religionem revocentur . . .' (Sepúlveda 1996: 124).

[11] 'And as we cannot doubt that all those who wander outside of the Christian religion are erred and walk infallibly towards the precipice, we must hold no doubt in banishing them from it using any means even if it is against their will . . .' (Sepúlveda 1996: 137).

[12] '. . . eodem jure, redigi barbaros in ditionem posse dico, quo ad Evangelium audiendum compelli. Nam qui jure finem petit, is eodem jure adhibet omnia quae pertinent ad finem; ut autem Evangelium infidelibus praedicetur, lex est [. . .] naturae et humanae charitatis . . .' (Sepúlveda 1996: 138).

Sepúlveda offers some incisive answers:

> Since the missionaries will have to carry out their work in the midst of barbarian and hostile peoples, in an aggressive environment, it is not possible to send them without first having conquered the barbarians: And how can they preach to these barbarians if they are not sent to them [. . .], and how are they to be sent if these barbarians are not conquered first? (Sepúlveda 1996: 141)[13]

But beyond this: if the Indians cling onto their ancient customs and traditions, if they are not motivated to change their habits, evangelisation will not bear fruit. That said, given that we are dealing with peoples that are only vaguely rational, due to their condition of natural slavery, this cannot be done by deliberative persuasion. It is not a question of reason, but rather one of fostering an affective disposition, which may ultimately be favourable to Christian ideas. Sepúlveda sees the solution in a certain ratio of fear and terror:

> . . . I say that the Barbarians should be controlled not only so that they can listen to our preachers but also to add threats to doctrines and advice and thus terror [. . .] not only to have the light of truth scatter the darkness of error but also that the force of terror may break bad habits . . . . (Translation taken from Rivera 1992: 220, citing Sepúlveda)[14]

Meekness Persuades: Las Casas

When we examine the proposition made by Las Casas regarding evangelisation and war, we can establish both his disapproval of Sepúlveda's theories and a pragmatic and realistic aspect. The use of violence and power is restricted, not because its use may ultimately not be legitimate, but rather because it may simply be unwise. That said, not only is the work of Las Casas very extensive, but it also took him various decades to write it. This may explain why some of his ideas changed and were reassessed over time. For this presentation, I base my work on his *Tratado*,[15] intentionally leaving aside other texts that may qualify his remarks.[16]

---

[13] 'Quomodo autem barbaris istis praedicabunt nisi [. . .] mittantur? Quomodo mittentur nisi prius barbari fuerint in ditionem redacti?' (Sepúlveda 1996: 138s).

[14] '. . . ego non solum ut praedicatores audient in ditionem barbaros redigendos esse dico, sed etiam ut ad doctrinam et monita addantur, et minae et terror incutiantur [. . .] [and the text goes on, citing Saint Augustine] ut non solum tenebras erroris lux veritatis expellat, verum etiam malae consuetudinis vincula vis temoris obrumpat . . .' (Sepúlveda 1996: 146).

[15] *Treatise Confining the Sovereign Empire and the Universal Princedom that the Kings of Castile and Leon Pursue over the Indians.*

[16] In relation to the obligation to hear to the preachers, in *De unico vocationis modo* (1525–6?) he states that the Indians are not obliged to hear them: '. . . apparet quod solum Christus Apostolis concedit licentiam et potestatem Evangelium volentibus illud audire praedicare, nolentibus autem vim aut aliquod molestum et ingratum non inferre' (Las Casas 1990: 178). However, in the Controvery at Valladolid (1550–1), his position in this respect seems doubtful: 'A lo que dice a la décima objeción, que el Papa tiene poder y precepto de predicar el Evangelio por sí e por otros en todo el mundo, concedámoslo; pero la consecuencia que infiere el reverendo doctor [Sepúlveda], conviene a saber, que puedan ser forzados los infieles a oír la predicación, no está del todo muy clara, y harto más delgada indagación de la verdad de la que hace el doctor conviene hacerse para que della se haga evidencia' (Las Casas 1997: 387). In *Tratado* (1552), as we will see, it is clear that the Pope has sufficient power to oppose any impediment that hinders contact between evangelisers and Indians in order to be able to evangelise.

Sepúlveda had already pointed out that no precept of natural law is denied by divine law[17] as both aim to determine good, and this notion is unique in the sense that it cannot cover any meaning that is contradictory or different to goodness. The effect here is, for example, that if natural law endorses war under certain conditions, the law of the Gospels cannot be read as a defence of pacifism at any cost. Christians must be allowed to kill in certain circumstances. Las Casas seems to provide a different reading of the relationship between natural law and that which results from the Bible; that is, that which affects the transcendent fate of humans, their lives in another world. In fact, he presupposes in his *Tratado* that anything required for the appropriate exercise of spiritual power, must be supported and allowed,[18] regardless of whether this goes against the authority of natural law. That said, as the head of this authority is the Pope with the support of the organisation of the Church – the Catholic and Roman – it could be asserted that the Supreme Pontiff is conferred unrestricted power:

> The Pope [. . .] has authority over the whole world which contains and comprises the faithful and the unfaithful, and over all the temporary goods and things and their worldly states, but only as far as right reason would dictate and which is needed and convenient to guide and put right or steer the faithful or unfaithful [. . .] on the path to eternal life and, in consequence, to remove the obstacles and impediments to its attainment, which is *in ordine ad finem spiritualem*. (Las Casas 1997: 925)

There is, therefore, nothing, in principle, that the High Priest is prevented from doing for the sake of attaining a spiritual objective. The supreme value of eternal life, which renders relative and conditional any value or aspect of life in this finite world, justifies the use of any means. And when we talk about any means, Las Casas observes that the Pope would have jurisdiction over any human in general, believer or unbeliever, which also seems to cover the orthodox, heretics, Jews, apostates and atheists, aside from any type of pagan. That is, any 'child of God', as they are all members of the same family affectable by the same fate of the descendants of Adam: mortal sin. The point is clear, although unbelievers have never been considered members of the Christian flock, the power of Rome would cover them anyway (Las Casas 1997: 927).

On the scope of means that could be used, he asserts:

> . . . the Pope [. . .] has the divine power to ready and steer men to said ultimate end of eternal life, inasfar as they are orderable, available and directable to said blessed end and, in consequence consider and judge their work, actions, and human operations, be they what may, when they are placed under reason of conveniences and inconveniences, impediments, and delays regarding the ultimate and eternal end [. . .] the pontiff, supported by divine law, therefore, has the right to judge and dispose of the temporary goods and states in that they can help or not in achieving this supernatural end . . . . (Las Casas 1997: 961)

That said, in choosing the means from this vast inventory, there are, however, some criteria that the Pope must respect: the means must be 'orderable, available and directable' towards the objective of eternal life. Thus, not everything is acceptable, although it is important to

---

[17] '. . . everything which is done in the name of natural rights or laws can also be done by virtue of divine rights or evangelical laws . . .' (Sepúlveda 1996: 59) (translation: T. Laudato).
[18] '. . . when a certain power is granted to a person by divine means, we necessarily have to allow for all the means necessary for the execution of that power to be conferred to him . . .' (Las Casas 1997: 955) (translation: T. Laudato).

note that the possible reasons on which to exclude a specific means are not, in themselves, prohibited by any law (civil law, the law of nations, and so on). As we can see, the choice of means is more a question of prudence than it is of justice. Clearly, among these means is the possibility to dispose of the goods and the political organisations of those affected (Las Casas 1997: 995).

The Pope would therefore have enough power to order any type of change of government, in the interest of what he considers to be convenient for the defence, preservation and extension of his Spiritual Republic. Applied to the case of the New World, this power is defined considering the need to evangelise. And from this point of view, the missionaries must be able to, in principle, preach, admonish and stay in an environment such that the unbelievers may ultimately come to accept the message of salvation. This would be the spiritual goal. The unbelievers' authorities hindering this process as far as impeding it, hampering it, or delaying it for more than a reasonable span of time would go against this end (see Las Casas: 1997: 999), and, in such cases, the Pope may induce war: 'In that case [if expansion is impeded or if one is a tyrant] the Supreme Vicar of Christ can order those tyrants who do not make amends or who resist to be compelled by war . . .' (translation taken from Rivera 1992: 312, citing Las Casas).

It is precisely in this context that we can introduce the problem of whether or not the Indians are compelled to hear the message of salvation. For Las Casas, it is clear that it is not possible to believe unless one has knowledge of the message of salvation; but to acquire this knowledge one has to hear it. Here, we should note that it is not assumed that the unbelievers are able to read. Thus, the question would be whether the Pope has sufficient power to compel the Indians to hear the message of salvation. The answer seems to be clear and consistent with earlier points:[19]

> [The Pope has power over] such works that may impede the principle and the gateway to the faith, which leads to the end, and the gateway becomes clear by hearing, because *fides ex audito, quomodo credent ei quem non audierunt*? (Romans 10) (Las Casas 1997: 1001)
>
> [. . .]
>
> if an infidel king or prince were to maliciously impede the opportunity and comfort of his people's hearing [. . .] it is the right of [the Pontiff] granted the power of Christ to judge and deprive any infidel king or prince from his royal dignity. (Las Casas 1997: 1001)

Las Casas is not asserting that the Pope can force individual Indians to hear the message, whether they want to or not, but rather that he can take forceful measures against infidel princes who impede a favourable encounter between preachers and Indians.[20]

To this point, there seems to be a convergence of ideas between Las Casas and Sepúlveda; both recognise the absolute moral importance for Christian Catholics to disseminate the faith to infidels at risk of eternal death. They seem affected by an implacable need to compensate for the loss of reformed Christians with the new followers in the New World. However, even in this topic, there are marked differences between one and the other: for Las Casas, it is clear that, although the Pope has extended powers that expressly include the possibility of making use of the instrument of war to change governments, it is not wise to do so. It deals with a possibility

---

[19] The point is, nevertheless, problematic for Las Casas. See Las Casas (1990: 387, 389).
[20] See Las Casas (1990: 395).

rather than a probability. In fact, he recommends a peaceful means to effective evangelisation: the path of meekness leading to persuasion:

> The peaceful, loving, humble, Christian, exemplary path, that raises no suspicion of covetousness, generous and selfless, that is conducive and provocative to invite the unbelievers to be Christians, is the necessary form and means to be used by those in charge of preaching and winning them to Christ. (Las Casas 1997: 981)

The arguments are different, but they have a notable common feature: they are supported by the criterion of convenience. A peaceful path is assumed because this is what is needed to 'win them to Christ'. This confirms that what we have is a kind of reasoning that is framed within the prudential: loving and humble actions that raise no suspicion of covetousness, that are generous, selfless and inclined to benefit others, and that are most likely to encourage infidels to hear and accept the Christian message, are, therefore, what should be applied. The reasons for which someone should actually convert to Christianity can come later, if necessary. Persuasion more likely occurs through the Indians' direct experience of a model of behaviour that reflects the ideal lifestyle that is being transmitted to them. The hypothesis behind the Christian propaganda of meekness would be as follows: if the Indians can come into contact with the Christian joy and goodness of this world, that is, with its best version, they will surely want to take part in it and be willing to convert to it. Merely in order to attempt to clarify this point, Sepúlveda proposes that the Christian message should be 'sold' by exposing the Indians to domination, fear and terror; that is, to the Christian reality of the damned, the expelled from Paradise and those close to the doors of Hell. Las Casas, in contrast, believes that the Indians of the New World are just a step away from the gateway to Heaven, given that they are not, in fact, very far removed from Paradise.

The Reasonable Persuades: Vitoria

Oddly enough, not only do both Las Casas and Sepúlveda recognise Francisco de Vitoria as an authority on theological-philosophical issues, but they also try to base themselves on his ideas to defend their own approaches (see Sepúlveda 1997: 219). However, their ideas take a different direction. I will highlight only two aspects regarding his conception on the relationship between evangelisation and war. First, the contact between evangelisers and Indians is set out in a context subject to the freedom of movement and trade, residence and the use of common resources for Spaniards on Indian lands. Second, in this environment, the evangelisers are compelled to present the message to the unbelievers who, in turn, are compelled to accept it to avoid committing sin due to vincible ignorance.

Basing himself on the principles of natural law and the law of nations (see Vitoria 1995), Vitoria maintains: 'The Spaniards have the rights to travel and dwell in those countries, as long as they do no harm to the barbarians and cannot be prevented by them from doing so' (translation taken from Baker 2013: 45, citing Vitoria).[21]

It is a remarkable assertion, as it formulates the freedom of movement and residence as a sort of general human natural law. In fact, this is something which has been endorsed by the law of nations, that is, as something that among different nations throughout history has

---

[21] 'Hispani habent ius peregrinandi in illas provincias et illic degendi, sine aliquot tamen nocumento barbarorum nec possunt ab illis prohiberi' (Vitoria 1960: 705).

been assumed as unjust: the mistreatment of travellers. In principle, travellers must be treated hospitably. With this in mind, the extent to which the Spaniards and the recently discovered Indians can conceive each other as pilgrims of some kind, it would be the duty of the Indians to open the doors to their realms and welcome them amiably.

But this is not only due to the above. The only kind of conduct that can be justly punished is one that somehow constitutes an offence. In other words, a human action that is condemned is one that involves damage to another. Thus, if the mere fact of travelling through new lands and to remain and reside in them, does not, in itself, cause damage, well then it should not be punished. For example, if the French were to impede the Spanish from travelling thorough their lands, under the understanding that they are not causing any damage by the mere fact of travelling through them, they would be unjustly harming them: 'It would not be lawful for the French to prohibit Spaniards from travelling or even living in France, or vice versa (. . .)' (Vitoria 1964: part 2, summary of the third section, para. 22).[22] This is a reciprocal or two-way right, so to speak: just as the barbarians cannot deny the Spaniards this right, the latter cannot do so to the former.

Among the other arguments developed by Vitoria, it would be regrettable not to fully cite the following: 'What race of men is this, or what barbarian nation, that allows such treatment? We are denied their hospitality on their coasts' (Virgil, *Aeneid*, I, vers. 538–40 cited by Vitoria [2012: 131]).[23] Freedom of movement is complemented by that of trade. In fact, it pertains to natural law to do everything possible to remain alive; and to do so it is necessary to be able to access the goods required to satisfy one's basic needs. But given that no place offers everything necessary, trade is lawful by natural law. Again, Vitoria uses the relationship between the French and the Spaniards as an example: '[. . .] It is clear that if the Spaniards were to prohibit the French from trading with the Spanish kingdoms, not for the good of Spain but to prevent the French from sharing in any profits, this would be an unjust enactment, and contrary to Christian charity' (Vitoria 1991: 280).[24]

Charity is one of the most basic natural laws: 'Love thy neighbour', which, in this case, materialises in the natural precept of 'Do not do to others what you would not want done to you' (Vitoria 2012: 133).[25] Trade allows people the benefit of enjoying a certain level of well-being; as such, just as everyone desires their own well-being, they should also allow it for others. Thus, it would not be proper to the general kinship between human beings for some to deny others the possibility of living reasonably.

As we can see, such arguments are supported by precepts that do not entertain a distinction between Christians and infidels. They are inherent to natural law, although they can also be recognised by divine law. Both the freedom of movement and that of trade demand that the New World should open its doors to the Spaniards, to integrate into a system of relationships of exchange of goods and people. Failing this, Spain could use war in order to defend these rights and take legitimate possession of the subjugated territories. This does not fall under

---

[22] '. . . non liceret gallis prohibere hispanos a peregrinatione Galliae vel etiam habitatione, aut e contrario . . .' (Vitoria 1960: 706).

[23] 'Quod genus hoc hominum, quaeve hunc tam Barbara morem / Permittit patria, hospitio prohibemur arenae?' (Vitoria 1960: 707).

[24] 'Clarum est autem quod, si hispani prohiberent gallos a commercio Hispaniarum, non propter bonum Hispaniae, sed ne galli participant aliquam utilitatem, lex esset iniqua et contra caritatem' (Vitoria 1960: 709).

[25] 'Non facies alteri quod tibi fieri non vis' (Vitoria 1960: 709).

the three basic reasons for just war that I mentioned earlier, and it is not a topic developed by either Las Casas or Sepúlveda. From this perspective, the legitimacy of a possible war on the grounds of trade involves the treatment of the barbarians on equal footing as though they were any other European nation.

However, this liberal air, so to speak, is strongly conditioned and qualified vis-à-vis religious considerations: the supposed freedom of movement and of trade does not imply, in itself, religious freedom. If the Indians were to impede the free divulgation, in a safe, obstacle-free environment of the message of salvation, they could declare just war: 'Christians have the right to preach and announce the gospel in the land of the barbarians' / In his mind this right can be inferred from the words of the Gospel: "Preach the Gospel to every creature . . ."' (Vitoria 1991: 284).[26]

This first argument includes most of what we have already seen: divine law, in relation to the Christian obligation to spread the faith, conditions and limits the rights recognised by natural law. Obviously, the Christians' right to spread their faith among infidels is not compensated by the reciprocal recognition for the pagan priests to have the same freedom to spread their idolisms in the very pious Spain. But, in addition, the war could have consequences similar to those proposed by Las Casas:

> . . . if there is no other way to carry on the work of religion, this furnishes the Spaniards with another justification for seizing the lands and territory of the natives and for setting up new lords there and putting down the old lords and doing in right of war everything which it is permitted in other just wars . . . . (Vitoria 1964: part 2, summary of the third section, para. 51)[27]

It is worth noting, however, a significant difference in the way in which they argue: whereas Las Casas's attitude is pragmatic and he focuses on practical considerations, Vitoria, in contrast, insists on that which is permitted by law.

Be that as it may, for Vitoria too, it is clear that conversion must be an act of free will, and not one marred by the pressure of fear and terror. The right to preach should only go as far as guaranteeing that the missionaries can adequately announce their message but not to the point of forcing a change of religion. In other words, if the Indians allow this dissemination but it does not lead to conversion, the latter would not constitute a just reason for war in this respect.

Apart from these points of contact with Las Casas, it is worth highlighting a significant difference that I have already pointed out: Vitoria inscribes the right to spread the faith within a context that already supports freedom of movement and trade. In his own words: 'For if the Spaniards have a right to travel and trade among the Indians, they can teach the truth to those willing to hear them' (Vitoria 1964: part 2, summary of the third section, para. 47).[28]

---

[26] 'Christiani habent ius praedicandi et annuntiandi Evangelium in provinciis barbarorum / Haec conclusio nota est ex illo: "Pradicate Evangelium omni creaturae", etc.' (Vitoria 1960: 715) (translation: T. Laudato).
[27] '. . . si aliter negotium religionis procurari non potest, licet hispanis occupare terras et provincias illorum et novos dominos creare et antiquos deponere et prosequi iure belli quae in aliis bellis iustis licite fieri possent . . .' (Vitoria 1960: 717s).
[28] 'Quia si habent ius peregrinandi et negotiandi apud illos, ergo possunt docere veritatem volentes audire . . .' (Vitoria 1960: 715).

Movement and trade are legitimised on the grounds of the well-being they can provide; they deal with activities that in one way or another lead to happiness, and the possibility to remain alive. If they are legitimised by natural law itself, how could it not also be possible, through the same law, to spread a message that, in Vitoria's opinion, can represent salvation and eternal happiness?

That said, the above accounts for the Christian obligation and the rights conceded to Christians to work towards the conversion of the infidels. However, it is important to also briefly consider the obligations and rights of the infidel Indians insofar as these announcements.

As already mentioned in relation to Sepúlveda, for Vitoria it is clear that mere infidelity is not a reason for just war. In fact, the infidels' ignorance of the Christian faith responds to a type of ignorance that they would be practically unable to overcome by their own means. This type of ignorance was known as 'invincible' (see Aquinas 1989: I-II, q. 76). Thus, if the Indians' infidelity was due to this type of ignorance, it could not be assumed as something voluntary, and, as the agent can have no responsibility in something that is not voluntary, this ignorance cannot constitute a sin. We are dealing, therefore, with a non-sinful infidelity, and, as such, one that does not imply any kind of offence. From this, we can conclude that no just war can be waged due to a mere difference of religion in cases influenced by invincible ignorance.

But Vitoria goes that bit further. The Indians cannot be expected to change their beliefs based solely on the first attempts at conversion:

> The Indians in question are not bound, directly [as] the Christian faith is announced to them, to believe it, in such a way that they commit mortal sin by not believing it . . . without miracle or any other proof or persuasion. (Vitoria 1964: part 2, summary of the second section, para. 64)[29]

This point is important as it suggests that conversion is a process and not merely the expected result of a specific and limited act of communication. It is reasonable for infidels to have their doubts when faced with a group of strangers that comes to question their general ideas of things, and unwise to believe them without corroborating the veracity of what they preach. What if the discoverers were Saracens? If this were so, the announcement would have had to have been duly supported by reasons that could persuade them, 'because they cannot and are not obliged to surmise which religion is most true, if they are not presented with more convincing reasons one way or another' (Vitoria 2012: 114).[30]

In fact, Vitoria is sure of the great effectiveness of the Christian argument to sell its faith to the infidels. It comes from a theological tradition firmly convinced not only of the power of reason but also of the inherent reasonableness of the Christian faith. And, for the same reason, it supposes that the Indians are, in principle, apt for deliberation and

---

[29] 'Barbari non ad primum nuntium fidei christianae tenentur credere ipsum, ita quod peccent mortaliter non credentes solum per hoc [. . .] sine miraculis, aut quacumque alia probatione aut suasione' (Vitoria 1960: 692).

[30] '. . . quia non possunt nec tenentur divinare utra sit verior religio, nisi appareant probabiliora motiva pro altera parte' (Vitoria 1960: 693) (translation: T. Laudato).

capable of enough understanding to recognise and accept the truth they are being conceded. He asserts:

> If the Christian faith be put before the aborigines with demonstration, that is, with demonstrable and reasonable arguments, and this be accompanied by an upright life, well-ordered according to the law of nature [. . .] the aborigines are bound to receive the faith of Christ . . . . (Vitoria 1964: part 2, summary of the second section, para. 68)[31]

In sum, as it is assumed that the Indians have a certain level of rational understanding, if the missionaries are diligent in their work then the Indians would be relieved of their invincible ignorance in relation to their condition of infidelity. In fact, they could hear if they wanted to, and there would be no impediment that would make it impossible or inconvenient for them to accept, through reason, the veracity of the message of salvation. However, if, given such conditions, they still refuse to hear and 'understand', they would be condemned for negligence. As their ignorance is vincible, they would be committing a mortal sin.

Conclusions

Although there are marked differences between Sepúlveda, Las Casas and Vitoria, all three coincide in that the moral duty to evangelise supposes extensive rights of the Spaniards over the Indians. It is important to highlight that, on the one hand, they understand the Christian message of salvation as something that has to reach all corners of the world, and, on the other, they assume love for one's neighbour as natural law. This combination of moral obligation together with fraternal love makes them prone to understanding their missional labour as an unconditioned superior value that is not subject to negotiation. The different arguments point out that much, if not all, is permitted in the interest of the freedom of communication of the Christian worldview, and the way in which natural law in general and divine law are understood serves to justify the legitimacy of this endeavour.

The fact of justifying the recourse to war and the possible change of political governments as a means to guarantee the comfortable and effective propaganda of faiths, supposes, in Vitoria and Sepúlveda, and with restrictions in Las Casas, that the spreading of the Christian religion is granted a higher value than that of the political and social order of the Indian communities. It does not matter if these have to disappear, as long as evangelisation takes place. Interestingly, there is little consideration that unbelievers may assume it as reasonable to reject the possibility of exposing themselves to the alien ideological message or that the fact of having organised societies is, in itself, something that should be respected and valued regardless of religious considerations.

In general terms, it can be said that there is no attempt whatsoever to question the truth of one's own creed, or, at the very least, to constrain its scope of legitimacy. This points to the importance of analysing the conceptual implications of assuming notions such as those pertaining to divine and natural law, under the assumption that there are or that there should be universal and necessary notions of good and evil that transcend all cultural and historical differences. In other words, if one is a Christian Catholic of sixteenth-century Spain and one

---

[31] 'Si fides christiana proponatur barbaris probabiliter, id est, cum argumentis probabilibus et rationabilibus et cum vita honesta et secundum legem naturae studiosa [. . .] barbari tenentur recipere fidem Christi . . .' (Vitoria 1960: 694).

discovers a New World abundantly inhabited by infidels, and if one assumes, at the same time, a conceptual system such as the scholastic as one's theoretical framework, to what extent could there have been the possibility to see and conceive things differently to how they were seen and conceived by thinkers such as Sepúlveda, Las Casas or Vitoria?

From a different perspective, the considerations of these authors on the way in which evangelisation should take place open a sparsely visited area of study: that of the analysis of the discourse of persuasion involving different images of the world for the sixteenth century. To use the terminology of Wittgenstein, how do we convince another society of the superiority of one's own ideas when there is no common language regarding what the world is in general, of its values, and so on? What is 'reasonable' in a meeting point of this nature? These Spanish authors combined the announcement of the message of salvation with the possibility of supporting it with arms, should that be necessary: does only violence convince? To what extent is the path of meekness and gentleness reasonable, and ultimately even that of the arguments and reasons in the style of Vitoria? All of these are questions pertaining to the philosophical considerations developed on the basis of the contact between different cultures, in which the problem of persuasive communication, under the shadow of war and violence, occupied a special place. Its current validity and pertinence probably lies precisely here.

Bibliography

Aquinas, Thomas (1989 [between 1265 and 1274]). 'Treatise on Law in General'. In *Summa Theologiae* I-II. Madrid: Biblioteca de Autores Cristianos, pp. 90–7.

Aristóteles (2004). *Política*. Madrid: Editorial Tecnos.

Aristóteles (2015). *Sobre la República – Libro I según la traducción Latina y escolios de Juan Ginés de Sepúlveda*. Bogotá: Ediciones Uniandes.

Baker, Gideon (2013). *Hospitality and World Politics*. New York: Springer.

Beuchot, Mauricio (1994). *Los fundamentos de los derechos humanos en Bartolomé de las Casas*. Barcelona: Ed. Anthropos.

Carriére, Jean-Claude (1998). *La controversia de Valladolid*. Barcelona: Ed. Península.

Castañeda, Felipe (2015). 'La esclavitud natural en Sepúlveda'. In *Aristóteles: Sobre la República – Libro I, según la traducción latina y escolios de Juan Ginés de Sepúlveda*. Ed. Felipe Castañeda and Andre Lozano. Bogotá: Universidad de los Andes. Ed. Uniandes, pp. 135–232.

Castañeda, Paulino (1996). *La teocracia pontifical en las controversias sobre el Nuevo Mundo*. México: UNAM.

Castilla Urbano, Francisco (1992). *El pensamiento de Francisco de Vitoria*. Barcelona: Ed. Anthropos.

Deckers, Daniel (1991). *Gerechtigkeit und Recht – Eine historisch-kritische Untersuchung der Gerechtigkeitslehre des Francisco de Vitoria (1483–1546)*. Freiburg: Universitätsverlag Freiburg Schweiz.

Gotthard, Axel (2014). *Der liebe und werthe Fried – Kriegskonzepte und Neutralitätsvorstellungen' in der frühen Neuzeit*. Köln: Böhlau Verlag.

Hensel, Howard M. (2016). *The Prism of Just War: Asian and Western Perspectives on the Legitimate Use of Military Force*. New York: Routledge.

Justenhoven, Heinz-Gerhard (1991). *Francisco de Vitoria zu Krieg und Frieden*. Köln: Bachem Verlag.

Las Casas, Bartolomé de (1990 [between 1522 and 1536]). 'De unico modo vocationis modo'. In *Obras Completas 2*. Madrid: Alianza Editorial.

Las Casas, Bartolomé de (1997 [1552]). 'Tratado comprobatorio del imperio soberano y principado universal que los reyes de Castilla y León tienen sobre las Indias'. In *Tratados de Fray Bartolomé de las Casas*, Tomo II. México: FCE.

Las Casas, Bartolomé de (1997). 'Aquí se contiene una disputa o controversia entre el obispo don fray Bartolomé de las Casas (...) y el doctor Ginés de Sepúlveda, coronista del Emperador (...)'. In *Tratados de Fray Bartolomé de las Casas*, Tomo I. México: FCE.

Luther, Martin (1983). 'Vom Kriege wider die Türken – 1529'. In *Luther Deutsch. Die Werke Martin Luthers in neuer Auswahl für die Gegenwart, Der Chirst in der Welt (Band 7)*. Ed. Kurt Aland. Stuttgart: Ehrenfried Klotz Verlag, pp. 94–118.

Maier, Hans (2008). 'Compelle intrare – Rechtfertigungsgründe für die Anwendung von Gewalt zum Schutz und zur Ausbreitung des Glaubens in der Theologie des Abendländischen Christentums'. In *Heilige Kriege*. Ed. Klaus Schreiner and Elisabeth Müller-Luckner. München: Oldenbourg Verlag, pp. 55–69.

Pagden, Anthony (1992). *The Fall of Natural Man*. Cambridge: Cambridge University Press.

Rivera, Luis N. (1992). *A Violent Evangelism: The Political and Religious Conquest of the Americas*. Louisville, KY: Westminster John Knox Press.

Schmitt, Carl (1966). *Teoría del partisan*. Madrid: Instituto de Estudios Políticos.

Schmitt, Carl (2002). *El nomos de la tierra en el Derecho de Gentes del Ius publicum europaeum*. Granada: Ed. Comares.

Schreiner, Klaus and Elisabeth Müller-Luckner (eds) (2008). *Heilige Kriege*. München: Oldenbourg Verlag.

Sepúlveda, Juan Ginés de (1946). 'Democrates Alter, Or, On the Just Causes for War Against the Indians'. In *Introduction to Contemporary Civilization in the West*. New York: Columbia University Press <http://www.columbia.edu/acis/ets/CCREAD/sepulved.htm> (last accessed 29 August 2018).

Sepúlveda, Juan Ginés de (1996 [1780]). *Tratado sobre las justas causas de la guerra contra los indios*. México: Fondo de Cultura Económica.

Sepúlveda, Juan Ginés de (1997). 'Apología en favor del libro sobre las justas causas de la guerra'. In *Obras Completas III*. Córdoba: Excmo. Ayuntamiento de Pozoblanco.

Sepúlveda, Juan Ginés de (2003). 'Exhortación a Carlos V'. In *Obras Completas VII*. Córdoba: Excmo. Ayuntamiento de Pozoblanco.

Tomás de Aquino (1995). *Suma de Teología III*, parte II-II (a). Madrid: BAC.

Vitoria, Francisco de (1960). *Obras de Francisco de Vitoria – Relecciones Teológicas*. Madrid: Biblioteca de autores cristianos.

Vitoria, Francisco de (1964). *De Indis De Jure Belli*. New York and London: Oceana Publications Inc., Wildy & Sons Ltd. <https://en.wikisource.org/wiki/De_Indis_De_Jure_Belli> (last accessed 29 August 2018).

Vitoria, Francisco de (1981). *Relectio de Iure Belli o Paz Dinámica*. Madrid: Consejo Superior de Investigaciones Científicas.

Vitoria, Francisco de (1991). *Political Writings*. Cambridge: Cambridge University Press.

Vitoria, Francisco de (1995 [1533–4]). 'La ley'. In *De lege – Commentarium in Primam Secundae*, qq. 90–108. Madrid: Tecnos.

Vitoria, Francisco de (2012 [1528, 1538–9, 1539]). *Sobre el poder civil, Sobre los indios, Sobre el derecho de la Guerra*. Madrid: Tecnos.

Vollerthun, Ursula and James L. Richardson (2017). *The Idea of International Society: Erasmus, Vitoria, Gentili and Grotius*. Cambridge: Cambridge University Press.

Wittgenstein, Ludwig (2000). *Sobre la certeza*. Barcelona: Gedisa ed.

Zavala, Silvio (1993 [1947]). *La filosofía política en la Conquista de América*. México: Fondo de Cultura Económica.

Part IV

Repetitions: Tradition and Historical Inheritance

16

A Gaping Lacuna: Gersonides's Apparent Silence About Aristotle's Ethics/Politics in the Context of the Judeo-Arabic Tradition

Idit Dobbs-Weinstein

The Torah is not a law (*nimus*) that forces us to believe false ideas [but] rather leads us to truth to the extent possible. (Gershom 1984–99: 98)[1]

True opinion follows reality rather than reality following opinions that are considered to be true, and thus dictate our rejection of the evidence of the senses for them. (Goldstein 1985: 42; quoted in Glasner 1996: 15)

Gersonides's strictly philosophical writings are constituted by extensive supercommentaries on Averroes's commentaries on Aristotle's works, a commentary on Averroes's writing on conjunction with the Agent Intellect, and an independent treatise on modal syllogisms. These ostensibly philosophical texts can be further divided into clearly logical ones and 'properly' philosophical ones. In the absence of an extant manuscript of the *Supercommentary on the Metaphysics*, the remaining strictly philosophical works can be grouped under the heading of physics, both in the form of supercommentaries on the biological works – including two on the *Physics*, one on the Epitome and the other on the Middle Commentary – and in the form of a *Supercommentary on the De Anima* which, properly understood, is a physics of animate entities capable of self-motion. In the light of the facts that (1) the text of the *De Anima* as well as Gersonides's supercommentary on it are concerned with causes of motion, ending with the centrality of desire/appetition to locomotion, and (2) the inseparability between the *De Anima* and the *Nicomachean Ethics* in Maimonides's and Averroes's extensive discussions of human felicity – both moral and intellectual, an inseparability implicitly acknowledged and even underscored in Gersonides's *Supercommentary on the De Anima* as well as throughout *The Wars of the Lord* – the absence of a supercommentary on the *Nicomachean Ethics* and relative

---

[1] With the exception of Book V part 1, all English references to *The Wars of the Lord* will be to (Gershom 1984–99). References to the English translation of *Wars* V.1 will be Gerson (1985). Since I have no access to the entire manuscript of *Wars* V.1, references to other chapters of *Wars* V.1, will rely on citations in Glasner's appendix and Harvey (1987). Hebrew references are to (Gershom 1966), which is a reproduction of Jacob Marciari (ed.) First printing of Riva de Trento, Editio Princeps, 1560. There is no published version of the Hebrew text of *Wars* V, 1, which is a long treatise on mathematical astronomy and trigonometry, and almost all the extant manuscripts omit it.

silence about Aristotle's ethics/politics in his *magnum opus* is, to say the least, striking. This silence is even more striking when we take into consideration Gersonides's stated apologia to the *Wars*, which he explains at length as being motivated by a concern for human flourishing, a concern that both there and in other works is expressed in classically practical idioms, namely as the *toʿelet* and *toʿalot*, תועלת, תועלות (utility or benefit) to the reader. Expressing this concern in strikingly desirative terms and in response to anticipated detractors, Gersonides states, 'my strong desire [ʿotzem tshukatenu] to remove obstacles that block the man of inquiry from attaining the truth on these questions leading to human happiness has led me to undertake this project' (Gershom 1984–99: 97). Insofar as the desire concerns human happiness, it is clearly an ethical/political one. And, finally, making the philosophical silence even more uncanny is the fact that a Hebrew translation of Averroes's *Middle Commentary on the Nicomachean Ethics*, by Samuel Ben Judah of Marseilles, was completed in February 1321. Seven years later in October 1328 Gersonides completed his *Commentary on Ecclesiastes* or *Qohelet*,[2] the text where the *Nicomachean Ethics* and Aristotelian politics finally make a stealthy appearance in a biblical commentary. Why here and nowhere else? And, more importantly, how does Aristotelean ethics affect Gersonides's readings of *Ecclesiastes* and vice versa? Before I turn to a preliminary consideration of this strange commentary on an exceedingly problematic biblical text, I wish to consider not only possible reasons for this silence, but the implicit complicity of its silencing by most Gersonides scholars.

At the outset I would like to 'confess' that it would be extremely tempting to explain away this uncanny silence, as well as some other surprising departures from a radically materialist physics, in Straussian terms, that is, as a prudent esoteric strategy. Tempting as this explanation may be, however, it is highly implausible, especially in light of Gersonides's totally imprudent practice of supercommentaries on most of Averroes's commentaries on Aristotle, including the *De Anima*, which was the main target of the condemnations of 1272 and 1277. Although there have been numerous attempts to 'force' Gersonides' *Wars* to support some form of individual immortality, not only does the *Supercommentary on the De Anima* belie such readings but so does Gersonides's denial of divine knowledge of particulars in the *Wars*. Nor can we explain away as esoteric the two other philosophical instances where Gersonides defends positions that are in tension with his thoroughly materialist commitments, dreams, divinations and prophecy, on the one hand, and creation from something, on the other. These inconsistencies are striking insofar as they concern *both* method *and* substance in a remarkably consistent philosopher, the former case arguing for a difference in kind among dreams, divinations and prophecy,[3] and the latter not only defending creation out of something but also claiming to have resolved all doubts about the question of origin (Gershom 1984–99: 6).

If the first 'esotericist' type of reading would conceal a tension between Torah and philosophy, another type would conceal a Platonic practical orientation to all knowledge – a claim often made about Alfarabi, Maimonides and Averroes, and against which Gad Freudenthal seems to argue when he insists upon the 'purely rational realism' of Gersonides in accord with which knowledge is an end in itself with no practical, that is, political significance (Freudenthal 1992). Freudenthal's radical depoliticising (and dehistoricising) of all knowledge is offered in support of an argument that there are two Gersonides, the one a philosopher and biblical exegete, the other a scientist, astronomer and mathematician, the latter of whom is a proto-modern. What is especially surprising about Freudenthal's position is not at all the claim to

---

[2] *Qohelet* is the Hebrew name of *Ecclesiastes*.
[3] See Dobbs-Weinstein (2006).

Gersonides's proto-modernism but rather Freudenthal's grounding of this position in the claim that Gersonides, like Alfarabi [sic] and Avicenna, and against Maimonides and Averroes, argued for individual immortality. I want to suggest that the coupling of modern science with individual immortality proposed by Freudenthal is a modern interpolation; Gersonides on this reading would be not only a proto-Cartesian dualist but also a pseudo-Christian. For, while the Christian origins of modern science have been amply and convincingly demonstrated,[4] and while I agree with the general claim, first advanced by Menachem Kellner, that Gersonides is a philosopher caught between two worlds, it is neither because he endorses individual immortality nor because he seeks to separate theory and practice, knowledge and action, as the *Qohelet* commentary will make amply evident. That there are sciences without practical utility, such as mathematics (but surely not astronomy) does not imply a tension between the theoretical and practical ends of any science – and certainly not for an Aristotelian who commented on the *De Anima* and read the *Nicomachean Ethics*. For, as Aristotle reminds us in *Nicomachean Ethics* 6.2 (1139a35–1139b1), 'it is not thought as such that can move anything but thought together with right desire, and that thought is practical' (Aristotle 1934, 1984). Moreover, and ironically, it is precisely at the level of indubitable science, the exemplary form of which is mathematics, whose objects do not exist by nature and hence do not undergo change, that individual immortality is both impossible and incoherent, since mathematical truths are indeed universal and eternal, and do not differ among individuals. It cannot be overemphasised, however, that although genuine human felicity consists in knowing the intellegibiles, in possessing them, and that such knowledge is the highest form of human perfection, it does not render the individual immortal, for, to recall Aristotle's *De Anima* 3 (430a23–24), 'we do not remember' (Aristotle 1957, 1981).

However we will come to understand the tension between the two worlds inhabited by Gersonides, a tension which is indeed evident in the articulation of the different human perfections, theoretical as well as practical, necessary for human felicity in the *Qohelet* commentary, that tension is not reducible to the radical differences between biblical exegesis, philosophy and science. On the contrary, and as Sarah Klein-Braslavy has made amply evident, Gersonides's commentaries on biblical texts follow the same procedures as do his philosophical commentaries precisely because Gersonides regards them *as philosophical texts*.[5] Finally, both Klein-Braslavy and Steve Harvey have argued and severally demonstrated that Gersonides's texts, especially in 'proemiums', that is, apologiae for writing, emphasise the utility or benefit of the subject matter, a benefit that is for the sake of human felicity (Klein-Braslavy 20005).[6] Finally, James Robinson outlines in detail the philosophical importance of the proemium in Samuel Ibn Tibbon's *Commentary on Ecclesiastes*, emphasising its origin in the Alexandrian tradition (Robinson 2000).[7]

Concealing Sources

Whereas in the *Wars* Gersonides's dialectical method not only mentions all possible opinions on the problems investigated in order to distinguish the true from the false and eliminate all doubt but also, and more importantly, he identifies all these sources, traditional as well as

---

[4] See Kojève (1984) and Funkenstein (1985).
[5] See Klein-Braslavy (2005).
[6] See also Klein-Braslavy (2011) and Harvey and Fontaine (forthcoming).
[7] In the introduction of her edition of 'Gersonides' Commentary on Ecclesiastes', Ruth Ben-Meir traces in detail the influence of Ibn Tibbon's commentary on that of Gersonides (Ben Meir 1993).

philosophical, in the *Qohelet* commentary, Gersonides does not identify his sources, with the exception of Solomon and Aristotle. Such silence notwithstanding, the influence of both Ibn Ezra's and Samuel Ibn Tibbon's Commentaries on Ecclesiastes are clearly evident.[8] In a manner consistent with his predecessors, especially Ibn Tibbon, Gersonides identifies the purpose of both texts as directing the wise to rise above all corporeal goods in deference to the fear of God, the necessary condition for human immortality.

Why does Gersonides refrain from identifying all his sources, including the traditional ones, in this instance? The most likely reason is the violent raging Maimonidean controversy and the virulent anti-Maimonideanism of the period,[9] especially the rejection of the unmitigated rationalism of first-generation Maimonideans, an exemplary representative of which is Ibn Tibbon. Concealing even traditional sources in this context, Gersonides can be seen to follow his two pre-eminent philosophical predecessors, Maimonides and Averroes. And unsurprisingly, both Maimonides and Averroes conceal their sources in their attempts to intervene philosophically in the traditional controversies of their times.

In the introduction to 'The Eight Chapters' – itself a lengthy preparatory introduction to his *Commentary on ʾAvot* tractate of the *Mishnah* – Maimonides underlines the fact that the text is of great benefit and leads to a great perfection, provided its seemingly clear diction does not cover over the difficulty in understanding its intentions or carrying them out without 'lucid explanation'. Following its teachings, according to Maimonides, leads to prophecy and 'encompasses a large portion of morality'. Maimonides is emphatic that the text presents no innovation – the traditional charge against philosophical interpretation – but rather is gathered from 'the discourse of the *Sages* in the *Midrash*, the *Talmud*, and other compositions of theirs, as well as from the discourse of both the ancient and modern philosophers, and from the compositions of many men. *Hear the truth from whoever says it*' (Maimonides 1983: 60; emphasis added).[10]

Following this emphatic admonition Maimonides presents two reasons for concealing sources, the first strictly practical, 'useless prolixity': the second, theologico-political, namely the likelihood that 'the name of such an individual might make the passage offensive to someone without experience and make him think it has an evil inner meaning of which he is not aware' (Maimonides 1983: 60–1). Seeking to be useful to the reader, Maimonides explains the inner meaning of the text after he provides the reader with a brief primer to the relation between Aristotelian epistemic/moral psychology and traditional aporiae, often by resolving apparent contradictions among them. As will become evident, there is a striking similarity between Maimonides's 'Eight Chapters' and Gersonides's *Qohelet* commentary both in terms of the subject matter and in terms of their method.

In a similar manner, in the *Decisive Treatise* Averroes seeks to defend the philosophers and philosophical enquiry into questions concerning which *is said to be* disagreements between tradition and philosophy, against charges of apostasy leveled by Abu Hamid al-Ghazali. In defence of philosophical enquiry, Averroes argues not only that it is (by law)

---

[8] See Ben-Meir (1993: 168–81). It is noteworthy that, in a striking departure from providing strictly philological commentaries on biblical books (a procedure lauded by Spinoza), in the case of Ecclesiastes and the Song of Songs, Ibn Ezra states that the text is multilayered and provides either allegorical or philosophical analyses. For Gersonides's sources, see also Weil (1991). It is clear, however, that Gersonides's library far from exhausts his sources.

[9] See Dobbs-Weinstein (2004).

[10] The original Judeo-Arabic (with facing Hebrew translation) of the 'Eight Chapters' can be found in Maimonides (1964).

obligatory but also that the obligation extends to the use of *ancient* philosophical sources. Whereas al-Ghazali accuses the philosophers of 'heretical innovations' in their deployment of syllogistic reasoning, Averroes argues,

> [i]f someone other than us has already investigated that, it is *evidently obligatory* for us to reply on what the one who has preceded us says about what we are pursuing, *regardless of whether that other person shares our religion or not*... And by 'not sharing [in our religion]' I mean those Ancients who reflected upon those things *before* the religion of Islam. (Averroes 2001: 4; emphasis added)[11]

Turning the tables on al-Ghazali, Averroes' claim that it is the one who discloses to the multitude and others incapable of demonstrative reasoning that there is a difference between the apparent meaning of the texts and the inner meaning, as al-Ghazali and other theologians had done, who should be accused of leading the multitude to disbelief about the 'roots of the Law'. Accordingly, interpretation ought not be declared to the multitude, nor established in rhetorical or dialectical books – that is, books in which the statements posited are of these two sorts – as Abu Hamid al-Ghazali did.[12]

Gersonides's Commentary on Ecclesiastes (*Qohelet*)[13]

Before proceeding, an important gloss: it took twenty-seven years before I could locate Aristotle's *Nicomachean Ethics* in Gersonides's corpus and discover it hidden in the *Commentary of Ecclesiastes*, a text fortunately edited by Ruth Ben-Meir as a 1994 PhD dissertation written under the direction of Zeev Harvey. It is also worth noting that, with the exception of Ben-Meir's analysis introducing her edition in this PhD thesis, to my knowledge no extensive work, philosophical or otherwise, has been done on this text. Certainly no philosophical study is available in print, with the exception of a very brief consideration of the prologue by Sarah Klein-Braslavy, and none is known to pre-eminent researchers on *Qohelet* commentaries – including James Robinson, the editor and English translator of Samuel Ibn Tibbon's *Commentary on Ecclesiastes* – which clearly influenced Gersonides.[14] More importantly, in a recent study of Gersonides's *Ethics*, which focuses on biblical commentaries (including the one on Proverbs), Gersonides's *Commentary on Ecclesiastes [Qohelet]* is deliberately ignored.[15] Is this the contemporary version of seeking to ban the book, let alone philosophical enquiry into it, as heretical? Perhaps. Given the heretofore 'hiddenness' of this text, the bulk of this chapter will be philological and paraphrastic, beginning with a detailed presentation and analysis of the prologue.

---

[11] Averroes follows this claim with examples from other sciences as well, for example, geometry and astronomy. Although truth may be a-temporal, knowledge of it is prefect and no one individual is capable of attaining it without the prior achievements of their predecessors.

[12] Averroes (2001: 26–7).

[13] *Qohelet* is the Hebrew title of the biblical texts translated into English as 'Ecclesiastes'. Since Gersonides emphasises the fact that the title refers to a *collection* of diverse opinions on good and bad – and therefore argues that the text proceeds dialectically – I shall henceforth refer to Gersonides's commentary as the *Commentary on Qohelet* (or *Qohelet* commentary), since the question of method is central to Gersonides's consideration of the *Commentary on Ecclesiastes*.

[14] See Robinson (2007).

[15] See Green (2016). Green mentions the commentary in passing but does not discuss it. This is not surprising since this commentary – as well as the one on the Song of Songs that, although mentioned, is largely ignored – puts into question Green's thesis and conclusion.

At the outset it is important to note that, at the end of the introduction, Gersonides identifies *Qohelet* as the first of Solomon's three ethical books, followed by Proverbs and concluding with the Song of Songs,[16] a progression that he argues establishes a descending order from general/universal *(kolel)* ethical problems to more specialised ones, and from the more to the less complete/perfect. The hierarchy of perfection established by Gersonides thus also establishes the *Qohelet* commentary as Gersonides's ethics/politics, an enquiry in which he addresses the most persistent and incalcitrant ethical aporiae in a comprehensive way. It is important to note that Gersonides's claim to the order of composition of Solomon's works is at odds with Gersonides's own order of commentary on them. His *Commentary on the Song of Songs* preceded *Qohelet* and was concluded in 1326, and his *Commentary on Proverbs* was not concluded until 1338.

Both Steve Harvey and Sarah Klein-Braslavy have examined in detail the philosophical importance of prologues in the Islamic and Jewish Alexandrian commentary tradition, Harvey focusing on Ibn-Rush, Klein-Braslavy on Gersonides. Succinctly but forcefully making the case for the pre-eminent importance of prologues to interpretation, Klein-Braslavy states:

> The introduction to books [is] one of the keys to understanding and interpreting them. When authors write an introduction they are telling readers what to expect and directing them toward how they should read and understand a book. The introduction to a commentary on a book by another author explains how the commentator views the work being glossed. Consequently the introduction is already *a part of the interpretation* and provides a lens through which readers should see the book. (Klein-Braslavy 2005: 257–89; emphasis added)

Given the importance of prologues for understanding commentary as interpretation,[17] and given the great difficulty of the biblical text of *Qohelet*, I shall examine the introduction in some detail.

As is his habit in all his writings, philosophical as well as biblical, Gersonides's prologues are classical apologia, explaining why he decided to comment on any given book, both on its terms and its substance. In the first sentence of the prologue to *Qohelet*, he immediately identifies the need for commentary to arise from the fact that the text embodies evident confusion, doubt and contradictions in a manner such that the letter of the book presents base things as desirable. Gersonides also immediately reminds the reader of the fact that the Sages debated whether or not to hide (or ban, *lignoz*) the book but refrained from doing so because its *arche* and *telos* concern Torah.[18] Gersonides also immediately identifies the source of the confusion prevalent in and generated by *Qohelet* with the nature of the subject matter of *Qohelet* rather than the thought of Solomon or the 'perfect' *(ha-Shalem)* as he presents him in the opening paragraph of the prologue. Further on in the introductory paragraphs, Gersonides interprets the word *Qohelet* to mean gathering, here a gathering of diverse opinions.

Whereas Solomon is the author whose perfection and wisdom authorises the biblical centrality of *Qohelet*, Aristotle is the philosopher whose philosophical authority both identifies the

---

[16] With respect to order, although for different reasons, Gersonides agrees with Samuel Ibn Tibbon and against Rabbi Jonathan. See Robinson (2000: 88–9).
[17] The Jewish tradition of biblical interpretation is divided into grammatical, philological and philosophical commentaries, the latter being rare. Gersonides often provides two of these methods in the same commentary.
[18] Note that Torah means instruction or teaching.

nature of the subject matter and the proper method of enquiry, namely dialectics. To identify Solomon's procedure with Aristotelian dialectics is to recognise not only the absolute agreement between the ethical teachings of the Tanakh (Hebrew Scripture) and of Aristotle, but also to identify Solomon as a philosopher. It is worth noting that the relation between Gersonides's Solomon and Aristotle is almost identical to that between Maimonides's Moses and Aristotle.[19]

In the second introductory paragraph, Gersonides proposes as a primary premise that the enquiry into good and evil (*tov va-r^{c}a*) belongs to political philosophy and it investigates what exists insofar as it exists and, as the philosopher explained, this subject does not lend itself to complete verification *(ha$^?$amatah)*, since whatever may be clarified in it proceeds by means of commonly held primary principles (*endoxa, mefursamot*) which principles prove one thing and its contrary, as has been explained in the *Topics* (Ben-Meir 1993: 1).

Already at this stage, it cannot be overemphasised that, for Gersonides, the aporiae of good and evil are ethical/political rather than metaphysical and that it is in this respect that he identifies the first and final causes/principles of Torah. For Gersonides, the enquiry into the question of human felicity is an enquiry into the *physis* of the specifically human psyche, which is precisely what the *Nicomachean Ethics* investigates or, as cited above, this is an enquiry into existents as they exist rather than as they should be (Averroes 2001: passim). Or again, in a classical Aristotelian manner, for Gersonides, the necessary precedes and determines the possible. Later on in the body of the *Commentary* Gersonides will indicate the proximity of Aristotelian physics and metaphysics.[20]

Although the aporiae encountered in *Qohelet* present special difficulties that arise from the nature and proliferation of the specific opinions about good and evil found in the biblical text, Gersonides is explicit, following Aristotle, that all philosophical enquiries must proceed dialectically first by gathering all the different, often contradictory, opinions specific to each discourse so as to distinguish the correct (*tsodek*) from the incorrect and in this manner attain first principles that will make possible the attainment of truth (*$^?$emet*).[21] He further argues that Aristotle advised following the same method even in demonstrative enquiries. Surprisingly, the example of a demonstrative science that he offers is physics, the exemplarity of which makes evident Gersonides's belief that dialectics not only lies on the way to first principles, as it does for Aristotle, but also can bring about their apprehension.[22] And, in a manner reminiscent of Maimonides, Gersonides views the question of proper procedure, of method – both its order and pace – to be an ethical question, since perplexity can lead not only to apostasy but also to improper conduct.

---

[19] Whereas for Gersonides Solomonic teachings here do not exceed Aristotelian wisdom, for Maimonides Mosaic perfection does. According to Maimonides, Aristotle is 'chief of the philosophers', whereas Moses is the 'pillar of human perfection'. Further discussion of this difference is beyond the scope of this chapter. Such discussion will have to take into account the differences between Maimonides and Gersonides on the relations among dreams, divinations and prophecy as well as the differences between their cosmologies, and Gersonides's rejection of emanation. See Dobbs-Weinstein (2006).

[20] As mentioned in the introduction, Gersonides composed supercommentaries on all of Averroes's commentaries on Aristotle's biological works, including two on the *Physics*. Unfortunately, his supercommentary on the *Metaphysics* is not extant.

[21] Klein-Braslavy carefully examines Gersonides's methodological procedure and further narrows the sense in which *Qohelet* is a dialectical enquiry to a 'diaporematic' method investigating all the possible opinions or *endoxa*, as hypotheses in order to distinguish the true from the false in them (Klein-Braslavy 2005: 283).

[22] While a discussion of Gersonides's departure form Aristotle and his Aristotelian predecessor with respect to noetics and science is beyond the scope of this chapter, it is important to indicate that, in his astronomy, we begin to see a breach with Aristotelian metabasis.

Following the careful clarification of the nature and method appropriate to political philosophy, namely dialectics, or as Klein-Braslavy argues convincingly in the case of *Qohelet* diaporematics, Gersonides posits a first general, comprehensive proposition about the precise aspect in which this book, *Qohelet*, is a study of good and evil. But, here, as in other enquiries, following Aristotle, Gersonides is at pains to foreclose a general understanding of dialectics, and thereby of method, insisting instead on specifying the precise, concrete or material aspect in which the question is to be investigated. He argues that the wise Solomon began his investigation with the question of whether the good is the pleasant or useful/beneficial, since preliminary or unreflective thought identifies the good with the pleasant and presents it as worthy of first choice, provided that there pre-exists no moral prohibition against this.

What is especially striking in these opening paragraphs is that Gersonides immediately attributes to Solomon the identification of the pleasant and its subsequent initial outright rejection with corporeal pleasure, an identification that leads to the conclusion that the good is the useful. The following discussion of the three useful goods makes amply evident a rather peculiar understanding of corporeal perfection, an entirely de-eroticised one, which is at odds not only with Aristotle and (to a lesser extent) Maimonides, but also and, more importantly, with Gersonides's own discussions of the human psyche in the *Supercommentary on the De Anima* as well as the *Wars*. Even on the basis of these few lines it becomes amply evident that, when Gersonides juxtaposes the pleasant as desirable or as first object of choice and moral prohibition, he views moral prohibition, that is, law and custom, not so much as a directing of desire/affect, both collective and individual, but precisely as its repression.

In this light, I want to suggest in a preliminary manner that, ironically, Gersonides's attempt to separate choice from desire in this commentary is a separation that is simultaneously in profound tension with his other works and may account at the end for this and the other striking tensions in his thought, that is, for the philosopher caught between two worlds, and two philosophical temperaments, respectively expressing a premodern ethos and a modern one. As will become evident, the de-eroticising – and thereby depoliticising of human felicity in the *Qohelet Commentary* – demonstrates in practice the manner and aspects in which Gersonides is a radical Aristotelian and those in which he departs from Aristotle. It may also serve to account for the absence of Aristotelian ethics/politics from the *Wars*.[23]

Having eliminated the pleasant as proper object of human pursuit in any form, Gersonides's Solomon identifies the good with the useful and the latter with the beneficial and distinguishes three forms of this good: (1) the striving (*hishtadlut*) to accumulate possessions (*harbot ha-kinyanim*); (2) the striving for excellence in practice (*kishron ha-ma'aseh*) so as to acquire useful moral virtues (*ha-moʿil ba-midot*); and (3) the striving for theoretical virtue (*Ha-hishtadlut ba-ʿiyyuniot*). To a philosophical, medieval Aristotelian ear trained in Hebrew, Gersonides's terminology is rather tortuous which, in my view, cannot be accounted for merely by the language of the biblical text of *Qohelet*, especially in light of Gersonides's use of Aristotelian terminology both in the prologue and throughout the text. Rather, I want to argue that the repression of desire/appetite in the constitution of goods, the disembodiment of the beneficial, in short, the displacement from or even loss of the body to the *Commentary* leads to a transformation and translation of Aristotelian and Maimonidean ethical language. The traditional consideration of human perfection in terms of the relation between the perfection of the body (*shelemut ha-guf*) and perfection of the soul (*shlemut ha-nefesh*) is no longer adequate to

---

[23] The other two striking tensions between Gersonides's scientific and philosophical and biblical interpretations concern the aporia of the origin of the universe and the respective relation among dreams, divinations and prophecy. I shall return to these in the conclusion.

Gersonides's ethical enquiry. Viewed in this light, however, how is this ethical enquiry a political enquiry? The answer to this question will depend upon the manner in which we interpret the relation between Gersonidean ethics and Torah, especially since the opening paragraphs seem to identify Aristotelian ethics/politics with Torah, at least with respect to their role as first and final causes of the attainment of human felicity, that is, perfection/happiness.

Asking which of the three goods is the true good, Gersonides's wise Solomon responds that, although each of these goods assists the others, the one most choice worthy is that of striving for wisdom. He adds that, insofar as Torah best directs its adherents to the right conduct most beneficial to the attainment of this good, Solomon instructs human beings to follow the ways of the Torah and obey the commandments by means of which 'the good which is the useful' will be attained most completely. The continuous repetition of the phrase 'the good which is the useful' (*ha-tov she-hu ha-moʿil*) in the space of the same paragraph in Gersonides has already determined that Solomon's good is not the pleasant, let alone corporeal pleasure, makes amply evident Gersonides's recognition that, by radically denigrating pleasure, he is departing from traditional Aristotelian, and even Maimonidean, ethics, and advocates for positions in tension with his other philosophical writings, especially the philosophical commentaries on Averroes's commentaries on Aristotle. And, if I may be permitted to psychologise, the phrase's repeated insistence also makes evident its non-philosophical dimension. In short, 'methink Gersonides doth protest too much'. Gersonides draws an astonishing conclusion from his claim that fulfilling the commandments is the best way to attain the perfect good, claiming that '[f]rom this it follows that the human being is provided by God with an individual providence (*hashgahah pratit*) and is safeguarded from many evils that may beset him, and this is the purpose of this entire book' (Ben-Meir 1993: 3). Whence individual providence? However we are to understand the Torah and the individual's possible relation to it, especially insofar as the emphasis here is on obedience to all the commandments as a way to the attainment of the complete human good, or the human good completely, surely it cannot be interpreted individually. The commandment to study the Torah – *Ve-hagitah bo yoman va-layla* or *thou shall study it day and night* – is not numbered among the 613 commandments and prohibitions, nor can it be.

The discussion of providence in Gersonides is clearly far beyond the scope of this chapter. In lieu of such a discussion let me recall that, for Gersonides, God does not know particulars as particulars, which clearly puts into question the meaning of particular providence. For, if providence is in accord with intellectual perfection, as it is in Gersonides, and even if we want to argue that the different proportions in which individuals attain intellectual perfection, or the different number of intelligibles each acquires, individuates them in a non-material way, it still does not follow from this that God watches over them individually, let alone that there is individual providence over all those who fulfil the commandments. For even in the case of those few who attain intelligibles, and they are but a few, their acquired intellect is but a proportion of the Agent Intellect, which is the only *self-subsistent*, existing individual.[24]

Before I turn to what I view as the central aporiae in the body of the commentary, a brief consideration of the prologue's final very short, concluding paragraph is called for, since it sheds further light on Gersonides's exegetical strategy. In the summary concluding statement about the nature of *Qohelet*, Gersonides once again emphasises the fact that the book is a comprehensive enquiry into 'the human conduct fitting to the pursuit of the different kinds of this good *which is the useful* [*minei ha-tov ha-zeh she-hu ha-moʿil*], and the shunning of its contrary in this [singular] respect [*b'tsad meyuhad*] in every one of its discourses [*davar davar mimenu*]' (Ben-Meir 1993: 3; translation modified).

---

[24] See Dobbs-Weinstein (1996: 191–213).

Having specified, once again, the respect in which *Qohelet* investigates the good, having stringently delineated the scope of the enquiry, which Gersonides identifies with Aristotle's ethics/political philosophy (*philosophia medinit*), Gersonides describes this enquiry as the universal enquiry (*ʿiyyun kolel*), that is, it is the architectonic ethical/political enquiry preceding and informing all others. I shall return to this in the conclusion because this emphatic delineation of ethics/politics not only instructs the reader about the precise way in which s/he is to interpret 'good and evil' in the body of this commentary (and perhaps by multiple repetition even warns her/him not to interpret it in any other way) but also distills the manner in which Gersonides's philosophy as a whole both follows and departs from that of Aristotle.

'The discourse of *Qohelet*, son of David, king of Jerusalem. Vapor vapors (or Vanity vanities) said *Qohelet*, vapor, vapors, all is vapor' (Ben-Meir 1993: 1–2)

If the prologue is a classical apologia, then the first paragraph of the body of the commentary is apologetic. In the opening statement, Gersonides claims that had the author's identity not been disclosed at the outset, or immediately, he would not have pursued the enquiry into *Qohelet* since its discourse would otherwise have appeared to be unseemly or improper (*bilti raʾui*) upon initial consideration. But, Gersonides adds that had he done so, he would have been prevented from deriving any benefit (*toʿelet*) from it. Clearly, this apology is also a warning to the readers not to hasten to conclusions about what follows, assuring them of the ethical appropriateness of the discourse of *Qohelet* by the double authority of Solomon and Aristotle. It is traditional authority that identifies the study of the book as a human good, a good that is useful. As such, the study of good and evil which is the subject matter of *Qohelet* is immediately identified as the good that is the useful. Ironically, as becomes evident in the opening paragraphs, the utility of the book derives predominantly from the fact that most of its discourse, that is, most of the opinions that are gathered in it, are incorrect *(bilti tsodkim* or *unjust)* so as to teach one how to avoid choosing the improper or unjust. The predominance, even pre-eminence, of the improper in the discourse of *Qohelet* upon this reading is announced again in the opening line by the term 'vapor' (*hevel*) which Gersonides identifies as a 'lie' (*khazav*). The more that lies are exposed as lies, the more what is fitting is disclosed.

And, indeed, as if the text itself does not already present enough perplexing opinions that could easily be interpreted as heterodox, many of Gersonides's interpretations and extrapolations of them are strangely perverse. For if to a large extent the difficulties in understanding *Qohelet* arise from its aphoristic repetitions, Gersonides's interpretation fleshes them out in the most extreme or base readings, as if to warn his readers against certain temptations when faced with the transitory nature of human life and all things in this lowly world (*ha-ʿolam ha-shafel*),[25] the subject matter and cause of the despair found in *Qohelet*. Briefly stated, in all of its variations – whether they are viewed from the perspective of physics, astronomy or ethics – Gersonides's presentations of the questions asked throughout the book are crudely reducible to a single question: 'what is the value of any human endeavor in the light of the transitoriness of this lowly world?' which, in the *Commentary*, is explored in terms of the relations among the three human goods identified in the prologue. More precisely stated, the question is: 'in light of the transitoriness of human life what are the benefits/or advantages in the pursuit of what are taken to be the three human goods?' – a pursuit that is presented by

---

[25] A stronger and starker translation of the Hebrew word *shafel* would be 'base'.

Gersonides in the language of striving or *conatus*, i.e., in *decidedly* materialist terms. To recall, these are: (1) the striving (*hishtadlut*) to accumulate possessions, (*harbot ha-kinyanim*); (2) the striving for excellence in practice (*kishron ha-maʿaseh*) so as to acquire *useful* moral virtues (*ha-moʿil ba-midot*); and (3) the striving for theoretical virtue (*ha-hishtadlut ba ʿiyyuniot*).

Before proceeding to an examination of the arguments against the striving for knowledge and Gersonides's Solomonic response to them, it would be helpful provide one example of the peculiar 'perversity' of Gersonides's interpretation or extrapolation of an instance of despair in the text of *Qohelet*. Glossing on *Qohelet* 2.20, 'I went about to cause my heart to despair of all the labor which I took under the sun',[26] Gersonides extends the despair to include the pursuit of wisdom, explaining the cause of the despair with an example of an evidently perfect individual. She has laboured in the acquisition of wisdom and knowledge (*hokhmah va-daʿat*) and virtuous action through study of the ethical virtues, striving to perfect both the political community and her soul, and has also laboured extensively to compose books on this subject and handed them down to another individual, who benefited from the fruit of this labour without extending any effort. Notwithstanding the great toil of the first individual, if she has not exhausted the enquiry in the most comprehensive way, the slothful heir (so to speak) using the fruit of her investigation will add to it and will be credited as the author who discovered this branch of wisdom or this ethics/political science (*nimus medini*). In the light of the likelihood of such an outcome, it is believed that it may, indeed, be beneficial for any individual to refrain from or even avoid the pursuit of knowledge, not only because s/he may not be credited for the beneficial fruits of her/his labor but also, and more importantly, because s/he may be striving in vain to attain it – however hard s/he tries and despite her/his desire for it.

I am hard pressed to think of a more petty, base or unworthy (*bilti raʾui*) (but not unrealistic) example of cause for despair than the first one presented by Gersonides. In light of the fact that he explicitly and repeatedly points out the incompleteability of all knowledge – let alone political science – were the pursuit of knowledge ever to be motivated by receiving credit for it (that is, by pride), it would clearly be pursued for the sake of another end/benefit. For even if, as in the case of political philosophy, enquiry/knowledge is not pursued as an end in itself but rather for the sake of action and the construction of the best possible political community, such that the benefit it provides extends far beyond the individual, it is beneficial to the individual as well. In contrast, Gersonides's second brief example of despair – philosophical and Aristotelian, as distinct from personal – is found numerous times in the *Wars* and is the focus of an extended discussion further on in *Qohelet* which investigates the nature of the human desire for knowledge, to which I now turn.

Commenting on *Qohelet* 4.1–12, which Gersonides interprets to reflect upon the relation between the three goods/benefits, he outlines here the seven prevalent opinions (*mahashvot*) enumerated by Solomon that lead to the conclusion that the human pursuit of knowledge is vain or useless, that is, without benefit. Before proceeding, it is important to underscore again the fact that pleasure in every instance of its mention is identified, quite emphatically, with corporeal pleasure. These are:

1. The human desire for knowledge is for naught (*le-batala*) since all things continuously undergo change and corruption and hence are unknowable. This opinion, Gersonides informs the reader, is one shared by many philosophers and is outlined in Aristotle's *Metaphysics*. Gersonides adds that the same opinion dismisses the striving to acquire the two other presumed goods as equally useless.

---

[26] Jerusalem Bible.

2. It is evident that the striving in the search for wisdom is accompanied by sadness and pain which, in aporetic enquiry, is constant; the more one engages in numerous such pursuits, the more one is prevented from *bodily* pleasure. Pain is to be avoided and pleasure pursued. QED. According to Gersonides's *Qohelet*, from this it also follows the opinion that folly is preferable to wisdom.
3. 'One should not tire with the acquisition of intelligibles, that is, with the apprehension of the plan (*nimus*) of the existents, their order, and perfection (*sidram ve-yoshram*) since humans cannot attain complete/perfect knowledge of this matter' (Ben-Meir 1993: 20). From this it follows that whatever partial cognition we do attain of the science of the existents (*hokhmat ha-Nimts'aot*), it is false.[27] To any reader of Gersonides's *Wars* it is not surprising that concerning this opinion he states: 'And this [opinion], upon my life, is a very profound first principle (*hakdamah*) and full of doubt, and it is fitting that we should endeavor to resolve it because of the high rank of this inquiry [*godel ma-ʿalat zeh ha-darush*]' (Ben-Meir 1993: 20). In light of the importance assigned to this problem by Gersonides and its centrality to Gersonides's entire work, I shall postpone a discussion of it, and its attempted resolution in the *Qohelet Commentary*, until I enumerate the other opinions and their resolution.
4. Sensible evidence falsifies the belief of followers of the Torah that God rewards the wise and punishes the fool with corporeal goods.
5. This opinion repeats the earlier example about the failure to acknowledge, let alone reward, the individual whose labour is credited to another who accrues all the benefits from it. Not only are benefits here explicitly identified with wealth but also Gersonides describes this outcome as an 'evil', vengeful cause of pain and suffering.
6. 'It is evident that were wisdom superior to folly, such superiority is psychic; that is, the soul will delight in her intelligible and will remain eternal' (Ben-Meir 1993: 21). Here again, Gersonides points out that this opinion expresses a very strong perplexity (*mebukhah*) or doubt about the soul's immortality. In light of the intimate relation between this opinion and the third one, their centrality to Gersonides's other works, let alone to the question of providence briefly raised above,[28] I shall postpone the discussion of it to the conclusion and to what I see as the central aporia as well as tension of the *Qohelet* commentary.
7. It is evident that, in the majority of cases the striving in pursuit of wisdom and perfection of action is the origin of envy which is a base vice. Whatever is base in its generation is base. Therefore, it is believed . . . QED.

Rather than respond to each 'objection' in the classic scholastic manner (and the presentation is strikingly scholastic, which is not without great historical importance[29]) Gersonides presents five contrary opinions that demonstrate that the pursuit of knowledge (*ʿiyyun*) is good. Awkward as the idiom of the commentary may be, I shall nevertheless use it in the

---

[27] It is noteworthy that Gersonides refrains from his predecessors' common reference to metaphysics as divine science.

[28] See above, p. 309.

[29] The extent of Gersonides's familiarity with scholastic works and his knowledge of Latin is a matter of dispute beyond the scope of this chapter. Charles Touati and Seymour Feldman have questioned his direct knowledge of Latin sources, let alone knowledge of Latin, whereas Shlomo Pines and I have argued to the contrary. See the introduction to Gershom (1984–99), Touati (1973), Pines (1966) and Dobbs-Weinstein (1991).

summary of the proofs and will translate it into philosophical language only in the subsequent discussion.

> First: The wise person directs her actions correctly to the chosen ends from the beginning and hence attains them, whereas the fool may attain them, if at all, only by accident.
> Second: It is reprehensible to neglect the pursuit of knowledge for the sake of corporeal pleasures since the latter are vain and empty and should be shunned.
> Third: Although it is true that each of these goods is transitory, each is good in its appropriate time. Likewise, the degree of knowledge of the order of the universe given to humans is *very good* even though it is incomplete.
> Fourth: Knowledge is necessarily incorruptible and permanent since it concerns common natures (species) which are incorruptible.
> Fifth: It is necessary that God rewards the righteous and punishes the wicked. Since it is sensibly evident that everything occurs at its appropriate time; even if reward and punishments may not always be sensibly evident, it follows that God metes them out at the appropriate time.

Gersonides concludes that these *sed contra* are valid and stronger than the previous objections and that on these bases Solomon rightly concluded that the pursuit of the three useful goods is beneficial and that each assists the others.

Given the brevity of their presentation, and that he makes no attempt at presenting arguments on their behalf, Gersonides's conclusion about the validity and forcefulness of these opinions is surprising, unless we assume that the commentary is written to a philosophically very well-informed audience, an audience familiar with his other works. Thus, indeed, the first opinion translates into the contradiction between chance and the choice which follows upon deliberation, the second would emphasise the extrinsic nature of corporeal goods, the third would underline the universal nature of knowledge, and so forth. But this very same audience will also notice the contradiction between Gersonides's earlier claim to individual immortality and the claim to the incorruptibility of knowledge in virtue of its universal nature. Likewise, only to a philosophically informed audience would the claim to reward and punishment be compelling, provided that it is interpreted philosophically in conjunction with the second opinion denigrating corporeal pleasure as well as his earlier de-eroticising of human choice and the human goods. Since these opinions focus on the status of the human soul and the nature of providence – since they concern questions central to both the *Wars* and the *Supercommentary on the de Anima* as well as the two profound difficulties that Gersonides underlines in objections 3 and 6 outline above – I shall now turn in a very brief conclusion to these. Given the extent of these discussion and given my previous work on these questions,[30] I restrict my concluding discussion to the text of *Qohelet*.

Conclusion

Gersonides's articulation of the nature of the difficulty presented by the third opinion is a brief summary of his lengthy arguments in *Wars* 1 to which he refers the reader, as well as an encapsulation of his *Supercommentary on the de Anima*. What is especially astonishing about it is the extent to which it is in profound tension with his repeated denigration of corporeal goods and

---

[30] See Dobbs-Weinstein (1991, 1996, 2015).

its proto-Spinozist aspectival materialism. He argues 'our apprehension of this plan (*nimus*) is from one aspect other than its intelligible in God, and from another aspect it is the intelligible in God as it is clear to whoever has studied our discourse in *Wars* 1' (Ben-Meir 1993: 20). Not only is Gersonides here the precursor of Spinoza's *Deus sive Natura* and the aspectival relation between body and mind, but also insofar as the discussion conflates God with the Agent Intellect, it also reflects a position in closer proximity to Aristotle and Averroes in the *de Anima*, where it is the *nous poieticos* that is divine and where intellect, which is the intelligible, is the divine aspect in humans. Gersonides continues:

> It is impossible to say anything other than what was stated in that place . . . And we say that it has been clarified that there is a wonderful difference [*hevdel nifla*] between one who attains the material (intellect) [*hyuli*] and one who attains it from the aspect in which it is material in virtue of its form . . . And in this manner what we apprehend of the science of the existents *is itself the intelligible in God*. (Ben-Meir 1993: 20)

The difference between the divine intelligible and the human intelligible is that in God it is the whole simple plan as a singularity,[31] whereas in humans it is composed of many intelligibles.

The elaboration of the difficulties and perplexities of the sixth opinion expressing doubt about the immortality of the soul follows a similar line as the argument just advanced. Gersonides argues that this confusion is based upon the failure to distinguish between the material nature of the form of the animal and that of the human soul; the former is perishable, the latter is not. Gersonides concedes the difficulty, arguing that because all these forms are material, they cannot exist without their subject. I quote at length in lieu of a detailed discussion which I have done elsewhere:

> Hence, it appears that this is also the case with the material intellect which is the human form, since it is the perfection of the appetitive soul; thus this human disposition [*hakhanah*] cannot subsist apart from the appetitive soul and therefore it is necessary that [ve-*lazeh yehuyav*] it will perish completely. It is further necessary that the acquired intellect is perishable, since it is believed that it is the perfection of the material intellect, and from this aspect it is conjoined to the soul that is the subject of this disposition, because it appears that the subject of the disposition is the subject of that which is generated from it into actuality. (Ben-Meir 1993: 21–2)

Before concluding, it should be noted that both in the *Supercommentary on the de Anima* and in the *Wars*, Gersonides's discussion of the subject of this disposition is long, tortuous and, in order to be consistent, must adhere to an aspectival materialist physics from which one may be able to argue for the immortality of the soul as the immortality of the intelligibile that does not differ among individuals. Gersonides's concluding remark on this profound difficulty is telling: 'And we have explained in book 1 of the *Wars* that the acquired intellect is indubitably immortal and we have resolved all the doubts about it' (Ben-Meir 1993: 22). Perhaps, but again this immortality is not individual.

Although a discussion of providence or reward and punishment is clearly beyond the scope of this very brief conclusion, the foregoing arguments should make clear that providence

---

[31] The same could be said about the Agent Intellect since it is a single intellect which, as intelligible, is the single *nomos* of the existents.

cannot be individual such that *hashgahah pratit* is at best modal; humans differ indefinitely in the number and types of intelligibles they possess and, hence, each can be said to differ from another indefinitely. Moreover, the more intelligibles one possesses, the more one knows the plan of the universe and its order, the more one can be said to be rewarded and be able to avoid pain. Indeed, reward and punishment, like providence, are thus worldly and proportionate to one's intellectual perfection. But this, of course, is at odds with some of Gersonides's other claims both in the *Qohelet* commentary and in the *Wars*.

Finally, Gersonides's *Qohelet* commentary embodies and underlines the tension also evident in his discussions of dreams, divination and prophecy where he insists on a distinction in kind rather than degree between dreams and divination, on the one hand, prophecy, on the other, in a manner that is irreconcilable with the substance of his physics and noetics.[32] His argument in defence of creation from something violates his painstaking methodological principles elsewhere, presenting as indubitable what is, indeed, most dubious.

By way of a brief conclusion, or as a concluding gesture towards further enquiry, I propose that on the basis of these three surprising inconsistencies in the thought of a most systematic and consistent thinker the only conclusion (without further argument here) is that Gersonides is not only a man caught between two worlds but that this duality can be characterised, all too briefly, broadly and crudely, as one between an Aristotelian materialist natural science and a modern ethics/politics. To be a follower of Aristotle in natural science is to be a materialist and empiricist rather than endorse pre-Ptolemaic (or even Ptolemaic) physics.[33] To be a modern in ethics/politics is to dissociate ethics and politics against Aristotle even when citing Aristotle. Unlike Aristotle, Averroes and Maimonides, Gersonides's primary concern is with individual felicity, *hatzlahah* or *eudaimonia*. Following the commandments and prohibitions assures the preservation and well-being of the community, which of course does not exist/subsist as a proper political community for Gersonides. This may also explain why, unlike Maimonides, al-Farabi and Averroes, Gersonides is not philosophically interested in the prophet, not even Moses, as a lawgiver.

References

Aristotle (1934). *Nicomachean Ethics*. Trans. H. Rackham. Cambridge, MA: Harvard University Press.
Aristotle (1957). *De Anima*. Trans. W. S. Hett. Cambridge, MA: Harvard University Press.
Aristotle (1981). *De Anima*. Trans. H. Apostle. Grinell, IA: Peripatetic Press.
Aristotle (1984). *Nicomachean Ethics*. Trans. H. G. Apostle. Grinell, IA: The Peripatetic Press.
Averroes (2001). *Decisive Treatise and Epistle Dedicatory*. Trans. C. Butterworth. Provo, UT: Brigham Young University Press.
Ben-Meir, R. (1993). Gersonides' Commentary of Ecclesiastes: Analysis and Text. Doctoral. Hebrew University of Jerusalem.
Dobbs-Weinstein, I. (1991). 'The Existential Dimension of Providence in the Thought of Gersonides'. In *Gersonide en son Temps*. Ed. G. Dahan. Louvain: E. Peeters, pp. 159–78.
Dobbs-Weinstein, I. (1996). 'Gersonides's Radically Modern Understanding of the Agent Intellect'. In *Meeting of the Minds. The Relations between Medieval and Classical Modern European Philosophy*. Turnhout: Brepols, pp. 191–213.

---

[32] See Dobbs-Weinstein (2006).
[33] It is worth noting that Gersonides expresses a desire to discover a mathematical model in astronomy, thereby violating Aristotle's strict prohibition against metabasis, despite the fact that in the introduction to the *Wars* he informs the reader that the book will present three distinct types of proof – mathematical, natural scientific and philosophical – according to the demands of the subject matter.

Dobbs-Weinstein, I. (2004). 'The Anti-Maimonidean Controversy'. In *History of Jewish Philosophy*. Ed. D. H. Frank and O. Leaman. London: Routledge, pp. 275–91.

Dobbs-Weinstein, I. (2006). 'Tensions Within and Between Maimonides' and Gersonides' Account of Prophecy'. In *Ecriture et réécriture des textes philosophiques médiévaux: Volume d'hommage offert à Colette Sirat*. Turnhout: Brepols.

Dobbs-Weinstein, I. (2015). 'Aristotle on the Natural Dwelling of the Intellect'. In *The Bloomsbury Companion to Aristotle*. Ed. C. Baracchi. London: Bloomsbury.

Freudenthal, G. (1992). 'Sauver son âme ou sauver les phénoménes: sotériologie, épistémologie et astronomie chez Gersonide'. In *Studies on Gersonides: A Fourteenth-Century Jewish Philosopher-Scientist*. Ed. G. Freudenthal. Leiden: Brill, pp. 319–52.

Funkenstein, A. (1985). *Theology and the Scientific Imagination: From the Middle Ages to the Seventeenth Century*, 2nd edn. Princeton: Princeton University Press.

Gershom, L. B. (1966). *Milhamot ha-Shem (מלחמות השם)*. Ed. J. Marciari. Leipzig: Leipzig Publishing Comapny.

Gershom, L. B. (1984–99). *The Wars of the Lord*, Vols 1–3. Trans. S. Feldman. Philadelphia: The Jewish Publication Society.

Glasner, R. (1996). 'The Early Stages in the Evolution of Gersonides' "The Wars of the Lord"'. *The Jewish Quarterly Review*, 87/1–2: 1–46.

Goldstein, B. R. (1985). *The Astronomy of Levi ben Gerson*. New York: Springer.

Green, A. (2016). *The Virtue Ethics of Levi Gersonides*. Basingstoke: Palgrave Macmillan.

Harvey, S. (1987). 'Did Gersonides Believe in the Absolute Generation of Prime Matter?' In *Shlomo Pines Jubilee Volume*, pt. I, at 307–18. *Jerusalem Studies in Jewish Thought*, No. 7. 1988 (Hebrew).

Harvey, S. and R. Fontaine (forthcoming). 'The Supercommentaries of Gersonides and his Students on Averroes' Epitomes of the Physica and the Meteorologica'. In *Gersonides through the Ages*. Ed. O. Elior, G. Freudenthal and D. Wirmer. Leiden: Brill.

Klein-Braslavy, S. (2005). 'The Alexandrian Prologue Paradigm in Gersonides' Writings'. *Jewish Quarterly Review*, 95/2: 257–89.

Klein-Braslavy, S. (2011). 'Dialectic in Gersonides' Biblical commentaries'. In *Studies in the History of Culture and Science: A Tribute to Gad Fruedenthal*. Ed. R. Fontaine, R. Glasner, R. Leicht and G. Veltri. Leiden: Brill.

Kojève, A. (1984). 'The Christian Origins of Modern Science'. Trans. D. R. Lachterman. *St. John's Review*, 35/1: 22–6.

Maimonides (1964). 'Nezikin'. Ed. Y. Qafih. *Perush ha-Mishnah*. Jersalem: Mossad ha-Ray Kook.

Maimonides (1983). 'Eight Chapters'. In *The Ethical Writings of Maimonides*. Ed. R. L. Weiss and C. Butterworth. Dover: Mineola, pp. 59–104.

Pines, S. (1966). 'Scholasticism after Thomas Aquinas and the Teachings of Hasdai Crescas and his Predecessors'. *Proceedings of the Israel Academy of Sciences and Humanities*, 1/10: 1–101.

Robinson, J. T. (2000). 'Samuel Ibn Tibbon's Commentary on Ecclesiastes and the Philosopher's Proemium'. In *Studies in Medieval Jewish History and Literature*, Vol. 3. Ed. I. Twersky and J. M. Harris. Cambridge, MA: Harvard University Press, pp. 83–146.

Robinson, J. T. (2007). *Samuel Ibn Tibbon's Commentary on Ecclesiastes: The Book of the Soul of Man*. Heidelberg: Mohr Siebeck.

Touati, C. (1973). *La pensée philosophique et théologique de Gersonide*. Paris: Gallimard.

Weil, G. E. (1991). *La bibliothèque de Gersonide d'après son catalogue autographe*. Ed. F. Chartain. Leuven: E. Peeters.

17

Founding Body in Platonism: A Reconsideration of the Tradition from Origen to Cusa

Wayne Hankey

Among leading contemporary Western philosophical and theological phenomena is making the ineffable immediately incarnate, i.e. the immediate union of the extreme ends of Platonist systems. The ineffable first is immediately joined to the material; intellect is pulled within soul, or life, spirit is bodily, and body has the attributes of mind. The shift from hierarchy of reality and value with graduated mediations as the all but exclusive paradigmatic structure for understanding the Platonic tradition has many consequences for philosophy, spirituality and religion. It challenges the dominant misrepresentations which come close to making Platonism a quasi-Manichean dualism, a source of hatred and fear of the body and the physical world, needy matter the cause of evil. Radically incarnational Neoplatonism goes with a reconsideration of past Platonisms which it enables and necessitates. My chapter points at some of this reassessment.[1]

I look at some causal connections between philosophers over the last 150 years, but mainly I treat the results of this change in perspective or mental climate by following my interests and those of my students and collaborators. I was struck by the effect on scholarship of this shift in perspective by the attention paid to body and sense in the Platonic tradition at my retirement colloquium in June 2017. Papers by former students now working independently displayed it. Besides those mentioned in what follows, Tim Riggs (2017) on sensing the good, Michael Harrington (2017) on the name of wisdom in the Dionysian commentary tradition, and Evan King (2017) on the Ground in Eckhart, all published in *Dionysius* for 2017, show this attention in some way. All three had looked at texts through the eyes of Jean Trouillard in the long course of their researches. The papers of Matthew Wood (2018) on Proclus's theory of the symbol, Daniel Heide (2018) on the fate of bodies in Origen and Eriugena, and Matthew Furlong (2018) on place in Eriugena, came out in *Dionysius* for 2018. They and other articles in that volume are part of this reassessment.

---

[1] For a treatment of the twentieth-century French Neoplatonism in these terms see Hankey (2016); for the phenomenon and its connection to engagement with Heidegger see Hankey (2008); for the shift among leading historians of Platonism see Hankey (2007a). A recent volume is dedicated to this reconsideration of ancient Platonism: see Marmodoro and Cartwright (2018). To avoid turning this chapter into a bibliographical list, I shall, when possible, refer to my publications where the citations required to establish my argument will be found. Versions of those which are in press can be found at <https://dal.academia.edu/WayneHankey>.

I begin here with the mystical vitalism of Henri Bergson, both instance and precursor, and move to Jean Trouillard (see Hankey 2019a). From this Sulpician priest and his little group of fellow Neoplatonic radicals, I go on to treatments of Proclus and Iamblichus they inspired. They are critical of Augustine, but others give relief from the slander that his Platonism was a continuation of his Manicheism, not a conversion from it. Boethius appears differently when seen in the sillage of a reconsidered Proclus and Iamblichus. I look at a recent retrieval of the corporeal in treatments of his *Consolation of Philosophy*. Finally, a more Procline Aquinas can be rescued from the idea that his is a Platonist rationalism with the Trinity and Incarnation as external additions. With such a liberation I conclude (see Hankey 1981 and 2017a).

Henri Bergson's Plotinian Vitalism

The advent of the twentieth-century's ineffable, immediately incarnational Platonism was announced by the mystical vitalism of Henri Bergson (1859–1941). Developed in reflections on Plotinus (205–70), his first *cours* at the Collège de France in 1897–8 was devoted to him, as were those in 1902–3. These lectures led the move of Neoplatonic studies from Germany in the nineteenth century to France where Bergson inaugurated what particularly characterises twentieth-century Neoplatonism. Among the auditors was the most important French scholar of Neoplatonism in the period, Émile Bréhier (1876–1952). Bergson's postmodern successors will seek to overcome what is for them the reductionist rationalism of modern metaphysics (see Hankey 2016: 110, 119, 232, and Hankey 2019b).

Bergson found in Plotinus not only a dynamic schema which corresponded to his own understanding of reality, but also what for him comprised the most fundamental error of the metaphysical tradition, viz. ignorance of the difference between intellect and the fluidity of reality. In consequence, life and movement are misrepresented in the fixity intellect gives its objects and seeks as its goal. Modern physics, which substitutes time-length for time-invention,

> calls upon the mind to renounce its most cherished habits. It is within becoming that it would have transported us by an effort of sympathy . . . The moments of time, which are only arrests of our attention, would no longer exist . . . It is the very flux of the real that we should be trying to follow. (Bergson 1911: 342)

Intellect must 'install itself within the moving', and creative intuition opens us to what intellect does not grasp (Bergson 1911: 343).

At this point what is for Bergson positive in Plotinus emerges. As opposed to the reification of oppositions, Bergson saw also how Plotinus united them in one movement, in the way both Gilles Deleuze (1925–95) and Jean Trouillard (1907–84) understand happens in Neoplatonism. Trying to approximate an idea of Spinoza, Bergson pulled much together when he wrote:

> the feeling of a coincidence between the act by which our mind knows truth perfectly, and the operation by which God engenders it; the idea that the conversion of the Alexandrians, when it becomes complete, is indistinguishable from their procession, that when man, sprung from divinity, succeeds in returning to it, he perceives that what he had at first taken to be two opposed movements of coming and going are in fact a single movement. (Bergson 1946: 133–4)

Crucially, with Trouillard, his associates,[2] followers and interlocutors like Deleuze, we have a reinterpretation of Neoplatonism through an understanding of the First Principle which does not put it on one side of a matter-mind, perception-intellect duality, but sees it founding and beyond both. By his reduction of intellect Bergson anticipates features of their understanding.

Deleuze sees the transcendence of the One. He writes of Plotinus:

> The participated does not in fact enter into what participates in it. What is participated remains in itself; it is participated in so far as it produces, and produces insofar as it gives, but it has no need to leave itself to give or produce . . . [T]he One is necessarily above its gifts . . . it gives what does not belong to it, or is not what it gives. (Deleuze 1990: 170–1)

This transcendent presence enables the mutuality of gathering, or conversion, and explication, or procession. Deleuze explains '*complicare* and *explicare*' in a way which reminds us of Nicholas of Cusa:

> All things are present to God, who complicates them. God is present to all things, which explicate and implicate him. A co-presence of two correlative movements comes to be substituted for a series of successive subordinate emanations . . . An equality of being is substituted for a hierarchy of hypostases; for things are present to the same Being, which is itself present in things. (Deleuze 1990: 175)

With this equality relative to the transcendent – immanent One, the intelligible is relativised. This enables Trouillard to retrieve Bergson without his opposition to Plotinus as Platonic idealist.

Jean Trouillard's Radical Neoplatonism

Bergson had little interest in the history of philosophy and used it polemically, but Jean Trouillard was both a creative Neoplatonist and a devoted scholar of the history of philosophy. For Trouillard, Plotinian mysticism 'is not a journey originating in philosophy and going to mysticism. It is more a mysticism which makes use of the philosophical circuit' (Trouillard 1961: 438–9). He represents Bergson's mysticism as using philosophy in this way but corrects Bergson's criticism of Plotinus on the relation of *praxis* and contemplation in order to see in Plotinus a unification of opposites like that identified by Deleuze. Trouillard writes: 'This is the paradox of Plotinus, which has not always been articulated well, even by Bergson. The action which is despised is an appearance of action' (Trouillard 1955: 41–2). He judges that Bergson 'did not arrive at the end of the Alexandrian's thought', who 'does not disdain one who is authentically active, that is, one who creates. He unmasks action that believes itself productive and free, while it is but agitation and servitude, because it does not have its center in spiritual self-collection.' For Trouillard, Plotinus points to 'a more autonomous spontaneity than calculation and choice' (Trouillard 1969: 899).

It was not until he moved on to Proclus from Plotinus that Trouillard's new theological structure really emerged – he published his translation, introduction and notes to Proclus, *Éléments de Théologie* in 1965, *L'Un et l'Âme selon Proclos* in 1972 and *La mystagogie de Proclos*

---

[2] Close are le r.p. Stanislas Breton, c.p. (1912–2005), Henry Duméry (1920–2012), who left the priesthood, le r.p. Joseph Combès (1920–2002). See Breton (1992) and Hankey (2005).

in 1982. He perceived that the universe was united in very different ways for Plotinus and Proclus. For Proclus, the One was present and powerful throughout the whole, even in the material. He writes:

> The important thing here is the repercussion of this difference in the system of Proclus as compared to the approach of the *Enneads*. Plotinus returns to the One through a severe negation, or, better, he gives way to a purifying motion which, springing out of the ecstasy hidden in each of us, detaches it first from the empirical world, and then from intellectual vision . . . If Plotinus ultimately saves nature and the forms, he keeps them at a two-fold distance. He goes to the divinity by night. Proclus shows rather a will for transfiguration. Without doubt his universe is arranged on horizontal planes like that of Plotinus, but it is also traversed by a series of vertical lines, which like rays diverge from the same universal center, and refer back to it the furthermost and the most diverse appearances. These chains tend to absorb the hierarchical ordering of the levels and to link them all directly to the One . . . The sensible is thus susceptible to a transposition and a purification. (Trouillard 1965: 23–5)

Trouillard concludes: 'Finally, translating the *Elements of Theology* . . . made me encounter the "self-constituting" character of all authentic being, and made it clear that, in a monadological perspective, the entire procession is intrinsic to each psycho-noetic subject' (Trouillard 1972: 3–4). When Proclus is properly understood, the Neoplatonic doctrines of transcendence and of the soul must be reconceived:

> Neoplatonic transcendence is not an absence, but an excess of presence, since it is for each spirit its interior home of liberation. It is less an end than a point of departure, less a superior term than a prior state, never participated, always communicated. It is only exterior to us inasmuch as we are exterior to ourselves . . . Since the soul is not only the term of the internal procession, but also the spontaneous recapitulation of the entire procession, from the One to matter, we are able to resume everything . . . in a single formula . . .: 'The soul is the perfect mediation because it is the plenitude of negations . . . It is in this that it is self-moving.' (Trouillard 1972: 4–8)

Trouillard's direct linkage between the One and the material, together with the mediation of soul to which everything is interior, has inspired a thesis by Matthew Vanderkwaak, 'Matter and the One in Proclus', from which an article for *Dionysius* 2019 will emerge: 'A Shrine for the Everlasting Gods: Matter and the Processions of the Gods in Proclus'. Trouillard led Vanderkwaak to what in Proclus the Sulpician identified as the authentic Neoplatonism of Eriugena (c. 810–80). The One and matter are both negations, the first by excess, matter by privation. These negations are relative to the affirmations of the intelligible and en-mattered forms. Soul alone is both negation and affirmation and thereby their resolution with one another (Vanderwaak 2019: 81).

Where Proclus places soul, Eriugena puts the human (see Hankey 2010a: 838–89). Understanding soul in this way involves a reach by Proclus back to Iamblichus. Martin Curran locates prayer in Boethius's *Consolation of Philosophy*, particularly its mediating metric prayer 'O qui perpetua', in this philosophical context. This was enabled by the work of Trouillard's last student, Gregory Shaw, and of Zeke Mazur (2004). Shaw approached Trouillard after reading about his work in *Dionysius* (specifically Hankey 1980). In the Anglophone world, Shaw helped in overthrowing the characterisation of theurgy as magical manipulation.³ Mazur built on Shaw when he attacked the established representation of Plotinus as an anti-religious rationalist.

Nathan McAllister's work on Iamblichus depends on Trouillard, Shaw, Mazur and Edward Butler. He quotes Trouillard's *La Mystagogie de Proclos*: 'The body that the soul animates, and through which it is placed in the cosmos, is not an extrinsic addition but the circuit that it travels in order to be united with itself' (as cited in McAllister 2018). So the universe of Iamblichus is a single living being, bound together by love in indivisible mutuality where the body is an integral part of the whole process of restoration. The divine is united with itself through the body and the bodily (McAllister 2014: 73). Rebecca Coughlin's (2006) work using Iamblichan theurgy, with sacred matter and the practice of prayer, to illumine Dionysius the Areopagite (sixth century) and Ficino (1433–99) depends on Trouillard, Shaw and Mazur. Vanderkwaak drew importantly on Edward Butler, whose work is in line with that of Trouillard, although determined to resist drawing Proclus into Christian monotheism.⁴

Michael Fournier's recent 'Epicurus' Panpsychism' (2018a) is part of his research on whether all matter is alive and has, in some sense, apprehension and freedom. He carries forward Bergson's vitalism based in the advances of physics, overthrowing the dead Newtonian world and the refusal of action at a distance. In this article contemporary philosophers of science, Democritus (460–370 BCE), Lucretius (99–55 BCE), Boethius (470–524 CE), Hegel (1770–1831), Bergson and Deleuze, belong to philosophical actuality together with Epicurus (341–270 BCE). I quote from Fournier's wrap-up:

> Hegel concludes that Epicurus banishes thought as implicit, without it occurring to him that his atoms themselves have this very nature of thought; that is, their existence in time is not immediate but essentially mediate, and thus negative or universal. Hegel does not attribute mind to Epicurus' atom, but discerns in the relation between the atom and the void described by Epicurus the elements of thought that he makes explicit in his own work. While Hegel detected an unrecognized resemblance, Marx articulated (in Hegelian terms) the explicit identification of the atom with abstract self-consciousness. My view is that Epicurus understood that blessedness and indestructibility both depend upon mind, and that true blessedness attends true indestructibility. The gods make this *visible* to us (via the *eidola* we receive from them), but there is also a more fundamental grasp of the imperceptible, the non-evident, by thought, which reveals the divine nature of the atom. (Fournier 2018a)

Body's Omnipresence in Augustine's *Confessions*

Although Augustine (354–430) knew about Iamblichus (250–330), had Proclus (412–85) as a junior contemporary, and supposed theurgy, which he condemned, to be the pagan equivalent of Christian sacraments, there is no reason to see the bishop as under the influence of these two great pagans. Nonetheless, there are parallels between some of his doctrines and some of theirs (Dodaro 1999; Feichtinger 2003; O'Neill 2008). His *Confessions* gives contrary evidence to the widely held view that he negatively evaluated matter and the body. His Platonism, like that of Iamblichus and his successors in the Procline tradition, e.g., Damascius and Dionysius, combines with his Christianity to set him against dualisms that denigrate the body and make matter evil or its cause.

---

³ Two of Gregory Shaw's publications were important for Martin Curran: the ground-breaking *Theurgy and the Soul* (Shaw 1995) and 'Eros and Arithmos' (Shaw 1999).
⁴ Vanderkwaak used extensively a series of articles on the intelligible gods in Proclus (Butler 2005, 2008).

Getting the *Confessions* right depends on looking at the work as a whole and seeing the personal autobiography in the cosmic return of all things to the One as their source, 'recurrens in te unum' (Augustine 1991). Modern centreing on the human self-conscious individual, together with sexual preoccupations, make getting inside the structure and argument of the work difficult. In fact, matter, spiritual and sensible, the corporeal rightly ordered, and the sacramental elements are from top to bottom, the foundation, the media of ascent, and the end. Both the personal conversion and the cosmic are contained within God's own Trinitarian conversion upon Himself. Augustine's individual return to rest in the One is framed within the exegesis of the first chapters of the Book of Genesis, the Hexameron. The Trinitarian conversions – divine, spiritual, psychological and physical – join the autobiographical and the exegetical books into one work (see Hankey 2017b). Henry Chadwick wrote:

> The last four books make explicit what is only hinted at in the autobiographical parts, namely that the story of the soul wandering away from God and then in torment and tears finding its way home through conversion is also the story of the entire created order. It is a favourite Neoplatonic theme, but also, as Romans 8 shows, not absent from the New Testament . . . So Augustine's personal quest and pilgrimage are the individual's experience in microcosm of what is true, on the grand scale, of the whole creation. (Chadwick in Augustine 1991: xxiv)

The work confesses this.

The result in the one confessing divine, cosmic, human conversion is immediate unification of God and the human in the knowledge and love of creation. As Elizabeth King writes: 'The return is not just that of the human and the cosmos together into God. It is also the self-return of God Himself, which enables and sustains the other returns and is in fact expressed through them' (Elizabeth King 2017: 103). Near the end of the final Book (XIII), Augustine discerns that God's being is that by which we are, God's judging is that by which we judge and God's love is that by which we love. The inverse is also made plain. God's being is our being, God's knowing is our knowing, God's loving is our loving. 'The things which by the help of your Spirit delight us are delighting you in us' (Augustine 1991: 13.31.46). The last words of the *Confessions*, devoted to the Sabbath rest, speak of the same union: 'we also may rest in you for the Sabbath of eternal life. There also you will rest in us, just as now you work in us' (Augustine 1991: 13.36–7). The *Confessions*, which began 'our heart is restless until it rests in you', has reached its conclusion (Augustine 1991: 1.1.1). On this divine-human conclusion Justin Wollf comments:

> A conclusion of the role of the physical in the *Confessiones* at the end of Book XIII is the near assimilation of God and the human in the spiritual cosmos of the church . . . At every step, the physical is necessary for the human's generation, bodily preservation, and conversions tending to, and assuming, its natural and expansive capacity as God's judge. At the same time, this *itinerarium* of the human is the discovery and realization of physical bodies, incorporeal mind, physical and spiritual matter, towards God Himself resting and working in the human. In this way, the physical is the positive and necessary means for the birth, growth, and assimilation of the divine-human mutuality by, and in comparison to, another. (Wollf 2019: 107–8)

The final Book is dominated by Genesis 1.2: 'Your good Spirit was borne above the waters' (Augustine 1991: 13.4.5). In it Augustine (1991: 13.2.2) gives creation and recreation the same structure, i.e., being is formed in the Verbum by returning to the One. Being, form and truth derive from the Unity which is also Goodness:

Your creation has its being from the fullness of your goodness . . . Formless physical entities are better than no existence at all. So formless things are dependent on your Word. It is only by that same Word that they are recalled to your Oneness and receive form. From you, the One, the supreme Good, they have being and are all 'very good'.

Matter and souls are both converted. Physical matter 'would have been dissimilar to you unless by your Word it had been converted to the same Word by whom it was made, so that, illuminated by him, it became light' (Augustine 1991: 13.2.3).

As Augustine meditates on the Spirit borne above the waters, his way to the dominance of love, he refers obliquely to the most obscure trace of Trinitarian life in the cosmos. The Holy Spirit is weight, who, as love, carries Augustine (1991: 13.9.10) to his rest, just as it carries every physical thing by its relative gravity. He had spoken of the vestige directly in Book V, devoted to natural philosophy and Skepticism: '[You] have disposed everything by "measure, number, and weight"' (Wisdom 11:21) (1991: 5.4.7). It is first encountered with the infant in Book I:

You, Lord my God, are the giver of life and a body to a baby. As we see, you have endowed it with senses. You have co-ordinated the limbs. You have adorned it with a beautiful form, and for the coherence and preservation of the whole you have implanted all the instincts of a living being. (1991: 1.7.12)

Book I concludes with a reformulation for the self-conscious child. 'For at that time I existed, I lived and thought and took care for my self-preservation (a mark of your profound latent unity whence I derived my being)' (1991: 1.20.31). The Trinity, as measure, number and weight, is the fundamental structure of every physical thing, and is confessed as sustaining sinners even in their sin.

Book XIII's 'My weight is my love' reminds us of the ascending fire of Book III where Augustine's first conversion to God (as immortal wisdom) was expressed in the language of sexual passion: 'I lusted (*concupiscebam*) for the immortality of wisdom with an incredible ardour of the heart' (1991: 3.4.7). 'How I burned, my God, how I burned' (1991: 3.4.8). Then, a self projected into the external corporeal, and supposing itself to be material, cannot escape speaking of God as if an object of sexual desire. Now, in the last Book, fire, love, spirit, passion return: 'Wherever I am carried, my love is carrying me. By your gift we are set on fire and carried upwards: we grow red hot and ascend' (1991: 13.9.10). However, here this image is juxtaposed to Augustine's most intellectual and adequate statement of the Trinity in the *Confessions* and is elevated by it (1991: 13.11.12).

Much attention is paid to the fall of the jealous infant in Book I (1.7.11), far less is given to what is more important, the harmony between God, physical nature and the human from which the descent happens; this enables restoration because it is the truth of human nature. The infant drinks from the woman's breast, filled by God. Both infant and nurses desire this giving and receiving and it is instinctually and internally moderated:

I was welcomed by the consolations of human milk. Neither my mother nor my nurses filled their own breasts, but you gave infant food to me through them in accordance with your ordinance and the riches distributed unstintingly to the bottom of things. You also granted me not to wish for more than you were giving, and to my nurses the desire to give me what you gave them . . . For the good which came to me from them was a good for them; yet it was not from them but through them. (Augustine 1991: 1.6.7)

Neither the human nor matter are originally evil or in conflict. Augustine does not change on this between Books I and XIII; we ascend through body to God who is its reality and is manifest in it.

I cannot give a detailed account of the bodily *Confessions* here, but I point to a few more demonstrative instances. In Book III, Manichean materialism is attacked, not by a turn against body, but by a true reasoning about it, and a right relation to it. In comparison with their 'false mythologies' Augustine (1991: 3.6.10) reflects: 'We have more reliable knowledge in our images of bodies which really exist, and the bodies are more certain than the images ... The life of bodies is superior to bodies themselves, and a more certain object of knowledge.' Just so, real poetry is better than Manichean stories (3.6.11). This is the approach also in Book V, where Augustine embraces Platonic natural science to enable comparison which moves towards truth:

> I compared some of the teachings [of the natural philosophers] with the lengthy fables of the Manichees. The philosophers' teachings seemed to be more probable ... The philosophers 'were able to judge the world with understanding' ... With the mind and intellect which you have given them, they investigate these matters. They have found out much. (5.3.3–4)

There are the ever-reiterated ascents to God which begin from sensible bodies and pass step by step, using them in their diverse kinds. The conversion to Platonism in Book VII enables these, as it does also the equation of being, truth and goodness, so matter cannot be evil (Augustine 1991: 7.15.21–7, 9.10.24, 10.6.10). The transition to sacramental body with the death of Monica at the end of his autobiography in Book IX keeps the *Confessions* with body after this life and prepares for its treatment in Books XII and XIII. There creation in the Book of Genesis is first read philosophically, beginning with the spiritual body of the first non-physical cosmos (12.2.2–12.9.9), and then as an allegory of the Church (9.2.4, 9.7.16, 9.13.36, 9.3.6–4.8, 13.20.26–23.34).

Book X has an orientation of mind to body that Augustine acquired from Plotinus: the spiritual senses. Augustine bequeaths them a long history, being found in Anselm and Bonaventure, for example (see Sastri 2006).

> There is a light I love, and a food, and a kind of embrace when I love my God – a light, voice, odour, food, embrace of my inner man, where my soul is floodlit by light which space cannot contain, where there is sound that time cannot seize, where there is a perfume which no breeze disperses, where there is a taste for food no amount of eating can lessen, and where there is a bond of union that no satiety can part. That is what I love when I love my God. (Augustine 1991: 10.6.10)

God is to be enjoyed sensually. The spiritual senses belong to the human as formed for that joy and the physical senses descend from them. These intimations serve here only as invitations to discover body affirmed and required everywhere in the *Confessions*.

Retrieving Corporality in Boethius's *The Consolation of Philosophy*

After Iamblichus, Augustine and Proclus comes Boethius with his work of ecumenical Platonism for pagans and Christians, *The Consolation of Philosophy*. Recent scholarship, remerging from the Dalhousie University Classics Department, using that of others, shows how for

Boethius consolation is corporeal, as well as rational, moral and emotional, all the way through: beginning, middle and end (see Hankey 2018a).

Six forms of physicality stand out in its operation. Their pervasive power for Boethius is owed to the same incarnational turn in Late Antiquity to which Iamblichan theurgy, its absorption into the Neoplatonic synthesis, Proclus's immediate passing back and forth between the One and matter, and the advance of the sacramental and hieratic Christian Church belong. The corporality of the theurgic operations of Lady Philosophy is indicated first by the *Consolation*'s reiteration of the mind-soul-body turning and movement out of the Cave to vision of the Sun-Good.

Second is the intricate textual structure of the *Consolation*, e.g., the correlation of the Books to the mathematical *gradus* pointed to by Michael Fournier (2012: 99), and the complex connection of prose and poetry in its movement. A third corporality is in the metres. They, their vocal character and how they alternate with the prose, are detailed by Dr Blackwood's 2015 monograph, *The Consolation of Boethius as Poetic Liturgy*.

The fourth physicality, the dependence of the *Consolation* on circular motions, is brought out strongly by Martin Curran in his 2012 Master's thesis on the theurgy of Boethius. There he analysed the roles of divine and cosmic circles, essential to its praying. 'O qui perpetua' effects union with the unified happiness, goodness, unity, divinity, thought and being of Parmenides's well-rounded sphere. On this Curran (2011) published 'The Circular Activity of Prayer in Boethius' *Consolation*'. His work rightly also draws Boethius back to Iamblichus and Proclus. Curran (2012: 82) argues:

> Iamblichus writes about the *sumbola* present in the human mind, which awaken only with the highest prayer. Boethius proposes that man's natural activity should activate these *sumbola*, represented as circles, at every level. The philosophical life is one that combines thought and prayer, but even the correct use of man's knowing faculties should be a kind of prayer. Similarly even the lowest prayers, if they are correct, are circular activities that should arouse the *sumbola* of the soul and provide a connection to the divine. In the fully philosophical life, thought is prayer and theurgy. The circles in the *Consolation* are an example of this unified process.

Fifth, the nursing of *Philosophia* and the conversion of the prisoner are enacted corporally by the gazing and touch, standing and sitting, movement and *stasis*, silence and speech of a healer and patient who are physical and emotional as well as sensing, reasoning and intellectual beings. Sixth, and most obviously, in respect to the incarnational physicality, is philosophy's personification which makes possible her corporeal and emotional interaction with the prisoner.

Her physical interaction starts at the beginning of the *Consolation*. A prisoner is bent over, eyes fixed on the earth in self-indulgent misery so that *Philosophia* must sit down on the side of his bed to come to him. There he feels her eyes gazing on his tear worn face. She wipes away his tears with a fold of the dress she wove herself and which maps in symbols the ascent she effects (Blackwood 2002: 151). His response is to turn up and fix his gaze on her instead of the earth. Throughout the five books, alternating poetry and prose, speech and silence, she modifies dramatically the tone of her address, the rhythms of her songs, the bitterness and sweetness of her medicines, and the character of her actions. In consequence, the prisoner ends, standing erect, in face to face mutual gaze with God, known as good providence and careful judge.

The final poem is constructed on the unique capacity of the human being to stand upright, erect. It urges humans to live in accord with the divine vocation inherent in their proper nature.

The unabashed corporality of antiquity comes out in the name of its metre, Ithyphallic, one used for the phallic performances which were part of Greek and Roman theatre:

> How many different shapes of life across the world! . . . Alone the race of men can lift its head on high, Can stand with body upright and disdain the ground. This picture warns – except to witless earthbound men, 'You who raise your eyes to heaven with thrusting face, Raise up as well your thoughts, lest weighted down to earth, Your mind sink lower as your body rises high'. (Boethius 1999: V, m. 5)

This exhortation anticipates the conclusion.

At its end the *Consolation* returns to the divine circle (or, perhaps better, spiral) closing the mediating poetic prayer, 'O qui perpetua', at its centre. This prayer was explicitly inspired by Plato's physics, the *Timaeus*, summarises its content, and draws us into the movement of the cosmic and divine cycles. It finishes: 'to see Thee is our end, Who art our source and maker, lord and path and goal (*te cernere finis, principium, uector, dux, semita, terminus idem*)' (Boethius 1999: III, m. 9). Its circle reiterated closes the dialogue by joining the downward gaze of God to the upward-looking knowledge, hope and prayer of humans (Boethius 1999: III, m. 9).

Because it shows the tight connection of content and form in these body affirming and corporally operating ancient works, it is important that the most recent analysis of the central and crucial 'O qui perpetua' suggests its shape is spiral. Cristalle Watson's paper 'The Structure of Boethius' *Consolation*: A Circle becomes a Spiral', found it to be the best figure for both the 'O qui perpetua' and the *Consolation* (Watson 2018). I judge that the spiral or ellipse are the best figures to image Neoplatonic systems. In them Aristotle's perfect circles are pulled, by Neoplatonic emanation, to greater embrace of otherness. There is a more radical *exitus* within them. That is what I found in Aquinas's *Summa Theologiae*.

Thomas Aquinas's *Summa Theologiae*: Structure and Content United

The independence of Scriptural exegesis which theology acquired in Boethius, Dionysius and Eriugena under the influence of Proclus enabled a unification of form and content in a landmark work of thirteenth-century scholasticism, the *Summa Theologiae* of Thomas Aquinas (1225–74) (see Hankey 1997: 63–4). His teacher, Albert the Great (died 1280), overthrew the dominance of Augustine among the Latins with a Peripatetic system drawing together Proclus conveyed in monotheistic form in the *Liber de causis* (identified as Aristotelian), in the Dionysian corpus (identified as the work of St Paul's convert on the Areopagus), and the Aristotelian corpus (reconciled with Neoplatonism through Averroes [1126–98] and Avicenna [980–1036]). Aquinas doubles down on Albert's revolutionary turn, maintaining the Proclus-Aristotle synthesis when, after seeing Moerbeke's 1268 translation of the *Elements of Theology*, he discovers the Platonism of the *Liber* and Dionysius (See Hankey 2016). In the *Summa Theologiae* this synthesis, with both a strong pull of the unknowable One and the relentless push of emanation (see Hankey 1987: 13–15, 2006: 163), even within the divine, enables a theology which proceeds 'briefly and lucidly according to the demands of the material' (Aquinas 1888, see Hankey 1987). The structure accomplishes the self-disclosure of *Ipsum Esse Subsistens* as Trinitarian and incarnational (see Hankey 2017a). Aquinas calls both the processions of the Divine Persons and of creation 'emanations' (see Hankey 2007b).

Sacred doctrine in the form of this *Summa Theologiae* is summary; although unfinished, it was intended to be complete, and is addressed to novices. Its author was assigned the post of Regent-Master in his Dominican Order. The *Summa Theologiae* originates in the demands of this non-university Dominican teaching position. Its prologue declares that to teach 'what pertains to sacred doctrine', 'according as it conforms to the way beginners learn' (Aquinas 1888: pr.) requires the unity of form and content. God is the subject of sacred doctrine and it treats its material 'according as it is ordered to God' (Aquinas: I, q. 1, a. 7). It describes a circle subordinate to the one which is God's self- knowing. As 'a certain stamp of God's knowledge' (Aquinas: I, q. 1, a. 3), the *Summa*, as a whole and in its parts, describes circles, spirals or ellipses of remaining, going out, return, by which all things come out from and revert to their beginning. Three parts of the *Summa* accomplish this: 'God'; the movement of humans in, towards and into God; and 'Christ, who, because he is human, is our way of journeying into God' (I, q. 2, pr.). The Third Part unites the other two, thus perfecting God's self-conversion. Following Augustine, Aquinas imported the circle of conversion into the First Principle by his understanding of the Trinity. The process of emanation from God is in the principle itself in a unified form. Thus, this theological circle, beginning and ending in God, and even within the Divine Essence, is total. The fluid movement prevents hierarchical difference and separation from engendering rigid horizontal planes; the sensible is present from the beginning and also emerges from within the self-othering of the Principle.

Sacred doctrine appears in relation to the philosophical disciplines, which seem to give a complete account of reality without Christian revelation. Sacred doctrine starts from the subject of theology, God. The other theology 'which is part of philosophy' (I, q. 1, a. 1, ad 2), e.g., Aristotle's *Metaphysics* and the *Liber de causis*, depends on the knowledge of creatures. The union of the two contrary logical motions produces the structure. Neoplatonic emanation within the deity, out from God to the creature, and from the creature back to God, shapes the particular character of the circling here. Thus, orientation to the creature, ultimately material, makes sacred doctrine. In contradistinction from, and containing philosophical theology, it is necessitated by the human desire for God 'as for an end which exceeds the comprehension of reason' (I, q. 1, a. 1, co.).

The Five Ways to the existence of God, beginning a science which must prove that its subject is, start with unreflective sensation (see Hankey 1987: 36–56). Relation to matter is present implicitly or explicitly throughout the *Summa*: the creature for whom the work exists is embodied, sensate rationality. The two ordering logics, descending and ascending, meet in the proof human theology needs to start. First, we have the ultimate authority for God's existence: God speaks: 'I am who is' (I, q. 2, a. 3, s. c.). Then comes the mere sensation of movement as the beginning of ascent.

My aim in briefly describing lesser circles within the treatise on God in himself (qq. 2–43) is to demonstrate how Thomas's multilayered thearchy manifests the God whose going out and return is a self-othering that embraces the human within a cosmos material and spiritual. The bottom of the system is with and in the top.

Final cause justifies the *Summa* as a whole. So that the natural desire of the rational creature is not vain, it must know the first cause of things (Aquinas: I, q. 12, a. 1, co.). In consequence, the principal aim of sacred doctrine is 'to transmit the knowledge of God, not only as he is in himself but also as he is the beginning and the end of things, and, especially, of the rational creature' (I, q. 2, pr.). This need, and its satisfaction, determine the whole: the connection between the Second and the Third Parts of the *Summa* lies here:

> After having shown in the Second Part the way in which the human, in so far as he is a rational creature, is capable of returning back towards his end, in the Third Part, Thomas shows us how this is possible within our actual human reality, through Christ and the mysteries of his human life, and through the sacraments which he has left us. (Oliva 2009: 245)

The resulting system has the finality of 'inclusive perfection'. By this I mean end as return to source, or beginning, but with this difference, the beginning as end includes what is traversed between the source and the end. Thus, God as end, attained in the *reditus* through Christ, is inclusive perfection vis-à-vis God as remaining. Oliva writes: 'Christ, in that he is human, is the way of our return (*tendendi*) to God, and, in that he is God, he is the goal of this very return' (Oliva 2009: 250). That is, God again, but now known as containing and redeeming, by the life, death and resurrection of the son of God and Man, the fall into alienated existence with its consequences. A passage from the *Compendium theologiae* sums up: 'The totality of the whole divine work is perfected by [the Incarnation], in that the human, which was the last to have been created, as if by a circling, returns to his beginning, united to the very principle of things by the work of the Incarnation' (Aquinas: lib. 1, ca. 201).

The inclusive finality which generates and moves the systematically connected spirals of the *Summa Theologiae* appears first in the circular movement from the question on the simplicity of God to the one on his unity (q. 3 to q. 11). Question 11 brings the circle of names predicated 'of the divine substance' back to the originating simplicity. This unity is above things, because of God's simplicity; in things, 'because of the infinity of the divine perfection'; and of things, because from it comes the unity of the world (ST, I^a q. 11 a. 3 co. For Proclus underlying this see Aquinas, *In De divinis nominibus*, I, ii, § 55, & XIII, ii, § 980; Proclus, *Elements of Theology*, prop. 6 with Vanderkwaak (2018: 30–1)). Unity is, thus, an inclusive perfection, containing the difference between simplicity as the exclusion of all composition, and the many and varied beings, that, implicit in it, came out from it. Unity is the beginning as goal.

The next steps in the divine self-differentiation come by God's circling upon himself in self-knowing and self-loving. In the questions on the activities of the divine substance, q. 12 to q. 26, we step out of the Procline-Dionysian circle dominated by the One, into Aristotelian self-reflexive knowing. There the divine ideas, God as truth and God as will explicitly contain a relation to creatures (see Hankey 1987).

Knowing is not ecstatic: 'it has to do with creatures as they are within God' (Aquinas: I, q. 14, a. 15), but, in contrast, his will regards creatures as they are 'in themselves' (I, q. 14, a. 15, ad 1). Thus, the procession of things existing in themselves outside God's essence requires the will of God. With will, God is moved by himself as if by an other: 'When the principal object of the will is a good outside the will, the will must be moved by another' (I, q. 19, a. 1, ad 3). Knowing is multiplied in the 'many Ideas' (I, q. 15, a. 2, co.). God's ideas are multiplied 'by the divine intellect comparing its own essence [which is the cause of things] to the things [it makes]' (I, q. 15, a. 2, ad 3).

Finally, because truth is in judgement, it requires reflective comparing: 'truth is defined as the conformity of knowing to what it knows' (I, q. 16, a. 2, co.). To be called truth, the divine intellect must circle around itself to compare what goes out from it to itself. The circle by which God is self-related has been stretched.

After the perfect activities which 'remain in the one who acts', is q. 25, on the power of God, the 'activity which goes out into an exterior effect' (I, q. 14, pr.). God's happiness, as another inclusive perfection, concludes the 'consideration of what belongs to the divine essence' (I, q. 26, pr.). Just as 'the divine perfection includes every perfection', so 'the divine happiness enfolds all happiness' (I, q. 26, a. 4, s. c.). This enfolding confronts us with a profoundly important difference between the medieval Latin Christian theologian and his Hellenic master (see Hankey 2018b). What belongs to the effect of the divine causation has been separated out from God and is then explicitly drawn back in.

By the self-othering or self-differentiation of the divine being through these interconnected progressive spirals, the Trinity and Incarnation are seen to be present in principle from the beginning. Neoplatonic conversion in the *Summa Theologiae* is elliptical, so strong is the outward force. It is most radical in the conversion of the divine essence upon itself by the movement in the Trinity from the Father to the Spirit. Here the divine essence is related to itself in the sheer opposition of given and received. The conversion of God upon himself in this complete self-othering is the basis of the *exitus* and *reditus* of creation and redemption. The end, or bottom, is present in the beginning, or top. We may regard Aquinas as a body affirming Platonist.

Conclusion

Western philosophy is not only a connected series of perspectives on the whole, it is also a series of diverse understandings of itself. Philosophy in our time, from at least Henri Bergson, by collapsing hierarchical differentiation and distance makes evident the likeness of the extremes of the Platonic systems so, at the very least, they are mutually known (and unknown). Nothing by excess and nothing by defect belong together. We cannot take Aquinas as the conclusion of Western philosophy. Trouillard who explained creation by negation regarded Eriugena, Eckhart and Cusa as more authentically Neoplatonic. Still, Thomas's intuition of the negation which is self-relation in the Principle and all the way down makes the material implicit in the ineffable first. Deleuze on *complicare* and *explicare* comes to mind. Released from spirit-matter dualism, we can discern throughout the history of Platonism important instances of how the One is immediately joined to the material; intellect is pulled within life, spirit is bodily and body has the attributes of mind.

Bibliography

Aquinas, Thomas (1888). *Summa Theologiae*. Corpus Thomisticum: online.
Augustine (1991). *Confessions*. Trans. Henry Chadwick. Oxford: Oxford University Press.
Bergson, Henri (1911). *Creative Evolution*. Trans. A. Mitchell. New York: Modern Library.
Bergson, Henri (1946). *The Creative Mind*. Trans. M. L. Andison. New York: Philosophical Library.
Blackwood, Stephen J. (2002). '*Philosophia*'s Dress: Prayer in Boethius' *Consolation of Philosophy*'. *Dionysius*, 20: 139–52.
Blackwood, Stephen J. (2015). *The Consolation of Boethius as Poetic Liturgy*. Oxford: Oxford University Press.
Boethius (1999). *The Consolation of Philosophy*. Trans. Victor Watts. London: Penguin.
Breton, Stanislas (1992). *De Rome à Paris: Itinéraire philosophique*. Paris: Desclée de Brouwer.
Butler, Edward (2005). 'Polytheism and Individuality in the Henadic Manifold'. *Dionysius*, 23: 83–104.
Butler, Edward (2008). 'The Gods and Being in Proclus'. *Dionysius*, 26: 92–114.
Coughlin, Rebecca (2006). 'Theurgy, Prayer, Participation, and Divinization in Dionysius the Areopagite'. *Dionysius*, 23: 149–74.
Coughlin, Rebecca (2018). 'Uniting with Divine Wisdom: Theurgic Prayer and Religious Practice in Dionysius and Marsilio Ficino'. *Dionysius*, 36: 142–55.
Crouse, Robert D. (1976). '*Recurrens in te unum*: The Pattern of St. Augustine's Confessions'. In *Studia Patristica* XIV. Ed. E. A. Livingstone. Berlin: Akedemie-Verlag, pp. 389–92.
Curran, Martin H. (2011). 'The Circular Activity of Prayer in Boethius' *Consolation*'. *Dionysius*, 29: 193–204.
Curran, Martin H. (2012). The Immaterial Theurgy of Boethius. MA thesis, Dalhousie University, Classics.
Deleuze, Gilles (1990). 'Immanence and the Historical Components of Expression'. In *Expressionism in Philosophy: Spinoza*. Trans. Martin Joughin. New York: Zone.
Dodaro, Robert (1999). 'Theurgy'. In *Augustine through the Ages: An Encyclopedia*. Ed. A. Fitzgerald. Grand Rapids: William B. Eerdmans.

Feichtinger, Hans (2003). 'Oudeneia and humilitas: Nature and Function of Humility in Iamblichus and Augustine'. *Dionysius*, 21: 123–59.
Fournier, Michael (2012). 'A *porisma* to Crouse on Boethius, Augustine, and the Mathematical Sciences'. *Dionysius*, 30: 95–100.
Fournier, Michael (2018a). 'Epicurus' Panpsychism'. *Dionysius*, 36: 25–37.
Fournier, Michael (2018b). 'Lucretius, Boethius and the Strong Freewill Theorem'. Boethius Study Day, University of King's College, Halifax, 27 October 2018.
Furlong, Matthew (2018). 'The Liturgy of Place: Theophany and Liberal Arts from Eriugena to Deleuze'. *Dionysius*, 36: 169–83.
Hankey, W. J. (1980). 'Aquinas' First Principle, Being or Unity?' *Dionysius*, 4: 133–72.
Hankey, W. J. (1981). 'The *De Trinitate* of St. Boethius and the Structure of St. Thomas' *Summa Theologiae*'. In *Atti del Congresso Internazionale di Studi Boeziani*. Ed. L. Obertello. Roma: Herder, pp. 367–75.
Hankey, W. J. (1987). *God in Himself, Aquinas' Doctrine of God as Expounded in the* Summa Theologiae. Oxford: Oxford University Press.
Hankey, W. J. (1997). 'Aquinas, Pseudo-Denys, Proclus and Isaiah VI.6'. *Archives d'histoire doctrinale et littéraire du Moyen Âge*, 64: 59–93.
Hankey, W. J. (2005). 'Neoplatonism and Contemporary French Philosophy'. *Dionysius*, 23: 161–90.
Hankey, W. J. (2006). *One Hundred Years of Neoplatonism in France: A Brief Philosophical History*. Leuven: Peeters.
Hankey, W. J. (2007a). 'Re-evaluating E.R. Dodds' Platonism'. *Harvard Studies in Classical Philology*, 103: 499–541.
Hankey, W. J. (2007b). 'Ab uno simplici non est nisi unum: The Place of Natural and Necessary Emanation in Aquinas' Doctrine of Creation'. In *Divine Creation in Ancient, Medieval, and Early Modern Thought*. Ed. Michael Treschow, Willemien Otten and Walter Hannam. Leiden: Brill, pp. 309–33.
Hankey, W. J. (2008). 'The Ineffable Immediately Incarnate. Interplay between 20th-Century French Neoplatonism and Heidegger'. In *Heidegger and Religion: From Neoplatonism to the Posthuman*. The Oxford Centre for Theology and Modern European Thought. <http://ora.ouls.ox.ac.uk/objects/uuid%3A05c4da8d-d3f0-44c2-b29c-12f8392b00e9/>.
Hankey, W. J. (2010a). 'John Scottus Eriugena'. In *Cambridge History of Late Greek and Early Medieval Philosophy*, Vol. II. Ed. Lloyd Gerson. Cambridge: Cambridge University Press, pp. 829–40.
Hankey, W. J. (2010b). '*Recurrens in te unum*; Neoplatonic Form and Content in Augustine's *Confessions*'. In *Augustine and Philosophy*. Ed. Phillip Cary, John Doody and Kim Paffenroth. Lanham, MD: Rowman and Littlefield, pp. 127–44.
Hankey, W. J. (2016). 'The Concord of Aristotle, Proclus, the *Liber de Causis* & Blessed Dionysius in Thomas Aquinas, Student of Albertus Magnus'. *Dionysius*, 34: 37–209.
Hankey, W. J. (2017a). 'The Conversion of God in Aquinas' *Summa theologiae*: Being's Trinitarian and Incarnational Self-Disclosure'. *Dionysius*, 35: 134–72.
Hankey, W. J. (2017b). 'Augustine's Trinitarian Cosmos'. *Dionysius*, 35: 63–100.
Hankey, W. J. (2018a). '*Ratio, Preces, Intuitus*: Prayer's Mediation in Boethius' *Consolation*'. In *Praying and Contemplating: Religious and Philosophical Interactions in Late Antiquity*. Tübingen: Mohr Siebeck, pp. 71–96.
Hankey, W. J. (2018b). '"Complectitur Omnem": Divine and Human Happiness in Aristotle and in Aquinas' *Summa theologiae*'. *Kronos*, VII: 187–205.
Hankey, W. J. (2019a). 'Jean Trouillard Authentic Neoplatonism in a French Seminary'. Preface for the Trouillard Translation Project at <https://www.academia.edu/31119354/>.
Hankey, W. J. (2019b). 'Henri-Louis Bergson and Plotinus'. In *Plotinus' Legacy: Studies in the Transformations of 'Platonism' from Early Modernsim to the Twentieth Century*. Ed. Stephen Gersh. Cambridge: Cambridge University Press, pp. 233–56.
Hankey, W. J. (forthcoming). 'Dionysius in Albert the Great and Thomas Aquinas'. In *Oxford Handbooks to Dionysius the Areopagite*. Ed. Mark Edwards, Dimitrios Pallis and George Steiris. Oxford: Oxford University Press.

Harrington, Michael (2017). 'The Divine Name of Wisdom in the Dionysian Commentary Tradition'. *Dionysius*, 35: 105–33.
Heide, Daniel (2018). 'σῶμα ψυχικόν, σῶμα πνευματικόν: The Fate of Bodies in Origen and Eriugena'. *Dionysius*, 36: 53–65.
King, Elizabeth (2017). 'Response to Dr. Wayne J. Hankey, "Augustine's Trinitarian Cosmos"'. *Dionysius*, 35: 101–4.
King, Evan (2017). '*Unum necessarium*: Meister Eckhart, the Ground and Theology in the Vernacular'. *Dionysius*, 35: 173–96.
McAllister, Nathan (2014). Systematic Theology: Iamblichus' Reception of Plotinian Psychology. MA thesis, Dalhousie University, Classics.
Marmodoro, A. and S. Cartwright (2018). *A History of Mind and Body in Late Antiquity*. Ed. A. Marmodoro and S. Cartwright. Cambridge, MA: Harvard University Press.
Mazur, Zeke (2004). '*Unio Magica*: Part II: Plotinus, Theurgy, and the Question of Ritual'. *Dionysius*, 22: 29–56.
Oliva, Adriano (2009). 'La *Somme de théologie* de saint Thomas d'Aquin: Introduction historique et littéraire'. *χώρα REAM*, 7–8: 217–53.
O'Neill, Seamus (2008). Towards a Retoration of Plato's Doctrine of Mediation: Platonizing Augustine's Criticism of the Platonists. PhD dissertation, Dalhousie University, Classics.
Riggs, Tim (2017). 'The Light of the Truth: The Role of the Good in Human Cognition in Late Ancient Platonism'. *Dionysius*, 35: 9–37.
Sastri, Martin (2006). 'The Influence of Plotinian Metaphysics in St. Augustine's Conception of the Spiritual Sense'. *Dionysius*, 24: 107–33.
Shaw, Gregory (1995). *Theurgy and the Soul: The Neoplatonism of Iamblichus*. State College: Pennsylvania State University Press.
Shaw, Gregory (1999). 'Eros and Arithmos: Pythagorean Theurgy in Iamblichus and Plotinus'. *Ancient Philosophy*, 19: 121–43.
Trouillard, Jean (1955). *La purification plotinienne*. Paris: Presses Universitaires de France.
Trouillard, Jean (1961). 'Valeur critique de la mystique plotinienne'. *Revue Philosophique de Louvain*, 59/63: 431–44.
Trouillard, Jean (1965). *Éléments de Théologie*. Paris: Aubier.
Trouillard, Jean (1969). 'Le néoplatonisme de Plotin à Damascios'. In *Histoire de la philosophie I, Encyclopédie de la* Pléïade. Paris: Gallimard, pp. 886–935.
Trouillard, Jean (1972). *L'Un et l'Âme selon Proclos*. Paris, Les Belles Lettres.
Trouillard, Jean (1982). *La mystagogie de Proclus*. Collection d'études anciennes. Paris: Belles Lettres.
Vanderwaak, Matthew (2018). Matter and the One in Proclus. MA thesis, Dalhousie University, Classics.
Vanderwaak, Matthew (2019). '"A Shrine for the Everlasting Gods": Matter and the Gods in Proclus'. Dionysius, 37: 87–113.
Watson, Cristalle (2018). Boethius Study Day. University of King's College, Halifax.
Wollf, Justin (2019). The Role of the Physical in Augustine's Return to God in the *Confessions*. MA thesis, Dalhousie University.
Wood, Matthew (2018). 'Similarity and Difference in Proclus' Theory of the Symbol'. *Dionysius*, 36: 125–41.

18

'Medieval Ethics' in the History of Philosophy

Mark D. Jordan

European philosophy that we call 'modern' was defined against its immediate predecessor, which it derided as 'medieval'. For influential early moderns, the *medium aevum* (middle or between time) separated the new dawn of philosophy in the Renaissance from an antiquity fantasised as unbroken day. The periodisation has been effective: it has sanctioned the dismissal of a millennium of European thinking on most philosophical topics, including ethics. It has also proved durable: almost half a millennium has passed since the periodisation was put into place, but it continues to influence the design of histories of philosophy.

A reader can verify this in the original version of Alasdair MacIntyre's *Short History of Ethics* (1966). As MacIntyre notes in embarrassed retrospect, that book devoted 109 pages to Greek ethics and 149 pages to Western European ethics from the Renaissance on. It allotted a mere twelve pages to the centuries between those two periods. What is worse, the allotted pages aimed chiefly to dismiss Christian authors while passing over Jewish and Islamic authors in silence. 'What an absurdity!', MacIntyre exclaims as he looks back. 'But it was not only my absurdity. This error of mine reflected a widespread, even if far from universal, practice in the then English-speaking world' (1998: v).

Much has been done since the 1960s to make medieval writings on ethics available to readers of English, not least by MacIntyre himself. Still, it is worth analysing the lingering 'absurdity' or popular 'error' for what it shows about prejudices lurking behind histories of ethics, perhaps especially those written in English. I will concentrate on two layers of the background before turning to illustrate an alternate story about 'medieval' ethical texts. The first layer appears when many modern philosophers set out to draw boundaries around medieval ethics. The second layer appears as a refusal to think more critically about historical mutations in ethics and what they imply for writing its history. This second layer raises questions about the ethics of a history of ethics.

Modern Historiography and Medieval Ethics

It is trite to complain that modern writers impose their prejudices on older philosophical texts. Still, it is worth seeing how far those prejudices can reach. For example, they touch on every part of the phrase, 'medieval philosophical ethics'. The prejudices dictate, first, that an account of medieval ethics should not trouble the prevailing chronological boundaries of the *medieval*. Second, they dictate that medieval ethics should *look like* whatever version of modern or contemporary philosophical ethics the writer endorses. Third, the prejudices hold that medieval philosophical ethics should treat *problems or topics* that interest recent academic ethicists. The three expectations may seem unobjectionable, but their unreflective application disfigures the older texts. Let me show this by going through them more carefully.

Periodisation, Language, Cultural Geography

However neat it may seem in its polemical origin, 'medieval' is in practice a fluid category. Writers on medieval philosophy regularly reach back into ancient, late ancient and early Christian texts. They reach forward into early modern writers. One of the founders of the contemporary study of medieval philosophy, Etienne Gilson, wrote his first two books on scholastic elements in Descartes, then returned years later to offer a more thorough treatment of the inheritance (Gilson 1913a, 1913b, 1930). With Gilson, other scholars of Thomas Aquinas go further: they trace a continuing reception of Thomas's ethical texts in some schools from his death in 1274 through a revival in the fifteenth and sixteenth centuries and a proclamation of Neo-Thomism in the nineteenth down to the present day.

If the chronology of the 'medieval' is in fact fluid, so too is the choice of languages and of religious traditions. Older accounts of medieval ethics tend to concentrate on works written by Christians in Latin. For example, Alois Dempf's *Ethics of the Middle Ages* traces the elaboration of various ethical 'systems' on the basis of 'the ethics of the Gospel' (Dempf 1927). The figures singled out for special attention are Augustine, Aquinas and Meister Eckhart. A similar emphasis on Christian texts can be found in older surveys – whether Tennemann's *Manual of the History of Philosophy* (1812) or Sidgwick's *Outlines of the History of Ethics for English Readers* (1886). In such books, 'Arabic' or 'Jewish' writers are mentioned in passing and mainly as sources for Christians. More recently, surveys of medieval philosophy have tried to incorporate other religious traditions and languages as integral parts of the history of *European* philosophy, but the main narrative remains centred in Christianity and Latin.

The word 'European' is significant. Linguistic exclusions have been reinforced by long-standing connections between the academic study of medieval philosophy and projects of European nationhood. Hauréau's *On Scholastic Philosophy* (1850), to take an early example, was composed for a competition that defined 'Scholastic Philosophy' as the teaching cultivated in Paris between the introduction of the new Aristotle and the fall of Constantinople (1850: 1:i–ii). Patriotic impulses for studying medieval philosophy were not confined to France. Modern editions of medieval texts were frequently included in series devoted to national literature.

There is a larger issue here, not confined to the 'medieval'. Among humanistic disciplines, philosophy is striking for its tight attachment to salient figures and canonical texts. The selection of figures and texts is inflected from decade to decade by prevailing fashions. Sometimes the whole scheme is rudely shifted by new programmes of thought – as when Neo-Kantians rewrote the history of philosophy. Still, the stability of 'Western' philosophy, its definitional identity, rests on a curious chrono-geography, by which ancient Athens and Rome are claimed as constitutively European while the Middle Ages are disclaimed, to one degree or another, as alien. This hopscotch produces absurdities. It also – and deliberately for some writers – hampers consideration of the relations of 'philosophy' to 'theology' or 'religion', even though such relations are central to much philosophical thinking in 'the West'.

Genre and Method

A similar prejudice operates through the modern distinction between philosophy and 'literature'. Writers of academic philosophy now compose within an impoverished set of genres: the lecture, the article, the monograph, and a few more. Students of the history of philosophy, especially ethics, need to remember how recent and parochial this set is. Even the approved canon of philosophy abounds in counter-examples. Plato's dialogues, to state the obvious, are not bare arguments so much as fully narrated scenes, with characters who perform ethics by speaking and acting. Aristotle was famous in antiquity for his logic and physics, but also for his rhetorical compositions, like the *Exhortation* or *Protreptic* to take up the study of philosophy. The *Consolation of Philosophy* by Boethius is written in both prose and poetry. Its sequence of poetic styles is essential to its ethical re-education. And so on. In the modern period, the boundaries separating ethics from literature are also more misleading than helpful. Samuel Johnson, whose works are typically allotted to curricula in English literature, often joins philosophical controversies, chiefly in ethics. He deserves to be counted as a leading figure in English-speaking philosophy.

What is true of writing in most periods of philosophy is especially true of the Middle Ages. (Having recognised the absurdity of that phrase, I am still compelled to use it.) The most famous medieval Latin authors employ a dazzling variety of genres: linked arguments and formalised disputes, of course, but also poetic allegory or drama, historical moralisation, legal interpretation, satire or denunciation, and hymnody or lament. A single author will write in different genres for different purposes, and some authors (such as Alan of Lille or Bonaventure) blend genres with enormous skill. All of the genres are counted as suitable for writing philosophical ethics.

Topics, Disciplines

The view that medieval ethics must treat topics that interest contemporary ethicists ignores large concerns in medieval texts: the relation of human action to divine influence, the limits on human self-reformation, the need for divine revelation of ethical instruction, the importance of ritual, and so on. The effects do not stop there. Even the topics that medieval writers seem to share with contemporary ethicists often carry other meanings not easily represented by prevailing methods or styles. Obvious examples are the central ethical notions, 'virtue' and 'law'. For many medieval writers, ethics presents special challenges to drawing a bright boundary between philosophy and theology.

'Philosophy', 'theology': those nouns point to other preconceptions. It is too easy for academic writers to take as given the prevailing table of academic disciplines. If most of us learned at some point that disciplines have histories and that disciplinary boundaries are always contested, we tend to speak as if philosophy and theology were stable things. In fact, they are equivocal terms: they contain multiple, changing meanings not held together by any unifying principle – not even a Wittgenstinian family resemblance. I would go further: the notion of what an academic discipline or field *is* changes with mutations in the assembly of what counts as knowledge.

How Ethics has History

A second layer of preconceptions behind the 'absurdity' or 'error' of skipping over medieval ethics is more elusive. I introduced it above as a refusal to think critically about historical mutations in ethics. I can put it now as a question: how should a writer of history conceive ethics to *have* a history? Tracing the history of any part of ethics demands choices about what in ethics can be expected to change and where to look for its evidence. The historiography of medieval ethics has too often appropriated techniques of textual philology or intellectual history uncritically – as if it were obviously no different from a history of grammar, mathematics or city planning.

Attempting to sketch a critique, I return to the opening of Michel Foucault's *History of Sexuality* 2.[1] Its stated aim is to explain his reorientation of a series of books already underway. In the first volume, Foucault had outlined five more that would tell the history of the category of sexuality from the beginning of the modern period into the twentieth century. By the time he publishes the second volume, he has pushed the chronological scope back to the ancient Mediterranean – not least in order to understand the difference that Christianity made for European morality. He prefaces the volume with a justification for moving the project's boundaries. He then describes some varieties of history that might be written about any teaching on human conduct.

Foucault begins by listing what he is *not* doing. To simplify: he is not writing a history of behaviours or their representations – that is, not acts or ideas about acts. He aims instead for a history of the 'experience' of a field of human action. By 'experience' he means the correlation of bodies of knowledge, types of norms and forms of subjectivity (Foucault 2015: 2:740). 'Forms of subjectivity', as Foucault explains in the next moment, refers to the 'shapes' human beings take on when they recognise themselves as subjects of a particular formation. For example, we must learn to see ourselves as subjects with a sexuality. We practise speaking that experience, matching it against approved rules and stories, cultivating it to improve ourselves. In Foucault's shorthand, we have to be constituted as subjects 'that can and must be thought about' in certain ways (2015: 2:742). The human being as ethical subject has a history – a personal history, of course, but also a longer history of types of subjectivation.

Once the ethical subject is put into history, the next question for Foucault is why certain topics become ethically salient for its formation in certain times and places. He is not asking about the basic prohibitions – say, murder or incest. On the contrary, he is curious about shifting preoccupations with areas of conduct not (yet) determined by strict codes, immemorial customs or severe religious prescriptions. Why is it that teachers of subjectivation become preoccupied with tasks *outside* the established prohibitions? Foucault calls their shifting preoccupation 'problematisation'. Since it occurs especially in under-regulated action or deportment, he links it to 'arts of existence' or 'stylisation'. The problematisation of a new area of conduct calls forth new ethical writing, but it also demands the improvisation or invention of new ways of shaping oneself. Many ethical texts in antiquity exhort their readers to such tasks, so Foucault borrows an ancient word to describe their aim: they are, he says, 'etho-poetic'. (*Poesis* is the Greek for making, but Foucault also puns on the modern sense of 'poetry'.) The old texts encourage the reader to re-make the reader's self.

The use of words like 'style' or '*poesis*' may suggest that Foucault regards ethical problematisation as superficial. On the contrary, he insists, etho-poetic texts concern the axes of human life: the self's relations to the body and death, to others, to one's self, and to the conditions for reaching truth. Foucault emphasises that ethical stylisation reveals the processes of self-shaping at the centre of ethical teaching or practice. To make the point plain, he draws out the consequences for any history of ethics.

There are, roughly speaking, three kinds of ethical history: a history of human behaviours or 'moralities'; a history of moral codes; and a history of how to conduct oneself (which Foucault calls ethics or ascetics). Foucault is quick to blur the boundaries among them. In particular, he notes that any code morality will have elements of the ethical, and conversely.

---

[1] I go to this volume only for help in conceiving other ways of writing a history of ethics. Foucault's writing is confined by other assumptions that I do not endorse – indeed, that I have just criticised. Of course, he follows a traditional canon of mostly elite, prescriptive texts as part of his rhetorical strategy. He is, after all, interested in archeologies of *power*.

Still, it is the third sort of history that he means to write – and that he commends. A history of how to conduct oneself must consider four things at least. First, there is the way in which a part of one's self is constituted as the primary material of moral conduct. Foucault calls this the determination of the *ethical substance*. The second aspect of a history of self-conduct is how one conceives one's subjection to the ethical demands. This is the *mode of subjection*. Third, there is the question of how you are to go about transforming yourself. Is your *ethical work* a long discipline under regular supervision, a sudden renunciation, a relentless combat with little perceptible progress? Finally, there is the *teleology* of the ethical subject. What is the goal of your ethical work? Do you seek more complete mastery over yourself, a sudden detachment from the world, a reliable tranquility, salvation?

Foucault's reinterpretation of the history of ethics is offered, as I said, to explain a change in the direction of his series of books. But it poses challenges, both general and specific, to any history of medieval ethics. A sharper challenge is posed by Foucault's techniques of composition. In and around the last three volumes of *History of Sexuality*, he labours to retell etho-poetic texts. When an author plans to write a history of books that both register ethical mutations at large scale and aim to encourage personal transformation, how does s/he represent the ethical ambitions of her/his own text? Where is s/he – *who* is s/he – in the ongoing mutations of the subject under ethics? And what transformation does s/he aim to produce in her readers? For Foucault, it can never be enough to say, 'I want to produce an objective, factual history of what these texts mean.' What counts as objective or factual mutates through history, and etho-poetic texts come to mean in the transformations they effect. A critical history of medieval ethics must negotiate both with the power in present configurations of knowledge and with the older powers projected through the texts it proposes to explain.

Illustrative Texts

In what follows, I offer just four illustrations from the range of etho-poetic projects that a critical history of medieval ethics should engage. My reading will not stamp Foucault's fourfold description of a history of self-conduct onto every text. Instead, I will begin from the notion of etho-poetic writing – or, rather, its transmutation into the rhetoric of pastoral care. I will assume that even the most code-like texts invite the reader to self-formation and so reveal the assumed ethical substance, mode of subjection, ethical work and teleology. But since I am concerned with the etho-poesis of a small handful of texts, I attend to what stands out in them rather than to generalisations about century-spanning movements or timeless ideas.

I restrict myself to familiar Christian texts even at risk of self-contradiction. Having criticised the narrow boundaries often set for medieval ethics, I now present a narrow selection of my own. The reader should remember that mine is only a little gallery of illustrations, not a well-bounded narrative. In fact, the gallery hopes to show that there cannot be such a narrative. Even the most familiar texts featured by the most restrictive histories resist the narratives they are enlisted to serve. There is no complete history of medieval ethics waiting to be told. There is only the assortment of surviving texts that call readers to be different sorts of ethical subjects by ceaseless shaping.

My gallery ends with a masterwork that still exerts some direct influence in philosophical discussion: the *Summa of Theology* by Thomas Aquinas. I set the *Summa* as the endpoint partly because of its influence, partly because its reception displays disciplinary shifts that inform modern ethics. But I do not subordinate earlier texts to Thomas's *Summa*, and I do not imply that his writing is a sharply demarcated end of medieval ethics. There are obviously medieval authors on ethics after Thomas – some would say, the most significant.

Scriptural Commentary: Gregory the Great, *Moral Teachings in Job*

One foundational cluster of genres for medieval ethics is commentary on revealed scriptures. For Christian authors, 'scripture' means the combination of disparate texts that make up the Christian Bible. The library of texts poses two notable problems for readers in search of ethics. First, there is relatively little detailed moral guidance in the paradoxical sayings of Jesus. The Gospel about Jesus Christ is offered as culmination of biblical teaching, but it hardly gives an ethical system or even a practicable set of rules. The bulk of New Testament ethical teaching is supplied in texts attributed to Paul, but even the Pauline texts offer more exhortation than daily guidance. Second, the most detailed guidance is found in the 'Old Testament' or 'Hebrew Bible'. There it is commingled with other prescriptions rejected by Christians – not least ritual directions and governmental provisions for the stages of Israelite history. There is no clear-cut way to detach the 'ethics' of the Hebrew Bible from ritual and legal parts of it, and there is no simple rule for determining which parts of the Hebrew Bible Jesus meant to impose on his followers. The obvious answer is, after all, the most disconcerting for later Christians: Jesus was a Jewish rabbi and his first followers were Jews.

The effort to find ethical instruction in the Bible for Christians who were not Jews (indeed, who rejected Judaism) led to Christian methods of exegesis that distinguished various levels of scriptural meaning. An influential distinction is proposed by Gregory the Great in his *Moral Teachings in Job* (finished in the 590s CE), one of the cardinal sources for later medieval writers. Gregory distinguishes three levels of scriptural meaning: historical, allegorical, moral (Gregory the Great 1979–85: 143–143b).[2] The historical is sometimes called the letter or the literal. It is praised as the foundation and root of other meanings. But when a passage fails to make literal sense, a reader must go to other meanings. Next beyond the literal is the allegorical. Gregory means by allegory the level on which a biblical figure or event foreshadows something in the future – say, Christ or the Church as an ark of faith. But the most important sense – for Gregory's text and later traditions – is the third, the moral. The moral sense of a passage is its lesson for present living. It is not a modern application of an old rule or story: it is an old anticipation of what moral teaching must be in the present. Within the divine providence, an event in ancient Israelite history was intended to become moral instruction for later Christian readers. A Christian teacher should bend the stream of scriptural discourse towards disclosing it.

With the distinction in place, Gregory undertakes to offer what no Christian author has yet attempted – a moral reading of the Book of Job. He begins with a set of assumptions. The first is that Job's life as retold in the scriptural text is exemplary. Job is a saint. He is not just a man of virtue but also a holy one. It is worth being struck by this claim because Job is a gentile. Indeed, Gregory argues that Job was chosen precisely as a pagan exemplar to rebuke those who have abandoned the law. But this also allows Gregory to stress that Job practises true philosophy. Job thus also stands as the figure of the ancient sage or the just pagan. Not only that: the character of Job embodies the relation of philosophical ethics to Christian ethics. On the one hand, Gregory enumerates Job's virtues: humility, hospitality, discipline, mildness, bountifulness (preface 3.7). Then, a few pages later, Gregory likens Job to Jesus (preface 7.16). This is one example of a textual gesture that recurs in medieval ethics: the claim that Christianity both corrects and completes ancient philosophy.

---

[2] Gregory the Great (1979–85), *Moralia in Job*, prefatory epistle 1–3. Here and in what follows, I cite medieval texts by their traditional textual divisions rather than the pages of a modern edition. This should allow the reader to track my citations in whatever edition is at hand. An English translation of this text, originally published in *A Library of Fathers of the Holy Catholic Church Anterior to the Division of the East and the West* (Oxford, 1884), has been recently reprinted (Ex Fontibus, 2012).

Gregory does not 'solve' this relation of supersession for later writers, since its terms continue to shift during the Middle Ages. He uses it to produce fused patterns for naming moral qualities. The patterns combine Scriptural passages with philosophical names for moral dispositions. The first pattern enumerates seven virtues of the Holy Spirit (1.26.36): wisdom, understanding, counsel, might, knowledge, piety, fear of the Lord. The list is drawn from Isaiah 11.2 and traditionally called the gifts of the Holy Spirit. But Gregory quite clearly calls these seven virtues, though they are also 'of the Holy Spirit', that is, given by God. Indeed, this list names the basic virtues for Gregory's teaching. To them Gregory adds three other virtues and then four more. The three are faith, hope, charity (1.27.38), drawn from 1 Corinthians 13 and traditionally called the theological virtues. The four are the cardinal virtues, adopted into Christian writing from various philosophical texts. What is clear in Gregory is that they are also gifts of the Spirit (2.49.76).

Lists of virtues may seem tedious. I suggest that they show how Gregory imitates the techniques he finds in the scriptural text. Gregory typically anchors his lists in an image. If the Scriptures add moral meaning to literal narrative, Gregory fastens his moral analyses to scriptural images or elaborates figures of his own. The mnemonic value of the list is reinforced by vivid imagery. Commenting on Job, Gregory can also ground the ethical analysis in a character that calls for imitation. If a reader has trouble holding on to argumentative elaborations, s/he can always return to Job as a desirable model. In addition to prompting imitation, the model consoles – because Job survived so much suffering to end in fulfilled hope. There is also the element of challenge: if a pagan can do this, think how much more a Christian ought to do!

Gregory's moral readings of Scripture provide patterns for shaping oneself as a subject. They teach as well how to read one's own experience. When a reader learns how to see divine shaping through a biography, s/he also learns how to see through the circumstances of her/his own life into moral patterns and possibilities for re-subjectivation. In Gregory, the most important ethical work is named *discretio, discussio, retractatio* (e.g., 1.30.42 to 1.34.47). The words describe a self that watches, reviews, reconsiders, examines itself. To do this, you must be able to read your experience through its letter to its moral sense. Techniques for finding moral lessons in Scripture give practice in ethical work on the self.

Confession and Legislation: The Penitentials

Christian ethics has long been concerned not just to propose ideals but to use punishment pedagogically. While many Christian writers relegate threats to the first stages of moral teaching, they are willing to resort to them as needed. The punishment is (officially) justified as a prelude to repentance. To have its intended effect, punishment has to be accepted and then appropriated by the errant Christian, who chooses to make amends and begin a better life. Christian communities have encouraged many kinds of bodily penance or mortification, but the goal has typically been verbal acknowledgement of sins and a public commitment to reform.

A reader in pursuit of medieval ethics might consider Christian codifications of penance mere background to theoretical arguments. Foucault rightly resists that judgement. The influence of some penitential texts affects not just the evaluation of whole classes of acts but the frames for understanding acts in relation to laws. A clear example is found in the early medieval texts known as Irish or Anglo-Saxon penitentials.[3] Many early penitentials arrange sinful acts by kind to assign graded punishments or penances. In their structure, they extend laws to a

---

[3] Penitentials take many forms in their long medieval history. I consider only one early form here. For an overview, see Vogel (1978).

punitive taxonomy of discrete acts. The claim that *acts* can be ranked by degree of ethical harm is not self-evident. Neither is the claim that they can be sorted with sufficient precision into species or kinds. These and other claims are embedded in the penitential codes.

I take as an example one of the earliest and simplest penitentials, the one named after Finnian, which is roughly contemporary with Gregory's commentary on Job.[4] This text explains, at its end, that it has tried to gather scriptural and authoritative opinion about 'the remedies of penance' and 'those to be treated' by them (canon 53). 'Remedy' (*remedium*) is a general term but it is also the technical word for a prescription or treatment. There are other traces of medical reasoning throughout the text. When he speaks of the five 'great and capital sins' (canon 29), Finnian recommends that they be cured by applying their contraries – an old therapeutic notion. Further: a penitential remedy is applied to inherited tradition, modified by local variation, the extraordinary variety of cases, the idiosyncrasies of individuals. The same qualifications are found in ancient and early medieval medical writing. Finnian's use of medical notions may even extend to a certain realism or perhaps pessimism about the efficacy of treatment. Relapses are to be expected; so too are long treatments with limited results.

If Finnian's penitential explains its teaching through a series of medical analogies, it then speaks, in a second conclusion, of destroying 'all the evil deeds of human beings'. There is no medical modesty here. Indeed, the notion of 'evil deeds' is surprisingly comprehensive: it combines what we would think of as religious sin, criminal offence and civil tort (as in canon 9). The range of particular evils is large: strife or quarrels, other violence, murder, theft, and a variety of 'sexual' crimes (to use our word). The sequence of presentation does not correspond to the gravity of the crime: that is inferred from the punishment imposed. The sequence is also complicated by an inconsistent division between punishments for clergy and those for laity. What is most striking is that the 'great and capital' sins are not assigned penances (canon 29). They are treated by cultivating their opposing virtues, not by fasting, public confession and a period of exclusion from the altar. Here the tensions between punitive and therapeutic understandings may collide. Or perhaps the anomaly suggests a certain hesitation about a closed system of ranking acts by assigned punishment. Is the classification of acts measuring ethical seriousness or amenability to correction? Still larger questions lurk in the combination of medical and legal metaphors. Both kinds imply a relatively passive subject – to whom treatments or punishments are prescribed. The passivity provides a key to this ethical subject and its work. The text attributed to Finnian is mostly silent about the kind of moral education that penance produces. One thing is clear: the body is a privileged medium for learning. The ethical work in this sort of penance is to learn from or through one's body. The passivity of Finnian's subject may be the body's vulnerability.

Pictures of Virtue and Vice: Alan of Lille, Anticlaudianus

In Gregory's *Moralia*, one of the scriptural senses was allegory, the prefiguration of later events. Moral figuration was, of course, used much more widely in 'medieval' ethical teaching, within and beyond texts. Medieval examples of allegorical teaching would include Romanesque façades on pilgrimage churches in Northern Spain; Giotto's frescoes in the Scrovegni or Arena chapel; some of the late medieval mystery plays; and so on. I concentrate on a single text: the *Anticlaudianus* of Alan of Lille – or, according to its full title, *The Anti-Claudianus about Anti-Rufinus* (around 1182 CE).[5] Already the reader is caught in a web of learned allusions. In Claudian's *Against Rufinus*

---

[4] For the Latin text and its dating, Bieler (1975). There is an English translation in McNeill and Gamer (1990: 86–97).
[5] There is a bilingual edition of the *Anticlaudianus* in Alan of Lille (2013).

(around 400 CE), an infernal council plots to install Rufinus as ruler to wage war on the earth. Claudian's text tells the failure of this plot and the ultimate triumph of good over evil. Alan of Lille reverses Claudian in a number of ways because he wants to tell about the making of a heavenly creature to restore the reign of the virtues on earth. Making a heavenly creature turns out to be rather like making a complex text, and so the *Anticlaudianus* becomes an allegory of its own moral teaching.

Why choose an allegory (to stick with that familiar word) for moral teaching? An obvious answer would be the need to represent what is happening invisibly within subjects. Alan keeps comparing his text to a painting because he is struggling to depict ethical conditions. At the same time, Alan appropriates through Gregory the idea that the moral lessons are both more memorable and more persuasive if attached to stories. Still there is something else – something odder – in Alan's complicated and self-delighted artifice. Alan wrote a series of texts in standard theological genres. In them, he quotes Scriptures and authoritative theologians to draw quite orthodox and even 'conservative' conclusions. Here, in the *Anticlaudianus*, he chooses to teach moral lessons through the luxuriance of classical – that is, pre-Christian – imagery. I say 'luxuriance' to suggest not only the excess of images but their sensuous or erotic qualities. Why would a theologian choose to write a poetic conceit that conceals the highest lessons of moral formation behind a dazzling procession of pagan images?

Here is the allegory in outline. Nature calls her sisters – a group of virtues corresponding to no traditional list – in order to heal human creation by making one perfect human. While Nature can make and remake a human body, only God can make a human soul. The council decides to send Providence – also known by the ancient philosophical terms *Fronesis* (Prudence or Foresight) and *Sophia* (Wisdom) – on a trip to Heaven to plead for God's help. The seven liberal arts build a chariot for Providence. Providence and Reason travel off, soon reaching the apex of the heavenly spheres where Providence meets Theology. Theology offers to act as tour guide so long as Providence leaves Reason with the horses (a caution for philosophers). After a tour of the heavenly dwellings, Providence approaches the throne of God, where she faints. She is revived by a potion and given a mirror in which to see the reflection of God. Steadied by Theology and Faith, she is finally able to stammer out her plea for help. God agrees to send down a new soul so long as Nature makes a suitable body. Back on earth, Providence joins the others in making a beautiful body, which receives gifts from each of the virtues. There are complications around the gift of Nobility, the daughter of Fortune – and so a lengthy side-trip to the house of Fortune, who finally comes to share in creating the new human. No sooner is the creation complete than Alecto gathers the forces of evil. There is an epic battle complete with just-when-you-thought-it-was-over moments. Finally, the forces of evil are defeated, the reign of the virtues established, and the book ends.

This story raises many questions for anyone interested in medieval ethical instruction, including the competing role of the liberal arts, reason and fortune. But I return to the question with which I began: why would someone versed in scriptural exegesis and earlier Christian forms of ethical instruction (like the penitentials) choose to write ethics in this sort of allegory? If the motive is vivid representation, why not return to the striking parables told by Jesus, to other examples of heroic virtue (like Job), or to the collected lives of more recent saints?

Alan's allegory frustrates simple answers, but I offer two responses to the question – both preliminary. The *Anticlaudianus* performs a unification of the many kinds of ethical teaching known to its author. It does not *argue* a hierarchy of arts and sciences in which literature, the arts and philosophy serve theology. The unification is performed in the structure of Alan's text – or, more exactly, in his experiment with using the variety of sources on the wager of their ethical persuasiveness. I then add, second, that the wager is complicated by the kind of ethical subject addressed by the *Anticlaudianus*. This subject is being shaped not by one pedagogy so much as a series of disparate pedagogies. Alan's ethical subject – exemplified by the narrator or Alan himself – is awash with patterns of moral formation. The battle in the subject is not just virtues against vices but contending pictures of the ethical work to be done. Alan's text offers a story in which the contention of means is aligned towards a single teleology.

An Introductory Moral Teaching in Outline: Thomas, Summa of Theology

Thomas Aquinas wrote about ethics in an enormous range of genres: sermons, various kinds of commentaries (not least on Aristotle's *Nicomachean Ethics*), advanced disputes, variously comprehensive treatments on the whole of theology. Of these, the most important is the (unfinished) *Summa of Theology* (probably 1268–73 CE). In it, a reader finds not only the most detailed elaboration around ethical topics but the sustained performance of an ethical pedagogy that subordinates other forms of ethical knowledge to theology in the very act of admiring their truths.

The *Summa* begins with the briefest of prologues. The Christian teacher is obliged to provide not only for the accomplished, but also for those just beginning. Thomas intends to hand down 'what belongs to the Christian religion [*Christiana religio*] in the way that befits the teaching of beginners [*incipientes*]' (*Summa Theol.* 1 prol). Readers are liable to suppose that 'religion' means doctrine and that the 'beginners' have undertaken to study it academically. Later in the *Summa*, 'religion' names both a virtue of devotion to God and vowed ways of life (2-2.81–91, 2-2.186–9). 'Beginners' refers to 'novices' under vows, as Thomas calls his readers a few lines later. What has the teaching of theology for novices to do with ethics? A first answer is that Thomas conceives a religious community as an ethical school. The *Summa* is a model curriculum for an intentional community dedicated to the pursuit of the fullest human life.

There are other answers. Thomas's curriculum is an invention that resolves a perennial difficulty. Most of the comprehensive works of theology before Thomas took as their basic pattern one of the familiar creeds or professions of faith. A creed teaches the history of creation, salvation and final judgement, but it does not provide moral guidance. Where does ethics fit within a creedal pattern? In the *Summa*, Thomas cuts the creed at its narrative centre by inserting an extended moral teaching between the creation and the redemption or restoration. The *Summa*'s first part treats God's essence and the distinction of persons in the Trinity, God as exemplar and the beings that proceed from God. The second or moral part considers 'the motion of the rational creature towards God'. It is subdivided into two sections. One presents moral matter generally or 'universally': the end of human life, the elements of properly human action, and the intrinsic and extrinsic principles of human acts. The second part's other section presents the main virtues in sequence before integrating them into states or ways of life. *Summa* 3, or the rest of the creed, narrates Christ's life, teaching and continuing presence as necessary means to enact the moral pattern set forth in *Summa* 2-2. The moral teaching remains incomplete until Thomas provides an account of incarnation and sacraments.

Still, *Summa* 2-2 is Thomas's most lucid and detailed representation of the complexities of embodied life. He begins by acknowledging that the great temptation for moral teaching is to run on endlessly, through every variety of virtue, gift, vice, precept and counsel, illustrating each with an excess of cases. Thomas proposes instead two simplifying principles. First, he unites in a single cluster of considerations a virtue, the corresponding gifts (recall Gregory), the opposed vices and the attached affirmative or negative laws or precepts. Second, Thomas traces all of the moral virtues back to the three theological and four cardinal virtues. He insists that vices – favoured by theatrical preachers – not distend this list of seven. Vices are treated compendiously in relation to virtues, and they are distinguished by real differences rather than accidental ones (2-2 prologue). This structure subordinates a number of traditional schemes for describing sins. For example, the 'deadly' or capital sins are not treated separately by Thomas; they are distributed across the *Summa* according to the list of virtues. Thomas also incorporates other Christian ethical taxonomies – many from Gregory – within the pattern of virtues. So, for example, the divine help traditionally called gifts of the Holy Spirit appear throughout the text rather than as a separate block.

Thomas's emphasis on the virtues is a pedagogical clarification that reinforces his main lessons. An evil act can be understood only as defect or derailment in regard to the good. The good abides, despite sin, as the human subject's ineradicable teleology: union with God. Thomas's sustained effort to teach about virtues presupposes that evil or vice is something from which human beings can turn. If the turn depends on divine grace, moral instruction can be – generally is – useful assistance. The analyses of virtues, vices or laws are subsumed by the arc of the *Summa*'s structure to a reader's moral re-education. The re-education summons every kind of resource available to Thomas, especially in law, philosophy and scriptural interpretation. (In contrast with Alan, Thomas is less confident about poetry – and apparently less familiar with it.) All of these ethical teachings are subsumed within a plot of Christian formation. That plot is also the pattern for a unified human subject,

The *Summa* is sometimes analysed as the reconciliation of Aristotle with scripture. The simplistic formulation is misleading on its face: Thomas knows much more philosophy than Aristotle and much more theology than the letter of Scripture. The formulation misleads in another way by suggesting that Thomas grapples with self-contained bodies of knowledge. On the contrary, he sees that philosophical ethics – like philosophical metaphysics – cannot be self-contained because it is inevitably incomplete. No comprehensive account of human lives can forget divine purposes and presences. No effective pattern of ethical formation can fail to invoke them. Human beings cannot reach their deepest ends without divine assistance – especially because human beings have fallen into ethical deformities from which they cannot rescue themselves. In response to these human needs, God replies with revealed law and Scriptures, but also with incarnation, sacraments and endless gift. These are necessary elements for the deepest human re-subjectivation.

Here a contemporary reader can glimpse an interesting reply to Foucault's notion of problematisation – or, more precisely, the notion that problematisation arises in spaces left relatively open by the prevailing moral codes. The *Summa* does not vindicate codes so much as extend problematisation. Foucault is, in some ways, much more optimistic about the ability of codes or disciplines or bio-power to form human beings. For Thomas, the challenges of subjectivation go so deep that they require not only divine incarnation but daily ministrations of divine love. Code gives way to stylisation or the art of living. That is another way of saying that the law is accomplished in grace.

Afterword

I have pointed to features in these four texts as illustrating the etho-poetic projects with which medieval ethics must be concerned. Illustrations need not imply an underlying narrative. In this case, I have argued, they cannot, since there is no well-bounded narrative of 'medieval ethics' to be told. Still, I can write this afterword most succinctly by indulging in a little storytelling.

There is evidence that Thomas wrote the *Summa* in part to overcome the scatter of ethical instruction within his own religious community – an order of preachers and teachers. If so, he failed. The reception of the *Summa* largely ignored its unifying structure to extract smaller or larger pieces for more specific use. Some of Thomas's ardent advocates undo what he most wanted to accomplish: they move moral theology into separate works, treating it as separate field. (The professional specialisation of contemporary ethics owes more to late medieval theology, I suspect, than to any close reading of the ancients.) At the same time, Thomas's texts were mined for a philosophical ethics, presumptively Aristotelian, that could be taught as preparation for theology or entirely apart from it. The *Summa*'s reception is a microcosm of the making of modern ethical disciplines and sub-disciplines.

We need not – should not – stop with lamenting a decline. At least, I refuse to recall medieval texts for the savour of reactionary nostalgia. Here again Foucault is helpful. In the introductory section of *History of Sexuality* 2, Foucault makes some unusually personal remarks about his motives for writing those volumes. He emphasises the importance of curiosity, but he also describes philosophic thinking as an art of living or exercise in self-conduct. 'There are moments in one's life when the question of knowing whether one can think otherwise than one does or perceive otherwise than one sees is indispensable for continuing to see or to think . . . [W]hat is philosophy today – I mean philosophical activity – if it is not the critical work of thought on itself?' The (ethical) work consists not of justifying what one already knows but of 'undertaking to know how or how far it is possible to think otherwise' (Foucault 2015: 2:744).[6] The critical work of philosophical thinking is an experiment in re-subjectivation conducted on oneself. It can begin from any number of topics or archives. It might begin, for example, by asking: how do I expect myself to be re-subjectivated by enquiring into the 'history of medieval ethics'?

References

Alan of Lille (2013). *Anticlaudianus*. In *Literary Works*. Ed. and trans. Winthrop Wetherbee. Cambridge, MA: Harvard University Press.
Bieler, Ludwig (1975). *The Irish Penitentials*. Dublin: Institute for Advanced Studies.
Dempf, Alois (1927). *Ethik des Mittelalters*. Munich: Oldenbourgh.
Foucault, Michel (2015). *Histoire de la sexualité*, Vol. 2. In *Oeuvres*. Ed. Frédéric Gros et al. Paris: Gallimard.
Gilson, Étienne (1913a). *Index scolastico-cartésien*. Paris: F. Alcan.
Gilson, Étienne (1913b). *La liberté chez Descartes et la théologie*. Paris: F. Alcan.
Gilson, Étienne (1930). *Études sur le role de la pensée médiévale dans la formation du système cartésien*. Paris: Vrin.
Gregory the Great (1979–85). *Moralia in Job*. Ed. Marc Adriaen. Turnhout: Brepols.
Haréau, Barthélemy (1850). *De la philosophie scolastique*. Paris: Pagnerre.
MacIntyre, Alasdair (1998). *A Short History of Ethics: A History of Moral Philosophy from the Homeric Age to the Twentieth Century*. London: Routledge.
McNeill, John T. and Helena M. Gamer (1990). *Medieval Handbook of Penance: A Translation of the Principal Libri Poenitentiales*. New York: Columbia University Press.
Sidgwick, Henry (1886). *Outlines of the History of Ethics for English Readers*. London and Edinburgh: Macmillan.
Tennemann, William Gottlieb (1812). *Grundriss der Geschichte der Philosophie für den akademischen Unterricht*, Part II. Leipzig: J. A. Barth. (English translation by Arthur Johnson and J. R. Morell, London: Henry G. Bohn, 1852.)
Vogel, Cyrille (1978). *Les 'libri paenitentiales'*. Turnhout: Brepols.

---

[6] Foucault, *Oeuvres* 2:744.

19

The Structural Causality of Specific Difference from Medieval Thought to Deleuze and Althusser

Eleanor Kaufman

Specific difference is not a term from medieval logic that is generally considered in and of itself. And it is certainly not a term that is ever highlighted as such in twentieth-century French philosophy. However, it *is* a term that is evoked in the latter context, at least in the work of Gilles Deleuze and Louis Althusser, and the concern here will be to review some of the ontological complexities of specific difference in its trajectory from Aristotle to the present, particularly as underscored in the critical literature on John Duns Scotus. While Deleuze is more attuned than Althusser to the ontological resonance of the medieval debates, and so will be considered in more detail here, the simple engagement with the medieval terminology itself indicates there is a period in French thought, at least into the 1960s, when questions of structure and being are not disavowed as they will be in the decades that follow. How that turn against structure and ontology took place is not the focal point here; at issue is simply establishing the linkage between medieval philosophical concerns and those of two giants of twentieth-century French thought, something which at least for most students of the later period would appear extremely counterintuitive.[1]

Of particular importance to an exploration of Aristotelian categories such as substance, quantity, quality, relation, time and place is the practice of predication in which a broader category is narrowed and ordered into more specific categories. The notion of a 'predicable', or something that can be predicated, dates to the third-century philosopher Porphyry whose *Isagoge* served as an introduction to Aristotle's *Categories* in the medieval curriculum. Specific difference, or *differentia*, might be considered the most challenging of the predicables to define and characterise, precisely because it is both a predicable and an instrument of predication. In Porphyry's model (referred to as the Porphyrian Tree), we start with the most general category of substance, which is taken as the operative genus and then divided into attributes of 'corporeal' and 'incorporeal'. Thus the genus 'substance' modified by the *differentia* 'corporeal' gives us the species 'body'. Taking 'body' as the new genus, it can be modified by the *differentia* 'animate' or 'inanimate'.[2] The animate body can be modified by sensitive and insensitive; the sensitive

---

[1] This is part of a larger study that examines Althusser's central role as both a signal thinker of 'structure' and a signal attacker of 'structuralism', the latter considered as a pejorative and imprecise designation of the thought of structure that reached its heyday in the 1950s and 1960s in France. Different connections between medieval philosophy and twentieth-century French thought have been put forward in Alliez (1996), Widder (2002) and Thacker (2010).
[2] See p. 7 of the Introduction to this volume for a diagram.

animate body by rational and irrational, until we arrive via this operation of predication at a 'rational, sensitive, animate, corporeal substance', or, the human. Often this is simplified as [genus=animal] + [*differentia*=rational] = [species=man]. This three-part equation has three predicables: animal, which is the broader genus; rational, which is the *differentia* or 'specific difference'; and man (changed to 'human' in what follows), which is the species. The fourth term is called the 'definition', and it comprises the entirety of the equation.[3]

As a term (for example, rational) which is added to a genus (for example, animal) so as to narrow it down by dint of a particular quality into a more particular species (for example, human), specific difference would seem to exist in an abstract or formal space. Whereas one can envisage a substantive entity that is an animal, or one that is a human, one does not usually entertain something like a 'rational' in and of itself. While arguably this makes it no less 'real' as a logical operator, it is hard to designate in what its being consists. Meanwhile, in a wholly different time and milieu, the field of twentieth-century French philosophy might be described as one that in large part questions the idea of any sort of coherent subject, truth, origin or being. Its terrain seems about as far from the categories of medieval logic and philosophy as one could be, rarely cites Aristotle sympathetically, and tends to favour existence over essence, becoming over being, difference over identity, and the like. Indeed, even to call this constellation of thought so often referred to as 'French theory', or simply 'theory', *French philosophy* is already to uphold a metaphysical dimension that this body of work, with Jacques Derrida as its most recognised figurehead, arguably calls into question. What do we make then, of a striking recourse to the terminology of specific difference in the work of two of twentieth-century French philosophy's most luminary figures, Gilles Deleuze and Louis Althusser?

It should be emphasised that what follows is not an influence argument, namely, that Deleuze's or Althusser's possible exposure to medieval philosophy – via a teacher such as Martial Gueroult or Ferdinand Alquié in the case of Deleuze, or a youthful Christian socialist orientation in the case of Althusser – led them to adopt this terminology. It is also not being argued that either French thinker employed this term with the rigour or specificity of their scholastic predecessors. Nevertheless, even though Deleuze and Althusser employ 'specific difference' in somewhat eccentric fashion and for fully different ends, it is striking that both draw on this phrasing in work from the 1960s to designate something that bears – or at least bumps up against – a structural-ontological register, and both abandon this terminology (along with denunciations of structuralism), some time after. This short-lived mobilisation of scholastic terminology will be considered as itself a marker of the *specific difference*, to employ the term in Althusserian periodising fashion, between a moment of twentieth-century French philosophy when structural-ontological thought was possible and a slightly later moment when it ceased to be thinkable in the same terms, both for the thinkers in question and for the larger field.

Before focusing on the French philosophical redeployment of this term, a brief overview of some of the difficulties and valences of specific difference, from its Aristotelian formulation to its appearance in high medieval polemics, and continuing to contemporary commentaries, is in order. Not only is specific difference hard to define in itself, but this very difficulty serves as a marker of its uneasy proximity to the highest and most simple entities, being and God. As indicated above, the most basic predication example is of the genus *animal*, which, if predicated by the *differentia* of *rational* results in the species *human*. Combined with the genus to form the

---

[3] The definition might be compared to the sign in semiotics insofar as it encompasses at least two other terms in structural relation to each other, such as 'signified' and 'signifier' for Saussure, but also serves as a signifying unit in its own right, for example, the unit 'animal + rational = man' signifies the Aristotelian categories logic as such.

species, the *differentia* is an important part of the definition, for without it the species could not exist in its specificity. But what is a *differentia*, or specific difference, in itself? In the few direct formulations from Aristotle's *Categories* devoted to *differentiae*, they are shown to have striking parallels to substance, the highest of the ten categories of being. Like substance, *differentiae* cannot be present in subjects, are not accidental, and are predicated univocally. While substance does not vary by degree, it would seem that *differentiae* might have this potential in the fashion of the category of *quality*. Aristotle's *Metaphysics* reformulates the question of substance into one of matter and form, in which matter would ostensibly correspond to genus and form to *differentia*, though this poses a whole new set of questions which strays from the particularity of specific difference and will not be considered here.[4]

Porphyry

Commentaries on Aristotle, both direct and indirect, highlight the complexity of this term that aligns sometimes with one predicable, sometimes with another, yet remains strikingly singular. Specific difference appears as something of a boundary case in its proximity both to quality and to being in Porphyry's *Isagoge*. On the one hand, specific difference (here 'difference') is similar to genus and does not vary in degree: 'genus is not predicated more and less, and neither are differences of genus' (Porphyry 1994: 8). On the other hand, difference is distinguished from genus in that it pertains to a quality of a thing rather than the thing itself: 'genus is predicated with respect to what the thing *is*, whereas difference is predicated with respect to what *manner* of thing it is' (12; emphasis added). Both aligned with and distinct from genus, difference's proximity to quality at once differentiates difference from genus and elevates it above genus, now on the side of species. Thus, there are two competing valences. Whereas difference is bound up with manner or quality, genus is closer to the 'being' of the thing; and specific difference itself facilitates this hierarchy that places genus in the originary and higher category; like genus, 'difference is prior to the species made in accordance with it' (16). However, and at the same time, the species surpasses the genus with respect to its closer proximity to substance, and presumably being. As Porphyry summarises it, 'genera surpass species by including the species under themselves while species by their differences surpass genera' (13). Differences, then, would seem to facilitate and align with what is loftiest in both the genus and the species.

Differences, however, are themselves different, as is the particularity of their role. Porphyry divides difference into different types, where specific difference is distinguished from the lower types of difference. The most basic type, or broad difference, is something 'distinguished in otherness, either from itself or from something else' (7). Such a definition would encompass most modern usages of this term, even in the bulk of the vast scholarship that draws casually on contemporary continental thinkers of difference, such as Derrida and Deleuze. A 'more proper' form of difference is the second sense, which is that of an inseparable accident, something not inherent to the being of a thing but which can't be separated from it, and to illustrate this Porphyry uses the example of the scar (7).[5] In other words, some accidental qualities are subject to modification, such as being healthy or ill, hence separable, whereas others are considered not capable of modification, such as the frequent Aristotelian example of being 'snub-nosed', or

---

[4] See Aristotle, *Categories*, and also *Topics* and *Metaphysics*, all in Aristotle (2001); see also Rorty (1973) and Greene (1974).

[5] Notably the scar is an example that is used in Stoic thought to illustrate *lekta*, or incorporeals, whereby the scar serves as the incorporeal mark of the wound that preceded it. See Bréhier (1928).

in Porphyry's example, having a scar. Of course, modifications of scars or noses may be quite possible with modern surgical techniques and might move the boundary between separable or inseparable in interesting ways. Here then is an early formulation of difference as the unseparated that is developed in the twentieth-century French tradition by Alain Badiou.[6]

Finally, we get to the third and 'most proper sense' of difference, which is specific difference. As distinguished from broad differences, and then more proper differences, both of which 'only make [something] otherwise', specific differences 'make it other' (7). What is the difference between being otherwise and being other? It would seem to pertain to something that is not just capable of minor modification but of a modification that alters its very being. And in fact, Porphyry proceeds to formulate it thus: 'difference is not just anything that separates but what pertains to the being of a thing' (10). Thus, despite its closer proximity to quality, specific difference nevertheless touches on ontological distinction, providing something of a glimpse into being. This least well-defined of the major predicables remains elusive for Aristotle and Porphyry, bound as it is so intricately in one direction or the other to genus and species, while entailing something of a purity or simplicity that none of the other terms has. In short, specific difference's conundrum is that it seems to be all these things at once, while itself serving as the highest in a hierarchy of types of difference, at least for Porphyry.

The question of specific difference's intricate if not exceptional status is put into distinctive relief in scholastic writings from the thirteenth and early fourteenth centuries, by which time more of Aristotle's corpus had become available in Latin, having passed in many instances by way of Arabic language intermediaries. Aristotle's oeuvre of course ranges over a vast terrain, from natural history to metaphysics to politics, but it is the writings categorised under the rubric of 'logic' that are the primary reference points for the training of students in the arts faculties at Paris and Oxford. While the 'logic' of the trivium – in its dissection and analysis of Aristotle's ten categories – might have little to do with what passes for logic now, my contention is that these debates shed light on the notion of specific difference which in turn brings into relief an important, though ultimately fleeting, current of twentieth-century French thought. This is a current concerned not just with epistemological questions of signification, or phenomenological questions of perception, but with unabashedly ontological conundrums such as whether being can be said in the same way for everything or varies according to the entity in question.

Scotus

Before considering the way Gilles Deleuze takes up this ontological vantage point in his early single-authored work, a quick survey of the major distinction between Aquinas and Scotus on univocity and analogy is in order. Whereas Aquinas propounds the analogical model of being – for example that God's goodness is not the same as human goodness, but although the two can't be measured in the same way we can still think of them analogically under the same concept – Scotus proposes, at least in certain logical if not metaphysical formulations, a univocal model, that being is said in a single sense of everything that is. This matters to the thought of difference in that specific difference or ultimate difference (differences pertaining

---

[6] Alain Badiou discusses the unseparated above all in *The Century* (Badiou 2007), where he contrasts the will to identity or fusion with the more desirable model of difference that exists within the structure of a political party, where members are different yet 'unseparated' (129).

to transcendentals such as goodness, truth and unity) are terms that complicate the extent of univocity's range, or more nearly indicate the point at which univocity may fall into analogy. Whereas a thinker like Gilles Deleuze will hail Scotus's intervention as the start of a univocal philosophical line that leads directly to Spinoza's unity between God and Nature, and beyond that to Nietzsche's notion of plays of force, most commentators on Scotus will qualify univocity's comprehensiveness in one way or another.[7]

These qualifications, which involve contradictory indications in Scotus's own oeuvre, as well as the question of this oeuvre's categorisation, are worth noting briefly here, insofar as specific difference plays a role in resolving conundrums in Scotus's thought noted by various commentators. Not only does Scotus's oeuvre give confusing and contradictory indications on these matters, but it also matters, as it did with Aristotle, whether we are dealing with a metaphysical or a logical question. As Giorgio Pini formulates it in *Categories and Logic in Duns Scotus*, 'only metaphysicians can speak of analogy, which is a real relation among essences, whereas the logician, who deals with the way things are understood and signified, only speaks of equivocity and univocity' (Pini 2002:178–9). Thus, metaphysics engages in ontology and considers being *per se*, as for example in Aquinas's *De Ente et Essentia*, whereas logic focuses on more epistemological questions of how the human mind observes and categorises being.[8] Étienne Gilson makes much the same observation in his seminal study of Scotus, citing a disjunction or 'décalage' (a term Althusser will employ extensively) between different ontologies that effectively reconciles Scotus and Aquinas.[9] In that regard, the Subtle Doctor's notion of univocity could be considered more of an epistemological tool than an ontological pronouncement. If this is the case, and being *per se* is more easily described analogically, why would this be so? One major reason is the difficulty of placing the *differentiae* themselves into the univocal framework.

As any number of commentators point out, the *differentiae* raise the problem of distinguishing between themselves and the entity they categorise. Or, we might ask, can the category by which we make a determination ever itself be part of the determination? As noted above, *differentiae* have commonalities with genus, species and even the simplicity of being itself, but does this mean they can be related to being in a univocal way? Scotus would seem to suggest that they can be, at the least, through their simplicity: '"being" is an irreducibly simple concept and consequently no middle term can exist between "being" and its attribute, for neither has a definition that might serve as a middle term'.[10] If specific or ultimate difference is not considered as a middle term, then it would seem it would also fall within Scotus's encompassing univocity. Étienne Gilson answers in the negative, arguing that 'being is not univocally predicable of its ultimate differences because, if it were, they could not be its "differences" . . . Being as being could not serve to differentiate being as being' (Gilson 1952a: 95; my translation).[11] As something that qualifies being, difference for Gilson does not share in the absolute potential of

---

[7] Deleuze's position on Scotus, culled from several works primarily from the 1960s that will be addressed below, seems remarkably close to that of Maréchal (1922).

[8] See Aquinas (1968) and Pini (2002: 19).

[9] See Gilson (1952a: 115). See also Gilson (1952b: 84–96).

[10] Duns Scotus, from *Opus Oxoniense* I, d. 39, q. 1, 137, translated (Scotus 1987: 8). Robert Prentice emphasises that 'Scotus has the emptiest possible notion of being' (24) and that for Scotus, 'the concept of being, while it is of reality, is such that its referent reality could not be less rich without being absolutely nothing' (41), both in Prentice (1970).

[11] He also writes that 'like transcendentals, ultimate difference is not included in common being but "essentially included" in certain beings' (99).

being but rather serves as a means of determination, just as Porphyry distinguished a quality of a thing from the thing itself. In thus falling into something of an analogous position because of this determining or modifying logical quality that distinguishes it from the thing itself, Gilson takes this as a stepping point to his Thomist reconciliation of Scotist univocity with Aquinas's notion of being as analogical.[12]

A somewhat different response to the problem of specific difference's potential interference with the univocity of being comes from Pini, who makes recourse to the theological problem subtending Scotus's model, namely how to categorise the divine and the human Christ, considered since the Council of Chalcedon in 451 as two natures in one person. For Pini, the key is to consider the *suppositum*, or the object a given term refers to. In this case, the two natures, though distinct, both refer to the same *suppositum*, Christ. Moreover, this serves as an example of 'identical predication' in which a distinct subject and predicate both refer to the same thing, as distinct from the standard model of 'formal predication' described above. As Pini glosses it:

> By applying the distinction between formal and identical predication to the differences of being, Scotus can conclude that the concept of being is common to everything. For being is common to all the things of which it is predicated *per se* by formal commonality. But being is also common to all the things in which it is included and to its differences by identical commonality, because each categorical item and each difference of being is identical to being, if we take 'being' not as a concept but as a supposit. (Pini 2002: 31)

In this fashion, like the human nature in its much-contested relation to Christ's divinity, specific difference is able, via identical predication, to maintain its differentiating function and still uphold univocity without falling into the redundancy Gilson points out.

These examples highlight the definitional fluidity of specific difference, how it functions simultaneously as a structural and an ontological category, indeed we might say something of a structural-ontological one. On the one hand it appears as something of a pure modifier apart from the things it modifies; yet on the other hand, as the above notion of identical predication underscores, its separability is fully bound up with a higher form of inseparability, whether with form, univocity or being itself. These same conundrums permeate what I am calling the structural moment, as distinct from structuralism, in twentieth-century French thought, insofar as the structures in question are not simple binary oppositions and epistemological tools, but themselves are the motor force enabling what they would purport to describe.[13]

A notable permutation of the conceptual openness of specific difference is that it arguably shares a number of features with an ostensibly different kind of difference, individuating difference, or *haecceity*. Rather than predicating genus in the fashion of specific difference, individuating difference allows for distinction of different individuals, such as Plato, Aristotle or Socrates. Richard Cross emphasises how Scotus himself, in the *Ordinatio*, introduces

---

[12] See also Scotus's *Ordinatio* I, d. 3, p. 1, q. 3, 618: 'First: concerning any of the aforesaid definitional concepts it happens that the intellect is certain that it is being, while doubting whether the differentia contracting being to such a concept is such a being or not. And so the concept of being, as it belongs to that concept, is different from those lower concepts about which the intellect is doubtful, and is included in each lower concept; for those contracting differentiae presuppose the same common concept of being which they contract.'

[13] See Kaufman (2013). See also Kordela (2018).

haecceity via analogy to specific difference, in that both are simple, indivisible and distinct from any other difference:

> It does not seem overly puzzling that a specific difference could perform these two functions: the absolute conceptual simplicity of any ultimate specific difference seems to entail both distinction from every other specific difference, and its indivisibility into any further species. And Scotus believes that these sorts of consideration can help explicate the function of a haecceity relative to individuation too. That is to say, he believes that something wholly devoid of common (shared) conceptual content – a haecceity – can explain not only indivisibility into further particulars, but also distinction from all other particulars. (Cross 2014)[14]

Cross underscores the structural similarity, if not analogy, between *differentia* and haecceity in terms of distinction and indivisibility. In this sense, it seems that specific difference and haecceity would stand against the more predicable genus and species on the grounds of their greater simplicity and inseparability.

Deleuze

Gilles Deleuze makes something of this same move in his 1968 *Expressionism in Philosophy: Spinoza*, but he voices it more as a polemic against the predicables, including to some extent against specific difference. Here, in tracing a direct line from Scotus to Spinoza, one that paints Descartes largely as the antagonist, Deleuze dismisses genus, species and specific difference as belonging to a logic of signs and possibility, which in turn makes real distinction merely numerical as opposed to fully expressive of possibility for difference in Being:

> There can be no necessity of existence in a substance of the same 'species' as an attribute – a specific difference determines only the possible existence of objects corresponding to it within the genus. So substance is once more reduced to the mere possibility of existence, with attributes being nothing but an *indication*, a *sign*, of such possible existence . . . Substance is not a genus, nor are attributes differentia, nor are qualified substances species. Spinoza condemns equally a thinking that proceeds by genus and differentia, and a thinking that proceeds by signs. (Deleuze 1992: 36)[15]

It would be hard to formulate a more succinct and overarching critique of an Aristotelian categorial logic, one in which Scotus momentarily drops out of the picture. It is noteworthy that the critique corresponds to similar attacks on the possible throughout Deleuze's oeuvre, as opposed to his preferred nexus of the virtual and actual.[16]

Given this denunciation, it is startling that in linking Scotist formal distinction to Spinozist non-numerical, real distinction in the subsequent chapter, Deleuze cites Gilson's monograph on Scotus in positive fashion in support of a formulation that largely coincides with the one developed above via Pini, Cross and Gilson, including the importance

---

[14] See also Scotus, *Ordinatio* II, d. 3, p. 1, qq. 5–6; Cross (2005: 60, 78) and (2014: 66–173).

[15] See also ibid.: 45 for another helpful overview of this non-transcendent, 'dynamic and active' Spinozist model that does away with genus and species.

[16] This critique is developed most fully throughout Deleuze (1995). Nevertheless, there are interesting fleeting moments where the Deleuzian virtual does not always appear as the favoured term.

of simplicity: 'Two attributes taken to infinity will still be formally distinct, while being ontologically identical . . . There are here as it were two orders, that of formal reason and that of being, with the plurality in one perfectly according with the simplicity of the other' (Deleuze 1992: 64). Indeed, Deleuze appeals to the same accord via simplicity of logic and metaphysics that has been mobilised above to align specific difference with univocity of being. Yet, following this Deleuze proceeds to denounce specific difference as inferior to Spinozist attributes while relying on a logic facilitated by its presence.[17] The resolution, if there is one, comes in the chapter's conclusion, where Deleuze concedes that the Subtle Doctor's need to avoid a pantheist heresy leads him into a path far too reliant on predicables, a path that Spinoza's variant of univocity fully avoids (Deleuze 1992: 67).

It is striking that in his magnum opus from the same year, *Difference and Repetition* (1968), Deleuze barely mentions Spinoza and only briefly references Scotist univocity, but continues to trace a lineage of univocity into the contemporary period, here via Darwin and Georges Simondon's notion of individuation.[18] In this instance, he contrasts haecceity and the process of individuation – something he takes more or less wholesale from Simondon[19] – in absolute terms from the process of predication into species. In his renewed polemic against species in *Difference and Repetition*, Deleuze makes the following oppositions:

> It is not the individual which is an illusion in relation to the genius of the species, but the species which is an illusion – inevitable and well founded, it is true – in relation to the play of the individual and individuation. The question is not whether in fact the individual can be separated from its species and its parts. It cannot. However, does not this very 'inseparability', along with the speed of appearance of the species and its parts, testify to the primacy in principle of individuation over differenciation? (Deleuze 1995: 250; hereinafter cited by page number in the body of the text)

Deleuze himself will distinguish between the higher and more virtual form of differen*t*iation versus differen*c*iation as it is actualised (written sometimes in the form of the differential calculus d(t)/d(c)), and it seems it is not a far stretch to correlate this pronouncement with the penchant outlined above, especially in the discussion of Porphyry, for locating inseparability as a function of the highest form of difference. Moreover, though without evoking formal distinction as he did in the first Spinoza book, this discussion of the primacy of individuation over differenciation mirrors the same primacy of identical over formal distinction that Pini locates in Scotus as a means of upholding the univocity of specific difference. In short, while denouncing specific difference in content, Deleuze, in a range of examples, extols the form of simple and unseparated difference that specific difference might arguably also evoke.

This section will conclude with two potential diagnoses for this impasse. In the same section of *Difference and Repetition*, Deleuze credits Darwin with 'inaugurating the thought of individual difference'. Following from Darwin and Weissmann, he emphasises how the embryo – also called the pre-individual or 'larval subject' – is able to sustain a form of life

---

[17] Deleuze (1992: 65): 'Substance is not a genus, nor are attributes specific differences.'
[18] This lineage, when expanded to other work, also includes Nietzsche, both as early as the 1962 *Nietzsche and Philosophy* (Deleuze 1983), and as relatively late as the 1970 *Spinoza: Practical Philosophy* (Deleuze 2001). See especially chapter 2, 'On the Difference Between the *Ethics* and a Morality' (pp. 17–29), for a discussion linking Spinoza and Nietzsche.
[19] See Simondon (1964).

at a limit beyond the 'species, genus, order or class' (249) and thus is the higher term. After a fashion, we might substitute 'specific difference' in many of Deleuze's statements, based on our analysis above, and perhaps come up with something close to his formulations, though admittedly with some distinctions. He writes that 'the highest generalities of life, therefore, point beyond species and genus, but point beyond them in the direction of the individual and pre-individual singularities rather than towards an impersonal abstraction' (249). Perhaps specific difference falls too close to something like an 'impersonal abstraction', two terms that are otherwise and generally read favourably by Deleuze, and, later, Deleuze and Guattari.

Even more speculatively, we might consider another formulation about difference in the same chapter of *Difference and Repetition*, 'Asymmetrical Synthesis of the Sensible', in which we see a static genesis that follows from difference that also leads to a separation not previously observed:

> Intensity or difference in itself thus expresses differential relations and their corresponding distinctive points. It introduces a new type of distinction into these relations and between Ideas a new type of distinction. Henceforward, the Ideas, relations, variations in those relations and distinctive points are in a sense separated: instead of coexisting, they enter states of simultaneity or succession. (252)

Quite remarkably, though this is as far as possible from Deleuze's overt orientation, we see something like a movement of emanation in which, as developed in theological discussions, we move from creator to creature, simple to composite, eternity to time, simultaneity to succession. This is a rare directionality for Deleuze, in that usually it is the later stage, such as the third (as opposed to the first and second) synthesis of time, elaborated in the 'Repetition for Itself' chapter of *Difference and Repetition*, that is more proximate to the empty, static, atemporal realm, one seemingly resonant with a theological model of eternity. Once again, it must be emphasised that this is not the terrain Deleuze sets out to uphold, but one that his frequent recourse to elements of its structural-ontological logic keeps ever-present on the horizon.

Althusser

The generation of separation and time as problems with which to contend forms the link to Louis Althusser's far less theologically inflected, though far more favourable, evocation of specific difference in several of his works from the mid-1960s. Whereas specific difference makes a cameo appearances as a serial 'bad guy' in a range of Deleuzian episodes or investigations, Althusser summons it to make a positive designation that is neither as separate nor as successively time-bound as it might rhetorically appear. To put it in different terms, it might seem like Althusser uses 'specific difference' as a means of achieving clear distinction and periodisation – but does it actually serve that end, or instead return us to the more heady ontological debates outlined above? Unlike Deleuze, Althusser makes no attempt to situate specific difference in its rich philosophical and theological lineage, but instead uses it to mark what he also refers to as an 'epistemological break' within his field of enquiry, namely, the oeuvre of Marx.

The term 'epistemological break' (*coupure*) is one that Althusser takes, or more nearly modifies from the pre-eminent French historian of science (and quasi-phenomenologist) Gaston Bachelard, and his several works on this topic mostly from the 1930s and

1940s.[20] Bachelard uses the term 'epistemological rupture' (*rupture*) to describe how, after a certain breakthrough such as that of Copernicus with astronomy or Lavoisier with chemistry, the whole previous framework for describing the centrality of the earth or the qualitative theory of elements disappears from the picture, and with this the historical narrative of these sciences changes fundamentally. Or, by contrast, it may be blocked from this change by what Bachelard terms an *epistemological obstacle*, that is, a way of thinking that serves as a barrier to the breakthrough of the properly scientific insight. As Mary Tiles helpfully glosses Bachelard, and drawing on an example from mathematics, to imagine that parallel lines do not converge is to think from a Euclidean perspective, which is an epistemological obstacle to the development of a properly non-Euclidean framework. By the same token, Althusser argues that Marx's early works are not yet Marxist and are still beset with epistemological obstacles; Marx's early works are only thinkable in the old ideological language, they are not yet properly scientific, to use Althusser's terminology. *The Theses on Feuerbach* and *The German Ideology* (1845) are still Hegelian, still ideological, and even the works of the transition (the *Grundrisse* from 1857–9 and *Contribution to the Critique of Political Economy* from 1859) have not yet reached an elaboration of the mode of production that is unmoored from its ideological underpinnings. This we find only in *Capital*, the first volume of which appeared in 1867. But even then, the first part of the first volume – which contains many of the most-cited passages on commodity fetishism and the mystical aspect of commodities[21] – is still ideological Marx. Althusser gives readers a strong directive, really an imperative: begin with the second section of *Capital* and continue, reread that four or five times, and only then read the first section (Althusser 1971: 81).

In his introduction to *For Marx* (1965), Althusser clarifies that his use of the term 'specific difference' pertains to the question of the *existence* of the epistemological break:

> The question of the specific difference of Marxist philosophy thus assumed the form of the question as to whether or no there was an *epistemological break* in Marx's intellectual development indicating the emergence of a new conception of philosophy – and the related question of the precise *location* of this break. (Althusser 2005: 32).

Whereas in the previous examples specific difference predicated an incontestable distinction between genus and species, with the question then turning to the structural ontology of specific difference itself, here the specific difference is the mark of proof, as it were, that a contestable distinction exists at all. It is not so much predicating genus into species as it is signalling the shift between two variants of Marxism, the ideological and the properly scientific (Althusser's terms), and this within Marx's work itself.

In the collaborative *Reading Capital*, also from 1965, Althusser's second entry, 'The Object of *Capital*', extends specific difference to mean that which distinguishes (and we could wonder if it also somehow predicates) classical political economy from Marx's variant. Once again, however, and unlike our previous examples, the difficulty is perceiving the distinction since it is considerably occluded at its own moment of formulation. Hence, as Althusser repeats in 'On the Materialist Dialectic', Marx's professed 'inversion' of Hegel did not itself understand the extent to which it had not simply reversed but had fully undone or 'eliminated' its object

---

[20] See especially Bachelard (1985, 2006).
[21] See Karl Marx, *Capital*, vol. 1, especially the section 'Commodities and Money'.

(Althusser 2005: 198). Marx, then, was not opposing Hegel, but was creating something of a new species. Similarly, in Althusser's reading, Marx does not have the language available to theorise his own difference from classical political economists such as Ricardo and Smith, and himself did not predicate as clearly as he might have, not having the language to classify the new species he had created, namely surplus-value and relations of production, though he was able to perceive his object more clearly than the others.

Althusser reiterates this problem in *Reading Capital* with repeated reference to Marx's wavering at the level of specific difference, able to predicate with more clarity than his cohort or than his earlier self, but not able fully to comprehend the logical and philosophical structure of the innovation he is making:

> Marx did not always define with the same precision the concept of its *distinction*, i.e., the concept of the *specific difference* between it and the object of Classical Economics. There can be no doubt that Marx was acutely conscious of the *existence* of this distinction: his whole critique of Classical Economics proves it. But the formulae in which he gives us this distinction, this specific difference, are sometimes disconcerting, as we shall see . . . Does not the difficulty Marx seems to have felt in thinking in a rigorous concept the difference which distinguishes his object from the object of Classical Economics, lie in the *nature* of his discovery, in particular in its fantastically *innovatory character*? In the fact that this discovery happened to be theoretically *very much in advance* of the philosophical concepts then available? (Althusser et al. 2016: 219–20)

Specific difference is here the mark of innovation in thought, or as Althusser defines it in *For Marx*, 'whether a new meaning has emerged' (Althusser 2006: 70). Like the ancient and medieval idea that the species is closer to substance or to simplicity and that the even simpler specific difference has aided in that sharpening, here too specific difference serves that function. The difference is that in Althusser's usage that *is* its sole function and hence even more its reality. It seems specific difference would not exist in this sense if it were not leading to conceptual innovation.

Specific difference also appears, at least in these examples, as something of a temporally based innovation. However, Althusser insists elsewhere in these works, though rarely in the same breath, that this is not a simple causal or temporal logic, that an entity does not precede its effects but a structure only comes to exist in the effects, however ordered or produced. As Althusser writes,

> we must regard these differences in temporal structure as, *and only as*, so many objective indices of the mode of articulation of the different elements or structures in the general structure of the whole . . . To speak of differential types of historicity therefore has no meaning in reference to a base time in which these backwardnesses and forwardnesses might be measured. (Althusser et al. 2016: 254)

In line with Althusser's more well-known concept of structural causality, in which the structure is 'immanent in its effects' (Althusser et al. 2016: 344) specific difference would here be something of the marker of that immanence, where it is at once a structure marking a distinction and itself indistinguishable from the thing it marks. Following from this, specific difference would not be a temporal marker *per se*, even though Althusser's examples would seem to lend it that valence since they generally move in chronological fashion (early to late Marx). Rather, and in line with the tenor of Althusser's entire oeuvre, the emphasis is always on the differentiating function of specific difference as such, and not a causal or temporal one. In this regard, Althusser retains the term's ancient and medieval role as a logical and ontological operator more faithfully than Deleuze. Nevertheless, such a notion is notably consonant with Deleuze's model of quasi-causality in his 1969 *The Logic of Sense* (in which the cause no more generates the effect than the effect generates the cause) with its equal favouring of immanence (Deleuze 1990). However, unlike Althusser, Deleuze shows a pronounced disinclination towards terminology from scholastic logic, while still affirming that logic by other means and in greater depth, or so it has been argued here.

Rather than a forward-progressing structure of innovation, marked by specific difference from the more inchoate structure from which it emerged, Althusser's notion of innovation evokes something of the simultaneity of an eternal structure, though this is not a term Althusser himself would favour. What is curious is that after about 1966, this vocabulary dropped entirely out of Althusser's lexicon, as it did out of Deleuze's by the late 1960s, leading one to speculate that perhaps in the larger field of contemporary French philosophy, something of the rigour and precision of the high medieval debates were in fact actually lost with the turn to so-called post-structuralism. But that is another story.

References

Alliez, É. (1996). *Capital Times: Tales from the Conquest of Time*. Trans. G. Van Den Abbeele. Minneapolis: University of Minnesota Press.
Althusser, L. (1971). *Lenin and Philosophy and Other Essays*. Trans. B. Brewster. New York: Monthly Review Press.
Althusser, L. (2005). *For Marx*. Trans. B. Brewster. London: Verso.
Althusser, L., E. Balibar, R. Establet, J. Ranciere and P. Macherey (2016). *Reading Capital: The Complete Edition*. London: Verso.
Aquinas, T. (1968). *On Being and Essence*. Trans. A. Maurer. Toronto: Pontifical Institute.
Aristotle (2001). *The Basic Works of Aristotle*. Ed. R. McKeon. New York: The Modern Library.
Bachelard, G. (1985). *The New Scientific Spirit*. Boston, MA: Beacon Press.
Bachelard, G. (2006). *Formation of the Scientific Mind*. Manchester: Clinamen Press Ltd.
Badiou, A. (2007). *The Century*. Trans. A. Toscano. Cambridge: Polity Press,.
Bréhier, É. (1928). *La théorie des incorporels dans l'ancien stoïcisme*. Paris: Vrin.
Cross, R. (2005). *Duns Scotus on God*. Aldershot: Routledge.
Cross, R. (2013). *The Medieval Christian Philosophers: An Introduction*. London: I. B. Tauris.
Cross, R. (2014). 'Medieval Theories of Haecceity'. *Stanford Encyclopedia of Philosophy*. Redwood City: Stanford University Press.
Deleuze, G. (1983). *Nietzsche and Philosophy*. Trans. H. Tomlinson. New York: Columbia University Press.
Deleuze, G. (1990). *The Logic of Sense*. Trans. Mark Lester with Charles Stivale. New York: Columbia University Press.
Deleuze, G. (1992). *Expressionism in Philosophy: Spinoza*. Trans. M. Joughin. New York: Zone Books.
Deleuze, G. (1995). *Difference and Repetition*. Trans. P. Patton. New York: Columbia University Press.
Deleuze, G. (2001). *Spinoza: Practical Philosophy*. Trans. R. Hurley. San Francisco: City Lights Publishers.
Gilson, É. (1952a). *Being and Some Philosophers*. Toronto: Pontifical Institute.
Gilson, É. (1952b). *Jean Duns Scot: Introduction à ses positions fondamentales*. Paris: Vrin.
Greene, M. (1974). 'Is Genus to Species as Matter to Form? Aristotle and Taxonomy'. *Synthese*, 28/1: 51–9.
Kaufman, E. (2013). 'Do Dual Structures Exist? Deleuze and Lacan in the Wake of Lévi-Strauss'. *Yale French Studies*, 123: 83–99.
Kordela, A. K. (2018). *Epistemontology in Spinoza-Marx-Freud-Lacan: The (Bio)Power of Structure*. Routledge Innovations in Political Theory. London: Taylor and Francis.

Maréchal, J. (1922). *Le Point de départ de la métaphysique*, Vol. 1. Bruges: Charles Beyaert.
Pini, G. (2002). *Categories and Logic in Duns Scotus: An Interpretation of Aristotle's Categories in the Late Thirteenth Century*. Leiden: Brill.
Porphyry (1994). 'Isagoge'. In *Five Texts on the Mediaeval Problem of Universals: Porphyry, Boethius, Abelard, Duns Scotus, Ockham*. Ed. P. V. Spade. Indianapolis: Hackett Publishing Company Ltd.
Prentice, R. P. (1970). *The Basic Quidditative Metaphysics of Duns Scotus as seen in his De primo principio*. Spicilegium Pontificii Athenaei Antoniani, Vol. 16. Roma: Antonianum.
Rorty, R. (1973). 'Genus as Matter: A Reading of Metaphysics Z–H'. In *Exegesis and Argument: Studies in Greek Philosophy Presented to Gregory Vlastos*. Ed. E. Lee, A. Mourelatos and R. Rorty. Assen: Van Gorcum, pp. 393–420.
Scotus, J. D. (1950–2013). *Ordinatio*. In *Opera omnia*, ed. Charles Balic et al., vols 1–14. Vatican City: Vatican Polyglot Press.
Scotus, J. D. (1987). *Philosophical Writings*. Trans. A. Wolter. Indianapolis: Hackett Publishing Company Ltd.
Simondon, G. (1964). *L'Individu et sa genèse physico-biologique: L'individuation à la lumière des notions de forme et d'information*. Paris: Presses universitaires de France.
Thacker, Eugene (2010). *After Life*. Chicago: University of Chicago Press.
Widder, N. (2002). *Genealogies of Difference*. Urbana: University of Illinois Press.

Notes on contributors

Jason Aleksander is Professor of Philosophy at San José State University. He works primarily in the areas of medieval and Renaissance philosophy, Dante studies, Cusanus studies and the philosophy of religion.

Peter Casarella is professor of Theology in the Divinity School at Duke University. He served from 2013–2020 as an associate professor of theology at the University of Notre Dame and before that as professor of Catholic Studies at DePaul University where he was also the founding director of the Center for World Catholicism and Intercultural Theology. He has published ninety-one essays in scholarly journals or books on a variety of topics, including a monograph, *Word as Bread: Language and Theology in Nicholas of Cusa* (2017), and edited or co-edited amongst other works: *Cusanus: The Legacy of Learned Ignorance* (2006), *A World for All? Global Civil Society in Political Theory and Trinitarian Theology* (2011), and, most recently, *The Whole is Greater than its Parts: Ecumenism and Inter-religious Encounters in the Age of Pope Francis* (2020). He is currently working on a book entitled *The God of the People: A Latinx Theology*.

Felipe Castañeda is currently a professor at the Universidad de Los Andes Faculty of Philosophy in Bogotá, Colombia. His research is focused on the philosophy of war, and specifically, to the philosophy behind the Conquest of America, and political colonial thinking derived therefrom.

Daniel O. Dahlstrom is John R. Silber Professor of Philosophy and Chair of the Department of Philosophy at Boston University. His Aquinas Lectures, 'Identity, Authenticity, and Humility', were published by Marquette University in 2017. His essay 'Scheler on Shame: A Critical Review' appeared in *Metodo* 5/1 in the same year.

Idit Dobbs-Weinstein is an associate professor of Philosophy, Jewish Studies and Graduate Department of Religion at Vanderbilt University. Her work is devoted to retrieving a materialist Aristotelian tradition whose impact on subsequent philosophy has been occluded by ecclesiastico-political prohibitions. Exemplary publications of this project include *Maimonides and His Heritage* (2009); *Spinoza's Critique of Religion and Its Heterodox Jewish Heirs* (2015); 'Tensions Within and Between Maimonides' and Gersonides' Accounts of Prophecy' (2006); 'Aristotle On the Natural Dwelling of Intellect' (2013); 'Praxis in the Age of Bit Information and Sham Revolutions: Adorno on Praxis in Need of Thinking' (2015); and 'Negative Dialectics as the Radical *or* Jewish *Species* of Negative Theology' (2017).

Emmanuel Falque is professor and honorary dean of the Philosophy Department at the Institut Catholique de Paris. He specialises in medieval and patristic philosophy, phenomenology and philosophy of religion. His works that have been translated into English are *The Metamorphosis of Finitude* (2012); *God, the Flesh, and the Other* (2015); *The Loving Struggle* (2018); *The Guide to Gethsemane* (2018); *Saint Bonaventure and the Entrance of God into Theology* (2018); and *Nothing to it, Reading Freud as a Philosopher* (2019).

Wayne J. Hankey (DPhil Oxon) is Emeritus Professor of Classics, Dalhousie University and Editor of *Dionysius*. He has published or has in press more than 100 scholarly articles and book chapters as well as scores of dictionary essays and reviews. His latest work concerns the connection of matter and the first principle in the Platonic tradition, the human and divine in Aristotle, Plotinus, Iamblichus, Eriugena, Anselm, Aquinas and Bonaventure, Trinitarian structure and the body in Augustine, procession and divine self-differentiation in Plotinus, Proclus, Aquinas and Jean Trouillard, prayer and thinking in Boethius, the meeting of Augustinianism and Dionysian peripateticism in Albertus Magnus and Aquinas, Henri-Louis Bergson's reworking of Plotinus, reason's self-transcendence, participation in Aquinas. Author of several monographs and edited volumes, the newest is *Aquinas' Neoplatonism in the Summa Theologiae on God. A Short Introduction* (2019).

Josh Hayes is an Associate Professor of Philosophy in the Department of Humanities at Alvernia University. He has previously taught at Santa Clara University, Loyola Marymount University, the University of San Francisco and Stanford University. His research interests include ancient philosophy, medieval Islamic philosophy, environmental philosophy and contemporary continental thought. In addition to publishing numerous articles in the history of philosophy, he has edited *Aristotle and the Arabic Tradition* (2013), *Heidegger in the Islamicate World* (2019), and *Philosophy in the American West: A Geography of Thought* (2020).

Mark D. Jordan is R. R. Niebuhr Professor in Harvard University's Divinity School. His recent books include *Teaching Bodies: Moral Formation in the Summa of Thomas Aquinas* (2017) and *Transforming Fire: Imagining Christian Teaching* (2021).

Eleanor Kaufman is professor of Comparative Literature, English and French and Francophone Studies at the University of California, Los Angeles. She is the author of *The Delirium of Praise: Bataille, Blanchot, Deleuze, Foucault, Klossowski* (2001); *Deleuze, the Dark Precursor: Dialectic, Structure, Being* (2012); and *At Odds with Badiou* (forthcoming).

Maggie Ann Labinski is an assistant professor of philosophy at Fairfield University where she also serves as the director of the Peace and Justice Studies Program. Her research focuses primarily on the intersection of feminist and medieval philosophies, with a special emphasis on sex/sexuality.

Andrew LaZella is an Associate Professor of Philosophy at The University of Scranton (USA). His *The Singular Voice of Being: John Duns Scotus and Ultimate Difference* was published in 2019. He is currently working on a book project on the problem of universals centered on the work of Peter Abelard.

Richard A. Lee, Jr. is Professor of Philosophy at DePaul University. He specialises in Medieval and Early Modern Philosophy as well as the Frankfurt School. He is the author of *Science,* *the Singular, and the Question of Theology*, *The Force of Reason and the Logic of Force* and *The Thought of Matter: Materialism, Conceptuality and the Transcendence of Immanence*.

Karmen MacKendrick is a professor of philosophy at LeMoyne College in Syracuse, New York (USA). Her work in philosophical theology includes *Failing Desire* (2018), *The Matter of Voice* (2016) and *Divine Enticement* (2012). With Virginia Burrus and Mark Jordan, she is a co-author of *Seducing Augustine: Bodies, Desires, Confessions* (2010).

Lisa Mahoney is an Associate Professor in the Department of History of Art and Architecture at DePaul University. Her articles on artistic production in the Latin Kingdom during the twelfth and thirteenth century have appeared in journals that include *Gesta* and collections such as *The Crusades and Visual Culture*. Together with Daniel H. Weiss, she has edited a volume called *France and the Holy Land*, which treats Frankish culture during and in the aftermath of the Crusades. Research for these projects has been supported by the National Endowment of the Humanities, the Andrew W. Mellon Foundation and the Samuel H. Kress Foundation.

Costantino Marmo is full professor in Semiotics and History of Semiotics at the University of Bologna. His bibliography includes numerous articles and books on medieval and contemporary semiotics and philosophy of language, published in Italian, English, French and Spanish; among them: '*Suspicio*: A Key Word to the Significance of Aristotle's Rhetoric in Thirteenth Century Scholasticism' (1990); *Semiotica e linguaggio nella Scolastica. La semiotica dei Modisti* (1994); *La semiotica del XIII secolo* (2010); *Segni, linguaggi e testi: semiotica per la comunicazione* (2015); *La semantica dei frame di Fillmore* (2017).

Alberto Martinengo is Assistant professor of Philosophy at the Scuola Normale Superiore (Italy). He has published essays in German, English, French and Spanish, on different aspects of the hermeneutical tradition. His most recent research deals with the philosophy of image and its political relevance. Martinengo is the author of a book on Martin Heidegger and Reiner Schürmann (*Introduzione a Reiner Schürmann*), a book on Paul Ricoeur (*Il pensiero incompiuto*) and a volume on the philosophies of metaphor (*Filosofie della metafora*). Among his edited books, *Beyond Deconstruction*.

Pascal Massie is associate professor of philosophy at Miami University of Ohio. He specialises in Ancient and Medieval philosophy and has published articles on Aristotle, Sextus Empiricus, Achard of Saint Victor, Duns Scotus, as well as Heidegger. He is the author of *Contingency, Time, and Possibility: An Essay on Aristotle and Duns Scotus* (2010).

Georgios Steiris is Associate Professor of Medieval and Renaissance Philosophy at the Department of Philosophy of the National and Kapodistrian University of Athens. He has also taught at the University of Peloponnese and the Hellenic Open University. Visiting Professor at the Department of Social Sciences and Philosophy of Jyvaskyla University. General Secretary of the Greek Philosophical Society (2015/16) and member of the Hellenic Unit of the UNESCO Chair in Bioethics.

Scott M. Williams (DPhil, Oxford) is an Assistant Professor of philosophy at the University of North Carolina Asheville. He publishes in the areas of medieval theology and philosophy, philosophy of religion, and philosophy of disability. He has published several articles on the philosophical theology of the Trinity, edited *Disability in Medieval Christian Philosophy and Theology* (2020), and recently co-edited a special issue of the journal *TheoLogica* on conciliar trinitarianism. He also has published on the history of personhood as it relates to Christian theology, 'Persons in Patristic and Medieval Christian Theology' (2019), and as it relates to philosophy of disability, 'When Personhood Goes Wrong in Ethics and Philosophical Theology: Disability, Ableism, and (Modern) Personhood' (2019). He is currently writing a book, *Henry of Ghent on the Trinity*.

Index

Abbāsid, 227, 229
Abegescheidenheit, 139, 187, 189, 191, 193–5
Abelard, Peter, 16, 75, 81–7, 926, 162, 164, 166–8
ableism, 37, 40–1, 44–5
Abraham, 60, 66, 221
accident, 6, 88, 149, 154, 162, 172, 221, 285, 313, 346
accidental, 164–7, 171, 176, 178, 187, 195, 202, 342
actuality, 7–8, 15, 210–12, 314, 321
adequation, 8, 120
Adorno, Theodor, 14
Aelred of Rievaulx, 117, 120–1, 139–41
affect, 15–16, 19, 134, 50–3, 97, 118, 120, 122, 126, 127, 133–7, 172, 176, 212, 245, 273, 285, 289, 302, 308, 338
affection, 42, 118, 120, 135–6, 229, 257
affectivity, 126
Agamben, 16, 201, 210–13, 269–70
agent, 101, 239, 260, 265–6, 294; *see also* intellect
akrasia, 235, 239
alchemy, 273–4
al-Farabi, 302–3
al-Ghazali, 13, 219, 224–5, 304–5
al-Kindī, 218–19
allegory, 324, 334, 337, 339–40
alterity, 126, 129, 132, 139
Althusser, Louis, 344–5, 348, 352–5
analogy, 12, 33, 66, 119, 138, 171–2, 175, 187, 196–8, 218–20, 273, 347–8, 350
Anaxagoras, 240
angel, 5, 22, 51–2, 149
anima see soul
Anselm of Canterbury, 9, 13, 117, 120–8, 324
   Proslogion, 13, 120, 122–8

aporia, 211, 304, 306–7, 308, 309, 312
Aquinas, Thomas, 1, 5–6, 8, 16, 41, 44–9, 75, 87–112, 123–4, 144, 171–2, 175, 196–7, 230, 242, 244–6, 250, 255–6, 258, 260–3, 276, 284–5, 294, 318, 326–9, 333, 336, 341, 347–9
Arendt, Hannah, 217
Areopagite *see* Dionysius the Areopagite
Aristotelian, 17, 53, 88, 110, 144–5, 147, 162, 164–5, 167, 170, 172–3, 175, 177–8, 188, 190, 195, 209, 211, 219, 225, 230, 234–6, 238, 240, 242, 272–3, 275–6, 302–4, 307–9, 311, 326, 328, 344–6, 350
Aristotle, 2, 5–6, 9, 17, 32, 87–8, 90, 98–102, 105, 109–13, 120, 130, 142, 144–5, 160–1, 164, 169, 172, 175, 196, 218–28, 230, 234–42, 244, 254–5, 261–2, 267, 272, 285–6, 301–11, 314–15, 326–7, 333–4, 341–2, 344–9
arithmetic, 153, 160
art, 3, 16, 28, 58–62, 64–5, 70–3, 98, 101–3, 109–10, 120, 130, 142, 153–4, 204, 226, 255, 261–2, 276, 326, 342–3
ascesis, 16, 117, 192–3, 185, 195
astrology, 273, 277
astronomy, 160, 229, 276, 301, 303, 305, 307, 310, 353
Augustine of Hippo, 5, 16, 21–33 41–6, 50, 59, 61, 75–82, 87, 92–4, 98, 108n36, 117, 123–4, 133, 142–51, 154, 160–1, 163–4, 169, 202, 211, 244, 250–1, 255, 257–61, 273, 285, 318, 321–4, 326–7, 333
   Confessions, 25, 30, 32–3, 97, 117, 143, 149–50, 244, 250–1, 321–4
autonomy, 196, 244

avarice, 257, 264, 274
Averroes (Ibn Rushd), 4, 225, 230, 244, 301–5, 307, 309, 314–16, 326
Avicebron (Ibn Gabriol), 4
Avicenna (Ibn Sina), 4, 303, 326

Bachelard, Gaston, 352–3
Bacon, Francis, 276–81
Bacon, Roger, 170, 173–1, 178
Badiou, Alain, 347
baptism, 13, 26, 41,479, 53, 163, 174
beautiful, 15, 26, 42–6, 59, 61, 66, 212, 218, 222, 323, 340
beauty, 15, 26–7, 29–30, 32–3, 42, 44, 46, 58–9, 106
belief, 40, 90, 124, 127, 200, 223, 226, 254, 283, 286, 307, 312
Benedict, 86, 128
Benedictine, 121–2
benevolence, 224, 227
Berengar of Tours, 162–4, 180
Bergson, Henri, 318–19, 321
Bernard of Clairvaux, 65, 117–22, 127, 130, 133–40, 192, 206
blind, 240, 269
blindness, 170
Blumenberg, Hans, 202
body, 2, 9–10, 17, 22–3, 25–31, 33–4, 39, 42–3, 45–6, 52–4, 64, 77, 79–80, 91, 99–100, 119–20, 128–34, 139–40, 144, 149, 155, 160–3, 180, 224, 228, 273, 277, 307–10, 314, 317, 321, 323–6, 335, 339–40, 344–5, 351
Boethius, 97, 142, 145–6, 149–50, 160, 164, 167–8, 172, 175, 177–8, 318, 320–1, 324–6, 334
Bonaventure, 144, 173, 192, 208–9, 250, 254, 257, 264–9, 324, 334

Cajetan, 2–3
Campanella, Tommaso, 276–81
caritas, 138, 187, 195–7, 259–61, 292
Cartesian, 2, 133, 303
Cassirer, Ernst, 201
categorial, 350
categories, 139, 132, 145, 147, 152–3, 165, 167, 170, 172, 178, 188, 344–8

cause, 13, 27, 39, 46, 50–3, 101, 143, 146–8, 150, 153, 155, 167, 172, 179, 205–6, 209, 218, 254, 257, 285–6, 292, 310–12, 317, 321, 327–8
certitude, 104, 133
chance, 14, 79, 87, 226, 313
change, 50, 65, 79, 86, 93, 120, 127, 139, 143, 163, 167, 174, 176, 178, 189, 200, 261, 288, 290, 293–5, 303, 311, 317, 324, 334, 336, 353
chastity, 264
Christ, 23, 27, 29, 42, 45, 47, 50, 65–6, 92, 160–3, 170, 188, 193, 242, 263, 290–1, 295, 327–8, 337, 341, 349
Chrysostom, John, 90
Cicero, 21–2, 24, 27, 32, 50, 117, 143, 169–70
classification, 2–3, 109–10, 160, 169–71, 173–4, 178, 273, 339
classroom, 74–5, 77–80, 83–4, 91
clergy, 69, 81, 206, 249, 339
cleric, 224
clerical, 249
cloister, 133
cognition, 51, 312
commandment, 46, 59, 136, 239, 287, 309
conatus, 163, 311
concept, 4, 6, 8, 16, 24, 120, 122, 125–6, 133, 147, 150, 154, 167–8, 170–1, 179–80, 195, 197, 203–5, 208, 211, 217, 225, 227, 262, 264, 273–4, 347–9, 354
Confessor, 142, 145, 152
conquest, 283–4
conscience, 133, 135, 284
consciousness, 3, 10–11, 98, 133–5, 212, 257, 321
consignification, 172, 177
contemplation, 25, 59, 75, 220, 236, 240–1, 261, 319
contemplative, 92, 201, 220, 261, 264
conversion, 22, 46, 80, 137, 162, 224, 244, 286–7, 293–4, 318–19, 322–5, 327–30
corporality, 324–6
corporeal, 22, 26, 33, 52–3, 75–6, 147, 268, 304, 308–9, 311–33, 318, 322–3, 325, 344–5
cosmology, 25, 28, 147, 201, 218–19
cosmopoiesis, 209, 211

cosmopolitan, 17, 217, 219, 221, 223, 225, 227–21
cosmopolitanism, 217, 219, 223–4, 228–32
cosmos, 5, 17, 23, 217–20, 321–4, 327
courage, 256
creation, 23, 25–7, 29, 33, 61–2, 65–6, 130, 143, 146–7, 151–3, 155–7, 189, 194–5, 209–10, 257, 273, 276, 278, 302, 322–4, 326, 340–1
creator, 23, 25, 27, 44, 61, 65, 127, 145, 147–8, 150, 153, 172, 174, 190–3, 195–7, 352
creaturality, 192
creature, 43, 52–3, 109, 127, 139, 150, 152–3, 190–3, 195–8, 242, 257, 273, 275–9, 293, 327–8, 340–1, 352
Crucifixion, 61–2, 70
culpa, 85, 103–4, 107
culpability, 110
Cupiditas, 259–60
Cusa, Nicholas of, 3, 16–17, 145–7, 200–5, 207–14, 317, 319

Damascene, John, 101, 103, 276, 321
damnation, 287
Dante Alighieri, 17, 230–1, 234, 242–7, 263
Darwin, Charles, 351
Dasein, 117, 210–12
deaf, 225
death, 2, 4, 15, 21, 26, 31–2, 45, 52, 79, 90, 134, 163, 174, 194, 201, 207, 290, 324, 328, 333, 335
definition, 8–9, 28, 32, 39, 58, 124, 129–30, 136, 160–1, 163–4, 169, 172–4, 177, 180, 204–5, 239, 251, 261, 265, 345–6, 348
deformity, 41–4, 101, 342
Deleuze, Giles, 318–19, 321, 344–8, 350–2
deliberation, 174, 217, 235–6, 245, 262, 294, 313
delight, 16, 30–4, 59, 78, 275, 312, 322
demiurge, 23, 218
democracy, 74, 223, 225
democratic, 222–3, 226
Democritus, 321
demonstration, 77, 87, 208, 226, 295
demonstrative, 133, 163, 305, 307, 324
denotation, 165, 175

depravity, 42
deprivation, 154
deprived, 249, 251, 257
Derrida, Jacques, 16, 202–3, 206–9, 212, 217, 230, 345–6
Descartes, 3, 10, 13, 17, 124, 137, 208, 333, 350
desirability, 226
desire, 15–16, 26, 28, 32–4, 37, 40, 43, 47–8, 75, 77, 84, 128, 150, 153, 205–7, 212–13, 221, 223, 228–9, 243–6, 249, 256, 259, 264–6, 301–3, 308, 311, 323, 327
detachment, 139, 187, 189–92, 194, 336
determination, 7–8, 111, 145, 176, 188, 194, 196, 202, 217, 244, 246, 263, 336, 348–9
determined, 7–8, 11–12, 50, 58, 60, 171, 174, 176–8, 194, 207, 211–12, 222, 226, 309, 321, 335
dialectics, 142, 307–8
différence, 18
difference, 5, 7–8, 38–43, 46, 50, 61, 78, 99, 101–3, 106–7, 109–12, 124–6, 161, 168, 171, 174, 176, 190, 193, 196–7, 207–8, 212, 234, 238, 253, 256, 265, 286–7, 293–4, 302, 305, 307, 314, 318, 320, 327–8, 335, 344–56
differential, 351–2, 354
differentiation, 2, 5–8, 102–3, 107, 111, 286, 328–9, 351
dignity, 42, 290
Diogenes, 257
Dionysius the Areopagite (Pseudo-Dionysius), 58–9, 125, 142–8, 151–3, 273, 317, 320–1, 326
disability, 16, 37–8, 40–2, 46–7
disabled, 38–40, 43, 46, 49
discernment, 132
disembodiment, 308
diversity, 2, 4, 11, 44, 46, 59, 172, 221, 223
divinity, 27–30, 139, 143, 146, 152, 162, 218, 318, 320, 325, 349
Dominic, 264
Dominican, 144, 201, 327
dominium, 90–1, 253, 256, 265–9
dreams, 168, 237, 276, 302, 307–8
dualism, 22, 25, 192, 303, 317, 321

earth, 25–6, 29, 58–9, 193, 221, 225, 251, 257–8, 261, 268, 277, 325–6, 340, 353
Eckhart von Hochheim (Meister), 2, 16, 139, 144, 150, 185–99, 202, 210, 333
ecstasy, 320
ecstatic, 59–60, 66, 328
ecumenical, 70, 219, 230–1, 324
education, 16, 21, 74–5, 77–8, 83, 86, 89, 91–6, 173, 277–8, 334, 339, 342
effect, 13, 31, 43, 45, 49, 51–2, 58–9, 61, 65–6, 86, 102–3, 109, 111, 148, 153, 205–6, 225, 289, 317, 328, 336, 338
effects, 13–14, 52, 106, 121, 148, 154, 172, 189, 210, 249, 262, 325, 334, 354
element, 13–14, 46, 177–8, 191, 194, 197–8, 338
elementary, 161, 229
elements, 3–4, 12–14, 52, 61, 87, 98, 180, 188–9, 193, 195, 275, 321–2, 333, 335, 341–2, 352–4
emanation, 25, 221, 307, 326–7, 352
embodiment, 15–16, 19, 21–2
embryo, 351
emendation, 101, 106
eminence, 257, 310
eminent, 150, 163, 204, 267, 304–6, 352
emotion, 16, 24, 27–8, 99, 104, 109–10, 174
empiricism, 4, 207–9
endoxa, 307
energeia, 193, 236
Enlightenment, 278
Epicurean, 209, 275
Epicureanism, 210, 273
Epicurus, 255, 321
episteme, 17, 234, 236
epistemic, 39, 47, 104, 304
epistemological, 9, 13, 180, 347–9, 352–3
epistemology, 179, 221
epoch, 2–6, 8, 10–15, 125, 201
epochal, 4–7, 10–14, 200, 209, 212
equality, 219, 221–3, 225, 227, 319
equivocal, 172, 176, 334
equivocation, 51, 87, 175, 239, 348
Erasmus, Desiderius, 2, 210, 275
Eriugena, John Scottus, 16, 142, 144–59, 162, 317, 320, 326
eros, 26–7, 30, 321

erotic, 28, 32, 84, 228, 340
eschatology, 8, 65
esoteric, 219, 302
esse, 44, 48, 51, 77–9, 86, 124, 126, 142–56, 167–8, 180, 210, 242, 288, 326
essence, 5–6, 8–9, 13–14, 51, 74, 88, 90, 106, 124, 145–9, 151, 153–5, 164, 167–8, 172–5, 179, 188, 194–8, 235, 327–9, 241
essential, 2, 4, 11, 13, 23–4, 26, 51, 58, 97–8, 100, 103–4, 109, 146, 148, 164, 173–4, 176–7, 188, 194, 198–9, 218, 220, 240, 249–51, 264, 278, 325, 334
eternal, 75, 143–4, 153–5, 191, 193, 196, 198, 210, 212, 226, 250, 260, 276, 287, 289–290, 294, 303, 312, 322
eternity, 25, 172, 191, 194, 209, 352
Eucharist, 47, 129, 160–3, 166, 180
eudaimonia, 221, 230, 234, 236
eugenics, 41
Eurocentrism, 4
Europe, 66, 201, 260, 272, 275
European, 2–3, 21, 122, 175, 202, 272, 293, 332–3, 335
event, 13, 16, 62, 65, 120, 122, 127, 174, 187, 193–5, 197–9, 228, 265, 337
evil, 23, 49, 51–2, 81, 99–105, 108, 110, 143, 149, 239–40, 251, 257, 284, 295, 304, 307–8, 310, 312, 317, 321, 324, 339–40, 342
exemplar, 2, 61, 337, 341
exemplarity, 307
existence, 13, 93, 98, 102, 109, 111–12, 123–6, 135, 143–4, 147–8, 150, 153, 163, 167, 179, 189–92, 201, 203, 205–6, 209, 218–20, 222, 227, 229, 252, 259, 262, 265, 269, 275, 286, 321, 323, 327–8, 335, 345, 350, 353–4
existential, 189, 191–2, 194
exitus, 142, 155, 326
Exodus, 58–9, 144
experiment, 244, 340

faith, 2, 23, 47–9, 53, 59, 61, 78, 111, 118, 124–5, 144, 218, 245, 254, 283–4, 286–7, 290, 293–5, 337–8, 340–1
Falāsifa, 2, 224
fantasm, 10–11, 15

fear, 25, 47, 60, 82, 99–112, 108–9, 120, 255, 259, 284, 288, 293, 304, 317, 338
female, 74–6, 82–3, 88–91, 278
Ficino, Marsilio, 2–3, 142–3, 321
finitude, 123, 139, 210
flesh, 10, 15, 22–3, 25–9, 31, 92, 102, 108, 119–20, 124, 129, 135–6, 188, 251, 277
force, 13, 23, 27, 66, 85, 88, 102–3, 109, 146, 164, 202, 209–10, 225, 229, 252, 284–5, 288, 302, 348–9
form, 15, 23–4, 26–7, 58–9, 70, 77, 80, 86, 101, 110–11, 128–9, 139, 146–7, 149, 155, 168–9, 171, 177, 179, 190, 192, 197, 201–3, 206, 208, 210–11, 229–30, 244, 247, 249, 253, 259, 261, 266, 269–70, 278, 291, 301–3, 307–8, 314, 322–3, 326–7, 338, 342, 345–6, 349, 351, 353
formless, 146, 149, 155, 323
fornication, 22
fortune, 340
Foucault, Michel, 12, 335–6, 338, 342–3
Franciscan, 2, 17, 249–50, 264, 266–71
freedom, 27, 51–2, 70, 82, 174, 188–9, 201, 212, 244, 256, 284, 291–3, 295, 321
friars, 264–6
friendship, 104, 206, 219, 221–2, 224, 227, 255

Gadamer, Hans-Georg, 16, 201–2
gender, 29, 74–6, 78–82, 84–9, 92–6, 177–8
genealogy, 124, 66, 210
genera, 7–8, 107, 167, 346
generation, 52, 66, 88, 153, 175–6, 178, 180, 189–90, 192–8, 201, 218, 221, 251, 272, 304, 312, 322, 352
generosity, 92, 227, 255
Genesis, 23, 75–6, 97–8, 151, 257, 261, 268, 273, 322, 324
genital, 27, 30, 32, 108
Gersonides, 17, 142, 301–15
Gilbert of Poitiers, 168–9, 172
Gilson, Etienne, 139, 144, 333, 348–50
girl, 74, 84
globalisation, 230
Gnostic, 25

God, 5–6, 13, 16, 22–3, 25–32, 42, 44–6, 49, 53–5, 59, 61, 65, 75–8, 80–2, 85, 87–8, 92–7, 101, 108, 118–30, 132–9, 143–58, 167–9, 172, 179, 187–200, 203–12, 218, 224–5, 236–8, 241, 244, 250–2, 257–61, 266, 268–70, 273–8, 285–7, 289, 304, 309, 312–14, 318–19, 322–31, 338, 340–2, 345, 347–8
Godhead, 152
godless, 286
goodness, 27, 40, 137, 147–9, 153, 155, 169, 172, 196–7, 205, 228, 260, 263, 287, 289, 291, 323–5, 347–8
grace, 46–7, 91–2, 124, 144, 202, 206, 244–5, 251, 269, 342
guilt, 99, 102–4, 107, 109–10

habit, 47–9, 51, 53, 105–6, 111, 130–1, 139, 170, 180, 234–5, 264, 284, 288, 306, 308
habitus, 105, 177, 265
Hadot, Pierre, 28, 30–4
haecceity, 6, 349–51
Haslanger, Sally, 2
health, 53–4, 172, 175–6, 223, 238, 277
heaven, 43, 58–9, 193, 218, 250–1, 291, 326, 340
Hegel, G. W. F., 155, 321, 353–4
Heidegger, Martin, 4–10, 13, 16, 97, 119–20, 127, 131, 186–7, 191, 198–9, 202, 206–7, 211–12
Heloise, 81–7, 92
Heraclitus, 4, 9
hermeneutic, 15–16, 38, 41, 83, 118–19, 128–30, 149, 202, 212–14, 219, 250
Hermeticism, 277
hierarchical, 221, 320, 327
hierarchy, 58, 82, 147, 152, 163, 190, 201, 225, 260, 306, 317, 319, 340, 346–7
Hobbes, Thomas, 225
homonoia, 221–2
homonym, 129, 175–6, 179
honesta, 295
honour, 84, 105–7
hospitably, 292
hospitality, 217, 230, 292, 337
Hospitaller, 64
humanism, 2–3, 123, 142, 203–6, 209, 212, 225, 230, 275

humanist, 203–6, 210–11
humanistic, 276, 333
humanity, 44, 123, 136, 162, 165, 171, 220–1, 223–4, 226, 257, 260, 272–9, 285–6
humility, 23, 109, 125, 127, 136, 211, 245–6, 264, 337
Husserl, Edmund, 97–8, 134, 203, 211
hylomorphism, 272
hypostases, 319

Iamblichus, 276, 318, 320–1, 324–5
icon, 41, 62
iconoclasm, 60, 62
iconography, 61
idea, 3–4, 21–2, 26–8, 30, 33–4, 59, 61, 70, 75, 80, 88, 92–4, 97, 109, 122, 124–5, 134, 145–8, 151, 161, 163–4, 174, 187, 195, 198, 200–1, 207, 209–11, 250, 253, 258, 269–71, 272–3, 283, 284–5, 288, 290–1, 294, 301, 318, 328, 335–6, 340, 345, 352, 354
idealism, 144, 185–6, 202, 319
identity, 3, 8, 16, 65, 119, 123–4, 139, 162, 164, 172, 185, 190–7, 264, 310, 333, 345, 347
ideological, 284, 295, 353
ideology, 32, 60, 186, 353
idol, 59
idolatrous, 240, 286
idolatry, 60
idolism, 286–7, 293
ignoble, 264
ignorance, 4, 145–6, 200–1, 204–5, 209, 212–13, 262, 286, 291, 294–5, 318
illness, 52–3
image, 13, 22, 58–62, 65, 69–73, 75, 121, 131, 143, 163–4, 167–8, 174, 185–6, 188–9, 193–5, 212, 323–4, 326, 338, 340
imaginary, 211
imagination, 50–3, 58, 70, 97, 209–10, 212, 229–30, 237, 243, 245, 247–8
imago, 75–6
Imām, 221, 224, 230, 237
imitation, 64, 70, 218, 238, 278, 338
immanence, 27, 319, 354–5
imposition, 160, 167, 171, 174–7, 180, 283–4
impossibility, 162, 193, 212, 243, 268, 286

impossible, 7, 93, 108, 154, 196, 198–9, 212, 251, 260, 266–7, 295, 303, 314
impotence, 81, 84–5, 108
incarnate, 119, 124, 148, 208, 317
incarnation, 25–6, 29, 144, 162, 193, 318, 328, 341–2
incarnational, 317–18, 325–6
incarnationalism, 17
incorporeal, 143, 253, 268, 322, 344, 346
incorporeals, 346
individual, 7–9, 16, 26, 28, 39–42, 46, 48–9, 51, 58, 64, 70, 77–8, 87–8, 93, 102, 104, 129, 165, 167–8, 171, 179–80, 196, 201, 220, 222–5, 228, 230, 239–41, 249, 252, 263, 290, 302–5, 308–9, 311–15, 322, 339, 349, 351–2
individuality, 153
individuating, 349
individuation, 350–1
ineffable, 125, 149, 152, 155, 317–18
infant, 47–8, 253–4, 323
infidel, 123, 287–8, 290–4
infidelity, 286, 294–5
infinite, 26, 122, 136, 143–4, 152–3, 155–6, 172, 201, 206–7, 210
infinity, 124, 146, 149, 203, 212, 328, 351
infirm, 41, 81, 85, 87
insane, 41, 50–1, 53, 253
insanity, 47–8, 51
intellect, 8, 16, 50–4, 91–2, 124–5, 128, 137, 142–3, 146, 152, 172–3, 179, 188–9, 195, 206, 218, 234, 236–8, 244–6, 277, 301, 309, 314–19, 324, 328–9, 349
  active, 237
  agent, 301, 309, 314
intellectual, 16–17, 22–3, 28, 32, 41, 51, 53–6, 77, 83–4, 93, 99–100, 162, 188, 195, 218, 234–43, 245–7, 250, 301, 309, 320, 323, 325, 334, 353
intellegibiles, 303
intelligence, 123–6, 128, 189
intelligibility, 4, 218
intemperance, 106
Intentio, 26
intention, 43, 75, 88, 130, 151, 173, 189, 191, 208, 228, 243, 253–4, 266
intentional, 31, 99–100, 107–8, 135, 207, 341
intentionality, 99–102, 163

intersubjective, 32, 104
intersubjectivity, 30, 99, 104
irony, 207, 235
Islam, 2, 15, 218–19, 224, 226–7, 305

Jesus, 29, 62, 64, 66, 69–70, 86–7, 92, 188, 194, 250–1, 337, 340
Jewgreek, 207
Job, 337–40
joy, 27–8, 30–1, 78, 127, 186–7, 193, 195, 273, 291, 324
joyful, 29
judgement, 27, 39, 52, 64–5, 99, 104–5, 111, 186, 190, 225, 234–6, 238–41, 243–6, 263, 328, 338, 341
justice, 15, 17, 45–6, 70, 85, 105, 108, 168–9, 197, 215, 219, 221–2, 224–5, 227, 229, 260–1, 267, 290
Justinian, 252–3

Kairos, 234, 247
Kant, Immanuel, 4, 13, 58, 60, 97, 124, 217
Kantian, 59, 201
knowledge, 9, 16, 21, 25, 27–8, 30, 37, 83–4, 92–3, 126, 133, 145, 153, 166, 172, 179, 190, 195, 197, 202, 205, 208, 225, 229, 234, 236, 242, 246, 250, 273, 276–80, 284–6, 290, 302–3, 305, 311–13, 322, 324, 326–7, 334–6, 338, 341–2

labour, 12, 220, 265, 276, 295, 311–12
language, 2, 6, 8, 11–12, 16–18, 29, 31–3, 37, 61, 88, 115, 134–5, 160–1, 164–6, 168–71, 174, 176, 179–84, 188, 190, 197–8, 200, 202–3, 206, 208–11, 243, 247, 267, 308, 311, 313, 323, 333, 347, 353–4
lapsarian, 27, 97, 108, 257, 260, 278
las Casas, Bartolomé de, 284, 288–91, 293, 295–6
laudable, 105–6, 110
laugh, 40
laughter, 131
law, 12, 26, 38, 65, 91, 118–19, 153, 164, 179, 191, 209, 222–4, 226–8, 230, 234–42, 247–8, 250, 252–4, 258–9, 262–5, 267–71, 277, 284–7, 289–96, 301, 304–5, 308, 327, 334, 338, 341–2
lawgiver, 221, 226

lawless, 31
lechery, 82
leisure, 221
Levinas, Emmanuel, 122, 202–3, 206–9
love, 22, 26–8, 31, 45, 79, 83–5, 100, 118, 127, 130, 134–9, 191, 195, 202, 212–13, 221–4, 227–9, 241–2, 251, 255, 259–61, 295, 321–4, 342
Luther, Martin, 2, 210, 283

Machiavelli, Niccolò, 2, 17, 211
macrocosm, 218, 273
madmen, 47
madness, 41, 47
magic, 224, 273–4, 321
Maimonidean, 304, 308–9
Maimonideans, 304
Maimonides, Moses, 2, 4, 17, 234–42, 244, 246–8, 301–4, 307–8
Manichaeaism, 22–4, 318
Manichaean, 22–3, 25, 27, 143, 317, 324
Marcuse, Herbert, 14–15
margins, 16, 58, 62, 65, 70, 76, 89
marriage, 22, 85, 263
Marsilius of Padua, 17, 249n3, 254, 256, 268
martyr, 4, 42–3, 45, 286
marvellous, 65
Marx, Karl, 12, 254, 274, 321, 352–4
masculinist, 29
Materia, 88, 93, 149, 151
material, 6, 17, 23, 25–9, 58–9, 61, 70–1, 76, 88, 162, 167, 170, 177, 235, 243, 251, 254, 263, 265, 277, 285–6, 308–9, 314, 317, 320, 323, 326–7, 336
materialism, 314, 324
materialist, 17, 25, 27, 302, 311, 314–15, 353
materiality, 25, 27
maternal, 24
mathematical, 160, 301, 303, 325
mathematicisation, 276
mathematics, 121, 276, 303, 334, 353
matter, 2–3, 16–17, 22–3, 25, 27–8, 30–1, 38–9, 47, 61, 70–1, 75, 78–9, 87, 97, 99, 101–2, 104, 106, 110, 127, 129–31, 136, 142, 144, 147, 149, 154, 177, 186–7, 189, 222, 240–1, 244, 246–7, 250, 254–6, 258, 262–5, 267–8, 295, 303–4, 306–7, 310, 312, 317, 319–25, 327, 341, 346
mechanism, 11, 16, 211

medicine, 38–40, 50, 53, 121, 172, 175, 273, 339
meekness, 288, 291
memory, 43, 142
men, 45, 89
mendicant, 98, 250, 254, 256, 264–6, 269–71
meontology, 16, 145, 148–9
mercy, 85, 105
mereology, 167
merit, 37, 222, 227, 229, 247, 255
meritorious, 77, 106
Merleau-Ponty, Maurice, 130–1, 134
metalinguistic, 166, 179
metamorphosis, 123, 139
metaphor, 14, 33, 146, 193, 195, 278
method, 29, 93, 120, 205, 208–9, 226–7, 274, 302–6, 307–8, 333–4, 337
metonymy, 169
minerals, 30, 277–8
miracle, 30, 162, 179, 224, 294
Mishnah, 234, 241, 304
misogynism, 28
misogynistic, 82
misogyny, 33, 76, 88
modal, 8, 136, 171, 301
modalities, 30, 38, 189
modality, 119, 138, 189, 196–7
mode, 8, 15, 107, 118–22, 125–6, 128–32, 134–5, 137–8, 149, 172, 177–8, 197, 203, 206, 208, 210, 212, 222, 246, 253, 259, 336, 353–4
modern, 3, 5, 11, 16–17, 33, 38, 40, 58, 61, 64, 177, 185–6, 198, 200–2, 206, 208–10, 212–14, 217, 249, 253, 265, 272, 274, 276–7, 284, 303–4, 318, 322, 332–7, 346–7
modernism, 303
modernist, 66, 201
modernity, 2–3, 10, 17, 200–3, 210, 212–14
modes, 5, 16, 27, 120, 132, 148, 150, 169–72, 177–8
modesty, 107, 208, 339
modification, 120, 346–7
modists, 175–8, 180
monarchy, 225, 230–1
monastery, 65, 81–2, 119, 132, 187, 261
monastic, 16, 66, 117, 119–22, 127–8, 132, 136, 139–41

monotheism, 321
monotheistic, 326
monster, 84
moral, 12, 16, 37–8, 31, 45–6, 99, 102–5, 107–8, 111–13, 194, 211, 218, 237, 240–1, 245, 249, 256, 260, 274–5, 278–9, 283, 287, 290, 295, 301, 304, 308, 311, 325, 335–43
Moralia, 337, 339
morality, 22, 108, 110–11, 260, 275, 304, 335, 351
mortal, 138, 289, 294–5
mortification, 338
motion, 99, 153, 155, 272, 278, 301, 320, 325, 327, 341
movers, 242
Muhammad, 60, 226
murder, 41, 239, 335, 339
music, 66, 160
mutation, 332, 334, 336
mystic, 16, 185–6, 210, 224–5
mystical, 32, 122, 125, 146, 185, 187, 194, 209–11, 243, 318, 353
mysticism, 16, 133, 138, 185, 187, 196–7, 206, 210, 272–3, 319

nameable, 172
nation, 15, 217, 219–22, 230, 284, 292–3
nationalism, 217, 230,
nationhood, 333
nations, 219–23, 230–1, 252, 262, 284–6, 290–1
natives, 283, 293
Natura, 11, 46, 85, 88, 136, 144, 148–51, 154, 167, 286–7, 295, 314
nature, 11, 13, 17, 27–9, 44–5, 60, 76, 83, 85, 88, 92–3, 99, 108, 123–4, 136, 139–40, 143–52, 154–6, 161–3, 167, 174, 176–7, 179, 186, 190, 192–3, 195–6, 198, 202–3, 206, 208, 210–24, 217–19, 221–2, 236–7, 240, 242–3, 245, 247, 249, 252, 256–7, 259–62, 264–5, 268–9, 272–6, 278–82, 284–6, 295–6, 303, 306–11, 313–14, 320–1, 323, 325, 340, 347, 349, 354
necessity, 13, 33, 128, 131, 144, 189, 249, 263–6, 350
negation, 100, 125, 146–7, 150, 154, 195, 204, 260, 320

negative, 2, 14, 27, 40, 110, 123, 125, 131, 137, 145–6, 164, 166, 168–9, 172, 188, 204, 209, 278, 321, 341, 348
neoplatonic, 17, 21, 25, 27, 142–4, 146–8, 169, 171–2, 219, 227, 318, 320, 322, 325–30
neoplatonism, 16, 21–2, 24–5, 27, 142–5, 151, 160, 273, 317–20, 326
neoplatonist, 17, 142–5, 147, 151, 276, 319
neopythagorean, 21, 276
Nero, 66–7
Nietzsche, 22, 207, 348, 351
nominalism, 209

obedience, 82, 87, 228, 239–40, 250, 256, 264, 269, 309
object, 10, 13–14, 31, 50–1, 53, 60, 62, 98–105, 108, 111–12, 125, 128, 166, 168, 173–9, 177, 180, 197, 207, 209, 211, 222, 228–9, 245, 253, 256, 259–60, 265, 267, 303, 308, 318, 323–4, 328, 349–50, 353–4
objectify, 256
Occam *see* Ockham, William of
occult, 273–4
Ockham, William of, 14, 17, 52–4, 178–83, 253, 268–9
oikeios, 219–21, 226, 229, 254, 256–7
omnipotence, 179
omnipresence, 321
omniscient, 143
oneness, 25, 152, 218, 227, 323
Origen, 145, 317
othering, 3, 327–9
otherness, 143, 193, 326, 346
ousia, 145–8, 153, 193, 196
ownership, 252–6, 258–60, 262, 264–5, 267–70

pacifism, 289
pagan, 17, 123, 142–3, 162, 250, 254, 287, 289, 293, 321, 324, 337–8, 340
painting, 62, 64, 341
panpsychism, 321
Pantheism, 196
paradox, 167, 208, 243, 264, 319
paraenetic, 188
Parmenides, 4, 146, 149, 325

participate, 49, 74, 77, 80, 105, 148, 171–2, 174, 241, 319
participated, 179, 319–20
participation, 76, 78, 168, 196–7, 205
particularity, 122, 230, 346
particulars, 88, 302, 309, 350
passion, 16, 59, 99–108, 110–12, 135, 145, 211–13, 323
passionless, 22
passions, 53, 99–100, 104–6, 108, 111, 134, 218
pedagogy, 87, 95, 341
Pelagius, 258
penitence, 99, 107, 110
penitent, 107, 110
penitential, 98, 338–9
penitentials, 338–40
penitus, 79, 83–4, 86, 168, 204
perception, 9, 79, 97, 131, 173, 230, 236, 257, 319, 347
person, 5, 27, 39, 43, 47, 49–51, 53, 61, 84, 100–2, 104, 106–7, 109–11, 122, 132, 161, 165, 167, 168, 170, 172, 174, 178, 191, 208, 222, 224–5, 227, 229, 239–40, 250, 253–4, 258, 262–3, 266–7, 289, 305, 313, 341, 349
Persona, 5, 167, 243
personhood, 53, 256
Petrarch, 209, 273
Phaedrus, 26
phallic, 326
phallocentric, 31
phantasia, 100
phantasms, 51, 52; *see* also fantasm
phronesis, 17, 234–6, 240–2, 244
pietist, 224
piety, 204, 338
pilgrim, 62, 121, 242–6, 292
pilgrimage, 228, 322, 339
pious, 76, 286, 293
Plato, 4–5, 9, 21, 23–4, 26, 32, 142–5, 147, 149, 167, 171, 207, 217–19, 221, 223, 225–6, 230–3, 247–8, 254, 256, 260, 273, 326, 334, 349
Platonic, 17, 25–6, 29, 142, 168, 171, 188, 195, 207, 211, 219, 275, 302, 317, 319, 324
Platonising, 275

Platonism, 21, 24–6, 146, 169, 206–8, 317–18, 321, 324, 326
Platonist, 17, 22, 24–6, 32, 142–5, 317–18
Platonists, 17, 24–6, 32, 142–3
Plotinian, 25, 212, 318–19
Plotinus, 24–6, 28–9, 32, 142–3, 145, 149, 218, 276, 318–21, 324
  Enneads, 26, 32, 142, 149, 218, 320
Plutarch, 273, 276
poesis, 335–6
Porphyrian, 6, 151, 344
Porphyry, 7, 24–6, 142–3, 145, 151, 160, 166–7, 221, 344, 346–7, 349, 351
  Isagoge, 344, 346
possibility, 11–16, 29, 31–3, 60, 92, 107–8, 119–20, 169, 186, 188–9, 193, 196, 198, 205, 210–13, 219, 221, 223, 225–6, 229, 234, 236, 240–1, 246, 249, 259–60, 265–6, 269–70, 285, 287, 290, 292, 294–6, 350
possible, 14–15, 24, 30–1, 42, 76, 80, 103, 105, 109, 111, 122–4, 126, 148, 150–1, 162–3, 166, 170–2, 174, 179, 187, 190, 192–3, 200, 202–3, 210–13, 218, 225, 229, 236, 238, 240–3, 245, 247, 251, 253–7, 263–5, 278, 285, 287–8, 290, 292–5, 301–3, 307, 309, 311, 317, 325, 327, 345, 347–8, 350, 352
potential, 40, 59–61, 65–6, 89, 106, 150, 198, 211, 238, 276, 346, 348–9, 351
potentiality, 7, 210–12
potentials, 168
poverty, 17, 226, 249–50, 257, 263–71
power, 12–13, 16–18, 22, 30, 48, 51, 53, 59–60, 64–6, 75, 80–2, 85–7, 92, 101, 106, 108, 139–40, 147, 188, 200, 202, 209–11, 215, 224–5, 235–6, 239, 243–5, 253, 256, 261, 265–6, 268–71, 278–9, 284–5, 287–90, 294, 325, 328, 335–6, 342
powerful, 26, 66, 100, 149, 194, 320
powerless, 83, 143
powerlessness, 85
powers, 45, 50, 53, 91, 100–2, 139, 220, 235–6, 242, 290, 336
praxis, 122, 130, 194, 319
prayer, 32, 62, 126, 133, 320–1, 325–6
predetermination, 97

predicables, 166, 344–5, 347, 350–1
Priscian, 160, 172, 178
privation, 143, 149–50, 153–5, 170, 189, 320
probability, 247, 291, 295
Proclus, 142–3, 146, 218, 317–21, 324–6
Procopius, 59, 66
profane, 70, 83, 251
prophecy, 90, 234, 236–9, 241–2, 247–8, 302, 304, 307–8
prophet, 122, 144, 224, 226, 237–8, 240
prosthesis, 39–40
protreptic, 234–5, 240, 242, 245, 334
providence, 148, 235, 238, 269, 309, 312–15, 325, 337, 340
prudence, 105, 230, 241–3, 290, 340
prudential, 291
prudishness, 109
Psyche, 33, 137, 143, 188, 255–6, 307–9
Purgatio, 230–1
purification, 320

Qohelet, 302–13
quiddity, 206, 237
Quine, W. V. O., 14–15

Rabbi, 2, 306, 337
race, 29, 44, 92, 223, 257–9, 292, 326
racism, 40
ratio, 90–1, 105, 175, 287
ratiocination, 262
real, 13–15, 17, 77, 92, 98, 101, 103, 108, 111, 162, 167, 189, 195–6, 200, 211–12, 318, 324, 341, 345, 348, 350
realism, 15, 64, 163, 166, 302, 339
realist, 167
reality, 12, 14–15, 63, 76, 121–2, 124–6, 128, 139, 143, 150, 166, 168, 175, 178, 191, 194, 197, 201, 203, 211, 218, 237, 243, 291, 301, 317–18, 324, 327, 348, 354
reason, 2, 23–5, 27–8, 31–2, 42, 44, 47–9, 53–5, 75, 89–91, 99–101, 105, 111–12, 118, 123–4, 135, 137, 152, 165, 191, 193, 195, 197, 205, 208, 218, 221, 224, 227, 230, 238–42, 256, 258–9, 261–2, 265–6, 269, 275, 284–6, 288–9, 293–5, 304, 321, 327, 340, 348, 351
rebel, 3
Reformation, 209, 334

refugee, 217, 230
reification, 179, 318
relation, 10–13, 16–17, 21, 43–4, 46, 48, 51, 53, 62, 98, 106–7, 125, 129–30, 132–3, 137, 147–8, 161, 170, 173–5, 178–9, 192, 198, 209, 250–1, 256, 259, 266–7, 269–70, 284, 288, 293–5, 304, 307–9, 311–12, 314, 319, 321, 324, 327–9, 334, 337–8, 341, 344–5, 348–9, 351
relations, 11–14, 30, 147, 167, 169, 173–4, 179, 221, 229, 264, 267–8, 307, 310, 333, 335, 352, 354
releasement, 187, 212
representation, 44, 50, 172, 174, 176, 246, 321, 340–1
Republic, 147, 223, 225–6, 230, 247, 254, 290
resurrection, 15, 26–7, 30, 41–2, 64, 139, 328
revelation, 9, 26, 65, 127, 155–6, 224, 228, 334
revolution, 198, 218
rhetoric, 21–2, 160, 202, 204, 207, 210–12, 226, 336
rhetorician, 207, 209, 211, 223
Ricoeur, Paul, 118–19
rights, 17, 38, 83, 217, 222, 249–50, 253, 255–6, 258–60, 264–5, 285, 289, 291–5
ritual, 334, 337
Roscelin, 166–7

sacrament, 38, 47–50, 53, 119, 129, 161, 163–4, 169–70, 180–1, 321, 327, 341–2
sacred, 59, 65, 70, 86, 92, 152, 321, 326–7
sacrifice, 62, 229, 259, 275, 285, 287
sadness, 107, 109–10, 134, 312
sage, 238–40, 304, 306, 337
St Monica, 77–80, 87, 324
salvation, 15–16, 48, 246, 251, 260, 290, 293–6, 336, 341
sanity, 47, 52
savage, 274, 278
scepticism, 13, 24, 32, 179, 323
Sceptics, 24
Schürmann, Reiner, 4, 10–12, 15–16, 186–99
science, 3, 17, 23, 42, 168, 179–80, 201, 220, 237, 240, 272–82, 303, 307, 311–12, 314–16, 321, 324, 327, 352

Scotist, 349–51
Scotus, Ioannis Duns, 6–8, 16, 46–9, 51–2, 175–6, 178, 247, 253, 344, 347–51
Scripture, 24, 26, 63, 81–3, 85–6, 92, 102, 122, 129, 133, 147, 151–2, 154–5, 162, 169–70, 172, 193, 206, 250, 258, 307, 337–8, 342
semiotician, 212
semiotics, 16, 160, 162, 169, 173–4, 180–1, 210, 345
Seneca, 27, 32, 117, 257–8
Sepúlveda, Juan Ginés de, 283–91, 293–7
sex, 22, 26–8, 32, 75, 79, 81–3, 85, 88–9, 91
sexism, 40
sexist, 88
Sextus Empiricus, 28
sexual, 16, 27–30, 74, 84–5, 97–8, 252, 322–3
sexuality, 27–8, 30, 32, 335–6
Shakespeare, William, 39
shame, 16, 87, 91, 97–114, 130, 229, 263
shamefaced, 91
shameful, 90, 91, 104, 106, 109, 131
shamelessness, 91, 105
Sherwood, William of, 170–1
signifier, 125, 162, 173, 180, 210–11, 345
signs, 42–5, 47, 121, 128, 150, 160, 162–4, 169–70, 173–5, 179, 225, 350
signum, 91, 161, 164, 173, 177
silence, 86–7, 90–2, 132, 205, 301, 302, 304, 325, 332
sinful, 25, 41, 44, 101, 137, 257, 260–1, 266–7, 294, 338
sinfulness, 88, 251, 257–8
singular, 11, 167–8, 224, 264, 310, 346
singularity, 6, 31, 87, 221, 227, 314, 352
sinner, 65, 123–4, 127, 138, 323
sins, 86, 102, 106, 338–9, 342
slave, 22, 220, 258, 268, 275, 285–6
slavery, 285, 287–8
Socrates, 4, 24, 26, 28, 163, 167, 171, 177, 205, 219, 223, 247, 349
solidarity, 39, 219–21, 225, 228–30
Sonhood, 172
Sophia, 17, 29, 59, 66, 234–8, 240, 242, 340
Sophistical, 175
sôphrosunê, 239
sorrow, 53, 100, 110, 263

soul, 16, 22–3, 25–6, 33–4, 37, 42, 45–6, 52, 76–8, 80–1, 89–91, 100, 104, 111, 115, 120, 139–40, 142, 144, 149, 173–4, 185, 187–97, 211, 218, 220, 223–4, 229, 235–6, 242, 251, 256, 264, 273, 275–6, 278, 284, 309, 311–14, 317, 320–5, 340
sovereign, 221, 223, 278, 288
sovereignty, 217, 221, 225, 230, 261
space, 10, 42–3, 62, 64–6, 80, 130, 132, 138, 152, 160, 192, 309, 324, 345
spaces, 59, 61, 65–6, 69–70, 132, 342
species, 7–8, 26, 29, 50, 99, 101, 103–6, 108, 110, 147–9, 153, 161–2, 166–7, 174–5, 235, 238, 246, 273, 276–9, 313, 339, 344–8, 350–5
speculative, 139, 175, 178, 201–3, 209, 237, 249
Spinoza, Baruch, 314, 318, 348, 350–1
spirit, 2, 50, 108, 121–2, 172, 187–8, 191, 197, 201, 210, 273, 276, 317, 320, 322–3, 338, 342
spirits, 51, 53, 286
spirituality, 117, 317
stasis, 221, 325
sterilisation, 41
sterility, 77
Stoicism, 22, 27–8, 230, 273
Strauss, Leo, 219
Straussian, 302
structuralism, 344–5, 349
structure, 2, 31, 66, 77, 84, 97, 126, 194–6, 211, 230, 235, 260, 317, 319, 322–3, 325–7, 338, 340, 342, 344, 347, 354–5
stuttering, 172
subjection, 89–91, 264, 336
subjectivation, 335, 338, 342–3
sublime, 194
sublimity, 147
substance, 6, 16, 45, 137, 139, 143–5, 147, 149, 154, 162–3, 165–6, 172–3, 178–80, 190, 196, 198–9, 268, 276, 302, 306, 328, 336, 344–6, 350, 354
substratum, 162, 165, 168
suffering, 41, 43, 45, 263, 266–7, 277, 312, 338
superabundance, 263
supererogation, 263, 266
superessential, 145–9, 151, 155

supposition, 170–1, 173, 176, 179–80
suppositum, 349
symbol, 127, 202–3, 317, 325
Symposium, 26, 227
syncategorematic, 179
syncategorems, 178

taste, 83, 206, 324
techne, 17, 234
techniques, 219, 243, 334, 336, 338, 347
technocracy, 272
teleology, 46, 191, 272, 336, 341–2
temperance, 104–8, 110–11, 240, 256
temporality, 189, 191
temptation, 23, 82, 201, 243, 310, 341
terms, 5, 11, 13, 15–17, 21, 33, 37, 41, 46, 48, 76, 79–80, 85, 91, 99, 103–4, 108–9, 111–12, 124–5, 146, 151–2, 162, 165–7, 171–3, 175–6, 178–80, 186, 189–90, 192–4, 196–9, 201, 204, 209, 211–12, 222, 237, 241–2, 247, 252, 262, 264–5, 283–4, 286, 295, 302, 304, 306, 308, 310–11, 317, 321, 334, 338, 340, 345, 347–8, 350–3
terror, 288, 291, 293
Thales, 240
theft, 239, 257–8, 263, 339
theologian, 2, 17, 22, 45, 47, 49, 53–4, 58, 60, 121–2, 150, 152, 160, 162, 168–9, 172, 185–6, 200, 204–5, 305, 328, 340
theology, 21, 28, 37–8, 41, 46, 49, 62, 88, 117, 119–21, 125, 128, 136, 139–40, 144–7, 149, 152–3, 160, 164, 168–70, 172, 185, 192, 194, 198–9, 203–6, 208–10, 218, 243–4, 320, 326–7, 333–4, 336, 340–3
theophanic, 120, 122, 125, 127, 243
theophany, 122, 124–6, 133, 146, 155–6
Theophilus, 61
Theophrastus, 221
theoria, 122, 148–9, 235–6, 242
theurgy, 320–1, 325,
Thomism, 144, 197, 276, 333
Timaeus, 143, 145, 217–18, 326
timeless, 33, 155, 336
timor, 101, 103, 105
tolerance, 261, 285

topography, 218, 230
Torah, 301–2, 306–7, 309, 312
totality, 121, 194, 198, 203, 220, 224, 328
touch, 30, 131, 284, 325, 332
tranquillity, 336
transcendence, 16, 58, 60, 66, 145–6, 152, 202, 206, 319–20
transcendent, 142–3, 145–8, 150, 152, 155–6, 207, 289, 319, 350
transcendental, 208
transfiguration, 26, 320
transposition, 169, 320
transubstantiation, 180
trauma, 27
triangle, 9, 175, 243
tribalism, 230
Triduum, 120
Trinity, 2, 5, 143, 145, 149, 161–2, 164, 167–8, 172, 191, 318, 323, 327–30, 341
trivium, 160, 204, 347
truth, 5, 8–10, 16, 22–4, 29, 76–8, 91–2, 127–8, 136, 143, 147, 152, 161–2, 164–5, 168, 170, 180, 187, 191, 197, 201, 205, 208–9, 226, 235, 242, 245–6, 276, 285, 288, 293, 295, 301–2, 304–5, 307, 318, 322–4, 328, 335, 345, 348
turpitude, 91, 97, 101–3, 105–9, 131
type, 2, 8, 16, 50, 60–1, 99, 126, 129, 169–72, 174–6, 178, 194, 197, 200, 229, 278, 283, 286–7, 289–90, 294, 302, 335, 346–7, 352, 354
typology, 178
tyrant, 89–90, 290

unbecoming, 91
unbelief, 123, 227
unbeliever, 283, 286–7, 289–91, 295
unborn, 143
uncaused, 143
unchanging, 143, 235
unconcealment, 9–10, 211
unconditional, 217, 272
uniformity, 76, 85
unity, 2, 11–12, 16–17, 22, 25, 100, 122–3, 130, 137, 139, 142–3, 155, 162, 187, 190, 193–4, 196, 201, 206, 218–19, 223, 228–9, 235–6, 322–3, 325, 327–8, 348

universal, 15, 17, 26, 45–6, 88, 147–8, 164–7, 171, 178–80, 196, 221, 223–4, 226–7, 230, 252, 257, 266–7, 278, 284, 288, 295–6, 303, 306, 310, 313, 320–1, 332
universe, 27, 29, 143, 147–8, 179, 194, 227, 273, 308, 313, 320–1
univocity, 6–7, 347–9, 351
unjust, 29, 222, 258, 261, 269, 292, 310
unknowability, 145
unseparated, 347, 351
usury, 261
utopia, 17, 274–5
utopias, 17, 272, 276

vacuum, 180
valour, 42, 44
value, 12, 17, 31, 41–2, 45, 50, 58, 60, 70, 93, 110, 161–2, 164, 168, 190, 195, 219, 222–3, 239–40, 246, 254, 259, 277, 289, 295, 310, 317, 338, 354
vanity, 310
vegetarian, 23
veneration, 10, 70, 228
veritas, 8–9, 23, 76, 92, 102–3, 106, 161, 163, 288, 293
vernacular, 2, 4, 11, 187
vestige, 201, 323
vices, 102, 105–6, 341–2
violence, 13, 81–2, 85–6, 202, 254, 257–9, 278, 283, 286, 288, 304, 339
Virgin, 64, 92, 188–9
virginity, 22, 188–90
virtue, 17, 23, 26, 42–5, 105–8, 110–13, 123, 173–4, 190, 202, 207, 209, 218, 221–3, 226–7, 229–30, 234–6, 239–41, 255–6, 263–4, 269, 275, 286, 289, 308, 311, 313–14, 334, 337, 339–41
  acquired, 106
vision, 25, 30, 38, 51, 87, 121, 142, 173, 211, 218, 227–8, 243, 274, 276, 278–9, 320, 325
vitalism, 318, 321
vivification, 52
vocation, 83, 288, 325
voice, 26, 33, 119, 121, 129, 134–5, 169, 187, 207, 211, 324
void, 188, 321

volition, 53–4, 106, 221–2, 266
vows, 82, 266

wage, 221, 283, 286, 294, 340
war, 15, 32, 38, 83, 87, 202, 221, 252, 283, 285–97, 340
wealth, 79, 201, 238, 249, 251–2, 254, 256–61, 312
well-being, 292
well-ordered, 295
wheelchair, 38–40
wickedness, 4, 149
wife, 28, 97, 188, 251, 263
wisdom, 28–9, 79, 85, 92, 117, 137, 154, 172, 188, 204–6, 208–9, 226, 234–6, 238, 242, 306–7, 309, 311–12, 317, 323, 338, 340

Wittgenstein, Ludwig, 283
woman, 16, 28–9, 31–3, 74–8, 80–2, 84–6, 88–94, 170, 188, 226, 254, 323
womb, 163
wonder, 7, 23, 29, 207, 353
wondrous, 224, 240
workshop, 61, 174
worldliness, 192
worldmaking, 209–10
worlds, 38, 201, 273, 303, 308
worldview, 4, 209, 272–3, 277–9, 283, 295
worship, 59–60, 273, 285
worshipper, 191
worthiness, 208
wound, 43–4, 346
Wyclif, John, 269

EU representative:
Easy Access System Europe
Mustamäe tee 50, 10621 Tallinn, Estonia
Gpsr.requests@easproject.com